sytex — Mac
Quadra 900

Sue Beaupre

Printing Technology

3rd Edition

J. Michael Adams, Dean
College of Design Arts, Drexel University
Philadelphia, Pennsylvania

David D. Faux, Professor
State University of New York at Oswego

Lloyd J. Rieber, Associate Professor
Drexel University
Philadelphia, Pennsylvania

 Delmar Publishers Inc.®

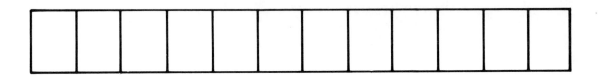

NOTICE TO THE READER

Cover photo courtesy of Brodock Press Inc., Utica, NY.

Delmar Staff

Associate Editor: Marjorie A. Bruce
Production Editor: Christopher Chien

Production Coordinator: Linda Helfrich
Art Production Coordinator: Linda Johnson

For information address Delmar Publishers Inc.,
2 Computer Drive, West, Box 15-015
Albany, New York 12212

Copyright © 1988 by Delmar Publishers Inc.

Printed in the United States of America
Published simultaneously in Canada
by Nelson Canada,
A division of The Thomson Corporation

10 9 8 7 6

Library of Congress Cataloging-in-Publication Data
Adams, J. Michael.
    Printing technology / J. Michael Adams, David D. Faux : with contributions by Lloyd J. Rieber.—3rd ed.
        p.   cm.
    Bibliography: p.
    Includes index.
        ISBN 0-8273-2775-7.   ISBN 0-8273-2776-5 (Instructor's guide).
ISBN 0-8273-2777-3 (Study guide)
        1. Printing, Practical.   I. Faux, David D.   II. Rieber, Lloyd J.
III. Title.
Z244.A515   1988
686.2'24—dc19   87-33032
                                                        CIP

Contents

Company Acknowledgments

The following manufacturers and associations provided technical information, art, and photographs. Their generosity helped ensure that the text reflects the current level of technology of the printing industry.

Eastman Kodak Company
Multigraphics, a Division of AM
    International, Inc.
Kroy, Inc.
Mackenzie and Harris, Inc.
Vandersons Corporation
Mergenthaler Linotype Company
SUCO Learning Resources and
    R. Kampas
Heidelberg Platen Press
C-Thru Ruler Company
Speedball
Connie Kindred
Schafer Machine Company, Inc.
Compugraphic Corporation
Alphatype Corporation
ItekGraphix Corporation,
    Composition Systems Division
Scangraphic Dr. Boger
Varityper, a Division of AM
    International, Inc.
Texet Corporation
Linotype
NASA
Spanish National Tourist Office

Smithsonian Institution
The International Museum of
    Photography at George
    Eastman House
ACTI Products, Inc.
nuArc Company, Inc.
Graphic Arts Manufacturing Co.
Stouffer Graphic Arts Equipment
    Co.
R. Kampas
Log E/LogEtronics, Inc.
Chris Savas
Richard W. Foster
Tobias Associates, Inc.
Beta Screen Corp.
Agfa-Gevaert, Inc.
James Craig, *Production Planning*
3M Company
DS America
Berkey Technical
Crosfield Electronics, Inc.
Kingsport Press, an Arcata National
    Company
Pre-Press Co., Inc.
GTI Graphic Technology, Inc.
Western Litho Plate and Supply
    Company
Rachwal Systems
Royal Zenith Corporation
Miller Printing Equipment Corp.
Graphic Arts Technical Foundation
Müller-Martini Corporation

Rockwell International Corporation,
    Graphic Systems Division
Solna, Incorporated
M.A.N.-Roland, USA, Inc.
Mead Paper
Micro Essential Lab., Inc.
Art Institute of Chicago
J. Ulano Company, Inc.
Naz-Dar Company
Advance Process Supply Company
Electronic Products Division, E.I. Du
    Pont de Nemours and
    Company, Inc.
Morrill Press
Southern Gravure Service
Gravure Association of America
Hewlett-Packard Corporation
Apple Computer, Inc.
Harris Corporation
Bell and Howell/Baumfolder
    Division/Philipsburg Division
Gane Brothers and Lane, Inc.
Plastic Binding Corporation
F.P. Rosback Company
Custom-Bilt Machinery, Inc.
Hantscho, Inc.
Kollmorgen Corp., Macbeth Color
    and Photometry Division
Enkel Corporation
Hell Graphic Systems, Inc.

Preface

Introduction

When *Printing Technology* was first introduced in 1977 it was one of a new generation of books that dealt with printing as a technology, rather than merely a process. The decade before had seen a revolution in the printing industry. Computer typesetting had become a commercial reality; presensitized litho plates had been introduced; offset printing had surpassed relief in percentage of sheets printed; web presses had grown in sophistication and acceptance. The first edition of *Printing Technology* covered the printing processes, but it also addressed the printing revolution and offered an introduction to the sophistication of printing.

We are still amazed by and appreciative of the reception of that first edition. Classroom teachers and their students reacted with enthusiasm. Instructors liked the combination of concepts with practice, and students liked the understandable language and contemporary illustrations. The second edition arrived in 1982, as a result of the encouragement of many individuals who offered suggestions for improvement. The second edition has been used at nearly every level of graphic arts education—in public, private and industrial training—and has found wide national and international acceptance.

Preparation of the Third Edition

As changes were planned for the third edition it became apparent the industry had experienced another revolution: The computer had entered every aspect of printing management and production, and had become the overriding element that guided all changes.

The third edition *Printing Technology* has been revised and updated to present the most current procedures and state-of-the-art materials in each phase of the printing process. The content has been reorganized to give students an understanding of the historical evolution of printing as well as knowledge about the latest equipment and processes. The third edition stresses computer applications in printing. Information about cold type composition has been totally rewritten to stress modern computer image generation and assembly, including full-page make-up and desktop publishing systems. The chapters on offset press operation have been rewritten to include web printing, computer-aided press control, and registration control devices commonly used in the industry. Flexographic printing is covered for the first time in the third edition, and an entirely new chapter on xerographic, laser, and ink-jet printing has been added. In addition to an integrated study of offset lithography—from the design through printing procedures—the text covers screen printing, gravure, and flexography. The information on color photography was strengthened and a major new section on camera calibration was created. Detailed discussions assume no previous knowledge about printing technology.
SPECIFIC CHAPTER CHANGES are as follows:

Chapter 3: Design Concerns for Printing has been rewritten to explain more about what a designer does and less about how to do design. It explains what the printer should know about design. Copyfitting and a thorough discussion on the preparation of both type and art copy have been added.

Chapter 5: The information which used to be "Cold Type Composition" has been totally rewritten into a new chapter called "Typesetting and Computer Image Generation." This chapter covers computer imaging, including basics of computer typesetting operations, computer typesetting terminology, fundamentals of computer imaging for graphic reproduction, automatic page make-up, integration of text and graphics, WYSIWYG and page display systems; output devices, microcomputer applications, and desktop systems.

Chapter 6: New information is provided on digital camera control, rapid access processing, and film processors.

Chapter 7: Expanded and simplified explanations of the main, flash, and bump tests (the three tests needed to calibrate for making a halftone negative) provided. These tests are directly applicable to areas of a continuous-tone print and the resultant halftone negative. Calculation for halftone exposures updated to include computerized calculation and on-line camera densitometers.

Chapters 8 and 9: Photography component upgraded to include the latest advances in processing.

Chapter 10: More information about color stripping and automated stripping added.

Chapter 11: Information about photopolymer presensitized surface plates added.

Chapter 12: New sections on multicolor sheet-fed presses, computer press monitoring sys-

tems (including plate and press sheet scanners and press consoles), and fundamentals of web presses added.

Chapter 13: New section on quality control devices for offset printing added.

Chapter 17: New chapter on "Other Printing Processes" added; includes fundamental information on flexography, xerography, laser printing, and ink-jet printing.

Chapter 19: New section on in-line finishing added.

Chapter 20: New section on Computer-aided production control, including automated data collection (ADC) added.

Special Features

The third edition of *Printing Technology* offers the following benefits:

- An excellent, comprehensive overview of the printing industry presented in an interesting, informative, and accurate manner.
- The text is organized to allow the teacher to focus student attention on the offset process, and achieve an overview of all of the major printing processes.
- Chapters contain objectives, key terms, questions for review, and informative anecdotes which present persons or events that have contributed to the development of the printing industry.
- Computer applications in printing are stressed throughout the text.
- Pre-press imaging—photocomposition, black and white camera work, color separation, and image assembly—has been

rewritten and updated to include information on the latest computer technology.

- Hundreds of new photographs and illustrations reflect state-of-the-art equipment, operations, and processes.
- In-depth procedures for offset lithography, including new information on color stripping and platemaking.
- Information about letterpress printing has been substantially reduced and moved to the front of the text to provide an historical overview of the development of printing, and introduce students to the many printing terms that originated with the letterpress processes.
- Extensive revisions have been made in the chapters covering careers in the printing industry, image generation, press operation, and new processes in printing.
- An eight-page full-color insert highlights color process printing, special effects photography, electronic color separation, color graphics work stations, and synthetic art.

Acknowledgments

Lloyd Rieber has joined Adams and Faux as an author for this third edition. Lloyd was a major partner in the preparation of the second edition and became the driving force behind the realization of the third edition.

The authors wish to express their appreciation to John Leininger, a former student and now a professional colleague, who reviewed the manuscript. During the course of the review he saw opportunities to improve the learning effectiveness of the text and gave freely of his time and talent to prepare material which is now part of the third edition, including new material in the color insert and new Appendix A, Determining Proper Film Exposure.

Appreciation is also expressed for the contributions of the reviewers who devoted many hours to careful examination of the manuscript. Their suggestions provided valuable guidance to the authors.

Ryan Smith, Milwaukee Area Technical College, Milwaukee, WI 53203

John Leininger, Clemson University, Clemson, SC 29631

Jerry D. Howell, Central Piedmont Community College, Charlotte, NC 28235

Frederick J. Reininger, Sidney Lanier High School, San Antonio, TX 78207

Richard Browne, Riverside City College, Riverside, CA 92506

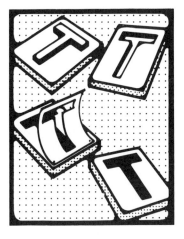

Chapter One

The Printing Industry

Anecdote to Chapter One

An Early Chinese Press The press was a low, flat table solid enough to hold the form in place.
The Bettman Archives

It is possible to trace the origins of printing to the use of seals to "sign" official documents as early as 255 B.C., during the Han dynasty in China. A ceramic stamp was pressed into a sheet of moist clay. When dry, the imprint served as a means of certifying the authenticity of the document. When paper was invented, around A.D. 105, the transition to the use of the seal with ink was a natural one.

Early documents and manuscripts were copied and recopied by hand. Frequent copying mistakes were made from one edition to the next; copies often differ significantly from the author's original. Around A.D. 175, the Chinese began the practice of cutting the writings of important scholars into stone. The stones were placed in centers of learning, and students made "rubbings," or copies on paper from the carvings. The process was faster than hand copying, and all editions were identical to the first.

No one knows when the ideas of the seal and stone rubbings came together, but in China in A.D. 953, under the administration of Fêng Tao, a large-scale block-printing operation was begun to reproduce the Confucian classics. Block prints were generally slabs of hard fine-grained wood that were carved to leave a well-defined raised image. The raised portions were inked, paper was laid over the block, and a pad was rubbed across the surface to transfer the ink to the paper.

During the Sung dynasty, around A.D. 1401, a common man named Pi Shêng invented movable type. Building on the ideas of block printing, he cut individual characters in small pieces of clay. The clay was fired to make it hard, and individual pieces were placed in an iron frame to create the printing form. Be-

cause the pieces did not fit together perfectly, they were embedded in a mixture of hot pine resin, wax, and paper ashes. When cold, all the pieces were held together perfectly tight, and the form was inked and printed. Reheating the resin mixture loosened the pieces of type so they could be reused.

Other materials, including wood, tin, copper, and bronze, were used for the same purpose. The idea of movable type traveled to neighboring countries. In Korea, in A.D. 1403, King T'aijong ordered that everything without exception within his reach should be printed in order to pass on the tradition of what the works contained. Three hundred thousand pieces of bronze type were cast, and printing began. It is interesting to speculate on the relationship between this event and a similar one that took place not more than fifty years later in Northern Germany, which brought Johann Gutenberg the title of "father of printing."

Objectives for Chapter One

After completing this chapter you will be able to:

- Discuss the development of graphic symbols from prehistoric times to the present through the evolution of the modern alphabet.
- List the major printing processes and describe the differences between them.
- List and describe the steps in the printing cycle.

- Rank the printing industry in terms of number of individual firms, number of employees, and "value added."
- Describe the structure and purpose of each level of a small- to medium-sized printing company.
- Compare the kinds of services provided by the different types of printing businesses.
- Describe the different ways to enter, train, and advance in the printing industry.

Introduction

Graphic messages are possible because lines can be made into shapes that have meanings to humans. As early as 35,000 B.C. people were drawing messages on cave walls (figure 1.1). These were probably intended to be temporary messages, but they became permanent. They were simple drawings—merely lines—but they carried meaning to the people of that period: "This is a mammoth," "Oh, what a feast we had," or "We hunted a great hairy beast."

Development of Pictographs. Drawings that carry meaning because they look like real objects are called **pictographs** (figure 1.2a). Pictographs have a one-to-one relationship with reality. To symbolize one ox (called *aleph*), draw one symbol of an ox. To represent five oxen, draw five symbols. It is difficult to use pictographs to communicate complex ideas, such as "I have six oxen—one brown, four white, and one white and brown." It is impossible to symbolize abstract ideas, such as love or hate, with a pictographic system.

About 1200 B.C., in a small country called Phoenicia (now a part of Syria), a group of traders began to realize the limitations of the pictographic system. They attempted to simplify the picture notations in their account books by streamlining their symbols. But however they drew the lines, *aleph* still symbolized one ox and *beth* still stood for one house (figure 1.2b).

Development of Ideographs. The next step was to have drawings symbolize ideas. These drawings are called **ideographs.** With this system *aleph* became the symbol for food and

Figure 1.1. An early message Pictured is a cave drawing (message made by prehistoric people) in the Altamira caves in Spain.
Courtesy of Spanish National Tourist Office, New York

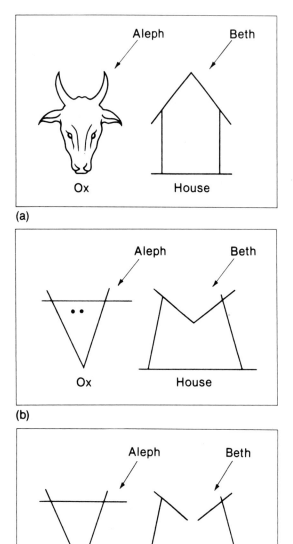

(a)

(b)

(c)

Figure 1.2. The development of ideographs Pictographs shown here in (a) and (b) were drawn to represent real objects. They were gradually simplified to represent general ideas and became known as ideographs (c).

beth represented a dwelling or shelter (figure 1.2c). **Ideographs** are simple drawings that symbolize ideas or concepts rather than concrete objects. They are a vast improvement over pictographs because complex or abstract ideas can be easily represented, but ideographs are still clumsy. The sheer number of symbols can be overwhelming. The Japanese and Chinese both still use ideographic symbol systems that contain over ten thousand different characters. It could take a lifetime to understand such a system.

Development of Phonetic Symbols. By 900 B.C. the Phoenicians had made another change. Instead of symbolizing the actual ox or food, the picture came to represent a sound. Whenever the readers saw the symbol, they could make the sound that the symbol represented. When the symbols were placed together, whole words could be repeated. This idea of representing sounds by symbols is known to us as a **phonetic symbol system** and is the basis for most modern written languages. The Phoenicians developed nineteen such symbols, but they were traders and were not concerned with recording all words used in everyday conversation. We form verbal symbols by combining consonants and vowels. The Phoenician system contained no vowels and was of little use in recording everyday speech.

By 403 B.C. the Greeks had officially adopted the Phoenician system, after adding five vowels and changing the names of the letters (figure 1.3). *Aleph* became *alpha* and *beth* became *beta*, which form our term *alphabet*.

About a hundred years later, the early Roman empire borrowed the Greek alphabet and refined it to meet its needs. It accepted thirteen letters outright, revised eight, and added *F* and *Q*, which gave it twenty-three—all that was necessary to write Latin. The Roman system stood firm for nearly twelve centuries. About one thousand years ago the letter *U* was added as a rounded *V*, and two *Vs* were put together to form *W*. Five hundred years later the letter *J* was added to give us a total of twenty-six letters that form our contemporary Latin alphabet.

There were still some problems to be worked out. Early Greek and Roman writing was done by scribes—all with different "penmanship." Some wrote from left to right, some from right to left. Combine these differences with the lack of punctuation marks or spaces between words or sentences, and the whole thing could be quite a mess.

It wasn't until movable metal type was introduced by Johann Gutenberg in the mid-fifteenth century that any true standard of punctuation or sentence structure was achieved. It took printing technology to stabilize the phonetic symbol system as we know it today. Slight changes have been made, but the basic composition of our alphabet has remained the same from the time of Gutenberg.

Printing Technology

Major Printing Processes

All printing processes reproduce lines and/or dots that form an image. **Printing** is the process of manufacturing multiple copies of graphic images. Although most people think of printing as ink on paper, printing is not limited to any particular materials or inks. The embossing process uses no ink at all, and all shapes and sizes of metals, wood, and plastics are common receivers of printed messages.

The following four major printing processes are used to reproduce graphic images:

Figure 1.3. The development of our alphabet Illustrated from top to bottom are the Phoenician alphabet (900 B.C.), the Greek alphabet (403 B.C.), and the Roman alphabet (300 B.C.).

- Relief printing
- Intaglio printing
- Screen printing
- Lithographic printing

Each of these processes is suited for specific applications, such as newspaper, book, package, or textile printing.

The **relief** process includes letterpress printing, flexographic printing, and all other methods of transferring an image from a raised surface (figure 1.4a). While once a major process in the printing industry, letterpress printing has been largely replaced by other printing processes. Most relief printing done today is done with flexography. Flexographic printing is used extensively in the packaging industry for printing on corrugated board, paper cartons, and plastic film. Flexography is also becoming a significant process for printing newspapers, newspaper inserts, catalogs and directories.

Intaglio printing is the reverse of the relief concept. An intaglio image is transferred from a sunken surface (figure 1.4b). Copper plate etching and engraving are two intaglio processes. One type of industrial in-

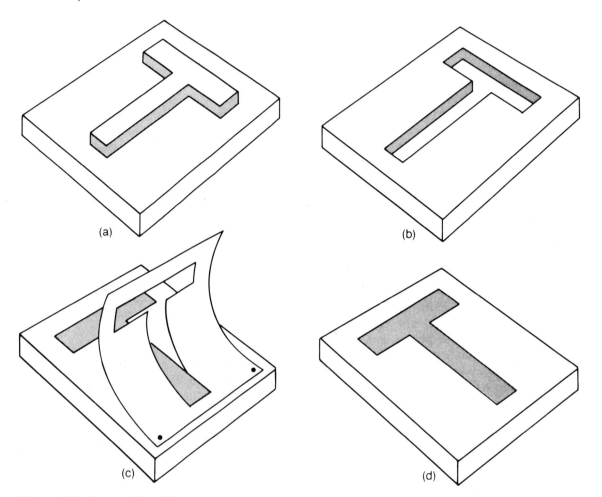

Figure 1.4. Four main printing processes Relief printing transfers an image from a raised surface (a). Intaglio printing transfers an image from a sunken surface (b). Screen printing transfers an image through a stencil (c). Lithographic printing transfers an image chemically from a flat surface (d).

taglio printing is **gravure.** Gravure is used for extremely long press runs. Cellophane and aluminum foil candy bar wrappers are two common packaging materials printed with gravure printing. *Readers Digest* and the *National Geographic* are but two of many national magazines that are printed with gravure.

Screen printing transfers an image by allowing ink to pass through openings in a stencil that has been applied to a screen mesh (figure 1.4c). The screen process is sometimes called "silk screen printing," even though silk is rarely used industrially to hold the stencil, because silk is not as durable as industrial screen materials. Some of the industrial uses for screen printing include printing on plastic, such as round plastic containers, printing large display signs and billboards, and printing on textiles. Another major use for screen printing is in the manufacture of printed circuit boards for electrical/electronic equipment.

Lithography as it is known today is a relatively new process, dating from around 1798. A lithographic image is transferred from a flat surface. Certain areas on the surface are chemically treated to accept ink, and other areas are left untreated so that they will repel ink. When the surface is inked, the ink remains in the ink-receptive areas, but not in the untreated areas. When a material such as paper contacts the surface, ink is transferred to the paper (figure 1.4d). This process is sometimes called planography, offset lithography, offset, or photo-offset lithography.

Offset lithographic printing is the most widely used printing process in the commercial printing industry. Its major application is for printing on paper, thus it is ideal for printing newspapers, books, magazines, pamphlets, and all other forms of paper publications.

Although there are several older printing processes (such as collography, which prints from a fragile gelatin emulsion), and also new processes (such as electrostatic printing and ink-jet printing, which form images by electromagnetic projection), the four major printing processes still account for most of the work done in the printing industry.

Printing technology has long been a powerful tool for social change. Edward George Bulwer-Lytton wrote, "The pen is mightier than the sword." But his statement assumes the distribution of the ideas that the pen recorded. Without printing, few would read the ideas, and the pen would become a rather weak weapon.

Printers have long been the most influential individuals in the community. Early colonial printers helped to shape our country by reproducing, recording, and distributing the ideas and events of the period. Benjamin Franklin, himself an early American patriot, was proudest of his role as a printer. After being active in the Revolution, a signer of the Declaration of Independence, a member of the First and Second Continental Congresses, founder of the first American library, an author, an inventor, a publisher, and ambassador to France, he directed that his epitaph should read "B. Franklin, Printer."

Printing Cycle

Since the time of Franklin, the basic cycle of the printing industry has not changed much from the following procedures:

1. Identifying a need
2. Creating an image design
3. Reproducing the image design
4. Distributing the printed message

The cycle begins with an identified need. The need might be as simple as the reproduction of a form or as sophisticated as a poster intended to change human attitudes. It could be as ordinary as a package designed to convince a consumer to buy one brand of cereal rather than another. Whatever the need, a graphic design evolves. Special design agencies are often set up whose sole purpose is to sell ideas and work closely with the printer as the design is turned into print for the customer.

The function of printing management is to be responsible for reproducing the image design. The most efficient printing process must be identified. Such variables as the type of material to be printed, length of run, number and types of colors, time requirements, desired quality, and customer's cost limitations must all be considered. An estimate must be made for each job. A profit must be made, and yet the estimate must be low enough to attract work in a very competitive market. If the customer approves the estimate, management must schedule the job, arrange for all materials, ensure quality control, and keep track of all phases of production so the job is finished on schedule.

The production phase of the cycle is often the only phase the customer, consumer, and printing student ever see. A large part of this book is concerned with production procedures, but it must be realized that the production process is only one part of the cycle.

The final test of the cycle is the method of distributing the printed message. Without an audience for the graphic images created by the artist and printer, the whole cycle is useless. Printing is mailed; handed out on busy streets; sold on street corners; and shipped to department stores, corner drugstores, and local newsstands. It is passed out in highway tollbooths, filed in offices, pasted on billboards, carried on placards, or even thumbtacked to poster boards. The purpose of all this activity is to place printed matter into the hands of consumers.

Sequence of Steps in the Printing Processes

The printing industry has long consisted of shops identified with a particular process, such as relief or lithography. Craftsmen were trained and then bound by union or guild structure to that particular process. More recently, it is common for a printing establishment to use a variety of printing processes. Regardless of the printing process used, however, there is a sequence of steps that all print-

ing follows. This sequence consists of the following:

- Image design
- Image generation
- Image conversion
- Image assembly
- Image carrier preparation
- Image transfer
- Finishing

The image is designed to meet a need. Sketches and final layouts are made, and design variables such as type style, visual position, type size, balance, and harmony are all considered. This is the **image design** step. After the customer approves the design, the image must be generated and made up into a final form. Specifications developed during the image design stage are carefully followed during **image generation.**

All printing processes now rely to a large degree on photography. Images are usually converted to transparent film in the **image conversion** step, placed in the proper printing order in the **image assembly** step, and then photographically transferred to an image carrier during the **image carrier preparation** step. The image carriers for each printing process may operate differently, but all must be prepared with the same general photographic considerations.

The image must be printed onto a receiver material during the **image transfer** step. **Finishing** is the last step which combines the printed material into a final finished form that can be delivered to the customer. This may include cutting, perforating, scoring, folding, inserting, stapling, binding, and/or packaging.

This book is designed to reflect contemporary printing technology. Letterpress printing is presented first to give an overview of the development of modern printing. Our discussion of letterpress will also introduce new terms and concepts that you will need in order to understand the other printing processes. All of the steps in the printing sequence for the lithographic process and for the screen process are examined in detail. The gravure process is only briefly discussed because the complexity of image carrier preparation and image transfer for gravure printing are beyond the scope of this work. Flexography is presented in some depth, because it represents the most contemporary relief process and is a significant part of the printing industry.

For years printing educators have realized that the printing industry is much larger than any particular printing process. The printing industry reflects a technology. A technology cannot be learned by examining tools or materials. A technology is mastered by understanding the concepts. The first ten chapters of this text provide the fundamental concepts needed for mastering the technology of printing. The remaining chapters cover the procedures used in each of the major printing processes.

Size and Scope of the Printing Industry

The U.S. Department of Commerce classifies all industries in the United States by Standard Industrial Classification numbers. In this classification system, the printing industry is part of Standard Industrial Classification (SIC) number 27 (Printing and Publishing). Department of Commerce information indicates that the U.S. printing and publishing industry consists of more than fifty-three thousand individual establishments that employ over one

million people. In 1985, industry yearly sales exceeded $100 billion. These figures place printing and publishing among the top five U.S. industries in terms of number of individual establishments and in terms of number of employees.

Economists use several measures to gauge the importance of an industry in a society's economy. The "gross national product" (GNP) is a figure that represents the overall annual flow of goods and services in an economy. In the United States, the printing industry is ranked among the top ten contributors to the GNP. "Value added" is a measure of the difference between the cost of raw materials and the final market price of a product. The higher the value-added figure, the more valuable the skills that went into the manufacturing of the product. Again printing ranks among the top ten.

Structure of Companies

The printing industry is dominated by small-to medium-sized companies that employ one to twenty-five people. There are "giants" in the industry that employ many hundreds of workers, but they account for a very small proportion (perhaps as small as 5%) of all the companies involved with the printing trade.

The structure of any individual printing company depends on many things, such as size, location, physical facilities, type of product, financing method (corporation, partnership, etc.), or management style. In fact, it is probably safe to assume that no two printing organizations are structured exactly alike. Figure 1.5 shows a possible structure for a small-to-medium-sized company made up of ten to twenty-five employees. In smaller organizations one individual might serve several functions. In larger concerns many workers might be assigned one area.

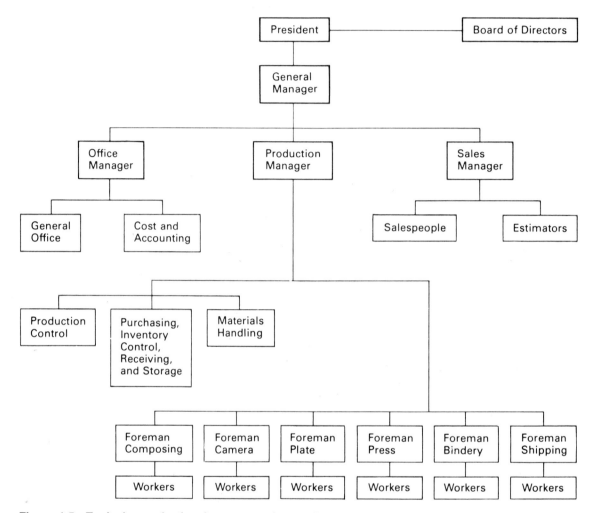

Figure 1.5. Typical organizational structure of a small- to medium-sized (ten to twenty-five employees) printing company.

Board of Directors.   The board of directors represents the financial control of the company. The board might be the actual owners or it might be an elected body, as in the case of large corporations. In either case, the board defines the scope and purpose of the company and deals with problems such as arranging for financing in the case of expansion.

The president is generally a member of the board of directors and acts as the board's representative to carry out its policies.

Management.   The president or Chief Executive Officer (CEO) delegates top-level management of day-to-day operation to the general manager. The office manager directs such important tasks as correspondence, record keeping, accounting, payroll, and customer billing. The sales manager directs an important part of the company; without something to print, the rest of the organization stands idle. Sales representatives make contacts with customers who require printing and with skilled estimators who calculate costs. The production manager is responsible for directing the materials, printers, and equipment so that a fine-quality printing job will be produced. Many managerial positions in the printing industry are filled by individuals who have moved up the ranks from the trade level.

Production. The production phase is generally divided into three categories:

- Production planning
- Manufacturing
- Quality assurance

One aspect of planning production control is scheduling work efficiently within the limitations of time, equipment, and human skills. People in charge of purchasing, inventory control, and receiving and storage are responsible for the advance ordering of all supplies. Some firms test incoming supplies such as ink, paper, plates, and films for quality assurance to guarantee that they meet quality standards. Costly press downtime can be avoided by assuring the quality of the materials used in the printing process. Accurate material handling ensures that supplies are delivered to the correct station (camera, press, etc.) as needed and that the finished product is removed from the last station. Production stations of composition, camera, plate making, press, bindery, and shipping must be directed by skilled supervisors who work to meet the schedules set up by production control. The actual production must be carried out by individuals who are highly skilled in the printing trades.

Although a worker's skill is not directly related to any form of organization or managerial control, it is important that employees understand the basic organization of their business. The efficiency of that organization directly influences continued employment.

Organization of Printing Services

There are several ways to categorize individual printing companies. An accurate reflection of industrial organization would categorize printing businesses according to the kinds of services they provide:

- Commercial
- Trade shops
- Special purpose
- Quick printing
- In-plant
- Publishing
- Packaging
- Related industries

Commercial Printing

The term **commercial printing** refers to a shop that is willing to take on nearly any sort of printing job. Commercial printers can usually handle a large variety of printing jobs, regardless of sheet size, number of ink colors, length of run, or even binding requirements. Typical products produced in the same shop might include small business cards, letterhead stationery, posters, and four-color glossy advertising sheets to be mailed. If a commercial printer does not have all of the equipment or skilled staff to perform the whole job, parts of the job, such as die cutting, foil stamping, or binding, may be subcontracted to a trade shop.

Trade Shops

Some shops provide services only to the printing trade. These are called **trade shops.** Not all commercial, special purpose, in-plant, publishing, or packaging companies can afford to own and operate all the equipment necessary to meet their total production requirements. For example, some printers may find it far more economical to contract with another company to produce all their composition needs. Another company might decide not to buy bindery equipment because only a small percentage of their work requires folding, collating, or binding. When they receive a contract that requires binding, they send it to a trade shop that specializes in this function.

Special Purpose Printing

Special purpose printing is defined by the limited type of jobs performed by a company. One printer might print only labels. The printer would purchase special equipment and accept orders for only one type of product. However, the printer would make labels to any size, shape, number of colors, length of run, or purpose. Another printer might specialize in business forms, such as order forms, estimate blanks, filing sheets, school note paper, or duplicate sales slips. Forms printing is an important area of the industry in terms of size and yearly sales. Yet another example of special purpose printing is called "legal" printing. It is concerned with reproducing such pieces as insurance policies, property titles, and loan contracts.

Quick Printing

Within the last several years, a whole **quick printing** sector of the printing industry has grown up around the use of the xerographic process (sometimes called electrostatic). More commonly known as photocopying, or simply copying, the xerographic process allows copies to be reproduced without the use of a printing plate or a true printing press (figure 1.6). The xerographic process has several limitations, but it is particularly valuable for producing short-run, low- to medium-quality reproductions in standard page sizes, such as 8 1/2" by 11" or 11" by 17". For these applications, the process can represent a considerable savings over any other printing process available.

In-plant Printing

Probably the fastest-growing area in the printing industry today is **in-plant printing.** It is defined as any printing operation that is owned by and serves the needs of a single company or corporation. A business might manufacture a variety of products that must each be packaged with an instruction sheet. The management might decide that it is more convenient and cost efficient to set up their own shop to print the instruction sheets themselves than to send the job to a commercial printer. The company would then also be able to produce in-house forms, company letterhead and stationery, time cards, and almost all of its printing needs.

Many in-plant printers use the lithographic process. Equipment manufacturers are currently marketing "systems" with a platemaker "in line" with a press, collator, and binder. With the systems approach, the in-plant printer can enter original copy (such as a typed form) into an automatic direct image platemaking system, select the number of copies to be printed and the preferred binding method, and produce bound copies in a matter of minutes (figure 1.7).

Figure 1.6. A xerographic (photocopying) system This 100-copies-per-minute photocopier allows users to reproduce standard sheet sizes with cover pages and wire staple binding. All machine functions are accessed through the control panel.
Courtesy of Eastman Kodak

Publishing

Another category of printing services that we use nearly every day is **publishing**. Within this group are the thousands of companies that produce daily or weekly newspapers, and the even larger group of companies that pro-

duces periodicals, such as *Time* and *Newsweek,* which sell to a national market. Consider also the group of businesses that produce and market books. The publisher of this book is a private company that produces textbooks. It is important to understand that printers don't usually make decisions to publish a book

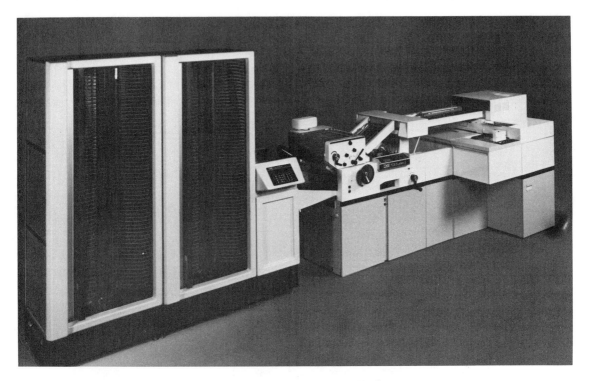

Figure 1.7. In-plant production equipment In-plant production is often done with a "systems" approach and with equipment that automates much of the time-consuming labor.
Courtesy of Multigraphics, a Division of AM International, Inc.

or magazine. Printers are rarely the publisher. Publishers, however, require the skills of the printer to manufacture their products.

Package Printing

Hundreds of different containers we use every day are produced by **package printing.** The idea of impulse buying (buying a product on the visual appeal of the package) has sky-rocketed the demand for high-quality multi-color packages that attract the consumer's attention. Package printers decorate and form hundreds of millions of folded paperboard boxes, flexible packaging, and corrugated

boxes each year. Millions of printed plastic bags are used every day in grocery stores and companies that distribute or package food. Corrugated boxes and thin plastic film are both printed by flexography. Packaging, however, is not restricted to paper or plastic containers. Think of all the steel and aluminum soft drink and beer containers sold every day. These packages are produced by a special process called "metal decorating."

Related Industries

The last category of services in the printing industry is called **related industries.** The raw materials of the printer are such things as ink, paper, plates, chemicals, and many other supplies. Printers also use special purpose equipment, such as presses, paper cutters, platemakers, cameras, and light tables, to produce their product. Companies that provide services to printers by either producing or selling these supplies and equipment are called related industries. Other businesses, such as consulting firms and advertising agencies that prepare designs for reproduction, might also perform a service, but they do not make or sell a physical product.

Preparing for a Career in Printing

Viewing the printing industry as made up of commercial, special purpose, quick printing, in-plant, publishing, package printing, trade shops, and related industries is only one way to look at a broad industry. The industry does not stand alone; it is carried by people. There is a need for skilled people power. There are no fixed paths to entering the printing industry, but a few general observations can be made.

Upper-Level Management Preparation

Managerial levels—specifically upper-level positions (see figure 1.5)—usually, but not always, require a college degree. There are several schools that offer degrees with an extensive specialization in printing technology. Printing specialization, however, is not an absolute requirement. Individuals with experience in such areas as art, journalism, engineering, chemistry, physics, research, data processing and computers, sales, marketing, and management are also employed in printing companies.

Middle-Level Management Preparation

Middle-level management, such as section foremen or production control people, and skilled crafts people enter the industry by a variety of routes. There are trade high schools designed to provide high school graduates with skills necessary for direct entrance into the industry. Other secondary school programs offer vocational or industrial arts classes combined with a cooperative work experience (where the student spends part of a day in a local printing company and part of the day in school). There are also technical printing programs offered in two-year community colleges that lead to an associate degree.

Craft-Level Preparation

Union membership may influence craft-level entrance into the industry. Printing establishments can be either closed or open shops. A **closed shop** requires union membership. An open shop does not have such a requirement. In an **open shop**, individuals can belong to a union, but they do not have to in order to keep their job.

Union Membership. There are several craft unions in the United States that represent the printing trades. Some reflect only one specific type of skill, such as press operators. Others extend across many craft lines. One advantage of union membership is a national negotiating power for wages and benefits. Another advantage of union membership is on-the-job training. In closed union shops trainees generally receive on-the-job training through a structured apprenticeship program.

Nonunion Organizations. Even though nonunion open shop workers are not represented in national-level collective bargaining, there are organizations that provide services such as retirement benefits and health insurance to nonunion printers. The advantage of open shop work is that the wage level is not necessarily linked to union pay scales. Open shops emphasize previous skills combined with knowledge learned on the job. There is a national nonunion certification called the Master Craftsman Program, coordinated through the Printing Industries of America. Many open shops also provide on-the-job training.

Career Advancement

Advancement in the printing industry is based on performance. The most skillful managers and workers gradually assume more responsibility through practice and additional training. A great many organizations provide continuing updating and training to the printing professions. Three examples are the Graphic Arts Technical Foundation (GATF), the Printing Industries of America (PIA), and the National Association of Printers and Lithographers (NAPL). All of these are nonprofit organizations designed to meet the research, technical, and educational needs of their members. They are supported by printers, suppliers, manufacturers, graphic arts educators and students. They are each involved in solving industrial problems, conducting applied research, publishing the results of their work in the form of books and audio visual aids, and conducting workshops.

Many other types of printing organizations serve both professional and social needs (See Appendix C). There are several management organizations, a number of fellowship groups, and even student clubs. The printing industry is made up of a vast group of people all devoted to the goal of fulfilling the graphic communication needs of a technical world.

Key Terms

relief	image assembly	in-plant printing
letterpress	image conversion	publishing
flexography	image carrier preparation	package printing
intaglio	image transfer	trade shops
gravure	finishing	related industries
screen printing	commercial printing	closed shop
lithography	special purpose printing	open shop
image design	quick printing	

Questions for Review

1. What is a pictograph?

2. What is an ideograph?

3. What is a phonetic symbol?

4. What are the four main printing processes?

5. What is the sequence of steps that all printers follow regardless of the printing process they are using?

6. What is the purpose of the board of directors of a printing company?

7. What is the task of the production manager in a printing company?

8. What is one job of the production planning department in a printing company?

9. What kind of printing services do trade shops provide for the printing industry?

10. What is the difference between a closed shop and an open shop in the printing industry?

11. List the different ways to enter, train, and advance in the different levels of the graphic arts industry.

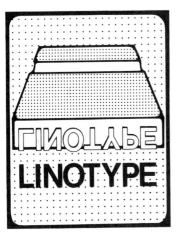

Chapter Two

The Tradition of Foundry Type

Anecdote to Chapter Two

Johann Gutenberg - The father of printing

The father of printing in the Western world is generally considered to be Johann Gensfleisch zum Gutenberg, who was born in the city of Mainz, Germany, in 1397. The wealth of the Gutenberg family freed Johann for a life of leisure and pleasure, during which he developed an interest in technology—primarily seal making and goldsmithing. In 1438 he started a business of producing religious mirrors in Strasbourg. By that time he was considered a master craftsman in metalworking.

There is evidence that by 1444 he had returned to Mainz to set up a printing shop. As a goldsmith he had cut letters and symbols in precious metals or in reverse in wax to form a mold to cast jewelry. The idea of casting individual letters for printing occurred to him. The casting process involved cutting a letter by hand in reverse on a piece of hard metal, then punching the letter shape into a soft copper mold to form a die, called a matrix.

Gutenberg next needed a suitable metal to cast in the mold. He experimented with pewter hardened with large quantities of antimony, but the material shrank when it cooled and pulled away from the matrix. The letters formed were imperfect. His experience with lead in mirror manufacturing finally encouraged him to try a combination of lead, tin, and antimony. Gutenberg's original formula (5% tin, 12% antimony, and 83% lead) remains nearly unchanged to this day. Characters can be perfectly cast with this alloy because it expands when it cools and forms an exact duplicate of the matrix cavity. Using his system, two workers could cast and dress (trim away excess material) twenty-five pieces of type an hour.

Gutenberg's most notable work, his forty-two-line Bible (a Bible with forty-two lines to the page), was begun in 1452 and completed by 1455. Each page contained around 2,800 characters. Two pages were printed at the same time, so 5,600 pieces of type were needed to make each two-page printing. It was the common practice for the next two pages to be composed during the press run, so at least 11,200 letters were needed even to begin printing. Working a normal workday (twelve hours), two craftsmen took more than thirty-seven workdays to prepare the initial type. At this rate of speed, over three years were needed to complete just two hundred copies of the Bible.

Much of the language of modern printing comes to us from the craft of foundry type composition, developed by Johann Gutenberg and his workers more than five hundred years ago. Terms such as "form," "leading," "uppercase," "lowercase," "type size," "impression," and "makeready" originated with Gutenberg. All printers today owe a debt to the hundreds of early craftsmen who followed Gutenberg in the tradition of hand-set foundry type and gave us both a language and an art.

Objectives for Chapter Two

After completing this topic you will be able to:

– Identify the major parts of a piece of foundry type.
– Describe the procedure for composing a line of foundry type.
– Compare the advantages of line-casting and character-casting composing machines over foundry type composition.
– Explain the difference between a duplicate and a primary relief plate.
– Outline the procedure to lock up and print a simple relief form.
– List and describe four special letterpress applications.

Introduction

Relief printing (printing from a raised surface) has long been one of the most important re- production processes. Until recently, all relief printing involved printing from lead-based metal type, called **foundry type** or **hot type.** Printing from lead-based hot type is often referred to as **letterpress** printing. For over 400 years after Gutenberg letterpress printing accounted for almost all of the industrial printing done in the world. With the introduction of other printing processes, particularly lithography, letterpress' share of the printing market has declined. Today letterpress printing accounts for only a small share of our industry. Most relief printing done today is done with flexography, a process that prints from a raised rubber surface, in much the same manner as reproductions are made from a rubber stamp. It is important, however, to understand the letterpress process. Much of the terminology used by printers comes from the tradition of foundry type and the letterpress process. There are also applications of letterpress printing in use today that cannot be accomplished by any other method.

Foundry Type Composition

Composition is the process of assembling type for printing. The methods used for hot type composition of foundry type for letterpress have changed little since the days of Johann Gutenberg. Individual characters are cast on separate bodies by type founders. The printer composes words and sentences by placing the appropriate cast characters, symbols, and spaces next to each other in a composing stick.

Identifying Foundry Type

To work with foundry type, it is necessary to be able to identify the significant parts of each cast character (figure 2.1). The actual printing surface is called the "face." The sides of the character are cast at an angle (called the "beard") for greater strength. The beard slopes

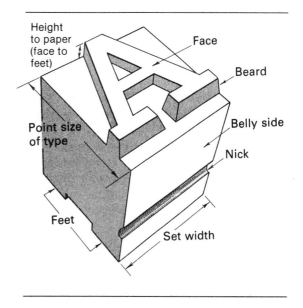

Figure 2.1. Example of a foundry type character Foundry type characters are cast on individual bodies.

down to the nonprinting shoulder and counter. The "feet" are perfectly parallel to the face. The distance from the face to the feet is the "height to paper" or **type-high.** For most English-speaking countries, it is 0.918 inches.

All characters in a single **font** (collection of type of the same style and size) have a nick cut in the same position on the type body. When setting a line of foundry type, it is easy to glance at the row of nicks. If one nick does not line up with all the rest, the printer knows it is probably a "wrong font" character. The nick side is often called the "belly side." The distance from the belly to the back side is the **point size** of the piece of type. Note that the type body in figure 2.1 is larger than the character "A." Type point size is defined by the point size of the body, not by the size of the character.

The distance across the nick or belly side

of the type is an important measure called the **set width.** The letter *m*, for example, is a wider character than the letter *i*. Therefore, the set width of *m* is wider than that of *i*, or stated in another way, the set width is proportional to the size of the letter on the type body. Most typewriters form "nonproportional" letters. This makes it possible to type the letter *m*, backspace, and type the letter *i* in the same visual space.

Special Characters

By using variations of the twenty-six letters of our Latin alphabet, many possible characters can be cast as foundry type to meet a special purpose. Gutenberg cast nearly two hundred and fifty different characters and symbols to be used in his Bible.

A **ligature** is two or more connected letters on the same type body (figure 2.2). The most common are *fi* and *fl* combinations. Whenever any portion of the printing face extends over the body of the type, the character is said to be **kerned** (figure 2.3). Kerns are very common in italic faces.

Type Storage Systems

The earliest relief printers stored identical characters in small compartments or bins. As the number of type styles grew, each font was stored in what was termed a "case."

A once-popular type storage system was

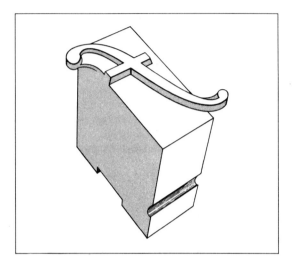

Figure 2.3. Example of a kerned letter

the **news case.** An entire font of letters was stored in two cases, capitals in one and small letters in another. The case with capitals was traditionally stored on a shelf directly over the case with small letters. Our terms *upper-* and *lowercase* to indicate CAPITAL or small letters date from the use of the news case.

The most popular type case is the **California job case** (figure 2.4). It is designed to hold one font of characters made up of upper- and lowercase letters, numerals, punctuation marks, ligatures, special symbols (such as $), and spacing material in a total of eighty-nine small boxes. Lowercase letters and symbols are assigned positions and space in the case according to the frequency of their use.

The Printer's Measurement System

Printers use a special system to measure almost all printed images. This system was developed from the measurement of foundry type and continues in use today. In this sys-

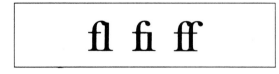

Figure 2.2. Examples of ligatures

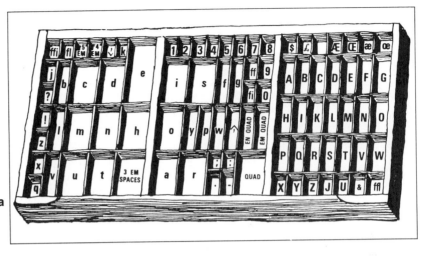

Figure 2.4. Example of a California job case
Courtesy of Mackenzie and Harris, Inc., San Francisco, CA

tem six **picas** equal one inch, and twelve **points** equal one pica (figure 2.5).

Printers use this special system to measure almost all printed images. Type size is almost always described in points. Common type sizes are 6, 7, 8, 9, 10, 11, 12, 14, 16, 18, 24, 36, 42, 60, and 72 points.

Space between lines of type is also measured in points. When a customer requests a type page to be set 10 on 12 (10/12), the printer understands that the letters will be 10 points high, with 2 points of space between each line (12 points − 10 points = 2 points).

Figure 2.5. Pica-inch ruler The printer's system of measurement is based on pica units of measure. The divisions shown on the bottom scale in this figure are 6 points and 12 points (1 pica).

Lines of type are specified in picas. Most newspaper columns are 13 picas wide. A 36-pica line is 6 inches long, since one inch equals six picas. Column depth is measured in picas from the top of the first line on a page to the bottom of the last line of type.

Word-Spacing Material

All hot type spacing material in a given font is of the same point size. Each space must match the point size of the type it is being used with and must be less than type-high (usually 0.800 inch or less) (figure 2.6).

Within any font size, then, is a collection of different pieces of spacing material. The basic unit of spacing material in each font is an **em quad,** sometimes called the "mutton quad." The em quad is a square piece of spacing material, each side of which is the point size of the font the em quad is from. For example, an em quad from a 12-point font of type would be less than type-high and would measure 12 points by 12 points on the face; an 18-point font would contain em quads that

Figure 2.6. Example showing spacing material between words Spacing material used between words must match the point size of the type and be less than the height of the type.

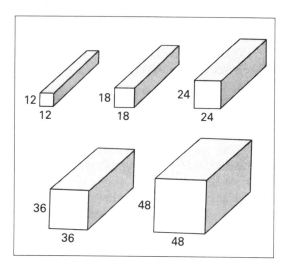

Figure 2.7. Examples of em quads The em, or mutton, quad is the basic word-spacing unit in each font.

are 18 points in each dimension on the face (figure 2.7).

All other spacing material in a font is based on the size of the em quad. Two **en quads,** or "nut quads," placed together equal the dimension of one em quad. For example, if the font size is 12 points, the en quad will measure 6 points by 12 points on the face. A 3-em space (abbreviated from "three to the em") is one-third of an em. The smallest space typically found in a job case is the 5-em space, which is one-fifth of an em. Some spaces, such as the 2-em quad or the 3-em quad, are larger than the em quad.

For most composition, the em quad is used to indent the first line of a paragraph, the en quad is used between sentences, and the 3-em space is placed between words. Combinations of all spacing material are used to adjust equal line lengths of type composition.

There is one more class of spacing material called thin spaces. The most common thicknesses of thin spaces are 1/2 point, generally made of copper, and 1 point, usually made of brass. Thin spaces are generally only used for spacing between letters (called "letter spacing").

Line-Spacing Material

In addition to spacing between words, the space between lines, called **leading,** must be controlled with line-spacing material. Line-spacing material is less than type-high and is generally cut from long strips to the length of line being set. All line-spacing material is classed according to thickness. **Leads** are generally 2 points in thickness, but anything from 1 to 4 points is termed a *lead*. **Slugs** are typically 6 points thick, but any piece up to 24 points (2 picas) is still labeled a *slug*. Both leads and slugs are made from type metal.

Any line-spacing material that is 24 points in thickness or larger is called **furniture.** Furniture is made from type metal, wood (generally oak), or an aluminum alloy.

Composing a Line of Type

Foundry type characters are placed in a **composing stick** to form words and sentences. The most common composing sticks have slots that seat an adjustable knee to exact pica or half-pica positions. Type is always set with the right hand. The stick is held in the left (figure 2.8).

Begin by adjusting the knee to the desired line length and placing a piece of line-spacing material in the stick. The first character of the first word is always seated against the knee of the composing stick, nick up. All other characters and spaces are set in order after this first character. The thumb of your left hand applies pressure against the last character set to keep the line from falling out of the stick.

When all characters have been set, it is necessary to fill out the remaining gap at the end of the line. The line must be held snugly in place within the preset line length. This is accomplished by filling the gap with spacing material. If the gap is large, begin with em quads or 2-ems until only a small space is left. Then select combinations of spacing to fill out the line perfectly. Ideally, the last space will slide in place with only slight resistance, and the entire composing stick can be turned upside down without the line falling out. This process of making the line tight in the stick is called **quadding out.** To set another line of type, insert a piece of line-spacing material and repeat the techniques used for the first line. The amount of line-spacing material added between individual lines of type determines the leading between the two lines.

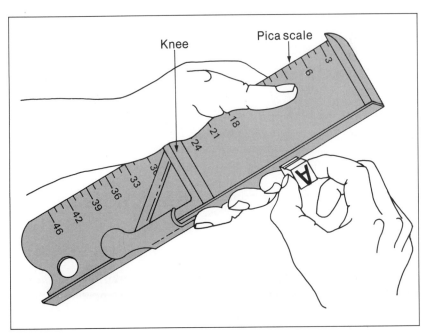

Figure 2.8. Example of a composing stick When using a composing stick, hold the stick in your left hand and place the first character, nick up, against the knee. Always compose from left to right.

Since cast characters are smaller than the type body, it is possible to set type with no leading without the letters from one line touching letters on the line below. Type which has been set with no additional leading between lines is referred to as "set solid."

Centering a Line of Type. The printer frequently wants to reproduce a series of centered lines, one over the other. To do this, set the entire first line in the stick against the knee. Quad the line out by placing equal amounts of spacing material on each side of the line.

Straight Composition. Straight composition or **justification** is the process of setting type so that both the left and the right margins form a straight line (figure 2.9). Hand-set straight composition involves setting each line of type against the knee of the composing stick, determining the amount of space left at the end of the line, and then dividing this space equally between the words in the line. Spacing material from the case is inserted between words in the line so that the words are separated from each other by a nearly equal amount and the line is tight in the composing stick.

Storing the Form. The process of composition creates what printers call a form. A **form** is the grouping of cast characters, symbols, and spaces that makes up a job or complete segment of a job (such as one page to be printed in a book). Composed forms are stored in shallow metal trays called galleys.

Proofing Techniques

Once set, hot type composition is difficult to read because the characters are cast in reverse. A sample print of type composition is called a **proof.** Printers check for typesetting

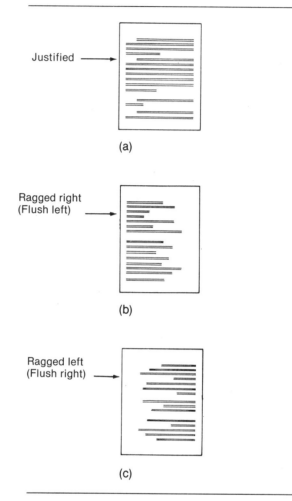

Figure 2.9. Examples of three styles of composition Justified composition is set flush left and flush right (a). Copy can also be set ragged right (flush left) (b), or ragged left (flush right) (c).

errors by "proofing," which means comparing composed copy to the rough or manuscript copy provided by the customer. Most companies employ proofreaders to proof copy for errors. Over the past century a collection of special proofreader's marks or notes have been developed to communicate to the printer what corrections to make on the proof (figure 2.10).

Galley Proofs. A galley proof is "pulled" on a device called a galley proof press. The name comes from the fact that the distance from the bed of the press to the roller that passes over the form is type-high plus the thickness of the metal base of a printer's metal galley. The thickness of a composing stick base matches the thickness of a galley (0.050 inch).

The galley press is designed so that during composition the printer merely places the composing stick or a galley filled with forms on the bed, inks the type with a brayer, sets the paper on the form, and pulls the roller over the paper. Galley proofs are typically delivered to the printing customer before the job goes to press.

Reproduction Proofs. Reproduction proofs are high-quality proofs made on a reproduction proof press (figure 2.11). There are primarily three considerations when pulling a reproduction proof: A precision press, quality type forms, and a good ink and paper combination.

Because they are designed to be photographed, reproduction proofs must be pulled from perfect pieces of type. Many companies reserve special fonts of foundry type to be used exclusively for "repro" proofs.

⊗	Defective letter	⊙	Colon
⊕	Push down space	*bf*	Boldface
#	Make paragraph	*9*	Turn over
⅃	Take out (delete)	⊢M⊣	Two-em dash
∧	Insert at this point	⊢M⊣	One-em dash
□	Em-quad space	//	Space evenly
⊏	Move over	#	Insert space
⌒	Close up entirely	‖	Straighten lines
⹀	Hyphen	⊙	Period
∨	Quotation	∧	Comma
∨	Apostrophe	*no* #	No paragraph
⅋	Semicolon	*lig*	Ligature
wf	Wrong-font letter	⌣	Less space
stet	Let it stand	*out-see copy*	Out—see copy
tr	Transpose	*spell out*	Spell out
⊘	Verify	*caps*	Capitals
lc	Lowercase letter	*sc*	Small capitals
ital	Italic	*rom*	Roman letter

Figure 2.10. Examples of commonly used proofreader's marks Proofreader's marks are used to indicate on proof sheets corrections that must be made in type.

Machine Composition of Hot Type

It probably wasn't long after the pages of Gutenberg's first Bible were dry that printers began thinking of ways to improve the speed of hand-set composition. Many ideas were tried even to the point of suspending a composing stick around the printer's neck so type could be set with both hands.

Machine hot type composition is a refinement of the hand-set foundry type concept. Instead of individual pieces of raised type, matrices (dies) are placed together to generate the words and sentences. Molten type metal is then forced into the matrices to form the raised printing surface. When the metal cools to form a solid cast character, each matrix is returned to a storage system to be used again. Most machines use a keyboard (like a typewriter) to control the position of each matrix. After the type has been used, it

Figure 2.11. A reproduction proof press
Courtesy of Vandersons Corporation, Chicago

can be melted and returned to the machine to be reused.

Line-Casting Machines.   On July 3, 1886, the first truly automatic typesetting machine was demonstrated in the composing room of the *New York Tribune.* The device was designed by Ottmar Mergenthaler. His invention, the Linotype machine, has been called one of the ten greatest in the history of the human race (figure 2.12).

The success of the Linotype is based on the concept of a recirculating matrix that is continually reused in the machine. The Linotype performs the following four basic operations with the matrices:

1. Matrices and spacebands are activated by keyboard control;

2. The line is justified;

3. The slug is cast;

4. Each matrix and spaceband is returned to its storage position.

The Linotype can be, and probably has been, set up to do nearly every typesetting function in almost every language.

A second line-casting machine (although not completely automatic) was the Ludlow, named after its inventor, Washington I. Ludlow. The device was designed around 1888 and can cast type from 8- through 144-point characters from hand-set matrices.

Character-Casting Machines.   The Monotype system was designed by Tolbert Lanston in 1889 to cast and assemble individual pieces

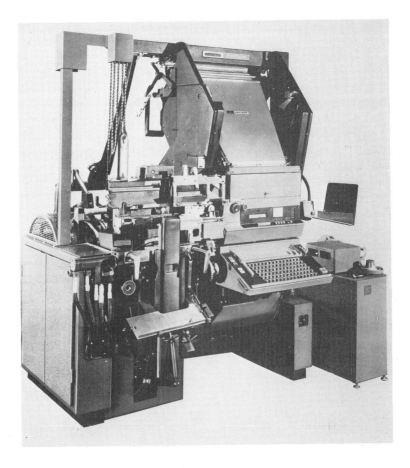

Figure 2.12. A Linotype machine
Courtesy of Mergenthaler Linotype Company

of hot type in a line. The system was made up of two machines: a keyboard device that punched holes into a long paper tape and a casting mechanism that cast type automatically from the information on the tape.

Character sizes up to 36 points and line lengths to 60 picas (90 picas with a special attachment) could be cast on the same machine. For small faces, up to 150 characters per minute could be cast. Because of the machine's speed and versatility, several keyboards could be constantly functioning to feed a single caster.

Relief Printing Plates

After the forms are composed, they must be assembled to make up a printing plate. There are only two main categories of relief plates: primary and duplicate (or secondary).

Primary plates can serve two functions. They can be prepared to be placed directly on the printing press or they can be used only as master plates from which duplicate plates are made. Primary plates can be prepared manually, by assembling composed type forms, or they can be made photomechanically as photoengravings or photopolymer (plastic) plates.

Duplicate plates are made from master forms that are not intended to be used as a printing surface. Copies or duplicates of the master are made for the actual printing operation. This method has several advantages. In extremely long runs, when a single plate would wear out long before the job is finished, duplicate plates are ideal. There are also instances, especially in newspaper production, where the master form is prepared in one location and duplicate plates are shipped to many plants across the country. Stereotyping is a very old process used to produce a duplicate relief plate. **Stereotypes** were once widely used in newspaper printing (figure 2.13). The procedures of preparing the relief plate to print are basically the same for both primary and duplicate plates.

Typical Lockup Procedures

Lockup is the process of securely locking in place a relief plate in some type of clamping frame or holding system, commonly called a **chase.** The following section examines one type of lockup, the chaser lockup procedures for use on a platen press. The procedures for any other press are similar.

Chases come in all sizes. The smallest is perhaps 3 by 5 inches; some chases are as large as 6 feet square. Whatever the size, the requirements remain the same: The chase must be sturdy, must be designed to fit exactly the specific printing press to be used, and must lie perfectly flat on a smooth surface without wobbling.

The process of placing the relief form in the proper position within the chase so the images will be correctly placed on the final printed sheet is called **imposition.**

Lockup is done on a special table called an **imposing stone** or simply a **stone** table (figure 2.14). The name ''stone table'' refers

Figure 2.13. A cast stereotype plate

Figure 2.14. An imposing stone or stone table
Courtesy of SUCO Learning Resources and R. Kampas

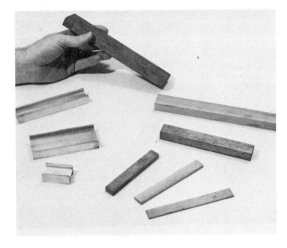

Figure 2.15. Examples of furniture
Courtesy of SUCO Learning Resources and R. Kampas

Figure 2.16. Examples of quoins and quoin keys
Courtesy of SUCO Learning Resources and R. Kampas

to early imposing tables that were made from polished granite. It is extremely important that the surface be perfectly flat. The granite was easily nicked, so it has been almost totally replaced by steel; but the original name remains.

Few relief plates are as large as the inside dimensions of the chase being used. Material called "furniture" (figure 2.15) is used to fill the unused portions.

The locks that hold the form in place in the lockup are called **quoins** (pronounced *coins*). Quoins are opened and closed by **quoin keys** (figure 2.16).

Reglets are thin pieces of wood that are always placed on either side of each quoin in a lockup. A printer never directly lifts a foundry typeform. You must slide it from place to place. To begin lockup, slide the form from the galley to the stone table surface; be sure there is no dust or lint under the form. Always place the chase over the typeform. Never place the chase down first and try to put the form inside it because the foundry type could be

easily spilled. Every chase has a top and a bottom. Always place the top of the chase away from you as you stand at the stone table. Place the chase over the form so that the form will be held slightly above center on the bed of the press when the chase is mounted in the press.

The next step is to block around the form with furniture. After the form has been surrounded, build furniture out to the sides of the chase from the bottom and left sides (figure 2.17). Then place quoins to the top and right of the form and build more furniture out from the form to the top and right sides of the chase (figure 2.18).

If the furniture has been properly placed, reglets should just slide into place on either side of each quoin. It might be necessary to vary combinations of furniture width in order to include the reglets, but they are a necessary addition.

The next step is very important. First insert a quoin key and tighten each quoin un-

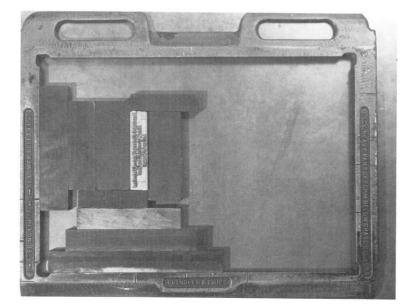

Figure 2.17. Building out the chase to bottom and left side From the blocked form, first build out with furniture to the bottom and the left side of the chase.
Courtesy of SUCO Learning Resources and R. Kampas

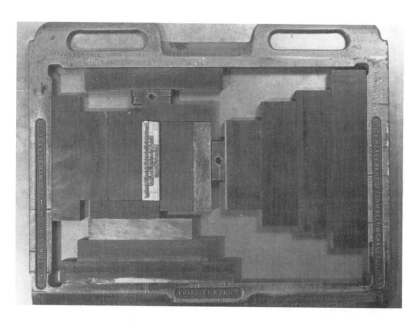

Figure 2.18. Building out the chase to top and right side With the quoins in place, build out the chase to the top and the right side.
Courtesy of SUCO Learning Resources and R. Kampas

til slight pressure is placed on the form and furniture. If any part of the form is not properly seated against the stone, the printing faces will not be on the same plane, and image quality will be difficult to control on the press. Place a planer block gently on the face of the form and sharply tap it several times with a quoin key to jog each character against the table (figure 2.19). Tighten the quoins a bit more, plane the form a second time, and turn the quoins to their outermost position with light resistance. Never force a quoin. It is possible to spring a chase out of flatness or even to damage it beyond repair by too much pressure. Be sure never to plane a form that has been completely tightened. Damaged type will be the only result.

The last step is to check that all parts of the form have been securely clamped in place, with a process called **checking for lift** (figure 2.20). Carefully lift one corner of the chase high enough to insert one part of a quoin key.

With your thumb, gently press down toward the table over all parts of the form. If any portion moves, the lockup is not acceptable and must be corrected. The problem could be because of poor composition techniques when setting the original form, because of faulty positions of furniture around the form, or simply because the quoins are not tight enough. If the lockup passes the test for lift, the job is ready for the press.

Traditional Hand-Fed Platen Press Operations

It is beyond the intent of this book to examine in detail the operation of all the different forms of relief equipment. Our goal is to provide enough information to allow the reader to transfer general understandings to specific operations with the assistance of a classroom

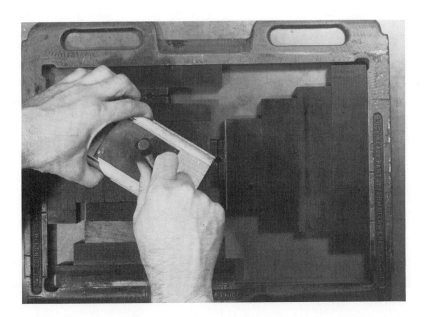

Figure 2.19. Using a planer block Gently place the planer block on the face of the form and tap several times with a quoin key.
Courtesy of SUCO Learning Resources and R. Kampas

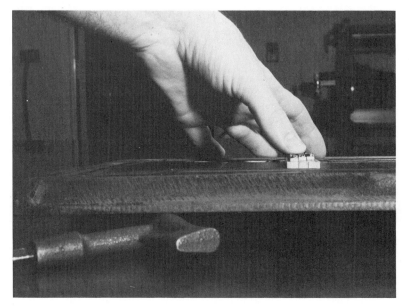

Figure 2.20. Checking for lift Check for lift by placing a quoin key under one edge of the chase and pressing with your thumb over the form.
Courtesy of SUCO Learning Resources and R. Kampas

instructor or a press operation manual. The following sections examine basic platen press techniques. The discussion is applicable to nearly any form of relief press used for letterpress printing.

Letterpress Machines

Letterpress is a common term that spans a wide range of devices and materials in the industry. In terms of machines, letterpress can be divided into three groups:

- Platen presses
- Flat bed cylinder presses
- Rotary presses

At one time the hand-fed platen press was the backbone of every job shop in America. Some hand-fed devices still remain, but, where letterpress is still used, hand-fed machines have been largely replaced by automatic devices.

Figure 2.21 illustrates the basic components of a power-operated hand-fed platen press. The size on any platen press is determined by the inside dimensions of its chase.

The flat bed cylinder press can print larger sheet sizes than the platen press. The image is transferred to only a small portion of the sheet at any given time by the force of the impression cylinder, so much less total pressure is needed and more printing area can be covered (figure 2.22).

Image transfer takes place on a rotary press as the paper passes between an impression and a plate cylinder. Rotary presses generally use cast duplicate plates (electrotypes and stereotypes).

Packing the Hand-Fed Platen Press

The platen press gets its name from the flat rectangular base that pushes the paper against the typeform during the printing operation. **Packing** is the material that is clamped on the

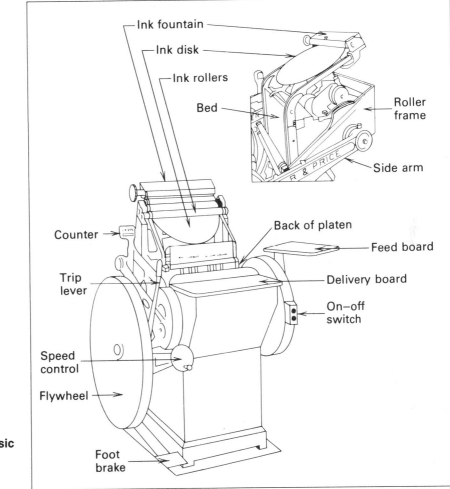

Ink fountain

Ink disk

Ink rollers

Bed

Roller frame

Side arm

Counter

Back of platen

Feed board

Trip lever

Delivery board

On–off switch

Speed control

Flywheel

Foot brake

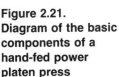

**Figure 2.21.
Diagram of the basic
components of a
hand-fed power
platen press**

platen by the bails (figure 2.23). Packing serves two functions. First, because the distance from the platen to the typeform is not easily altered, packing is the only means of controlling the overall impression (amount of pressure) that the press sheet receives. Second, the top sheet of the packing holds the mechanical fingers (called **gauge pins**) that hold the press sheet in place during the printing operation.

If impression is too heavy, the type will emboss the paper, or punch through it. If impression is too light, a poor image will result. For impression to be perfect, the form must press against the paper hard enough to reproduce characters clearly and sharply, but not so hard that the image can be felt on the back of the printed sheet.

The process of placing packing on the platen is called **dressing the press.** The first sheets to be positioned are the **hanger sheets.** The hanger sheets are cut so that they will

Figure 2.22. Example of a traditional flat bed cylinder press design
Courtesy of Heidelberg Platen Press

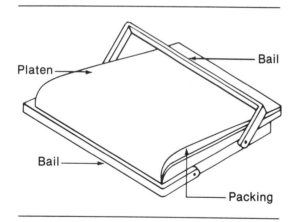

Figure 2.23. Diagram of press platen and bails

extend under the bottom bail but will not reach the top bail of the platen (Fig. 2.24a). Next the oil-treated manila **tympan sheet,** or **drawsheet,** is cut long enough to be held by both

bails and is clamped with the three hanger sheets under the bottom bail (figure 2.24b). The last addition is the pressboard, which is cut to the size of the chase and placed under the last hanger sheet but is not held by either bail (figure 2.24c). The **pressboard** is a heavy, hard paper sheet that gives a firm, flat, accurate base to the packing. With all materials in place, the tympan paper is drawn smoothly under the top bail and is clamped in place.

Inking the Press

Most power platen presses are equipped with an ink fountain that will automatically add ink to the ink disk during a long run. When setting up the press for a short-run job, the ink disk can be easily inked by hand. The procedure is to distribute a small quantity of ink over several areas of the ink disk. Then turn the motor on and allow the press to idle

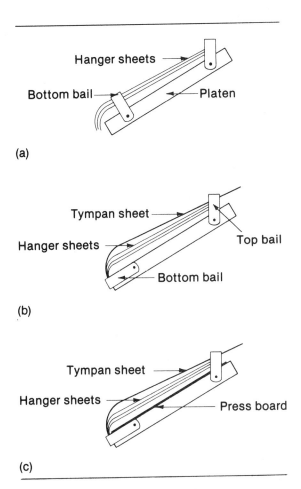

(a)

(b)

(c)

Figure 2.24. Diagram for dressing the press Insert the hanger sheets under the bottom, but not the top, bail (a). Position the tympan paper over the hanger sheets and secure the bottom bail (b). Place a sheet of pressboard under the last hanger sheet (c).

at a slow speed until the ink is evenly distributed over the entire disk.

Novice printers sometimes have difficulties judging the amount of ink to place on the disk. Too little ink will produce a gray,

fuzzy image. However, it is always better to start with too little ink than too much. Additional ink can be added later if needed. Too much ink will plug the type form and result in a dense, blurred image.

Inserting the Chase

After the press has been properly inked and dressed, it is ready to receive the chase. Turn the flywheel by hand until the platen is at its farthest point from the bed and the ink form rollers are in their lowest position. At the stone table, test the form for lift. Then move the chase to a vertical position and wipe the back of the form with a clean rag to remove any dust or lint that might prevent perfect contact against the bed of the press.

While the chase is still in the vertical position, carefully carry it to the press, place the frame against the bed, and lock it in position (figure 2.25). It is important that the chase be firmly held by the clamping device and perfectly seated against the bed's frame.

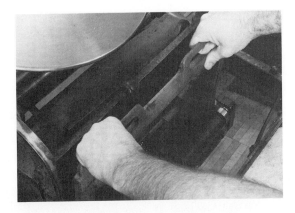

Figure 2.25. Inserting the chase Seat the chase in the bed of the press and lock it in place.
Courtesy of SUCO Learning Resources and R. Kampas

Controlling Image Position on the Press Sheet

Because the surface of the drawsheet on the platen is perfectly flat and smooth, some device is necessary to hold the press sheet in the proper printing position during the printing operation. On automatic presses this is accomplished by mechanical grippers. On hand-fed platen presses gauge pins are used (figure 2.26). The basic problem is to attach the pins to the drawsheet so that each press sheet will be held in the same position and so that the printed image will appear in the correct position on every press sheet.

To determine the proper gauge pin positions, the form must first be printed on the clean drawsheet. This is called **pulling an impression.** The press should be operated by hand for this impression. On the drawsheet, print an image that is clear enough to determine the exact position of the form.

Next it is necessary to draw two lines the proper distance from the printed image on the drawsheet. These two lines represent the position of the top and left edges of the press sheet during the printing operation (figure 2.27).

In order to hold the sheet on these lines, attach gauge pins to the drawsheet. Place two on the lead edge (front edge) and one on the left-hand side (figure 2.27).

When all three gauge pins have been inserted in the tympan, check to ensure that the grippers do not line up with any gauge pins. Then place at least one gripper in a position to catch part of the press sheet (figure 2.28). The grippers prevent the sheet from

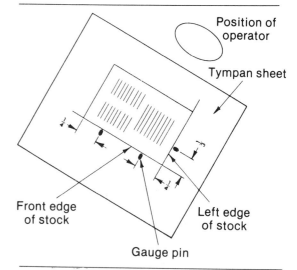

Figure 2.27. Determining the press sheet position Identify the position of the stock on the tympan by drawing lines to the front and left edges of the image. Place two gauge pins on the front edge of the stock at a distance of 1/4 the length of the sheet in from each edge. Place one on the left edge of the stock at a distance of 1/3 the width of the sheet in from the front edge.

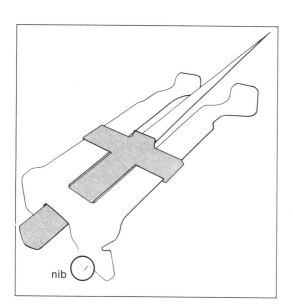

Figure 2.26. Diagram of a gauge pin

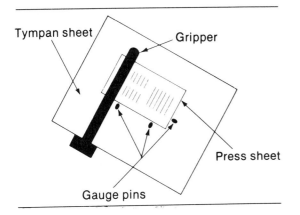

Figure 2.28. Using a gripper A gripper is placed in line with part of the sheet but not touching a gauge pin.

Figure 2.29. Throw-off lever The impression control for most hand-fed platen presses is a throw-off lever located at the side of the machine. Courtesy of SUCO Learning Resources and R. Kampas

moving during the printing operation and keep the sheet from sticking to the inked form as the platen moves back to deliver the printed sheet.

The final gauge pin positions are located after a proof has been taken on an actual press sheet. Small adjustments of one or more pins are always necessary so that the image appears parallel to one edge of the sheet and is in proper printing position. Once the exact locations are defined, push the nibs or feet of the gauge pins into the tympan paper so the gauge pins will not shift during production.

Final Make-Ready

Final make-ready is the process of adjusting impression to obtain the best possible image quality. This is done by printing an impression on a press sheet and examining the image for print quality. On most platen presses, the operator pulls a lever forward to print an impression. Pulling the impression lever may be the origin of the term, "pulling an impression" (figure 2.29).

If the press is properly inked, and the overall image on the press sheet is too light, overall impression can be improved by adding press packing. If the image is light in only certain areas, overlays, underlays, and spotting up must be used. In these procedures, tissue paper is used to build up the areas where impression is low.

Feeding the Press

Several steps can be taken to feed the power platen press smoothly and without difficulty. First, fan the paper to remove any static electricity and then slant the pile to make it easier to lift only one sheet at a time. Place the stack on an easy-to-reach spot of the infeed table. Stand comfortably in front of the platen section within easy reach of both the paper and the platen areas.

The actual feeding, printing, and delivering for a platen press is a two-hand operation, with the right hand feeding a sheet into the gauge pins while the left removes a printed sheet and stacks it on the delivery table. Inexperienced operators should practice feeding stock with the chase removed from the bed and with the press in an off-impression position. Skillful printers can feed some jobs at the rate of 5,000 impressions per hour, but the novice should concentrate on consistency, not on speed.

Cleaning the Press

To clean the press, remove the chase and place it on the stone table to be knocked down or store it for future use. Then wash the ink disk with a rag saturated with wash-up solvent. Next turn the flywheel by hand until the ink rollers move to the top of the bed. With a cloth saturated with wash-up solvent, clean the rollers.

Special Letterpress Applications

Up to this point in the discussion of relief presses, we have discussed only the use of ink to form the image. Several other operations can be performed with a relief press that use no ink but create an image or contribute to the final image design. Some of the possible techniques are creasing, perforating, embossing, die cutting, hot foil stamping, and numbering. These specialty operations help letterpress continue to play an active role in modern printing technology.

Perforating is a common requirement in jobs where portions of the piece are to be removed by the consumer (such as a ticket with a removable stub). In the perforating process, a series of very short slits are cut in the stock, leaving only a small bridge of paper in place. A perforating rule is a strip (generally about 2 points thick) of hardened steel that is made up of a series of equally spaced teeth that are driven through the stock by the motion of the press.

Creasing is a process that uses a solid strip of hardened steel to crush the grain of the paper to create a straight line for folding. The process is also referred to as **scoring.** A ragged or cracked fold can occur when the printer tries to fold a heavy paper or when the job requires that the sheet be folded against the grain of the paper.

Embossing is a process that creates a three-dimensional image by placing a sheet of paper between a concave and convex (sometimes called female and male) set of dies (figure 2.30). The concave die is usually made of 3/16-inch or 1/4-inch brass and is mounted

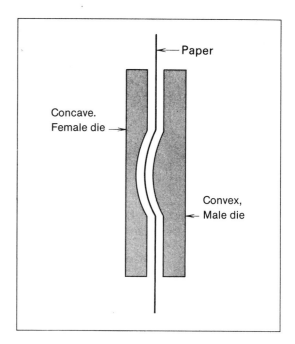

Figure 2.30. Diagram of embossing dies Embossing creates a three-dimensional image between a male and a female set of dies.

on a metal plate so that the topmost surface is type-high. The convex die is usually formed from the concave die, which has been mounted in a chase and placed on the press.

Die cutting is a process that uses a razor-sharp steel rule to cut or punch various shapes (typically irregular) in the press sheets. It is possible for the printer to produce basic die forms, but complicated designs should be prepared by commercial firms that are tooled-up to work with the hard steel rule.

Hot foil stamping is a form of specialty printing that uses the platen press to its full advantage. In this process, the relief type form is locked into a special chase which can be heated while on the press. The ink rollers are removed from the press and replaced with a device that holds a plastic ribbon in front of the type form. The ribbon is available in a variety of metallic colors, including gold and silver. As an impression is made, the heated type plus the pressure of the press during impression causes the metallic color from the ribbon to be transferred to the press sheet. Hot foil stamping is often used on greeting cards, business cards, and book covers.

Numbering is a process used to print a sequential number on each press sheet. The pressure produced during each impression causes the numbering machine to advance to and print each sequential number. Raffle tickets are one example of a job that can be numbered, printed, and perforated with the relief process.

Key Terms

letterpress
hot type
type-high
set width
ligature
news case
California job case
em quad
en quad
slug

lead
furniture
composing stick
quadding out
justification
ragged right
ragged left
form
galley proof
chaser lockup

platen press
press packing
make-ready
impression
perforating
creasing - scoring
embossing
die cutting
hot foil stamping
numbering

Questions for Review

1. Identify the major parts of a piece of foundry type.

2. What dimensions of a piece of foundry type determine set width and point size?

3. What is the point size of an en quad in a 12-point font of foundry type?

4. What thickness are leads and slugs, and what are they used for?

5. What is meant by quadding out?

6. What is the difference among justified, centered, ragged right, and ragged left composition?

7. What is the function of lockup?

8. What does the term imposition describe?

9. What does the expression "dressing the press" mean?

10. How is image position controlled on a platen press?

11. What do the terms creasing, perforating, embossing, die cutting, hot foil stamping, and numbering mean?

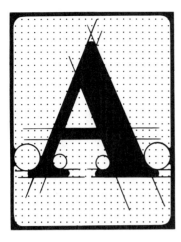

Chapter Three

Design Concerns for Printing

Anecdote to Chapter Three

On March 9, 1972, an unmanned U.S. rocket—*Pioneer 10*—began a half-billion-mile journey to the planet Jupiter and beyond. It was our first effort to leave this solar system. Along for the ride were a robot and a six-by-nine-inch gold-plated aluminum plaque attached to the rocket's antenna supports. The plaque carried a message for any extraterrestrial creatures that might encounter it. The message explained the robot's purpose and who its builders were.

Once the decision had been made to send a message with the rocket, the problem was what to say and how to say it. If there were other creatures like us in the universe, what language would they speak—English, Russian, French? What experiences could we share with creatures that were not from Earth?

The solution was to use lines to draw the basic shape of a man and a woman standing in front of a scale outline of *Pioneer 10*. That could communicate what sort of animal we are and show our size. A code was then devised that used the wavelength of radiation given off by a hydrogen atom (the most common element in the universe). The code described where the rocket came from and how far our sun is from the center of the galaxy.

Traveling at a speed of seven miles a second, it should take *Pioneer 10* more than eighty thousand years to reach the nearest star. The chances that the message will collide with an inhabited planet are slim. But that small grouping of lines and symbols stands as our first attempt to communicate with and confirm the existence of humanity to the rest of the universe.

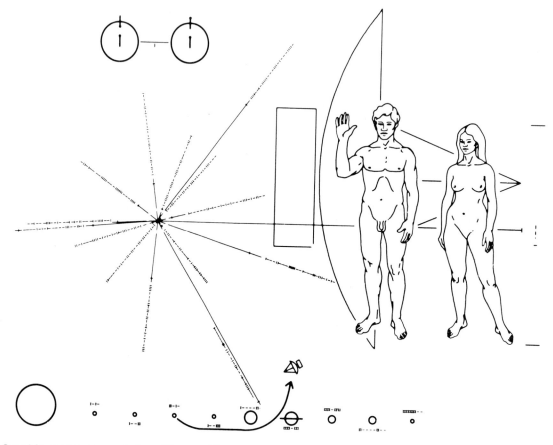

Graphic message carried on Pioneer 10.
Courtesy of NASA

Objectives for Chapter Three

After completing this chapter you will be able to:

– Recognize and explain the design considerations of balance, dominance, proportion, and unity.

– Identify the common elements of alphabet design.
– Define the terms stroke, stress, and serif, and explain how they can be used to identify a typeface.

- Discuss the six basic type styles.
- Measure and copyfit type.
- Describe several manual image generation techniques for art copy.
- Explain the three basic types of color print- ing, and identify tints, surprints, reverses, and bleeds.
- List and explain the design steps used to produce a printed product.

Introduction

As mentioned in Chapter 1, printing is the process of manufacturing multiple copies of graphic images. Image design is the first step in a typical printing job. The purpose of image design is the creation of an image which meets the customer's needs. The purpose of print- ing is the reproduction of this image. The im- age may be created by the customer or by a professional designer. It may be a simple page of text, or it may be a complex color printing job, requiring several colors, scoring, em- bossing, and folding. Whether the job is sim- ple or complex, the printer must provide reproductions that meet the customer's needs, at a price the customer can afford. Thus, to compete, the printer must be efficient and must provide quality work. But efficiency and quality cannot be achieved by the printer alone; the printer and the designer must work together. The designer must create an image that can be printed efficiently, and provide the printer with specifications for the printing job. The printer must understand and satisfy the designer's specifications during printing. It is not necessary for a printer to be a de- signer, but some knowledge of design is im- portant for a printer. This chapter will introduce you to some of the language, tools, and concepts of the designer's art.

Design Considerations

It would be impossible in a book of this nature to give you more than a brief introduction to the graphic design process. Graphic design is an art and a skill, both of which are mastered only after years of study and practice. A graphic designer's art is in imagining and cre- ating a graphic image that will meet a specific need. Artistic decisions about balance, dom- inance, proportion, and unity must be made. The purpose of the printed piece influences design decisions about the type of illustra- tions, paper, and binding it requires. All of these decisions are influenced by the budget for the piece.

A graphic designer's skill is in present- ing the image design to the printer properly, and with clear specifications and directions, so that the printer can reproduce it. More printing jobs are sent back to the printer for rework due to misunderstandings between the designer and the printer than because of printing errors. Type measurement and spec- ification, copyfitting, and the ability to pre- pare both type and illustrations for printing are among the many skills needed by a graphic designer.

Balance

Balance is concerned with the equilibrium and visual weight of the image. The visual weight of an image on the printed sheet depends on the image's size, color, and density in relation to other images on the sheet. Solid areas have more visual weight than outlines. Circular forms generally appear heavier than rectangles. Color can be used to make an image visually heavier or lighter.

Equilibrium refers to the balance of visual weight on either side of a visual center line. Visual equilibrium is often compared to the idea of a balance scale, on which actual weights are placed on each side of a center point, or fulcrum.

There are three kinds of balance:

– Formal balance
– Informal balance
– Subjective balance

Formal balance (figure 3.1a) places identical visual weight on the top, bottom, and both sides of a visual center. Designers often use formal balance in situations that demand dignity. Wedding and other formal invitations often have formal balance. Designs in which images create a sense of visual balance around a visual center because of their size, weight, and position have **informal balance** (figure 3.1b). **Subjective balance** (figure 3.1c), as the name implies, allows the designer complete freedom with the design's equilibrium. The visual fulcrum may be shifted from the center, or the piece may be designed deliberately out of balance.

Dominance

Dominance refers to the main purpose of the printed piece—to communicate a message. If

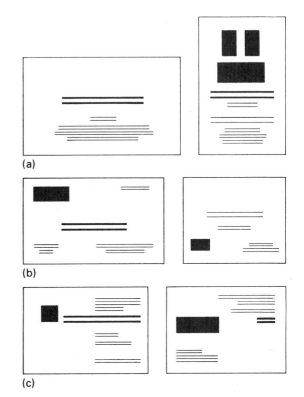

(a)

(b)

(c)

Figure 3.1. Examples of visual balance
Examples of balance shown here are formal (a), informal (b), and subjective (c).

the message did not dominate, the reader would have to search for meaning.

Dominance can be achieved by contrasting the most important parts of the message with the rest of the sheet. Some lines of type can be set larger than others. Boldface, italic, or underlining can help create dominance. Words can be printed in special colors or tints, reversed, or dropped (figure 3.2).

Good control of contrast can also direct the eye to the most important part of the message, even though it might not be the largest part. A prime example of contrast is the use of white space around densely set copy.

Screen tint

Drop

Reverse

Figure 3.2. Examples of a screen tint, a drop, and a reverse

Proportion

Proportion is concerned with size relationships. Both the sheet size and the size and placement of the images on the sheet are important when proportion is considered.

Proportion plays in important part in the selection of margins during page design. In most page designs the two side margins are set equal, the top margin is wider than the sides, and the bottom margin is larger than the other three (figure 3.3).

Unity

The idea of **unity** connects all the design functions. It is concerned with how the entire piece flows together into a complete message. Sev-

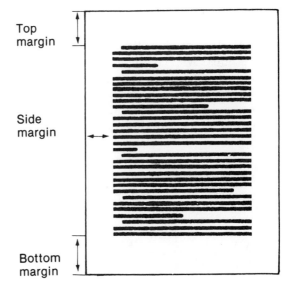

Top margin

Side margin

Bottom margin

Figure 3.3. Margin proportions Margins must appear proportionally correct on the page. The top margin is usually larger than the side margins, and the bottom margin is usually larger than the top margin.

eral ideas should be considered under this label. One is called theme and deals with the selection of appropriate typefaces and art for the message being printed. Letterforms create feelings and moods by their characteristics. We enjoy certain books and magazines without being aware of the contribution of the type, art, and page arrangement, which are independent of what the author has to say.

Alphabet Design

Symbol Characteristics

Graphic designers work with the placement of images and the manipulation of white or open space. The most basic group of images used in graphic design is the twenty-six symbols of our Latin alphabet. Just as each individual person possesses a different and distinctive handwriting style, printers can reproduce the alphabet in many different **typefaces.**

All alphabet characters in every typeface are designed with common elements (figure 3.4). Our alphabet is made up of uppercase (capital) and lowercase (small) characters. Both upper- and lowercase characters are formed along a common base line. The **x-height,** or

body height, of a typeface is the distance from the base line to the top of the lowercase letter *x*. The body height of a typeface can affect how large characters appear on the printed page and how easy they are to read (figure 3.5). For this reason, typefaces with a large body height are often used in children's books. Any part of a letter that extends below the x-height is called a **descender;** letter parts that extend above the x-height are called **ascenders.** Accurate recognition of words depends on the visual impact of the ascenders and descenders (figure 3.6).

Individual typefaces all use the same character symbols with the same common ele-

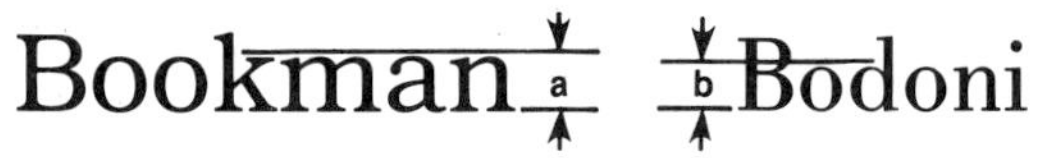

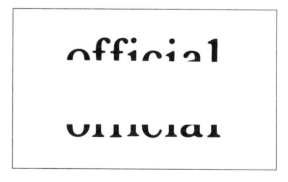

Figure 3.5. Comparison of body heights The body height of the Bookman typeface (a) is higher than that of the Bodoni typeface (b).

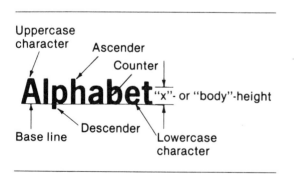

Figure 3.4. Elements of typeface design

Figure 3.6. Recognizing words by their ascenders Cover the top line and ask someone to read the bottom. Then reverse the procedure. Which was easier?

ments. Typeface designers create unique typefaces by varying the stroke, stress, and serif of the alphabet characters. **Stroke variation** refers to the thickness or weight of the lines that form the character (figure 3.7). The stroke might be perfectly uniform, as with the Helvetica typeface, or contrasting line weights may be used, as on characters from the Bodoni typeface. **Stress** refers to the slant of the character. It is easy to visualize stress as the angle of a line that passes through the center of a character (figure 3.8). **Serifs** are the small strokes that project out from the top or bottom of the main letter strokes (figure 3.9). Serifs can be simple square lines placed at right angles to each main stroke; they can vary in thickness; they can be stressed; they can form a **fillet** (an internal curve) between the serif stroke and the main stroke; or they can be rounded instead of squared.

Alphabet Categories

By observing variations in stroke, stress, and serif, it is possible to group all typefaces into the following categories:

- Roman
- Sans serif
- Square serif
- Text
- Script
- Occasional

Roman. The text in this book is set in a Roman typeface. The Roman design is based on the characteristics of letterforms cut into granite by early Roman stonemasons. Iron chisels were used to cut horizontal and vertical lines. Where strokes did not intersect, the tool left a ragged appearance at the end of a line. A cut made with the tool straightened the un-

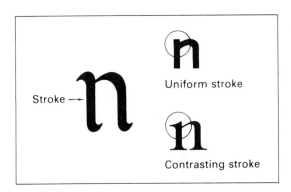

Figure 3.7. Stroke The stroke or thickness of typeface designs varies among designs.

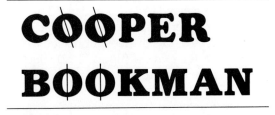

Figure 3.8. Comparison of stress The Bookman face has vertical stress. The *os* in the Cooper typeface are stressed (slanted) from the upper left to the lower right.

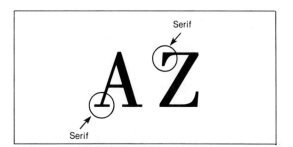

Figure 3.9. Serifs Serifs are often the distinguishing feature between similar typefaces.

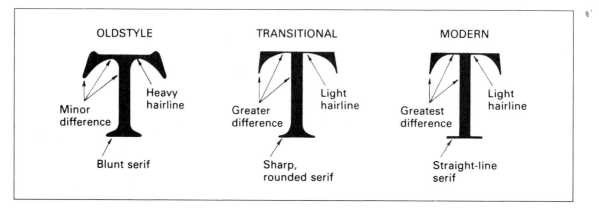

OLDSTYLE   TRANSITIONAL   MODERN

Minor difference — Heavy hairline
Blunt serif

Greater difference — Light hairline
Sharp, rounded serif

Greatest difference — Light hairline
Straight-line serif

Figure 3.10. Roman designs Roman designs can be oldstyle, transitional, or modern.

evenness. The cut was called a serif. Today we define any design that has the main characteristics of stroke variation and serifs as a Roman typeface.

There are three subcategories of the Roman design—oldstyle, transitional, and modern (figure 3.10). An "oldstyle Roman" has little stroke variation. There is usually a slight rounding of the serif base, and fillets fill in the area between main and serif strokes. A "modern Roman" character is formed from thick strokes contrasted with almost hairline strokes. There is generally no rounding or filleting of the serif. Between the two is the "transitional Roman," with greater stroke variation than oldstyle but less variation than a modern Roman face. Most alphabets with a Roman design are considered easy to read. Many books, magazines, and newspapers are set in a Roman typeface.

Sans Serif.   Sans serif means "without serifs" (figure 3.11). Sans serif characters are typically formed with uniform strokes and with perfectly vertical letter stress.

Triumvirate

Avant Garde Gothic

ALDOUS VERTICAL

Figure 3.11. Examples of sans serif typefaces

Square Serif.   Square serif typefaces are sometimes referred to as "Egyptian." The serifs on square serif typefaces are not pointed but appear as blocks or slabs connected to the main character strokes (figure 3.12). Square serif faces are often used in larger point sizes for display type. When set in smaller sizes, they tend to make the printed page appear dense and black.

Text.   Text typefaces attempt to recreate the feeling of the era of medieval scribes (figure

Lubalin Graph Book

Figure 3.12. An example of a square serif typeface

Figure 3.14. An example of all uppercase text Words in a text typeface that are set in all capital letters are almost unreadable. This word is Diane.

Wedding Text

Figure 3.13. An example of a text typeface

Figure 3.15. An example of a script typeface

Comstock

Funky

Figure 3.16. Examples of occasional typefaces

3.13). They are generally used in very formal situations, such as wedding invitations. Text characters are difficult to read and become almost illegible when set all uppercase (figure 3.14).

Script. Script (or cursive) designs give the feeling of handwriting (figure 3.15). As with text, script is not easy to read when set in all uppercase.

Occasional. The last classification, occasional, is really an "other grouping" (figure 3.16). Anything that cannot be classed in one of the first five categories is labeled occasional. Some **typographers** (type designers) use the labels "novelty" or "decorative," but whatever the typeface is called, there are no design limits. Occasional typefaces are usually created to meet a specific design need. Companies often design and copyright a particular letterform so that consumers will associate it with their product or service.

Each **type family** has a unique combination of stroke, stress, and serif. The design of these elements is similar in each letter of the alphabet in the type family. There are thousands of different type families, each identified by a specific name. Each type family can be classified under one of the six type categories. Just as human families are made up of various members—sisters, brothers, cousins, aunts, and so on—who all carry a family resemblance, type families are made up of letterform variations. These variations are all based on and resemble the main type family characteristics of stroke, stress, and serif (figure 3.17). A type family variation may be created by making the characters in the basic family design bold, light, condensed, expanded, extra bold, extra light, italic, or combinations of several variations, such as "extra bold condensed." The word that describes the variation—for example, bold or italic—is added to the type family name to distinguish between each member in the type family. Nine different members of the Century typeface are shown in figure 3.17.

Alphabet point size is measured with the printer's measurement system, explained in Chapter 2. Every member (variation) of a type family can be reproduced in a range of point sizes (figure 3.18). A **font** is a collection of all of the characters of the alphabet, including punctuation marks and symbols, of one type family variation that are the same point size. All of the characters and symbols in a font of 10-point Century Bold, for example, make up a *font* of the Century Bold variation of the Century *type family*, which is one of many type families in the *Roman* type category.

Most commercial typesetting establishments provide type specimen books which display the typefaces that they can typeset. Typically each typeface is shown in a variety of sizes from 6 to 48 or 72 points.

Century Light
Century Light Italic
Century Bold
Century Bold Italic
Century Bold Condensed
Century Bold Extended
Century Textbook
Century Textbook Italic
Century Textbook Bold

Figure 3.17. An example of a type family The family name of this type is Century. Its variations are combinations of different weights—light, bold, regular—and different stress.

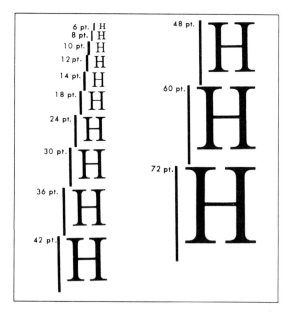

Figure 3.18. Type size Type size is measured in points, shown here from a small letter of 6 points to a display letter of 72 points.
Courtesy of Mackenzie and Harris, Inc., San Francisco

Type Copy

Type copy is all copy that will appear as type in the printed piece. Much of what is printed is type copy, which is "set into type" through phototypesetting, as explained in Chapter 5. Designers use their knowledge of type design and typesetting to select and specify the typefaces and sizes to be used on the printed piece. All type copy is either display type or body copy, depending on its size and function.

Display Type. Display type is typeset in a large point size—typically 14-point type or larger. Uses for display type include newspaper headlines, book chapter headings, and book covers. Most printed advertisements include some display type. The words "Type Copy" in the heading that introduces this section of this chapter are an example of display type.

Transfer Type. Designers often use transfer type to generate display type during the design stage. Transfer type consists of a transparent sheet of transfer paper with a selection of type printed on it. Transfer sheets typically contain a complete alphabet of characters printed in one typeface and size. Characters are printed on the transfer sheet with a carbon-based ink, and can be transferred by rubbing the face of the transfer sheet over the selected character after the character has been positioned on the paper (figure 3.19).

Some design studios have headline machines, with which they can generate display type photographically (figure 3.20). These devices vary in the typefaces and sizes which they can set, but they all operate on the same principle. Individual negatives of type characters are aligned under a light source, light passing through the negative exposes a strip of photographic paper in the exposure unit,

Figure 3.19. Transfer type Many typefaces are available in different sizes in transfer type.

Figure 3.20. An example of a headline device
Courtesy of Kroy, Inc.

the paper strip is developed in photographic chemistry, rinsed, dried, and the type is ready for use.

Body Copy. Copy that makes up the text of the printed piece is considered body copy. The words you are reading right now are an example of body copy. Body copy is generally set in smaller sizes than display copy (14 points or less). Copy in the body of this text is set in 10-point type.

Type Measurement

A designer must specify the sizes in which the display type and body copy are to be typeset. Selection of type size is a design decision, but it is based in part on the amount of space available for type matter on the printed piece. Display type for a business card, for example, probably would be too large if it were set in 72-point type; 24-point type might be more appropriate for this applica-

tion. If this textbook were set in 14-, instead of 10-point type, many more pages would be required to set the same amount of copy, because less characters would fit on each text page.

Type rulers, similar to the one shown in figure 3.21, aid in type specification. Most type rulers offer scales for measuring inches, picas and points. The rule shown in figure 3.21 has additional aids for measuring the thickness of typeset rules and the leading (distance from base line to base line) between lines of type.

Measuring Type Point Size. There is a difference in the actual height of a typeset character and the point size of the character. Recall from our discussion of foundry type that type point size is the size of the foundry type body from the belly to the back side (figure 2.1). Thus the height of a typeset foundry type character is actually less than the point size of the lead body on which it is cast. A small amount of white space remains above and below the character when the character is

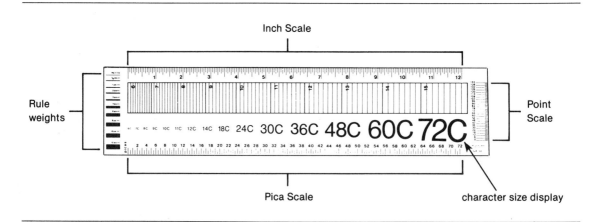

Figure 3.21. A type rule Note, rule has been photographically reduced for use in this text and is not shown in accurate scale.

Courtesy of C-Thru Ruler Company

typeset (figure 3.22). This extra space above and below typeset characters exists whether the characters are generated from foundry type or through phototypesetting. Thus, even if lines of type are set solid (with no extra leading between them), there will always be some space between each line of type (figure 3.23). The amount of space above and below the typeset character depends on the point size in which the character is set. A 48-point character will have more extra space above and below it than will a 24-point character. Measurement is the only way to precisely determine the actual height that a 48-point character from a specific typeface will be when it is typeset. Type measurement in points is taken with the point scale on the type rule by measuring from the baseline to the top of an uppercase character that has been typeset in the required typeface. Type specimen books, supplied by type houses and typesetting equipment manufacturers, can be used for this measurement.

The typeset height of a character in relation to its specified point size can be approximated by applying the "two-thirds rule." On the average, the height of a typeset character will be approximately 2/3 of its specified point size. Applying this rule, an uppercase character specified at 48 points will be approximately 32 points high when typeset (48 points multiplied by 2/3, equals 32 points).

Most type rulers offer a visual means of estimating the typeset size of a character. A display of the uppercase C, typeset in point sizes from 6 to 72, is printed across the face of the rule in figure 3.21. A designer can compare a C in this display to a typeset uppercase character. The number on the rule face printed next to the C that most closely matches the

A small amount of white space remains above and below the character when the character is typeset. Thus, even if lines of type are set solid (with no extra leading between them) there will always be some space between the lines of type.

(a)

Copy set 9/9, Century Book

A small amount of white space remains above and below the character when the character is typeset. Thus, even if lines of type are set solid (with no extra leading between them) there will always be some space between the lines of type.

(b)

Copy set 12/12, Century Book

Figure 3.23. Type set solid The first paragraph above is set solid in 9-point type; the second paragraph is set solid in 12-point type. The amount of extra white space between the lines depends on the point size of the type.

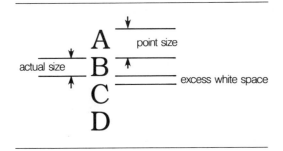

Figure 3.22. Comparison of actual size and point size The characters above are all set in 24-point type with no leading. Their actual size is about 16 points, which leaves about 6 points of excess white space between them.

height of the typeset character gives an approximation of the typeset character's point size.

The length of a typeset line, called the **line measure** or **line length,** and the vertical distance that type occupies on the typeset page, called the **depth,** are both specified in picas. Picas can be converted to points by multiplying the total number of picas by 12. Conversion charts, similar to the one shown in figure 3.24, can be used to make pica-to-point conversions.

Copyfitting

Copyfitting is used to determine the space that one or more lines of type copy will occupy after typesetting. Most type copy is delivered to a designer as typewritten copy with nonproportional characters. Through copyfitting, the designer can predict how much space the typewritten copy will occupy after it is typeset. Without copyfitting, the designer would have no idea how much type would fit in any area on the design.

In Chapter 2 we mentioned that foundry type has proportional set widths. This is also true of most phototypeset type. Thus a 10-point *m* in one typeface, such as Century, will be wider than a 10-point *i* in the same typeface. Not only does the set width of each character within a specific typeface vary, but the set width of the same character varies from typeface to typeface. A 10-point *e* in the Century typeface is likely to have a different set width than a 10-point *e* from the Helvetica typeface. Variations in both the set width and point size of a typeface must be considered during copyfitting.

To copyfit, you must know the number of characters to be typeset; the measure of the typeset line; and the typeface, point size, and

leading to be used. Copyfitting involves three basic steps:

- Counting the typewritten characters
- Determining the number of typeset lines required
- Calculating the depth that the typeset material will occupy

For our example, we will set the copy shown in figure 3.25a, in the Century Book typeface, on a 17-pica measure, in 8-point type with 10-point leading. A designer would specify this as "8/10 x 17."

Step 1: Counting the Typewritten Characters. For small amounts of copy, as might be required for a one-line headline, the total number of characters to be typeset can be determined by simply counting the characters. For larger blocks of body copy, such as a typewritten paragraph or page, it is easier to estimate the total number of characters. The paragraph in figure 3.25a contains ten lines of typewriter copy. Note that the copy is flush left (ragged right), so each of the ten lines is a different length. We must account for these differences in line length by identifying an average line of copy. To do so, find an average length full line of copy and draw a pencil line along the right side of the copy after the last character in the line. Count the number of typewriter characters—all alphabet characters, punctuation, and spaces—to the left of this averaging line to get the average number of characters in a full line of copy.

In figure 3.25a, the averaging line was drawn after the *m* at the end of the fifth line in the copy. The fifth line looked to be about the average line length; some lines were shorter, some longer. There are 54 characters to the left of the averaging line in the fifth

Pica to Point Conversion Chart

Picas	Points 0	1	2	3	4	5	6	7	8	9	10	11
0	0	1	2	3	4	5	6	7	8	9	10	11
1	12	13	14	15	16	17	18	19	20	21	22	23
2	24	25	26	27	28	29	30	31	32	33	34	35
3	36	37	38	39	40	41	42	43	44	45	46	47
4	48	49	50	51	52	53	54	55	56	57	58	59
5	60	61	62	63	64	65	66	67	68	69	70	71
6	72	73	74	75	76	77	78	79	80	81	82	83
7	84	85	86	87	88	89	90	91	92	93	94	95
8	96	97	98	99	100	101	102	103	104	105	106	107
9	108	109	110	111	112	113	114	115	116	117	118	119
10	120	121	122	123	124	125	126	127	128	129	130	131
11	132	133	134	135	136	137	138	139	140	141	142	143
12	144	145	146	147	148	149	150	151	152	153	154	155
13	156	157	158	159	160	161	162	163	164	165	166	167
14	168	169	170	171	172	173	174	175	176	177	178	179
15	180	181	182	183	184	185	186	187	188	189	190	191
16	192	193	194	195	196	197	198	199	200	201	202	203
17	204	205	206	207	208	209	210	211	212	213	214	215
18	216	217	218	219	220	221	222	223	224	225	226	227
19	228	229	230	231	232	233	234	235	236	237	238	239
20	240	241	242	243	244	245	246	247	248	249	250	251
21	252	253	254	255	256	257	258	259	260	261	262	263
22	264	265	266	267	268	269	270	271	272	273	274	275
23	276	277	278	279	280	281	282	283	284	285	286	287
24	288	289	290	291	292	293	294	295	296	297	298	299

Figure 3.24. A pica-to-point conversion chart

Averaging
Line ————→

This is the number of characters that will fit on

a line of type from my typewriter. On my typewriter, I

get ten characters per inch, because I have a "pica"

typewriter. If I had an "elite" typewriter, I'd get

12 characters per inch. Note that all the copy from my

typewriter is flush left (ragged right). When I copyfit

this copy, I must account for the fact that all of the

lines of copy are not the same length. I have to either

count all of the characters in the copy individually, or

I have to average them up.

(a)

This is the number of characters that will fit on
a line of type from my typewriter. On my typewriter,
I get ten characters per inch, because I have a "pica"
typewriter. If I had an "elite" typewriter, I'd get 12
characters per inch. Note that all the copy from my
typewriter is flush left (ragged right). When I copyfit this
copy, I must account for the fact that all of the lines of
copy are not the same length. I have to either count all
of the characters in the copy individually, or I have to
average them up.

(b)

Figure 3.25. Copyfitting typewriter copy The paragraph in (a) contains
approximately 512 typewritten characters. This paragraph is typeset in the
Century Book typeface on a 17-pica line measure in 8/10 (b).

line of copy. The first line of copy is indented, but since it will be typeset as an indented line, we can count it as a full line. The last line of copy is not a full line, so there are only nine full lines of typewritten copy. Thus, there are a total of 486 characters in the full lines to the left of the averaging line (54 characters per line, multiplied by 9 full lines of copy, equals 486 characters). The last line of copy has only 26 characters, including spaces and punctuation. When added to the 486 characters that we have already calculated, this brings the total to 512 characters.

This estimate alone would be good enough for many copyfitting purposes. More precision can be attained by adding the number of characters to the right of the averaging line and subtracting the number of blank spaces at the end of lines that fall a few characters short of the averaging line, but this precision is seldom necessary.

Step 2: Determining the Number of Typeset Lines Required. To determine the number of lines required to set the type, you must know how many characters are to be typeset, the number of characters that will fit on a typeset line, and the leading to be used. In Step 1 we

found that there are approximately 512 characters to be typeset. Our line measure is to be 17 picas. Information about the number of characters that can be typeset per pica is supplied in type specimen books. A character per pica chart for the typeface Century Book is shown in figure 3.26. This chart shows the number of characters per pica that can be typeset in four variations of the Century Book typeface, when set in various sizes from 6 points to 24 points. If we set our copy in Century Book, in 8-point type, approximately 53 characters will fit on a 17-pica long typeset line (3.09 characters per pica, multiplied by 17 picas per line, equals 52.53 characters per line). If we divide the number of characters that can fit on a typeset line (53) into the total characters to be typeset (512), we find that our copy will require 10 typeset lines (512 characters, divided by 53 characters per line, equals 9.66 typeset lines). This is the number of lines our copy will take up, when set in 8-point Century Book, on a 17-pica measure.

Step 3: Calculating the Depth that the Typeset Material Will Occupy. All that remains now is to calculate the depth of the copy. This is done by multiplying the leading for the copy

	Characters Per Pica									
	6	7	8	9	10	11	12	14	18	24
Century Book	4.12	3.53	3.09	2.75	2.47	2.25	2.06	1.77	1.37	1.03
Century Bold	4.09	3.50	3.07	2.73	2.45	2.23	2.04	1.75	1.36	1.02
Century Italic	3.83	3.28	2.87	2.55	2.30	2.09	1.91	1.64	1.28	0.96
Century Bold Italic	3.86	3.31	2.89	2.57	2.31	2.10	1.93	1.65	1.29	0.96

Figure 3.26. Character-per-pica chart for the Century Book typeface

(a)

(b)

Figure 3.27. Two types of art copy Line copy, shown in (a), consists entirely of lines and/or dots. Continuous-tone copy (b) consists of shades from white to black and must be converted to a halftone for printing.

by the number of typeset lines required. In our example, the number of typeset lines required was determined in Step 2 to be 10. The leading to be used is 10-point. Multiplying the leading value (10-point leading) times the number of typeset lines required (10 lines) gives us a copy depth of 100 points. There are 12 points in a pica. Dividing 100 points by 12 gives us a depth for our copy of approximately 8 picas (100 points, divided by 12, equals 8.33). Thus our 512 characters, set in 8-point Century Book, with 10-point leading, on a 17-pica line measure will occupy an area 17 picas wide and approximately 8 picas in depth (figure 3.25b).

Art Copy

In addition to type copy, most printing jobs include art copy. There are two basic types of art copy: line copy and continuous tone copy. **Line copy** (figure 3.27a) is composed entirely of lines or dots. An illustration drawn with technical pens is a good example of line copy. The lines can be drawn in a variety of thicknesses, but all of the lines drawn are the same tone, thus each line is just as dense and black as all the other lines on the drawing. **Continuous-tone copy** consists of images made up of a variety of tones. One common type of continuous-tone copy is a black-and-white photograph, made up of many tones, from white, through grey, to black.

No printing press can print more than one tone in one ink color from a single printing plate. Thus it is not possible to print all of the tones in a continuous-tone photograph as a range of tones from white to black. To print a black-and-white continuous-tone photograph, it must be photographically converted into a halftone. Halftone conversion is explained in detail in Chapter 7. Through halftone conversion, all of the different tones on the original black-and-white photograph are converted to dots on the halftone. The different sizes of these dots gives an illusion of various tones. Many large dots appear on the printed piece as a darker, black area; small dots appear as a lighter, grey area (figure 3.27b).

Manual Image Generation

Hand Techniques. Images for art copy can be created by hand with such instruments as a pen, pencil, or brush. We all understand how to use these devices, but there are some special considerations when drawing for printing production.

The use of any pencil image should be avoided, because graphite does not photograph well. All drawings should be prepared with a pen and black india ink. A variety of devices are designed for hand illustration with

ink. Some are as simple as the traditional ruling pen. Others have interchangeable quill points (figure 3.28). Still others have ink reservoirs and interchangeable floating points. Whatever pen is used, however, the concerns are the same. The lines should be dense, with sharp, uniform edges. It is better to draw illustrations larger than reproduction size and then photographically reduce them than to draw them small and enlarge them. Reduction always sharpens an image; enlargement decreases line quality.

Paper influences the quality of any drawing. Uncoated papers such as newsprint tend to absorb ink rapidly into the paper fibers and give a ragged edge to any inked line. Coated papers generally have a slick, shiny surface that does not absorb ink. The ink dries by evaporation and produces nearly ideal line quality. Most hand-drawn images are drawn on coated stock or on special layout illustration board.

Pressure-Sensitive Materials. Several types of material are designed to transfer an image

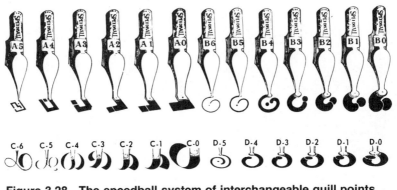

Figure 3.28. The speedball system of interchangeable quill points
Courtesy of Speedball

to illustration board or paper by means of adhesion. One type uses a plastic support sheet that carries a dense image on one side and an adhesive layer on the other. Many special-effect tints or images are available in sheet form (figure 3.29). A large piece of this material can be placed over an inked image, the plastic cut to the image outline, and the unwanted materials removed. The plastic-based image will be nearly permanently affixed if it is then burnished (pressed flat) with a roller or blunt instrument. Sheet pressure-sensitive materials should always be cut in the center of any inked image lines (figure 3.30).

Adhesive alphabets can be purchased on large acetate sheets. Individual letters will adhere to nearly any surface. Letter spacing of characters depends on the designer's visual judgment.

Other forms of adhesive image generation material are available on rolls, like cellophane tape, with an image affixed to the base side. The roll form is typically used to create decorative borders, but tapes of varying widths can be used to generate black lines on any layout (figure 3.31).

Prepared Images.   For a small subscription fee, printers can purchase books of camera-ready drawings, supplied on a monthly basis. With the fee comes certification that the designs are copyright-free to the printer. Most prepared-image or **Clip-Art** services are nationwide organizations that mass produce printed illustrations on coated papers. Figures are usually provided in several different sizes, so enlargements or reductions are not necessary.

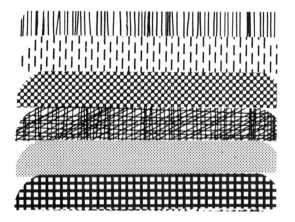

Figure 3.29. Pressure-sensitive images and tints These are some examples of special-effect images or tints that are available as pressure-sensitive materials.

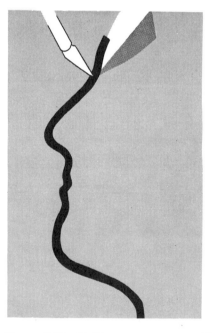

Figure 3.30. Cutting pressure-sensitive materials The proper place to cut pressure-sensitive materials is in the center of the inked image line.

Figure 3.31. Pressure-sensitive tape Examples of pressure-sensitive images that are available on rolls include rules and borders.

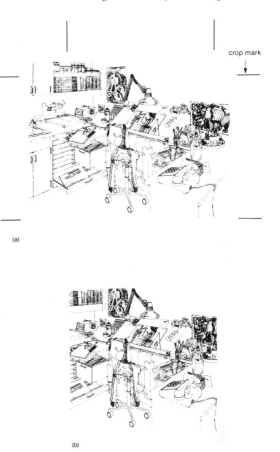

crop mark

(a)

(b)

Figure 3.32. Crop marks Crop marks are used to indicate the part of the photograph to be printed (a). The cropped photograph is shown in (b).

Cropping

It is quite possible that all of the image on an original photograph or illustration is not wanted on the printed reproduction. **Crop marks** are used to indicate the part of the original art that is to be reproduced on the printed sheet. An example of a cropped original and the final image reproduction is shown in figure 3.32. Crop marks are never drawn directly on the original. Instead, the original is mounted on a separate board, and the crop marks are placed on the board near the top and bottom and to the sides of the original or are marked on a tissue overlay. Most designers also specify the measurement in inches between the crop marks. It is important that crop marks be dense black, so that they will reproduce on the film negative. For this reason, crop marks are typically made with a grease pencil, such as a china marker. Once recorded on the negative, they provide a reference during stripping (Chapter 10) for positioning of the cropped image.

Scaling Art

It is often necessary to enlarge or reduce the size of display type, illustrations, or photographs to fit a certain space on the design. Enlargements and reproductions are typically produced photographically, either as negatives which are assembled with the type image during stripping, or as paper positives which can be pasted up on a mechanical (Chapter 4). The industry refers to these paper positives as **photostats,** or simply **stats.** The production of stats with the diffusion transfer process is discussed in Chapter 6.

Designers use a **proportion scale** to determine and specify the actual percentage that the image should be enlarged or reduced. The camera operator sets the camera to reproduce the image at the specified percentage of its original size. To use a proportion scale, first measure an existing dimension (called the original size) of the copy to be enlarged or reduced, and then determine the desired new dimension.

Consider the example in figure 3.33. The line length is 5 inches but must be reduced to fit an area on the copy that is only 3 1/2 inches long. Locate the original size, 5 inches, on the inside scale of the proportion scale. Then find the desired final measurement, 3 1/2 inches, on the outside scale. Rotate the wheel until the inside measurement (5) lines up with the outside measurement (3 1/2). With the original and final dimensions in line, read the percentage size difference, 71, at the arrow pointer. A stat must be made at a 71% reduction to reproduce this image in the correct length.

All scaling is based on 100% being considered the original size. If the example in figure 3.33 was copied at 100%, then the stat image would be 5 inches long. A 50% reduction would give an image 2 1/2 inches long. A 200% enlargement would be 10 inches long.

Camera enlargements or reductions alter the size of the copy in two directions, not just in the calculated one. Figure 3.34 illustrates the **diagonal line method** of predicting two-dimensional size changes. Affix to a drawing board the art work to be scaled, tape a sheet of tracing paper in place over the copy, and draw a rectangular box around the edges of the image. Draw a diagonal line from the

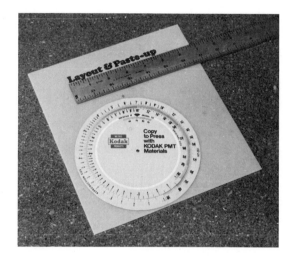

Figure 3.33. Using a proportion scale This job requires a size change from 5 inches to 3 1/2 inches. A 71% reduction is calculated by lining the original width of 5 on the inside scale with the final size of 3 1/2 on the outside scale.

lower left corner through the upper right corner and continue it across the page. Measure the desired width along the base of the first rectangle, and from that point draw a vertical line until it intersects the diagonal line. The place where the diagonal and vertical lines meet defines the new height and width of the scaled copy. The same information can be obtained by reading the proportional scale.

Use of Color

With rare exceptions (such as embossing), all printing is color reproduction—because printers count black as a color. When the term "color printing" is used, however, the printer is generally referring to multiple colors on the same sheet. Printing with more than one color is expensive because each additional color re-

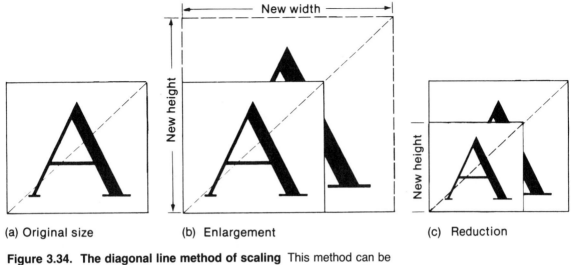

(a) Original size (b) Enlargement (c) Reduction

Figure 3.34. The diagonal line method of scaling This method can be used to predict the dimensions of the original (a) after enlargement (b) or reduction (c).

quires an additional printing plate and an additional impression on the printing press. Ink and paper considerations (Chapter 8) also affect the cost of color printing.

Printers classify color printing in the following three groups:

- Fake color
- Flat color
- Process color

Fake Color. A one-color reproduction printed on a colored sheet is known as **fake color.** Any color of ink or sheet combination could be used, but the sheet must carry only one layer of ink.

Flat (or Match) Color. Inks the printer purchases or mixes for a specific job are called **flat colors.** Flat colors can be specified from

a color-matching system or hand mixed to match a color submitted by the designer. A color-matching system generally employs a swatchbook with samples of ink colors printed on both coated and uncoated papers. All colors are numbered, and mixing formulas are included. If the designer specifies a particular swatchbook number, the printer can easily mix the required color. Hand mixing of colors to match a color sample is a more difficult trial-and-error process.

Process Color. The term **process color** refers to the use of four specific colors: process blue (cyan), process red (magenta), process yellow, and black. **Four-color process printing** is used to reproduce continuous-tone color images, such as color photographs. Chapter 9 deals with the use of four-color process printing to create the illusion of nearly any color on the printed sheet.

Tints, Surprints, Reverses, and Bleeds

An interesting technique for creating the illusion of different tones or color hues with a single color is the use of a **screen tint**. Tints break up solid areas into uniform series of dots. The size of the dot is specified as a percentage of the paper area that is covered with ink. A 60% screen tint places dots over 60% of the image area (figure 3.35).

Both **surprints** (often called **overprints**) and **reverses** are images positioned over another design. Surprints are reproduced as solids; reverses, as open areas. Both techniques are often used to set words over a picture or illustration. It is important to consider the density of the background area when deciding whether to use a reverse or a surprint (figure 3.35). A surprint will not show up well in a dark background, and a reverse will not show up well in a light background.

A common printing design is to "bleed" an image off the edge of the page. A **bleed** is a design that extends an image to the edge of the printed sheet. The technique is not difficult, but it is often confusing to novice designers. During printing, the bleed edge of an image is actually printed beyond the dimensions of the trim size for the printed sheet. When the printed sheets are trimmed to final size, the part of the bleed that was printed beyond the trim sheet size is cut away, leaving the image printed to the edge of the trimmed sheet (figure 3.36).

Image Positions on the Printing Plate

Most presses ink printing plates by means of ink rollers. The rollers pick up ink from a reservoir system, pass over the plate to ink the image areas, then return to the reservoir to re-ink. Halftone images require more ink during printing than does type copy. If several halftone images are placed so that they fall in a line at right angles to the ink rollers, it is difficult to obtain uniform ink coverage across the printed sheet (figure 3.37). One common result of improper image placement, particularly on small presses, is **ink depletion.** As the ink roller revolves over the sheet, it has enough ink to properly print the first halftone on the lead edge of the sheet, but not enough ink to print the remaining images located in line with the halftone on the tail edge of the

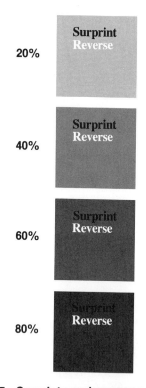

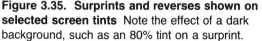

Figure 3.35. Surprints and reverses shown on selected screen tints Note the effect of a dark background, such as an 80% tint on a surprint.

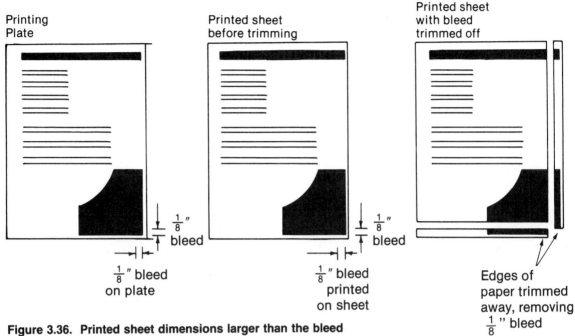

Figure 3.36. **Printed sheet dimensions larger than the bleed image** When a bleed is required, the image is printed beyond the trim size and then trimmed.

sheet. That is, the ink becomes depleted from the ink rollers faster than it can be replaced from the ink reservoir. The result is good ink coverage on the lead edge of the sheet, but poor ink coverage on the tail edge of the sheet. Correct image position during the design stage can balance ink distribution needs to avoid ink depletion (figure 3.38).

Design Steps

The basic task is to produce an image that will communicate the desired message to the intended audience. The steps that graphic artists have traditionally followed to accomplish this task consist of the following:

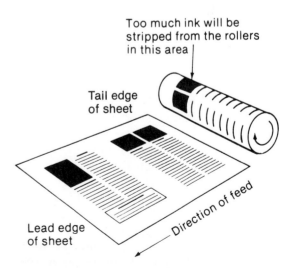

Figure 3.37. **Image position that can result in ink depletion.**

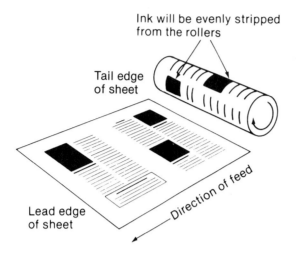

Ink will be evenly stripped
from the rollers

Tail edge
of sheet

Lead edge
of sheet

Direction of feed

**Figure 3.38. Image position that will help
avoid ink depletion.**

1. Preparing a set of thumbnail sketches
2. Preparing rough layouts based on the preliminary thumbnail sketches
3. Preparing a comprehensive layout
4. Preparing a final layout or mechanical

To illustrate this process, let's follow each step on a typical printing assignment.

Assume that we have been contracted to produce an announcement of a local printing association meeting. There will be a dinner followed by a presentation entitled "Role of the Artist." The announcement is to be a self-contained mailer. The body copy and meal information have been provided (figure 3.39). Our task is to design a mailer that will attract attention, communicate the feeling of the title of the presentation, and carry all the necessary information.

Thumbnails

The process begins with a series of **thumbnail sketches** (small, quick pencil renderings that show the arrangement of type, line drawings, and white space). They are in proportion to, but always smaller than, reproduction size. Thumbnails do not necessarily carry the actual wording that will appear on the final product. Penciled lines are frequently used to indicate type placement. A straightedge is rarely used, and the designer concentrates only on the overall visual effect of the printed piece.

Figure 3.40 shows two of the many thumbnails produced for this job. It was decided to prepare a cover that showed an artist at a drawing board, with the title of the presentation carried on the board. Notice that these examples meet the criteria for thumbnails: they are in proportion to, but smaller than, final size; they are quick sketches; and they do not carry all of the message. From the thumbnails the designer selects the one that he or she thinks will best meet the assignment. For this job, figure 3.40b was chosen.

Roughs

A **rough layout** is a detailed expansion of the thumbnail sketch that carries all the necessary printing information. Any printer should be able to produce the final reproduction from the directions on the rough. The rough layout is generally the same size as the final product, contains the actual wording (if there is a great deal of body copy, typewritten copy is sometimes attached and the rough indicates where it is to be placed after typesetting), margin specifications, image placement for any line drawings or halftone photographs, and type specifications (typefaces and sizes to be used).

TYPE AND ILLUSTRATION SPECIFICATIONS
for "Role of the Artist" mailer (inside)

1. ROLE OF THE <u>18 pt. Spartan Book, caps (all capitals)</u>
2. Artist <u>30 pt. Brush, C & C.L. (caps and lowercase)</u>
3. Body composition <u>Bodoni & Bodoni Bold, 9 pt.</u>

About the speaker: (Bold) Art's formal preparation in advertising design began with a year at Pratt Institute in Brooklyn. He left Pratt to enter the army in 1952. After completing intelligence school at Fort Riley, he went to Germany with the Second Armored Division. Completing his hitch with the army in 1955, he did design drafting for Oneida Products. In 1956 Art entered Mohawk Valley Technical Institute to further his education in the area of design. He received his AAS degree in 1958 at the top of his class. While attending MVTI, Art completed his work experience program at Canterbury Press and was immediately hired by the company. Concentrating mainly in the art area, he also gained experience in single- and multicolor stripping, specification and production scheduling, estimating and full-service sales. He also became involved in the first phototypesetting establishments in Central New York. While at Canterbury Press Art increased his education by receiving a certificate in Commercial Art and Illustration from the Famous Artist School.

In 1966 Art accepted a position as an artist with Concord Studios, Ltd., of Syracuse—a subsidiary of Midstate Printing Corp. His present responsibilities include the design and preparation of commercial brochures and catalogs.

Supported by his charming wife Sheila, he became active in the Syracuse Club in 1966 and has served as rough proofs editor, table host, treasurer, second and first vice president, president, and currently is chairman of the board of governors.

We are pleased to have a talented, local craftsman make a presentation about a controversial and misunderstood area of our business.

Come witness a verbal and visual presentation of the <u>ROLE OF THE ARTIST in the printing industry. (Bold)</u>

4. EXCELLENT LADIES PROGRAM 9 pt. Bodoni Bold
5. at <u>Raphaels Restaurant,</u> (Bold) Tuesday, February <u>19, 1974</u>
State Fair Boulevard, Lakeland, New York
6. <u>COCKTAILS 6:30</u>　　　　　DINNER 7:30 (Bold)
7. Hot Buffet Dinner—only <u>$5.00</u> (Bold)—includes tax and gratuity
Reservations Please: To your key man or Gene Cook (472–7815)
8. Support Graphic Arts Education
Cover by H. Rose—Student, Oswego State University
9. Halftone of artist
10. Speaker (Bold, C & L.C.)
ART LANGE (Bold, Caps)
11. 20% background tint

Figure 3.39. Copy for "Role of the Artist" mailer Type and illustration specifications for use by the printer are marked on the copy.

(a)　　　　　　　　**(b)**

Figure 3.40. Two thumbnail sketches for "Role of the Artist"

In addition, if any special operations, such as folding, trimming, or perforating, are to be performed, they are so indicated. The drawing is done in pencil and may be sketched, but it must be an accurate representation of the final printed sheet.

In our example several decisions were made after the thumbnail sketch was produced. It was judged to be most economical to produce the job as a single sheet folded and stapled, with one side, after the fold, left blank for the mailing address. The final trim size was to be 4 1/2 x 6 1/4 inches. The rough layout for the cover of this job, therefore, was constructed so the image would fill only half of one side of the press sheet (figure 3.41a).

To produce the rough layout, the outline

of the paper size to be run through the press was first placed on a clean sheet of white drawing paper. This outline forms the **paper lines.** It was decided to bleed the image off three edges of the sheet, so **trim lines** were drawn to represent where the press sheets would be trimmed after the job was printed. The image is generally allowed to bleed into the trim area from 1/16 to 1/8 inch. A line was also drawn to indicate the position for the final fold. The fold line is important for this type of job because it becomes the top image limit for the cover. After all guidelines were positioned, the thumbnail idea was transferred in detail to the rough. The wording was actually placed on the drawing. Although it is not necessary to duplicate the type styles to be used, it is important that the style and size specifications be included. The complexity of this cover warranted the use of numbers to indicate printing instructions and type specifications on a second sheet (figure 3.41b).

All image positions, whether type or illustrations, should be accurately indicated. In the case of photographs, the image is generally sketched in place, and the original is placed in a work envelope with the rough.

In addition to the rough layout, the graphic designer prepares a detailed work sheet for the job (figure 3.42). A work sheet should contain any information not specifically used for detail images on the rough but necessary for the job to be printed.

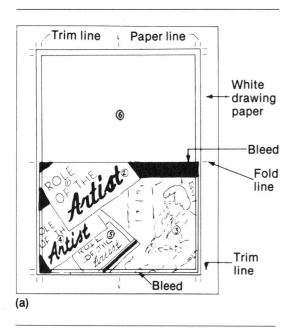

(a)

TYPE AND ILLUSTRATION SPECIFICATIONS for "Role of the Artist" mailer

1. Role of the *36 pt. Spartan Book*
2. Artist *60 pt. Brush*
3. Two-tone posterization of artist
4. Lettering to represent rough layout
5. Lettering to represent thumbnail layout
6. Space for the address

(b)

Figure 3.41. The rough layout for "Role of the Artist" mailer

Comprehensives

In most instances the customer approves the rough, and the design immediately goes into production. In some cases, however, such as for expensive multicolor jobs, the customer expects to see a comprehensive layout. Most printing customers have had little experience

WORK SHEET FOR "Role of the Artist" mailer

1. Type of stock: Warren, Cameo Dull Cover
2. Weight of stock: Cover 80
3. Color of stock: White
4. Finish of stock: C2S (coated two sides)
5. Basic sheet size: 20 × 26
6. Number of basic size sheets needed: 500
7. Process of production: Offset
8. Finish trim size: 5 5/8 × 7 1/2
9. Ink color: Black
10. Length of run: 4,500
11. Imposition: 1-up
12. Finishing techniques: Score for fold
13. Special processing: Trim

(a)

Figure 3.42. Job work sheet for "Role of the Artist" mailer The work sheet contains all printing and materials specifications.

interpreting roughs and are unable to visualize the final product from them.

A **comprehensive** is an artist's rendering that attempts to duplicate the appearance of the final product. It is drawn to final size, it carries no guidelines or printing instructions, display type is hand lettered or shown with transfer type that resembles the actual type styles and sizes, and any illustrations are drawn in place. Figure 3.43 shows the comprehensives for the cover and the text of the printing association's meeting.

Many techniques are used to indicate detailed body copy. In figure 3.43, a razor blade was used to shave a pencil point to the x-height of the type, the line spacing was accurately measured, and the lines were drawn with the chiseled pencil to represent body composition. With this method the customer gets an impression of the type weight on the page, yet the artist does not have to spend time hand lettering a great deal of body copy.

(b)

Figure 3.43. Comprehensive layouts for "Role of the Artist" mailer The cover layout is illustrated in (a). The text copy comprehensive is illustrated in (b).

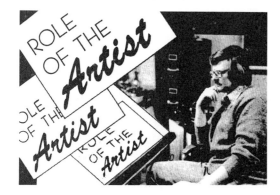

Figure 3.44. Camera-ready copy for "Role of the Artist" mailer

Final Layout

If the job is to be produced by hand-set foundry type or by some form of machine hot type composition method, the type form is prepared directly from the rough layout.

If the printing process relies on printing plates produced from film negatives, one or more mechanicals must be produced. The **mechanical** is a camera-ready layout, made from detailed information on the rough. A negative made from the mechanical is used to make the actual printing image. Figure 3.44 shows the camera-ready layout for the sample job. Chapter 4 deals with the process of preparing mechanicals.

Dummy

Jobs that are made up of signatures formed by folding one or several press sheets can be very confusing in the final layout stage. To simplify the process, a **dummy** is usually prepared. A blank press sheet that is identical in size to the paper that will be used for the job

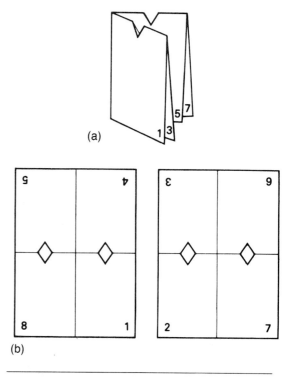

(a)

(b)

Figure 3.45. Preparing the dummy The press sheet is folded, numbered, and notched at the top (a). The opened sheet, which is numbered on the front and back, is a guide to correct position of the pages (b).

is folded in the order that it will be folded after the press run. The sequence of folds is important and will influence page placement.

Without trimming the folded sheet, the printer numbers each page and cuts a notch through the top of the folds. When the dummy is unfolded, the notch indicates the head of each page and the pages appear in their proper order for the final layout. Figure 3.45 illustrates this process.

Key Terms

x-height
descender
ascender
stress
stroke
serif
fillet
type style
sans serif typeface
square serif typeface
text typeface
Roman typeface
script typeface
occasional typeface

type style
type family
type series
type font
pica
point
display type
body copy
transfer type
copyfitting
line copy
continuous-tone copy
cropping
halftone

scaling
proportion scale
fake, flat, and process color
screen tint
surprint
reverse
bleed
thumbnail
rough
comprehensive
mechanical
dummy

Questions for Review

1. Define x-height, ascenders, and descenders.

2. What are the six typeface categories?

3. What can be done to a type family to produce a variation of the family?

4. Define the term "font."

5. What is the difference between display type and body copy?

6. How many points are there in 2 picas? How many picas are there in 252 points?

7. Why is a typeset character actually smaller than its specified point size?

8. Copyfit 15 lines of typewritten copy containing 840 words. The copy is to be set in 10-point Helvetica, which will average 2.62 characters per pica. The copy is to be set 10/12 on a 20-pica line measure.

9. Using a proportion scale, give the percentage reduction needed to reduce a 5 1/2″ image to 3 1/2″.

10. Describe the difference between halftone and line copy.

11. What is the difference between fake, flat, and process color?

12. Describe a screen tint, a surprint, a reverse, and a bleed.

13. Thumbnails, roughs, comprehensives, mechanicals, and dummys are all used during image design. Discuss the purpose and preparation of each.

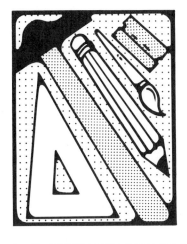

Chapter Four

Layout and Paste-up

Anecdote to Chapter Four

Before World War II, almost all printing was done with the letterpress process, utilizing cast metal type. The growth of offset lithography after World War II forced the development of

Paste-up artists working at a layout board
Courtesy of Connie Kindred

alternative methods of setting type. No longer were all images printed directly from raised metal type. Instead, most images to be printed were arranged on a flat paper surface and photographed to produce a film negative. The negative was used to produce a printing plate. The name "hot type composition" had been used to describe cast type images, so it seemed natural to give the name "cold type composition" to this new photographic method of producing images.

Cold type composition has several advantages over hot type. A major advantage is that artists have far more flexibility and ease in producing images for printing. Almost any two-dimensional image can be photographed and printed. In addition, cold type images can be enlarged, reduced, or cropped without being recast. A second advantage of cold type is the speed with which images can be produced. The step of casting the image onto a type-high lead body is completely eliminated with cold type. Finally, cold type made it possible for printers to greatly expand their type libraries. Heavy type cases and banks of type cabinets were replaced by computers that could reproduce hundreds of different typefaces at speeds impossible to achieve with cast type.

One early method of producing cold type images was to compose hot type images and pull reproduction proofs on a special proof press that produced exceptionally high-quality images. The reproduction proofs were then pasted up on a piece of paper and photographed to produce the cold type image. As computer-based photocomposition systems became available, the reproduction proof process was replaced with more direct methods of cold type image generation.

With the development of cold type composition came a new occupation in the printing industry, that of paste-up artist. The paste-up artist is responsible for arranging cold type images into their proper printing position and pasting them up on a flat surface so that they can be photographed. Early paste-up artists used paper as a base to carry the image. However, it was soon discovered that paper was not dimensionally stable. With a change in temperature or humidity, the size of the paper would change, causing a shift in image position. This produced registration problems for the printer, particularly when printing multi-color work. To overcome registration problems, some paste-up artists used plate glass for paste-up. Glass was stable, but it was expensive, awkward, and difficult to handle. Modern paste-up is done on stiff paperboard or plastic sheets which are specially formulated for dimensional stability.

New developments in electronics have brought about more changes in layout and paste-up. As you will see in Chapter 5, composition systems now exist that allow an artist to compose total pages electronically on a computer screen—including rules, line drawings, halftones, and type. Once set on the screen, the complete page can be produced as photographic output, thus eliminating layout and paste-up entirely. Some composition systems can even output the page directly onto a printing plate, eliminating the need to produce film negatives. Even though full page make-up on computer composition systems is refining and changing the paste-up artist's job, many printers still rely on traditional paste-up techniques. On some printing jobs, especially where the image arrangement is complex or requires last-minute changes in position or corrections before going to press, traditional paste-up techniques are the most efficient method available.

Objectives for Chapter Four

After completing this chapter you will be able to:

- Identify common layout and paste-up tools and materials.

- Identify the three techniques for dealing with photographs on a paste-up.
- Describe the procedure of working from a rough layout.

– Describe the steps for preparing a single-color paste-up, including mounting the board, adding layout lines, and attaching the copy or artwork.
– Describe the procedures for cutting a mask.

– Describe the steps for preparing a multi-color paste-up.
– Describe the steps for preparing a reverse.
– Describe the steps for preparing a surprint.

Introduction

The goal of layout and paste-up is to bring all the different pieces of composition together into a final form that meets job specifications and is of sufficient quality to be photographically reproduced. Printers generally refer to this camera-ready copy as a **paste-up**, or a **mechanical.**

Materials for Layout and Paste-up

Surfaces for Layout

There are three basic types of paste-up surface:

– Drafting board
– Glass-top table
– Light table

The least expensive surface is the common **drafting board** (figure 4.1). The surface is usually set at an angle to eliminate light reflection from the paper or board and to reduce back strain for the paste-up artist. Many companies cover the wooden board with thick, coated paper or with a special adhesive-backed plastic. Any surface is acceptable as long as it is

Figure 4.1. Drafting board A drafting board is an acceptable paste-up surface.

flat and smooth and the edges are perfectly straight.

The second common type of paste-up surface is a **glass plate** mounted on an **angled table** (figure 4.2). The main advantage of the glass is that it is hard and will not be damaged when pieces of copy are trimmed with a razor blade or Exacto knife.

The third type of surface is a stripper's **light table** (figure 4.3). Light tables are used during stripping to bring together pieces of transparent film (see Chapter 10). A light ta-

Figure 4.2. Glass-top table Some layout artists use a glass surface for paste-up.

Figure 4.3. Light table A light table is also used for paste-up.

ble is made from a sheet of glass with a diffusion sheet beneath it. Light shines up through the glass from beneath the diffusion sheet. With a light table it is possible to see through most layout paper. When preprinted layout sheets are used, it is possible to see through the copy to line up images with the printed guidelines.

Paste-up Board

Several different materials are used by the industry for paste-up board. The most stable and expensive material is called **illustration board.** Different manufacturers use their own trade name, but their products all have the same general characteristics. Illustration board is smooth, white, and has a finish that allows for ruling of inked lines without feathering. **Feathering** is the tendency of ink on a rough, porous surface to spread, which is undesirable because it results in uneven weight lines. Illustration board is formed from laminated layers of board stock and paper. It is a thick, strong material that is not easily damaged with handling.

While many people use 110-pound index or even heavier material for paste-up, an increasingly common paste-up material is 60- or 70-pound **offset paper.** Offset is a paper grade widely used in the printing industry. The pound measure refers to paper weight and is a general description of paper thickness. Sixty- or 70-pound paper is thinner than the stock used for business cards but thicker than most office typing paper.

Companies with jobs that all conform to the same column or page size, such as newspapers, usually print guidelines on offset paper to receive the paste-up. With this technique, the layout artist does not have to redraw guidelines for every job. **Preprinted paste-up sheets** are widely used for this purpose.

Offset paper is popular as a paste-up board material because it is inexpensive and can be used on a light table. Use of preprinted sheets with the light table usually cuts down on labor costs, because paste-ups can be produced very rapidly.

Yet another type of paste-up material is stable-base **polyester** or **acetate** (plastic) **sheets.** Some clear sheeting is used, but the most common type has a frosted surface. The main use of this material is as an overlay to carry images for a second color.

Stable-base means the size of the sheet will not change with moderate changes in temperature and humidity. Dimensional stability is very important with jobs involving the register of two or more colors or with work that requires critical size tolerances. The Uniform Product Code is an example of an image that must be held to exact size specifications (figure 4.4). Of the three major paste-up materials, illustration board and polyester are the most stable.

Paste-up Tools

Most tools used for layout and paste-up are common artist or drafting equipment. The three most basic are a **T-square, triangle,** and **ruler** (figure 4.5). Both plastic and steel tools

are commonly used. Plastic edges are easy to look through when positioning lines of type, but they are easily damaged. This is a special problem when the tools are used for ruling. A nick in the plastic edge can ruin a carefully inked line. A plastic edge should never be used as a guide for cutting. Steel tools are more expensive than plastic but are nearly indestructable under normal use. Layout rulers are supplied with both English (inch) units and printer's (pica) units.

Several different types of cutting tools are used by the paste-up artist. **Exacto knives** and **single-edged razor blades** are the two most common hand-held cutting tools (figure 4.6). It is always best to hold the blade as low as possible when cutting paper. This technique shears rather than stabs through the paper and prevents ripping or wrinkling the sheet. Rapid cuts can be made with a small table-model **guillotine cutter** (figure 4.7) or with a specially designed cutting device such as the one shown in figure 4.8.

Adhesive tape is used to hold both the board and overlay material in place during

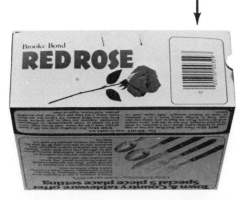

Figure 4.4. Printing the Uniform Product Code (UPC) Printing this code imposes critical size tolerances for the printer because variations in code bar thickness will result in inaccurate readings at the cash register.

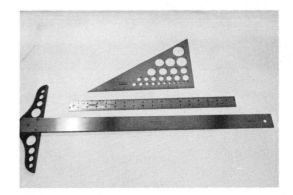

Figure 4.5. Three basic layout and paste-up tools T-squares, triangles, and rulers are available in various lengths in both plastic and steel.

Figure 4.6. Cutting tools Exacto knives (or other stick-type cutters) and single-edged razor blades are commonly used to cut pieces of art. The blades should be replaced often to ensure clean, smooth edges.

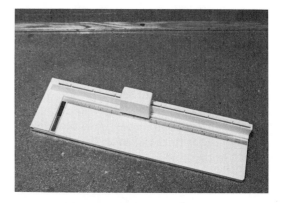

Figure 4.8. Compugraphic's Easy Trimmer

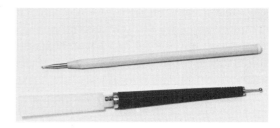

Figure 4.9. Two types of burnishers

Figure 4.7. A table-model guillotine cutter

paste-up. Designers commonly use masking tape, clear cellophane tape, and white tape. Masking tape is used to secure the board to the working surface. Cellophane tape is used to tape clear plastic sheets in place. White tape is often used to hold large pieces of copy to the paste-up board.

Burnishers are used in the layout room to adhere dry-transfer images or small pieces of pressure-sensitive materials to the paste-up board. Burnishers come in several different shapes (figure 4.9). Ball-pointed tools can be purchased in many styles. Some are spring loaded, so uniform pressure can be applied to any surface. Straight burnishers are also available, but they are not as popular as the ball type.

Part of the layout artist's job is to add layout and image lines to the paste-up. All guidelines not intended to print are drawn with a light blue (nonrepro) pencil or pen.

Light blue lines on the layout will not be recorded on the film used to make the negative for the printing plate. For lines that should be recorded on the film, such as trim or fold marks, special instruments are used (figure 4.10). The most common is a technical pen with black **india ink.** India ink is especially dense and forms perfect film images. A new tool gaining wide acceptance is called a **repro-quality** (reproduction-quality) **disposable drawing pen.** This inexpensive, felt-tipped pen is available in a variety of line widths. Most ballpoint or office-grade felt-tip pens are not acceptable for paste-up work.

Types of Art

Jobs for paste-up come to the layout room in several forms. Most are black images on an opaque paper base. **Opaque** means that under normal viewing it is not possible to see through the sheet. You can read the words on this page without seeing through to the page on the other side of the sheet because the paper is opaque. As mentioned in Chapter 3, line copy (such as type, ink drawings, and clip art) and **continuous-tone photographs** are the two most common sorts of copy (figure 4.11). **Clip art** is copyright-free material supplied to printers and designers in forms ready for paste-up.

Jobs sometimes arrive with black or red images on a transparent base. Red reproduces the same way black does for most graphic arts films. **Transparent-based images** can be seen through the backing sheet. These images are typically used for multicolor work.

The term "copy" is commonly used in the layout room. In this situation copy refers to the pieces of art and galleys of type that will be applied to the paste-up.

Adhesives for Paste-up

The main job of the layout artist is to adhere the different pieces of copy to the paste-up board in the proper printing positions. Several different adhesives are used to hold the images in place.

Figure 4.10. Technical and felt-tip pens Two devices used to create dense black lines on a paste-up are technical pens (a) and reproduction-quality felt-tip pens (b).

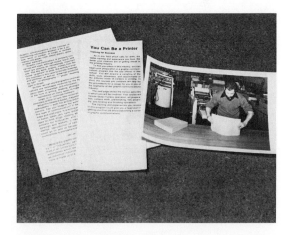

Figure 4.11. Paste-up copy The copy for paste-up is either line work or continuous-tone photographs.

A **wax coater** (figure 4.12) is a device designed to place a uniform layer of wax material on one side of a sheet of paper. The side to be coated is placed image up on the feeder side of the machine. As the sheet is pushed against the drive rollers, it is drawn through the device, against the wax drum. After coating, the pieces may be laid aside and used at any time. The advantage of using a wax coater is that the adhesive can be pushed in place on the paste-up and then removed to be repositioned any number of times. The adhesive continues to work as long as it remains free of lint or dirt and does not dry out. The wax coating does eventually dry; but its useful life is several weeks, well beyond normal paste-up requirements.

Rubber cement is an inexpensive adhesive that is applied wet to the back of the copy. To use rubber cement, place the copy image down on a sheet of scrap paper and, with a small brush, carefully cover the back of the copy (figure 4.13). Be sure the copy does not shift and that no thick areas of cement remain on the sheet. The drying time of rubber cement is short, so immediately place the copy on the paste-up board, cement-side down, and position the image with a T-square and triangle.

It is not easy to remove images that have been adhered with rubber cement. The liquid is also messy. The wet cement sometimes creeps out around the edges of the paper. As it dries, it tends to pick up dirt that can form an image on the film when the paste-up is photographed. It is easier to remove excess rubber cement when it is dry than when it is wet. Use a soft eraser to rub away dried areas of cement from the paste-up.

Some artists use **tube** and/or **stick adhesives** to mount copy on the paste-up (figure 4.14). These are available in a variety of forms. Most, however, are applied by coating the back of the paper with a liquid or paste that dries rapidly. Before purchasing, care should be taken to read the product directions and specifications. For example, one popular brand specifies that for permanent mounting, the copy should be applied while the solution is

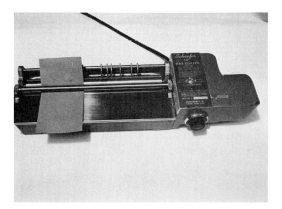

Figure 4.12. A wax coater The drive roller pulls the paper through the wax in the wax coater.
Courtesy of Schafer Machine Company, Inc.

Figure 4.13. Using rubber cement Cover the back of the copy with a thin coating of cement. Use a piece of paper under the copy so that the cement can be applied evenly to all edges without getting onto the layout area.

Figure 4.14. Examples of stick and liquid adhesives

ut
rb
sn
tr·
yh
id{
vi1
yg

eu
tr:
ig
yg
ot:
yg
sb
gh
··¡·
y

Benson Franklin Faux
Agyrt skk vinoiduyuib gsd nrrb syysvgrf y
frdutsnkr yi otivbufr frysukrf otubyubh ubdy·
ib ygr osdyr-yu. Ydyskktm s dgrry ig ytsvubh

Figure 4.15. A prescreened print pasted on a mechanical Random letters are used here to visualize copy applied to a typical job.

wet. If the coating is allowed to dry before mounting, then it can be positioned, removed, and attached again, like a wax coating.

Working with Photographs

It is often necessary to allow for the inclusion of continuous-tone photographs on the mechanical. There are basically three ways for the layout artist to handle the problem at this stage:

- By using prescreened prints
- By forming a window on the negative
- By drawing holding lines

It is possible to prepare an opaque halftone that can be pasted directly onto the mechanical and rephotographed with the rest of the job as line copy. This procedure is called copy dotting (figure 4.15). These prescreened halftone prints are referred to as stats or photostats.

The second technique is to place a layer of red or black material, sometimes called a "blockout," in the area on the mechanical where the photograph is to appear in the final reproduction (figure 4.16). Black acetate may be used, but the most common material is transparent red. It is possible to see guidelines through the red material and, therefore, to make a more accurate cut. When photographed, the black or red blockout will form a clear area (called a **window**) on the negative. A halftone negative can then be attached under the window prior to making a printing plate.

The last approach to allow for photographs on the mechanical is to draw **holding**

F
ub(
rbg
snr
trv
yhr
idg
vin
ygr
)
euy
trs
ig)
ygr
otr
ygr
sbf
ghi
vin
Benson Franklin Faux   ygr
Agyrt skk vinoiduyuib gsd nrrb syysvgrf yi
frdutsnkr yi otivbufr frysukrf otubyubh ubdyty
ib ygr osdyr-yu. Ydyskktm s dgrry ig ytsvubh o·

**Figure 4.16. A blockout on a
mechanical** When this layout is photographed,
the black area will appear on the negative as a
clear rectangle window into which the halftone
negative will be positioned.

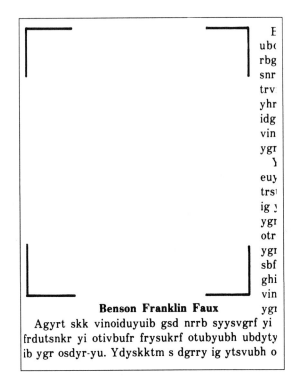

F
ub(
rbg
snr
trv
yhr
idg
vin
ygr
)
euy
trs
ig)
ygr
otr
ygr
sbf
ghi
vin
Benson Franklin Faux   ygr
Agyrt skk vinoiduyuib gsd nrrb syysvgrf yi
frdutsnkr yi otivbufr frysukrf otubyubh ubdyty
ib ygr osdyr-yu. Ydyskktm s dgrry ig ytsvubh o

**Figure 4.17. Holding lines drawn on a
mechanical** These lines serve as a guide in the
placement of the halftone negative.

lines (figure 4.17). The lines will act as a guide for positioning a halftone negative during stripping, when film images are positioned together on a light table. The holding lines can be simple corner marks or they can be bold inked lines that will act as a border on the final reproduction.

Working from the Rough

Reviewing Instructions

The first step in beginning any paste-up job is to examine the rough layout. The rough is the detailed guide used to identify and position every piece of art on the paste-up. Recall from Chapter 3 that the rough is a sort of "floor plan" that predicts and describes the final product. It should contain all the information necessary to produce the job.

It is important to carefully review every part of the rough before beginning any work. The rough should contain several categories of information. The five most common are the following:

- Type content and specifications (size, style, etc.)
- Product dimensions

- Image positions for all elements
- Finishing operations (such as folding, trimming, scoring, or perforating)
- Press specifications (including paper, length of run, imposition, and ink color)

The layout artist must consider every part of the rough in addition to image positions. For example, if finishing operations, such as folding and trimming, are indicated on the rough, then lines must be added to the paste-up that can be used in the bindery as guides for the finishing operation. If the layout department forgets to add them, problems may occur.

The sequence of paste-up operations can vary depending on job requirements. The ability to read a rough and look ahead to anticipate the order of steps is important. This ability is developed with experience.

Checking for Completeness

After reviewing the specifications, it is important to ensure that all necessary pieces are in the job packet. It is frustrating and costly to begin a paste-up and then, when nearing completion, discover that one piece of copy is missing. It is difficult and confusing to remove the job from the layout board, set it aside, and begin another while waiting for the missing copy.

Check the composition against the rough layout. Check that all type composition is complete and in camera-ready form. Examine the artwork and review each piece. Measure each piece and determine whether enlargements or reductions are necessary.

Before beginning any work on the paste-up, make sure that everything is ready. Be sure that all instructions are clear and understood. A few minutes' delay at this point prevents problems later on.

Trimming the Copy

The last step before beginning the paste-up is to trim all pieces of art copy and type galleys to a workable size. Use a razor or Exacto knife with a steel ruler to trim each piece within 1/4 to 1/2 inch of the image size. It is better not to use a guillotine paper cutter for this operation, since it is easy to make a mistake and cut through an image.

When cutting copy, always place the ruler over the nonimage area rather than on top of the copy. The back side of the metal might scratch a photograph or a type character. The ruler also has a tendency to carry dirt, which can spot the copy. If the amount of trim is too small to support the ruler, then place a piece of clean scrap paper under the ruler, on top of the image.

When all copy has been cut to size, place the pieces of copy on the layout table in the positions in which they will appear on the paste-up (figure 4.18). This technique saves time and prevents confusion. Some layout artists wax coat each piece before trimming. The hot wax does have a tendency to flow

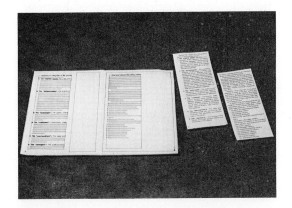

Figure 4.18. Laying out the copy Lay the pieces of copy on the layout table in the order they will appear on the paste-up as determined by your rough layout.

over the edge of the paper. If enough wax becomes attached to the edge, it will pick up dirt when mounted on the board and will photograph as a line.

Preparing a Single-Color Paste-up

Novice layout artists should begin to develop paste-up skills by working on simple, single-color jobs. Basic layout skills should be developed before attempting multicolor work or single-color jobs that require overlays. The purpose of this section is to review basic paste-up procedures. More sophisticated techniques are discussed in the following sections.

Mounting the Board

The first step is to select and mount the paste-up board on the layout table. If preprinted sheets are used, then the selection process is simple. If illustration board, offset paper, or a plastic sheet is used, then the material must be cut to size. Cut a piece that is slightly larger than the press paper size. A good approach is to cut the board at least 1 inch larger in each dimension than the press sheet. For example, if the press sheet size is to be 8 1/2 x 11, then cut the paste-up board at least 9 1/2 x 12. Board that is a great deal larger than the job dimensions is cumbersome to work with. A very large board is sometimes impossible to position on the graphic arts camera and is also difficult to store when the job is finished.

Be sure the layout table is clean, without spots of rubber cement or dirt. Position the board near the head of the T-square, to the left side of the layout surface if you are right-handed, to the right if you are left-handed (figure 4.19). The position of the T-square is

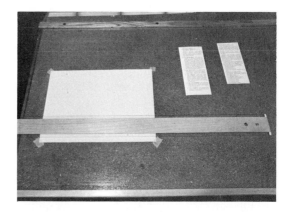

Figure 4.19. Position of the layout board and the head of the T-square This position of the board and the head of the T-square on the left of the table is correct for a right-handed person.

important because the blade of a T-square is more stable close to the head than it is out near the end of the blade. This arrangement also allows space to lay the rough and pieces of copy within easy reach. If a preprinted layout sheet is used, then position the sheet so the guidelines are in line with the T-square edge.

When the board is in position, secure it to the table with pieces of masking tape at each corner. It is important that the paste-up board not shift during paste-up. If the board moves in the middle of the job, then the different elements will be crooked and unacceptable to the customer.

Adding Layout Lines

The next step in the paste-up process is to add layout lines to the board (figure 4.20). Preprinted layout sheets already have layout lines. When working with blank board, it is necessary to add the lines. Begin by drawing light **center lines** for each dimension. Next,

Figure 4.20. Adding layout lines to the board Using a triangle and T-square, draw the dimensions of the press sheet in light blue pencil so that the rectangle formed is centered on the layout board.

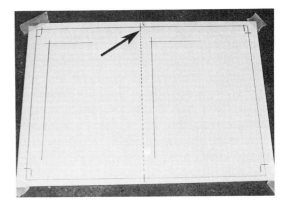

Figure 4.21. Adding fold lines Fold lines are drawn in light blue pencil, but small black marks are added at the edge of the sheet as guides for the bindery.

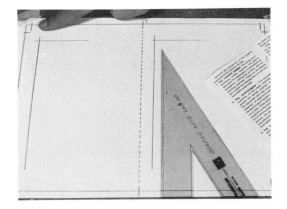

Figure 4.22. Adding trim marks Trim marks must be added if the job is to be trimmed during the finishing operation.

add **paper lines.** Carefully measure the dimensions of the press sheet and position the guidelines the proper distances from the center lines. Paper lines should be drawn in light blue pencil because they are not intended to print. Nonprint (nonrepro) blue lines are used by the layout artist as a guide and are not needed after the paste-up is finished.

Next, add any **fold lines.** These are also drawn in blue pencil and appear as dashed lines. Small fold lines are sometimes drawn in black on the edge of the paper dimensions as a guide for the bindery (figure 4.21). Use india ink or a repro felt-tip pen to make fold lines on the board. These fold lines will print but are usually cut away when the job is trimmed to final size.

If the job is to be trimmed, then small black **trim marks** should be placed on the board (figure 4.22). Trim marks are used by the paper cutter to accurately cut the final job to the desired size. Trim marks are cut away during the operation and do not appear on the sheets delivered to the customer. The marks must, however, appear on the press sheet and are therefore added to the paste-up in black ink.

Image guidelines are added in nonrepro blue. These lines are used by the layout artist to position pieces of copy. Measure in from the paper lines to define the image margins (sometimes called image extremes) (figure 4.23). Always follow specifications listed on the rough. Then add any special measurements to position the different elements of the job. If a headline is to appear a certain distance from the top of the sheet, draw a blue line to indicate its position. Do the same for the positions of all pieces of art.

Attaching the Copy

Begin mounting copy at the top of the sheet and work down. Moving the T-square back and forth over the copy can smudge or scratch it. By beginning at the top, each piece is positioned and then not touched again. Use blue image guidelines to position each piece. Use the plastic edge of the T-square to ensure that each piece is straight (figure 4.24). It is also wise to check image position with a triangle to make sure that both horizontal and vertical dimensions are straight and line up perfectly with all other pieces.

If the sheet has a wax coating, gently position it and use the point of an Exacto knife to shift it into position. Slight pressure against the T-square will then secure it in place. After checking the vertical edge with a triangle, the sheet can be lifted and repositioned again if necessary.

Some layout artists use a rubber roller to attach the copy firmly to the board. To use this technique, place a piece of clean paper over the image and move the roller firmly against the surface (figure 4.25). The paper keeps the copy clean and ensures that the image will not be scratched during the operation.

The same technique of checking alignment and pressing in place is used for every element on the job. When every piece is positioned, carefully check the placement by referring back to the rough layout. Next, cut a sheet of tracing paper to the same size as the board and tape it in place along one edge so it can be hinged back. Add any directions from the rough that are important for the darkroom or stripping tasks (figure 4.26).

Some layout artists add a cover sheet to

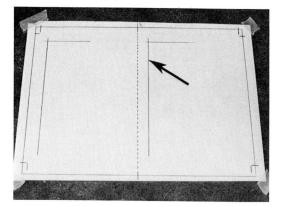

Figure 4.23. Adding image guidelines Image guidelines are drawn in nonrepro blue and are used as guides to position the copy.

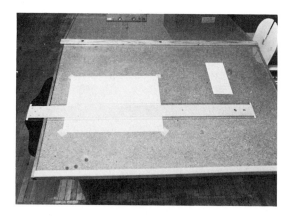

Figure 4.24. Positioning the copy Use the plastic edge of the T-square to position and straighten each piece of copy

Figure 4.25. Attaching the copy Use a scrap of clean paper over the copy and move the roller over the image to be adhered to the paste-up board.

Figure 4.27. Adding a cover sheet A cover sheet is often used to protect the finished paste-up.

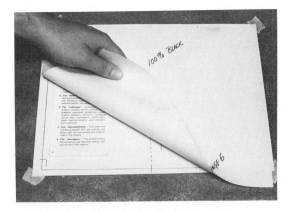

Figure 4.26. Adding directions for shooting the copy A tissue overlay is added to the board and used to specify directions for the camera operator or the stripper.

protect the art (figure 4.27). Cut a piece of tissue or cover paper to the size of the layout board, but add one inch to the hinge edge. Fold the sheet at the one-inch point and slide

it over the board. Tape it on the back side with masking tape.

Cutting Masks

A **mask** is material that blocks the passage of light. The most common masking material used in layout is red masking film. This type of film is not light sensitive, but it does have a thick emulsion that can be cut away with a razor blade or knife, leaving a clear plastic support sheet.

Masks are commonly used to cut half-tone windows, to create open areas for screen tints, to drop out areas around a photograph, and to create special overlay images.

To prepare a mask, cut a piece of masking film larger than the image dimensions of the job. Use an Exacto knife or other sharp instrument to cut through the emulsion, but not through the plastic base (figure 4.28). Keep the blade angle low, to make a shear cut. Always cut to the center of any image line. With

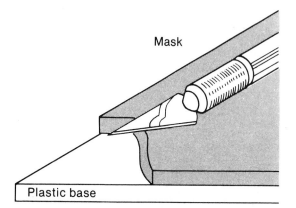

Figure 4.28. Cutting masking material Cut through the emulsion layer, but not through the plastic support sheet.

Figure 4.29. Adding masks to the board Cut a piece of masking film and hinge it in position along one edge on the paste-up board.

this technique, images will overlap and "fit" together well. After the mask is cut, position it over the layout, with the emulsion up, and tape it along one edge so it can be hinged back out of the way (figure 4.29).

After an area has been cut out and the mask has been positioned, stab the emulsion with the point of the knife. By gently lifting, the unneeded portion can be lifted away (figure 4.30).

Preparing a Multicolor Paste-up

Multicolor jobs are more complex than single-color work, and require a thorough understanding of paste-up procedures.

Begin the job by setting up the board as with single-color work. Draw paper lines, fold lines, and image guidelines in nonrepro blue. Place all image guidelines for both colors on the same paste-up sheet. Add trim or fold marks for the finishing room in black india ink or repro felt-tip pen.

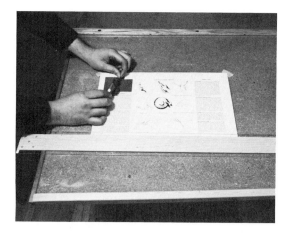

Figure 4.30. Removing excess mask from the board Stab a corner of the masking film and gently lift the excess mask area from around the desired window.

Adding Register Marks

For multicolor work it is necessary to add **register marks** (figure 4.31). Register marks can

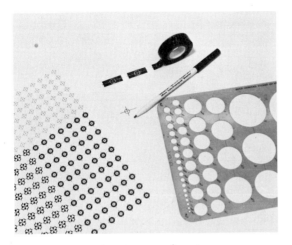

Figure 4.31. Register marks Register marks can be purchased in pressure-sensitive or preprinted form, or created by hand with a ruling pen.

Figure 4.32. Placement of register marks Place register marks in areas of the press sheet that will be cut away in the finishing operation.

be purchased commercially on pressure-sensitive tape, as preprinted transfer material, or they can be created by drawing with a black layout pen.

Register marks help the press operator align one color over another in perfect register. On single-color presses, one color of a multicolor job is printed first. The paper is then returned to the press, and another color is printed. The operator adjusts the paper or printing plate so the register marks from the second color print precisely over those from the first.

A minimum of three register marks should be placed on the board to ensure good registration. Register marks should always be placed in areas that will be trimmed off after the job is finished (figure 4.32). Some companies prefer to place register marks in the image area and then to remove them from the plate after the first sheets have been checked for register. Always follow shop guidelines in the placement of register marks.

Working with an Overlay

Most two-color jobs involve black and some other color. Most layout artists place the images to be printed in black on the illustration board or base sheet. In most cases, the color used for the greatest number of images (or that covers the greatest surface area) will be placed on the board. Position the first set of images by using normal single-color procedures. Check to ensure that all pieces are straight and firmly attached.

The second-color images are placed on a special **overlay sheet.** Place a piece of clear or frosted plastic over the board. Tape one edge of the plastic sheet in several places to create a hinge (figure 4.33). It should be possible to look through the plastic sheet and see the blue pencil image guidelines for the second set of images.

Mount each piece of copy on the overlay as with board material. Use rubber cement, a wax coater, or dry adhesives. Use the guide-

Figure 4.33. Adding the color overlay Hinge a piece of plastic over the board to receive the second set of images. Be sure to cut away the areas over the register marks.

Figure 4.34. Mounting the second-color copy Adhere the second set of images to the overlay sheet, following the image guidelines on the first sheet.

lines on the board to make sure the new images are in their proper positions and are straight with the first images (figure 4.34).

If they are not using a transparent overlay material, layout artists cut away the overlay in the register mark areas. When the camera room photographs the paste-up, two separate pieces of film will be used. The first will be of the board paste-up, with the overlay hinged back out of the way. Next, the overlay will be hinged back and a white piece of paper placed between the board and overlay. If the register marks can clearly be seen, they will be recorded on both the first and the second pieces of film. Since the marks are in identical positions for both exposures, they will appear in the same position on both negatives. They will then appear in the correct position on two printing plates and can be used on the press to check register.

Again check both the board and the overlay to make sure that all copy is in the correct position, is straight, and is tightly bonded, and that the whole area is free from dirt or scratches. After the tissue or cover sheet have

been added, the job is ready to be sent to the camera room.

This technique can be used for three- and four-color jobs or for work that uses an overlay for several different screen tints. For each additional color, another overlay is hinged from an edge of the board.

Preparing Reverses and Surprints

Many jobs require the use of reverses or surprints to create a special image or effect. Paste-up techniques for reverses and surprints are similar.

Reverses

A **reverse** is a recognizable image created by the absence of a printed image. Copy preparation for a reverse involves the following three steps (figure 4.35): (1) paste-up, (2) film positive, (3) stripping assembly.

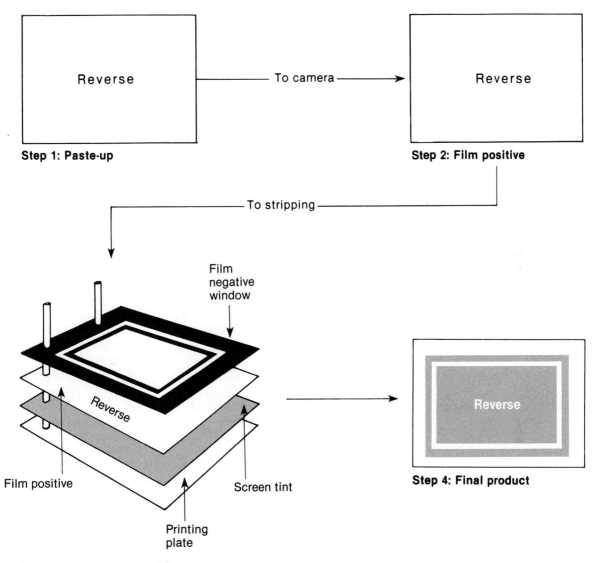

Step 1: Paste-up

Step 2: Film positive

Step 3: Stripping assembly

Figure 4.35. Preparing reverse copy for printing A reverse is a recognizable image created by the absence of a printed image. In this example, a screen tint is used with a film negative window to create the reverse image.

First, the desired reverse image is prepared as if it were a normal one-color paste-up. Black or red copy is positioned on the board in the desired printing position. Second, the paste-up is sent to the camera room to be produced as a film positive. The film positive blocks the "image" area and creates the desired reverse image. The third step is done during stripping, when the pieces of film are assembled for plate making. From directions specified by the layout artist, the film positive will be positioned over another image, usually a film negative. If light is passed through both the positive and the negative to the plate, a reverse image will be created by the positive.

An alternative method of preparing a reverse is with red masking film. It is possible to cut a design by hand then to use the mask in the stripping operation. The choice of technique depends on the type of image being reversed. If the image can easily be cut by hand, then the masking-film method is acceptable. Reverses that involve type or special designs with complex images require the paste-up technique.

Surprints

A **surprint** is an image that is printed over another image. Surprints are commonly used to print dark type over a light area of a halftone photograph or a screen tint. The technique used to prepare a surprint is similar to that for preparing a two-color paste-up by using an overlay.

The base image (usually a photograph) is mounted on the paste-up board, and the surprint image (usually type) is positioned on the overlay sheet. The camera room prepares separate film images and sends the job to the stripper. Two separate exposures—the first is the base image, and the second is the surprint

Paste-up with overlay and register marks

Film negative of base   Film negative of overlay

Final printed sheet

Figure 4.36. Preparing surprint copy for printing A surprint is an image that is printed over another image. The two film negatives are separately exposed to the printing plate in a single-color surprint.

image—are used to prepare the printing plate. These images are combined to form a single image on the final printed sheet (figure 4.36).

A simpler way of making a type surprint is to use dry-transfer letters. The layout artist can carefully burnish the characters directly onto the photograph. Another method is to use a clear plastic overlay sheet to hold the characters. When the job goes to the camera room, it is shot as a single halftone. The first method of using separate exposures, however, is preferred, since it makes for a denser surprint on the final press sheets.

Key Terms

paste-up
mechanical
preprinted paste-up sheets
T-square
triangle
ruler
opaque

line work
transparent-based images
wax coater
clip art
stats
window
holding lines

center lines
paper lines
trim marks
mask
register marks
overlay sheet

Questions for Review

1. What are the three types of table surface used for paste-up?

2. What are three common paste-up board materials?

3. What is a burnisher?

4. What does the term "opaque" mean?

5. What are the two most common types of image in paste-up?

6. What is the purpose of a wax coater?

7. Why is a blockout used on a paste-up to produce a window?

8. Why is nonrepro blue used for paper lines, fold lines, and image guidelines?

9. What is the purpose of trim marks on a paste-up?

10. What is a mask?

11. When are register marks used?

12. What is the purpose of an overlay?

13. What is a reverse? a surprint?

Chapter Five

Typesetting and Computer Image Generation

Anecdote to Chapter Five

The introduction of the first successful typewriter—then called a writing machine—in the fall of 1867 began a series of important changes in this country and the world. The typewriter contributed to a revolution in the printing industry. What is such a common-place printing tool today was feared as a threat to the printers of the 1800s.

Christopher Sholes and several associates built the first successful typewriter in Milwaukee in the summer of 1867. Sholes began as a printer's apprentice and later became a successful editor and publisher. By the time he perfected the first typewriter, he had already invented several other machines that had an impact on the printing industry. One example was an automatic labeling-pasting machine that was the forerunner of the high-speed machines used today to address newspapers, magazines, and envelopes for bulk mailing. Another example of Sholes's work was a numbering machine that could be mounted in a press to automatically number each successive press sheet.

The first writing machine was a cumbersome tool that "typed" under the page, so the writer could not see what had been produced until the sheet was removed from the machine. Only thin tissue paper could be used because the characters, or keys, hit the paper from the back and pushed the sheet against a piece of carbon paper to form the image.

One of the first persons to purchase a commercially manufactured typewriter was the printer-author, Mark Twain (Samuel Clemens). Despite the machine's disadvantages, Twain thought it was a marvelous device, much preferable to handwriting. He managed to reach a typing speed of twelve words per minute.

The writing machine was not well received by all printers when it first began to enjoy acceptance by the business world. Before that time all letters were handwritten. If more than two or three copies were required,

An early writing machine
Smithsonian Institution, Photo No.
38–785F

as in law offices or the courts, a printer would hand set the job and make copies on a printing press. By the early 1900s the typewriter was so popular that several type founders cut typefaces that duplicated typewriter copy. With such fonts of type, jobs could be run on the press but would look as if they were typewritten, with ribbon marks, imperfect alignment, and inconsistent impression. There was great fear that much of the printer's work would be taken over by the typewriter. In 1885 the *Inland Printer* wrote that the time might come when each printing office would have a type writing machine and could execute jobs on it as well as on any other printing apparatus.

This did happen. High-quality typewriters that could produce dense, consistent images linked with the tool of photography were once used for cold type composition. Printers could "set type" by typing it on a piece of paper, photographing it, and transferring the image to a printing plate, all without touching a type case. Later developments in computers teamed the typewriter keyboard with photographic output in a process known as phototypesetting. The typewriter keyboard is now an important part of almost every type composition device.

Objectives for Chapter Five

After completing this chapter you will be able to:

- Discuss the three major components in a computer system and explain the difference between hardware and software.
- List and describe the components of a typical computer composition system, including typical input/output devices.
- Describe how a computer represents information in memory, and explain the terms "dot matrix," "bit," and "pixel."

- Describe three methods of providing input to a computer composition system.
- Discuss the differences between paper tape, magnetic tape, and magnetic disk storage.
- State the differences between code- and menu-driven composition systems.
- Describe the differences between first-, second-, third-, and fourth-generation phototypesetters.
- State the differences between traditional composition systems and desktop systems.

Introduction

Most type images used for printing are generated with the aid of computers. In the printing industry, computer-aided imaging devices are often referred to as "composing" or "composition" systems. The people who operate these devices are called **compositors.** The first composition systems could generate only the characters and symbols that made up the text of the printed page. More recently, systems have become available that can generate graphics, in the form of line art and halftones, as well as text.

The primary advantage of computer-aided image generation is speed. Foundry type can be composed by a "quick" (an early term for a skilled compositor) at the average rate of perhaps 4 characters per minute. Line-casting hot type machines might average 6 char-

acters per second (CPS). An expert typist on a good day can generate perhaps 8 CPS (100 words per minute). But a typical computer composition system can typeset well over 1,000 CPS. Some composition systems can typeset over 64,000 characters each second.

It is not our intention in this chapter to provide details for the operation of any specific computer composition system. Manufacturers supply documentation giving specific operating procedures for their equipment. It is possible, however, to provide a general understanding about how composition systems operate and to describe some of the functions that they can perform. This general understanding may make the manufacturer's documentation easier to follow and apply.

Computer Operation

Computers have had a profound effect on every aspect of the printing industry, from composition through press work and bindery. To understand computer imaging, you must have some understanding about how computers operate. A computer is basically an adding machine which can perform the arithmetic operations of addition and subtraction at very rapid speeds. Much has been said about how simple computers are, but they are actually quite complex.

A computer system is made up of hardware and software. **Hardware** is the physical wires, motors, screens, keyboards, and cases from which the computer is made, and the disks, paper, ribbons, and other supplies used with the computer. To do anything useful, a computer must have software. **Software** is the instructions that direct the computer to perform specific tasks. These instructions are recorded on computer disks or tapes as computer programs. Information that is placed into the computer by the operator, such as all of the characters and symbols that make up a page of this book, is called **data.**

A computer system actually contains two types of software: system software and application software. **System software** provides the programmed instructions needed for the computer to perform a system function, such as writing data on a disk or sending data to an output device. **Application software** is used to process data. Application software is typically programmed for a specific function, such as word processing, mathematical computation, graphics, or typesetting. System software and application software work together to perform any operation on data. A thorough understanding of what each type of software does and how to make it operate can be acquired through manufacturer's documentation.

Components of a Computer System

A computer system consists of three major components:

- Memory
- Central processing unit
- Input/output devices

Each of these components is housed in some type of hardware. The core of the system is the memory and central processing unit (CPU), without which the computer could not compute. The circuit boards and computer chips that make up the central processing unit and memory are often housed in a separate piece of hardware. Almost all computers are configured with a keyboard for input and a screen for data display. Together, the screen and keyboard are referred to as a **terminal.** On most typesetting systems it is possible to attach several terminals with a single CPU. A number of other input/output devices can be attached to most computers. These additional input/output (or "I/O") devices are called **peripherals** (figure 5.1).

Memory. Memory can be viewed as a set of locations, like mailboxes. Each of these locations is capable of holding a number. These numbers can represent data or they can represent instructions provided by software. Memory does not process data; that is, it does not add or subtract. Memory can only receive data and store it. Data processing and the execution of software instructions is performed in the central processing unit.

Central Processing Unit. The central processing unit can be thought of as a huge switching station, containing thousands of electronic switches which can be turned either on or off. Any operation performed by the

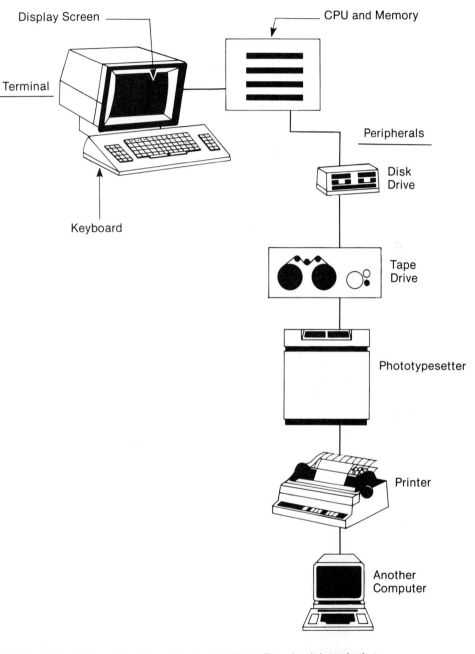

Display Screen

CPU and Memory

Terminal

Peripherals

Keyboard

Disk Drive

Tape Drive

Phototypesetter

Printer

Another Computer

Figure 5.1. Schematic of a computer system The circuit boards that make up the CPU and memory control the system. The terminal consists of the screen and keyboard. A variety of input/output devices can serve as peripherals.

central processing unit is performed through the unique routing of electronic impulses through these switches.

Input/Output Devices.   Information is placed into memory and gotten out again through input/output devices. Most input systems utilize a keyboard similar to a standard typewriter keyboard. The keyboard is connected, through the computer, to a video screen. Each time the operator presses a key on the keyboard, an alphanumeric code for that key's character is placed into memory, and the symbol for that keystroke is displayed on the video screen. An **alphanumeric code** contains a unique code symbol for each of the letters of the alphabet (both upper- and lowercase), and for the numbers. Alphanumeric codes also include standard punctuation and symbols, such as the dollar sign ($). All data entered into the computer by the operator, and all instructions entered by the software are converted to alphanumeric code and placed in memory, as numbers. The numbers are a binary (two-number) sequence made up of the two digits *0* and *1*. Each *0* or *1* is called a **bit** (short for "binary digit"). Individual bits cause the switches in the central processing unit to turn on or off. Information that is represented as a sequence of digits is said to be **digital** or **digitized** information. Digital information can be sent to an output device, such as a printer or a computer screen.

Storage of data in computer memory is temporary. When the computer is shut down, the information in memory is lost. All computers provide some type of more permanent information storage to which data can be output. The most common type of storage is storage on magnetic media, such as computer tapes or disks. **Magnetic media** store information as electromagnetic impulses on a special recording surface. These impulses are converted to numbers for use in the central

processing unit when the tape or disk is "read" by the computer.

A computer disk can contain a great deal of information. This information must be divided up in some manner, so that it can be located easily by the computer operator. Information is divided up by placing it on the disk or tape in separate areas, usually called **files.** To understand the concept of a file, think about the individual file folders in a filing cabinet. All of the information for one topic is stored in one file folder. The file folders are organized in some manner in the file drawer, so that they can be located easily. In a similar manner, all of the information in one computer file is typically related to one job, such as one typesetting job for one customer. Each file is given a unique name by the operator who creates the file and puts information into it.

To put information into a file, an operator opens the file, through a typed command, which causes the information in the file to be placed into memory and displayed on the computer screen. Once the file is open, changes can be made to the information on the screen and the file can be rewritten onto the disk. It is important to understand that when a file is opened, the actual information in the file is *not taken from the disk file and placed on the screen*. Instead, a *copy* of the information in the disk file is made and put into the computer's memory. It is this copy that is displayed on the screen, and this copy that the operator changes. The original information on the disk file remains unchanged until the operator directs the operating system to replace it with the new information from the screen. In most systems, this process is called "saving a file." When a file is saved, the computer erases all of the original information from the file on the disk and replaces it with the information in memory which has been edited on the screen.

Classifying Computers

There are many types of computers available. The major differences between computers are the number of different operations that they can perform and the speed at which they can perform these operations. Both of these differences are based, in part, on the amount of memory they have.

The largest and fastest computers, often called **mainframe** computers, have the ability to handle extremely large amounts of software and data, such as all of the tax data from all taxpayers and the programs for calculating tax returns. A mainframe computer can serve a large number of users simultaneously, and is **multitasking;** that is, it can perform more than one task at a time. Thus with a mainframe composition system, many operators can be simultaneously entering and storing data, and having data typeset. Extremely large, high-volume composition systems are often controlled by mainframe computers.

Minicomputers are used to drive many typesetting systems (figure 5.2). These computers are generally smaller and less powerful than mainframes and are typically dedicated; that is, they are used for only one specific operation, such as typesetting, rather than being used for typesetting and a variety of other functions. With the development of microcomputers, which today are as powerful as the minicomputers of only a few years ago, the term "minicomputer" is losing its meaning and will probably disappear altogether in the near future.

Microcomputers, also known as Personal Computers or PCs, have found wide application in the printing industry (figure 5.3). They are small, inexpensive, and can be supplied with software for typesetting, estimating, quality control, inventory, and almost every other function of a printing business. Most microcomputers can have only

Figure 5.2. A dedicated typesetting system driven by a minicomputer.
Courtesy of Compugraphic Corporation

Figure 5.3. A microcomputer Printing estimating, billing, inventory, and process control software is available for microcomputers such as the one shown here.
Courtesy of Alphatype Corporation

a limited amount of software available at any one time, most are designed to serve only a few users at a time, and most are not multi-tasking. For high volume data processing, microcomputers are much slower than mainframes. However, where computing requirements are within the capabilities of a microcomputer, it is far less costly to purchase a microcomputer than to purchase a mainframe or rent time on one.

Computer Composition Systems

All modern composition systems rely on computers for their operation. Each component of a typical computer composition system can be categorized by the function it performs (figure 5.4):

- Input
- Information storage
- Editing
- Composition
- Output (image generation)

Figure 5.4. Essential components of a computer composition system Input and editing is done at the computer terminal (the keyboard and screen). The disk drive, printer, and typesetter are input/output devices. Composition is accomplished by the control unit (CPU and memory) which is located beneath the printer. Courtesy of Compugraphic Corporation

The equipment that performs the first four of these functions—input, information storage, editing, and composition—is commonly referred to as the "front end" of the system, because it assembles information and sends it to the output device. The output device is typically a separate piece of hardware. It could be a phototypesetting machine, a laser printer, or a computer graphics device. It is common to **configure** (link together) one manufacturer's front end composition system with a variety of output devices.

Input

One method of getting information into a composition system is by typing it in at the keyboard. Anyone who has seen a composition system keyboard knows that it contains far more keys than a standard typewriter. All keyboards have an alphanumeric keypad which contains keys for all of the alphanumeric (alphabet and number) characters, arranged as they would be on a standard typewriter. In addition to these standard keys, the alphanumeric keypad may contain special keys for common typeset symbols, such as long and short dashes (called "en" and "em" dashes), and keys for fixed spaces such as the en, em, and thin space. Along with the alphanumeric keypad, most typesetting keyboards have a separate command keypad which is used to direct commands to the operating system (figure 5.5).

While operator keyboarding is probably

Figure 5.5. A composition system keyboard This keyboard has different keypads for various machine functions and operation.
Courtesy of Compugraphic Corporation

the most common method of entering data into a computer composition system, three other methods of "inputting" information are also used: optical character recognition, image scanning, and telecommunication.

Optical Character Recognition (OCR). Optical character recognition (OCR) is a process in which a computer can "read" copy from an original. OCR machines use an optical character scanner that can scan a page of type, convert the characters on the page into alphanumeric code, and place them into the computer for use by the composition system. The first OCR machines developed were only able to read copy typed in a limited number of specially designed typewriter fonts (figure 5.6).

As OCR technology developed, machines were produced that could accept a wider variety of fonts and could read typeset as well as typewritten material. However, in addition to the many different type styles that can be produced as typewriter copy, there are thousands of different typefaces that can be typeset. One of the major limitations of OCR technology has been the limited number of

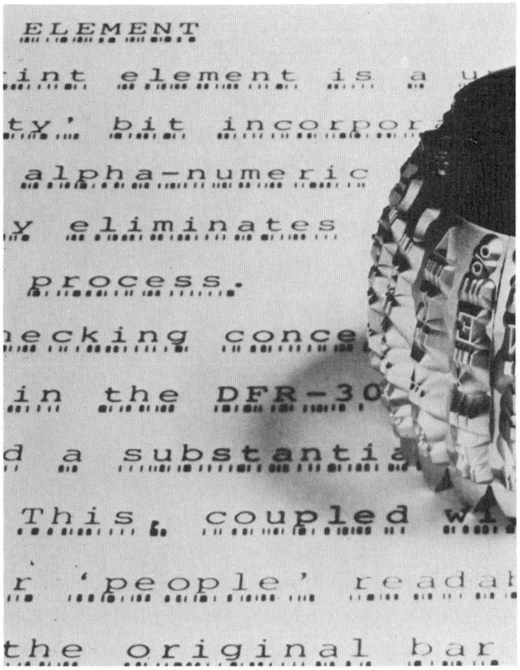

Figure 5.6. Special OCR characters This type ball produced a special OCR font with a machine-readable bar code under each character.

typefaces that could be accurately scanned and recorded. Even an OCR device that can accurately read over 100 different typefaces is of little use when presented with a new typeface that its software cannot read.

The most recent generation of OCR machines, known as **Intelligent Character Recognition (ICR)** devices (figure 5.7), were designed to overcome this limitation. These devices are considered "intelligent" because they can be "taught" to recognize new fonts of type. With an ICR machine, the operator directs the scanner to scan a page of type. The computer then "reads" each character on the page and displays the way its software interpreted each character. When a new font of type that the computer software is not programmed to recognize is scanned in, the com-

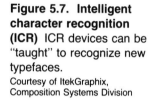

Figure 5.7. Intelligent character recognition (ICR) ICR devices can be "taught" to recognize new typefaces.
Courtesy of ItekGraphix, Composition Systems Division

puter must "interpret" the characters on the page. It does so based on software instructions which provide information about the general shapes of characters. No matter what the typeface, a lowercase *d* will have an ascender on the right side of the character, and a closed loop on the base line. The computer will interpret characters with this general shape as *d*'s. This interpretation may not always be accurate. If the first character on the page was an uppercase *Q*, based on the general shape of the character the computer software might interpret the character as an uppercase *O*. In this situation, the compositor could instruct the computer through keyboard commands to interpret all characters shaped exactly like the first character on the page as *Q*s, not *O*s. The computer would then recognize and read all uppercase *Q*s scanned in the new typeface as *Q*s, not *O*s.

There are several applications for OCR. Many original manuscripts are written with typewriters rather than word processors. Without OCR, such manuscripts would have to be keyboarded into the composition system. It is also possible to use OCR to read previously typeset material, such as a book

that has gone out of print. Again, keyboarding can be eliminated. Where it is appropriate, the major advantage of OCR is speed: Characters which have been typewritten or typeset can be scanned into a computer at a much faster rate of speed than they can be keyboarded. Typical scanners for OCR and ICR can read and record nearly 2,500 characters a minute.

Image Scanners. Image scanners are similar in function to the scanners used for OCR, except they read and store information as graphics, not as alphanumeric codes (figure 5.8). An operator can insert a piece of line art into an image scanner. The scanner will record the lines on the original art and place them into the computer as binary numbers that can be used by an output device, such as a printer or a typesetter, to represent the image as a series of small dots. These dots, called picture elements or **pixels,** can be thought of as a grid of individual "yes-no" or "on-off" switches in computer memory. All pixels that define a line on the original art will be turned "on" in the grid; those representing white space are turned "off."

Figure 5.8. An image scanner This graphics workstation uses an image scanner (to the left of the desktop) to scan an image and display it as part of the data file on the computer screen.
Courtesy of Scangraphic

Image scanners are becoming quite common in the printing industry. Some composition systems offer both text scanning through OCR or ICR and image scanning, making it possible to produce all of the text and graphics for a page of a book without ever keyboarding a single text character or hand drawing an illustration. Modern image scanners can scan continuous-tone photographs and reproduce them as halftones. Large composition systems may be configured with color scanners, which can scan continuous-tone color images and reproduce them as color separations.

Telecommunications. Telecommunications provides a method of sending data from one computer to another over the telephone lines. Telecommunications requires software that allows the computer to send and receive data, and a phone modem (figure 5.9). A **modem**

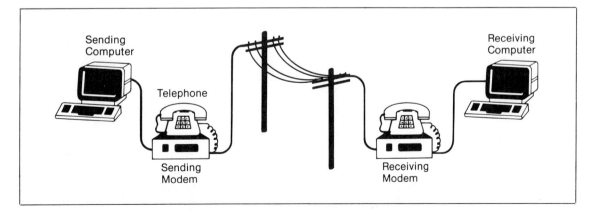

Figure 5.9. Telecommunications setup Two modems are needed for telecommunications.

converts electronic impulses from the computer into sound impulses that can be sent over the telephone lines. The computer receiving the data must have a second modem to convert the sound impulses back into electronic impulses for use in representing data. The speed (number of bits per second) at which the modem can send or receive data and convert it is the **baud rate** of the modem. With a high-speed modem, many pages of text can be sent from one computer and received by another in just a few moments.

Telecommunications is an obvious outgrowth of the use of computers for information storage and processing. The advantages of telecommunications are the speed at which information can be placed in computer memory, and the elimination of most data keyboarding by the operator. Once information is stored as data in any computer, it is often foolish to re-keyboard the information for use in another computer. For large quantities of data, it is much less costly to telecommunicate the data from one computer to another.

Three problems can occur in telecommunication. The first problem occurs when the sending computer does not represent data in the same alphanumeric code as the receiving computer. The most commonly used alphanumeric code is the ASCII code (pronounced "As-Key"). IBM computers use the EBCDIC code (pronounced "Ebsee-dick"). Most telecommunications software contains programs which convert the alphanumeric code sent from one computer into the proper alphanumeric code for the receiving computer.

A second problem with telecommunications is that alphanumeric codes are only standardized for a limited number of characters. For example, there are only about 100 standard characters in the ASCII character set. Each of these characters is represented by a unique ASCII code, which is made up of a unique bit sequence. The ASCII code that represents each of these characters will be exactly the same, regardless of the computer used to store or generate the character. Any two computers utilizing the ASCII code set will represent the lowercase "e" or the number "1" with the same unique bit sequence. A lowercase "e" sent from one machine will be recorded as a lowercase "e" when it is received by the other machine. However, there are over 15,000 unique characters that can be typeset. Thus, even if both the sending and the receiving computer are utilizing ASCII code, there are approximately 14,900 characters which are not included as standard characters in the ASCII code set. The bit sequence for an open box ("□") on the sending computer might be the bit sequence for a plus sign ("+") on the receiving machine. In this situation, the compositor must display on the computer screen the information that was received and then change the plus signs into open boxes. Some telecommunications software offers translation instructions with which a "translation table" can be produced. The translation table will make these changes automatically.

A final problem with telecommunication is transmission errors from electronic "noise" (interference) on the telephone lines. Most telecommunications software has transmission protocols (instructions) which the computer can use to automatically check for transmission errors. If data is received that does not correspond exactly to the transmission protocol, the computer will alert the operator to a possible transmission error by placing a flag, such as a string of question marks, in the file at the point where the interference occurred.

Many telecommunication programs can be used to send and receive both text and graphics. The newspaper *USA Today* is a good example of the use of telecommunications. All composition for *USA Today* is done in a central location, then telecommunicated via satellite to several printers for simultaneous output and printing in many locations across the country.

Information Storage

All computer composition systems store information on some storage medium, such as paper tape, magnetic tape, or magnetic disk (figure 5.10). Paper cards, called punch cards, were one of the first forms of computer information storage. Continuous paper strips in which holes are punched that correspond to a particular keyboard symbol are an extension of the punch card system. Image generation

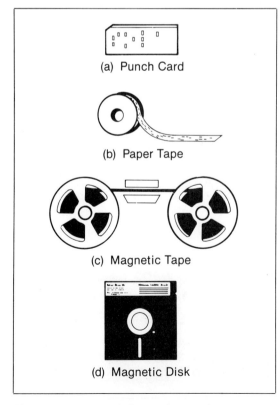

(a) Punch Card

(b) Paper Tape

(c) Magnetic Tape

(d) Magnetic Disk

Figure 5.10. Types of storage media

devices were designed that could "read" the punches in a paper tape and output the appropriate characters. While paper tape storage is still used in the printing industry for some types of information storage, composition systems typically store information on magnetic disks or tapes.

Magnetic Tapes. Magnetic tapes can be used to receive keyboard input directly, but are more often used to "back up" (duplicate) information from disks. Magnetic tapes can be read by machine at a faster rate of speed than paper tapes and tend to hold up longer under use. Paper tape can tear easily. Magnetic tapes can also be erased and reused to store new information. Information on paper tapes cannot be erased or recorded over.

Magnetic Disks. Most composition systems store information on magnetic disks. With magnetic disks, instead of storing the information on a rolled tape, like a tape recorder tape, information is stored on a round disk. The major advantage of disk storage over tape storage is that information stored on disk can be retrieved for use far more quickly than information stored on tape. The disk spins quite rapidly, and the disk drive reading head can quickly jump from one unique piece of information to the next on the disk. To retrieve information from a computer tape, the operator must cause the tape to be rewound or advanced until the required information is positioned under the tape reader heads. Even before the tape can be positioned, it must be mounted by hand on a tape drive. With disks, which are always in a disk drive when in use, information is always "on-line" and readily accessible. Information stored in magnetic disk storage is often referred to as "disk-based" information.

Two types of magnetic disks are common: floppy disks and hard disks. **Floppy**

disks are thin, flexible plastic disks that are small in diameter, typically eight inches or less (figure 5.11). They are mounted in a paper or plastic cover and, owing to this protection and their small size, are quite portable. A **hard disk** consists of several rigid disks which are thicker than floppy disks and are stacked one on top of the other. Disk reader heads are positioned so that they can read and record information on the top or bottom of each disk. Hard disks are typically supplied as a separate component in a separate piece of hardware (figure 5.12). A major advantage of a hard disk over a floppy disk is that a hard disk can hold much more information than a floppy disk. An operator can also retrieve information faster from a hard disk than from a floppy disk, because a hard disk spins much faster—over ten times faster—than a floppy disk.

Editing

Editing is the process of adding, changing, or deleting information in a file. During editing, the compositor can make corrections to information in a file as well as add and change typesetting commands in the file. Composition computers allow the operator to make changes to the original file by selecting, on the computer screen, the word or words to be changed, deleting them, and typing in new copy. Most systems use a cursor to select specific screen areas. A **cursor** is typically a blinking rectangle or short blinking rule that can be moved up, down, or across the screen with special cursor movement keys on the keyboard.

Typesetting Commands

Traditional computer composition systems are **code-driven;** that is, the operator enters unique combinations of keystrokes that make up a unique typesetting code for each typographic operation the system is to perform. A typical typesetting code specifying type at 12-point size might be ⟨PT12⟩. The actual commands utilized on each composition system are unique to the system and must be learned by the operator. All commands, however, consist of a unique character string (grouping) that specifies an operation, such as *PT* for point selection. This character string is combined with one or more **parameters.** In the example above, *12* is the parameter that determines the point size selected.

Figure 5.11. Floppy disk storage
Courtesy of Compugraphic Corporation

Figure 5.12. A hard disk
Courtesy of Compugraphic Corporation

More than one parameter may be required for a specific typographical operation. Instructions that will cause the composition system to generate a horizontal rule (line) are a case in point. To produce a rule, the computer must know where to begin the rule, how thick the rule is to be, and the measure (length) of the rule. The typesetting command for drawing a 1-point rule, 30 picas long, indented 2 picas from the left margin of a type column might be ⟨DHR1,30,2⟩. Individual parameters are generally separated from each other by commas or some other separator. If a parameter is not supplied by the compositor, the computer will either fail to execute the command, or will supply a parameter to complete the code. Parameters supplied by the computer are called **default** parameters.

Commands are typically surrounded on each side by a delimiter, such as the symbols "⟨" and "⟩" in the examples above. **Delimiters** alert the composition system that the information contained within them is a typesetting command, not text to be typeset.

The operator specifies point size, line length, leading, font selection, and all other typographic operations with typesetting codes. These codes can become quite involved and, in many ways, can be considered a computer language of their own. The commands needed to typeset a simple line of type might read: ⟨LL36⟩⟨PT12⟩⟨LD14⟩⟨FT21⟩. This line of code commands would specify type to be set with a line length of 36 picas, a point size of 12 points, with 14-point leading, in font number 21. In this case, the number 21 is assigned to a specific type font, such as Century Book. Commands could be added to this line to control the depth of the page; the spacing between individual characters and words; the amount of extra space that the computer can place between lines of type to fill out the page depth; or virtually any typesetting function the composition system can perform. A certain amount of study and prac-

tice is required before an operator can learn all of the typesetting codes for even the simplest composition system.

A screen filled with typesetting codes and characters to be typeset can appear confusing at first glance. Most typesetting screens provide some method of distinguishing between the typesetting commands and the text to be typeset. One common method is to display typesetting codes in a different intensity, either brighter or dimmer than the text (figure 5.13).

Code Syntax. The placing of commands in their proper form and sequence to perform a typographical operation is called **syntax.** Syntax can be compared to the rules of grammar in a spoken language. Proper syntax allows the computer to go from one command to the next, executing each command in its proper order. Most composition systems are syntax specific: If the syntax requires that point size

Figure 5.13. Code and type on a computer screen Note that lines of code are displayed in less intense light than the characters to be typeset.
Courtesy of Compugraphic Corporation

be specified before line length, for example, and this order is reversed, the computer will not be able to compose the job until the syntax is corrected. On code-driven composition systems, an operator must learn both the code format and the code syntax.

Menu-Driven Systems.   Composing systems which are menu-driven instead of code-driven are becoming popular. On these systems the compositor selects typographical features such as point size, font changes, and other selections from a list of possible operations displayed in a menu on the computer screen

Figure 5.14. Menu display The operator selects an operation from among the menus or "icons" (pictures) displayed on the right side of the computer screen.
Courtesy of Varityper, a division of AM International, Inc.

(figure 5.14). Menu items are selected by moving a pointer on the screen. The pointer is typically controlled with a hand-held device, called a "mouse," or with a special "pen." The pointer can also be used to move the cursor on most menu-driven systems. Menu selection eliminates the need for memorizing commands and can speed up operator training. However, trained operators can generally enter codes faster than they can make selections from a menu or series of menus.

Composition

During composition the composition system executes all of the typesetting commands that arrange the information in the file as it will appear on the output. On some typesetting systems, composition occurs as characters are keyboarded. On other systems, composition is a separate function, activated by the operator after the text and typesetting commands are entered. On all machines, composition is a calculation process.

It is probably easiest to understand composition through an example. Assume that a page of type is to be typeset following the command string given in the previous example, ⟨LL36⟩⟨PT12⟩⟨LD14⟩⟨FT21⟩. During composition, the computer calculates the number of characters from font 21 that can fit on a line of type 36 picas long when set in point size 12. If the type is to be set flush left or flush right, the computer calculates the width of each individual character and the width of each individual word, and places each word on a single output line until there is no more room on the line measure to fit the next word. The computer then places the next word on a new line and begins the calculation process again. This sounds simple enough, but it involves thousands of calculations. Remember that typeset characters are proportionally spaced. Not only does the *m* in a specific typeface have a wider set width than the letter *i* in that typeface, but a bold face, condensed, or italic *m* in the same typeface will all have different set widths. During composition the computer must calculate the set width of every character, from every font specified, in the specified point size to determine how many characters will fit on a line of a specified measure.

Justification.   If the typeset copy is to be justified, instead of set flush left or right, the composition process becomes more involved. For justified copy, the line of type must be both flush left and flush right on the measure. To justify copy, the computer must locate the last word that will fit on the line, calculate the space remaining on the line, then insert the space remaining evenly into the existing spaces between words and characters in the line. Most systems perform this function by inserting the bulk of the remaining line space evenly between the words on the line. Any space remaining after this initial division is inserted evenly between all of the characters on the line. Parameters, entered by the operator, specify the maximum and minimum amount of space that the computer can insert between words and characters to justify a line.

Hyphenation.   Hyphenation further complicates the composition process. Figure 5.15 shows an example of justified copy without hyphenation, and the same copy with hyphenation. As can be seen, hyphenation makes the copy tighter, easier to read, and more visually appealing. Without hyphenation, all of the space remaining between the last full word that can fit on a line and the next word to be typeset must be inserted in the line as white space. If the next word to be typeset is short, this does not present a problem. But if the next word to be typeset

(a)

    The word "technology" has become a common part of the vocabulary of this society. Technology is often discussed as if it were some mythical beast that could be coaxed or caged into submission. We tend to view it as a physical object or living being that we can blame for most of our social ills.

(b)

    The word "technology" has become a common part of the vocabulary of this society. Technology is often discussed as if it were some mythical beast that could be coaxed or caged into submission. We tend to view it as a physical object or living being that we can blame for most of our social ills.

Figure 5.15. Justification The first three lines of copy in (a) show pronounced rivers of white space; hyphenation (b) eliminates this problem.

is a long word, a great deal of white space will be inserted in the line, and the output copy may end up with **rivers** of white space. To avoid these rivers, an end-of-line hyphenation decision must be made for each line of type.

On the first computer composition systems, all end-of-line decisions were made by the operator. During composition, the computer first calculated the words that would fit on a line, then alerted the operator through an audible "beep" or a flashing light to hyphenate the next word. The operator then determined whether the word could be hyphenated and, if so, inserted a hyphen from the keyboard.

Automatic Hyphenation and Justification.   Hyphenation software for automatic hyphenation during justification is available on most modern composition systems. Such software is commonly referred to as **H&J software.** With automatic hyphenation, when the composition system locates the last word that will fit on the line, it can "look the word up" in its hyphenation dictionary software, locate the proper hyphenation point, and hyphenate the word, putting all of the characters before the hyphen on one line, automatically inserting a hyphen, and placing the remaining characters on the next line to be typeset.

Automatic hyphenation software typically provides the computer with instructions, based on the rules of grammar, for hyphenating words. This software cannot cover all hyphenation possibilities, however. For example, H&J software can rarely identify words that should never be hyphenated. A case in point would be a proper name, such as the name "Sunfield." Based on the rules of grammar, the hyphenation software would recognize "Sun" and "field" as two separate syllables, and attempt to hyphenate the word after the first syllable, "Sun." To overcome this and other limitations, exception word dictionaries are provided with most H&J software to give special instructions for problem words. Words that the standard hyphenation dictionary does not hyphenate properly, or words that should never be hyphenated can be placed in the **exception dictionary** through the keyboard. During composition, the last word in each line is compared with every word in the exception list. If the word is located in the exception list, the exception dictionary hyphenation is used. If the word is not included in the exception list, it is hyphenated according to the rules in the standard hyphenation dictionary. Most H&J software also allows the operator to manually insert a keyboard hyphen in a word, even though the use of a hyphen at this location in the word may not follow the rules in the hyphenation dictionary. Because automatic hyphenation requires few end-of-line decisions from the operator, it greatly increases the speed of the composition process.

Composition Software

In addition to hyphenation and justification software, software is included on most modern composition systems to perform many of the following typographical operations:

- Set type in various sizes, typically from 6-point up to 72-point or larger
- Set type as a reverse (white type on a black background)
- Set characters slanted to the right or left, as outline type, or as shadow type to produce decorative type or type which appears italic
- Typeset vertical and horizontal rules and decorative borders
- Typeset grids of rules for business forms
- Alter the set width of characters to typeset them as condensed or expanded
- Set type in columns and tabs

Most systems offer **automatic kerning** of selected letter pairs (figure 5.16). Some composition systems also offer additional software, such as spelling checkers and code syntax checkers. This type of software greatly increases the accuracy of keyboard input and eliminates the need for correcting typing errors in the file. Increased keyboard accuracy represents a significant increase in productivity.

Automatic Page Make-Up.   Advanced composition systems feature software for auto-

(a) Warren Peace

(b) Warren Peace

Figure 5.16. Automatic kerning Kerning decreases the visual space between selected character pairs. The *W* and the *a* are a character pair that would appear too far apart if set without kerning (a). Kerning brings such character pairs closer together (b).

matic page make-up. With page make-up software, a compositor can cause the computer to compose a file and automatically divide it up into individual typeset pages, based on the designer's specifications. In addition, page make-up software can be used to typeset trim marks at the top and bottom of each page, automatically number the pages in sequential order, ensure that the top and bottom lines of type on each page are set at the same depth on each page and, in short, make all of the decisions that a layout artist would make during paste-up.

Text and Graphics Integration. Systems with automatic page make-up often feature **text and graphics integration;** that is, they can include both text and graphics on a typeset page. On some systems, graphics are scanned as the job is typeset. In such systems, keyboard code instructions for illustrations are placed in the file along with the copy to be typeset. The illustration code identifies the illustration to be scanned and specifies the physical size it should be and its position on the typeset page. When the output device encounters this code, it alerts the operator that a scan is required. The operator then inserts the required illus-

tration into a graphic scanner, which scans it and sends it to the output device (figure 5.17).

On larger text and graphics systems, both the graphics and the text can be placed in disk storage and manipulated on the display screen (figure 5.18). With these systems, the image is pre-scanned before typesetting starts, digitized, and placed on disk. During output, both the graphics and the text to be typeset are on-line as digitized information ready for use by the output device. Pre-scanning speeds up the typesetting process, because the output device does not have to stand idle while the image is scanned. However, digitized storage of graphic images requires a great deal of disk space, far more than is required for storage of alphabet character and symbol information. This storage requirement limits the use of on-line graphic storage to only the largest composition systems.

Page Display. On code-driven composing systems, the computer screen, cluttered with text and typesetting codes, generally bears no resemblance to the typeset page. The compositor must interpret the typesetting codes to visualize how the page will look after it is typeset. To help with this visualization process, some composition systems provide a means for the operator to "preview" the page before typesetting. On such systems, a page to be typeset can be composed and sent to the computer screen for previewing. Most preview screens will display the images in their proper location, show differences between bold and roman type and between different typefaces (figure 5.19). Many devices will display both text and graphics. After the operator has checked the copy on the preview screen, it can be sent to the output device. If the preview screen displays an error in the copy, the error can be corrected before typesetting. Preview capabilities can mean a savings in both time and money, because accurate

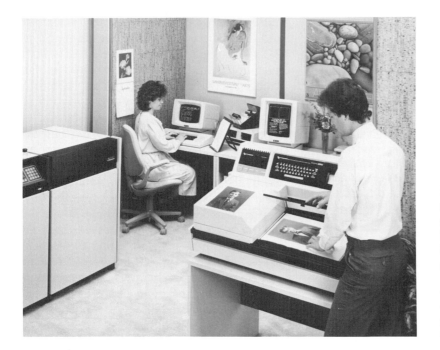

Figure 5.17. Graphics scanning for inclusion in a typeset job As the job is being typeset, graphic images are scanned and sent to the typesetter. Note areas (boxes) left in the screen display of the file for the graphics.
Courtesy of Compugraphic Corporation

Figure 5.18. Text and graphics integration Both text and graphics can be arranged on the screen, made-up into a page, then sent to the output device.
Courtesy of Texet Corporation

copy can be typeset the first time through the phototypesetter, without needing to be typeset a second time to correct formatting errors.

WYSIWYG. WYSIWYG (pronounced "wizzy wig") is an abbreviation for "What You See Is What You Get." WYSIWYG systems take the notion of the preview screen a bit further. On a WYSIWYG system, as they are keyboarded, images appear on the computer screen almost exactly as they will appear on the typeset output. On code-driven WYSIWYG systems, the screen is generally split so that one area on the screen shows the code and text and another area shows the made-up page (figure 5.20).

Figure 5.20. WYSIWYG display This screen is split, with the WYSIWYG display above and the typesetting code below.
Courtesy of Compugraphic Corporation

Figure 5.19. A preview device With a preview screen, the operator can view the job before outputting it to the phototypesetter.
Courtesy of Compugraphic Corporation

On many menu-driven WYSIWYG systems, the pointer used to select commands from the menus displayed on the computer screen can also be used to select, move, and arrange individual characters or groups of characters. To put more space between two letters, for example, a compositor simply selects one letter with the pointer, and moves it away from the other. With such systems the type displayed on the screen can be tilted, set backwards so that it is wrong-reading or flipped upside down, and lines of type can be set at an angle on the page, without ever entering a single command code. The relative

simplicity of menu-driven WYSIWYG systems, coupled with the ability to manipulate screen images and see how they will appear before they are typeset, is an obvious improvement over code-driven composition systems with no previewing capabilities.

Output Devices

A photocomposition system is of little value without some type of output device. We have already discussed one type of output, output which is displayed on the computer screen. Screen output is often referred to as **soft copy.** Most images for printing are assembled as **hard copy** to be pasted up on a mechanical and converted onto photographic film for platemaking. For an image to reproduce well on film, the original copy must be high-contrast. That is, the images on the mechanical must be dense black, surrounded by white. The images on the printed sheet will appear as exact duplicates of the images on the mechanical. Thus, the cleaner and sharper the original image—that is, the clearer it is and the smoother and better defined its edges are—the better it will appear as a reproduction on the printed sheet.

Most computer output devices form text and graphic images as a series of either dots or lines. Dot formation is typically referred to as **dot matrix.** A matrix is a grid consisting of horizontal and vertical lines. If you overlay a matrix on a character, the character can be broken up into a pattern of individual squares on the matrix. Dot matrix output utilizes this pattern to generate an image. To the central processing unit, the matrix is a grid of bits (binary numbers *0* and *1*) which activate "yes-no" switches. To reproduce a letter such as an uppercase *M*, these individual bits cause the central processing unit to turn on only the switches in the matrix that define the letter *M*. The individual bits in the matrix can be thought of as forming a map of the bits that cause the output device to produce the dots or squares (pixels) that form the image (figure 5.21). For this reason, dot matrix representation of images is often referred to as **bit mapping. Raster** imaging is basically the same process. The computer divides the image up into a bit map, but the output device uses the bit map to reproduce the image as a series of lines, instead of dots or squares.

One important concern when selecting an output device for a composition system is resolution. For computer output, **resolution** can be described as the smoothness of the image's edges. As will be seen, the more dots or lines used to generate an image, the higher the image's resolution will be.

A computer composing system can typically output information to a variety of output devices. Among these are strike-on printers, line and ink-jet printers, and photo-

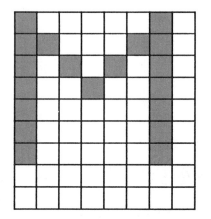

Figure 5.21. Dot matrix image formation The letter *M* can be reproduced as a series of pixels mapped by an electronic grid. The unused pixels provide space below and to the right of the character.

typesetters. Phototypesetting produces a clean, sharp, high-contrast image, and is the most common method of producing type images for printing. Strike-on, line, ink-jet, and laser printers cannot be considered phototypesetting devices because they do not reproduce images photographically. However, these output devices are frequently found on composition systems, and our discussion would not be complete without at least a brief explanation of them. Further information about ink-jet printers and laser printers is contained in Chapter 17.

Strike-On Printers. The first hard copy output devices utilized on computer systems were strike-on printers. These devices do not use either dot or raster image formation. Instead, they use strike-on character formation, similar to typewriter strike-on characters. With a strike-on printer, all of the characters and symbols that can be displayed by the printer are arranged on a type ball or on a wheel, called a "print wheel" or "daisy wheel" (figure 5.22). The computer sends the alphanumeric code representing a keyboard character to the printer. This code causes the ball or wheel to force the appropriate character against a ribbon which is impregnated with ink, or coated with carbon. When the character strikes the ribbon, an ink or carbon image of the character is transferred to the printer paper.

While some strike-on printers can produce fairly high-quality images, they have two major disadvantages. One drawback is the time required for the mechanical action of locating the correct character in front of the ribbon, then striking it against the ribbon. Thus, strike-on printers are slow, far slower than modern phototypesetters. Another drawback is that the printer can only reproduce the characters on the ball or wheel that is mounted in the printer head. Each time a new font is required in the job, the operator has to stop the printer, change the ball or wheel, and restart the printer. Some symbols, such as foreign language or mathematical symbols, cannot be reproduced at all. Except for the printing of horizontal and vertical lines, which can be formed by repeated dashes or periods, no graphic images can be produced.

Line Printers. Line printers generate dot matrix images. The printer head on a line printer contains a column of small wires, called "striker-wires" that are activated by the computer to strike against a ribbon. As the printer head moves across the printer paper, the individual wires are activated independently to produce the dot matrix pattern that defines the image. When the wires strike the printer ribbon, the image is transferred to the printer paper as a series of dots. Because several wires must be activated to form any character, line printers generate images only slightly faster than strike-on printers.

Line printer output is often used as proof copy for proofreading. On some composing systems, line printer output displays both the text to be typeset and the typesetting codes. On other systems, printer output displays characters that are visually representative of the typeset output. Bold characters, for example, will appear more bold on the output; italic characters will appear slanted (figure

a

b

Figure 5.22. Strike-on printer fonts Fonts for strike-on machines are arranged on print wheels or type balls.

Top–Courtesy of Compugraphic Corporation
Bottom–Courtesy of IBM

Sans Serif Regular

Sans Serif Bold

Sans Serif Regular Italic

Sans Serif Bold Italic

Serif Regular

Serif Bold

Serif Regular Italic

Serif Bold Italic

Figure 5.23. Line printer output

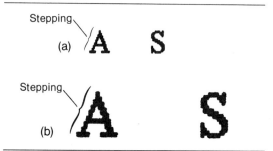

Figure 5.24. Stepping Low-resolution line printer output shows stepping (a). With 200% enlargement (b) stepping is quite pronounced.

5.23). Line printers on some composition systems can produce a fairly wide range of typographical features.

Line printer copy is rarely used for preparing mechanicals. Not only does it lack the high contrast characteristic of phototypeset copy, but it has very low resolution. On a typical line printer, 72 wire strikes may be made to generate a line 1 inch long. Such a printer would have a resolution of 72 dots per inch (DPI). This is an extremely low resolution for printing purposes. Note the jagged edges on the enlarged image of line printer output shown in figure 5.24. This jaggedness, called **stepping,** is quite pronounced on line printer output, and is one major reason that line printer output is typically used for proofing copy and not for mechanical preparation.

Ink-Jet Printers. Dot matrix image formation is also used by ink-jet printers. However, instead of generating an image by forcing wires against a ribbon, ink-jet printers transfer tiny droplets of ink from the printer head to the printer paper to form the image. The ink droplets are not transferred mechanically; no wires are moved. Thus, ink-jet printers tend to be considerably faster than line printers. However, like line printer images, ink-jet images tend to be low-resolution and are not used for producing images to be photographed for printing purposes.

Laser Printers. Laser printers are a marriage of two technologies: xerography (Chapter 17) and the laser light source. A laser beam in the printer is used to project the pattern of a character onto a revolving drum. The pattern is recorded on the drum as electrostatic charges. These electrostatic charges are then transferred from the drum to the printer paper. Toner is attracted to the paper in the charged image areas. The toner consists of tiny particles which melt when heated and adhere to the printer paper to produce the final copy (figure 5.25).

The formation of images with a concentrated light beam rather than a wire-strike gives laser printers several advantages over

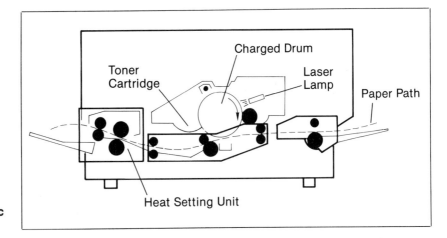

Figure 5.25. Schematic of a laser printer

Figure 5.26 Laser printer Low-speed laser printers like this one are a common peripheral on computer composition systems.
Courtesy of Linotype

Figure 5.27. Laser output Under 200% enlargement, laser output shows less stepping than line printer output.

up to eight 8½″ × 11″ pages per minute. Many laser printers can reproduce type in a variety of typefaces that duplicate the appearance of phototypesetter typefaces.

Even with these advantages, laser printers are not phototypesetters. While laser printer resolution is adequate for some printed images, it falls far short of the resolution produced by most phototypesetters, as can be seen in figure 5.27. Most laser printers reproduce only a limited number of type fonts in only a limited number of sizes, and most are not equipped to perform all of the typographical operations available on a modern composition system.

One common use for laser printers in

line printers. Laser printers can form images with much greater contrast, at much faster speeds, and with much higher resolutions than can line printers. Resolutions of over 300 DPI are common. Small laser printers, such as the one shown in figure 5.26, can output

composition systems is the use of laser printer output as proof copy. During full page make-up, a compositor can produce page proofs on a laser printer. The proofs will show image position, font changes, and many other typographical features. After the proof corrections are made, the operator can send nearly perfect copy to the phototypesetter. A sheet of paper for a laser printer costs only a few pennies; the photographic paper used in a phototypesetter costs approximately a dollar per foot. Laser proofing can mean a considerable savings in proofing costs for a 100-page typesetting job.

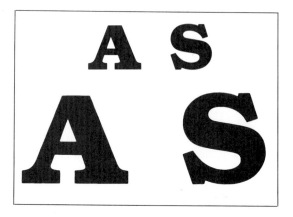

Figure 5.28. Phototypesetter output Even when it is enlarged 200%, it is difficult to see any signs of stepping in phototypesetter output.

Phototypesetters

A phototypesetter sets type by exposing individual characters and symbols onto light-sensitive media, such as photographic paper. Photographic paper is coated with a light-sensitive emulsion. During exposure, light strikes the paper and produces an image on the emulsion. This image cannot be seen until after the paper is developed in photographic chemistry. After development, the paper is rinsed, dried, and is ready for use on a mechanical.

Images produced through phototypesetting are extremely high-contrast: the images are dense black, and the paper is bright white. The resolution of phototypeset images is also quite high, much higher than the resolution available from any output devices we have so far discussed (figure 5.28). High contrast and high resolution make phototypeset output ideal for printing purposes.

The mechanical operation of a phototypesetter is not complicated. All that is required is an exposure unit that controls a light source which can project light onto the light-sensitive paper, and a means of positioning the paper in front of the exposure unit. On most machines, drive wheels are used to position the paper and advance it each time a new line of type is to be set. The exposure unit moves across the paper, exposing the individual characters and symbols that make up the line of type. Both the exposure unit and the paper drive wheels respond to commands sent from the composition system.

Paper for most devices is supplied in rolls, contained in light-tight boxes, ready for mounting in the phototypesetter (figure 5.29). During typesetting, the paper is fed from the box, past the exposure unit, into a light-tight take-up cassette (figure 5.30). Any light, including room light, will expose the paper. Thus the paper supply, the exposure unit, and the take-up cassette must all be housed in a light-tight area of the phototypesetter. After exposure, the take-up cassette is removed from the phototypesetter and placed in a processing unit for development (figure 5.31). The processing unit automatically draws the paper through baths of development chemicals and through a rinsing bath. Many processors have a drying unit that dries the paper after development. Typeset output is proofread, corrected, and delivered as typeset galleys to a layout artist for paste-up.

Figure 5.29. Phototypesetter paper Paper and film for phototypesetters are supplied in light-tight containers.
Courtesy of Compugraphic Corporation

Figure 5.30. Take-up cassette The light-tight take-up cassette receives the paper or film after exposure.
Courtesy of Compugraphic Corporation

As has been mentioned, many composition systems can process both text and graphics, and have page make-up capabilities. Machines of this type can assemble type and graphics into the exact position required on the printed page. Phototypesetters used with composition systems that offer full page make-up of text and graphics can often expose images on photographic film, as well as paper (figure 5.32). Full page make-up with exposure directly onto film eliminates the need for both layout and negative generation. Layout is accomplished by the composition system during page make-up. The film produced by the typesetter can be used to produce a printing plate. Elimination of both the layout and negative generation steps can mean considerable savings.

Film and paper are supplied by individual manufacturers in a variety of widths and with a variety of photographic emulsion characteristics. Development chemicals are also supplied by film or paper manufacturers. The types of development chemicals required is

Figure 5.31. Processing unit Film and paper can be developed, rinsed, and dried automatically in this unit.
Courtesy of Compugraphic Corporation

Figure 5.32. Film output This phototypeset film negative is ready for plate making.
Courtesy of Compugraphic Corporation

based on the characteristics, such as emulsion surface and coating, of the film or paper. Often, one manufacturer's film or paper cannot be developed in another manufacturer's chemicals. Some manufacturers require different chemicals for developing film than for

developing paper. Individual manufacturers provide information about their products, including the compatibility of their film, paper, and development chemicals. This information should be checked carefully before processing typeset output to ensure that a dense, high-resolution image is produced.

There have been many advances in the way images are actually projected in the exposure unit. Phototypesetting machines are classified into "generations," based on the manner in which they project an image during exposure. Four generations of phototypesetters have been developed.

First-Generation Phototypesetters. The first phototypesetter, produced in 1946, used the idea of the Linotype casting system. Instead of using a die to cast molten metal and form a character, each individual character was carried on a separate film negative in a small metal frame. As a character key was pressed on the keyboard, the frame carrying that character would fall into place in front of the light source. The light would then be projected through the film onto a sheet of photographic paper. Typesetters that utilize this type of character formation are called first-generation phototypesetters. Because a character could not be typeset until the frame that carried the character was positioned in front of the light source, first-generation phototypesetters were slow. Because of this limitation, first-generation phototypesetters have been replaced with second- and third-generation devices.

Second-Generation Phototypesetters. Second-generation phototypesetters place an entire font of characters on a single film strip and move each symbol in front of a light source as directed by the computer. One system rotates the font to position the image, then flashes the exposure lamp when the image is positioned (figure 5.33). Characters are en-

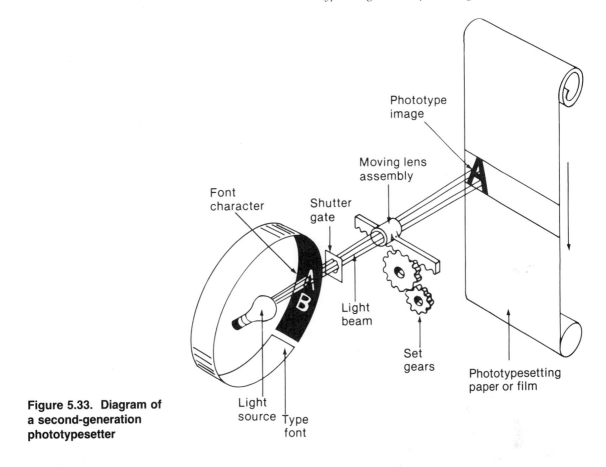

Figure 5.33. Diagram of a second-generation phototypesetter

larged, reduced, or slanted through the use of a moving lens assembly.

Some models can carry several variations of a typeface on the same film strip. A typical film strip might carry a font such as Helvetica in bold, italic, and condensed. Movement of the lens assembly for enlargement and reduction is limited, so more than one film font may be required for a particular job. One film font may product Helvetica in a range of sizes, perhaps 6-point to 24-point; another font is required to produce larger sizes.

There are several disadvantages to second-generation phototypesetters. The me-

chanical operation of positioning characters carried on a film strip is considerably faster than the positioning of individual film negatives used in first-generation machines. However, the rate of speed with which a film strip can be rotated to position a character is considerably slower than the rate of speed with which most composition computers can send information to a phototypesetter. Thus, the speed of the output device limits the overall speed of the photocomposition process. Second-generation phototypesetters can only typeset copy at a rate of 25 to 150 characters per second (CPS). An additional limitation is that only a few film strips can be loaded into the typesetter at a time. If a character is required that is not on a loaded film strip, the operator has to change the film strip before typesetting can proceed. This process of loading and unloading film strips also limits output speed. A final disadvantage is that the only images that can be produced are the letters and symbols contained on the film strips. It was not until the development of third-generation devices that complex graphic images could be phototypeset.

Third-Generation Phototypesetters. Third-generation phototypesetters form images on a cathode ray tube (CRT), similar to the way a picture is formed on a television screen. All CRT character generation is either dot matrix or raster formation. The individual lines that make up a raster image are called "scan lines." The number of scan lines or dots used to make up an image determines the image's resolution. Extremely high-resolution images with over 15,000 lines or dots per inch can be produced.

There are two basic techniques for transferring the CRT image to a sheet of photographic paper or film. In the first, light from the CRT screen is focused through a lens, then reflected from a moving mirror onto the film or paper (figure 5.34). The mirror directs each character into its proper position on the typeset line. With the second technique, a fiber optics bundle, consisting of thousands of fiber optic strands, carries the light to the photographic material. The fibers run from the CRT screen to a glass plate. As the film or paper is moved across the plate, the composition system sends light through individual fibers in the bundle to expose the film or paper and form the image.

Third-generation phototypesetters do not require film strips or film negatives to produce characters or images. Type fonts for these devices are supplied as digitized information

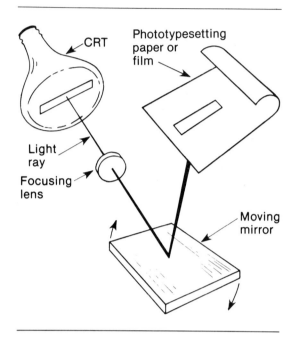

Figure 5.34. Diagram of a third-generation phototypesetter with CRT image projection

which is sent to the exposure unit from computer disks. Because font information is digitized, the speed with which information for forming individual characters can be sent to the CRT is limited only by the speed with which the typesetting computer can read information from the font disk. As a result, characters can be typeset at extremely high speeds. Font disks can be loaded individually, or placed on-line in the typesetter. Many third-generation machines can store over 500 digitized fonts on-line. On-line font storage eliminates the need to change font disks during typesetting, which further increases output speed.

Along with increased speed, third-generation machines offer the ability to typeset almost any image. Type can be produced in a large variety of sizes, from 6 points or less to over 100 points high. In addition, type can be slanted, reversed, expanded, condensed, or set in any manner that the composition computer can instruct the CRT or fiber optics bundle to display it. With the addition of a graphics scanner to scan graphic images and reproduce them as digitized information, CRT machines can typeset both line illustrations and halftones. A photocomposition system with full page make-up software and the ability to combine text and graphics can be configured with a third-generation photo-typesetter to generate images that are literally "ready for press." Some machines can even expose images directly onto a printing plate.

Fourth-Generation Phototypesetters. Fourth-generation phototypesetters typeset raster images from digitized information. However, instead of utilizing a CRT tube or fiber optics bundle to project the image, fourth-generation machines utilize a laser beam for image formation.

The laser exposure unit shown in figure 5.35 splits a laser beam into two separate

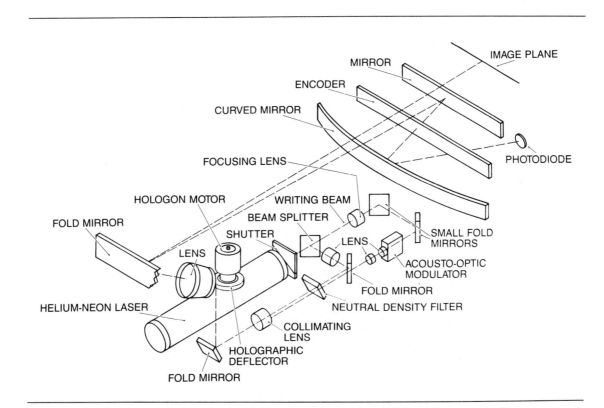

Figure 5.35. Schematic of a fourth-generation phototypesetter with a laser exposure unit.
Courtesy of Compugraphic Corporation

beams: a writing beam and a reflectance beam. The writing beam exposes the image; the reflectance beam is read by an internal control system, and controls the placement, accuracy, and consistency of the writing beam. In its path to the photographic paper or film, the writing beam is reflected off mirrors, and is filtered through an acousto-optic modulator which adjusts beam intensity for proper exposure for the film or paper being used. The beam then passes through a deflector which positions it in the proper location along the horizontal plane and moves it horizontally to produce scan lines.

Only image areas are exposed; light which would expose nonimage areas is directed away from the film or paper. Beam movement is only horizontal. Once all image areas on a horizontal axis are exposed, the film or paper is advanced and exposure begins along another horizontal axis. Thus all images, both text and graphics, consist of a series of horizontally drawn scan lines.

Fourth-generation phototypesetters of-

fer several advantages over third-generation devices, especially for the generation of graphic images. For this reason, fourth-generation phototypesetters are often referred to as **imagesetters.** One major advantage of fourth-generation devices for type production is the almost complete elimination of all stepping in type formation. Before fourth-generation machines, there were two methods used for character creation: dot matrixing or vectoring. As previously explained, dot matrixing composes characters based on a bit map of square dots. This technique reproduces curves as stair steps (figure 5.36a). **Vectoring** creates characters as the linear connection of a series of points. This technique reproduces curves as angles connected by straight lines (figure 5.36b). With fourth-generation laser imaging, it is possible to produce true curves, based on mathematical formulas. With this technique, called **curvilinear type generation,** a character's outline is defined as a complex mathematical expression rather than as a bit map or as a series of points. This makes it

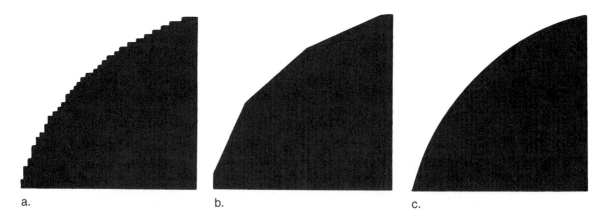

a.   b.   c.

Figure 5.36. Curve formation with dot matrix (a), vectoring (b), and curvilinear type generation (c).
Courtesy of Compugraphic Corporation

possible to output characters with true curves rather than approximated curves. Even when greatly magnified, laser imaged characters exhibit smooth curves, almost entirely free from stepping (figure 5.36c). In addition, the mathematical formulas used to create characters can be mathematically manipulated by the computer to enlarge, reduce, or modify them. Thus type can be output in much larger sizes than could bit-mapped or vectored characters while still maintaining their design integrity.

Graphic imaging is also greatly enhanced with imagesetters. One reason is that the exposure precision of the laser light source is much higher than that which can be achieved by either a cathode ray tube or a fiber optics bundle. No matter how many individual fiber optic strands in the bundle, or how many individual pixels on the CRT, each individual strand or pixel would be much larger than an individual flash from the laser exposure unit.

A final advantage of laser imaging is that it makes possible the use of a page description language during image generation. To understand the effect of a page description language, think of the operations that a third-generation device with CRT exposure would go through to typeset a page containing two columns of type. The text for the type to be produced would be contained, along with codes for all page formatting and typographical operations, as digitized data in the composition file, and passed to the typesetter as a continuous stream of information. The typesetter would start typesetting with the first character in the first column of type and proceed typesetting the characters to the bottom of that column. The paper or film would then have to be reversed to the proper location to start typesetting the second column at the same page depth as the first. Reversing the paper or film could result in improper align-

ment of type and images; the more frequent the reversals, the higher the chance of improper image alignment. While slight variations in alignment will have no significant effect on line art or type, such variations could seriously affect the appearance of a halftone image.

With a **page description language,** the total page is laid out in computer memory before typesetting starts. Thus the typesetter never needs to reverse the film or paper because all of the text and graphics are constructed in horizontal exposure sweeps that cover the width of the page. When all of the exposures for one sweep along one horizontal axis are complete, the film or paper is advanced and the next horizontal sweep is made. The page is exposed in the image areas along its complete page width with each sweep. Because the film or paper moves at a steady rate in only one direction, image placement is much more precise than could be achieved if the film or paper direction had to be reversed.

Composition software which uses page description languages is becoming common on both large and small composition systems. Not only do page description languages offer the advantage of increased image accuracy during full page make-up, but most languages provide compatibility among a variety of devices. That is, when a page description language is used, the output device does not have to be completely compatible with the front end composition system. If the output device can read the page description language, it can format the page. Thus the page description language can be viewed as a translator through which output from a variety of composition systems can be made compatible with a variety of output devices. This feature increases options in equipment configuration, flexibility for the customer in purchasing typesetting services or equipment, and flexibility for the compositor in the overall typesetting operation. From the customer's point of view, the text and graphics for the job can be entered in a word processing program on a microcomputer. The information can be formatted into a page description language and telecommunicated (or simply given as disk-based information) to any compositor who has equipment that is compatible with that page description language. From the compositor's point of view, any information can be typeset without re-keyboarding, providing it is formatted into the page description language used by their equipment. In either case, as there are far fewer different page description languages than there are different composition systems, the problem of the compatibility between input and output device is greatly reduced by the use of page description languages.

Microcomputer Applications

The microcomputer is becoming a common component in many composition systems. One of the first applications for microcomputers in composition systems were as "dumb terminals." To serve as a dumb terminal, a microcomputer requires software, called "terminal emulation" software. **Terminal emulation** makes the keyboard and screen on the microcomputer appear and behave in every way exactly as do the keyboard and screen on the composition computer. Thus the microcomputer can be used as an input and editing terminal for the composition system. Data input into the microcomputer can be sent to the composition computer for composition. With terminal emulation software and a suitable microcomputer, an additional input terminal can be added to a composing system at a relatively inexpensive price.

Desktop Composition Systems.   When compared to the microcomputers available only a few years ago, today's machines have more memory, greater data storage capacity, more software available, and the ability to output to a greater variety of output devices. They are also easier to learn and use, and are less expensive.

Several companies provide software that makes microcomputers perform like composition systems. These small, relatively inexpensive microcomputer-based composition systems have become known as "desktop composition" or "desktop publishing" systems. Advanced composition software for desktop systems includes hyphenation, justification, and many other typographical features; menu selection; text and graphics processing; page make-up; and preview or WYSIWYG capabilities. Software is also available for many microcomputers that allows them to output to phototypesetters, typically through the use of a page description language (figure 5.37).

One advantage a desktop system has over traditional composition systems is that the word processing software for text input and editing available on most desktop systems is far less complicated and much easier to learn than are the word processing programs on most large composition systems. Therefore, less training is needed to operate most desktop systems.

There is no question that a desktop composition system is less expensive than most larger, high-production composition systems. However, desktop systems have their limitations. They are generally much slower than larger systems. Thus, dollars saved on equipment and training may be lost in increased production time. Also, while most desktop publishing software can perform *some* of the functions available on larger composition systems, few desktop systems can perform *all* of

Figure 5.37. A desktop publishing system This microcomputer system has a mouse, located to the right of the keyboard, WYSIWYG screen display, an external disk drive, a raster image processor (RIP), located under and to the right of the computer, for processing images and sending them to the typesetter, which is located to the left of the computer.
Courtesy of Linotype

the functions a larger system is likely to offer. Even with these limitations, a desktop composition system can be a good alternative to a larger system if the work load is not heavy, and the numbers of typographic operations needed are few.

Key Terms

hardware
software
data
memory
central processing unit
input/output
peripheral
alphanumeric code
digitize
mainframe

microcomputer
optical character recognition
pixel
telecommunications
modem
baud rate
floppy disk
hard disk
code-driven
menu-driven

hyphenation & justification
automatic page make-up
text and graphics integration
WYSIWYG
dot matrix
raster imaging
phototypesetting
desktop publishing

Questions for Review

1. What are the three major components of a computer system, and what functions do they perform?

2. What three methods are used to enter data into a computer composition system, and how is each accomplished?

3. Describe four types of information storage media used on computer systems, and state the differences between each.

4. What operations are performed during editing and during composition?

5. Describe the elements of a typical typesetting command.

6. What is the difference between code-driven and menu-driven computer composition systems?

7. What is the advantage of automatic page make-up with text and graphics integration?

8. What does the term WYSIWYG mean?

9. Explain the terms binary, bit, dot matrix, bit mapping, and pixel as they relate to computer image generation systems.

10. How do strike-on, line, and laser printers generate images? What is the difference in resolution between these images?

11. How does a phototypesetter generate an image? Why are phototypeset images most often used for printing purposes?

12. Discuss the differences between first-, second-, third-, and fourth-generation phototypesetters.

13. What are the advantages and disadvantages of a desktop composition system?

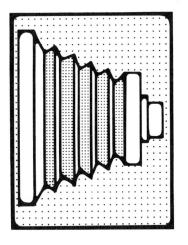

Chapter Six

Line Photography

Anecdote to Chapter Six

A gun camera
Courtesy of the International
Museum of Photography at
George Eastman House

Cameras have been produced in all shapes and sizes for purposes from the sublime to the ridiculous. One of the most entertaining periods of photographic history was the brief vogue of "detective cameras." These devices were not intended for police detectives but rather were designed for amateur photographers who wished to disguise the fact that they were taking a picture. Such cameras were the first attempt at candid or unstaged photography. Cameras were hidden in strange places such as flowers and hats, camouflaged as neckties, and even concealed in walking-stick handles.

Perhaps the strangest detective camera was the gun camera, built around 1882. This camera looked exactly like a gun. It is interesting to speculate how long an individual would stand still if he thought he was being shot at instead of merely having his picture taken.

The gun camera is a part of photographic history, but it is still a common event for a photographer to "shoot a picture."

Objectives for Chapter Six

After completing this chapter you will be able to:

- Classify photographic films.
- Identify the basic parts of any camera and recall their names and purposes.
- List the basic line photography tools.
- Define basic exposure.
- Recall the steps in making a basic line exposure on a process camera.
- Identify the variables in photographic chemical processing.
- Recall the steps in chemical processing for line photography.
- Explain the process of making film duplicates.
- Explain the process of making diffusion transfers.

Introduction

When the term *photography* is used, we tend to think first of pictures processed at our corner drug store, school pictures, or perhaps a family portrait. This kind of photography is called "continuous-tone photography" and is an important part of our world. However, the applications of photography are much more far reaching than continuous-tone photography. Infrared photography can predict crop production from photographs taken from airplanes or detect cancer in the human body. X-rays have long been used to assist in setting bones. Photography is used to produce miniature electronic circuits, and photofabrication is a growing part of the metal-working industry.

As we learned in Chapters 4 and 5, most type images for printing production are generated photographically, through typesetting. In addition, negative and positive film images are used to record images on the plate or image carrier. All images carriers—whether used for relief, screen, or lithographic printing—can be photographically prepared.

All of the major printing processes place a single consistent layer of ink on some receiver, such as paper. This idea cannot be overemphasized. *Printers reproduce only lines.*

These lines can be so big that we see them as huge ink areas or so small that we need a magnifying glass to see them, but they all have the same ink density (figure 6.1). The primary concern of this chapter is the production of line images that can be used with the printing processes. This process is called **line photography.**

Except by special techniques, it is not possible to print a **continuous-tone** photograph, such as the pictures used in this book. Continuous-tone photographs have the characteristic of varying shades of gray, called tones. A picture reproduced in a book or magazine is not a continuous-tone image. Such a picture is reproduced through **halftone photography.** This process breaks the tones of a picture into small, dense dots that trick the eye into seeing what appear to be various tones. Chapter 7 deals with halftone photography.

The Nature of Light

The basis of photography is a chemical change caused by the action of light on a light-sensitive material, called an emulsion. It is generally agreed that light is electromagnetic radiation measured in wavelengths emitted from either a natural source (the sun) or an artificial source, such as a camera light (figure 6.2). All electromagnetic radiation, whether gamma rays, visible light, heat, or radio and television signals, travels in waves. The effect produced by radiation is determined by wavelength, which is measured by the distance from one wave crest to the next (figure 6.3). The top scale in figure 6.2 shows that X-ray radiation has a very short wavelength and that radio waves have a long wavelength. Figure 6.2 also illustrates the relationship of visible light to the spectrum of known electromagnetic radiation. What we see as vis-

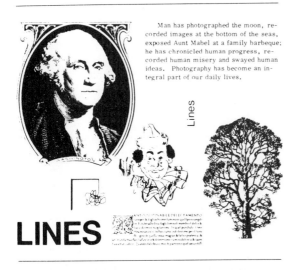

Figure 6.1. Examples of line reproduction This illustration shows some different images that are reproduced by lines.

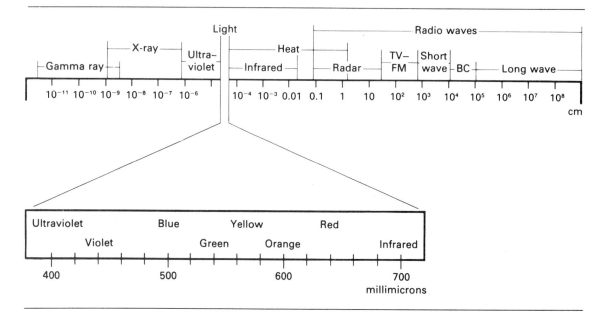

Figure 6.2. Wavelengths of different colors of the visible light spectrum

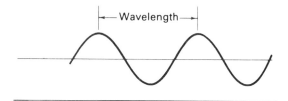

Figure 6.3. Diagram of wavelength

ible light is the wavelengths in the light spectrum that are of the proper length to stimulate the optic nerve.

Because light waves are small, they are generally measured in millimicrons (mµ) (one millimicron = one billionth of a meter, or twenty-five millionths of an inch) or in Angstrom units (Å or A.U.) (one millimicron = ten Angstrom units). Each color of the visible spectrum has a unique wavelength. White light is the balanced presence of all radiation from the visible spectrum.

The human eye can perceive wavelengths from about 400 millimicrons to about 700 millimicrons. The shorter wavelengths (closer to 400 millimicrons), produce the colors on the blue end of the spectrum, and longer wavelengths (closer to 700 millimicrons) produce the colors at the red end of the spectrum. The maximum sensitivity of the human eye is in the green portion of the visible spectrum.

Radiation in the visible spectrum produces a chemical reaction on a light-sensitive emulsion. It is this reaction that makes photography possible. As explained in Appendix B, graphic arts photographic processes use artificial light sources which vary in the range of wavelengths of visible light they produce. Some light sources produce wavelengths high in the blue end of the spectrum; others produce wavelengths high in the red end. As will be seen in what follows, light-sensitive emulsions are formulated to record selected wavelengths of light. That is, emulsions are produced that are sensitive to some colors in the spectrum but not to others.

Light-Sensitive Materials

All light-sensitive materials, whether films or plates, can be classified according to three main variables:

- Color sensitivity
- Contrast
- Film speed

Color Sensitivity. **Color sensitivity** describes the area of the visible electromagnetic spectrum that will cause a chemical change in a particular emulsion. A **wedge spectrogram** is often used to show a film's reaction to light across the visible spectrum (figure 6.4). There are basically three types of light-sensitive emulsions: blue-sensitive, orthochromatic, and panchromatic materials.

Blue-sensitive materials are often called "color blind" because they react to only the blue end of the spectrum (figure 6.4b). On a negative they record high densities from blue light, but they record very little from the green or red end of the spectrum. Roomlight film, which can be used outside the darkroom, is blue light sensitive.

Orthochromatic material is not red-sensitive, but it is sensitive to all other portions of the visible spectrum (figure 6.4c). Because they are not sensitive to red light, "ortho" films can be safely handled under a red darkroom safelight.

Most film manufacturers provide a wedge spectograph for each of their films.

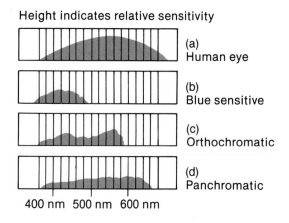

Height indicates relative sensitivity

(a) Human eye
(b) Blue sensitive
(c) Orthochromatic
(d) Panchromatic

400 nm 500 nm 600 nm

Figure 6.4. Examples of wedge spectrograms
A wedge spectrogram shows a film's reaction to light across the visible spectrum.

Figure 6.5 illustrates the sensitivity of one type of ortho film. The most efficient and accurate photographs will always be obtained when the peak sensitivity of a film's spectograph corresponds to the peak output of a light source (See Appendix B).

Panchromatic films are sensitive to all visible colors, and approximate the sensitivity of the human eye (figure 6.4d). Because they are sensitive to all of the colors that humans see, "pan" films can be used to record vari-

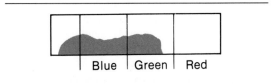

Blue | Green | Red

Figure 6.5. Wedge spectrogram for Kodak Kodalith Ortho film 2556, type 3 (ESTAR base)
Courtesy of Eastman Kodak Company

ations in tone, and are ideally suited for continuous-tone photography. Sensitivity to all wavelengths of light also means that a panchromatic emulsion will be exposed by any visible light that strikes it. Therefore, pan films must be processed in total darkness.

Contrast.   **Contrast** is a term that describes the compression or expansion of the shades or tones of the original copy on the film or plate. Contrast is described by a film's **characteristic curve,** also called a "Log E curve," "H & D curve," "Density-Log E curve," "D-Log_{10} E curve," or "sensitometric curve" (figure 6.6).

Film manufacturers provide characteristic curves for each of their films. Figure 6.7 illustrates the curve of Kodak's Ortho 3, an extremely high-contrast film. This curve reveals that a very slight change in exposure will provide a rapid jump in film density. This characteristic is ideal for printing production because the film will record sharp, clean lines between image and nonimage areas of the original copy.

Film Speed.   **Film speed** is the third main variable that can be used to classify light-sensitive materials. Each film or plate material requires a different amount of light to cause a chemical change in the emulsion. Emulsions that require little light are called "fast" and

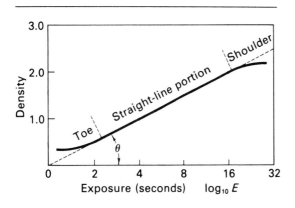

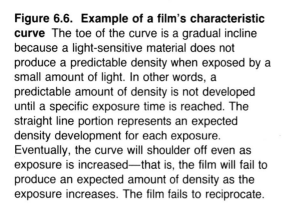

Figure 6.6. Example of a film's characteristic curve The toe of the curve is a gradual incline because a light-sensitive material does not produce a predictable density when exposed by a small amount of light. In other words, a predictable amount of density is not developed until a specific exposure time is reached. The straight line portion represents an expected density development for each exposure. Eventually, the curve will shoulder off even as exposure is increased—that is, the film will fail to produce an expected amount of density as the exposure increases. The film fails to reciprocate.

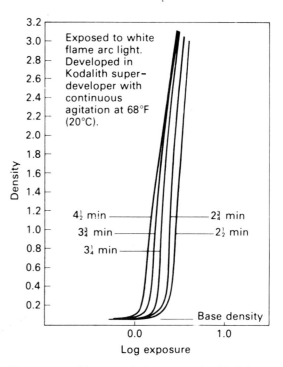

Figure 6.7. Characteristic curves for Kodak Ortho film
Courtesy of Eastman Kodak Company

Table 6.1. Exposure Indexes for Meters Marked for "ASA" Speeds or Exposure Indexes.

White-Flame Arc	Tungsten or Quartz-Iodine	Pulsed-Xenon*
10	6	10

* This value indicates the relative speed of this material to pulsed-xenon illumination as measured by a conventional time-totalizing device.

Note: Example of Exposure—When making a same-size (1:1) line reproduction under average shop conditions, with two 35-ampere arc lamps about 48 inches from the copyboard, expose for about 10 seconds at f/32.

Source: Eastman Kodak Company.

those that require much light are called "slow." Because there are so many different emulsions, each requiring a different amount of light, the concept of "fast versus slow" becomes meaningless. For that reason, an "exposure index" is assigned to each film by the manufacturer. The ASA system (developed by the American National Standards Institute) applies a number scale to relative film speed—the higher the number, the faster the film. For example, a film with an ASA rating of 25 will require twice as much light to create the same image density as does a film rated at ASA 50. Exposure index is assigned as a function of the type of light source used to expose the film. Table 6.1 lists the ASA ratings assigned to Kodak's Ortho 3 for several lighting conditions.

It is important to understand that color sensitivity, contrast, and film speed are unrelated variables that cannot be directly compared. It is possible to produce films that exhibit any combination of the three characteristics.

Film Emulsions

All photographic films use some type of light-sensitive material called an **emulsion** to re-

cord an image. The characteristics of the light-sensitive emulsion as well as the quantity and type of light reaching that emulsion will determine the sort of image recorded on the film. Most film emulsions are formed from a silver halide suspended in a gelatin compound (this is easy to picture as fruit suspended in a bowl of gelatin). The most common film emulsion is silver bromide (AgBr), which reacts rapidly and with predictable results. Silver iodide (AgI) and silver chloride (AgCl) are less common and are almost always used in combination with silver bromide to produce different film characteristics.

Whatever their chemical differences, all films are structured in the same general manner (figure 6.8). Glass was long used as a

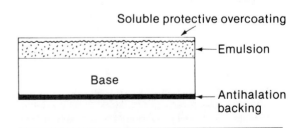

Figure 6.8. A typical film structure

transparent, extremely stable base material. It is still used in topographic mapping, electronic circuitry, or some color work—uses in which perfect registration (image location) is critical and in which the size of the film must not change with humidity, temperature, or age. Graphic arts films are generally made from a cellulose-ester- or polystyrene-based material. The advantage of these materials over glass is that they are flexible and much less expensive. Several patented flexible bases, such as Cronar, have been developed. These

materials compete with glass in dimensional stability.

The gelatin compound containing the silver halide emulsion is bonded to the base material by an adhesive lower layer. An additional stability problem is caused by this lamination of two chemically dissimilar materials, each of which is affected differently by the environment and by age.

For many years film was formed from only the base and emulsion material. This type of film had several problems. During exposure the light would pass through the camera lens, strike and expose the emulsion, and then pass on through the base material. Unfortunately, the light would not stop there. It would be reflected from the back of the base material and would again pass through the emulsion, reexposing it (figure 6.9a). To prevent this effect, an **antihalation dye** is now placed over the back of the film base. Instead of being reflected, the light is absorbed and exposes the film only once (figure 6.9b). With flexible base films, the antihalation dye also serves as an anticurl agent. The antihalation dye dissolves during chemical processing.

The second problem with a film made up of only an emulsion and a base was the frailness of the gelatin material in the emulsion. To overcome this problem, the emulsion is now blanketed with a transparent protective layer called **overcoating**. This overcoating protects the gelatin material from fingerprints and adds an antistress factor during handling. The overcoating also dissolves during chemical processing.

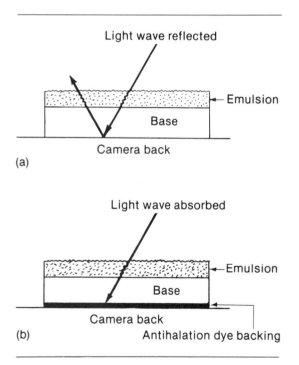

(a)

(b)

Figure 6.9. Comparison of light rays through two types of film structure Without the antihalation dye layer, light reflected from the back of the film base could reexpose the emulsion (a). The antihalation dye absorbs the light rays and prevents the problem of reexposure (b).

Camera Fundamentals

The intent in line photography is to record an accurate reproduction of an image (the copy) on the film emulsion. In order to do this, a device called a **process camera** is used. Process cameras vary in type, size, complexity, and cost. Regardless of their differences, all cameras serve three basic functions:

- They provide a place to mount the light-sensitive film
- They provide a means of focusing an image on the film
- They provide a system that controls the amount of light that reaches the film emulsion

It is possible to understand how a process camera works by building a general understanding of how any photographic system operates. Then we can move on to how line photography uses the same approach. All that is required for photography is some light source, a light-tight box to hold the film, a way to focus an image on the film, some way to control the amount of light that reaches the film, and, of course, something to photograph.

Whatever the light source, it should be directed at the object to be photographed. What the film records is reflected light. If we use artificial light, it is easy to position the light source so that all areas of the object receive the proper amount of light. If we use natural light (the sun), we have to position the object itself to get the proper illumination. In line photography, artificial light is always used to illuminate the image because uniform illumination across the whole image is required.

Process cameras all have the same characteristics and controls. There must be some sort of opening through which to pass and aim light. This is called a **lens.** It is necessary to be able to move the lens so the reflected light from the object will be sharp and clear on the film—this is called **focusing.** If the image is not in focus, a blurred picture will be produced.

After the image is focused, there must be a way to control the amount of light that passes through the lens. This is important. If not enough light reaches the film, no image will be recorded. It too much light strikes the film, an unacceptable image will be recorded. The two ways to control this passage of light are:

- By controlling the size of the lens opening **(aperture)**
- By controlling the amount of time the lens is open **(shutter speed)**

A simple way to understand the concept of controlling light is to think of a camera lens as a water faucet and of light as the water that passes through the pipe. First, consider the size of the pipe. It seems logical that a 2-inch pipe will pass nearly twice the amount of water as a 1-inch pipe in the same amount of time. If we run water through the 1-inch pipe for twice as much time as through the 2-inch pipe, the same amount of water should pass through each pipe. This example is not exactly accurate in terms of the specific amount of water passed, but it does show the importance of the relationship between time and area.

The light controls for a camera operate in a similar manner. We can, in effect, control the amount of time the lens stays open by means of the **shutter,** a timing mechanism that accurately measures the amount of time the lens passes light. This amount of time is called shutter speed. It is also possible to vary the size of the "pipe" or lens opening. This control is referred to as the **diaphragm.** The diaphragm controls the aperture, which is the size of the lens opening. This size is based on the f/stop system (figure 6.10).

The **f/stop system** is based on a ratio of aperture opening diameter to the focal length of the camera lens. **Focal length** is the distance from the node, or center, of the lens to

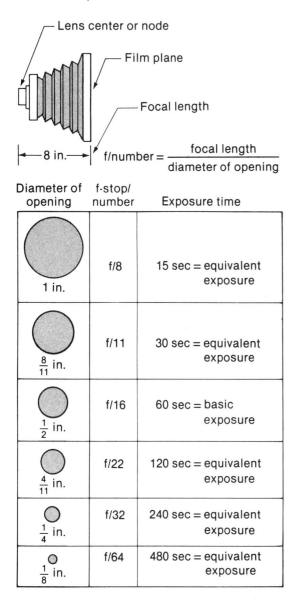

Lens center or node

Film plane

Focal length

8 in.

$$\text{f/number} = \frac{\text{focal length}}{\text{diameter of opening}}$$

Diameter of opening	f-stop/ number	Exposure time
1 in.	f/8	15 sec = equivalent exposure
$\frac{8}{11}$ in.	f/11	30 sec = equivalent exposure
$\frac{1}{2}$ in.	f/16	60 sec = basic exposure
$\frac{4}{11}$ in.	f/22	120 sec = equivalent exposure
$\frac{1}{4}$ in.	f/32	240 sec = equivalent exposure
$\frac{1}{8}$ in.	f/64	480 sec = equivalent exposure

Figure 6.10. Camera f/stops Camera f/stops are the relationship between focal length and lens opening sizes. In this figure, the focal length is 8 inches and the lens opening sizes vary from 1 inch to 1/8 inch. The basic exposure time is 60 seconds at f/16. Equivalent exposure times are given for the remaining f/stops.

the film board when the lens is focused at infinity (maximum reduction for graphic arts cameras) (figure 6.10). If the lens has an 8-inch focal length, a 1-inch opening is assigned the f/stop value of f/8; a ½-inch opening is f/16. Notice in figure 6.10 that the larger the f/stop number, the smaller the aperture opening. For example, changing the f/stop from f/32 to f/22 will double the aperture opening. Moving from f/16 to f/22 will halve it. This is because the numbers and openings that designate the f/stop are selected so that adjacent f/stop numbers differ by a factor of two in the amount of light they pass.

The aperture and shutter controls work together. Each f/stop either doubles or halves the cross-sectional area of the preceding f/stop. Thus the shutter speed can be halved or doubled to correspond with a one-stop diaphragm change. (Remember, when you change the f/stop, you are actually changing the diaphragm.) For example, if the film were being correctly exposed at f/16 for 40 seconds, an equivalent exposure could be made at f/8 for 10 seconds. The same amount of light would hit the film, and the film record would be the same. An understanding of this relationship is a powerful tool for any photographer. A camera operator often seeks to reduce the exposure time to save time and also to save camera lights, which, like any artificial light source, wear out with use.

Process Camera Controls

Line photography is also called "process photography," "reproduction photography," or "high-contrast photography." Whatever label is applied, the goals are the same: the camera operator makes precision enlargements and reductions, and critically controls line dimensions with a process camera (figure 6.11). The

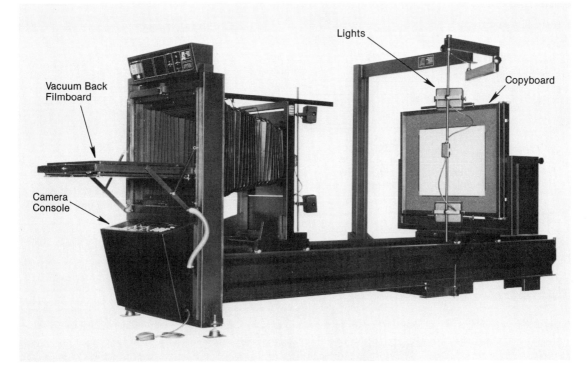

Figure 6.11. A horizontal process camera
Courtesy of ACTI Products, Inc.

process camera is large because it must be able to hold large sheets of film.

Process cameras can be classified according to where they are intended to be used or according to their basic shape. A **galley camera** is designed to operate in normal room light, so the film has to be loaded in a darkroom and then carried in some light-tight container to the camera. A **darkroom camera** is designed to operate in a safelight situation, so the photographer can load the film directly into the camera without leaving the darkroom. A **horizontal process camera** has a long stationary bed, with the film end usually in the darkroom and the lights and lens protruding through a wall into a normally lighted

room (figure 6.12). A **vertical process camera** is a self-contained unit that takes up little space in the darkroom itself (figure 6.13). Whatever type is used, all process cameras have the same general controls and characteristics.

A process camera is nothing more than a rather sophisticated light-tight box. The film end of the camera opens to show a **filmboard** (figure 6.11), which holds the film in place during the exposure. A vacuum back filmboard is generally used to hold the film flat on the filmboard and ensure that it will not shift during exposure. The filmboard hinges closed and is perfectly parallel to the copyboard, located at the opposite end of the camera. The **copyboard** is simply a glass-covered

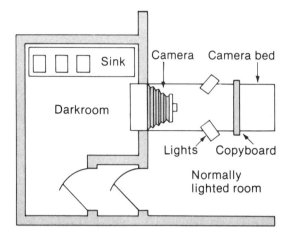

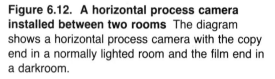

Figure 6.12. A horizontal process camera installed between two rooms The diagram shows a horizontal process camera with the copy end in a normally lighted room and the film end in a darkroom.

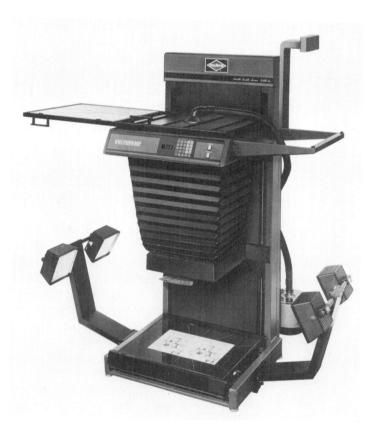

Figure 6.13. A vertical process camera
Courtesy of nuArc Company, Inc.

frame that holds the copy that is to be photographed. There are generally guidelines on both the film and the copyboard that, if followed, ensure that the image will be recorded in the center of the film.

Process cameras have an artificial light source that directs light at the copyboard. Most light systems are controlled by the camera shutter, which controls the passage of light through the lens. When the timer opens the shutter, the lights go on. They are automatically shut off when the timer closes the shutter.

The main advantage of the process camera is that it can make enlargements and reductions of the original copy. Size changes are referred to by the percentage size of the original that is to be recorded on the film. A 100% or 1:1 reproduction will expose an image on the film that is the same size as the original copy. A 25% reduction will expose an image that is one-quarter the original size. A 200% enlargement will expose an image that is twice the size of the original copy. The percentage of enlargement or reduction is controlled by changing the positions of the camera lens and copyboard. On some cameras the adjustment is made manually by lining up percentage tapes (see figure 6.14) or by following guide numbers provided by the camera manufacturer. Newer cameras, such as the one shown in figure 6.11, have digital readout devices that can be used to set the lens and copyboard automatically through the camera console.

The amount of light necessary to produce a quality image on the film is calculated at a 100% (or same-size) reproduction called "basic exposure." Whenever the positions of the lens and copyboard are changed for enlargement or reduction, the distance the reflected light from the copyboard must travel to reach the film, and thus the amount of light that will reach the film, is also changed. How-

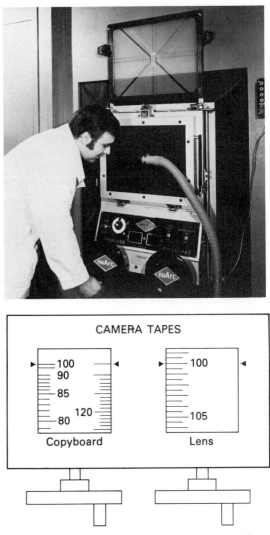

Figure 6.14. Adjusting the distance between the camera lens and the copyboard Before exposing the film, the operator must adjust the camera for the correct size of the final image. On some cameras, this is done by moving the percentage tapes until both are set at the desired reproduction size.
Courtesy of nuArc Company, Inc.

ever, whatever the percentage of enlargement or reduction, the quantity of light reaching the film must remain the same as for a 100% reproduction to produce an acceptable exposure. Most process cameras have a **variable diaphragm control** which increases or decreases the amount of light reaching the film. The control changes the f/stop (aperture opening) to correspond to the percentage of enlargement or reduction. For example, if a 67% reduction is to be made, the diaphragm control is moved in line with 67%. With this method, the exposure time will always remain the same and only the aperture opening will vary to provide the correct exposure.

A more accurate method of controlling film exposure is with a **light integrator** (figure 6.15). A light integrator uses a photoelectric cell. The cell is connected to a device that measures the units of light reaching the film. With a light integrator, the camera operator simply dials in the desired amount of light. The lens will automatically close when that quantity of light has reached the photoelectric cell. Any variation in light characteristics, such as changes in the voltage in the power source

that operates the camera lights, will automatically be accounted for.

Basic Exposure and Camera Operation

In general, **basic exposure** is the camera aperture and shutter speed combination that will produce a quality film image of normal line copy with standardized chemical processing. The basic exposure will vary from camera to camera, depending on many variables, such as energy level of the light source, color temperature (see Appendix B), processing chemicals, temperature control, rate of agitation, copy characteristics, and type of film. Whenever one of the variables is changed, however slightly, the basic exposure must be recalculated. Once the basic exposure has been determined, it can be used to accurately predict new exposure times for any change in reproduction size or in copy characteristics. The procedures for determining basic camera exposure are explained in detail in Appendix A.

Let's work through a practical example

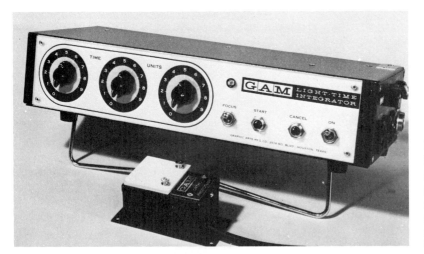

Figure 6.15. A light integrator This machine automatically controls the amount of light used to expose the film in the camera.
Courtesy of Graphic Arts Manufacturing Co.

using the concept of basic exposure to make a typical line exposure. Assume that our task is to produce a high-contrast negative, such as the copy shown in figure 6.1, which can be used to expose a printing plate. In order to meet rough layout specifications, we are told to provide a 53% reduction. Our process camera is a horizontal model with a basic exposure of f/16 for 22 seconds. (The explanation that follows can also be applied to a vertical camera.)

Mounting the Copy

Begin by mounting the copy in the copyboard. Swing the copyboard to a horizontal position and open the glass cover. Spots of dirt or dust can interfere with image quality, so the glass should be thoroughly cleaned before each use. There is usually some sort of guideline system that will allow the original to be placed nearly perfectly in the center of the copyboard (figure 6.16). The copyboard guidelines are in line with guidelines on the filmboard. Because the camera lens reverses the image, place the copy so that it will be upside down when the copyboard is in a vertical position. This will help if fine focusing is necessary.

A graphic arts **step tablet** or **gray scale** is a tool used by camera operators as an aid in judging the quality of a film image (figure 6.17). With every exposure, the camera operator places the gray scale on the copyboard next to the material being photographed (figure 6.18). The specific position does not matter, but it is important that the gray scale not cover any line detail, that it receive the same light as the copy, and that it be in a position to be recorded on the film. As the film is developed, both the copy image and the gray scale will become visible. As individual density steps on the scale darken and fill in during

Figure 6.16. Mounting copy in the copyboard
The copy is centered on the copyboard guidelines and positioned to be upside down when the frame is in the vertical position.
Courtesy of nuArc Company, Inc.

development, they serve as a visual cue that indicates the stage of film development. After development, the gray scale image on the film serves as a means of judging the film's usability, and if unacceptable, of indicating the change needed to correct the shortcomings.

When the copy and gray scale are in position, close the glass over the copyboard and turn on the vacuum pump. Check again for lint or dust in the image area, and make sure that the copy has not moved. Swing the copyboard into a vertical position so that it is parallel to the filmboard.

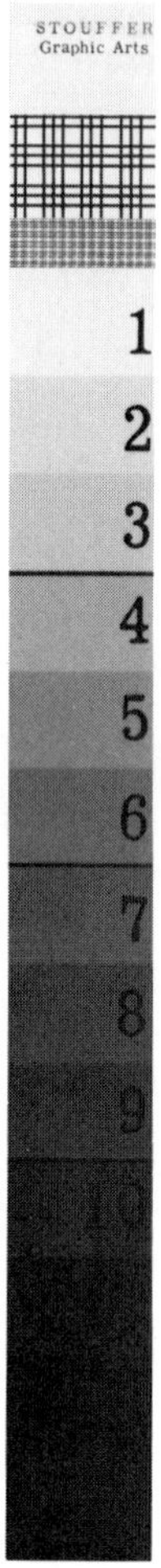

STOUFFER
Graphic Arts

Figure 6.17. A gray scale
Courtesy of Stouffer Graphic Arts Equipment Co.

Focusing

Enlargement and reduction on our camera are controlled by percentage tapes. By moving the tapes, the relative positions of the lens and copyboard are changed so that the image will be in perfect focus and at the same time will be reproduced in the required size. To make a 53% reproduction, both tapes are positioned at 53%.

Some cameras have ground glass screens that can be used to check both image position and focus. Swing or place the ground glass into position. When the camera lights are turned on, the reflected image is projected through the lens onto the inside layer of glass. It is then possible to use a magnifying glass to check for focus.

It might be necessary to adjust the camera lights for even illumination across the image. A general recommendation is to set the lights at a 45° angle from the copyboard frame (figure 6.19). The ground glass image can be used to judge evenness of intensity across the image. Some types of reflection densitometers (see Chapter 7) can be used to make the same, but more precise, measurement.

Setting the Aperture and Shutter Speed

Next, prepare the aperture and timer controls. Set the timer for the basic exposure time, which for our example is a 22-second exposure. Because we are making a 53% reduction, move the variable diaphragm control arm to 53% on the f/16 scale (figure 6.20). This setting automatically adjusts the lens opening (aperture) for the proper quantity of light at a 53% reduction.

It is important to understand that when you move the variable diaphragm control along this scale, you are changing the f/stop setting so it corresponds to the basic camera exposure. The f/stop setting for the basic exposure is determined at a 100% (same-size) exposure. In this example, a 53% reduction is being made. When the percentage tapes are set at 53%, the relative position of the lens, filmboard, and copyboard are different from what they would be at a 100% reproduction

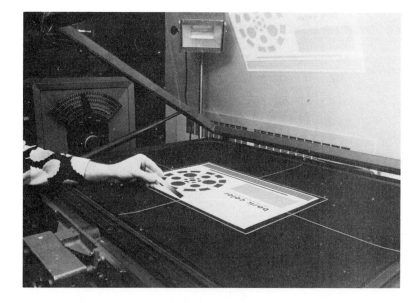

Figure 6.18. Using a gray scale Place a graphic arts gray scale next to the copy, but do not allow it to cover any image area.
Courtesy of R. Kampas

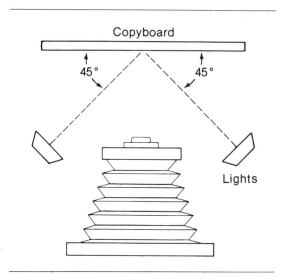

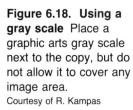

Copyboard

45°   45°

Lights

Figure 6.19. Position of camera lights The camera lights are usually positioned at 45° angles from the copyboard.

(figure 6.21). Thus, the intensity of the light striking the film will be different as well. An adjustment will have to be made to either the exposure time or the aperture opening to allow the proper amount of light to reach the film. If the exposure time is kept the same, the variable diaphragm control can be used to change the aperture opening. Without a variable diaphragm control, a new calculation for exposure time would have to be made each time an enlargement or reduction was made. This calculation would compensate for the light intensity change at the filmboard which would result from each change in lens and copyboard position. The variable diaphragm control provides a scale with these calculations already made.

Digital Control. On cameras with digital control, it is often not necessary to manually adjust the copyboard or filmboard, or to man-

Figure 6.20. Setting the aperture control Adjust the aperture by moving the diaphragm arm to the reproduction percentage size in line with the f/stop size for the basic exposure.
Courtesy of nuArc Company, Inc.

ually set the aperture opening. Instead, the camera operator keyboards in information about the enlargement or reduction required. A microcomputer in the camera automatically makes the required camera adjustments. The most sophisticated digital cameras have memory storage, and can remember the exposure times and conditions used for producing a variety of exposures. With these cameras, the operator need only enter enlargement and reduction information, then call for the appropriate exposure program by entering a keyboard code. The microcomputer sets the camera according to preprogrammed information.

Mounting the Film

In most cameras, the film is held in place on the filmboard by a vacuum system. It is necessary to adjust the filmboard so that vacuum pressure will be applied over the entire area of the film sheet and will not lose holding power by pulling in air where there is no film. Individual cameras are adjusted differently, but most are designed to accommodate the most common film sizes.

All these first steps of setting up the camera for making a line exposure can be performed in normal room light; the last steps cannot. The process darkroom is normally equipped with a dual lighting system. Use the red light, or **safelight,** when working with high-contrast orthochromatic film. Use the white light for setup only.

With only the red safelight on, carefully open the film box, remove one sheet of film, and replace the cover. A common error for new photographers is to forget to close the box until after the camera exposure has been made. With some darkroom designs, most of the film in the box has been ruined by that time.

Handle film only by the outside edges.

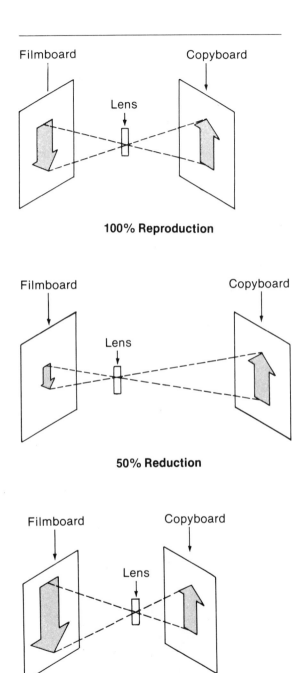

100% Reproduction

50% Reduction

150% Enlargement

Figure 6.21. Adjustments for enlargements or reductions The relative position of the filmboard, lens, and copyboard are changed for enlargement and reduction. This change effects the intensity of light striking the filmboard. To maintain the same intensity as a 100% reproduction, adjustments must be made to exposure time or aperture opening.

If a wet or even moist finger touches the emulsion, a fingerprint can appear on the developed film and ruin the image's usability.

Center the sheet of film on the guidelines on the filmboard with the emulsion side up (so that it faces the copyboard when the filmboard is closed). There are rare instances when the emulsion side is placed down, but in general the film is always exposed through the emulsion. Even in the red light of the darkroom, it is easy to identify the emulsion side of the film.

There are three basic ways to identify the emulsion side of a piece of film. The easiest is simply to look at the sheet. The darker side is the antihalation dye layer, and the lighter side is the emulsion (figure 6.22). This is easy to remember because the antihalation dye is dark to absorb the light that passes through the film. A second way to identify the emulsion side is by remembering that most films tend to curl into the emulsion side. Be careful, however, because the heat of your hand can cause curling in either direction. The third method of identifying the emulsion side of a piece of film works only for film material that is intended to be used in total or nearly complete darkness. On such film, the manufacturer uses a notching system. Each different type of film has a unique pattern of notches so that the photographer can identify different materials in the dark by using only

Figure 6.22. Identifying the emulsion side by its color The emulsion side, or the lighter side of the film, is placed up on the filmboard.

a fingertip (figure 6.23). The notches also serve to identify the emulsion side. If the sheet is held so that the notches are in the upper right-hand corner, the emulsion is facing the photographer.

With the film in place, turn on the vacuum pump and carefully roll the film with a roller to remove any air pockets that might be trapped under the sheet (figure 6.24). Be extremely careful; the emulsion is a very fragile material and is easily scratched. As an alternative to this practice, many photographers turn on the vacuum and then roll the film itself into position, thereby eliminating the possibility of air pockets.

Exposing the Film

The last step is to make the actual exposure. Swing the filmboard into position so that it is parallel to the copy, and lock the entire frame in place. When you push the timer control button, the camera lights automatically go on and the shutter opens. When the preset ex-

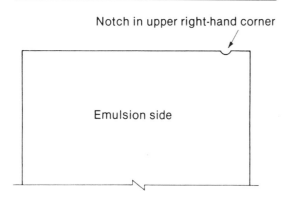

Figure 6.23. Using notches to identify the emulsion side When the film notches are in the upper right-hand corner, the emulsion side is up.

Figure 6.24. Removing air pockets from the film After positioning the film on the filmboard, turn on the vacuum and carefully roll the sheet to remove any trapped air.
Courtesy of R. Kampas

posure time has been reached (for this example, twenty-two seconds), the shutter closes and the lights go off. Open the camera back, turn off the vacuum, and remove the film. The film appears no different than it did before the exposure, but it now carries an invisible, or latent, image. Chemical processing is necessary to make the latent image visible and permanent.

Chemical Processing

Processing Chemicals

When light of the proper quantity and quality strikes the light-sensitive silver halide emulsion on the film, a change takes place. It is a subtle change in the chemical structure of the halide crystals, a change that cannot be detected by the human eye. Because this change is invisible, it is said to produce a **latent image.**

Light passes through the lens to the film and selectively alters portions of the emulsion according to the amount of light reflected from the copy on the copyboard. The white areas of the original copy (generally, nonimage areas) reflect a great deal of light, which changes many halide crystals. The black or pigmented areas (generally, the image areas) absorb most of the light, reflecting little back to the film and thus changing very few halide crystals. This is a very important concept. Photography depends on reflected light from the original copy to record a reverse (or negative) image on a sheet of film (figure 6.25).

Remember, where light is reflected from the original copy, halide crystals are changed. Where light is not reflected from the copy, halide crystals are not changed. Where halide crystals are changed, the film will be black after processing. This will be the film record image of the white (nonimage) areas on the photographed copy. Where halide crystals are

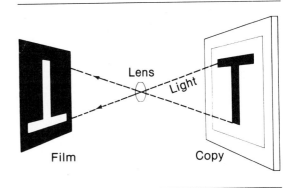

Figure 6.25. Film exposure The light reflected from the nonimage or light portions of the original copy exposes the film and results in a negative image where the reflected light was not absorbed by the film.

not changed, the film will be clear after processing (because the unchanged halide crystals are washed away during processing). The clear areas on the film will be the film record of the dark (image) areas on the copy. This is why a film image is a "negative" of the original copy.

The purpose of film development during chemical processing is to change the latent or invisible image on a sheet of exposed film to a visible and permanent image.

Processing Steps

For orthochromatic, lith films, at least three chemical solutions and a water bath will be used during film processing. The steps in film processing are as follows:

1. Developing the film
2. Stopping the development
3. Fixing the image
4. Washing away the chemicals

Developing the Film. The **developer** is a complex solution designed to make the latent image visible. The solution contains an organic compound, called the developing agent, dissolved in water. The developer changes each exposed silver halide crystal to a grain of black metallic silver (which is why exposed areas of the film turn black during processing). The change takes place very slowly, so an activator (usually sodium hydroxide) is added to speed things up. An additional problem with the developing agent is that it oxidizes (loses its ability to work when exposed to air). When a developer has turned brown, oxidation has broken down the activity level of the developer and no film can be processed in it. To delay the effects of oxidation a preservative, usually sodium sulfite, is added to the developer solution. The final weakness of lith developer is that it is "infectious." Thus, after all the exposed silver halide crystals have been changed to black metallic silver, the solution begins to work on the unexposed crystals. If the process were to continue, the entire sheet of film would be a solid layer of black silver and would be unusable. This is why lith film must be removed from the developer as soon as all the exposed silver halide crystals have changed to black metallic silver.

An unexposed area of film that does not appear clear is "fogged." Fog can be caused by accidental exposure to light or by developer agents. To prevent fog, a restrainer, generally potassium bromide, is added to the developer solution.

Although the actual compounds differ depending on the characteristics of the chemical emulsion of the film, all developers are made up of the following five parts:

- Solvent (water)
- Developing agent
- Activator
- Preservative
- Restrainer

Developer manufacturers always recommend development procedures for their chemicals. For example, Kodak recommends that Kodalith, a high-contrast lith developer, be stored in two separate solutions and mixed in equal parts to form the working solution. Once mixed, oxidation exhausts the activity of the working solution in several hours. Manufacturers also recommend the maximum number of square inches of film that should be processed in a quantity of developer solution before new developer should be mixed. Most lith developer solutions are designed to function at exactly 68°F (20°C). Any temperature fluctuation will decrease the predictability of results.

Stopping Development. Once the desired level of development has been reached, the developing action must be halted immediately. Plunging the film from the developer (a base) into an acid solution will stop all developer activity. This acid solution is called the **stop-bath** or **short-stop.** It is usually made up of a small quantity of acetic acid combined with a large amount of water. The stop-bath really serves two functions:

- To halt the development
- To extend the life of the third solution, the fixer

Fixing the Image. After development and stop, the image on the piece of film is visible but not permanent. The silver halide crystals that were not exposed are still present in the emulsion and are visible as cloudy areas in the clear areas of the film. These unexposed crystals are still sensitive to light. The fixing bath removes all of these unexposed silver crystals and makes the film image permanent.

The **fixing bath** is a chemical solution nearly as complex as the developer. As with all photographic chemicals, the main solvent is water. Water does not dissolve unexposed halide crystals, but a compound called **hypo** or sodium thiosulfate does. This is such an important ingredient of the fixing bath that the term "hypo" is often used interchangeably with fixer. Acetic acid, the primary ingredient of the stop-bath, is also added to the fixing bath to neutralize any developer that the film might still carry. However, the acetic acid has a tendency to affect the hypo by turning it into small pieces of sulfur and thus rendering it useless as a fixing agent. To overcome this difficulty, a preservative called sodium sulfite, which combines with the sulfur and changes it back to hypo, is added. During development, the gelatin of the film emulsion swells up because the main solvent is water. To harden the gelatin again, a hardener, such as potassium alum, is added to the fixing bath. If a hardener is used, then a pH of 4 must be maintained (pH is a measure of acidity of a solution). To accomplish this, a buffer, such as boric acid, is used.

After development and the stop-bath, the unexposed portions of the film negative appear milky white under red safelight conditions. This milk-white color is actually the unexposed silver halide crystals remaining in the clear areas of the film. Fixing time is generally determined by leaving the film in the hypo twice the length of time required to remove these unexposed crystals and make the film clear.

Washing Away the Chemicals. During chemical processing, some of the processing solutions become attached to the film base and emulsion material. If they were allowed to remain, the image could yellow or gradually begin to fade. The fourth step for all photographic processes is to wash away all traces of the processing chemicals. Because water is the main solvent for all the processing solutions, a simple running-water bath will remove all objectionable chemicals. Depending on the rate of water change, ten minutes in a strong water flow should be sufficient for films, and thirty to forty-five minutes for any other photographic materials.

Controlling Chemical Processing

There are many ways, such as shallow-tray, deep-tank, or automatic processing, to store and work with the chemical baths. Whatever the method, there are three processing variables that must be controlled:

- Agitation
- Time
- Temperature

Agitation.   **Agitation** refers to the flow of the solution back and forth over the film during processing. If the film were allowed to sit in the solution, the chemicals immediately in contact with the emulsion would quickly become exhausted. Agitation during development ensures that new chemicals are continually flowing over the film, giving constant chemical action. The rate of agitation is not important, but the consistency of the motion is. By being consistent, the photographer can duplicate results for every piece of film that is processed.

Consistency is important. If the right and left pages of this book were each made from two different pieces of film, and the piece of film that recorded the right page had been agitated more frequently or rapidly than the piece of film that recorded the left page, the images on the right would appear lighter than the images on the left. This would be true even if both pieces of film were agitated for the same length of time! This is because the film for the right page, being agitated more frequently, would be overdeveloped, and the images would "fill in" (some of the unexposed silver halide crystals in the image areas would start to turn to black metallic silver). All the images on the right page would appear thinner and smaller than all the images on the left page.

Time and Temperature. Processing time and processing chemical temperature must also be controlled. The film's manufacturer provides recommended processing times. For example, Kodak recommends that with the shallow-tray method, their Ortho 3 film be developed for 2¾ minutes with 10 seconds in the stop bath. It should be fixed twice as long as it takes to clear the film. Several different types of darkroom timers are available to assist photographers in controlling processing times. If the temperature of all chemicals is within ± ½° of the optimum (68°F or 20°C), the temperature is usually considered "in control" for line photography. Temperature control sinks are generally used to control chemical temperatures.

Shallow-Tray Chemical Processing

The following steps are necessary for chemical processing with the shallow-tray method (figure 6.26). All these steps, except washing and drying, are carried out under safelight conditions. Before placing the film in the developer, set the timer for the recommended time (usually 2¾ minutes).

1. Place the dry exposed film from the camera into the developer with the emulsion side up and the film completely covered by the liquid. Place the film emulsion-side up in the developer so that you can inspect the image as it becomes visible during development.

You could see the image develop even if the film were emulsion-side down in the developer; but because you would be looking through the antihalation backing, the image would appear to be developing more slowly than it is actually doing. Remember to handle the film as little as possible; touch it only along the outside edges. As soon as the film is covered by the developer, turn on the timer and start agitating the film. Keep your agitation as consistent as possible. As the film develops, the latent image will become visible. As soon as you can see the image, look for the image of the gray scale.

Visually inspecting the gray scale on the film as it is developed, will allow you to correct for slight variations in time, temperature, or agitation during development, and for variations in copy. For normal line copy, a solid step 4 should usually be obtained on the scale. Extremely fine-line detail should be developed less (steps 2 or 3), and bold lines could be developed much further (steps 5 or 6) (figure 6.27). If for some reason the development time has reached the recommended length and with normal copy the scale shows a solid step 3, then the processing should be extended, because optimal results have not yet been obtained. This could happen if the developer was old and almost exhausted. But development should not be extended much beyond the recommended time. If the recommended time is 2¾ minutes and a solid step 4 has not been reached after 5 minutes, discard the film and expose a new sheet. You may need either to increase the exposure time because some variable is not in control or to mix new developer.

2. When the correct gray scale step appears on the film, move the film to the stop-bath. To do this, lift the film by one corner out of the developer and let it drain briefly over the developing tray; then place it in the stop-bath. Agitate the film in the stop-bath at

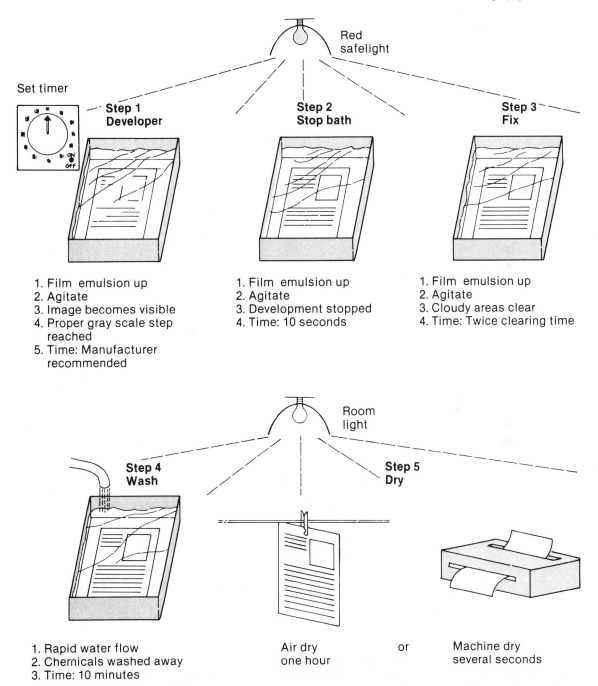

Set timer

Red safelight

Step 1
Developer

1. Film emulsion up
2. Agitate
3. Image becomes visible
4. Proper gray scale step reached
5. Time: Manufacturer recommended

Step 2
Stop bath

1. Film emulsion up
2. Agitate
3. Development stopped
4. Time: 10 seconds

Step 3
Fix

1. Film emulsion up
2. Agitate
3. Cloudy areas clear
4. Time: Twice clearing time

Room light

Step 4
Wash

1. Rapid water flow
2. Chemicals washed away
3. Time: 10 minutes

Step 5
Dry

Air dry one hour   or   Machine dry several seconds

Figure 6.26. Shallow-tray method of developing film

NORMAL COPY

Most line copy can be handled as step 4 copy, that is to be exposed and developed to step 4 on the gray scale shown below.

You will notice, when developing, that step 1 developes very quickly. Step 2 will turn black about 15-20 seconds after 1. Step 3 follows and by the end of the recommended development time step 4 will be black. When step 4 blackens, transfer the film to the stop bath and continue to process as recommended by the film manufacturer.

FINE LINE COPY

When photographing grey or fine line copy a change in exposure is recommended to hold a step other than 4.

The screened art below (85 lines per inch) must be handled as line copy. To develop the negative to a solid step 4 would result in loss of detail.

BOLD OR HEAVY COPY

In order to insure excellent density in the non-image area of a negative containing only bold copy, or when making an extreme enlargement, an increase in exposure is recommended. This would result in producing a step higher than 4 on the gray scale.

Figure 6.27. Using a gray scale to gauge development of film
Gray scales can be used to gauge the stage of development for a piece of film. Different types of copy are developed to different steps. In this example, normal copy is developed to step 4, fine line copy is developed to step 3, and heavy copy is developed to step 6.

the same consistent rate that you agitated it throughout development. Leave the film in the stop-bath for at least 10 seconds.

3. Pick the film up by one corner and let it drain into the stop-bath; then move it to the fixer. Again, the film should be placed in the fixer emulsion-side up. Watch the clear areas on the film as you agitate it in the fixer. Make a mental note of the time that it takes these clear areas to go from cloudy to completely clear. Agitate the film in the fixer for twice the length of time that it takes for the unexposed areas to lose the cloudy appearance. If it takes 20 seconds for the unexposed areas to completely clear, a 40-second fixing bath with constant agitation should be sufficient.

4. When the film has been fixed for the proper amount of time, lift it out of the fixer, let it drain, then put it into a running-water bath. Ten minutes of strong water flow should wash away all chemicals remaining on the film.

5. After the film is washed, either hang it up to air dry or put it through a film dryer. Air drying will usually take up to one hour. Automatic film dryers can reduce this time to less than a minute.

Figure 6.28. An automatic film-processing unit
A unit such as this machine provides greater accuracy and control of agitation, time, and temperature than is possible by manual processing methods.
Courtesy of Log E/LogEtronics, Inc.

Automatic Processing

An automatic film-processing unit provides an alternative to shallow-tray processing (figure 6.28). Most machines are designed for dry-to-dry delivery in 4 to 5 minutes. This is a tremendous advantage over tray processing because the photographer never gets wet hands, and can be making another exposure in the camera room while a sheet of film is being processed.

Common feeding methods use a continuous belt or roller system that passes the film through a developer, a stop-fixer, a washing tank, and a dryer (figure 6.29). With deep-tank chemical storage, there is little problem with oxidation, although long periods of disuse will cause some activity change. Chemical exhaustion as a result of film processing is controlled by the addition of a small quantity of replenisher after each piece of film enters the machine. Replenisher is generally added automatically as a function of the area of the sheet of film being processed. With the use of replenisher, the chemical solutions generally need be removed from the tanks only several times a year for machine maintenance.

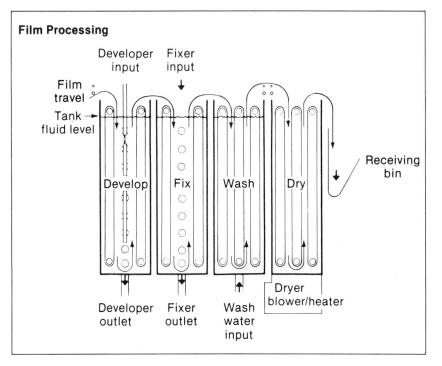

Film Processing

Figure 6.29. Side view diagram of a typical automatic film processor Rollers move the film from tank to tank.

Automatic processing can provide accurate time-temperature-agitation control, can free the photographer for increased camera work, and can reduce production costs through faster processing. However, automated processing cannot be viewed as a solution for all production problems. It can, in fact, cause more problems than it solves.

There is no single chemical solution that can process all photographic materials a printer might use. If any material that the developer was not designed to process is passed through the processor, the material will not be developed properly, and the chemical balance of the machine may change.

Further, adding replenisher to the developer to keep the activity level correct is not a simple process. With most machines, huge quantities of replenisher must be added after

even an overnight shutdown. **Control strips** (controlled density wedges from the film manufacturer that have been exposed on pieces of film of the type the printer is using) are used to measure developer activity. Several times a day the camera operator must feed a control strip through the machine to check the developer. If the strip is overdeveloped, the activity is too high. If it is underdeveloped, the activity is too low. Too low an activity is corrected simply by manually dialing in replenisher, but too high an activity level is a problem. The general technique for reducing a high activity level is to expose several sheets of film to room light, send them through the machine without replenisher, and then process another control strip. While all this is going on, no productive processing is taking place, film is being wasted, and the average cost of all the day's processing is mounting.

Whether shallow-tray or automatic processing is used, the problem of controlling chemical processing remains a primary concern. If the camera operator is not aware of all the variables and the ways to control them, consistent high-quality results become an impossibility.

Film-to-Film Processes

While much graphic arts photography involves making transparent negatives from opaque positive originals, it is often necessary to produce film positives or negatives from previously exposed and developed film materials. Two common film-to-film processes are used in the industry:

- Camera copying from a back-lighted copyboard
- Contact printing

Back-lighted Copyboard. Process cameras can have two types of copyboards. The one we discussed previously was a **solid-back copyboard,** probably covered with black material. We have already discussed producing a film negative from positive, opaque copy mounted in a solid-back copyboard. In this process, light reflected from the opaque copy passes through the camera lens and exposes a sheet of film. The second type of copyboard is called a **back-lighted copyboard.** With this design, a transparent film negative or positive is placed in the copyboard, over a sheet of frosted glass (figure 6.30). Lights, located behind the frosted glass, project light through the open (nonemulsion) areas of the transparent material to make the exposure. If a positive is placed in the copyboard, and a negative film is used in the camera, a negative

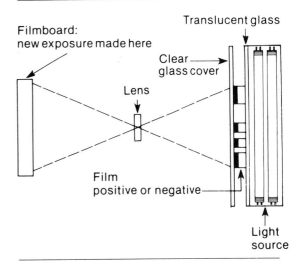

Figure 6.30. Diagram of a back-lighted copyboard A back-lighted copyboard is needed to photograph transparent negative or positive film.

will be produced. A negative transparency placed in the copyboard will produce a positive on the film. With this method the production of a duplicate negative from an original negative transparency requires two steps. The operator must back-light the original negative to produce a positive, then back-light or contact the positive to expose a new negative.

Duplicating Film. A duplicating film is designed to produce either duplicate film negatives from original negatives or duplicate film positives from original positives. Duplicating film can also be used to produce film positives from opaque originals. By using duplicating film, it is possible to produce a duplicate negative or positive in one step.

Contact printing. Contact printing is the process of exposing a sheet of film (or other light-sensitive material) by passing light directly through a negative or positive to an unexposed sheet of film. To make a contact positive from a negative, the emulsion side of a film negative is placed against the emulsion of an unexposed sheet of film (figure 6.31). The two sheets are then pressed together, usually in a vacuum frame, until there is no air gap between them. Light is projected through the open, image areas in the negative to the emulsion of the unexposed film. Light is blocked by the emulsion in the nonimage areas on the negative. Thus the image produced on the contact printed film is a positive. Contact printing can also be used for making negatives from positives by passing the light

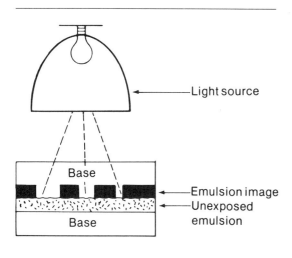

Figure 6.31. Contact printing This diagram shows the proper placement of the film negative against a fresh sheet of film to make a contact positive. Note that the two pieces of film are placed emulsion to emulsion and that the positive produced will be right-reading through the emulsion.

through a positive film image, or for making duplicate images in one step with duplicating film.

A gray scale is usually not used with contact printing, so there is no visible guide to film development. In general, films that have been contact printed are processed in the same manner as camera-produced films, following manufacturer time, temperature, and agitation recommendations. However, film made through a contact exposure has a wider latitude (less crucial development conditions) during development than does film made through a projection exposure. This wider latitude is due in part to the fact that, with contact printing, there is no possibility of light reaching the film from a nonimage area during exposure, because the exposed and unexposed film are in "intimate contact" (pressed tightly together). Thus a gray scale image is not required to control development.

Lateral Reverse. A transparent film negative that has been correctly exposed in a process camera is **right-reading** through the base side. In other words, as the printer looks at the film with the base side up, the copy reads from left to right (figure 6.32a). Right-reading film images are required for most printing operations. There are, however, several situations, such as photoengraving for relief printing, preparation of screen printing stencils, and some printing plates, that require exposures made through film positives. These situations often require the film to be **wrong-reading** (the copy does not read from left to right through the base, as shown in figure 6.32b).

Changing a right-reading sheet of film to wrong-reading or vice versa is called a **lateral reverse.** It can be accomplished on the camera by reversing the right-reading sheet on the back-lighted camera copyboard. A lat-

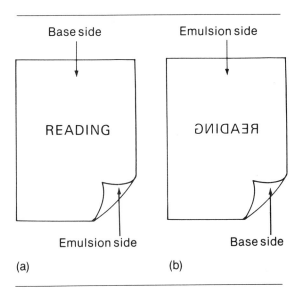

Figure 6.32. Right-reading transparent film
Transparent film that has been correctly exposed
in a process camera is right-reading through the
base side (a) and wrong-reading through the
emulsion side (b).

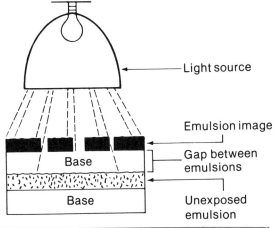

Figure 6.33. Making a lateral reverse This
diagram shows the placement of the base side of
the exposed film against the emulsion side of an
unexposed sheet of film for producing a lateral
reverse.

eral reverse can also be produced through
contact printing by placing the base side of
the right-reading film against the emulsion
side of the new sheet (figure 6.33). There is
a slight spreading of light between the two
sheets of film because of the gap between
emulsions, but it is expected and can be di-
minished by allowing for the spread when
preparing the original film negative.

Rapid Access Processing

Up to this point we have been discussing traditional graphic films and processing. These
films are commonly called **lith** films, and the
developers used with them are called lith developers. The primary disadvantage of lith
processing is the lack of latitude during development. That is, the two-part developer
has to be mixed in the correct proportions
immediately before development and replaced or replenished frequently to ensure
proper development. In addition, development time, temperature, and agitation have
to be critically controlled. If all of these conditions are not met, the film will be over- or
underdeveloped and the image will not be
acceptable.

Recently a new type of non-lith processing, called **rapid access,** has been introduced. Rapid access processing offers a much
wider latitude than lith, which gives it several
advantages. The developer requires only one

solution and the fixer is simpler in chemical composition than that used for lith. Thus, whether shallow-tray or automatic processing is used, no replenishment is needed. The camera operator need only keep the developer and fixer "topped off" to the appropriate level. In addition, because of the differences in developer chemistry, the developer is not easily exhausted through oxidation. Though rapid access developer will eventually become exhausted from processing film, it can be left in the development tray, exposed to air, for a day or more without becoming exhausted through oxidation.

Latitude is also increased by the fact that the three major development variables (time, temperature, and agitation) are far less crucial for rapid access development than for lith development. If properly exposed, film developed in rapid access chemistry will almost completely stop developing at the proper point, with almost no chance of over- or underdevelopment. For example, most rapid access chemistry requires a minimum development time of ninety seconds. However, the film will not be overdeveloped if it is left in the developer for several times this amount. Because the film stops developing at the proper point, development time does not need to be controlled for copy variations. A piece of film used to record fine line detail can be developed for the same length of time as a piece of film used to record normal detail. One additional advantage of rapid access is that it can be used to process a range of film materials, including process camera films, contacting films, duplicating films, and even some typesetting papers.

All of these advantages add up to processing simplicity and productivity in the camera room, particularly with automatic processing. Critical chemical replenishment and monitoring through control strips is not needed with a rapid access film processor, and the processor can be used to process a wide range of film materials without changing chemistry. Productivity is also increased by the speed of development time. Automatic processors can process rapid access materials from dry-to-dry in two minutes or less. Many automatic processors designed for lith processing can be easily converted for rapid access processing.

When they were first introduced, rapid access materials and chemistry proved excellent for line work but not for halftone reproduction. Within a few years manufacturers introduced halftone screens specially designed for use with their rapid access materials. Halftones produced with these screens and developed in rapid access chemistry are acceptable for a variety of applications where reproduction quality need not be the highest possible.

To meet the need for high-quality halftones, manufacturers have introduced a new product, called **high-speed lith,** that represents a cross between traditional lith and rapid access. High-speed lith is said to offer the same high-quality development available with traditional lith, but at much faster speeds and with simpler processing procedures.

Diffusion Transfer

Diffusion transfer is a photographic process that produces quality opaque positives from positive originals. Diffusion transfer has widespread applications for printing production in such areas as copy preparation, proofing, and lithographic plate making.

Basically, the concept involves the use of a light-sensitive negative image sheet and a chemically treated receiver sheet which is not light-sensitive. The negative sheet is exposed to the camera copy through normal line photography techniques. Wherever light is reflected from the camera copy (the nonimage areas of the copy), an image is recorded on the receiver sheet. Wherever light is absorbed by the camera copy (the black image areas of the copy), no image is recorded on the receiver sheet. After exposure, the negative and receiver sheets are placed in contact and passed through a processor that contains an "activator" solution. The image recorded on the negative sheet from the nonimage areas of the copy acts as a chemical mask and prevents any image from being transferred to the receiver sheet in these areas. Where no image was recorded on the negative sheet (that is, the dark areas of the copy where no light was reflected from the copy to the negative sheet), the activator or developer bath causes an image to be transferred to the receiver sheet. In this way a positive image is produced on the

receiver sheet. In other words, wherever chemicals are transferred, an image is formed; where no chemicals are transferred, no image is formed (figure 6.34).

Several characteristics of diffusion transfer material should be mentioned. Because it is a transfer process, the camera exposure results are reversed from a direct line photograph. To increase the density of the image on the receiver sheet, decrease the exposure time; to decrease density, increase the exposure. When processing the materials, place the negative sheet under and before the receiver sheet with the emulsions of the two together. The sandwich is then inserted into the processor, where it is passed between a separator rod through the activator bath and is brought into intimate contact by two pressure rollers. The transfer actually takes place in five to seven seconds, but the sheets should not be separated for at least thirty seconds (figure 6.35). Once the transfer has taken place, the negative sheet cannot be reused and should be discarded. The receiver sheet is still chemically sensitive and can be reused any number of times if multiple images are required, but it must be washed in running water for several minutes after exposure to prevent a slight yellowing from age.

Diffusion transfer materials can be used to produce stats during copy preparation to enlarge or reduce headlines, copyfit text material, clean up soiled original copy, convert color line material to black-and-white copy, make reverses, and, with special screens, prepare halftones. Diffusion transfer materials can also be used to make reflex proofs (contact proofs from opaque paste-ups). Lithographic printing plates and transparent films have been developed that will accept a diffusion transfer image.

Figure 6.34. Example of diffusion transfer sheets The sheets that have been through the activator bath can be separated after thirty seconds.

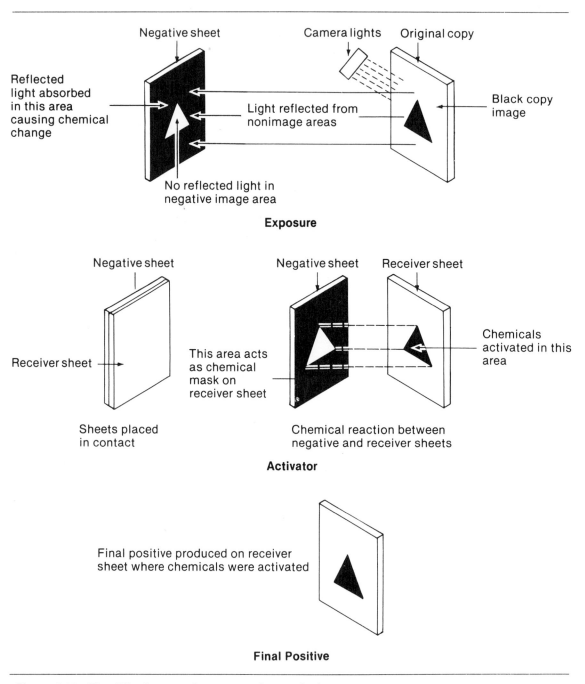

Negative sheet   Camera lights   Original copy

Reflected
light absorbed
in this area
causing chemical
change

Light reflected from
nonimage areas

Black copy
image

No reflected light in
negative image area

Exposure

Negative sheet

Negative sheet   Receiver sheet

Receiver sheet

This area acts
as chemical
mask on
receiver sheet

Chemicals
activated in this
area

Sheets placed
in contact

Chemical reaction between
negative and receiver sheets

Activator

Final positive produced on receiver
sheet where chemicals were activated

Final Positive

**Figure 6.35. The diffusion transfer process for producing an opaque
positive from a positive original.**

Key Terms

line photography
halftone photography
emulsion
antihalation dye
overcoating
process camera
lens
focusing
aperture
visible spectrum
color sensitivity
blue-sensitive
orthochromatic

panchromatic
film speed
shutter speed
shutter
diaphragm
f/stop system
focal length
filmboard
copyboard
basic exposure
gray scale
latent image
developer

stop-bath
fixing bath
agitation
back-lighted copyboard
duplicating film
contact printing
lateral reverse
rapid access
right-reading
wrong-reading
diffusion transfer

Questions for Review

1. What is the common characteristic of all printing processes that forms the primary concern of line photography?

2. What is the basis of photography?

3. What determines the effect caused by electromagnetic radiation, such as light?

4. What colors is panchromatic film sensitive to? What colors is orthochromatic film sensitive to?

5. What does film speed tell us about a film emulsion?

6. What is the purpose of the antihalation backing (or dye) on any piece of film?

7. What is the change in quantity of light passed through the lens when the aperture is changed from f/16 to f/22?

8. What is the difference between a galley camera and a darkroom camera?

9. Why are process cameras so large?

10. What does "basic exposure" mean?

11. What is the purpose of a camera light integrator?

12. Why is it important to clean any dirt or dust from the glass cover of a camera copyboard when making an exposure?

13. What is the purpose of a graphic arts step tablet (sometimes called a gray scale)?

14. What happens to the film emulsion during exposure?

15. What is the purpose of each of the chemical baths—developer, stop, fixer, and wash—used in processing film?

16. What are the three major concerns that the photographer always tries to control during chemical processing?

17. What is the importance of agitation of photographic chemical baths in film processing?

18. Describe the process of contact printing.

19. What is the difference between a right-reading and a wrong-reading film image?

20. How does rapid access processing differ from lith processing?

21. Describe the diffusion transfer process.

22. For how many seconds should developed film remain in the stop-bath?

23. How long should film remain in the fixer?

24. What effect does a longer exposure time have on the density recorded on diffusion transfer materials?

Chapter Seven

Halftone Photography

Anecdote to Chapter Seven

The first commercial halftone illustration reproduced in a mass circulation publication appeared in the March 4, 1880 issue of the New York *Daily Graphic*. It was a picture of a scene in Shantytown, New York. As the byline advertised, it was a "reproduction direct from nature." Even before the first halftone illustration, however, the New York *Daily Graphic* was a startling venture in both design and manufacture. An editorial from the same period observed that "the boldness of the experiment, when it was proposed to start and maintain in the city of New York a daily illustrated newspaper, was well fitted to take away the breath."

Before halftones, the only way to add illustrations to a printed piece was to include line drawings by artists. It was the day of the "sketch artist" or the "artist on the spot," as many newspapers advertised. The task of providing enough artist's illustrations to fill twelve pages of newspaper was a mammoth undertaking.

The person responsible for the *Daily Graphic*'s success was a young man named Stephen H. Horgan, then twenty-six years old. As early as 1875 Horgan conceived of a method to make gradations in density of a photographic negative into lines. His first commercial halftone was made with a negative screen formed from a series of fine rulings, all slightly out of focus. A print was made by projecting the original photographic negative through the negative screen. The result was then treated exactly like a line drawing by the production workers.

Horgan's early work was with a single-line screen. In other words, the gradations from opaque to transparent on the screen ran in parallel lines. The resulting reproduction looked, to many printers, somewhat like the artist's drawings that they had been working with for many years. The single-line ruling was coarse and well suited to reproduction on fast letterpress equipment using inexpensive pa-

**The first commercial
halftone illustration**
Courtesy of Smithsonian
Institution, Photo No. 73–5138

per. The single-line illustrations were all right, but every press operator said that only a fool would suggest that a cross-line halftone could be printed without looking like a "puddle of mud."

The "foolish" ideas of people like Stephen Horgan have contributed to the growth and refinement of halftone photography, the subject of this chapter.

Objectives for Chapter Seven

After completing this chapter you will be able to:

– Explain the difference between density, contrast, and tone.

– Discuss the purpose of a reflection, transmission, and dot area densitometer.
– Discuss the significance of a gray scale in the photomechanical process.

- Explain the difference between a halftone screen and a screen tint.
- Explain how a halftone screen produces dots of varying sizes.
- List standard screen rulings.
- Explain how to determine appropriate highlight and shadow dot sizes.
- Discuss the difference between various types of halftone screens.
- Identify continuous-tone copy.
- Identify highlight, midtone, and shadow areas of continuous-tone copy.

- Select the proper instrument for measuring highlight and shadow densities.
- Describe the data needed to calculate halftone exposures with a halftone computer.
- Discuss the concept of contrast and explain how contrast is controlled in the halftone process.
- Explain the purpose of a main, flash, and bump exposure.
- Identify the characteristics of a quality halftone negative.

Introduction

Much discussion has been devoted in this book to the idea that the major printing processes work exclusively with lines. Lines can have meaning, depending on how they are drawn. High-contrast photography is well suited to line work. A line negative either passes light (in the image area) or blocks the passage of light (in the nonimage area) to a printing plate. If all images that needed to be reproduced were made up only of lines, then simple line exposures would meet all printing needs. There is, however, a large group of images that do not have line characteristics.

A continuous-tone image is not made up of lines. It is formed by a combination of varying shades of gray. The typical photograph is made up of a gradation of tones ranging from "paper white" through grays to the darkest black. Examples of other continuous-tone ma-

terials are ink and brush washes, charcoal sketches, watercolor paintings, soft-pencil drawings, and oil paintings. If we attempted to reproduce a continuous-tone print on high-contrast film, we would lose detail (figure 7.1). To reproduce such a print with the use of one of the major printing processes, it is necessary to change it into a special type of line image called a "halftone."

This chapter is divided into three major sections. Section 1 is an introduction to the basic ideas of halftones. Section 2 examines in detail the necessary concepts of halftone procedures. Section 3 discusses methods of evaluating halftone negatives and relates to the materials on densitometry discussed in Section 1. It is assumed that not all readers will want to deal with all the information in the last section.

Figure 7.1. A high-contrast reproduction of a continuous-tone image We see in this type of print only black and white areas. There are no gray tones reproduced.
Courtesy of Chris Savas

SECTION 1

Density, Contrast, and Tone

In Chapter 6 we discussed how to make a line photograph of a high-contrast image. Before proceeding to a discussion of halftone photography, it is necessary to establish a basic understanding of the terms "density," "contrast," and "tone," and of what they mean to the graphic arts photographer.

Density. In the most general terms, **density** describes the ability of a material to absorb or transmit light. It is well known in the construction industry that a house with a white roof is much cooler in the summer than one with a black roof. The white shingles reflect a great deal of light and, consequently, heat. The black shingles absorb the light and store the sun's heat in the house. In the tropics, light-colored clothing is much cooler and more comfortable than dark because it reflects light and heat. Density is not such a strange concept.

In printing production, the density of the copy, film emulsion, and printing plate emulsion are all important. In printing production, a film negative is used either to pass or to absorb light. If properly exposed and processed, the negative should pass light in the image areas and block light in the nonimage areas to expose a light-sensitive printing plate. In other words, the film emulsion must have more density in the nonimage areas than in the image areas. Thus the density of the film emulsion in the nonimage areas directly influences the quality of the printed piece.

While standing over the washing sink examining a wet negative, however, the photographer is hard pressed to make an accurate judgment about the density of the emulsion on the piece of film. The negative could be examined with a magnifying glass on a wet light table. If the copy were grossly over- or underprocessed, the photographer might be able to detect the problem (figure 7.2). However, the film could appear acceptable but still not be giving the best possible results. The photographer has available several tools to ensure that a negative is of truly acceptable quality and will faithfully reproduce the original copy. The gray scale used during devel-

opment of a line negative, which we discussed in Chapter 6, is one such tool. When we watch the gray scale during film development, while waiting for a step 4 to go solid, we are waiting for the film emulsion to reach a specific level of density.

The printer is concerned with both the density of the image on the original copy and the density of the emulsion on a piece of film. The density of the image on the copy is defined by the term "reflectance." The density of the film emulsion is defined by the term "transmittance."

Reflectance is a measure of the percentage of directed light, called **incident light,** that is reflected from an area of the copy. **Transmittance** is a measure of the percentage of directed light that is passed through an area on a piece of film. For example, if 100 units of light are directed from the camera lights to the copy and only 50 units of light are reflected back from an area on the copy to the camera lens, reflectance for that area of the copy is 50%. If 100 units of light are directed at an area on a piece of film and only 50 units of light pass through the area of the film, transmittance in that area of the film emulsion is 50%. See figure 7.3.

Tone and Contrast. Up to this point in our discussion of line photography, we have been concerned only with copy that is either all black in the image areas or all white in the nonimage areas. Our object has been to reproduce every area with no density (nonimage area) on the copy as an area of density on the film emulsion, and every area with density (image area) on the copy as an area with no density on the film emulsion. During processing we have examined the gray scale and accepted development of the gray scale image to a solid step 4 as adequate density for the nonimage areas on the film emulsion.

CORRECT EXPOSURE	UNDEREXPOSURE	OVEREXPOSURE
This segment was exposed correctly. The negative areas are either clearly transparent or densely opaque. Edges are sharp, and detail proportions are true to the original.	This segment was underexposed. Although transparent areas are clear, the dark areas have low density. A positive made from a negative of this type shows thickening of all detail.	This segment was overexposed. Although dense areas are opaque, density appears in some areas which should be clear. A positive made from a negative of this type shows loss of fine detail.

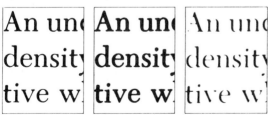

Figure 7.2. Examples of correct exposure, underexposure, and overexposure It is possible to judge underexposure or overexposure by comparing the reproduction with the original copy.

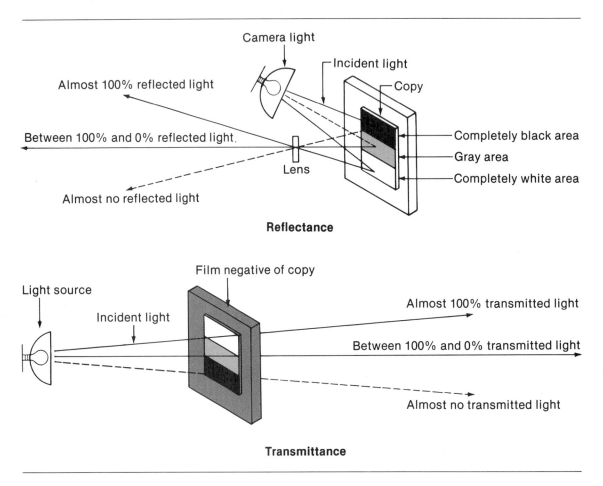

Figure 7.3. The relationship between incident light and reflectance or transmittance From the diagram we can see that there is an inverse relationship between the light reflected from the original image area and the light transmitted through the negative. That is, from the black area of the image, almost no light is reflected. However, in the corresponding area of the negative, almost 100% of the light is transmitted.

This simply means that when the gray scale is solid to a step 4, the nonimage areas on the film are dense enough so that they will not pass light when the negative is used to produce a printing plate.

Copy such as a snapshot is not composed of only white and black areas. Halftone copy is made up of white areas, black areas, and shades of gray. These differing shades from white through grays to black are called **tones.** Different tones have different densities.

Line copy that is either all black or all white is called high-contrast copy, because the two tones of the copy (white and black) are far apart. **Contrast** is simply a measure of how far apart the different tones on a piece of copy are from each other. The two tones on line copy can be said to be discontinuous. There is no continuum of varying tones from white through grays to black. Halftone copy is said to be continuous tone because all (or most) of the tones on such copy are on a continuum from white to black. Each of these tones has a different density on the copy. In fact, it is the differing densities in these tones that give the copy contrast and detail (figure 7.4).

Recall from Chapter 6 that in graphic arts photography we use high-contrast film. When exposed and processed, high-contrast film emulsion will have only two tones (areas of density). The emulsion will be either clear and transmit light or it will be black and transmit no light.

Graphic arts film has to be high-contrast because printing presses cannot print varying tones. A printing press puts ink density in the image areas and no ink density in the nonimage areas. This is the printer's problem when dealing with a continuous-tone photograph: How do you record a continuous-tone image on a high-contrast film? In fact, it cannot be done. What we can do is to break up a high-contrast image into a series of dots of varying shapes and sizes (but all of the same density) and give the illusion of tone

(a)

Figure 7.4. Comparison between a normal-contrast picture and a high-contrast picture. A normal-contrast picture (a) shows shades or tones from white through gray to black. A high-contrast picture (b) shows only two colors, white (no ink) and black.

Photograph of Dr. Charly Schindler by Richard W. Foster

(b)

variations. The dot patterns are produced by using a special screen.

Densitometry

Measurements of density belong to an area called **densitometry.** Transmittance and reflectance can be expressed algebraically as shown below:

$$Reflectance = R = \frac{I_r}{I_{rw}}$$

where:

R = reflectance,

I_r = intensity of light reflected from a tone,

I_{rw} = intensity of light reflected from white paper.

$$Transmittance = T = \frac{I_t}{I_i}$$

where:

T = transmittance,

I_t = intensity of transmitted light,

I_i = intensity of incident light.

The screen used to produce halftone dot patterns will be discussed later in the chapter. But densitometry is easy to understand without mathematics. A variety of tools measure transmittance and reflectance, expressed in logarithmic scales.

Logarithms are a way to express large quantities by using small numbers. Logarithmic information is readily available from tables in any mathematics book. As printers, we don't have to be able to manipulate logarithms in order to work with optical density. Densitometric tools read transmittance and provide readings that are already translated to logarithmic numbers.

Table 7.1 shows some common transmittance and density relationships. Although in theory there is no maximum density read-

Table 7.1. Some Common Transmittance and Density Relationships

Transmittance	Density
100%	0.0
10%	1.0
1%	2.0
0.1%	3.0
0.01%	4.0
0.001%	5.0
.	
.	
.	
0.0000001%	9.0
.	
.	
. and so forth	

ing, realistically, for printing, there is no need to measure an optical density much greater than 3.0.

A density reading is nothing more than a logarithmic scale ranging from 0.0 to around 3.0 that equates a numeric value to the relative ability of a material to absorb or transmit light. The higher the density reading, the denser the material. Dark areas on a piece of copy are denser than light areas.

Densitometers

Density is measured by a tool called a **densitometer**. The first densitometers were visual densitometers which operate on the basis of human judgments (figure 7.5). In the device is a set of known density wedges. The printer inserts the material to be measured and visually compares it to the known densities. After identifying a wedge that is identical in density to the test material, the printer records the logarithmic value printed on the wedge.

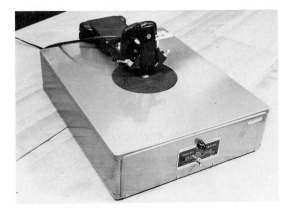

Figure 7.5. A visual densitometer Visual densitometers allow the operator to compare copy, which is placed under the probe, to labeled densities that are seen through the viewing element.

A **photoelectric densitometer** generally operates on a logarithmic measure of incident light. A controlled beam is projected onto the material to be tested, and the transmittance or reflectance is measured. Most have a readout device that immediately reports the logarithmic density.

Visual densitometers are the least inexpensive and most rugged of the two types, but they depend too much on the operator's judgment. Most individuals become tired after twenty to thirty visual measurements on continuous-tone black-and-white material. Color densities are even more difficult to perceive. With the photoelectric densitometer, there is no dependence on the operator's judgment, results are extremely consistent, and most have color heads that will accurately read primary color densities.

Densitometers can be classified according to the type of materials they are designed to measure: opaque or transparent. Any ink or emulsion on a solid base (such as paper) that is not designed to pass light is called opaque copy. Several examples of opaque materials are drawings, paste-ups, continuous-tone paper prints, or sheets of paper from a printing press. Density of opaque materials is measured by reflected light with a device called a **reflection densitometer** (figure 7.6). This tool directs a narrow controlled beam of light at a 45° angle onto an area of the opaque material. The amount of light reflected back is measured photoelectrically and translated to a logarithmic number. Before any reading is taken, the device is always calibrated to the same reading (usually 0.0, but for some devices 0.10) with the use of a standard white opaque wedge to ensure accurate measurements. The calibration process is called **zeroing.**

Any ink or emulsion that is on a clear base (such as glass) and is designed to pass light is called transparent material. Graphic

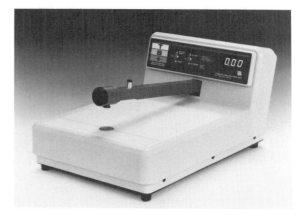

Figure 7.6. A reflection densitometer The reflection densitometer probe is placed over a specific area of the copy. Light is projected from the densitometer and reflects back into the densitometer probe. This reflected light is measured and displayed digitally as density units. The last reading taken on this densitometer represented 0.07 units of density.
Courtesy of Tobias Associates, Inc.

Figure 7.7. A transmission densitometer A negative or positive film image can be placed between the densitometer probe and the densitometer table. Light is passed (transmitted) through the film to the densitometer probe. The amount of light transmitted through the film is read and recorded on the densitometer display.
Courtesy of Tobias Associates, Inc.

arts film is an example of a transparent material. The density of transparent material is measured by light passing through the base with a device called a **transmission densitometer** (figure 7.7). A transmission densitometer passes a narrow beam of light at a 90° angle onto an area on the transparent film. The amount of light that passes through the film is measured and then translated to a logarithmic number. Care must be taken when zeroing a transmission densitometer. The base material of all transparent film always has some small amount of density, and the film's fog is always a concern. The device should be zeroed on a clear area on the piece of film being measured.

Gray Scale and Density

It is important to realize that the graphic arts gray scale discussed in Chapter 6 is nothing more than a visual description of the logarithmic density scale. Each step on the gray scale is an area of a specific measurable density. Scales are commercially available in opaque or transparent forms. The number of steps is arbitrary. Most printers use 10-, 12-, or 21-step gray scales. The opaque scale can be used as a crude sort of visual densitometer, but its best use is as an indicator of film density during and after chemical processing.

Examine the step tablet in figure 7.8. It is actually only an approximation of a 12-step

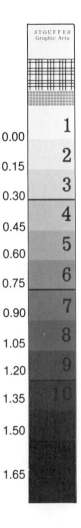

0.00 1
0.15 2
0.30 3
0.45 4
0.60 5
0.75 6
0.90 7
1.05 8
1.20 9
1.35 10
1.50
1.65

Figure 7.8. A 12-step gray scale This scale is calibrated into 12 steps representing densities from 0.00 to 1.65.
Courtesy of Stouffer Graphic Arts Equipment Co.

calibrated scales can be measured with a reflection densitometer.

From the calibrated scale it can be seen that step 4 represents a density of 0.45. If this small scale were placed on the copyboard and photographed, the light reflected by step 4 would be the same as any part of the copy having a density of 0.45, *and this is the key*.

The white nonimage areas for high-contrast copy such as line copy all have about the same density. This density is 0.45 or less. When determining the basic exposure for line shots on the process camera (see Appendix A), we select an exposure time and aperture opening that will cause step 4 on the gray scale to fill in (go solid) at optimum development time (usually 2¾ minutes) and optimum development conditions (usually constant agitation, with fresh developer, at 68°F or 20°C). In doing so, we ensure that all white nonimage areas on the copy will record as solid black areas on the film negative when a solid step 4 is reached during film development. Any images on the copy (lines, dots, or even fingerprints and smudges) with greater than 0.45 density (darker than a step 4 on the opaque gray scale) will record as clear areas on the film negative when the film is developed to a solid step 4.

An understanding of the gray scale steps as specific blocks of density is a powerful tool for the graphic arts photographer. With it the photographer can predict the effects that different camera aperture openings or shutter speed changes will have on the density of the film emulsion. Graphic arts photographers have learned that a change of one f/stop number on the camera will produce a 0.30 density shift on the sheet of film. For example, assume that after time-temperature-agitation processing of a line negative, a solid step 2 with a density of 0.15 was produced from an exposure of f/16 for 20 seconds. If develop-

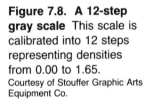

gray scale (an opaque tablet could not be reproduced here because it is made up of different tones), but it can illustrate the usefulness of the tool. Each step represents an increase in density from around 0.00 (no density) to 1.65, evenly divided into twelve steps. Figure 7.8 shows an uncalibrated scale (each step has, printed next to it, the manufacturer's values in increments of 0.15). Un-

ment of a step 4 (density of 0.45) was desired for normal copy, changing the exposure to f/11 for 20 seconds (or f/16 for 40 seconds) will add 0.30 density to the film (0.15 + 0.30 = 0.45). This one f/stop change in exposure will produce a solid step 4 which is appropriate for normal copy.

This concept of a predictable density shift as a result of exposure can be used in all phases of photography, whether continuous-tone, line photography, halftones, special effects, or color separation.

Extending the concept of a gray scale a bit further is the idea of a device called a sensitometer. A **sensitometer** is an instrument that accurately exposes a gray scale of density from 0.0 to 3.0 in increments of 0.30 or 0.15 density steps. The device has its own calibrated light source and shutter. In practice, an unexposed edge of a sheet of film is inserted under a cover and an exposure is made.

If that portion of the film is covered during camera exposure, two separate images will be recorded on the emulsion—a sensitometric step tablet and the reproduced camera image. During processing the step tablet can be checked to judge the stage of development. The advantage of this technique is that if the film is processed to the same step each time, the processing conditions will always be the same and the results on the film will be absolutely consistent. This is not the case for a camera-exposed gray scale because its density is a function of the camera exposure—the smaller the exposure, the longer the development necessary to produce the same density step. The sensitometer is ideal for processing images that require absolutely consistent development, such as halftones or color separations. A sensitometer can also be used to produce control strips for checking the activity level of automatic film processors.

Figure 7.9. Halftone reproduction A halftone photograph is a series of lines or dots so small that they trick the eye into seeing a continuous effect. Note that the dot pattern is visible in the detail enlargement on the left of the halftone.
Courtesy of Chris Savas

Halftone Screens

Screen Rulings

The most common method of printing a continuous-tone image is to convert the continuous-tone image into line copy by a process called "halftone photography." With this technique, the continuous-tone image is broken up into a series of dots of varying size but of the same density. The dots combine in such a way as to trick the eye into believing that the picture is still continuous-tone (figure 7.9). This trick is accomplished by placing a ruled halftone screen between the copy and

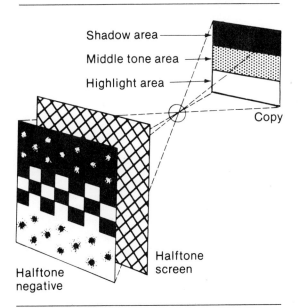

Shadow area

Middle tone area

Highlight area

Copy

Halftone screen

Halftone negative

Figure 7.10. Diagram of halftone screen use A halftone screen is placed between the continuous-tone copy and the film when exposing the film to break the continuous tone image into dots of varying sizes and shapes. White or highlight areas of the copy produce big dots of black on film. Middle tone areas produce intermediate size dots, and black or shadow areas produce small dots on the film.

the film in a process camera (figure 7.10). On the camera, light is reflected from the white highlight areas of the copy and is absorbed by the black shadow areas. The middle tones (gray areas) absorb light to varying degrees, depending on their density. The reflected light then passes through the openings in the screen and forms dots on the film. The relative size of each dot is controlled by the amount of light that passes through the screen, which is controlled by the amount of light reflected from the different areas on the copy.

It is perhaps easiest to conceive of a halftone screen by picturing crossed solid lines. The openings between the lines pass light; the lines do not. If we were to count the number of parallel lines in an inch of the screen, we would have a simple idea of the size of dot that would be produced with that screen. The more lines per inch, the smaller the average dot produced. This measure is referred to as **screen ruling** and is the method the industry uses to roughly define the dot size a screen will give. Figure 7.11 was produced by using a 65-line screen (there were 65 parallel lines in any given inch in the screen that produced the halftone negative). Figure 7.12 is an example of the same photograph produced by using a 133-line screen. It is apparent that for this book the finer screen ruling produces a more effective picture.

The following variables suggest what screen rulings to use for any particular halftone photograph:

– Normal viewing distance
– Process of reproduction
– Type of paper or material being printed

A halftone photograph appears continuous because at a normal viewing distance the eye cannot detect minute line detail. What is a "normal viewing distance"? It varies with the function of the printed piece. This book

Figure 7.11. Example of a 65-line screen halftone This halftone was reproduced from the original with the use of a 65-line screen.
Courtesy of Chris Savas

Figure 7.12. Example of a 133-line screen halftone This halftone was reproduced with the use of a 133-line screen. Compare the difference between this halftone and figure 7.11.
Courtesy of Chris Savas

is intended to be read at about 14 inches (about 36 centimeters) from your eyes. Therefore, the normal viewing distance for this book is 14 inches. A billboard you might see along a busy highway is designed to be read from approximately 300 yards (about 275 meters). That measure, then, is the normal viewing distance for the billboard. The effective halftone screen ruling for a billboard might range as coarse as 10 lines per inch. Screen rulings range from the huge dot size of a billboard to the fine dots produced from a 300-line screen.

The method and material of reproduction also influence the selection of screen ruling. For example, with current technology, a 300-line halftone is much too fine to be used with screen printing. For other methods, that same ruling is possible, but it becomes a test of sophisticated reproduction control. The ink-absorbing characteristics of papers vary widely. Newsprint rapidly absorbs ink and tends to spread or increase dot size. Clay-based or gloss-coated papers do not absorb or spread ink at all and can "hold" fine detail with little trouble. For most processes and paper characteristics, screen rulings of 85, 100, 120, 133, and 150 lines per inch are the simplest to manipulate and are the most widely used.

Screen Structure

Although a mesh of crossed solid lines is easy to visualize as the structure of a halftone screen, it is not an accurate idea of how the most commonly used screens are made. The dots formed by the clear openings produced between solid line rulings would all have the same shape and size, but to produce a halftone, we need dots of varying shapes and sizes. There are solid line screens, called **screen tints,** but they are not used to produce halftone photographs. The typical halftone screen is constructed with a photographic emulsion to form a **vignetted screen pattern.** Let's examine the difference between one intersection of two crossed lines on a screen tint and the same area on a vignetted halftone screen. Figure 7.13 is an artist's rendering of what a magnified view of these two areas looks like.

Screen tints have rigidly controlled openings. They are classified according to the amount of light they pass to the piece of film. A 40% screen tint will pass through its openings 40% of the light and will block, by solid lines, 60%. Figure 7.14 shows the range of typical screen tints. Some solid line screens are not crossed line. Screens containing such solid line screen patterns are generally referred to as "special effect screen tints." Screen tints and special effect screen tints are not used to produce halftones.

To appear continuous, a halftone must be formed from dots of varying shapes and sizes. Figure 7.13(b) illustrates the vignetted structure that produces these variations. The

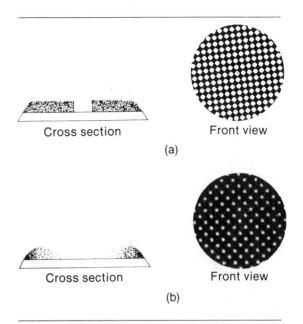

Figure 7.13. Comparison of a solid line screen with a vignetted screen A solid line screen with evenly shaped and sized openings is used to produce an even tone tint. A vignetted screen produces variations in the size and shape of the dots that result in the continuous-tone appearance of the halftones.

center portion of the screen opening (the area between the intersection of two lines) is clear, but the density of the emulsion increases as the diameter of the opening grows larger. When reflected light from the copy passes through the screen opening, a dot the size of the clear part of the opening is formed immediately on the film. As the quantity of light reaching the screen increases, more light penetrates the denser portion of the opening and the dot recorded on the film becomes larger. Within any halftone photograph, there is a wide range of individual dot variations. These variations are directly related to the amount of light reflected from the copy and focused through the camera lens onto the halftone screen. The more light that is reflected from

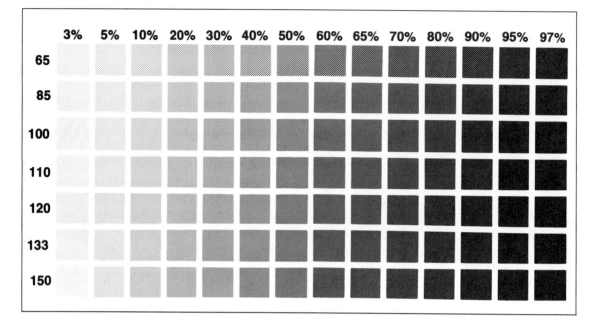

Figure 7.14. Screen tints In this example of screen tints, the horizontal rows show screen ruling and the vertical columns describe dot size.
Courtesy of Beta Screen Corp.

the copy, the more light that will penetrate the denser portions of the vignetted dots and the larger the dot recorded on the film. This makes sense if you remember that more light is reflected from the white highlight areas of the copy and less light is reflected from the dark shadow areas. You would want larger dots in the highlight areas on the film negative in order to block more light from reaching the printing plate, thus producing small dots on the plate. These small dots would print as small dots on the final page, thereby providing highlight areas on the printed page that have little density because little ink is printed in them.

Dot Size and Shape

To control individual dot variation, it is necessary to identify and measure dot size (the area the dot covers on the printed sheet). Dot size is measured in terms of percentage of ink coverage. Thus a printer will speak of a printed halftone as having a 5% or 10% dot in the highlight area, and a 90% or 95% dot in the shadow area. What is actually meant is that 5% of the highlight area is covered by dots and 95% of the shadow area is covered by dots.

The actual dot size varies according to screen ruling. A 20% dot produced from a 65-line screen would be larger than a 20% dot produced from a 133-line screen. This presents no problems for the printer, however, because a 20% dot produced from a 65-line screen would cover 20% of the printed area with ink. Likewise a 20% dot from a 133-line screen would cover 20% of the printed area with ink. One dot would be smaller than the other, but the percentage of actual ink coverage produced in each area would be the same. Comparisons of dot size between different lined screens is made only when printers are selecting the correct screen for a job. Comparisons of dot percentage sizes produced by the same screen, however, are made whenever printers are attempting to assess the results of a halftone they have made, to decide whether they have put the correct-sized dot in the highlight and shadow areas of the negative or whether they are actually printing the correct-sized dot in the highlight and shadow areas of a halftone reproduction.

Halftone screens are designed to produce one of two different types of dot structure:

– Square dots
– Elliptical dots

Figure 7.15 illustrates the typical range of dot sizes for a conventional "square dot" structure. Although the square dot screen is commonly used, there are some problems with it. In the area of the 50% dot there is a sudden visual jump in dot size that does not accurately reproduce the original photograph (figure 7.16). Figure 7.17 shows the elliptical dot size range that was developed to overcome the square dot limitations.

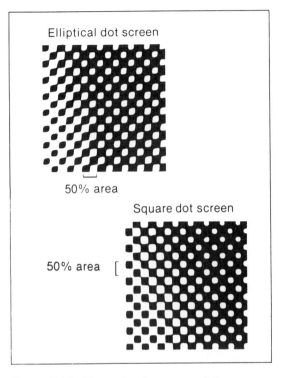

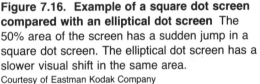

Figure 7.16. Example of a square dot screen compared with an elliptical dot screen The 50% area of the screen has a sudden jump in a square dot screen. The elliptical dot screen has a slower visual shift in the same area.
Courtesy of Eastman Kodak Company

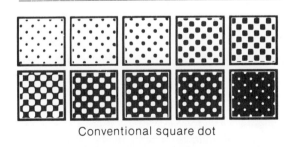

Conventional square dot

Figure 7.15. Examples of square dot sizes A typical range of dot sizes for a square dot screen is 5% to 95%.

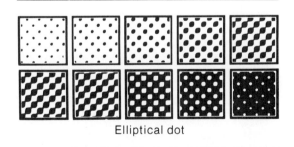

Elliptical dot

Figure 7.17. Examples of elliptical dot sizes Shown is a typical range of dot sizes (5% to 95%) for an elliptical dot screen.

Notice in figure 7.16 that in the 50% area the elliptical dot structure provides a smooth transition to where one dot finally touches another on all four sides. Both the square and the elliptical dots are produced with a halftone screen in exactly the same manner.

Whatever dot structure is used to produce the halftone, there are two ways that printers measure dot area:

– By a visual inspection technique
– By an optical dot area meter technique

It is possible with the use of a **linen tester** or magnifying glass to view dots of any ruling size (figure 7.18). By comparing figure 7.16 or 7.17 with a halftone negative, we can approximate dot size. This is done less by comparing the actual size of the dot to the illustration than by comparing the configuration of an area of dots to the illustration. As has been mentioned, the 50% dot is easy to

recognize. If a square dot screen was used to reproduce the negative, a 50% dot is found on the negative in an area where the dots just start to touch on all four corners. If an elliptical dot screen was used to produce the negative, the 50% dot is found in an area on the negative just before the dots start to touch on two corners. By viewing the amount of white space around a printed 10% dot, an area on a negative that will produce a 10% dot will become easy to identify.

Visual dot size identification is not as complicated as it may seem. When they are making halftones, graphic arts photographers are mainly concerned with the dots that will reproduce the highlight areas of the copy

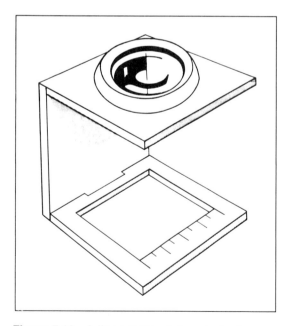

Figure 7.18. A linen tester A linen tester is used to view dot structure.

Figure 7.19. Example of a dot area meter This transmission dot area meter measures dot sizes on transparent materials. A reading of 0.10 indicates a 10% dot from the shadow area of a halftone negative. A 10% negative shadow dot produces a 90% shadow dot on the printed sheet.

(typically around 5% to 10% dots) and the dots that will reproduce the shadow areas of the copy (typically around 90% to 95% dots). Some practice is required, but an experienced printer can give at least a rough visual estimate of highlight and shadow dot size. However, this becomes somewhat of a subjective problem. Is a dot a 9% or an 11% or perhaps even a 13% dot? As much as a 7% variation in visual judgment among even experienced camera operators is possible. Although we can work with this inaccuracy, a solution is to use a **dot area meter** (figure 7.19). This device "integrates" or averages the amount of light passing through a selected area on a halftone negative and equates that measure to a dot area reading. It is possible to adapt the information from a transmission densitometer for the same function with some slight loss in accuracy (table 7.2).

Table 7.2. Conversion from Density Readings to Percent Dot Area

Integrated Halftone Density	Percent Dot Areas	Integrated Halftone Density	Percent Dot Areas
0.00	0	0.36	56
0.01	2	0.38	58
0.02	5	0.40	60
0.03	7	0.42	62
0.04	9	0.44	64
0.05	11	0.46	65
0.06	13	0.48	67
0.07	15	0.50	68
0.08	17	0.54	71
0.09	19	0.58	74
0.10	21	0.62	76
0.11	22	0.66	78
0.12	24	0.70	80
0.13	26	0.74	82
0.14	28	0.78	83
0.15	29	0.82	85
0.16	31	0.86	86
0.17	32	0.90	87
0.18	34	0.95	89
0.19	35	1.00	90
0.20	37	1.10	92
0.22	40	1.20	94
0.24	42	1.30	95
0.26	45	1.40	96
0.28	48	1.50	97
0.30	50	1.70	98
0.32	52	2.00	99
0.34	54		

Use this table to convert integrated halftone densities (halftone densities with fringe area of dots compensated for) into percent dot area.

General Types of Halftone Screens

There are several basic methods for preparing halftone negatives from continuous-tone originals. The earliest technique was a glass ruled screen. Parallel lines were etched on two sheets of glass, which were then cemented together with the sets of lines at right angles to create individual dot-forming openings. In the production of a halftone, the glass screen was placed a predetermined distance from the film in the camera. The camera image was then focused on the screen and finally refocused onto the film. The size of the gap was critical. It was a measure of the ratio of the lens-to-copy and copy-to-screen distance. Halftone negatives produced with such screens were traditionally thought to be of the highest quality. However, the high cost of the screens, the high level of sophistication required to use them, and the development of high-quality vignetted contact screens have resulted in a decline in their use.

The simplest method of halftone preparation is the use of "prescreened film," which allows for production of halftone negatives without the use of a halftone screen. A piece of prepared film, simply exposed and processed, gives an acceptable halftone reproduction. The screen is, in a sense, "built into" the prepared film. Prescreened film is ideal for simple exposures. Halftone exposures can be produced without a vacuum frame-holding system, and the film can be used in any portable camera (such as a press camera) to make halftones of three-dimensional scenes. However, the control limitations restrict the use of prescreened film. It cannot be used for high-quality halftone reproductions.

Contact halftone screens have revolutionized the industry. They are inexpensive and simple to use, and they require no sophisticated equipment or manipulation. As we have seen, they form dots using a vignetted structure. All further explanation of the production of halftones will assume the use of a contact screen.

Types of Contact Halftone Screens

There are two basic types of contact screens, classified according to the color of dye used to produce the emulsion. The two colors are magenta and gray. Within both categories are special purpose screens. Table 7.3 outlines these variations and defines the intended use for each. In general, any screen may be used with any sort of copy. However, if a screen is not used for its intended function, special manipulation may be necessary to produce optimum results.

Magenta screens are designed to work with monochromatic (black and white) originals. Filters may be used to change the basic density range of the screen (see Section 2). Magenta negative screens are used on a process camera to produce halftone negatives from opaque (paper) positives. Magenta positive screens are designed to make halftone positives in a contact printing frame from continuous-tone negative transparencies.

Gray screens are popular for reproducing black and white photographs and are also designed to work with colored continuous-tone originals. Gray screens do not respond to filter control of the basic density range of the screen. Gray negative screens are intended to be used to make negatives from either opaque or transparent copy. Photogravure gray screens have a special structure to produce a "hard dot" for the gravure printing process. Diffusion-transfer gray screens are designed to make positive opaque halftones from positive opaque originals by using the diffusion-transfer process.

Whatever the type of contact screen used, the basic processing steps are exactly the same.

Table 7.3. A Classification of Vignetted Contact Screens for Halftone Photography

MAGENTA

Negative	Camera negatives from positive black and white originals
Positive	Contact positives from continuous-tone separation negatives
Photogravure	Intermediate halftone negatives for the gravure process

GRAY

Negative	Halftone negatives from positive color originals (transparency or print)
Diffusion Transfer	Opaque camera positives (stats) from black and white positive originals using the diffusion transfer process

SECTION 2

Section 1 gave some basic ideas about halftone photography. Now our attention turns to more specific understandings of procedures. This section examines some terminology, shows how exposures can be determined, and provides enough information so that the reader will actually be able to produce an acceptable halftone negative.

Areas of a Continuous-Tone Print

There are three areas that both printers and photographers identify as the most significant measures of the quality of a continuous-tone print (figure 7.20):

– Highlight area
– Shadow area
– Middle tone area

The **highlight area** is that portion of the picture that contains detail but has the least amount of density. There is a special kind of highlight, called a "spectral highlight," that has no detail or density. This will be dealt with later in this chapter. The darkest areas of the print are called the **shadow areas**. All the shades of gray between the highlights and shadows are called the **middle tone areas.**

It is possible to compare the density of these three areas of the print with the density of the steps on any graphic arts gray scale. We can also equate these densities with the size of halftone dots on the film negative and on the final printed sheet. For example, in figure 7.20:

1. The highlight detail begins in step 1, or with a density near 0.05. The highlight dots begin with the smallest reproducible dot (generally about 5%) and extend to about a 20% or 25% dot.
2. The shadow detail ends in step 10, or with a density of about 1.45. The shadow dots extend from about 75%

Figure 7.20. Areas of a continuous-tone print
In this continuous-tone print, the highlight areas correspond to steps 1 and 2 on the gray scale. From the gray scale, we see that the middle range is from 3 to 7. The shadow area ranged from 8 to 11 on the gray scale.
Courtesy of Chris Savas

Several things need to be emphasized with respect to this comparison. Printers do not typically measure a particular highlight, middle tone, or shadow density. They are primarily concerned with the density extremes (the amount of density from the lightest highlight to the darkest shadow). This measure is called the **copy density range (CDR)** of the photograph. The CDR is equal to the shadow density minus the highlight density. This is an important relationship to remember. The copy density range of figure 7.20 is 1.40 (1.45 minus 0.05). The typical continuous-tone photograph has a density range of approximately 1.70.

Comparing the dot size and the gray scale tonal area should not be taken to mean that a certain dot size should be formed in any particular part of the gray scale for every halftone negative. Printers are concerned that the smallest dot appear in the highlight step and that the largest dot appear in the last shadow step. The placement of all dot sizes between these two extremes controls the contrast of the halftone and depends on the particular photograph being reproduced. There is no rule that states in what step any dot should be placed.

Understanding Halftone Exposures

Two simple exposures are generally used to produce a halftone negative from a vignetted contact screen:

– Main exposure
– Flash exposure

They both are relatively straightforward and easy to understand.

The only required exposure is called the **main exposure.** Sometimes referred to as the

or 80% to the largest reproducible dot (generally about 95%) before a solid black is reached.

3. The middle tone area for this photo is probably from step 3 to step 7 but is not a definite range. Middle tone dots typically range from about a 25% dot to a 75% dot.

highlight exposure or detail exposure, it is simply an exposure on film through a contact screen using a process camera. Just as each continuous-tone photograph has a different density range, so does each halftone contact screen. The **basic density range (BDR)** of a halftone screen is that density range reproduced on the film with one main exposure through the halftone screen. This density range is also called the **screen range.** It is the main exposure that controls where the smallest highlight dot will be placed on the gray scale and in the corresponding areas of the negative. Figure 7.21 illustrates three different exposures of the same gray scale. Notice how increasing the exposure moves the highlight dot up the scale, but the basic density range recorded on the gray scales remains the same. Each gray scale shows discernible dots throughout the range of seven steps. The difference in the three scales is simply the difference in the placement of the highlight dot. In each gray scale, the highlight dot has moved down the gray scale. The main exposure, then, controls the placement of the highlight dot.

Assume that we have a halftone screen that produced a highlight dot in the density value of 0.05 and a shadow dot in the density value of 1.05. The BDR of this screen would be 0.90 (1.05 − 0.05 = 0.90). This simply means that our particular screen can record no more than a basic density range of 0.90 with only a main exposure. If the CDR of the photograph we are shooting is smaller than the BDR of the screen we are using, one main exposure will reproduce the original. But if the BDR of the photograph is larger than that of the screen, there will be problems.

As we have already mentioned, the typical continuous-tone photograph has a density range of 1.70. This difference between copy density range and screen density range is called **excess density.** It must be handled with a secondary exposure.

The **flash exposure** is a nonimage exposure on the film through the contact screen. Light may be flashed through the lens, but a special yellow flashing lamp is typically used. Nearly all the identifiable detail of a continuous-tone photograph is found in the highlight to middle tone areas. A single main exposure will record most of the detail of a typical photograph. However, there is still some detail in the shadow areas and this density affects the contrast of the final product. Most halftone screens are not equipped to record the entire range of shadow density and detail. Because shadows usually absorb more light than they reflect, the film records shadow detail long after any reflected highlight detail has been recorded. The main exposure typically cannot form reproducible shadow dots on the film and still faithfully reproduce the highlight detail. The function of the flash exposure is twofold:

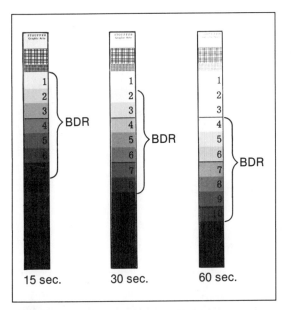

Figure 7.21. Three main exposures of a gray scale Three different main exposures were made of the same gray scale. Notice that the basic density range does not change as the exposure is increased; it just moves down the scale.

– It adds density to the weak shadow dots, bringing them up to a reproducible size.
– It adds uniform exposure to the entire negative, increasing the size of all dots, especially those representing the shadow areas.

The flash exposure is needed to make the final halftone reproduction match as closely as possible the density range of the original print.

This is not difficult to understand if you remember the vignetted dot pattern on the halftone screen. The highlight areas of the copy are going to reflect the most light back to the camera lens. In just a few seconds of main exposure, the reflected light from the highlight areas of the copy will pass through the clear areas in the center of the elliptical dot and produce a dot on the film emulsion. As the main exposure continues, reflected light from the highlight areas will penetrate the denser portions of the vignetted dot, and the highlight dots will grow in size. At the same time, some of the middle tone areas will reflect enough light to penetrate the vignetted dot and they, too, will record an image. However, the shadow areas of the photograph, being dark, absorb most of the camera light and reflect back only a small amount. During the main exposures, this small amount of light reflected from the shadow areas may penetrate only the very center of the vignetted dot, which is clear. The dots produced by the reflected light from the shadow areas during the main exposure are so small that they cannot be printed.

The flash exposure is made directly through the halftone screen and does not rely on reflected light from the copy. Therefore, an equal amount of light is passed through all parts of the screen. The flash exposure increases the size of all the dots recorded during the main exposure, but it has more of an effect on the shadow dots than on the highlight dots.

This is because the highlight dots, having been formed from the reflection of the white camera light, are about as large as they can get. Enough light penetrated the vignetted screen dots in the highlight area to almost completely expose the film emulsion in the highlight areas. The yellow flash light will not have much effect in these areas; there just are not many unchanged silver halide crystals left to change. However, the flash exposure greatly affects the shadow area because the shadow area was not affected much during the main exposure. The small dots made in the shadow area during the main exposure are enlarged during the flash exposure. This is why the

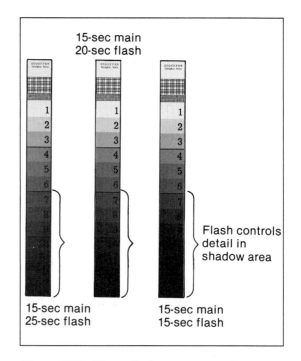

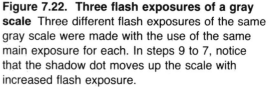

Figure 7.22. Three flash exposures of a gray scale Three different flash exposures of the same gray scale were made with the use of the same main exposure for each. In steps 9 to 7, notice that the shadow dot moves up the scale with increased flash exposure.

flash exposure is said to control the placement of the shadow dot.

Figure 7.22 illustrates three different flash exposures of a gray scale, with the use of the same main exposure. Notice that the position of the highlight dot does not significantly change, but the shadow dot moves up the scale as the flash exposure increases. The length of the flash is calculated from the amount of excess density of the print (CDR of print minus BDR of screen). The goal is to print a 95% dot (or largest reproducible dot) in the darkest shadow area containing detail.

Controlling Halftone Contrast

The placement of the middle tone dots in a halftone photograph affects contrast. The term "contrast" is bantered about frequently by both printers and photographers, but what does it really mean? Figure 7.23 is an example of a "contrasty" print. Figure 7.24 shows a normal photograph. Examine each reproduction. Figure 7.23 has fewer visible tones than figure 7.24. Also, figure 7.23 has a greater shadow density with no detail. In other words, a high-contrast photograph is usually one with a compressed tonal range and not much detail in the highlights and shadows. It is actually the compression or expansion of tones that defines contrast.

We can control contrast on the final printed sheet when we produce a halftone. By compressing or expanding the tonal range, we shift the middle tone dots up or down the scale. There are two common ways of controlling contrast:

- By using a filter
- By using a special camera exposure

When using a magenta contact screen, it is possible to shorten or lengthen a tonal range by using a yellow or magenta filter. The

Figure 7.23. A contrast image A print or its reproduction is considered to have contrast when there is very little detail in the highlights and shadows and when there are few intermediate tones.
Courtesy of R. Kampas

Figure 7.24. A normal image A normal print or reproduction has highlight detail, shadow detail, and a range of intermediate tones.
Courtesy of R. Kampas

filter is placed in front of the camera lens during the main exposure. What the filter actually does is change the screen's BDR. The following list shows the degree of change of a screen's BDR through the use of this method:

- CC-50M   1.15
- CC-10M   1.35
- NO-FILTER   1.40
- CC-10Y   1.45
- CC-50Y   1.60

(CC = color correcting filter, M = magenta, Y = yellow.)

The most frequently used technique to increase contrast is to use a **bump** or **no-screen exposure.** With this technique, a second image-forming exposure is made on the camera without the contact screen in place. This exposure must be made either before or after the main and flash exposures, but not between the two. The actual exposure time is expressed as a percentage of the main expo-

sure. Figure 7.25 illustrates two different bump exposures of a gray scale, with the use of the same main and flash exposures. The bump compresses the screen range and therefore increases contrast. Figure 7.26 shows how the use of a bump can improve a previously flat image.

Again, this is not difficult to understand if you think about what is actually being recorded on the film during the bump exposure. After the main and flash exposures, the highlight areas on the film are almost completely filled in, and the shadow areas have recorded a printable dot. The bump exposure is made without the halftone screen, with the use of reflected light from the copy that is in the exact location it held during the main exposure. Unlike the flash exposure, the bump exposure is going to affect the highlight areas of the film. These areas have been almost completely exposed during the main exposure and would require only a small additional exposure to completely fill in. The

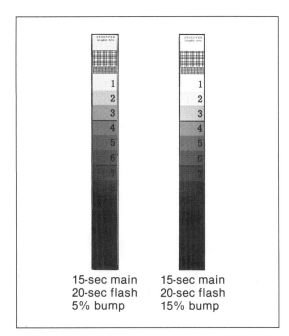

Figure 7.25. Two bump exposures of a gray scale Two different bump exposures of the same gray scale were made with the use of the same main and flash exposures for each. Notice that a 5% bump produces detail from steps 1 through 8. A 15% bump produces detail from steps 2 through 7. An increase in bump exposure has eliminated two tones from the gray scale. Instead of eight tones there are now six tones. Contrast has been increased.

shadow areas will be relatively unaffected by a small additional amount of exposure.

A bump is a very short exposure. As a small burst of light strikes the copyboard, it is immediately reflected by the extreme highlights and almost completely absorbed by the shadows. The result, when the reflected light passes through the lens to the film, is to close dots in the highlight areas, but dots in the shadow areas are not affected. When the film is processed, the ultimate effect is to compress the tones of the original by reducing the num-

ber of density steps between the highlight and shadow areas.

Understanding Halftone Dots

The density variations in a continuous-tone original are represented in a halftone reproduction as dots of various sizes. The size of these dots in any area of the halftone negative is determined by the amount of light reflected from the original to that area during the main and bump exposures, and the amount of exposure produced by the flash. Halftone dots show detail. Where there are no dots on a printed halftone, there will be either completely open, uninked areas or completely filled in, inked areas. No individual dots will appear to show detail in these areas.

The object of making a halftone is to produce a printed piece that reflects the tonal range of the original, through variations in dot size and placement. The more closely the halftone approximates the tonal range of the original, the more closely it will show detail from the original. Looking back at figure 7.20, even in the lightest areas of the subject's left shoulder we can see the weave of her sweater. This is a highlight area with detail. A shadow area with detail is located at the top of the subject's right shoulder. Above this shadow detail area, the dots have disappeared, and solid ink is printed. Because no dots are printed in this area, no detail from the original can be shown. Thus, the smallest dots on the printed halftone will represent detail in the highlight areas of the original. The largest dots on the printed halftone will represent detail in the shadow areas of the original. In the lightest highlight areas (called the **spectral highlights**), where there was no detail in the original, there should be no dot detail on the

(a)

(b)

Figure 7.26. Example of use of a bump to increase contrast Only main and flash exposures were used to produce the print in (a). To increase contrast, a 3% bump exposure was made to produce (b).

printed piece. In the deepest shadows, where there was no detail on the original, there should be no dot detail on the printed piece.

Printable Dots. It is impossible to observe all of the dot sizes on a halftone negative during film development to check for accurate dot size. Instead, we use aim points, typically at either extreme of the original's density range. We try to place the smallest dots we can print in the detail highlight areas of the original, to show highlight detail in the print, and the largest dots we can print in the detail shadow areas. Thus the position of the smallest and the largest printable dot on both the negative and the printed piece is a concern.

Remember that on the negative, the *smallest* printable dots will appear as small clear openings surrounded by black, exposed emulsion (density). During plate making, these small openings will expose only small dots on the printing plate, which will transfer small dots to the printing paper. These small dots (highlight dots) will reproduce detail in the highlight area of the printed piece.

The *largest* printable dot will appear on the negative as a small area of density, surrounded by a large clear opening. During plate making, these large openings will expose large dots on the printing plate, which will transfer large dots to the printing paper. These large dots (shadow dots) will reproduce detail in the shadow area of the printed piece.

A press operator refers to a dot that is printable as a dot that the press can "hold," or a dot that can be "held" on press. A 5%

to 10% highlight dot can be held with most offset presses. Dots smaller than this size will be too small to print accurately and consistently, and may not print at all. The largest printable shadow dot that can be held with most offset processes is a 95% shadow dot. On press, these dots will appear as tiny, unprinted areas, surrounded by ink. Shadow dots larger than 95% will tend to fill in on press and go solid.

The smallest and largest printable dots are a concern to the camera operator. If the highlight dots on the negative (small open areas, surrounded by density) are too small, they will not pass enough light during plate making to expose a printable dot on the printing plate, and detail will be lost in the highlight areas. If the large open areas on the negative that produce shadow dots in the print are too large, they may fill in during plate making and become plugged with ink on press.

To make an acceptable halftone, the camera operator must know something about printable dot size. The correct size of a printable dot (5%, 10%, 95%, etc.) is determined through knowledge about the printing process to be used, the working conditions in the printing plant, and the ink and paper (or other substrate) to be printed. This information is given to the camera operator before the halftone is made.

Dot Gain. One very important consideration when determining printable dot size is dot gain. Halftone dots tend to gain in size during plate making and on press. Critical exposure and development control is needed during plate making to accurately reproduce the dot structure on the negative. Improper plate exposure or processing will produce dot sizes on the plate that are different in size from those on the negative. If larger dots are recorded on the printing plate than those on the negative, larger dots will be printed and detail will be lost. Dot growth during plate making is one cause of dot gain.

Even if the dots' sizes are recorded accurately on the plate, dot gain can still occur on press. In the offset process, improper ink and water balance can cause dot gain (or loss). The type and condition of the press can also affect dot gain, as can the paper and ink combination being printed. Uncoated papers, such as bond or newsprint, absorb ink (see Chapter 18, *Ink and Paper*). A dot printed on uncoated paper tends to spread out and grow larger. Small highlight dots get bigger; large shadow dots fill in. Coated paper has better "ink holdout," it does not absorb as much ink, and dots do not spread as much as they would on uncoated paper.

Dot size is determined by visual inspection with a magnifying glass, or through readings taken with a dot area meter. The size of the smallest and largest dots that can be reproduced (plated and printed) is determined by comparing dot size on the negative to the actual dot size printed. Through this comparison, a historical record of expected dot gain for a variety of processing and printing conditions on a variety of paper and ink combinations can be developed. Equipped with this knowledge, the camera operator can recognize the smallest and largest printable dot for particular processes and working conditions, and place them in the correct density areas on the negative.

If no information is known about dot gain, shop tests must be run. One common test is to plate the negative made during the main test (described below), print it on a number of paper types commonly used in the plant, and measure for dot gain. In practice, a variety of control devices are available to the camera operator, plate department, and press operator to monitor and control dot gain.

Camera Calibration for Halftone Exposures

It is possible to produce a halftone negative by trial and error. In other words, we can guess at the main and flash exposures, produce a halftone, evaluate the results, and then try to compensate for any limitations on the negative by changing our exposures. The problem with a trial and error method is that it leads to a great waste of both film and time. Every original photograph is likely to have a slightly different copy density range (CDR) than the next. Likewise, each halftone screen will have a slightly different basic density range (BDR) than every other. Even if we could, through trial and error, come up with exposure times for the main, flash, and bump that would produce an acceptable halftone for the majority of our continuous-tone originals, there would always be problem photographs (such as an especially flat or contrasty original) that our trial and error exposure times would not reproduce correctly. That is, our results would not be predictable. Predictable results are required in halftone photography, for the purposes of both quality control and reducing waste in the camera room. To achieve predictable results, we must have densitometric information about our working conditions and about our original copy. Information about our working conditions—the BDR of our screen, and the effects upon film density recorded during the main, flash, and bump exposures—is gathered during camera calibration for halftones. Information about the original copy—the CDR and the actual density of the highlight and shadow areas—is read from the original photograph with a densitometer.

Through camera calibration we will determine the following:

- The basic density range of the halftone screen we are going to use
- The minimum flash required to record density in the shadow areas on the negative
- The effect that a bump of a specific duration will have on the highlight area of the negative

These three pieces of information are determined from three tests, one each for the main, flash, and bump exposures. During these tests, only exposure is changed. All other darkroom conditions, including camera lighting and chemical control—time, temperature, and agitation—are kept as consistent as possible. If shallow-tray processing is used, it is advisable to mix fresh developer after each test, to keep a consistent level of developer activity.

Main Test

The main test is used to determine the BDR of the halftone screen. This test requires a visual gray scale with steps of known density, such as the 24-step reflection density guide shown in figure 7.27. In addition, a basic knowledge of camera operation is needed (Chapter 6).

1. Place a step-calibrated gray scale in the center of the copyboard.
2. Set the lens for an aperture opening that is two f/stops smaller than the largest opening.
3. Place an unexposed sheet of film on the filmboard, emulsion up.
4. Place a halftone screen over the film, emulsion down.

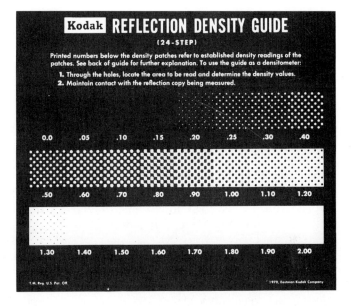

Figure 7.27. Twenty-four-step reflection density guide The main exposure test shows a range from 20 to 1.20, or a basic screen density range of 1.00 with a 30-second exposure.
Courtesy of Eastman Kodak Company

5. Set the camera exposure for a test exposure. A 30-second test exposure is generally a good starting point.

6. Develop the negative according to the manufacturer's recommendations, keeping processing conditions absolutely consistent.

7. Look for the smallest printable highlight dot on the negative. For this test, the smallest printable dot should fall between the 0.00 density step and the 0.30 density step on the negative image of the gray scale.

8. Observe the density step on the negative image of the gray scale that contains the smallest printable highlight dot. Read the corresponding density of this step on the calibrated gray scale. In the example in figure 7.27, the smallest printable dot was produced in the fifth step, representing 0.20 units of density. Record your results.

9. Now examine the remaining steps in which dots were recorded on the gray scale negative. Note and record the density step that carries the largest printable shadow dot. For this test (figure 7.27), the dots recorded in the 1.30 density step appeared too large to be printable; those in the 1.20 step were too small. We determined that the largest printable dot would be recorded at about a density step of 1.25.

10. Obtain the BDR of the screen by subtracting the density reading in the density step that contains the smallest printable dot (highlight) from the density reading in the density step that contains the largest printable dot (shadow).

The BDR of the screen we tested was 1.05:

Shadow Density	1.25
Highlight Density	−0.20
Basic Density Range (BDR)	1.05

A BDR of 1.05 means that if we make an exposure through that specific screen, in the camera that was used to test the screen, with the same film, under the same processing conditions, from a continuous-tone original that has a copy density range of 1.05, then all of the image density—from whitest white, through midtones, to black—can be recorded with only a main exposure. Most continuous-tone originals have a longer density range than 1.05. Using the screen tested, a flash will be required to accurately reproduce the detail displayed in the complete tone range of any continuous-tone original which has a CDR greater than 1.05.

Main Test Adjustments.   It is worth noting that locating the smallest printable dot in a step between 0.00 and 0.30 with the main test exposure is important. No attempt is being made in the main test to match the density steps of the reflection gray scale to the density recorded on the gray scale negative step-for-step. But it is important to locate the first step of density reflected from the original somewhere near the low density end of the negative gray scale. If the first printable dot was located in the 1.40 step of the negative gray scale, and the screen BDR was 1.05, the largest reproducible dot would have to be recorded in the 2.45 density step (1.40 + 1.05 = 2.45). Most reflection density guides, such as the one shown in figure 7.27, do not have steps this high in density, and the screen BDR could not be determined from the test. This would be the case if an extremely long trial main exposure were used. An overly short trial main exposure would have the opposite result, and a midtone dot, larger than the smallest reproducible dot, would appear in the 0.00 density step of the negative gray scale. Again, the screen BDR could not be determined because the smallest printable dot would not show on the gray scale.

If a dot larger than the smallest printable dot is recorded in the 0.00 step, re-run the test with an increase in exposure time. Increasing the exposure will move the dot sizes recorded in each step up the scale, toward 0.30. If the smallest printable dot is recorded above the 0.30 density step, decrease exposure time. Decreasing exposure will move the dot sizes recorded in each step down the scale, toward 0.00.

If the first test exposure did not place the smallest printable dot in the 0.00 to 0.30 density range, it is possible to predict a new test exposure. Doubling the main exposure will shift all halftone dots up the scale 0.30 units of density. Halving the main exposure will shift all halftone dots down the scale 0.30 units of density. Thus, if the smallest printable dot is found to lie in the 0.40 density step, exposure with the same aperture opening but for half the exposure time will place this dot in the 0.10 density step. Repeat the main test until the required highlight dot placement is achieved.

Flash Test

Results from the flash test are used to calculate the amount of flash exposure needed to extend the density range in the shadow area of the negative by an amount consistent with the shadow detail density range on the original. To make this calculation we must determine the minimum flash required to produce a printable shadow dot on the negative. The flash test is made with a step-exposure. Use the same type of film and the same screen used in the main test.

1. Position the screen and film emulsion-to-emulsion on the filmboard, under the flash lamp. Turn on the vacuum.

2. Cover most of the sheet of film with an opaque sheet of paper (such as cardboard), leaving about one fifth of the sheet uncovered.

3. Expose the uncovered area for 5 seconds.

4. Without moving the film or screen, shift the opaque paper so that it uncovers another fifth of the sheet of film and expose for another 5 seconds.

5. Continue this process until the whole sheet of film has been uncovered during the last 5-second exposure.

6. Process the film using standard conditions and methods.

7. Examine the negative for the largest printable dot, and record the flash exposure needed to produce it.

The results of our flash test are shown in figure 7.28. Five steps were used. The first step was exposed 5 times for a total of 25 seconds; the last step received only one 5-second exposure. For our test, a printable shadow dot was produced with 10 seconds flash exposure. Dots were produced with the 5-second exposure, but these dots were too large and would fill in during plate making and printing.

Flash Test Explanation.   Recall that the flash exposure extends the density range recorded on the negative by increasing apparent density in the shadow area, the area which received the least reflected light from the copy. Density is added in the shadow area during the flash by making an exposure with a flashing lamp, directly through the negative onto the film emulsion. During the main exposure, the highlight areas of the copy reflect a great deal of light. Thus the amount of light added to the negative highlight dots during the flash will produce almost no further exposure, and the flash will have little effect on the highlight dots. However, only a small amount of light is reflected from the shadow areas of the original during the main exposure. Thus the amount of light received in the shadow areas during the flash will produce much more exposure in these areas on the film. This is the reason that the flash extends density mainly in the shadow area: it increases dot size mainly in shadow areas, which were least affected by the main exposure.

When exposure calculations are made for a halftone, a balance is struck between the exposure times such that the main exposure produces the smallest printable dots, which reproduce highlight detail in about the same density as the highlight detail on the original,

Figure 7.28. Flash exposure test The negative produced during the flash exposure test shows that a reproducible shadow dot was obtained at 10 seconds.

and the flash extends density only in the shadow areas. In the illustration shown in figure 7.20, if a highlight density reading of 0.10 was recorded from the woman's right shoulder on the original, and step 2 on the gray scale at the bottom of the picture contained 0.10 units of density, we would expect to see the smallest printable dots printed in the woman's right shoulder. We would expect to see about the same size dots in step 2 of the gray scale.

The main exposure produces the highlight dots and continues producing midtone dots up the scale until the BDR of the screen is reached. The BDR of our screen was 1.05, which means that the density range of the original will be reproduced only up to 1.05 units of density. Density over this amount will appear as completely open, unexposed areas on the negative. Thus it will not be reproduced with dots on the print and will appear on the printed piece as a solid ink mass. If the copy has a CDR of 1.70, and the screen has a BDR of 1.05, there are 0.65 units (1.70 − 1.05) of "excess density" which will not be reproduced by the main exposure only. Without a flash to extend the density range in the shadows, a print with a very short density range would be produced.

This idea of extending the recorded image range should not be confused with the basic density range of the screen. A flash exposure adds density in the shadow areas of the recorded halftone image, and thereby "extends" the image density range. It does not, however, affect in any way the basic density range of the screen.

Bump Test

We have seen that a flash is used to extend density into the shadow areas when the copy density range exceeds the screen density range. There are occasions, however, in which the screen BDR exceeds the CDR. When the screen BDR exceeds the CDR, it is impossible to produce both an acceptable highlight dot and an acceptable shadow dot with a single main exposure. If the exposure produced an acceptable highlight dot, the shadow dot would be too large. If an acceptable shadow dot were produced, the highlight dot would be unacceptable. A bump exposure is required in these situations, to increase exposure in the highlight areas. This has the effect of compressing the screen density range to more closely match the copy density range.

Another use of the bump exposure is to improve the appearance of an unacceptable original photograph. By compressing the copy density range, the bump increases contrast, giving the image what is often called "more snap." "Snap," it should be noted, is not a characteristic that can be accurately measured. The bump exposure tends to close the small negative highlight halftone dots; the result is a more appealing image.

The bump is a no-screen exposure, generally made after the main and flash. The bump is a very short exposure during which light reflected from the copy exposes the negative. The shadow and midtone areas of the copy will reflect very little light during this short exposure, thus the bump has no effect upon the shadow areas of the negative, and little effect in the midtones. The highlight areas, on the other hand, will reflect the most light and are most affected by the bump.

Use the same screen and processing conditions for the bump test that were used in the main and flash test.

1. Place a sheet of film on the filmboard, emulsion-to-emulsion with the contact screen.

2. Position a calibrated gray scale on the copyboard.

3. Expose the film through the lens, using the main exposure time that was determined during the main test to give the correct highlight dot location (0.00 to 0.30).

4. Open the camera back, keeping the vacuum on, and remove the halftone screen, being careful not to shift the film, then close the camera back.

5. Expose the film through the lens for 5% of the main exposure (10% if a gray positive halftone screen is used). Neutral density filters can be used instead of varying exposure for the bump. Use a 1.3 ND filter for a 5% bump; a 1.0 ND filter for a 10% bump.

6. Process the negative.

7. Locate the smallest printable highlight dot on the negative, and record the density of the step in which it appears.

8. Compare this density with the density step in which the smallest printable highlight dot occurred during the main exposure test, and record the difference in the two densities.

The difference between these two numbers is called the "highlight shift," because it represents the shift in highlight density, up

the density scale, that will result from a no-screen, bump exposure. Accurate information about the highlight shift will be needed when calculating halftone exposures for a given piece of copy.

Bump Test Adjustments. Bump exposure time is expressed as a percentage of main exposure, and can range from about 3% to about 10% or more of the main exposure. If a halftone required a 40-second main exposure with a 10% bump, the bump exposure would be 4 seconds (40 seconds × 10% = 4 seconds). An exposure this short can be accurately reproduced on cameras equipped with light-integrated exposure systems—in which the actual amount of light striking the film is used to control exposure—rather than a timer. Cameras not equipped with light integration often require neutral density filters fitted in front of the lens during the bump. These filters reduce the intensity of the light passing through the lens, thus increasing bump exposure times. Recommended neutral density filters for a range of bump exposures are shown in Table 7.4. The correct filter allows you to use the same f/stop and main exposure. Bump exposure time is increased by the filter factor, which is determined by the amount of exposure the filter blocks. The more exposure the filter blocks, the higher the filter factor.

Table 7.4. Neutral Density Filters for Selected Bump Exposures

Percent Bump	Neutral Density Filter
3%	1.50
5%	1.30
10%	1.00
15%	0.80
20%	0.70

Use this table to select the proper neutral density filter for the bump.

Calculating Halftone Exposures

Exposure calculations must be made for every halftone produced to determine the correct main, flash, and bump (if required) exposure needed to reproduce the original. As previously mentioned, during exposure calculation, a balance is struck between all exposure times. This balance assures that the correct size dots will be placed in all areas of the negative to accurately reproduce the densities found in corresponding areas on the original. Correct dot placement almost always requires adjustments to exposure times for individual copy.

For example, even though the flash exposure has little effect on dot size in the highlight areas of a halftone, it can be sufficient to increase the effect of the main exposure, producing overexposed highlight areas. To compensate for this effect, main exposure must be decreased by the correct amount so that the total exposure (main plus flash) will not overexpose the highlight dots and cause them to fill in on the negative. There is also an interaction between the bump and main exposure times. If a bump is used, the main exposure must be reduced in proportion to the effect that the bump will have on dots produced by the main.

These calculations can be made mathematically; however, several halftone computers have been developed that make halftone calculation a relatively simple process. All that is needed for halftone calculation are the results from the halftone calibration tests (main, flash, and bump) and readings of the CDR—the detail highlight and the detail shadow density readings from the original. The halftone computer adjusts all exposures for shop conditions using the results of the calibration tests, then adjusts these exposure times for particular copy requirements.

The first step in halftone calculation is accomplished by calibrating the computer for shop conditions. During calibration, the computer is supplied with information from the calibration tests—the BDR of the screen and the effect upon density of the flash and bump. After calibration, the computer can predict the required exposure times for any original, based on information that the operator enters about the CDR of the original.

A manual halftone computer is shown in figure 7.29. This device displays a number of scales which revolve around a central pin. The computer is calibrated and information about the CDR is entered by selecting and rotating the appropriate scales. This manual computer is inexpensive and comes supplied with thorough directions for calibration and use. However, it does have some disadvantages. It is not as accurate as modern, digital devices because it is hand manipulated and relies on visual readings. In addition, manual computers of this type can only be calibrated for one set of working conditions (screen and processing) at a time. They must be recalibrated each time the camera-screen combination is changed.

Small, hand-held digital halftone calculators, similar in operation to pocket calculators, are also available. These devices offer the advantage of more accurate readings than can be obtained with manual computers, but they generally rely on correct operator entry of information. For each halftone produced, the operator must take accurate density readings from the original and accurately enter them into the calculator, along with calibration information.

Microcomputers are also used for halftone calculation. While these devices are more expensive than hand-held manual or digital calculators, they offer several advantages. All

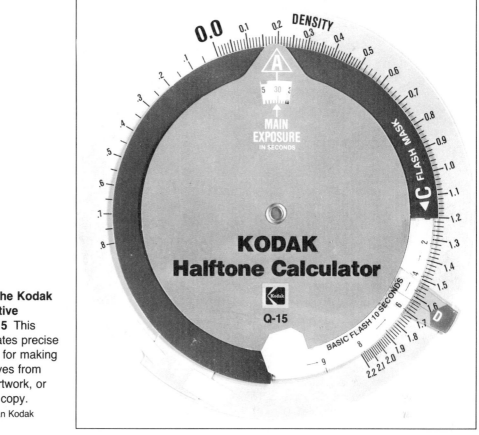

Figure 7.29. The Kodak Halftone Negative Computer, Q-15 This computer indicates precise exposure times for making halftone negatives from photographs, artwork, or other reflection copy.
Courtesy of Eastman Kodak Company

of these advantages are related to the microcomputer's ability to store information and to process it quickly. Most microcomputers programmed for halftone calculation have memory storage that allows them to store information about several sets of working conditions. A computer might be able to store information about two to forty or more different camera-screen combinations. Thus it could be used for making a variety of halftones without recalibration. The operator would simply call up the correct calibration for the camera-screen combination to be used,

then enter information about the CDR of the original to be reproduced (figure 7.30). Advanced systems can apply CDR readings to information about ink and paper combinations, press, and other process conditions, as well as camera-screen combinations. All of this amounts to an increase in accuracy, predictability, quality control, and a reduction of waste. Calculation speed is increased as well; on most computers, final exposure settings can be determined in a matter of seconds.

The most recent improvements in halftone computers have led to the development

Figure 7.30. Microcomputers for halftone calculation This vertical camera has a built-in microcomputer for halftone calculations. The operator keys in information about the highlight and shadow density of the original. This information is used in conjunction with preprogrammed information to calculate exposure for a particular screen and film material.
Courtesy of Agfa-Gevaert, Inc.

Figure 7.31. A process camera configured with a densitometer This process camera features an on-line densitometer, which can pass density readings directly to the camera computer.
Courtesy of Agfa-Gevaert, Inc.

of microcomputers which can accept density readings directly from the original copy, without the need for operator entry. Such devices connect a densitometer directly to the computer through a serial interface. The interface consists of a port (socket) on the computer into which a plug from the densitometer can be inserted. Densitometric readings are passed directly from the densitometer head to the computer memory for use in exposure calculations. The densitometer can be positioned manually by the operator on the detail high-

light and shadow areas of the original, or a scanning densitometer can be used to read and record original copy densities.

Often the densitometer is built right into the darkroom camera (figure 7.31). This configuration eliminates the need for the operator to enter any density readings. The microcomputer receives density readings directly from the densitometer. Exposure adjustments are made automatically, based on information supplied to the camera console from the microcomputer.

Processing Considerations for Halftone Photography

General film processing was explained in detail in Chapter 6. Here we will only emphasize the great importance of being able to repeat exactly every processing step from one negative to the next. With simple line negatives, the extent of development can be judged visually, making it possible to compensate for a slight variation in time, temperature, or agitation and still produce a usable negative. Such visual judgment is difficult when tray processing halftone negatives.

Automatic processors provide the greatest consistency in development. Unfortunately, such processors are not always available. There are several important considerations in tray processing of halftones.

A major problem with shallow-tray development is chemical exhaustion. Once the two parts of the high-contrast developer have been joined, the exhaustion process begins. Even if the mixture is not used, it becomes exhausted in a matter of hours. This is partly a result of solutions being combined and partly a result of the surface of the chemicals coming into contact with room air (aerial oxidation). The developer also becomes exhausted through use because it reacts with the emulsion of the film, and both the developer and the film change chemical structure. Chemical exhaustion radically affects the quality of the final halftone.

The following suggestions diminish the effects of developer exhaustion:

- Don't mix the developer until just before processing the negative.

- Mix a sufficient quantity to cover the negative in the tray completely.
- Don't reuse the same chemicals for additional halftone negatives.
- Discard the developer and mix a fresh batch if another halftone is to be produced.

Temperature control is a variable that is often overlooked with halftone processing. Even one degree of difference can result in extreme halftone variation.

The final consideration is the rate of tray agitation. Several techniques discussed in Chapter 6 are not applicable to halftone work. Still development (a technique that uses no agitation) is perfectly suited for critical development of extremely fine-line detail in a high-contrast negative. But with halftone negatives, the same technique lowers negative contrast and produces a softer, less defined dot. A mechanical tray technique leaves streaks in halftone negatives because currents of chemicals flow in the same paths over the film.

Try to agitate in at least three directions at a consistent rate. The actual speed is not significant, only the fact that the rate is always the same for every piece of film. Watching a sweep second hand on a darkroom timer is helpful. Some photographers even use a metronome to ensure a consistent rate. Another alternative is to use a sensitometer after any camera exposures. By this method it is possible to use visual judgment with tray development of halftones.

Typical Halftone Procedures

Let's tie together the information of this section by following through with the typical procedures for making a halftone negative from a continuous-tone original, using a manual or digital hand-held computer.

1. With a visual or reflection densitometer, determine the highlight and shadow densities. Be sure to measure the lightest area with detail for the highlights and the densest area (whether there is detail or not) for the shadows. With that information, determine the main and flash exposure times from a halftone computer. If a bump exposure is necessary, identify the time with the same tool.

2. Set up the process camera by using the procedures described in Chapter 6. Clean the copyboard glass, mount the original photograph and gray scale centered on the guidelines, close the frame (turn on the vacuum system if the camera has one), and move the copyboard so that it is parallel to the film plane. Adjust the diaphragm control to the percentage of enlargement or reduction desired at the f/stop opening that the computer was calibrated for (the photographer generally writes the f/stop on the computer as a reminder). Then move the percentage tapes so that they are balanced at the correct reproduction size. Set the camera timer at the main exposure time. Then adjust the flash timer to the flash exposure time. It is wise to check for even illumination by viewing the image through a ground glass screen. Aim the camera lights if necessary. Check for correct image position and camera focus. Adjust the vacuum system on the filmboard to the size of the contact screen, not to the size of the piece of film. (The contact screen must always be larger than the piece of film that is being used.)

3. To make the halftone exposures, first turn off the normal room lights so the darkroom is under safelight. Remove a sheet of high-contrast film from the storage box (be sure to close the box immediately—this is a good habit to develop) and mount the piece of film on the camera filmboard, emulsion up. If both the copy and the film are centered on the guidelines, there is little chance of ruining a sheet because the image missed the film. Next, position the halftone contact screen over the film so that the emulsions of the two pieces are touching (figure 7.32). Turn on the vacuum system and carefully roll out any air pockets that are trapped between the film and the screen. A loss of detail will occur if an air gap between the emulsions is allowed.

Close the camera back and turn on the timer to make the main exposure. When the shutter closes, open the camera back and, without touching the film or screen, make the flash exposure (figure 7.33). If a bump exposure is to be made, reset the camera timer, remove the halftone screen (carefully so the film does not shift), close the camera back, and make the through-the-lens bump exposure.

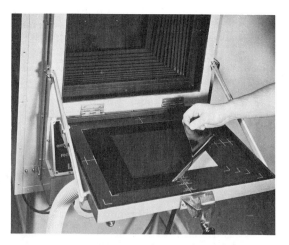

Figure 7.32. Adding the halftone screen to the film sheet Place the emulsion of the contact screen in contact with the emulsion of the film. Courtesy of nuArc Company, Inc.

Figure 7.33. Making the flash exposure After making the main exposure, open the camera back, turn on the flashing lamp, and make the flash exposure.

4. Remove the exposed film from the camera and process it by standard shop procedures. When the film is dry, evaluate the gray scale and image areas for usability. In the most general terms, the negative should carry a printable highlight dot in the same area of the image that was measured on the densitometer for highlight detail and a printable shadow dot in the corresponding shadow

area. Increasing the main exposure will move the highlight dot farther up the gray scale.

Evaluating the usability of halftone images and making knowledgeable changes to correct defects in the halftones are the most important parts of the photographer's job. The following section takes a closer look at these processes.

SECTION 3

Evaluating Halftone Negatives

The major variables involved in halftone production have now been introduced. The central purpose has been to deal with the basics of the process. The ultimate goal has been, of course, to be able to produce the best possible halftone from any continuous-tone image. We have talked of end-points (highlights and shadows) and suggested that the placement of middle tone dots was an important control of contrast. However, no concrete method of interpreting the true usability of a halftone or of correcting inaccuracies was presented. The interpretation is vital.

It should be obvious that there are some problems with any visual interpretation of a halftone. Most people have difficulty making a judgment of any negative image and sometimes become confused with the difference between shadow and highlight dots. Another problem is that the actual picture is made up of dots that can usually be viewed only through a magnifying glass, and they are of random shape and size.

The solution to these problems is not to deal with the individual dots as they appear in the image itself but rather to be concerned with their positions on the gray scale that was photographed along with the continuous-tone photograph. The gray scale is simply a numeric measure of density, and each step can easily be equated to a corresponding area of density on the print, so interpretation becomes much easier. The actual technique is to compare the gray scale that was photographed along with the continuous-tone print to the print itself. Assume that when the original highlight and shadow density readings from the continuous-tone print were taken, they were 0.10 for the highlight area and 1.40 for the shadow area. On the gray scale pictured in figure 7.8, 0.10 density lies somewhere between step 1 and step 2; 1.40 density lies in about step 10. (If you do not have a calibrated gray scale, you can calibrate the one you have with a reflection densitometer by simply reading the density in each step.) If your halftone negative (and, consequently, your printed halftone positive) is going to have the same density range as your continuous-tone original, you would expect to see the gray scale almost completely filled in at step 1 or 2 and almost completely clear at around step 10. Actual dot size in these steps can be determined by looking at them with a magnifying glass. Again, the key is not to look at individual dots but to look at an area of dots. An area of dots on the negative film image of the gray scale that will produce 10% highlight dots on the printed piece will appear mostly black with a uniform pattern of small, clear openings. An area of dots on the negative film image of the gray scale that will produce 95% shadow dots on the printed piece will appear clear with a uniform pattern of small black dots. If the placement of your shadow and highlight dots on the film image of the gray scale corresponds to the density recordings of

the shadow and highlight areas from the original photograph, you can have some confidence that your final printed halftone will accurately represent the continuous-tone original. This should be the case if the halftone negative computer was calibrated and used accurately, and all exposure and processing steps were carried out correctly.

Correcting Defects

What if your dots fall in the wrong place? This is where the concept of a predictable density shift discussed in Section 1 of this chapter becomes important. Let's assume for the example above that your highlight dot did not fall in step 2 but instead appeared in step 3. You know that the highlight dot is controlled by the main exposure. If your highlight dot was recorded in step 3, you must have had too long a main exposure. You also know that a change of one f/stop number on the camera will produce a 0.30 density shift on the film emulsion. You know further that halving or doubling the shutter speed is the same as changing the f/stop one stop up or down. If you were using the calibrated gray scale in figure 7.8, you would see that the density difference between step 3 (where your highlight dot appeared) and step 2 (where you want your highlight dot to appear) is approximately 0.15 (0.32 − 0.14 = 0.18). This means that you would have to decrease your main exposure by ¼ in order to move the highlight dot from step 3 to step 2. By making this exposure adjustment and reshooting the picture with all other conditions (f/stop, flash, chemistry, and processing conditions) equal, you can shift the highlight dot down one step.

A halftone negative computer should eliminate the need of reshooting to produce perfect results. But even a halftone computer cannot account for differences in individual processing techniques and conditions. Visual inspection of the gray scale is one method of correcting for improper dot placement. But when you reshoot the photograph, you must vary only the shutter speed and keep all other darkroom conditions constant.

It is worth noting here that a very accurate measure of the dot size on the actual halftone negative can be achieved with a dot area meter or a transmission densitometer. As mentioned in Section 1 (figure 7.19), a dot area meter reads the dot coverage in an area of a piece of transparent film material. By measuring the dot area on the halftone negative that corresponds to the areas you identified as the highlight and shadow areas of the continuous-tone original, you can establish whether you have placed the correct sized dots in the proper location. Measures taken with a dot area meter can be used directly. Measures taken with a transmission densitometer (figure 7.7) can be converted as shown in table 7.1.

Key Terms

density
reflectance
transmittance
tones
screen ruling
screen tints
vignetted screen pattern
dot area meter

copy density range
basic density range
main exposure
excess density
contrast
densitometry
reflection densitometer
transmission densitometer

highlight area
shadow area
middle tone area
flash exposure
bump exposure
spectral highlight
dot gain

Questions for Review

Section 1

1. Name several examples of continuous-tone images.

2. In general terms, what does the term *density* describe?

3. What does the term *contrast* describe about tones on a piece of photographic film?

4. What is the difference between a transmission densitometer and a reflection densitometer?

5. What does the term *screen ruling* describe?

6. To what does the term *normal viewing distance* refer?

7. What is the difference between a vignetted screen structure and a solid line screen structure?

8. Which will produce a larger dot on the printed page, a 40% or a 60% screen tint?

9. What is the purpose of a dot area meter?

10. Name the two basic types of contact screens.

Section 2

1. What three areas of a continuous-tone photograph are probably the most significant measures of print quality?

2. What is meant by the BDR (basic density range) of a photograph?

3. What two types of halftone exposures are almost always used to reproduce a continuous-tone image?

4. What is the purpose of a bump exposure?

5. What is the major problem when using shallow-tray development to process halftone images?

6. Briefly outline the typical procedures when making a halftone negative from a continuous-tone original.

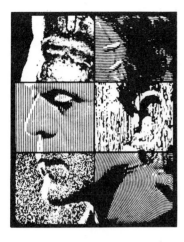

Chapter Eight

Special Effects Photography

Anecdote to Chapter Eight

Photographers and printers have gone to great lengths to create special photographic effects. One of the early ideas was to create huge illustrations that would dazzle the layman's mind. At a photographic exhibition in Vienna in 1864, an enlargement of a flea was entered that was more than "a metre" in height. The picture startled those who saw it because they could not imagine how the print was made. Oversized prints of that time were usually made on several pieces of paper joined together. They were usually of such poor quality that elaborate retouching was necessary at the joints.

In 1899, the Chicago and Alton Railroads commissioned the Pullman Train Works to build an elaborate passenger train to celebrate the coming turn of the century. The company also wanted to exhibit a massive photograph of the train at the Paris Exposition the following year. Mr. George R. Lawrence, the company's photographer, was asked to build the largest cam-

era in the world so that the "Alton Limited" could be photographed on one negative.

J.A. Anderson of Chicago, under Lawrence's supervision, spent two and a half months building the camera. When fully extended on four 2- × 6-inch beams, the completed device was almost 20 feet long. It was constructed completely from solid cherry. The heavy rubber bellows took 40 gallons of glue to prepare. A special hinged frame on the back held the 8- × 10-foot glass negative. The two Zeiss lenses used in the camera were specially made. One was wide angle, with a 5½-foot focal length. The other was telescopic, with a 10-foot focal length. The camera with one lens weighed 900 pounds. With the plate holder and plate, it weighed over 1,400 pounds. It was so large that the front lens panel was a hinged door through which the photographer could climb into the device to clean the interior.

In the spring of 1900 the finished camera

The Mammoth
Courtesy of Smithsonian
Institution, Photo No. 72-10645

was placed in a padded van and mounted on a flatcar for a short journey to Brighton Park, where the exposition photo was to be shot. It took fifteen men to set up "The Mammoth," as it was officially named. A special focusing screen was hinged in the back, and the image was "focused" by several men pushing the lens forward or backward on the wooden track.

The exposure took 2½ minutes to make. It took 5 gallons of developer to process the image. Three prints were made from the 5- × 8-foot plate. One was placed on a wall in the train's grand salon. The second was given to the U.S. government as a gift for a new building. The third was sent to the Paris Exposition. The exposition officials found the photograph so remarkable that they required a certified affidavit specifying the details of its manufacture before they would accept it as "the world's largest photograph."

Objectives for Chapter Eight

After completing this chapter you will be able to:

- Outline the procedure for producing a duotone.

- Define the term "moiré pattern."
- Describe how to make a simple line conversion.
- Explain how photoposterizations are classified.

– Outline the procedure for making a three-tone posterization.
– Outline the procedure for making a two-color, three-tone posterization.

– Outline the procedure for making a three-color, four-tone posterization.

Introduction

It should be apparent from Chapters 6 and 7 that the nature of photographic materials requires exacting and critical processing controls. This does not mean, however, that all darkroom techniques for printing technology are fixed and allow for no creative individual expression. In the darkroom it is the human element, not the materials, that produces results. A wide variety of problems is continually encountered in an industrial or production situation. The camera operator must be observant and able to creatively apply knowledge and skills to produce optimum results. There is a category of darkroom procedures labeled "creative" because the results require subjective decisions on the part of the photographer. This is not to imply that the processes involve guesswork or trial and error—only that the images can be manipulated to produce a wide range of pleasing and usable results.

Special photographic effects are produced to meet two general goals. The first is to work within material or equipment limitations (or advantages) to produce more economical or effective reproductions. As has been mentioned in Chapter 7, printing presses can reproduce only a limited density range. With a "double dot black duotone" it is possible to overprint a second, specially produced halftone in register with the first normal halftone on the printed sheet. The result is to increase the shadow density and, therefore, enhance the appearance of the final image. Another powerful communication technique is the use of color. However, four-color process reproduction is time consuming, exacting, and expensive (see Chapter 9). In many cases the creative use of two colors, as with a "duotone" or a "posterization," can be as effective as four colors (plates A and B).

The second goal of any special photographic effect is to be able to generalize an idea or an image rather than to reproduce exactly some specific picture or to create a pleasing visual impression. "Posterizations" can generalize ideas and also produce an attractive image.

Of the many special photographic techniques, this chapter will examine only duotones and posterizations. The bibliography provides resource material on more sophisticated or advanced techniques.

Duotones

Understanding Duotones

The duotone process is one method the printer can use to overcome the basic inability of printing presses to reproduce long tonal

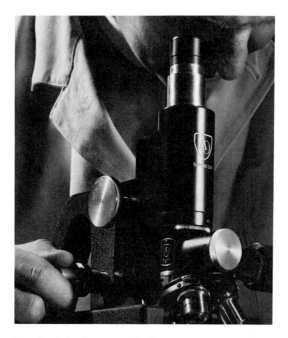

Figure 8.1. A normal halftone conversion This illustration is an example of a normal halftone conversion.

ranges. The term **duotone** implies the use of two layers of tones to produce one final image. Duotones were once nothing more than the same halftone printed in two colors, one in register over the other. The result was colorful, but it did nothing to change the basic printed halftone density range.

Duotones still involve the use of two halftones, called **printers.** However, the two negatives are made to different specifications. The first halftone, or **light printer,** is produced to carry highlight and upper middle tone detail (see plate B). The second, or **dark printer,** is made to carry the lower middle tone and shadow detail. When these two halftones are overprinted, the result is a reproduction with a longer density range than a single halftone can produce. This type of re-

production approaches the actual tonal range of the original photograph.

The duotone color combination is extremely important. Most duotones are produced by using black or some other dark color for the dark printer and a light color, chosen to allow for contrast, for the light printer. The subject of the original photograph should suggest appropriate color combinations. The customer wouldn't choose green to reproduce a beach scene duotone or red as the second color in a picture with a lot of snow.

An effective duotone can also be produced when both halftones are printed in black (a **double dot black duotone**). The result increases the reproduction density range, intensifies the shadows, and still holds accurate highlight detail without creating a "flat" reproduction.

There is also a special class of reproductions called **fake duotones,** in which a single halftone is printed over a block of colored tint or even over a solid block of color. However, such duotones do not involve the manipulation of the original tonal range of the print and will not be considered in this discussion.

Duotones can be effective if properly used. A two-color duotone will attract more attention than a single-color image, and yet it can be produced less expensively and with less difficulty than can a four-color process print (see Chapter 9). A double dot black duotone contains more detail and is a more attractive image than a single black halftone reproduction.

Selecting the Photograph

A duotone can be produced from any black-and-white continuous-tone photograph. However, not all pictures will make effective use of the process. The photograph should have normal contrast and a long tonal range (figure 8.1). There should be no large monotone areas, and significant image detail should extend from the highlight areas to the shadow areas. The original should be big enough that an extreme enlargement is not required for the final print size. Finally, as with all processes, it is difficult to produce a quality reproduction from an inferior original.

Screen Angles

A complication is introduced whenever two different screen patterns (or dots) are overprinted. If two screens are randomly positioned over each other, an objectional **moiré** (pronounced *more-ray*) **pattern** could form (figure 8.2). The problem is caused by individual dots overlapping at an inappropriate angle. The typical contact screen, whether solid line or vignetted halftone, has a built-in 45° angle. When overprinting two screen patterns, you must angle the second screen pattern 30° from the first, a difference that could

be produced by any of the following three methods:

1. Using preangled screens
2. Changing the angle of the screen
3. Rotating the angle of the copy

The most efficient method is to purchase specially preangled screens: a normal 45° screen and another screen angled at 15° or 75°. This method makes more use of available screen area because the screen itself does not have to be angled over the film on the filmboard.

A second possibility would be to actually change the angle of the screen on the vacuum back of the camera (figure 8.3). However, this method can cause vacuum problems, such as a loss of contact between the film and screen. The vacuum openings on most camera backs are designed to hold sheets of film and screens square to the board. When the sheet is angled out of this position, not all the openings are covered and holding power diminishes. This problem can be overcome by using a clear

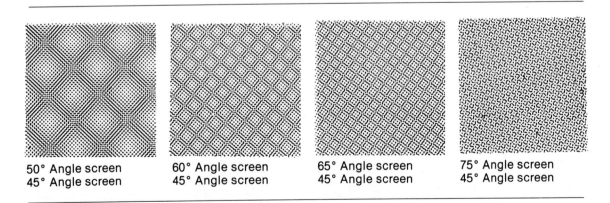

50° Angle screen
45° Angle screen

60° Angle screen
45° Angle screen

65° Angle screen
45° Angle screen

75° Angle screen
45° Angle screen

Figure 8.2. Moiré patterns The moiré patterns were formed by a 33-line screen at approximately 20% tone value.

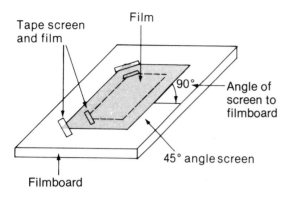

Tape screen and film

Film

90° — Angle of screen to filmboard

45° angle screen

Filmboard

First exposure: Taped screen and film are held in close contact by the vacuum system

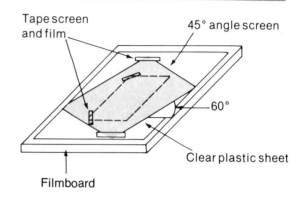

Tape screen and film

45° angle screen

60°

Clear plastic sheet

Filmboard

Second exposure: A clear plastic sheet ensures holding power by covering vacuum openings missed by the angled screen

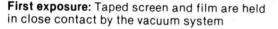

Figure 8.3. Angling the screen on the filmboard Working on the filmboard of the camera, the operator moves the screen 30° between exposures. Both film and screen have been taped in position to prevent accidental movement.

acetate or plastic sheet over the contact screen (figure 8.3).

The third method to control screen angle of the two printers is to rotate the angle of the copy itself. Figure 8.4 illustrates a simple method that can be used to hold the screen stationary and to shift the angle of the original. A cardboard guide is used to change the angle of the photograph on the copyboard. The first screen exposure is made with the center wheel in line with the 45° mark. For the second screen exposure the wheel is rotated 30° to the 15° or 75° mark. It is important that the contact screen not change position between exposures, because a slightly changed screen angle could cause a moiré pattern when the two negatives are printed. For this reason, the edge of the contact screen is usually taped to the filmboard, and the film

is slid out and reinserted under it for the second exposure.

Producing the Light Printer

The choice of color combinations and tonal range positions is almost totally subjective, so there are no set rules to direct the printer in making these duotone separations. The following general set of procedures is presented only as a starting point for the printer who has never before attempted the duotone process. With experience, printers develop their own approaches.

In any duotone the light printer carries the most significant detail of the original photograph, thus influencing the appearance of the final product much more than does any

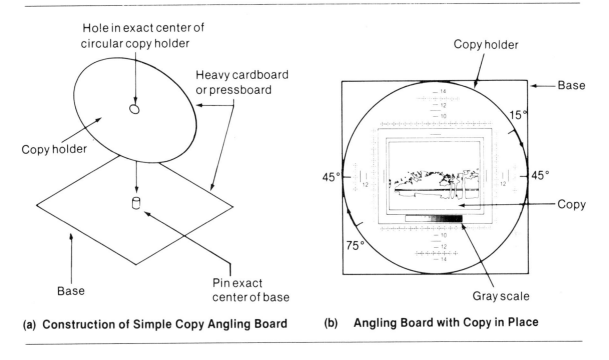

(a) **Construction of Simple Copy Angling Board**

(b) **Angling Board with Copy in Place**

Figure 8.4. Diagram of a simple copy angling board This diagram is an example of a frame made of pressboard with a wheel that can be rotated to the desired angle for each camera exposure.

other factor. A good starting procedure when making a duotone is to calculate a main exposure as would be done for a normal halftone (see Chapter 7). This exposure should accurately record the highlight and upper middle tone areas of the continuous-tone print.

The choice of color for this light printer will influence the use of a flash exposure. If a dark color (such as black for a double dot duotone, or even a strong orange) is to be used, a normal flash is called for. It is even possible to increase the flash to build a larger shadow dot. The important consideration is

that no shadow area should reproduce as a solid on the final printed sheet.

If the light printer is to carry a light color, such as yellow or blue, it is desirable to reduce or even drop the flash exposure. This procedure will allow some shadow areas to print solid, which is desirable in this case because the shadows will appear to carry stronger detail when the second color is overprinted and will thus create a duotone with a long tonal range.

After the main and flash exposure times have been determined, the camera procedures are simple. The following general procedure assumes the use of the copyboard angling system:

1. Mount the copyboard angling device on the camera copyboard and tape it securely in place. Then tape the photograph in the center of the board; be sure to add register

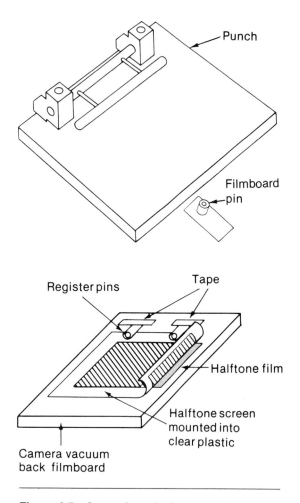

marks and a gray scale. Set the angle pointer to the 45° position and close the copyboard frame.

2. Set the camera to the desired reproduction size and lock that size in position. It is important that these settings not be touched until both the light and the dark printers have been produced. Any change, however slight, will make accurate registration of the two halftones on the light table or the press impossible.

3. Because the angle of the screen is going to be controlled on the copyboard, you must ensure that the angle of the screen on the filmboard remains constant. You can use a punched tab system (see figure 8.5) or tape one side of the screen to the board (figure 8.6). A clear plastic mask can be put around the halftone screen. This will provide a handling area and a place to punch or tape the screen (figure 8.7). Whatever system you use,

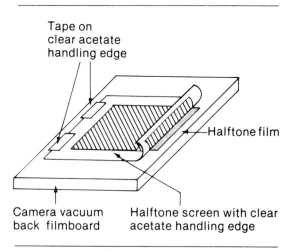

Figure 8.5. A punch and tab system A punch tab system can be used to control the angle of the screen on the filmboard.

Figure 8.6. Taping the screen to the filmboard Taping the screen will ensure that it does not move between exposures.

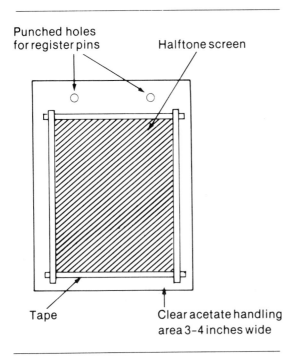

Punched holes
for register pins

Halftone screen

Tape

Clear acetate handling
area 3–4 inches wide

Figure 8.7. A clear acetate sheet put around a halftone screen This use of an acetate sheet will provide a handling area and a place to punch the screen for tab registration.

you must position the screen for good vacuum control and must not change the screen's position between the light and dark printer exposures. As with any halftone, the screen should be emulsion-side down on the filmboard so that the screen and the film will be emulsion-to-emulsion during the shot.

4. Place a sheet of halftone film emulsion-side up on the vacuum back, place the contact screen in place over the film and obtain perfect vacuum contact between the two. Turn the copy- and filmboards into position and expose the light printer using the times you previously determined.

5. You can place the exposed film in an empty film box or develop it immediately. To ensure accurate and reproducible results with tray processing, process the film by the time-temperature-agitation method explained in Chapter 6 (see "Controlling Chemical Processing"). Use an automatic processor if one is available.

Producing the Dark Printer

The dark printer carries the shadow information of the original photograph and provides a significant increase in contrast and density. Using a normal halftone as this second printer would present problems. Not only would the shadow density be increased, but so would the highlights and middle tones. The result would be unpleasant and would defeat the purpose of the duotone process, which is to extend the total tonal range of the final print.

In general, the dark printer should carry no highlight detail. Rather, the entire halftone dot structure is shifted to a higher step on the gray scale to record lower middle tone through shadow detail. One method to accomplish this is to greatly increase the main exposure. A good starting point is to double the amount of light that reaches the film. A simple technique is to open the lens one stop and keep the same exposure time. A suggested starting point for the dark printer flash exposure would be ½ the light printer exposure.

1. Change the copy angle 30° from that of the first exposure. Open the copyboard frame and rotate the angle pointer to 15° or 75°. Be certain that the board, photograph, and register marks do not shift from their taped positions. Only the center dial should move (figure 8.8). It is vital that the camera

Figure 8.8. Changing the angle of the copyholder When the angle is changed for subsequent exposures, use care to ensure that only the center dial moves and not the frame or photograph.

size settings and the contact screen positions not be changed from those of the first exposure. If any movement has taken place, discard the first negative and repeat the light printer procedure.

2. Place a fresh sheet of halftone film on the filmboard, sliding it under the taped contact screen, and again obtain perfect vacuum contact between the two. Turn the copy- and filmboards into position and expose, using the exposures determined for the dark printer.

3. After exposure, process the film by using the time-temperature-agitation method explained in Chapter 6.

4. When both the light and the dark printers have been developed and fixed, the halftones can be inspected on a wet light table. The gray scale on the light printer should carry a reproducible dot in the highlights, and the dot formation should extend down the scale according to the colors chosen (figure 8.9). The dark printer gray scale should have the first reproducible dot appear at least 3 or 4 steps farther down the scale than the light printer, on a 12-step gray scale.

These procedures are only suggestions designed to introduce the duotone process. The experienced photographer will be able to vary these suggested exposures to obtain the most effective duotone possible from the original photograph.

Any multicolor separations should be proofed before printing plates reach the press. Proofing techniques are discussed in detail in "Multiple-Color Photomechanical Proofing," Chapter 10.

Photoposterization

During the early days of photography, the sensitivity of most orthochromatic film was so limited that a long range of tones could not be accurately recorded on a single sheet. The solution to this problem was to divide the tonal range of an original into several groups and to deal with each group as a separate exposure on a new piece of film. They were then recombined on the printing plate. The images produced by this method had a poster-like quality, and so the term **posterization** was used. With subsequent film emulsion improvements, this technique was quickly forgotten.

The process has been revived as a simple and economical technique that creates an attention-getting visual effect—or changes a specific photograph into a generalized image. The most elementary posterization is a simple line conversion.

Light Printer

Figure 8.9. Examples of light and dark printers The gray scale can be used to identify the areas of the original that have been reproduced for each printer. Here we can see that in the dark printer the first reproducible dots appear at step 4. The dots appear in step 1 in the light printer.

Dark Printer

A Simple Line Conversion

A line exposure of a continuous-tone photograph actually is a sort of posterization. It does not accurately represent the tonal range of the photograph and communicates only a general idea or impression. Line photography produces a one-color, two-tone conversion (paper color as one tone and ink as another).

A similar conversion could be produced by placing a solid line screen or special effect screen tint over the film before it is exposed. The resulting image would again record only the highlight detail of the original. Although not a common technique, the conversion would have all the characteristics of a line negative except that the image areas would be broken up into mechanical lines or dots instead of solid ink.

There are two problems with the use of line conversions of continuous-tone originals. Because they contain only two tones, the results from some photographs might be unrecognizable. Also the film exposure determines what tones of the original are recorded. Because not all photographs have the same basic density range and the significant detail is not always located in the same density step, it is difficult to calculate a proper exposure for a line conversion.

Classifying Photoposterizations

Posterizations are classified according to the number of colors and the number of different tones reproduced on the final press sheet. When counting colors, only the number of different ink colors is counted. Although it is possible to print a single ink color on a colored sheet (other than white), the result is still classified as a single-color posterization because there is only one layer of ink on the paper. Figure 8.10 shows a one-color posterization.

Plates A and C show two- and three-color posterizations.

The second classification of posterizations is the number of tones contained in the image. Unprinted paper areas (generally assumed to represent the highlight areas of the original) are counted as one tone; solid ink areas (shadows), as another; and any line or tint variation (representing middle tones), as the third. Plates A and C show a three- and four-tone posterization. Notice that in the figures, it is possible to count the distinct tones produced by the different colors. A simple way to remember this is that the number of colors is equal to the number of printed colors, and the number of tones is equal to the number of printed colors plus one (the paper tone).

Any more than two tones generally represent the middle tone area of the photograph and are produced by an additional exposure through a solid line or special effects screen tint. Any variation of the number of tones and colors is possible. The main problem, however, is to produce the tonal separations. The following sections explain and detail the procedures for producing a three- or four-tone posterization.

Understanding Three-Tone Posterizations

Recall that a two-tone conversion (a line photograph) is produced with a single camera exposure. A three-tone conversion or posterization is produced with two camera exposures (figure 8.11). The first exposure records the extreme highlights (as does a normal line photograph). The second records the middle tone area on the same sheet of film.

In the actual production of a normal three-tone posterization, a solid step 4 on a 12-step gray scale as a reflection of highlight detail is too far down the scale. That density

Figure 8.10. Example of a one-color posterization
Courtesy of John N. Schaedler, Inc.

extends too far into the detail area of most photographs for effective reproduction. The first exposure should record only the extreme highlights.

It is possible to predict the amount of density that will be recorded from any original at a particular exposure. Recall from Chapter 6 that a change in camera exposure results in a density change on the film. Reducing the basic exposure time by one-half will reduce the density of the negative by 0.30. Doubling the basic exposure time will increase the density of the negative by 0.30. With this information, it is possible to control

Step 2 negative

Step 5 negative

Step 8 negative

Step 1
Create negative images from continuous tone original

Positive of Step 2 (30%)

Positive of Step 5 (30%)

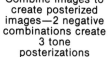
Positive of Step 8 (solid)

Step 2
Add screen tints to distinquish tones (shown in positive form here)

Combination of Step 2 & 5

Combination of Step 2 & 8

Combination of Step 5 & 8

Step 3A
Combine images to create posterized images—2 negative combinations create 3 tone posterizations

The halftone reproduction at the right illustrates the appearance of the original continuous tone image.

Halftone

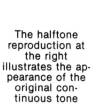
4 tone posterization

Step 3B
Combining all three images creates a four tone posterization.

Figure 8.11. Example of tone posterization process

the density of any original recorded as a solid area on the negative.

The authors have had great success producing the highlight image for a posterization by merely reducing the basic camera exposure for line film by one-half. As an example, if the basic exposure was f/16 for 20 seconds, the first exposure for our posterization would be f/16 for 10 seconds (or at f/22 for 20 seconds—the results would be the same). In figure 8.12, the basic exposure, with normal processing, produced a solid step 4, or a density of 0.45. When the exposure is decreased by one-half, we can subtract 0.30 from the density of the last solid step (0.45) to find that any highlight detail with a density of 0.15 or less will be recorded. This density equals a solid step 2 on the gray scale in figure 8.12. This, then, is a first visual cue for shallow-tray processing of the negative.

The three-tone effect is produced with a second camera exposure. A separate image is recorded on the film for the density range that extends from the last highlight record of the first exposure into the middle tone areas of the original. To keep the second film exposure visually separate from the first, a solid line screen is placed over the film before the middle tone exposure is made.

In Chapter 7 we discussed the differences between a solid line and a vignetted

contact screen. Halftone screens should not be used to produce the second tonal separation. The result would look like a shoddy halftone attempt. Only a solid line screen tint or a special effects screen tint will give the desired results. Recall that screen tints are rated in terms of the amount of light they pass. A 40% tint passes 40% of the light and blocks 60%. Figure 8.13 shows a variety of screens used with the same original image. The choice of which tint or special effects screen to use is a subjective decision.

Because a screen, which will absorb some of the light reflected from the copy, has been placed over the film, and because the purpose of the second exposure is to record detail from the middle tone areas, the second exposure should be longer than the first exposure. The authors recommend a second camera exposure four times longer than the first or highlight exposure. Continuing the same example, if the first exposure were f/16 for 10 seconds, the second exposure would be f/16 for 40 seconds (or any combination of f/stop and shutter speed that produces the same quantity of light).

It is also possible to predict the density range of the second exposure. Increasing the quantity of light by four times adds 0.60 density to the film. In figure 8.14 we found that the first exposure would produce detail with

Figure 8.12. Example of calculating the highlight detail based on a ½ basic exposure The computation shown is used to predict the highlight detail that will be recorded from an exposure that is ½ the normal line or basic exposure.

Mahogany

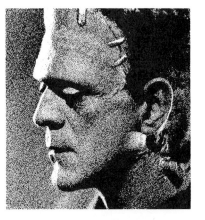

Mezzotint

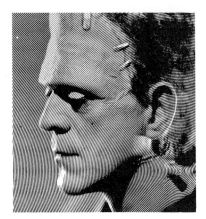

Circleline

100 Straightline

Wavyline

50 Straightline

Figure 8.13. Examples of special effect tints
Special effect screen tints can be used to create different impressions with the same image.
Courtesy of James Craig, *Production Planning*

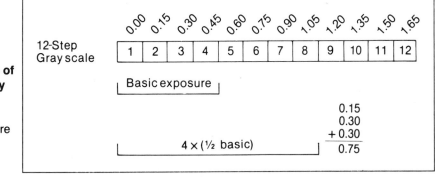

Figure 8.14. Example of calculating the density range of the second exposure The computation is used here to predict the density range of the second exposure.

a density up to 0.15. Therefore, the second exposure should record detail of the original that has a density of 0.75 or less (or 0.15 + 0.60), which equates to a solid step 6–8 depending on the real density recorded from the gray scale being used. This step then provides a second visual cue for shallow-tray development.

Single-color posterizations can be produced by placing all exposures on a single sheet of film and printing with one press run (see figure 8.11). Multicolor posterizations can be prepared by two methods. The simplest is to print a block of color on the press sheet, then overprint the posterization as a second color. An alternate method for color is to record separate tones on individual sheets of film. Each separation is plated and run as a different color printed in register on the final sheet. Two methods of producing a three-tone posterization are explained below.

Procedures for Making a Three-Tone Posterization

Method One: Single-Color, Three-Tone

1. Center the copy on the copyboard of the process camera. Position a gray scale next to, but not covering, the copy.

2. Place a sheet of high-contrast film on the camera and make a line exposure sufficient to record the extreme highlights of the photograph. Try an exposure that is one-half the basic line exposure.

3. Carefully open the camera back and place a solid line screen tint or special effects screen over the film. Be sure not to shift the position of the film. Expose the film a second time to record an image from the middle tone area of the photograph. Try an exposure that is four times the exposure used in step 2 above. For a first attempt, use a 40% screen tint.

4. Process the film as you would normal line film. Use the visual cues explained in the previous section to determine adequate development.

5. Proof or examine the negatives, particularly the gray scale:

   i. If it appears that not enough highlight detail was recorded, increase the first exposure.

   ii. If large clear areas with no detail are produced, decrease the first exposure.

   iii. If the black area is excessive, increase the second exposure.

   iv. If there is too little black in the shadow areas, decrease the second exposure.

Method Two: Two-Color, Three-Tone

1. Place a register mark in each corner of the continuous-tone photograph. Center the copy on the copyboard of the process camera. Position a graphic arts gray scale next to, but not covering, the copy.

2. Place a sheet of high-contrast film on the camera and make a line exposure sufficient to record the extreme highlights of the photograph. Try an exposure that is one-half the basic line exposure.

3. Open the camera back and remove the exposed piece of film. Place it in a light-tight container (such as a film box) and position a new sheet on the camera. Expose the film to record an image from the middle tone area of the photograph. Try an exposure that is four times the exposure used in step 2 above. Do not use a screen tint when making the second exposure.

4. From this point follow steps 4 and 5 of method one.

Key Terms

duotone
light printer
dark printer

double dot black duotone
fake duotone
moiré pattern

posterization

Questions for Review

1. What are the two general purposes of special photographic effects?

2. What does the term *duotone* imply?

3. What is the purpose of the dark printer in a set of duotone halftone negatives?

4. What is a double dot black duotone?

5. What is a fake duotone?

6. Why is it necessary to change the dot angle between the light and dark duotone printers?

7. How many tones are carried in a simple line conversion photoposterization?

8. How are photoposterizations classified?

9. How many camera exposures are necessary to produce a one-color, three-tone posterization?

10. Doubling the quantity of light that strikes the film adds how much density to the film?

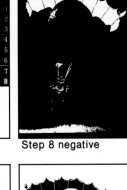

Step 2 negative

Step 5 negative

Step 8 negative

Step 1

Create negative images from continuous tone original

Positive of Step 2 (Cyan)

Positive of Step 5 (Mag)

Positive of Step 8 (Black)

Step 2

Determine color selection for each negative (shown in positive form here)

Combination of Step 2 & 5

Combination of Step 2 & 8

Combination of Step 5 & 8

Step 3A

Combine images to create posterized images—2 negative combinations create 2 color posterizations

The halftone reproduction at the right illustrates the appearance of the original continuous tone image.

Halftone

3 color posterization

Step 3B

Combining all three images creates a 3 color posterization.

A

EXAMPLES OF POSTERIZATION

232

LIGHT PRINTER

B
DUOTONE
(Dark plus
light printer)

DARK PRINTER

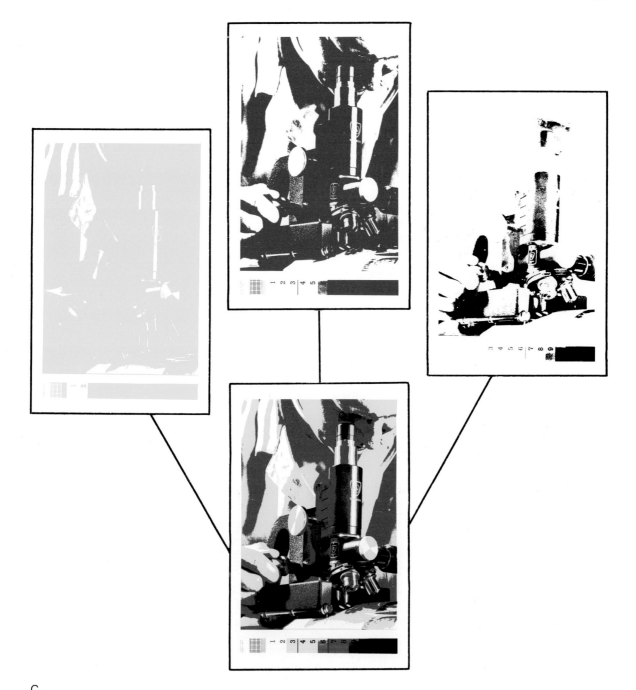

C
THREE-COLOR POSTERIZATION

D

IVES EARLY TRICOLOR EXPERIMENT.
Original proof of tricolor halftone
reproduction made by Frederic E.
Ives about 1893. Perhaps the first
three-color illustration ever
produced with a crossline halftone
screen. Courtesy of 3M Company,
from the Joseph S. Mertle Collection.

E   PRISM

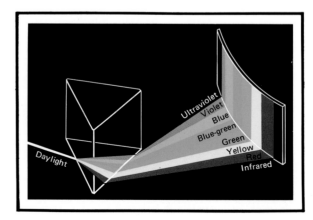

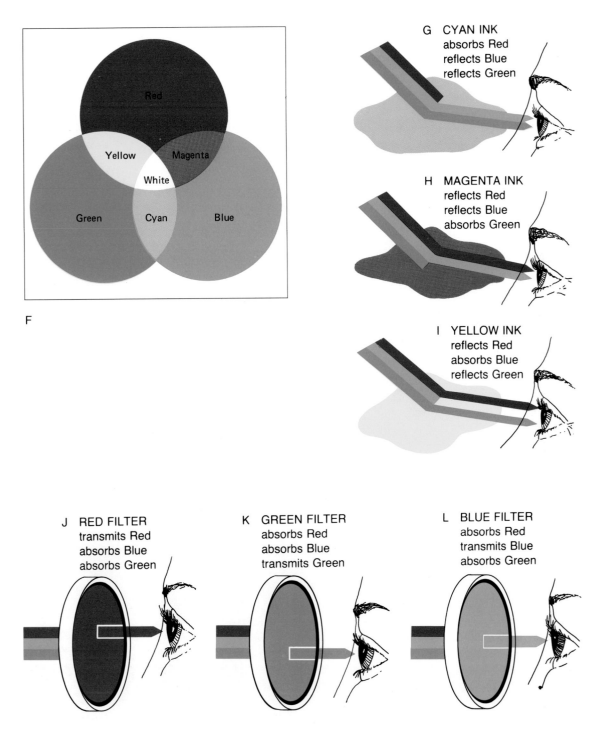

F

G CYAN INK
absorbs Red
reflects Blue
reflects Green

H MAGENTA INK
reflects Red
reflects Blue
absorbs Green

I YELLOW INK
reflects Red
absorbs Blue
reflects Green

J RED FILTER
transmits Red
absorbs Blue
absorbs Green

K GREEN FILTER
absorbs Red
absorbs Blue
transmits Green

L BLUE FILTER
absorbs Red
transmits Blue
absorbs Green

Yellow proof

Magenta proof

M
SEPARATIONS (above)
PROGRESSIVE PROOF (below)

From The Metropolitan Museum
of Art, the Michael Friedsam Collection, 1931. (Detail)

Yellow plus Magenta

Cyan proof

Black proof

Yellow, Magenta plus Cyan

Yellow, Magenta, Cyan plus Black

238

BEFORE

AFTER

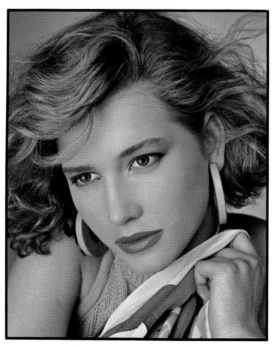

N   EXAMPLES OF ELECTRONIC COLOR-IMAGE EDITING

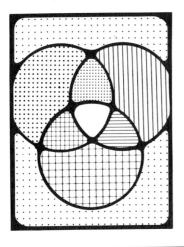

Chapter Nine

Color Separation

Anecdote to Chapter Nine

In 1862, Louis Ducos du Hauron sent a letter to M. Lelut of the Academie de Medecine et Sciences describing his ideas for a "Physical Solution of the Problem of Reproducing Colors by Photography." Hauron said:

The method which I propose is based on the principle that the simple colors are reduced to three—red, yellow, and blue— the combinations of which in different proportions give us the infinite variety of shades we see in nature. One may now say that analysis of the solar spectrum by means of a glass which passes only one color has proved that red exists in all parts of the spectrum, and the like for yellow and blue, and that one is forced to admit that the solar spectrum is formed of three superimposed spectra having their maxima of intensity at different points. Thus one might consider a picture which represents nature as composed of three pictures superimposed, the one red, the second yellow, and the third blue. The result of this would be that if one could obtain separately these three images by photography and then reunite them in one, one would obtain an image of nature with all the tints that it contains. [*]

It was Hauron's ideas that were, in part, responsible for the later development of successful additive color plates and film.

A man named Frederick E. Ives was a journeyman printer who became interested in photography. In 1880 he moved from Ithaca, New York, to Philadelphia. From that time on he only did research in color photography and photomechanical printing. He was familiar with Hauron's early ideas and worked to refine them.

By the end of 1881 Ives had received

---

[*]Louis W. Sipley, *A Half Century of Color* (New York: Macmillan, 1951), p. 22.

two U.S. patents for a specialized halftone printing process and was beginning to spend most of his energy on color. In 1885, at the Philadelphia "Novelties Exhibition," he exhibited a process of photographing colors and a photomechanical method for reproducing them.

In May of 1892, Ives was invited to present a paper outlining his ideas before the Society of Arts in London. At that time he displayed the Photochromoscope camera he had invented. Using a single exposure, the device recorded a three-color image on three separate plates. The transparent separations could then be viewed through red, green, and blue color filters.

The illustration on page 240 was produced by Ives in 1893 with his tricolor process. It is perhaps the first photomechanically printed color image. It is uncertain whether it was reproduced by using a relief plate or a rotogravure cylinder, but the halftones were certainly made from crossline screens. By the turn of the century, almost all printers and photographers understood the color separation process, and national publications such as the *National Geographic* used full-color picture printing.

Objectives for Chapter Nine

After completing Chapter 9 the student will be able to:

– Define process color photography.
– Explain additive color theory.
– Discuss how subtractive colors are related to additive colors.
– Explain how a color filter works.
– Explain the reason for concern about screen angle on process color separation negatives.
– Discuss how four black and white halftones can produce a full color reproduction.

– Briefly describe the purposes of a mask.
– Describe the difference between direct and indirect color separation methods.
– Explain the purpose of dot etching.
– Explain the four primary steps in electronic color separation, including scanning, analysis and modification, storage and image editing, and exposure.
– Explain the difference between traditional electronic separations and Achromatic separations.

Introduction

Around 1454 Gutenberg printed his famous 42-line Bible. He printed almost all of the lines of type with black ink. The initial letter on opening pages, however, was hand-painted in multiple colors by special artists called "illuminators." Gutenberg was attempting to duplicate the work of scribes who illustrated their finest work in decorative colors.

For nearly three centuries after Gutenberg, most printing was done in a single color—black. By the nineteenth century, color plates and inserts in books were becoming more common, although it was only flat color (recall the three types of color printing: flat color, fake color, and process color). By the beginning of this century, printers and photographers clearly understood the color separation process, and they were printing "color photographs" in a wide number of publications. Books or magazines filled with process color, however, were not the commodity available today at every newsstand, book store, or grocery store.

Since the end of World War II there has been an accelerating increase in the use and sophistication of printed color images. Color printing has now become the expectation rather than the exception. There are literally thousands of weekly or monthly magazines with color illustrations on every page. Every major metropolitan newspaper features process color in its Sunday edition, and there is a national daily newspaper printed in four colors.

As people become accustomed to color illustrations, their demands increase for more and higher-quality color reproductions. It is no longer sufficient that a page merely carry several colors. Now the goal is to eliminate printing defects, such as poor fit, inaccurate color balance, or insufficient ink density, and to produce a perfection color reproduction matching or enhancing the quality of the color original.

Within the last decade there have been major advances in color separation, color correction, and color reproduction technology. The purpose of this chapter is to introduce the basic concepts of color separation, discuss the significant use of scanners, and explore the potential of color correction and color editing.

Basic Color Theory

Light and Color

Isaac Newton demonstrated the hues of the visible spectrum by passing a light through a glass prism (plate E). He not only produced a rainbow of color but passed the rainbow through a second prism and reconstructed the original beam of light. Newton therefore proved that color is in the light and what we see as white light is really a mixture of all colors.

The idea of wavelength was introduced in Chapter 6. Recall that the visible spectrum is that portion of electromagnetic radiation from approximately 400 mμ (millimicrons) to around 750 mμ (figure 9.1). Every distinct color in the spectrum, from blue at one end to red at the other, has a unique wavelength. However, we rarely see a single wavelength color; we more commonly perceive the effect of combinations of different wavelengths. Sunlight is natural white light, made up of relatively uniform amounts of each wavelength in the spectrum.

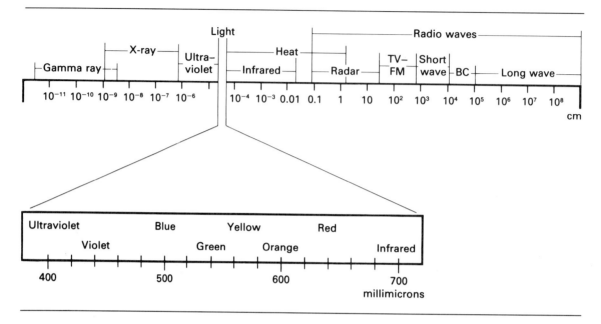

Figure 9.1. Plot of the visible spectrum compared to the electromagnetic spectrum

Remember also the difference between reflected and transmitted light. If you look up at the sun, you are seeing transmitted light— light directed at you from a light source. If you hold a color slide between you and the sun, you are viewing the image by transmitted light. Light passed in a straight line from the sun, through the slide, to your eye.

If you look down from the sun to any object, you are seeing by reflected light. White light travels from the sun to the object and bounces back to your eye. Every object absorbs or reflects different wavelengths of light, and in different quantities.

For example, an apple might appear as a strikingly bright red or look dull red. As the white light strikes the apple it absorbs most of the wavelengths below around 600 mμ on the visible spectrum and reflects most wave-

lengths above that point (figure 9.2). This combination of reflected wavelengths creates the color impression humans see as "red." The brightness depends on the quantity of wavelengths reflected. The wavelengths reflected define color, the quantity of wavelengths reflected defines intensity.

Additive Primary Colors

The visible spectrum is often described as being made up of three colors: blue, green, and red. Actually, they are the combination of wavelengths in each third of the spectrum. Red, green, and blue are called the **additive primary colors,** because they can be combined to form every other color of light in the spectrum. Figure 9.3 shows the plot of re-

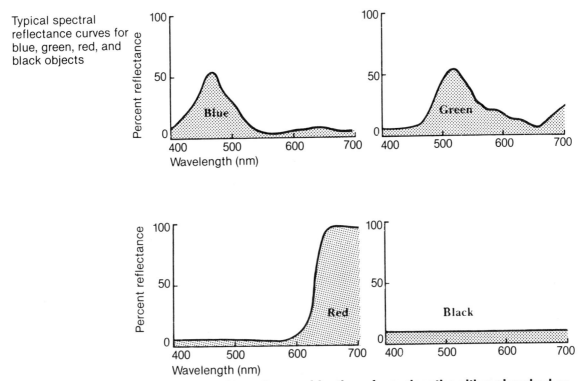

Typical spectral reflectance curves for blue, green, red, and black objects

Figure 9.2. The color we see depends on the combination of wavelengths either absorbed or reflected from objects An apple appears red because it reflects wavelengths of light in the 600-700 nm range and absorbs wavelengths in the 400-600 nm range. Black objects absorb all wavelengths of light; white objects reflect approximately equal amounts of all wavelengths.

flected light for each of these primary colors. It is very important to understand this fundamental idea: Objects display color by absorbing and reflecting different wavelengths of light in the visible spectrum. In the case of transmitted light—looking through a color slide—the idea is the same. We perceive color because portions of the slide absorb certain wavelengths of light and pass (transmit) others.

Subtractive Primary Colors

The three **subtractive primary colors** are cyan, magenta, and yellow. They are formed from the combination of two of the additive primary colors. For example, a banana appears yellow because it absorbs wavelengths at the blue end of the visible spectrum and reflects light at the middle (green) and red ends (figure 9.3). Yellow light is a combination of green and red light (plate F).

In a similar manner, when an object absorbs red and reflects green and blue, the color **cyan** is formed (figure 9.3)(plate F). When green is absorbed but blue and red are reflected, we see **magenta**.

Plate F is an important visual to understand. It shows what happens when the three additive colors of light overlap. Where all three touch, white light is formed. Where any two

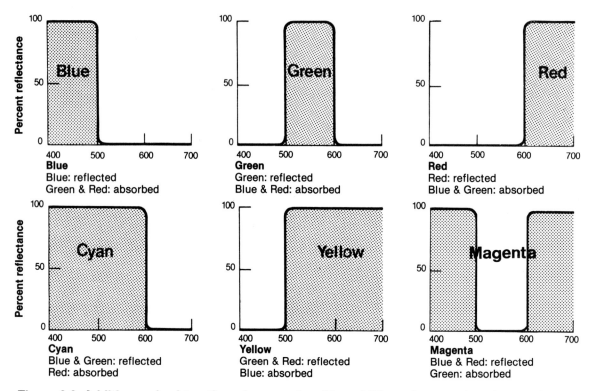

Blue
Blue: reflected
Green & Red: absorbed

Green
Green: reflected
Blue & Red: absorbed

Red
Red: reflected
Blue & Green: absorbed

Cyan
Blue & Green: reflected
Red: absorbed

Yellow
Green & Red: reflected
Blue: absorbed

Magenta
Blue & Red: reflected
Green: absorbed

Figure 9.3. Additive and subtractive primary colors The additive primary colors (top row) each reflect about one-third of the wavelengths of light in the visible spectrum and absorb the other two-thirds. The subtractive primary colors (bottom row) each reflect about two-thirds of the wavelengths of light in the visible spectrum and absorb the other one-third.

overlap, one of the subtractive primaries is created. Printers use magenta, cyan, and yellow inks to create the reflected colors of the spectrum. These are called **process inks**. Process inks are specially formulated so that they are somewhat translucent. That means that they both pass and reflect light.

Plate G illustrates that when white light hits cyan ink, the color reflects blue and green (blue and green create cyan) and absorbs red. Plates H and I show a similar relationship for magenta and yellow inks. Process inks are translucent, which means that there is an ad-

ditive effect if two process colors are printed one over the other. If equal amounts of magenta and cyan process ink overlap, the visual effect is blue. Look at plates G and H. Compare what each color absorbs and reflects; only blue is reflected by both magenta and cyan, therefore blue is the only color you see. If less magenta is printed, and more cyan, then the result will be a greener blue (see plate F). By controlling the amounts of cyan, magenta, and yellow (and black for density), we can form the illusion of any color of the visible spectrum.

Basic Separation Theory

The task, then, of color separation is to separate the hues of a continuous-tone color original into four negatives to prepare cyan, magenta, yellow, and black printing plates.

Figure 9.4 illustrates the basic concept of color separation.

When viewing this figure, it is important to keep two ideas firmly in mind:

1. A color filter transmits its own color and absorbs all other hues.

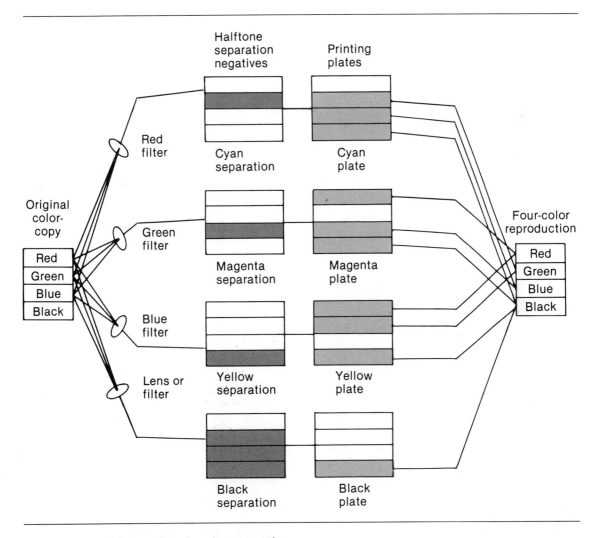

Figure 9.4. A diagram of basic color separation

2. Light that reaches the film exposes the emulsion and becomes nonimage area; the actual reproducible image is that area of the film that has not been exposed to light. This is a record of the two additive colors that were absorbed by the filter.

In the color separation process, the primary additive colors—red, blue, and green—are used as filters to prepare cyan, magenta, and yellow separations. The separation process begins with a color original. The light from the original is directed through a red filter to produce the cyan separation negative (figure 9.4). Because a red filter (plate J) transmits its own color, the red patch is the only area of the original to form density on the film. The unexposed areas then represent the combination of blue and green, which were absorbed by the red filter. We see this color as cyan. The magenta printer is made by using a green filter (plate K). The wavelengths reflecting from the green patch of the original will be transmitted through the filter and will expose the film. Red and blue light will be absorbed by the filter and will not expose the film. Red and blue combine to form magenta. The blue filter (plate L), transmitting only blue light, will produce the yellow printer by exposing the negative in all but the red-green areas (figure 9.4). The black printer is exposed in such a way that shadows or dark areas of the original are not recorded on the film, but the primary hues are recorded as density on the negative.

After the negatives are exposed to printing plates, the clear areas on the film become areas of density on the plate. When the four plates are printed together in their proper combinations on a single sheet, the result should duplicate the range of hues of the original copy.

Halftone Dots and Color

Although figure 9.4 is a good conceptual view of the color separation process, it represents flat color and does not accurately show how the full range of hues is produced on the final printed sheet. Most color separation is done from continuous-tone color originals and must be screened during the reproduction process. Recall from Chapter 7 that halftone photographs form the illusion of tones by the use of dots of varying sizes. For example, 15% dots surrounded by 85% white space will appear as light gray; 35% dots with 65% white space will appear to be a darker gray. That same dot structure will produce a range of values within a given subtractive color for process color reproduction. It is the overlapping of dots of varying size from the four different printers that produces the accurate representation of the color original. It is possible to illustrate this concept with a set of "progressive color proofs" (plate M).

The yellow printer is actually a halftone represented in one hue (yellow), consisting of a limited range of values. The values of yellow are produced by many halftone dots of varying sizes. When the magenta printer is added to the yellow printer, additional hues and values become noticeable. By adding a cyan printer, the image looks complete. All the hues and values of hues seem to be visible. By adding a black printer, density will be increased in the shadow areas and the values of each hue will be strengthened.

Because the various values of each hue are produced by an overlapping dot structure, it is important that each halftone separation be prepared with dots at differing screen angles. If these angles are not properly controlled, an objectionable moiré pattern (see figure 8.2) could be formed. The cyan separation is typically made at a 45° angle, the magenta at 75°, the yellow at 90°, and the black at 105°. Angle control is discussed later in this chapter.

Masking

Color masking has three distinct goals in color reproduction:

- To compress the density range of the color original (called tone correction)
- To compensate for color deficiencies in process inks (called color correction)
- To enhance the detail of the final reproduction (called sharpness enhancement)

The term "masking" is still widely used, and is an important photographic process. Traditionally, a color mask is made by exposing the color original to **pan masking film** (a continuous-tone film) through a special filter. The mask was then physically placed over unexposed film during the separation process. However, electronic color scanning is doing the masking step electronically. A computer can be programmed to adjust the final separated digital images before they are output onto film or printing plates. Whether a physical film mask or electronic adjustments, the three goals remain the same.

Color transparencies typically have a maximum density of around 2.60, and color prints may reach 2.00 (refer to Chapter 6 for a discussion of density measurement). Four layers of ink on a printed sheet of paper can match a 2.00 reflection density; but a 2.60 density of a transparent image cannot be reproduced on the press. A mask allows the tonal range of the image to be compressed to a usable range without causing color imbalance.

A second problem is the inherent limitations of printing inks. While color theory says that cyan ink is a combination of blue and green pigments, in practice it is impossible to manufacture cyan ink without some

red. Figure 9.5 shows plots of each process color. Each figure compares the ideal ink with real inks. If cyan ink absorbs green and blue, as expected, but also a bit of red, then it is necessary to reduce both the magenta and yellow separation negatives in areas where cyan is printed on the final reproduction. This interaction occurs between all colors. The process of masking (whether photographic or electronic) reduces selected areas of the separation negatives in an attempt to compensate for the deficiencies of process inks.

The third purpose of a color mask is to

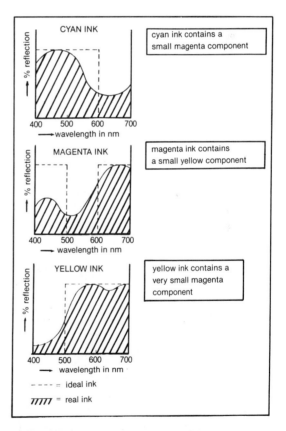

Figure 9.5. Comparison of real inks with theoretically ideal inks
Courtesy of D.S. America

enhance the detail of the individual separation. An unsharp photographic mask will produce a sharp separation. A photographic mask is produced by placing a diffuser sheet (generally frosted acetate) between the original and the pan masking film during the mask exposure. The diffused mask then slightly increases the contrast of the edges of the images, which in turn gives more detail to the reproduction. Electronically, the computer exaggerates the density difference (contrast) of the image edges.

Methods of Producing Color Separations

There are basically only three methods of making color separations. They are:

- direct screen photographic color separation
- indirect screen photographic color separation
- electronic color separation by scanner

The following sections briefly introduce each method.

Direct Screen Color Separation

The direct screen method produces color separation halftones in one step. In other words, the halftone and the color separations are made at the same time. This method has both cost and time advantages. Because the color separated halftone is produced in one step, fewer pieces of film are exposed, and operators spend less time producing a set of separations. Figure 9.6 illustrates the basic steps

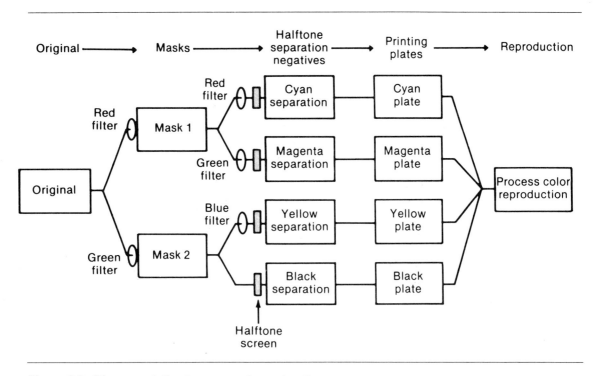

Figure 9.6. Diagram of direct screen color separation

involved in the direct screen method. This method can be used with a contact system, an enlarger, or a camera.

The first step in any photographic separation process is to produce the masks. Only two masks are made for direct screen separations. Figure 9.7 shows how each of the three systems—contact, enlarger, and camera—is set up to produce masks. These setups will be discussed in detail later in this chapter. The next step is to make the halftone and color separations using light that comes from the original and passes through the color separation filter, mask, halftone screen, and

onto the film (figure 9.8). The order of the items, through which light passes, will depend upon what type of equipment is used. Finally, the plates are made from the stripped negatives and run on the press.

Direct Screen Method—Transparent Copy. Using the direct screen method to make separations from transparencies is a very popular technique. The separations can be made in one of four ways: a contact system, an enlarger, a camera, or a scanner. The contact process requires only a point light source with filter capability, filters, gray contact screens, and a vacuum frame or easel with a simple register system. The process is popular because the equipment is inexpensive to set up and frees the process camera for other production work.

With both the contact and the projection techniques, it is first necessary to produce a two-color correcting mask by contact printing from the transparency (figure 9.9a). The final halftone separation negatives are made on high-contrast panchromatic film by using a sandwich of the transparency, mask, and gray screen with appropriate filtration (figure 9.9b). This process is described in detail in the last half of this chapter.

The projection direct screen method is generally used when a change from the original size is desired (figure 9.9c). The procedure is very similar to the contact method, except that an enlarger projects the masked transparent image to the proper size through the halftone screen onto the film. An industrial enlarger is shown in figure 9.10 (see p.252).

If a change in size is necessary and no projection system is available, a duplicate transparency can be made to the proper size from the original and then separated by the contact technique. Several transparencies can be ganged together and separated at one time with the contact system, whereas only one

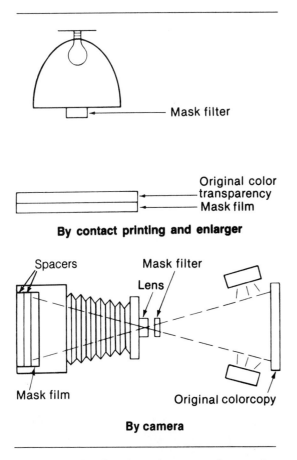

Mask filter

Original color transparency
Mask film

By contact printing and enlarger

Spacers   Mask filter
           Lens
Mask film   Original colorcopy

By camera

Figure 9.7. Making the color separation mask

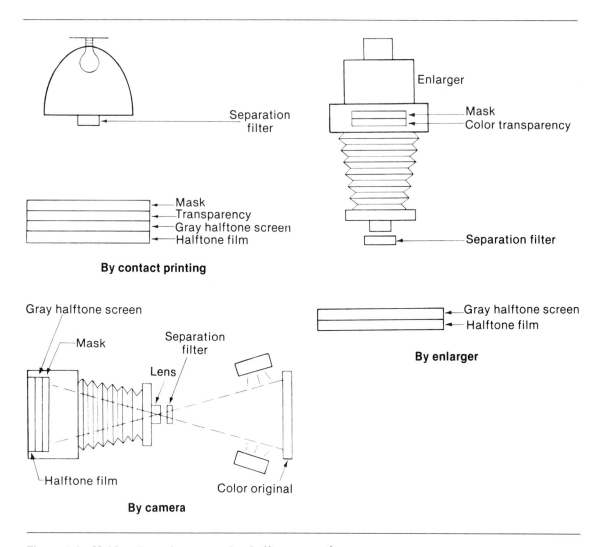

By contact printing

By enlarger

By camera

Figure 9.8. Making the color separation halftone negative

image can be handled at a time with the enlarger.

Direct Screen Method—Reflection Copy. A process camera (or a scanner, but the scanner concept will be discussed separately) must be used to prepare color separations of reflection copy. Direct screen with a camera is not a popular method. With this process, the copy is placed in the camera copyboard and masks are produced to the desired size (figure 9.11a). Each halftone negative is made in a single step by exposing a sandwich consisting of the mask, halftone screen, and film through the appropriate filter (figure 9.11b). The main disadvantage is that the camera cannot be used

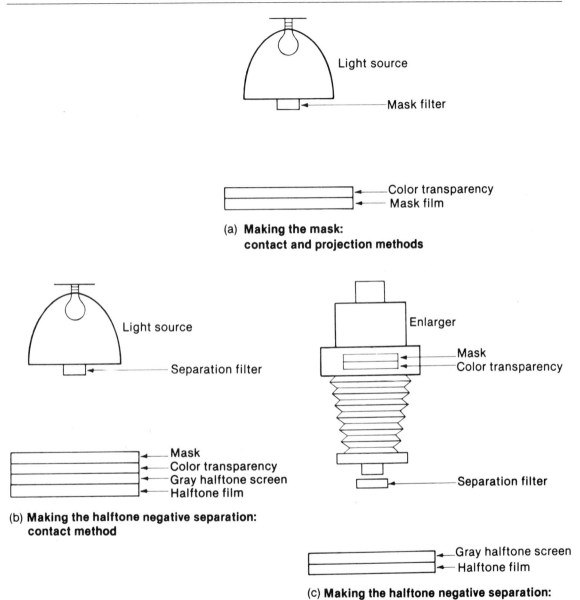

(a) **Making the mask:
contact and projection methods**

(b) **Making the halftone negative separation:
contact method**

(c) **Making the halftone negative separation:
projection method**

**Figure 9.9. Contact and projection methods of direct screen color
separation** When the original copy is a transparency and the size of the
reproduction is the same as that of the original, the contact method of
separation is used. When the original is a transparency, but the size is
changed in the reproduction, the projection method of separation is used.

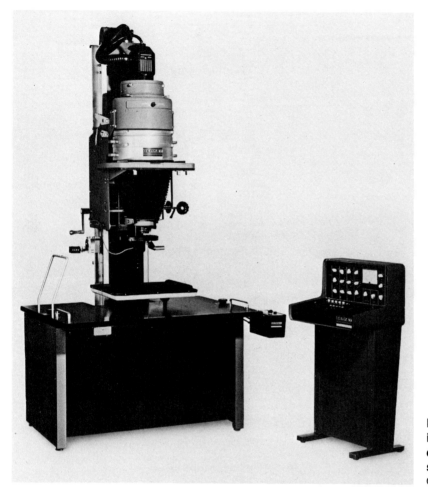

Figure 9.10. An industrial projection enlarger and color separator
Courtesy of Berkey Technical

for any other purpose until the entire set of separations is produced and approved. If the camera were moved, it would be impossible to reset it to the exact enlargement or reduction ratio. Due to a size or dimensional consideration, some jobs require the use of a process camera for color separations. Such cameras are either computer controlled or use dial micrometers to ensure an exact return to size if necessary.

Indirect Screen Color Separation

The indirect screen method first produces a continuous-tone separation negative (figure 9.12). Next, the continuous-tone negative is screened to produce a halftone positive. The screened positive is then contact printed to make the final separation negative.

Each mask for this method is made exactly like direct screen separation masks are

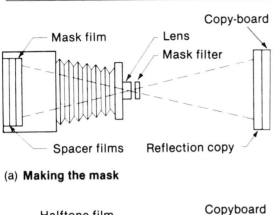

Copy-board

Mask film

Lens

Mask filter

Spacer films   Reflection copy

(a) Making the mask

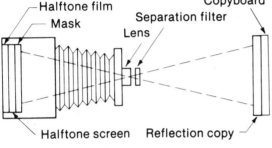

Halftone film

Mask

Copyboard

Separation filter

Lens

Halftone screen   Reflection copy

(b) Making the negative separation

Figure 9.11. Direct screen color separation from reflection copy

An enlarger is usually not used to produce the halftone positives because the continuous-tone negative is too large to fit in the negative carrier. Advantages of the indirect method are that the negatives can be retouched or enlarged. The opportunity to enlarge, for the second time, during the separation process allows the printer to produce large posters and display work.

Direct and indirect color separation can be done with a variety of equipment (such as a process camera, an enlarger, a contact printing system, or even an electronic scanner). A process camera can be used to separate either reflection copy, such as a color print, or transparencies (with a back-lighted copyboard). An enlarger or a contact printing system can only be used to separate transparent copy. A scanner can be used to separate either transparent or reflection copy.

Several variables need to be considered when selecting the method and equipment to use for color separation. Typical considerations include available money, type of copy to be separated, the enlargement-reduction factor required, and ultimate use for the separations. Fewer steps are involved with the direct method, so it is obviously faster than the indirect process. The additional steps can, however, be used to advantage for color correction and proofing. The fact that indirect separations are finally contacted to give the halftone negatives also produces a better dot structure.

Indirect Screen Method—Transparent Copy. One of the oldest techniques of making color separations is with transparencies on a back-lighted process camera copyboard. Size changes can be made with an enlarger or can be allowed for on the camera. Masks are made with the proper filter by transmitting light through the transparency and the mask filter

made (figure 9.7). The difference in making masks with the indirect screen method is that usually four masks, one for each separation negative, are made. After the masks are made, the indirect method completely differs from the direct method. A continuous-tone separation negative is now made from the original by using the appropriate mask and separation filter (figure 9.13). The continuous-tone separation negative is contacted or projection printed to produce a halftone positive. The halftone positive can be made in a contact system or with a process camera (figure 9.14).

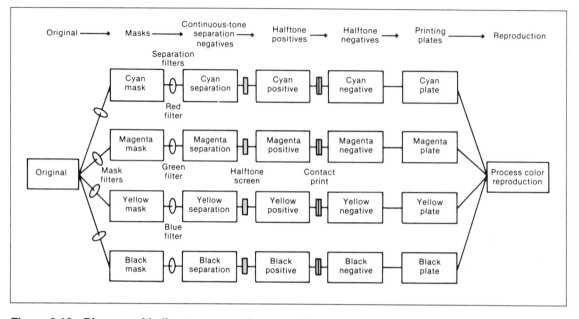

Figure 9.12. Diagram of indirect screen color separation

and onto the masking film (figure 9.15a). Spacer film is used between the mask film and camera back. Spacer film moves the mask material away from the camera vacuum board a distance equal to the thickness of separation film. When the actual separations are made, the spacer film will be replaced by film material. In this way, there will be no size or focus distortion in the final product. Next, separation negatives are made by exposing continuous-tone film through the proper filter and mask (figure 9.15b). The separation negative is then placed on the copyboard and exposed to ortho film through a halftone screen (figure 9.15c). The separation positive is then contacted to produce a halftone negative. Again, this technique requires that the camera be maintained at the required size during the entire process.

Indirect Screen Method—Reflection Copy. This technique is very similar to the indirect method for transparent copy. Masks are exposed by light reflecting from the copy (figure 9.16a). A spacer film is placed behind the masking film so that the mask will be in focus when it is placed in front of the separation film in the following step. Next, continuous-tone separation negatives are made by photographing the original through the appropriate filter and mask (figure 9.16b). Positives can be made by contact printing or by placing the positives in the back-lighted copyboard (figure 9.16c). The final halftone negative separations are made by contact printing (figure 9.16d).

Electronic Color Separation

Electronic color separation is commonly called color scanning. A scanner is a device that electronically measures color densities of a color original (such as a slide, photograph, or paint-

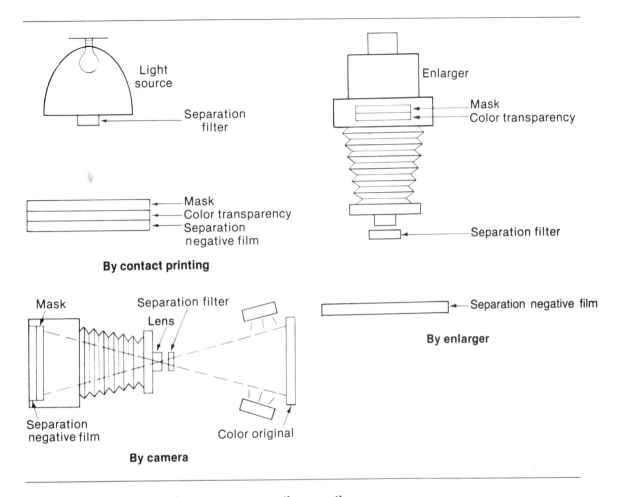

By contact printing

By enlarger

By camera

Figure 9.13. Making a continuous-tone separation negative

ing), stores those measurements as digital information in computer memory, manipulates or alters the digital data to obtain the best printing results, and uses the new information to create four film separations (figure 9.17).

The original concept of an electronic color scanner dates to 1937, but it wasn't until 1949 that the first successful scanner was actually put into commercial operation. Until recently, industrial acceptance of scanners has been slow. It was the general feeling of the industry that contemporary photographic methods and color scanners were about the same in terms of final quality and cost. It was also obvious that scanners required a substantial initial investment. American printers did not accept the concept as readily as did the rest of the world. However, it is rapidly becoming the standard method for producing screen separation negatives directly from original color copy.

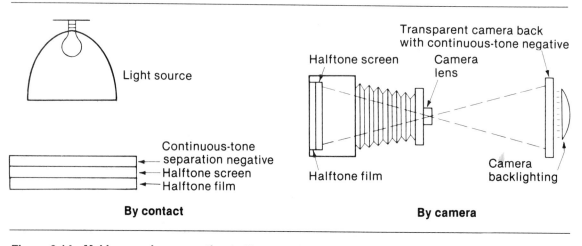

Figure 9.14. Making a color separation halftone positive

This acceptance is due to several factors. Computers are commonly used to measure and control ink densities on a printing press. With the ability to measure the strengths and weaknesses of each individual press, that information can be used to make sets of separations that deliver maximum quality. Scanners can individualize results for any specific printing press. The last decade has seen an increase in sophistication and power of computer systems. In many instances these came with a reduction in costs. A widespread cultural acceptance and use of computers has helped change attitudes about scanners. Finally, the development of powerful color editing systems lead to an increase in the use of scanners. Color editing requires and uses the data that can only come from a digital color scanner.

Basic Scanner Operation. Figure 9.18 is a simplified schematic of a scanner. The color transparency is mounted on a rotating cylinder. A portion of the cylinder is clear glass or plastic. An unexposed sheet of film is mounted on the other end of the same cylinder. As the cylinder spins, a narrow beam of light is passed through the transparency to a measuring device inside the cylinder. The computer takes those color and density readings, and electronically stores data for cyan, magenta, yellow, and black separations. Simultaneously, the computer directs a beam of light at the unexposed sheet of film. The film is exposed in direct proportion to the density of the area being measured on the original, but for only one separation.

This is, of course, a very simplified explanation of a complex and sophisticated technology. It is possible to have many variations of this basic approach. Four sheets of fresh film can be mounted on some scanners so the cyan, magenta, yellow, and black printers are produced at one time. Another design uses a single large sheet of film, and the scanner records each separation at different positions. The computer can also store the data for output on a separate machine after color editing.

Both color transparencies and color

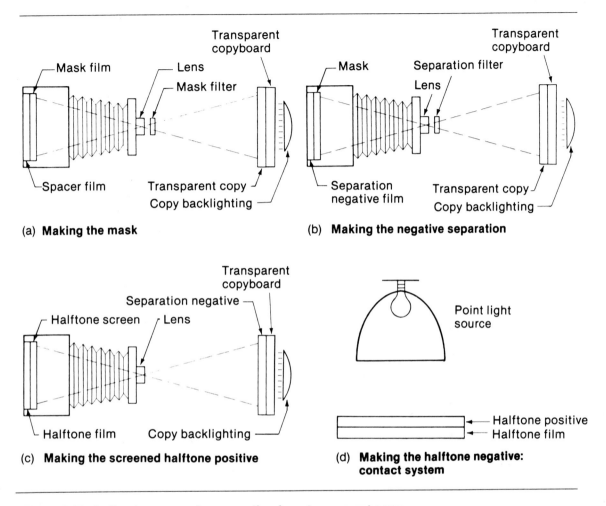

(a) **Making the mask**

(b) **Making the negative separation**

(c) **Making the screened halftone positive**

(d) **Making the halftone negative: contact system**

Figure 9.15. Indirect screen color separation from transparent copy

prints can be scanned. Although the rotating cylinder form is the most common design, an alternative is the flat-bed scanner. The flat-bed design is especially useful for originals that cannot be curved around a cylinder.

The color scanning process involves four steps. They are: scanning, analysis and modification, storage and image editing, and exposure. The following discussion describes scanning a color transparency. The proce-

dures are slightly different for reflection copy. However, the concepts remain the same for either type of original. This explanation is a generalized description and does not apply to any specific manufacturer's machine.

Scanning. The color transparency is first mounted on the transparent revolving drum. Some devices have a vacuum system, and others use a plastic sheath, but it is most com-

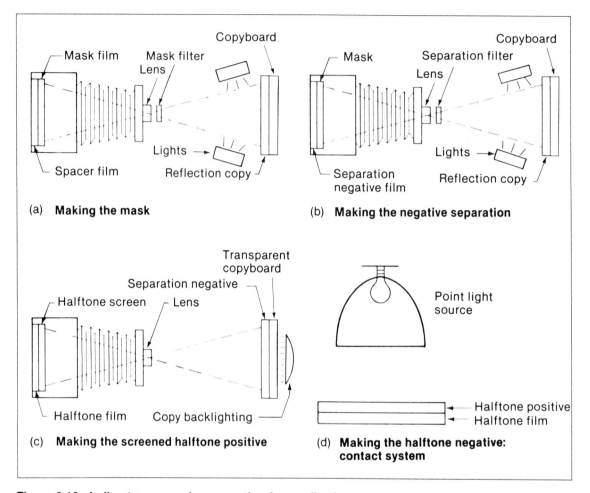

Figure 9.16. Indirect screen color separation from reflection copy

mon to simply tape the sheet in place with clear cellophane tape. Position is not of crucial importance, but the transparency must not move or shift as the drum rotates.

The most important element of the scanner is the **photomultiplier tube (PMT)**. The PMT has the ability to change light into an electrical signal. The PMT can send a signal that varies in strength with variations in the light it receives.

The lamphouse contains a light source and lenses. The two most common light sources are high-pressure xenon or a tungsten-halogen lamp. The light is passed through a condenser lens and is deflected by a mirror. The mirror is set at a 90° angle to the drum surface. The narrow beam of light from the mirror passes through the color transparency and is split into four light paths by microscopic optics. Each light path enters a pho-

Figure 9.17. An electronic rotating-cylinder color scanner
Courtesy of Crosfield Electronics, Inc.

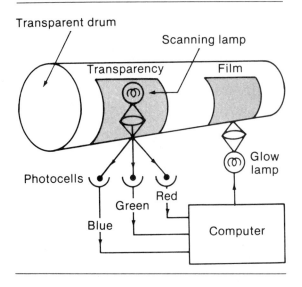

Figure 9.18. A schematic of scanner operation
Courtesy of Eastman Kodak Company

tomultiplier tube (PMT). Three PMTs are covered separately with red, green, and blue filters. The amount of light passing into any single PMT is proportional to the density of a primary color from a spot on the color transparency. The PMT sends the computer a signal that controls the amount of light used to expose the separation film at the other end of the rotating drum (figure 9.19).

These red-, green-, and blue-filtered PMTs provide information to the computer to expose the cyan, magenta, and yellow separations. The fourth light path enters a PMT to provide unsharp masking information. That masking data is used by the computer to control the exposure of the final film sheets. The black printer is created by the computer, using information from the cyan, magenta, and yellow signals. This entire operation occurs as the transparency drum rotates at high speed.

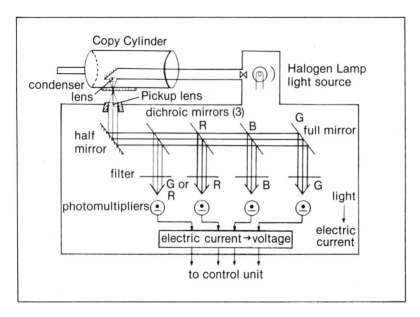

Figure 9.19. Pickup head schematic
Courtesy of D.S. America

The lamphouse and the PMT units must be in perfect synchronization with each other. A common design is to place the lamphouse on the inside of the drum and the analyzing unit on the outside, connected together by a U-shaped rod. As the drum rotates, the light and analyzing units move horizontally across the transparency.

Scan rate is typically listed with two numbers, one over the other, such as 70/150. The first number gives the number of seconds it takes to scan one inch. In this example, the light and PMTs would have moved horizontally one inch in 70 seconds. The second number refers to **scan pitch**. Scan pitch is the number of exposing lines per inch. Exposing lines is not comparable to the more familiar halftone dot screen rulings, also measured in lines per inch. Scan pitch describes the degree of detail the computer is measuring. The choice of precision depends more on enlargement requirements than halftone ruling.

Most scanners allow for overlap of information. While scan pitch refers to the actual number of scan lines per inch, in reality each scan both gathers new information and confirms a portion of the previous pass. This allows the computer to expose a continuous film image rather than what would appear as distinct visual lines.

Analysis and Modification. The electronic signals from the photomultiplier tubes must pass through the computer control system. It is at this point that the operator can directly control the output variables. The most common areas of concern are color correction and undercolor removal.

One purpose of masking, as discussed in the previous section, was to adjust for the differences between ideal and real printing inks. For example, ideal cyan ink will absorb red light and reflect blue and green. In reality, while cyan ink does reflect most blue and green, it also absorbs some blue and green. This gives the practical appearance of contamination with magenta and yellow inks. The solution is to reduce magenta and yellow ink wherever cyan is also printed. The computer is ideally suited to automatically make such adjustments for all color interactions. Once the operator has set the machine for the actual press conditions, ink, paper, and press printing characteristics, the computer can take information from the color transparency and modify the data to produce the best possible set of separations.

Another reason for **color correction** is intended use. A printed sheet will look different depending upon its viewing situation. For example, supermarkets always place warm (slightly red) lights over their meat counters. Customers tend to buy more when the meats appear rich red at the point of purchase. If a package with a process color image is to be placed in or near the meat counter (such as a box of frozen shrimp), then the color separations should be adjusted with a reduction in the magenta printer. However, an adjustment in the magenta printer will affect every other color separation; therefore, the cyan and yellow printers must also be corrected where the two overlap with magenta. The scanner's computer can be set up to make such corrections, and with the operator's direction, produce a set of four appropriate printers.

The operator may also make adjustments to actually improve the color balance of an inferior color original. The system may be used to adjust for the type of paper to receive the image. The separations used to print a color image on newsprint should be different than those used for a high quality coated offset paper (see Chapter 18).

Undercolor removal (UCR) is the process of diminishing the amount of cyan, magenta, and yellow ink printed in the shadows, and increasing the amount of black ink in the reduced areas. Equal amounts of cyan, magenta, and yellow create a neutral gray. The basic idea is to remove equal amounts of the three colors to the extent that each individual color's clarity is retained, but to diminish neutral gray, which adds nothing to the image (figure 9.20).

The result of undercolor removal is to prevent ink buildup, which tends to cause picking (see Chapter 13), and actually increase detail in the shadow areas because of added density in the black printer. The goal is increased image quality, but one important result is the savings gained by reducing use of expensive color inks and replacing them with relatively inexpensive black ink.

Since the scanner makes UCR adjustments electronically, and in proportion to the actual data received from the color original, it tends to give more control than is possible with any photographic process.

Storage and Image Editing. Not all scanned images are stored within computer memory.

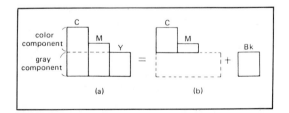

Figure 9.20. Equivalence of three-color gray and black
Courtesy of D.S. America

Only scanners that use a video display terminal store the entire transparency. Most systems store only one scan line of data at a time. The data is modified and directed to the exposure unit. For example, on the first revolution of the drum, one scan line is recorded. As the second scan line begins, the computer adjusts the first line's digital data to the specifications the operator has set. After modification, the information is removed from computer memory, sent to the exposure unit to expose the film separations, and data from the second scan line is replaced in computer memory. The process continues until the entire transparency has been scanned and the last line has been removed from memory and sent to the output exposure unit.

If there are few changes from the original photographic image, this approach works very well. The photograph is reproduced exactly as created, with the best possible separations given the printing conditions. However, few printing jobs have that ideal situation.

A customer is selling contact lenses and wants an existing photograph modified so the model has one green eye and one blue. A client wants an image of King Kong climbing a building in Chicago (King Kong never visited Chicago). A company in Virginia has decided that the image of a lawn in its annual report should appear gold because of a very successful financial year. All of these changes are possible by traditional photographic printing processes, but are extremely time consuming and, therefore, very costly.

Image editing and color editing are relatively new terms that describe the ability to store and then electronically modify the original image using a video display terminal and a computer. The computer storage requirements for even an 8- × 10-inch color photograph is immense. This decade has seen a

major advance in storage media, making full-page color and image editing possible.

Plate N shows an example of color-image editing. Two unrelated images have been combined electronically to create an illustration that has never existed in reality. With color-image editing, any color image may be modified to meet a customer's needs. Even if such changes were possible photographically, the effort involved would require far more time and resources than most could afford. Electronic color and image editing has created an environment in which customers can specify major and minor changes, and designers can move beyond what can be created in the studio or the real world.

One interesting outgrowth of image editing has been the creation of a new term—synthetic art. **Synthetic art** describes any image created electronically that was either developed by the artist/operator from imagination—and, therefore, no piece ever existed in reality—or is a combination of several real-time images, but assembled together in a manner that never existed before. Plate N is a clear example of synthetic art.

Exposure.   Color scanners may also be classified by type of output. There are three basic methods of electronic image output: continuous-tone, contact screen halftone, and dot-generated halftones.

All early electronic scanners produced continuous-tone separations. The final printable separations were converted to screened halftones on a process camera. In general, continuous-tone separations require a finer scan pitch than any other method. The continuous-tone scanned image is most practical where it is necessary to produce the same image in different sizes. The continuous-tone negatives are mounted on the camera and enlarged or reduced to meet design needs. Consider a situation in which the advertising agency has set up a studio photograph for a breakfast cereal product. They want the same image to appear on the cereal box in the supermarket, on billboards, on discount coupons, and in newspaper ads. Rather than paying to scan four distinct sets of sized color separations, only one continuous-tone set is made, and then separation halftones are enlarged or reduced to meet the customer's needs.

Continuous-tone scanners are the least expensive devices for initial purchase. Increasingly, however, there is more emphasis upon machines that can produce separations for a variety of purposes.

Contact screen scanners, in theory, only add a physical contact screen between the unexposed film and the exposing unit. The contact screen used on a scanner is less dense than the traditional halftone contact screen. The same screen can be used to produce either halftone postives or halftone negatives. There is little output change between a continuous-tone scanner and a contact screen scanner. The light output must be adjusted to the spectral sensitivity and intensity requirement of lith or rapid access film rather than a continuous-tone emulsion.

Dot-generating scanners are equipped to take the electronic signal that has been modified from the photomultiplier tubes and form a computer-designed halftone dot pattern on the unexposed lith film. The terms **electronic dot-generation** and **laser scanning** are sometimes used to describe the same output system. The dot pattern and screen angle are controlled by the computer, with the specific dot shape described mathematically by the original software program (figure 9.21). The computer can form round, elliptical, square, or rectangular dots.

Dot-generated halftones tend to produce hard, individual dot patterns. They resemble the sharp edges of a contact dot (contacting a halftone negative to produce a halftone positive gives sharp edges), rather than the more common soft-edged patterns exposed through a contact screen.

Achromatic Color

A new color separation technique that is unique to the modern electronic color scanner is **Achromatic Color.** The technique is also known as **Gray Component Replacement (GCR).** GCR is an extension of UCR (undercolor removal). While UCR only removes cyan, yellow, and magenta in the darker neutral gray areas of the separation, GCR replaces cyan, yellow, and magenta wherever they overprint to produce a neutral gray, even in the highlights. Traditional electronic separations produce a (ghost) black printer that prints from the midtones into the shadows. GCR produces a more full-range black. With GCR, the black printer is responsible for producing a full range of neutral gray tones from highlight to shadow. The result is that the process inks—cyan, yellow, and magenta—will only print where necessary to produce the color portion of the image. Where black is required, black will be printed, rather than building the color black with equal parts of each process color as is done with traditional separations. The press is now able to lay down a heavier film of the process inks without fear of upsetting the gray balance of the separation. In addition, much of the more expensive process inks is replaced by the less expensive black.

Dot Etching

It is frequently necessary to alter individual separations to emphasize or deemphasize in-

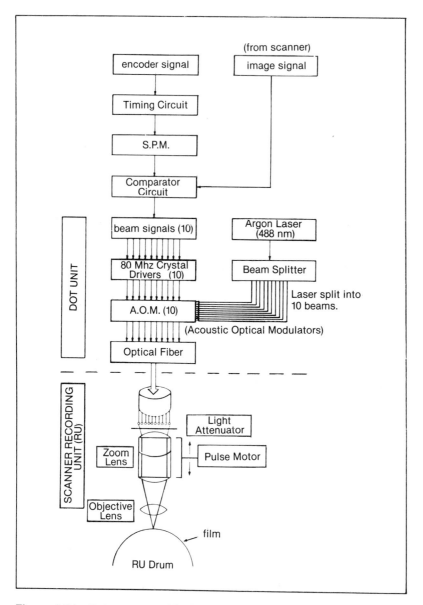

Figure 9.21. Dot generator block diagram
Courtesy of D.S. America

dividual sections of color. The need for changes does not necessarily imply frequent errors or inexact processing controls, but rather is often done to specifications defined by the customer after seeing color proofs. **Dot etching** is a process that changes dot sizes on color separations with a liquid etch (a combination of potassium ferricyanide and sodium thiosulphate) that reduces the developed silver of the film emulsion. There are two basic techniques: wet etching and dry etching.

Wet Etching

With wet etching, both halftone and continuous-tone separations can be etched. Due to the shape of the halftone dot, the etch first affects the outer edges of the dot. Etching continuous-tone separations changes tonal values on the separation in order to obtain the desired dot size on its halftone reproduction. A diluted etch must be used because continuous-tone emulsions reduce rapidly.

Stain, a thin black liquid, is often used for adding highlight and shadow detail in small areas on continuous-tone images. Stain can also be used to reduce color on negatives or to add color on separation positives. **Retouching pencils** are used to add fine line detail or to repair damaged film.

Once halftone positives are made, a set of proofs will indicate any necessary corrections. The areas needing correction are then marked. If the color needs to be increased in an area, a **staging solution** (an etch resist) is applied with a brush to all other parts of the film. To reduce the unstaged area, the film is immersed in a tray of etch solution (start with one-quarter potassium ferricyanide, one-quarter hypo, and one-half water).

Occasionally an area becomes over-etched. It is possible to bring up or restore an etched dot by an intensification process. The process requires two solutions: a bleach and a developer. The bleach is first applied to the dot area needing intensification. The developer is then applied to the bleached area, and the original dot structure is made visible.

Dry Dot Etching

Dry etching has several advantages over wet etching. Dry etching is nondestructive to the original separation films. It is generally a faster process that requires less artistic skill of the etcher. The disadvantage is that the process can be more time consuming, especially when a small change in one area of the film is required. Dry dot etching is a two-step process that requires a contacting station and a pin register system. The process can add or reduce color locally or overall. Prior to contacting, a cut and peel mask must first be made which is open only in the areas to be etched.

Color Reduction. The percentage of color in an area can be reduced by first contacting the original separation film, emulsion to emulsion, to contact (reversal) film using a normal contact exposure time. This will produce a normal positive, wrong-reading through the base, of the entire separation film. After the normal positive is processed, a second contact is made from this positive.

Place the normal positive, in the contact frame, the mask on top of the positive, and the unexposed contact film below the positive. Again, the films must be emulsion toward emulsion. Expose this second contact for an exposure time which will produce the degree of reduction required in the color. This time is expressed as the number of times greater than a normal contact exposure. For instance, a minor color change may only require a 1.5-times exposure. A major change may require as much as twelve times the normal exposure. The amount of change per increase in exposure is determined through a series of test exposures. The number of times beyond the normal exposure is determined by the color evaluator. It is his or her judgment which will determine the amount of change needed.

After the additional exposure is made, the mask is removed and a normal exposure is given to the film. This exposure will transfer the rest of the color information, which is to receive no color change, to the contact film. After processing, this film will contain all the original information plus the reduced dot size required in the masked area.

Color Addition.   Adding color or increasing dot size in a specific area is similar to color reduction, with the difference that the mask is used in the first step when the contact positive is being exposed. The second step produces a normal contact of the positive, which received the color addition, because of the mask. A right-reading film negative is then produced.

Key Terms

process color photography
subtractive primary colors
additive primary colors
masking
direct screen color separation
indirect screen color
  separation

dot etching
staging solution
scanner
electronic color separation
photomultiplier tube
scan rate

scan pitch
color correction
undercolor removal (UCR)
synthetic art
electronic dot-generation

Questions for Review

1. What are the subtractive primary colors?

2. What are the additive primary colors?

3. When using subtractive primary inks, what color would result from a combination of yellow and magenta?

4. What is the purpose of adding a black printer if a combination of three subtractive inks will approximate all colors?

5. What are the three purposes of masking in color separation?

6. What are the three general methods of making color separations?

7. What is the advantage of the direct screen contact technique of color separation?

8. What are several advantages of color separation by electronic scanning over other techniques?

9. What is scan pitch and how is it related to final print quality?

10. What is the purpose of dot etching color separations?

11. Outline the steps in adding color density in a specific area of a separation using the dry dot etching method.

12. GCR is an extension of what masking function of the electronic color scanner?

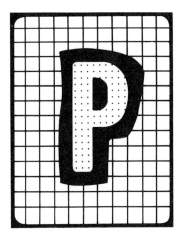

Chapter Ten

Image Assembly: Stripping and Proofing

Anecdote to Chapter Ten

Stripping refers to the process of preparing and positioning a piece of film for exposure to a printing plate. The term originally described a process, commonly used as recently as the 1950s, in which a wet emulsion was removed from a special "stripping film." Stripping film was cumbersome to work with when compared to today's flexible, stable-base photographic materials, but at the time it was considered an efficient, simple process.

The stripper could use a variety of techniques. One of the most common was to manufacture the film from existing materials in the darkroom. The process started with the careful cleaning of a sheet of glass. The glass was then polished with a soft rag and a powder called "French chalk." Next, substratum of rubber solution or egg albumen solution was poured on the glass, followed by a layer of rubber and naphtha. The final layer was a light-sensitive stripping emulsion.

While the emulsion was still wet, the plate was rushed to the camera and an exposure was made of the image to be reproduced. The plate was then taken to the developing area and processed. The wet plate then went back to the stripper, who immersed it in an acetic acid-water bath.

When the emulsion began to lift, the stripper started at one corner and actually stripped the membrane from the plate. While this was going on, another worker prepared a new glass plate by covering it with a small pool of gum solution. The wet emulsion was positioned on the second plate and finally squeegeed into place. Depending on the printing process used, the emulsion could be placed on the plate either right- or wrong-reading. If a half-tone or new piece of line work needed to be added, the stripper used a sharp knife to cut away the unwanted area and put a new wet piece in its place.

Even though wet strippers would probably not recognize the materials used today,

Stripping film on a light table
Courtesy of Kingsport Press, an Arcata National Company

it would take little retraining for them to function at a modern light table. The task of positioning film images remains the same, and they would probably feel accepted because they would still be called "strippers."

Objectives for Chapter Ten

After completing this chapter you will be able to:

- Understand the purpose of stripping and proofing in the printing processes.
- Recognize the equipment and supplies used in stripping and proofing.
- Recall and explain the basic stripping steps.

- Describe several methods of multiflat registration that include common edge, snap fitter and dowel, and punch and register pin.
- Recall and explain the basic methods of preparing single-color proofs.
- Describe the techniques of preparing both opaque and transparent color proofs.

Introduction

This chapter is divided into two main sections. The first section describes the sequences of steps used to work with film, prior to making a printing plate. This operation is called stripping. The second section deals with methods of checking the quality and the accuracy of the position of the stripped film images. This process is called proofing.

Stripping Transparent Materials

The Purpose of Stripping

After the final layout has been completed and converted to transparent film, the film image must be photographically transferred to the printing plate. Although the type of plate used will differ according to the method or process of reproduction (relief, lithography, screen, or gravure), the stripping and proofing steps from the darkroom to the plateroom are basically the same.

Stripping is the process of assembling all pieces of film containing images that will be carried on the same printing plate and securing them on a masking sheet that will hold them in their appropriate printing positions during the plate-making process. The assembled masking sheet with attached pieces of film is called a **flat.** After the flat is stripped, it is generally tested on some inexpensive photosensitive material to check the image position and to ensure that no undesired light reaches the plate. This process is called **proofing.** If the proof is approved, the flat can be placed in contact with a printing plate, light passed through the film, and the plate exposed.

Most printers view the stripping process as the most important step in the printing cycle. The stripper can often correct or alter defects in the film image by etching away undesired detail. The stripper also directly controls the position and squareness of the image on the final page. If the film is not stripped square in the masking sheet, the image will appear crooked on the printed page. However, the stripping process cannot correct poor work that started on the mechanical or in the darkroom, no matter how skillful the stripper.

Equipment and Supplies

The stripper uses a variety of tools that center around the use of a quality T-square and triangle. Tools made of plastic or other easily nicked materials are not used because the tools must serve as cutting edges for razor blades or Exacto knives when trimming pieces of film or masking sheets. Most printers use one quality steel T-square and one steel 30°-60°-90° triangle. Measurements can be made with an architect's scale and an engineer's scale. Stainless steel straightedges with fractional gradations to one-hundredth of an inch are also commonly used. For greater accuracy, an ordinary needle or a special purpose etching needle is used to mark the masking sheet when laying out a flat. The etching needle can also be used to remove unwanted emulsion from a film negative or positive. Detail is added to a piece of film with a brush. Most strippers have an assortment of red sable watercolor brushes on hand. Start your collection of brushes with # 0, 2, 4, and 6 brushes. In addition, the stripping area should have such things as a scissors, a supply of single-edged razor blades, a low-power magnifying glass (10X), pencils (# 2H and 4H), erasers, and several felt-tip marking pens for labeling flats.

Almost all stripping is done on a glass-topped light table (figure 10.1). One side of the glass is frosted, and a light source (generally fluorescent) is located under the glass so that the surface is evenly illuminated. When a film negative or positive is placed on the lighted glass, it is easy to view the image and to detect any film defects. A variety of light tables are available. Most are equipped with accurately ground straightedges on each side so that if a T-square is placed on any side, lines will always be at right angles to each other. More sophisticated models, called mechanical **line-up tables** (figure 10.2), come equipped with rolling carriages, micrometer

Figure 10.1. A glass-topped light table On this light table, negatives for a 32-page signature are being assembled and stripped.
Courtesy of Pre-Press Co., Inc.

adjustments, and attachments for ruling or scribing parallel or perpendicular lines.

Several types of supplies are needed for the stripping operation. For negative stripping, **masking sheets** that do not pass light to the printing plate must be used. The most common material is "goldenrod paper," which blocks **actinic light** (any light that exposes blue-light and ultraviolet light sensitive emulsions) because of its color. For jobs that require greater dimensional stability, orange colored (sometimes red) vinyl masking sheets are typically used. When you are stripping positives, the masking sheet and film must pass light in all but the image areas. Most positive stripping is done on clear acetate support sheets, although some special function shops use glass plates. In most positive stripping, tracing paper is used for the initial image layout. Transparent tape is used to secure the film to the flat. Special "red" translucent tape can be used to secure film negatives during stripping. This tape blocks actinic light. Opaque is a liquid material used to cover pinholes and other unwanted detail on film negatives. Red opaque is easier to apply, but black colloidal-graphic opaque is thinner and thus more efficient for extremely small areas, as when retouching halftones. Both water- and alcohol-based opaques are available.

All tools and supplies should be centrally located near the light table so the stripper can reach any item easily. If each item is located in a particular spot and is always returned there after use, much time can be saved. Disorder causes wasted motion and, over a period of time, increases the cost of each job.

Imposition

Imposition refers to the placement of images in the correct positions on the printing plate so they will be printed in the desired location

**Figure 10.2. A
mechanical line-up table**
Courtesy of nuArc Company, Inc.

on the final printed sheet. Several types of imposition are commonly used. The type of imposition used depends on several factors:

- The design of the printed piece (whether it is multicolor, process-color, or single-color; whether one or both sides of the sheet are to be printed; whether one or several duplicate images are to be reproduced on the same sheet; and the type of finishing operations, such as folding, trimming, and binding that are required)
- The type and size of the press to be used (whether the press is sheet-fed or web-fed, and the size of the press sheet)
- The type of paper to be used during printing (whether image position in relation to grain direction will effect folding operations)

In general, the best imposition is the one which will most efficiently produce a quality job with not only the minimum press time and minimum amount of paper but also the minimum time in the finishing operations that follow. Without careful planning in the stripping operation, a job could be stripped, plated, and run on the press only to discover that it cannot be folded correctly.

One-Side Imposition.   The simplest form of imposition is one-side imposition. In one-side imposition, one printing plate is used to print on one side of the sheet as it passes through the printing press. This type of imposition is common in small offset press operations.

Sheetwise Imposition.   Two printing plates are used in sheetwise imposition. One printing plate is used to print on one side of a press sheet. A second plate, containing different information, is made, the sheets are turned over, and are printed on the other side from the second plate.

Ganged Imposition.   Often the size of the job to be printed is smaller than the press can handle or is so much smaller than the standard press sheet size that printing only one job on each press sheet would be a very inefficient use of equipment. To overcome this problem, several jobs are often "ganged" together, reproduced on a large sheet, and then

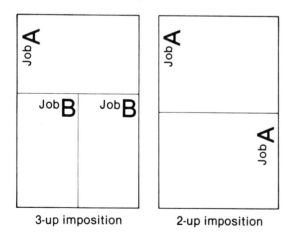

3-up imposition   2-up imposition

Figure 10.3. Ganged imposition Images or pages are ganged on the press sheet for more efficient use of materials and equipment.

cut to the final trim size with a paper cutter (figure 10.3). When a press sheet carries only one job, it is called "1-up" imposition. When more than a single job is run on the same sheet, it is called "2-up," "3-up," "4-up," and so on, depending on the number of final jobs run on each press sheet. It makes no difference if the same or different images are printed; the same terms are used.

Signature Imposition.   A large single sheet is frequently passed through a printing press and then folded and trimmed to form a portion of a book or magazine. This process is called **signature imposition.** Four-, eight-, twelve-, sixteen-, twenty-four-, and even forty-eight-page signatures are common press runs (figure 10.4). The printer must impose the pages in the proper position so they will be in the correct sequence when folded in the final publication.

Work-and-Turn Imposition.   Another common form of imposition is the work-and-turn. **Work-and-turn imposition** employs one printing plate to print on both sides of a single piece of paper (figure 10.5). The sheet is first printed on one side, the pile is turned over, and the sheet is fed through the press again with the same **lead edge** (first edge that enters the press).

Work-and-Tumble Imposition. **Work-and-tumble imposition** also uses one plate; but on the second pass through the press, the pile is tumbled (or flopped) so that the opposite edge enters first (figure 10.6). Both techniques are more efficient than sheetwise imposition because only one printing plate is prepared. Work-and-tumble imposition is generally not used where **fit** (critical image position) is desired—such as in multicolor jobs—because using two different lead edges requires additional press adjustments.

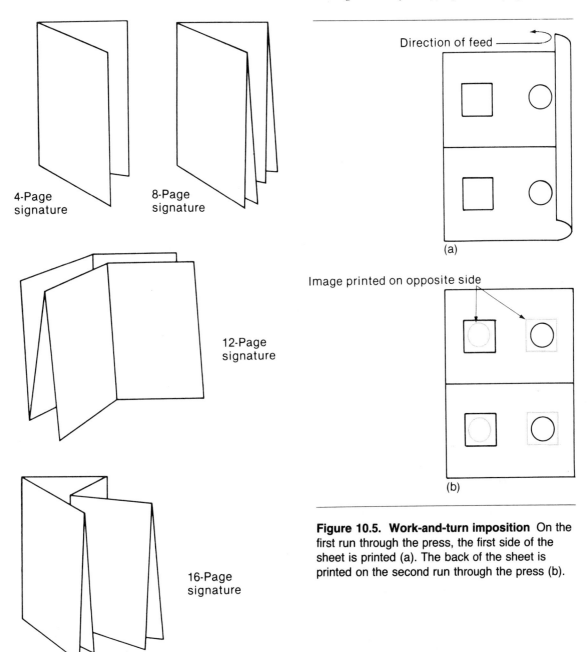

4-Page
signature

8-Page
signature

12-Page
signature

16-Page
signature

Figure 10.4. Folded signatures A predetermined folded signature of several pages is the result of signature imposition.

Direction of feed

(a)

Image printed on opposite side

(b)

Figure 10.5. Work-and-turn imposition On the first run through the press, the first side of the sheet is printed (a). The back of the sheet is printed on the second run through the press (b).

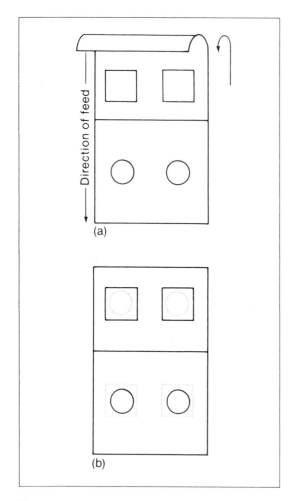

Figure 10.6. Work-and-tumble imposition showing first run (a) and second run (b)

Elementary Stripping Techniques

It is important to keep in mind that there is no single "correct" way to strip a flat. In fact, it sometimes seems that there are as many different stripping methods as there are strippers. The techniques presented in this section are intended to introduce some basic strip-

ping procedures, but it should be understood that they represent only one approach.

Several things must be considered before the actual stripping operation begins. Most jobs arrive at the stripper's in a work envelope with a work order attached. The work order has been completed from information contained on the rough layout and from the printing customer when the contract was awarded. The rough should provide detailed specifications for all phases of production, but the stripper is concerned only with such things as the process of reproduction, plate size, paper size, final trim size, image position specifications, and a detailed list of all pieces of film to be stripped. The stripper should check the contents of the packet against the list and examine each piece of film for quality. It is an expensive delay if the stripper has nearly completed a flat and then discovers that a piece of film is missing or is of inferior quality.

The more complex the stripping job, the more important it is for the stripper to plan the stripping operation. Often it is the stripper's responsibility to make or request the various film images that may be required for the job. In addition, the stripper must plan the contents of each flat so that the minimum number of flats are used for the job.

Masking Sheets

The position of the images on the printing plate is determined by the film positions on the masking sheet. Thus the masking sheet "represents" the printing plate and must be at least the same size as the plate. Care must be used in placing the film images on the masking sheet to ensure that they are in the correct printing position and are parallel to the lead edge of the masking sheet. Identifying the following four areas on the masking sheet will help you accurately position the film images in their correct printing position:

- The cylinder line
- The gripper margin
- The plate center line
- The point where the image begins on the printed piece (figure 10.7a)

The **cylinder line** identifies the area of the masking sheet that covers the part of the lithographic plate clamped onto the press to hold the plate on the plate cylinder. Most offset lithographic plates are flexible and wrap

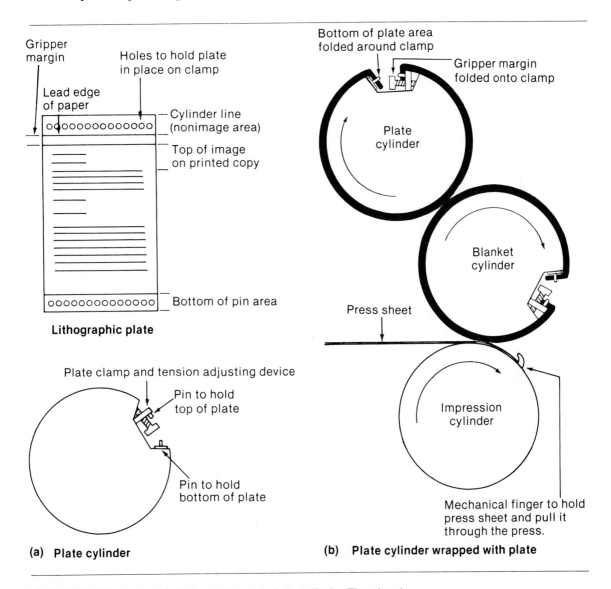

(a) Plate cylinder

(b) Plate cylinder wrapped with plate

Figure 10.7. Diagram of printing plate and plate cylinder The plate is wrapped around the plate cylinder and held in place on the top and bottom with clamps.

around a press cylinder called the "plate cylinder." The lead edge and tail portions of the plate are covered by the clamps that hold the plate in place, so no image can be printed from these areas (figure 10.7b). The **gripper margin** is the area of the paper held by the mechanical fingers that pull the sheet through the printing unit (figure 10.7b). Since these fingers cover part of the paper, it is not possible to print an image in the gripper margin area.

The top of the uppermost image on the printed piece dictates how far down from the bottom of the gripper edge the film image is stripped onto the masking sheet. Information on this dimension should be included on the rough. The center line of the masking sheet is used to line up the center of the film image area so that it is exposed squarely in the center of the lithographic plate and consequently prints in the center of the press sheet. (There are instances when an image is to be printed off center on the final press sheet; but for these images, too, the center line of the masking sheet must be identified in order to correctly position the film.) Once these four areas are marked on the masking sheet, film can be stripped onto the sheet with confidence that the images will appear in the correct location on the printing plate and the final press sheet.

Masking sheets can be purchased with or without preprinted guidelines. Preprinted masking sheets are typically made in specific sizes for specific presses. For example, preprinted masking sheets can be purchased for an 11- × 17-inch offset duplicator. These numbers indicate that the press can print a page up to 11 inches wide and 17 inches long. The plate for such a press would be about 11 inches wide and slightly more than 17 inches long. The plate is longer than 17 inches to allow for space to clamp it to the plate cylinder.

The stripper's job is to create a flat by positioning the film on the masking sheet so that the plate will transfer images in the required locations on the final press sheet. Press adjustments to change image location are possible, but they are time consuming and costly. Press adjustments for image location are also limited. For example, it is difficult, if not impossible, for a press operator to salvage a plate that has an image above the cylinder line. Often an incorrectly stripped flat must be completely restripped, and a new plate made. This wastes both time and money. The problem becomes even more critical when several flats are used to expose images on the same plate (see "Multiflat Registration").

Preprinted masking sheets of the type mentioned above are generally made only for small duplicator presses (images up to 11 by 17 inches in size). Stripping for larger presses requires the use of unlined masking sheets. Whether or not the masking sheets have preprinted guidelines, the stripper's tasks remain the same: The cylinder line, center line, gripper margin, and top image must be identified, and the images must be stripped into their correct printing position (figure 10.8). Stripping for both lined and unlined masking sheets will be discussed. We will cover stripping procedures for lined masking sheets first.

Laying Out a Preprinted Masking Sheet

To begin our discussion, let's pick a simple one-color, single-flat stripping problem: a single image to be printed on 8½- × 11-inch paper on an 11- × 17-inch duplicator. For this example, we will be stripping a negative film image.

The stripper's first job is to select the correct masking sheet. If there is only one size of press in the shop, this presents no problem. However, if the shop has several different-sized presses, careful masking sheet selection becomes necessary. Our job requires

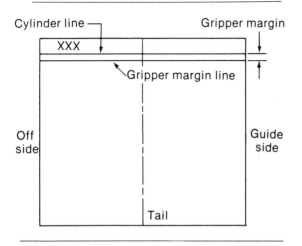

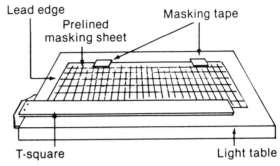

Figure 10.9. Placing the masking sheet on the light table Line the masking sheet up against the edge of a T-square and tape it on one side.

Figure 10.8. Marking blank masking sheets Many strippers lay out blank masking sheets using the specifications for a particular press. The cylinder line, gripper margin, and center line are carefully located. All layout is made from these three lines. Preprinted masking sheets are also used with these guidelines provided.

a preprinted masking sheet for an 11- × 17-inch duplicator. Often the masking sheet will carry the name of the press manufacturer and a symbol code or size marking to identify which press the masking sheet is designed for. If your shop does not have masking sheets with this information, a simple measurement will help you locate the correct sheet; or you can compare the sheet to a plate from the press on which the job is to be run. The masking sheet should be the same size as or slightly larger than the plate that will be used with it.

Place the masking sheet on a light table and line up one edge of the sheet with a T-square. Tape the sheet securely in two places on the edge opposite the T-square (figure 10.9). Masking tape can be used for this purpose.

Our masking sheet is prelined in a ¼-inch grid. This grid can be used as a rough

indicator of measurements on the sheet, but exacting measurements should always be carefully made with a ruler. Not only is the ¼-inch grid not perfectly accurate, but we taped the masking sheet in place based on the location of the edge of the sheet against our T-square, not the printed grid. There is no reason to assume that the grid printed on the masking sheet is parallel to the edge of the masking sheet. It may be close, but probably not perfectly parallel. Using the T-square and ruler for all image location ensures that the images will end up correctly positioned and straight on the sheet.

After the masking sheet is taped in place, look it over carefully. As shown in figure 10.8, the cylinder lines, gripper margin, and center line should be clearly identified. It is often a good idea to draw a line over the bottom of the gripper margin line and down the center line on the masking sheet. This will help you refer back to these locations as you lay out the sheet.

Now check the rough layout to determine top margin: the distance from the top of the paper to the top of the image on the printed piece (figure 10.10). A line representing the top of the image should be drawn across the masking sheet, below the bottom of the gripper margin; lines representing side and bottom margins should also be drawn (figure 10.11).

For this example, there will be only one film negative. Lay it emulsion-side down near the masking sheet on the light table. Examine the negative carefully. Corner marks that indicate image extremes or center lines (or both) should be recorded on the negative (figure 10.12). These marks will help you position the film negative in the proper location under the masking sheet.

Attaching Film Negatives

With rare exception, all printing plates are exposed with the emulsion side of the plate against the emulsion side of the film. Recall from Chapter 6 that negatives are right reading through the base. In other words, if the piece of film is placed on the light table so that the image can be read from left to right, the base side is up and the emulsion side is against the glass. If there is any question about which is the emulsion side of the film negative, the emulsion side can be identified in one of two ways: by comparing the finish or by scratching the film edge. If the film is folded over on itself, the emulsion side will be the duller of the two sides. Also, the emulsion side of the film can be scratched. A small pin scratch on the edge of the film outside the

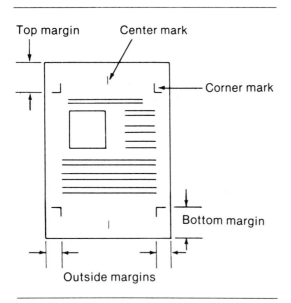

Figure 10.10. Rough layout with margins identified

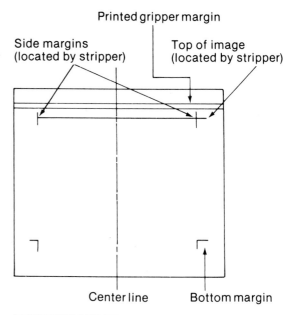

Figure 10.11. Diagram of a masking sheet
Lines representing the top, side, and bottom margins are first drawn on the masking sheet. The top image margin should always be below the gripper margin.

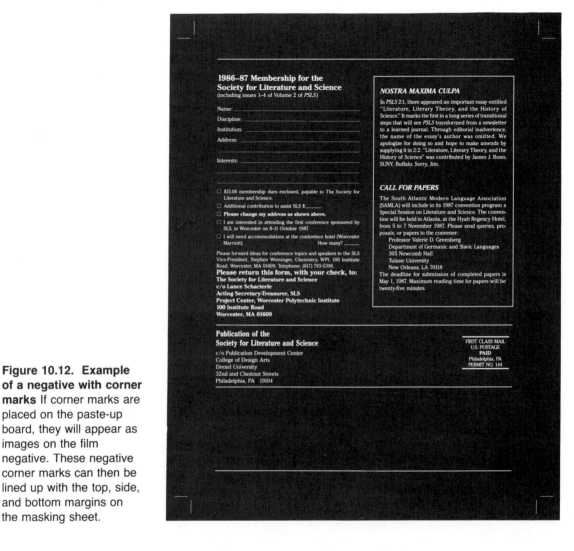

Figure 10.12. Example of a negative with corner marks If corner marks are placed on the paste-up board, they will appear as images on the film negative. These negative corner marks can then be lined up with the top, side, and bottom margins on the masking sheet.

image area will quickly determine which is the emulsion side of the film.

Begin by placing all negatives emulsion-side down on the masking sheet in their appropriate positions, with the images roughly falling in place with the image margins. Never allow pieces of film to overlap on the flat. If the overlap is near an image area, there may be some distortion as the plate exposure is made. With all negatives in place, mark where any pieces overlap. If possible, cut any over-lapping sheets to within ½ inch of any film image. If, because of imposition (image location on the final press sheet), the cut must be less than ½ inch from an image area, delay trimming the film until both pieces have been attached. That procedure will be discussed shortly. After trimming, the negatives should

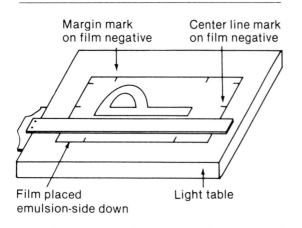

Margin mark on film negative

Center line mark on film negative

Film placed emulsion-side down

Light table

Figure 10.13. Positioning the negative on the light table

be removed and set aside until they are needed again.

Because the masking sheet is translucent, it is possible to see through the material to the glass surface below. With right-reading stripping, untape the masking sheet and set it aside or flip it back out of the way. Place the negative, emulsion-side down, on the light table. Accurately align the image margins or tick marks with a T-square and triangle, and tape the film in place (figure 10.13). Next, move the masking sheet over the film until the image lines are positioned with the image margins on the negative. It should be easy to see both marks line up as you look down through the flat. Use a T-square to ensure that the margins and type lines run parallel to the edge of the masking sheet. After the nega-

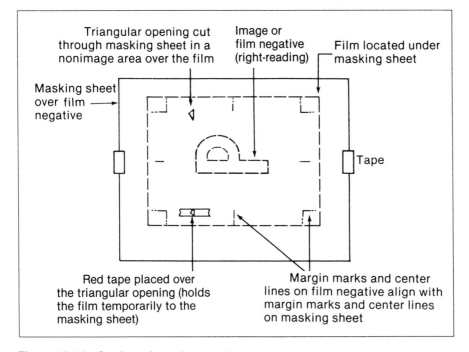

Triangular opening cut through masking sheet in a nonimage area over the film

Image or film negative (right-reading)

Film located under masking sheet

Masking sheet over film negative

Tape

Red tape placed over the triangular opening (holds the film temporarily to the masking sheet)

Margin marks and center lines on film negative align with margin marks and center lines on masking sheet

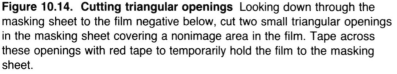

Figure 10.14. Cutting triangular openings Looking down through the masking sheet to the film negative below, cut two small triangular openings in the masking sheet covering a nonimage area in the film. Tape across these openings with red tape to temporarily hold the film to the masking sheet.

tives are in place, smooth the masking sheet down and cut two small triangular openings over the negative in the nonimage areas (figure 10.14). It is important that you cut only through the masking sheet and not into the film. Practice several times on a scrap sheet. Still holding the film in position under the masking sheet, place a small piece of red tape over each triangular opening and apply pressure. This will temporarily attach the negative to the flat (see figure 10.15). Continue the same procedure for all other negatives.

Before untaping the flat from the light table, again check all film images for position and squareness. Improper image placement at this stage will be reflected throughout the rest of the job.

After all negatives have been temporarily attached and checked for accuracy, release the flat from the light table and carefully turn

it over. Each negative should now be secured to the masking sheet at each corner with a small piece of cellophane tape (figure 10.15). Be sure to smooth each negative as the tape is applied to ensure that there are no buckles in the film. Once the film is securely taped in place, turn the masking sheet over again (lined side up) and recheck the image placement.

If two pieces of film overlap, it is necessary to cut the negatives so they will butt against each other. To do this without cutting into the masking sheet, insert a piece of scrap film or acetate beneath the overlapping portions and with a steel straightedge and a single-edged razor blade or frisket knife cut through both pieces of film (figure 10.16). Do not remove the straightedge until you are certain that you have cut completely through both sheets of film. Remove the loose pieces and the scrap of film and tape the negatives to the masking sheet. Tape the negatives on the nonimage edges only. Do not put tape over the image areas on a negative.

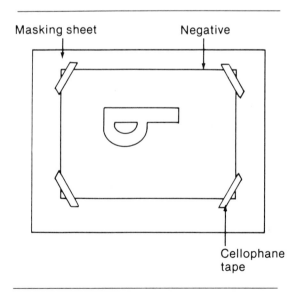

Figure 10.15. Taping the negative to the masking sheet Turn the masking sheet over and tape each corner of the film negative with cellophane tape. For larger films, tape the long edges at their centers.

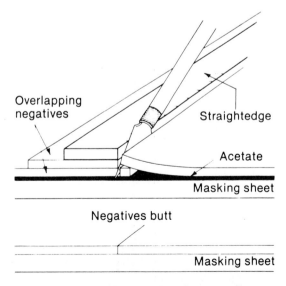

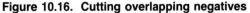

Figure 10.16. Cutting overlapping negatives

After all the negatives have been located and taped in place, turn the flat over again so that the film emulsion is against the light table and cut away the masking sheet in the image areas. Some strippers slide a piece of scrap plastic between the masking sheet and the film during this operation to ensure that only the masking sheet is cut. With practice and a sharp cutting tool (a single-edged razor blade or frisket knife), however, lack of a plastic insert should cause no problems. The masking material should be removed to within ⅜ of an inch of the image areas. The less open nonprinting area exposed, the better (figure 10.17).

Opaquing and Etching the Flat

Although theoretically the flat is now ready to be sent to the plating room, in actual practice there are usually small defects that must be corrected. The most common defect is **pin-**

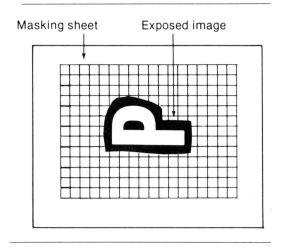

Figure 10.17. Exposing the image area The masking sheet is cut away to expose the image area of the film negative.

holes. These are small openings in the emulsion that pass light. They may be caused by dust on the copyboard when the camera exposure was made or by dirty original copy. Whatever the reason, any openings in the film will pass light to the printing plate and will ultimately appear as ink on the final press sheet. Pinholes are undesired images and, therefore, must be blocked out with **opaque.**

Most opaques are water based. Alcohol-turpentine-, or petroleum-based materials are also available. These opaquing materials dry more rapidly than water-based opaques. The opaque should be applied in as thin a coat as possible yet still block light through the negative. If properly mixed, water-based materials should dry on the film in 15 to 30 seconds. Although some printers opaque on the emulsion side of the film, the authors recommend opaquing only on the base side. The emulsion of any film is frail and cannot stand a great deal of manipulation. If opaque is mistakenly placed over a desired image on the base side of the film, the opaque can be washed off or scratched away with a razor blade without damaging the film emulsion. Such scratching on the emulsion side of the film would destroy the emulsion. Also, opaque on the emulsion side of the film will come into contact with the plate emulsion, thereby producing thick areas that could hold the film emulsion away from the plate emulsion during plate making and introduce image distortion (figure 10.18).

Novice strippers often have trouble deciding whether or not to opaque an area. As a rule of thumb, when someone standing over a light table looking straight down at an eye-to-flat distance of about 2 feet can see light through a pinhole, then the pinhole will probably pass enough light to expose the plate.

The fact that a film's emulsion is fragile can be used to advantage. There are frequent situations when detail needs to be added to

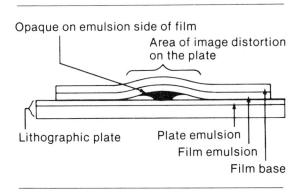

Figure 10.18. Opaque-caused image distortion
Opaque used on the emulsion side of the film can hold the film away from the plate emulsion during exposure and thereby distort the image.

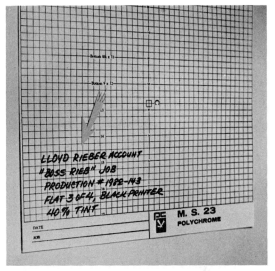

Figure 10.19. Identifying the film flat

a negative. Images can be created in the film emulsion by scraping away the emulsion with an etching tool.

The final step, after all opaquing and etching are complete and checked, is to label the flat. The platemaker typically handles many flats in a single day, so each must be identified. Place all information in the trailing edge of the masking sheet, out of the paper limits. The notations made depend on the individual shop, but such things as the name of the account, job title or production number, sequence of the flat, ink color, or any special instructions such as the inclusion of a screen tint are all commonly included (figure 10.19).

Attaching Film Positives

There are several advantages to stripping film positives instead of negatives. Because a positive has the image as a black emulsion on a clear film base, it is easier to position the film on the support sheet and to register additional pieces of the film to the first piece for multicolor work. It is also possible to work with many small pieces of film, which would be difficult with negatives and goldenrod masking sheets. Finally, a positive halftone produces a higher-quality printing plate and is easier to strip than a negative halftone. This is because a negative halftone, made with a vignetted contact screen, produces a ghost image around each dot. When a negative is contacted to a new piece of film to make a film positive, a well-defined hard dot is produced.

The initial layout of all guidelines is made on a piece of tracing paper instead of a goldenrod or yellow vinyl masking sheet. When complete, the tracing sheet is turned over and mounted on the light table with the T-square. A clear sheet of transparent base material is then taped in place over the reversed layout. The film positive will be placed on top of this support sheet. For low-quality jobs, a second sheet of tracing paper can be used. But a clear, stable plastic, such as vinyl, acetate, or a polyester-based material, is typically used. Notches are cut to indicate the plate limits to aid in placing the flat on the plate in the plate-making department.

All positives must be adhered emulsion-side up and in reverse on the support sheet so that all images will be exposed emulsion to emulsion in the platemaker. The emulsion of a positive is right-reading when produced by contact printing from a film negative. For that reason, it is necessary to laterally reverse the image during contacting so that the final stripped flat will be emulsion to emulsion with the plate during plate making. "Duplicating Film Materials" in Chapter 6 outlines the process in detail.

Trim each positive to within ⅜ inch of the image, position it on the support sheet in line with the margin marks, and tape it in place with clear cellophane or polyester tape. The tape should not extend over any image area. When the film is too small or is too close to another piece of film to allow for taping, rubber cement can be used to secure the positive to the support material. To do this, position the positive and then lift one corner. Place a small quantity of thin rubber cement on the base side of the film and press the corner back into position. Repeat the operation with each corner of the positive. Be sure to use the cement sparingly and avoid any contact with the film emulsion. As with negative stripping, individual pieces of film should not be overlapped.

Stripping Halftones

Several techniques for adding halftone images to printed materials were discussed in Chapter 4. One method suggested the inclusion of a red or black pressure-sensitive material on the paste-up that would reproduce on the film negative as a clear, open window.

A halftone negative could then be added to the window at a later phase in production. It is the stripper's responsibility to combine the halftone negative with the negative holding the window on the flat. This must be done in such a way that the halftone will appear in the proper position on the final printed sheet and the added piece of film that carries the halftone image will not interfere with the existing images on the negative that has the window.

To add a halftone negative to a window in a main negative, first prepare the masking sheet, add the main negative(s), and complete all cutting, opaquing, and etching. Then turn the flat over on the light table so that the film is emulsion-side up. Trim the halftone that is to be stripped into the window so that it is larger than the window opening and yet does not overlap any image detail near the window. Position the trimmed negative over the window emulsion-side up, in line with the rest of the image detail on the flat, and tape it in place with clear cellophane tape. The halftone must be mounted in this position because the emulsions of both the main negative and the halftone negative must be in contact with the printing plate when the plate exposure is made (figure 10.20).

Check to be sure that the halftone image completely fills the window. Any open area around the edges of the window will print as a solid line on the final reproduction.

When you are stripping positive flats, treat a halftone exactly as you would all other pieces of film. Cut it to size and secure it in place with clear tape or a thin layer of rubber cement.

It is often not possible to add a halftone negative to an existing flat without overlapping image detail and creating an area of image distortion. This happens when two halftones are to be butted together on the final printed sheet or the halftone window is po-

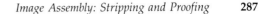

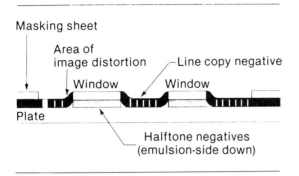

Figure 10.20. Positioning the negatives The emulsions of both the line copy and the halftone negatives must contact the emulsion of the printing plate.

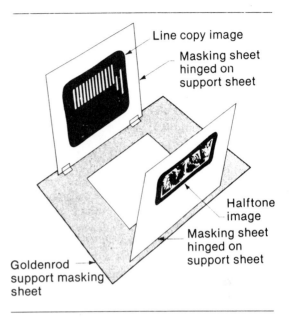

Figure 10.21. Complementary flats In this example of complementary flats, the two masking sheets are hinged on a larger support sheet.

sitioned too close to other image detail. In such cases, the stripper cannot work with the halftone on a single flat. The solution is to use two **complementary flats.** One flat carries the main printing detail; the second holds the halftone image (figure 10.21). If properly stripped, each flat can be exposed in succession in the platemaker in order to combine the two images in their proper positions on a single printing plate (figure 10.22). The section titled "Multiflat Registration" in this chapter is concerned with this problem of controlling the positions of film images that are mounted on more than one flat.

Laying Out Masking Sheets for Larger Presses

Masking sheets for offset presses larger than 11 by 17 inches are generally unlined. However, the stripper is still concerned with the four major areas on the sheet: the cylinder line, the gripper margin, the top of the image area, and the center line of the masking sheet. All images are positioned from these four dimensions.

The initial layout lines are located from specifications provided by the printing press manufacturer. Table 10.1 shows the specifications for the Harris LXG offset lithographic press. The following example will assume use of the Harris press, although the process is applicable to any printing process or press.

Begin by cutting the masking sheet equal to or slightly larger than the plate size. If you are doing positive stripping, cut a piece of tracing paper instead of goldenrod masking sheet. Tape the paper securely in place in the center of the light table; use a T-square to line up the top edge of the sheet accurately. Be sure that there are no buckles or loose portions that will cause inaccurate line rulings.

Mark the edge closest to you with three Xs to identify the lead or gripper edge of the plate. Label the off (left), tail (back), and guide

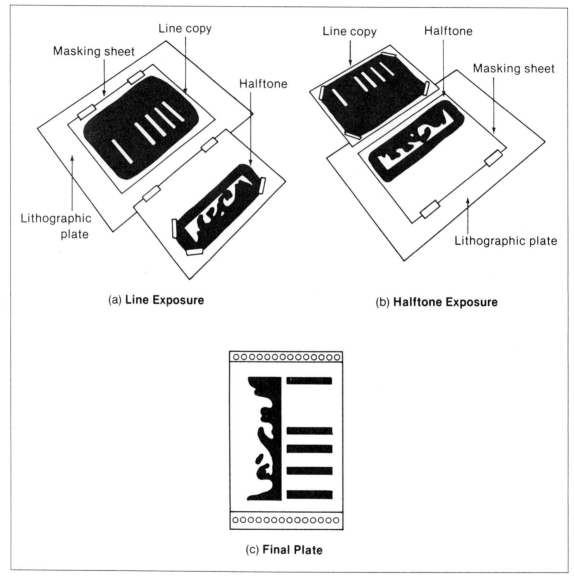

(a) **Line Exposure**

(b) **Halftone Exposure**

(c) **Final Plate**

Figure 10.22. Using complementary flats for double exposures The complementary flat uses one exposure to record the line copy (a) and one exposure to record the halftone (b). The final plate carries both images (c).

Table 10.1. Harris LXG Press Specifications

Maximum Printing Area	22⅝ × 30
Maximum Sheet Size	23 × 30
Minimum Sheet Size	9 × 12
Plate Size	27 × 30
Distance from Lead Edge of Plate to Cylinder Line	1¹³⁄₁₆
Gripper Margin	⁵⁄₁₆

(right) sides (figure 10.23). From the press specifications, measure from the lead edge of the sheet the position of the cylinder line, and prick the goldenrod with a needle or etching tool. Then draw a line through the point (figure 10.24). From the same specification list determine the amount of gripper margin (or bite); mark the distance from the cylinder line to the bottom of the gripper margin, and draw a second line parallel to the first (figure 10.25). The area between the cylinder and gripper line represents the gripper margin. The area varies in size from press to press, but the width is generally from ³⁄₁₆ to ⅜ of an inch. It is important to remember that the gripper margin represents nonprinting area and can carry

no printing image. The last initial layout line is a vertical line drawn in the center of the masking sheet (figure 10.26). All vertical measurements will be made from this center line, and all horizontal measurements will begin from the cylinder line. With this technique there is little chance of error in image placement.

From the center line, measure one-half the length of the plate in either direction, then cut notches as illustrated in figure 10.27. The lead edge of the masking sheet and these two notches will serve as guides when the flat is placed on the printing plate during the plate exposure.

The next concern is to define the press

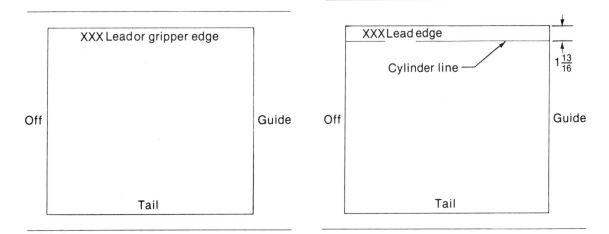

Figure 10.23. Goldenrod sheet with labeled edges

Figure 10.24. Goldenrod sheet with labeled cylinder line

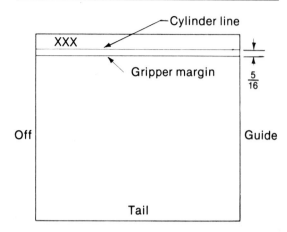

Figure 10.25. Goldenrod sheet with labeled gripper margin

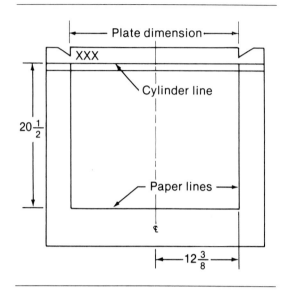

Figure 10.27. Goldenrod sheet with paper dimension added

sheet area. The work order should identify the paper size and the way in which the sheet is to be fed through the press. If a sheet is to be trimmed after printing and a choice is possible, lay out the masking sheet so that the lead or gripper edge of the paper will be

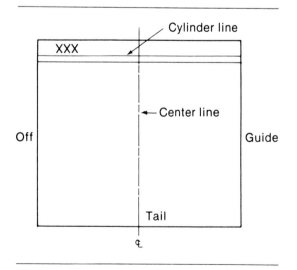

Figure 10.26. Goldenrod sheet with labeled vertical center line

trimmed. Position any register marks (for multicolor registration) or test scales in the trim area. Assume for this example that a 20½- × 24¾-inch sheet is to be fed through the Harris LXG. Measure 20½ inches from the cylinder line and 12⅜ inches on each side of the vertical center line, and draw the paper lines (figure 10.27). You must position all film images within this area, but do not extend them into the gripper margin.

With large sheet presses but small final printed sheet size, most companies gang several jobs on the same flat, with the intention of cutting the paper pile after printing. In large companies the ganging positions are decided by the planning section; in most small organizations the stripper makes all these decisions. Figure 10.28 illustrates the ganging of several sheets on a larger press sheet. Notice that identical jobs are identified by similar numbers and that image margins are defined by the use of corner ticks. Again, measuring

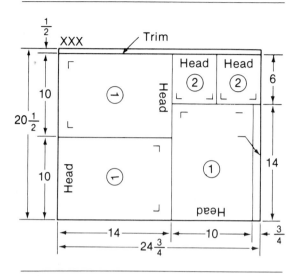

Figure 10.28. A press sheet layout

from the cylinder and vertical center line, the stripper places all final paper lines within the large press sheet paper lines and steps off the margin marks for each sheet (figure 10.29). After one check of all dimensions is made, the masking sheet is ready to receive the film negatives.

Most industrial stripping is done with the film negative emulsion-side up, facing the stripper. Begin by turning the masking sheet over on the light table. Accurately position the cylinder line with a T-square and tape the sheet in place. Check to be sure you can see the layout lines through the masking sheet (figure 10.30).

Position the first negative in the correct area, emulsion-side up, after checking the rough layout. Place the side margins and top image in line with the head and side guide-lines on the flat. Check with the T-square to ensure that the image is parallel to the cylinder line and then tape each corner of the negative with cellophane tape. Repeat the same procedure for the remaining negatives (figure 10.31).

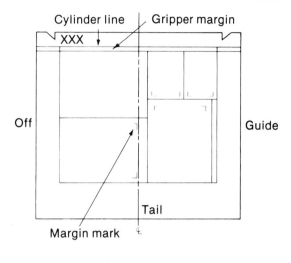

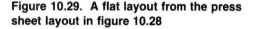

Figure 10.29. A flat layout from the press sheet layout in figure 10.28

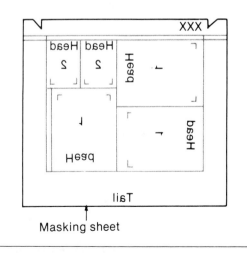

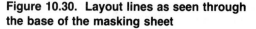

Figure 10.30. Layout lines as seen through the base of the masking sheet

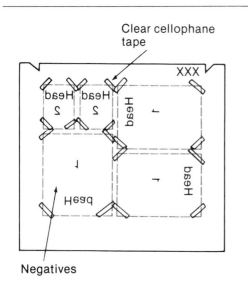

Clear cellophane tape

XXX

Negatives

Figure 10.31. Positioning negatives on the masking sheet Position negatives emulsion-side up in line with head and side guidelines. Secure the negatives with cellophane tape.

When all negatives have been attached and checked for accurate position, turn the flat over and cut windows through the masking sheet to expose the film image openings. Opaque and etch as necessary.

Multiflat Registration

The Purpose of Registration Systems

It is important to realize that almost all printing plates can typically be exposed from five or six different flats before the sum effect of light passing through the goldenrod or yellow vinyl masking sheets begins to expose the plate emulsion in nonimage areas.

The problem of multiflat exposures is that of registration. The stripper must place the separate film images on each flat and then control the placement of the images from each flat on a single plate. When the plate is proc-

essed, all images must appear in their proper printing positions in relation to each other and to the limits of the printing press. Some form of mechanical punch or guide is generally used to aid in the multiflat registration process. These techniques will be discussed shortly.

Many situations besides complementary halftone flats require the stripper to deal with the multiple flat process. Commonly the stripper must print two separate screen tint values in the same color with the use of the same plate. It is possible to place both images on a single negative and to use folding masks to make the plate exposure (figure 10.32). Two separate exposures would be made with a screen tint between the flat and the plate during each exposure. Only the desired areas

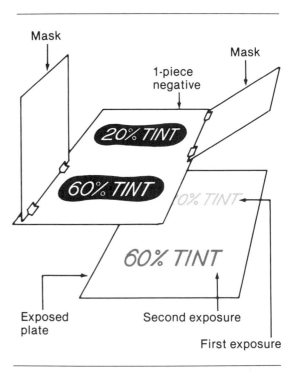

Mask

Mask

1-piece negative

20% TINT

60% TINT

0% TINT

60% TINT

Exposed plate

Second exposure

First exposure

Figure 10.32. Using folding masks to control multiple plate exposures

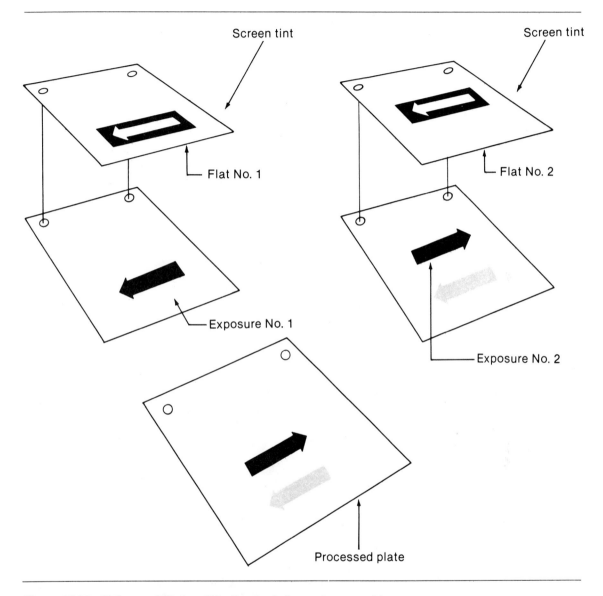

Screen tint

Screen tint

Flat No. 1

Flat No. 2

Exposure No. 1

Exposure No. 2

Processed plate

Figure 10.33. Using multiflat registration techniques to assemble different screen tints on the same plate

would be opened for each exposure, and the proper screen would be placed between the flat and the plate each time the plate was exposed. If the images are extremely close together, however, or if many different areas are spread over the entire flat, this technique is not usable. It is then necessary to place all images of common screen tint values or sizes on separate flats. With proper multiflat registration techniques, these images can be assembled on a single plate in the proper tint values, screen angle, and position (figure 10.33).

Surprints and reverses were introduced in Chapter 3 as a part of the design phase, but they are actually assembled by the stripper. Figure 10.34 illustrates the use of two flats with two separate exposures to produce a surprint over an image on a single plate. Figure 10.35 shows the registration of a positive image to create a reverse in an area during a single plate exposure. Multiple flats are often used to provide a mask or frame for a larger image (figure 10.36).

Certainly the largest application of multiflat registration techniques is in the area of process color reproduction. The four primary

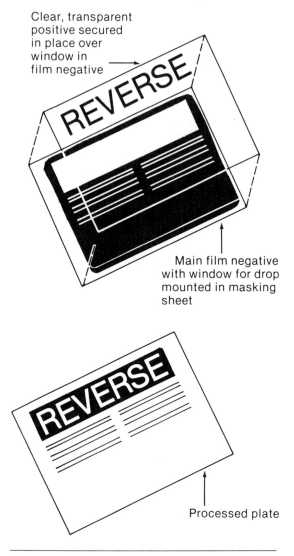

Figure 10.35. Film positive positioned over a window in a flat to create a reverse

flats, representing cyan, magenta, yellow, and black detail, must be stripped so that the plates, when placed on the printing press, can be adjusted to ''fit'' the four colors together on the printed sheet, duplicating the original as closely as possible.

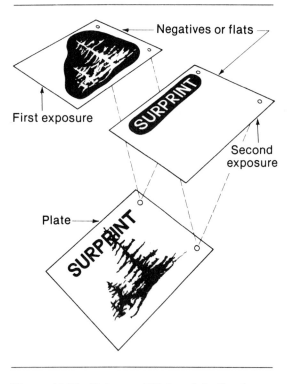

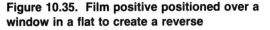

Figure 10.34. Using multiflat registration to place a surprint over another image

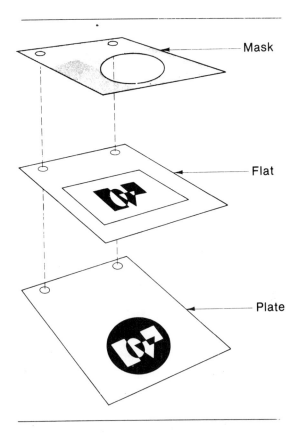

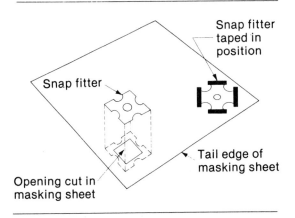

Figure 10.37. Using snap fitters on a masking sheet

Figure 10.36. Using multiple flat registration to create a mask or frame for a larger image
The mask is registered in place over the film positive. Only one exposure is made.

Basic Registration Methods

Several methods are used for multiflat registration. The ones discussed here include:

– The common edge method
– The snap fitter and dowel method
– The prepunched tab strip method
– The punch and register pin method

Common Edge Method. The simplest system is the **common edge** method. With this method the flat containing the greatest amount of de-

tail is first stripped by using ordinary layout and assembly procedures. This first flat is called the main or **master flat.** All remaining flats are aligned with it. The second negative (or set of negatives) is then placed in position over the completed master flat and attached to a second masking sheet. It is important that both flats have at least two edges (generally the top and right or gripper and guide sides) that line up perfectly. Any number of flats can be registered with this method as long as each image on each flat is registered to the master flat and the masking sheets have a minimum of two common edges. When the plates are exposed, the top and right edges of each flat are placed in line with the top and right edges of the plate.

Snap Fitter and Dowel Method. A second technique is the use of **snap fitters and dowels.** With this system the main or master flat is stripped as usual. At the tail edge of the masking sheet, well away from any image or paper limits, two openings are cut and plastic snap fitters are taped in place (figure 10.37). The flat is then positioned on the light table with a T-square, and soft adhesive-backed pins

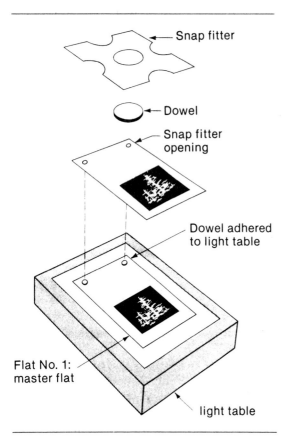

Figure 10.38. Positioning flat using snap fitters and dowels The snap fitter slides over the dowel and controls flat position.

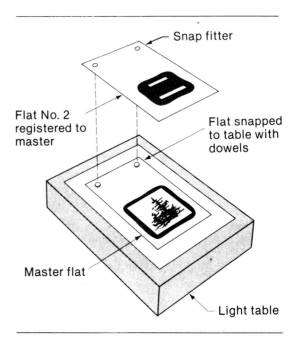

Figure 10.39. Registering additional flats

(dowels) are pressed through the fitter openings onto the glass table surface (figure 10.38). The flat can then be removed, but the dowels will remain in place on the light table. When the snap fitters are inserted over the pins a second time, the flat has been returned to exactly the same position. To register additional flats, new snap fitters are cut into separate masking sheets and are stripped so that image detail registers to the first master flat (figure 10.39).

Prepunched Tab Strip Method. A less expensive method for control of multiflat registration is the use of **prepunched tab strips.** Most companies that employ this technique save their scrap or discarded sheets of film material and cut them into tabs approximately 3 inches wide and as long as their masking sheets. Three holes are then punched into each tab with a special mechanical punching device (figure 10.40). Special register pins (generally, metal) are then taped to the light table so that the punched tabs fall perfectly in line with the pins (figure 10.41). After the master flat has been stripped, a punched tab is taped to the tail edge. All subsequent flats are stripped in register to the main flat while it is secured to the register pins. Tabs are added to the tail of each additional flat to hold it in register with the master.

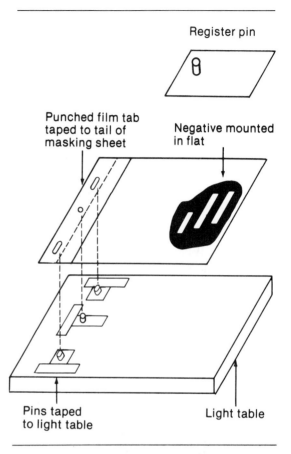

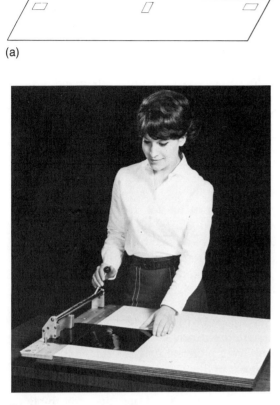

Figure 10.40. Example of a punched tab (a) and a mechanical tab (b)
Courtesy of Dainippon Screen Mfg. Co., Ltd., distributed by DS America, Inc.

Figure 10.41. Using register pins to secure a flat to a light table Register pins are taped in place on the light table in line with the holes in the punched film.

Punch and Register Pin Method. The most efficient approach for controlling registration is to apply the **punch and register pin** method from the camera to the press. With this method the camera operator uses a mechanical punch on each piece of film as well as register pins to hold it in position on the camera back. This is especially effective for process color separation work where the copy is not moved be-

tween exposures. Once the film is processed, the stripper works with opaquing and etching, and mounts the film on a punched masking sheet if necessary. When used as a total system approach, the printing plate is also punched to line up with the film or masking sheet holes before plate exposure, and register pins are placed on the printing press to receive a punched plate. If used throughout the process, the technique results in printed images that line up perfectly with few press adjustments. This significantly reduces costs in all areas.

Multiflat Stripping for Process Color Work

This section is primarily concerned with the specific techniques involved in stripping for four-color process printing. The general procedures are applicable to all other multiflat stripping, whether it is flat color, more than four colors (such as topographic mapping where five are used), or single color with the use of several flats to generate one plate.

It is generally accepted that registration for process color work is too critical to employ the common edge registration method. Some form of pin or dowel register system must be used. The most accurate method of positioning multiple flats is to use some type of master image stripped into a master flat as a guide for all subsequent images and flats. There are two basic approaches: blueline flats and single master flat.

Blueline Flat Method.   With the **blueline flat** system a special flat is prepared. This flat holds any detail needed to position all film images for the job and includes all necessary registration marks. Negatives are generally used to assemble the blueline flat. The blueline master flat is then exposed to a special light-sensitive solution that has been coated on a piece of clear plate glass or plastic. The processed emulsion produces a blue image that will not expose a printing plate if the clear base is used for positive stripping. If you are stripping negatives, you can use the blueline image as a guide to register all flats. For positives, prepare a laterally reversed blueline for each flat. Then take the master flat apart and strip all pieces of film with their appropriate color.

Single Master Flat Method.   The most common registration technique for color negative stripping is the use of a single master flat as a guide for all other flats in the job. For flat color, the master flat is generally the one that carries the greatest amount of detail. For four-color process work, the cyan, magenta, or black printer can be used, depending on which color carries the greatest detail. Four-color stripping with a master flat will be covered here.

Prepare the master flat by using common stripping techniques. After opaquing and etching, apply some type of pin register device and turn the flat over on the light table with the emulsion side of the film facing you. Apply the pin system to a second masking sheet and position it over the first flat. Then place the second set of negatives, emulsion-side up, in register with the first image.

Recall from Chapter 9 that register marks were placed with the original during the color separation process. Each piece of film carries duplicate halftone and register mark images for each of the four color printers. The register marks become your first guides. As you superimpose the second negative over the first, the register marks on each negative are lined up. With four-color reproductions made up of halftone images, the alignment tolerance is extremely critical. If you view register marks on any but a 90° angle, the thickness of the film might cause a distortion that will put the two images out of register. To eliminate the possibility of this type of error, some strippers use a sighting tube to view the register marks (figure 10.42).

After all register marks are in line, hold the negative in place with some weighted material (often a leather bag filled with lead pellets is used) and examine the detail registration in the halftones themselves. The register marks should always be ignored in preference to accurate image alignment on the different negatives.

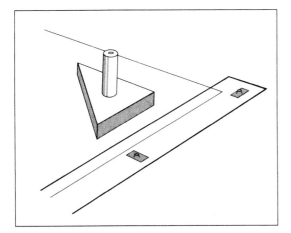

Figure 10.42. Example of a sighting tube

If the job is made up of only four flats to print as four different colors, all flats are individually registered to the master flat. If there are more than four flats to be reproduced with only four colors (such as when using two different screen tint percentages in the same color, or when line copy falls too close to a halftone image to include it on one flat), the sequence of flat registration is important. Examine each color grouping. For each color, the flat that contains the greatest amount of image detail becomes the key flat for that color. Register each key color flat to the master flat and register all other flats in the color group to the key (figure 10.43).

A method of color stripping that produces high accuracy is stripping with clear mylar. Accuracy is improved with mylar stripping for two reasons:

1. Clear mylar is easier to see through than orange masking sheets.
2. Mylar is very stable; thus, it is affected very little by changes in temperature or humidity.

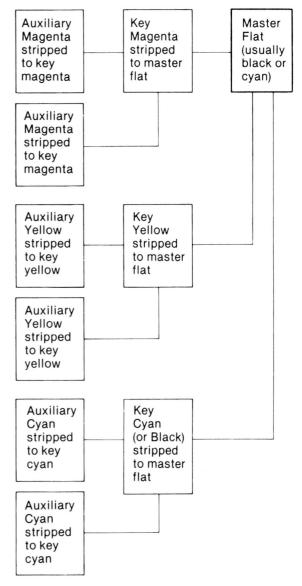

Figure 10.43. Example of a sequence of color flat registration for more than four flats A four-color reproduction may require more than four flats if two different screen tint percentages in the same color are specified or if line copy falls too close to a halftone image to include in one flat.

The use of clear mylar allows the stripper to work on top of the flat with the film pieces emulsion up. Each mylar flat is punched and registered to the key flat. Since the process films are stripped to a clear base, a mask must be made to block unwanted light in the nonimage areas during plate exposure. For example, a page of text that contained one four-color illustration would require a mask that would allow only the illustration to be exposed on the printing plate for the yellow, magenta, cyan, and black negative. Each of these images will be in the same location on each printing plate, so a single mask can be used for all exposures. This mask is sometimes called a **traveling mask** because it is placed over each flat for each color as the flat is exposed to the plate. After exposure, it "travels" to the next flat for exposure on the next plate. If the type on the page were to be printed in black, the plate for black ink would be exposed twice. The first exposure would be made with the traveling mask to produce the black printer for the four-color illustration. In the second exposure, a flat would be produced that blocked exposure in the illustration area but allowed the type to be exposed.

Automated Stripping

Stripping can be a time-consuming and expensive process, especially where complementary flats have to be assembled and masks have to be made for multiple-color work. **Automated stripping** can greatly speed up the stripping process.

The simplest automated stripping systems use a digitizing tablet to place information for mask cutting into a computer. With such systems, the operator places a layout of the job, or the actual job mechanical, on the tablet. The digitizing tablet consists of a surface under which there is an "electronic grid." The operator activates an electronic pointer to record image positions into computer memory. If a rectangular mask for a halftone window is needed, for example, the operator points the pointer at two opposite corners of the rectangle. The computer can then define the actual size of the rectangle and send this information to an automatic mask cutter. The mask cutter will cut the window into peelable masking film. Because masks are cut automatically, based on digitized information, they can be cut extremely accurately. In addition, difficult-to-cut geometric shapes, such as circles and ellipses, can be made with ease. With most systems, the pointer can be also used to produce irregular mask shapes.

Advanced automated stripping systems utilize graphic workstations that are linked with a color scanner and a composition system. These systems can produce composite film negatives of text and graphics, as well as masks. Most true graphics workstations are designed so that the operator can take images from a variety of sources—type from the composition system, continuous-tone color from the color scanner, and line art from a graphics scanner—and make them up into pages. Such systems use a CRT screen through which the operator can check image placement and registration during page make-up. These systems can output made-up page negatives with the text and graphics and all register marks in place. Where more than one color is required, these systems will provide separate negatives for each color. The negatives will all be in exact register because they are generated electronically.

Automated stripping systems are expensive; however, they do greatly decrease the amount of time needed to strip a complex job. In addition, once they contain the information for the job, alterations can be made without returning to the stripping table. The information in computer memory need only be changed to meet the alteration, and a new set of negatives is produced. Rapid turn-around time during stripping is important, particularly when corrections have to be made to a job that is on press. Much money can be saved if the press does not have to sit idle while the job is restripped.

Proofing Transparent Materials

The Purpose of Proofing

After the job has been stripped and checked, it is ready to be converted to some form of plate or image carrier. Generally, however, another step, proofing each flat, occurs before plate making. It is difficult to interpret the image on the flat. Both printers and printing customers are distracted by such things as the masking sheet, tape, opaque, notations, or instruction marks. Moreover, the image on the flat is often a negative. It is also not possible to fold a flat to check for accuracy of image position for a work-and-turn or a signature job. The function of proofing is to check for image location and quality, and to obtain the customer's final approval to run the job. There are basically two ways to proof transparent materials: by using press proofs and by using photomechanical proofs.

Press proofs are made using the same types of ink and paper that are to be used on the final job. Press proofing has the disadvantage of high cost. The costs of press time (set-up, make-ready, actual running time, and clean-up) and materials involved in press proofing must be borne by the customer. Therefore, press proofing is reserved for extremely high-quality, long-run jobs. However, with press proofing the customer can see how the final job will actually look (including the final colors).

Photomechanical proofs, on the other hand, require no large investment in special proofing equipment and generally use existing plate-making equipment (see Chapter 11). Most photomechanical proofing systems use a light-sensitive emulsion coated on some inexpensive carrier, such as paper or plastic, which is then exposed through the flat in the same way the plates will be exposed. The emulsion is then chemically processed to produce an image that represents the final press sheet. Contrary to what many proofing manufacturers claim, no photomechanical proof will match the quality and color of a press proof. However, the low cost of photomechanical proofs vastly outweighs this disadvantage. Photomechanical proofs are generally classified as either single color or multiple color.

Single-Color Photomechanical Proofing

Single-color photomechanical proofing is the least expensive of all proofing systems. Most methods use a vacuum frame to hold the flat in contact with a light-sensitive coating on a sheet of paper and a light source to expose the emulsion. This equipment is discussed in detail in the following section. Single-color proofs do not show the actual ink color of the final press run. They are used only to check on such things as imposition, masking and opaquing, and image position. Four common types of materials used for single-color proofs are blueprint paper, brownlines, diazo, and instant image proof papers.

Blueprint paper is a low-cost material that produces positive images from transparent film negatives. The paper is coated with an organic iron compound (potassium ferricyanide) that changes structure when light strikes it. The proof is developed in water and dried by hanging it in the air. Unfortunately, blueprint paper is not dimensionally stable (which means that it can easily change size) and the image recorded on the blueprint tends to lighten with age.

Brownlines are formed on papers coated with a silver salt compound similar in structure to that used on photographic films. Brownlines form an image that becomes more intense the longer the exposure to the development chemicals. The proof is developed in water, fixed in hypo, washed in water to remove the fixer, and air dried. Although the image formed on a brownline is permanent, the paper is not dimensionally stable.

Diazo papers produce a positive image when exposed to transparent film positives. The exposed emulsion is developed when placed in contact with a special liquid or gas (generally ammonia fumes). The material has the advantage of relative dimensional stability because the paper is not moistened with water during development.

Instant image proof papers produce dry image proofs without the aid of processing equipment and chemicals. One example is DuPont's Dylux materials, which are exposed with ultraviolet light and produce a visible image without chemical processing. The proof can be fixed, or deactivated, after exposure by placing the proof under a bright white light. Dylux papers are available coated on one or two sides, with either a blue or near-black image. The material can be handled under normal room light for several minutes. Typical exposure light sources are Sylvania BLB lamps, pulsed xenon with an ultraviolet filter, mercury vapor with a UV filter, or carbon arc with a UV filter. Different colors can be proofed for fit by using different screen tint values to represent each color.

Blueprints, brownlines, diazos, and instant image proofs can all be used to check imposition for jobs that involve image alignment on both sides of a press sheet. Most papers can be purchased from the manufacturer with both sides sensitized. The first flat to be proofed is positioned on the paper, small notches that line up with the center lines of the flat are cut—or the proofing material is punched with the same punch system used for flats—and an exposure is made. The proofing paper is turned over, the center lines of the second flat are placed in line with the small notches, and the second exposure is made. When processed, the proof can be folded or cut to approximate the final job. If paper that is sensitized on both sides is not available, two separate sheets can be glued together for the same effect.

Multiple-Color Photomechanical Proofing

It is possible to proof some types of multicolor jobs, such as jobs requiring flat color (Chapter 3), on a single-color photomechanical proofing material. Brownlines are often used for this purpose. Color variations on a brownline can be shown by varying the exposure time for each color. The intensity of the image recorded on a brownline varies with exposure time. Thus, if each color is exposed with a different exposure time, each color will be recorded as a different shade on the brownline. Similar effects can be achieved by using various screen tint values to expose each individual color on a single-color proofing material. Both of these techniques for showing color are acceptable for checking registration and the fit of one image with another.

While registration and fit are important concerns from the printer's point of view, the designer or customer is primarily interested in what the job will look like after printing. Thus the typical use for multicolor proofing is to proof the job in color so the printer and customer can predict how the colors—whether flat or process colors—will appear on the final press sheet. Therefore, the proofing system's ability to produce an image as close as possible to the image that will be printed on the final press sheet is important. A press proof can provide a nearly exact duplicate of the image that will be printed during the actual press run. Photomechanical color proofs cannot make this claim because they are rarely made from the actual paper that will be used in the press run, and because they use colored emulsions or colored toners, rather than process inks, to produce colors. Photomechanical color proofing materials can be grouped as either transparent or opaque based.

Transparent color proofs. These proofs are generally formed from separate sheets of clear-based plastic (each carrying one color image) that are positioned over each other so that the total effect approximates the printed job. Many companies produce these materials. A commonly used product is Color-Key, manufactured by the 3M Company. Color-Key sheets are available as negative or positive acting. They produce transparent colors on a clear polyester backing. The sheets are exposed to a high-intensity light source with the emulsion of the negative or positive being proofed against the base side of the proofing sheet. The image is processed with a special 3M Color-Key developer, rinsed in water, and allowed to air dry (figure 10.44). When used for proofing four-color process negatives, the exposed and developed sheets are sandwiched yellow first, then magenta, cyan, and black

last. Each sheet is placed in register with the previous sheet and is fastened on one side to hold all the sheets in register. One advantage of transparent proofs is that the potential press sheet can be placed under the transparent sandwich of colors to obtain an approximation of the appearance of the final job. One disadvantage of this type of proofing system is that the proof takes on a color cast from the polyester backing.

Opaque color proofs. This type of proof is prepared by adhering, exposing, and developing each successive color emulsion on a special solid-based sheet. A typical product is Cromalin by the DuPont Corporation. The Cromalin system uses a patented laminator to apply a special photopolymer to the proof stock. The laminated sheet is then exposed through a film positive by using a conventional plate-making system. After exposure, the top mylar protective layer is removed and the entire sheet is dusted with a color toner, which only the exposed areas accept. The dry toners are available in a wide variety of colors and usually can be mixed to match any press ink color. After all surplus toner powder has been removed, the proof sheet can be relaminated and exposed to additional flats to produce other color images on the same sheet.

It is important that all color proofs be viewed under a common light source. Any variation in color temperature, light intensity, amount of reflected room light, evenness of illumination, or surrounding color environment will change human judgment concerning color values. Many problems result when the printer and the customer use two different light sources or viewing situations to view color proofs. The industry has generally accepted 5,000K color temperature emitted from an artificial source as the standard for color viewing. Several companies have developed

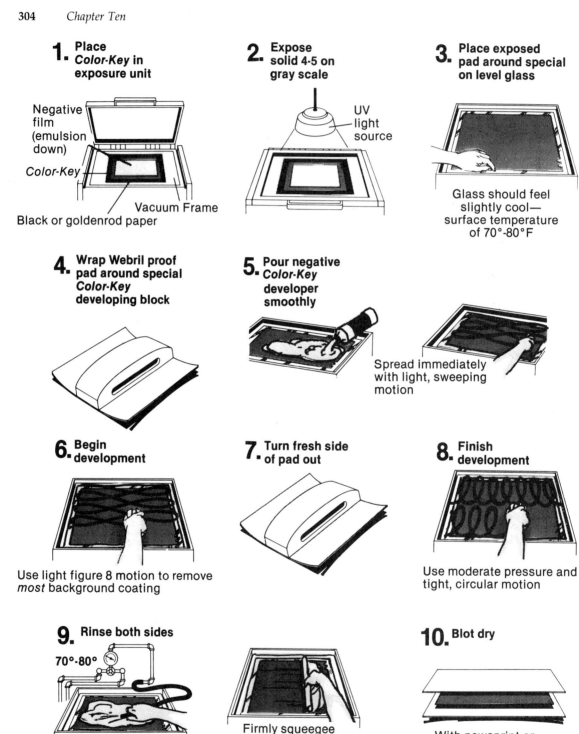

1. Place *Color-Key* in exposure unit

Negative film (emulsion down)

Color-Key

Black or goldenrod paper

Vacuum Frame

2. Expose solid 4-5 on gray scale

UV light source

3. Place exposed pad around special on level glass

Glass should feel slightly cool— surface temperature of 70°-80°F

4. Wrap Webril proof pad around special *Color-Key* developing block

5. Pour negative *Color-Key* developer smoothly

Spread immediately with light, sweeping motion

6. Begin development

Use light figure 8 motion to remove *most* background coating

7. Turn fresh side of pad out

8. Finish development

Use moderate pressure and tight, circular motion

9. Rinse both sides

70°-80°

Firmly squeegee uncoated side

10. Blot dry

With newsprint or other absorbent paper

Figure 10.44. Processing steps 3M Color-Key negative material
Courtesy of Printing Products Division, 3M Company

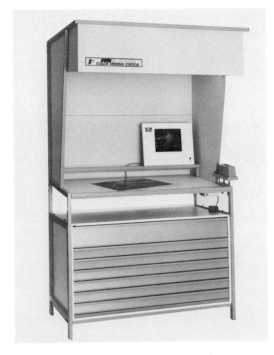

Figure 10.45. Example of a color viewer
Courtesy of GTI Graphic Technology, Inc.

viewing systems that meet the industry's specifications (figure 10.45).

Digital Proofing

Digital proofing is a relatively new development in color proofing that promises to overcome some of the limitations of transparent and opaque color proofs. With **digital proofing,** digitized color separations are electronically sent from a color scanner or a graphics workstation to a proofing mechanism that makes a color proof directly from the digitized information (figure 10.46). The device operates by recording the digitized image as electronic charges on an image carrier, typically a chrome drum. The charged areas of the drum then cause a liquid color solution to be transferred to a sheet of paper.

Digitized proofing can provide process color proofs, for four-color process printing, that are remarkably similar in color to those that will be produced during the actual press run. They have several advantages over transparent or opaque proofing materials. The liquid color solution can be formulated to duplicate process colors produced by press inks, and the sheet of the paper that the job is proofed on can be the same stock that will be used in the final press run. Thus, color fidelity is quite high; that is, the colors on the proof are "true" to the colors that will be produced on the press. In addition, because digital proofing requires no camera work, the process is faster than any photomechanical proofing process when several proofs have to be made. Digital proofing systems are quite expensive; thus they are suitable only for high-production applications.

Figure 10.46. Digital color proofing This digital color proofing system can produce up to four 30″ × 40″ proofs an hour.
Courtesy of Eastman Kodak Company, Graphic Imaging Systems Division

Key Terms

stripping
flat
proofing
cylinder line
pinholes

complementary flats
master flat
snap fitters and dowels
photomechanical proofs
blueline flat

brownline
diazo
transparent color proof
opaque color proofs
digital proofing

Questions for Review

1. What is the task of the industrial stripper?

2. What is the purpose of the masking sheet when preparing a negative flat?

3. What does the term "imposition" mean?

4. What is a signature?

5. What does the cylinder line represent on a flat?

6. Why can no printing image be placed in the gripper margin?

7. What is the purpose of opaquing a film negative?

8. What is the purpose of etching a film negative?

9. What are some advantages to stripping film positives rather than film negatives?

10. Why must a halftone negative be mounted in a window on the flat so that the halftone emulsion is facing in the same direction as the emulsion on the negative that carries the window?

11. What are complementary flats?

12. Briefly describe the approach of using the punch and register pin technique from the camera to the press in order to control registration.

13. What are the two basic approaches of multiflat stripping for process color work?

14. Describe the difference between a key flat and a master flat for multiflat stripping for process color work.

15. What is the purpose of proofing?

16. What are the three common types of single-color, photomechanical proofing?

17. What are the two basic groups of multicolor photomechanical proofs?

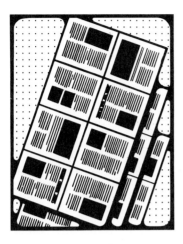

Chapter Eleven

Offset Plate Making

Anecdote to Chapter Eleven

In 1789 a law student at the University of Ingolstadt in Bavaria, Germany, wrote a play entitled *Die Maedchenkenner* and had it published. After all printing costs were subtracted, he made a sizable profit and was convinced his fortune was to be made on the stage. Alois Senefelder is little known to us today as a playwright, but he is recognized as the inventor of lithography.

After *Die Maedchenkenner,* Senefelder's plays were not well received, and he lost money on them. He was convinced, though, that it was not the quality of his writing but rather the high cost of the printing that caused his financial strain. After viewing printers at work one day, he decided printing was a simple task and resolved to learn the craft so he might write, print, and publish his own works. The common printing process where he lived was copperplate engraving. The images to be printed were carved in reverse into soft copper plates with a flexible steel tool.

Senefelder purchased the necessary tools and materials and began to learn the printer's craft. He soon learned that it was not as simple as he had assumed. He made many errors on the copper and finally had to invent a correction fluid (made from three parts wax and one part soap, mixed with a small quantity of lampblack, all dissolved in rain water) to use to correct his mistakes.

Unfortunately, even with the correction fluid, Alois's skills and finances were so small that he could not afford to continue practicing on actual copper plates. He tried tin as a substitute, but his resources dwindled with even that inexpensive material.

By chance he learned of a material called Kellhein stone—a limestone quarried at a local site. The stone had the unique quality that slabs of nearly any thickness could be easily cut. Kellhein stone, in comparison to copper, could be polished to a perfect surface with little effort. He resolved to practice writing in reverse

Alois Senefelder
Courtesy of Smithsonian Institution, Photo No. 10577A

on the stone to develop the skill necessary to be able to return to copper. With the stage set for a discovery, Senefelder relates in his book:

> I had just succeeded in my little laboratory in polishing a stone plate, which I intended to cover with etching ground, in order to continue my exercises in writing backwards, when my mother entered the room, and desired me to write her a bill for the washerwoman, who was waiting for the linen; I happened not to have even the smallest slip of paper at hand,

as my little stock of paper had been entirely exhausted by taking proof impressions from the stones; nor was there even a drop of ink in the inkstand. As the matter would not admit of delay, and we had nobody in the house to send for a supply of the deficient materials, I resolved to write the list with my ink prepared with wax, soap and lampblack, on the stone which I had just polished, and from which I could copy it at leisure.*

The result of that experience was an idea. Making a border of wax around the stone, Alois allowed an acid solution to stand on the entire stone surface for a short period of time and thereby etch away the limestone in any areas on which he had not drawn an image. The wax writing solution resisted the acid. After he removed the acid, he found that the coated, or image, areas were raised about 1/10 inch above the rest of the stone. By carefully rolling ink over the surface, he could ink only the image and easily transfer this ink to a sheet of paper with a little pressure.

Senefelder had invented an adaptation of the relief process—printing from a raised surface. Because of the low cost of stone, the ease of creating an image, and the simplicity of transferring the image to paper, he felt he could easily compete with local printers for jobs. He contracted with several people, notably music sellers, to produce musical scores, and he continued to experiment with his invention.

Senefelder called his invention "lithography," based on the Greek words *lithos,* meaning stone, and *graphein,* meaning to write. Although his discovery was a significant ad-

*Alois Senefelder, *A Complete Course of Lithography,* reprint of 1819 edition (New York: DaCapo Press, 1968), p. 9.

vance beyond copperplate engraving or even hand-set relief type, his greatest contribution was the refinement of what he called "chemical lithography."

After several years of experimentation, he observed that a solution of gum (gum arabic) and water, when coated over the stone, would clog the pores in the stone and would repel ink. As long as the gum-water mixture remained moist, an ink brayer rolled over the entire stone surface would deposit pigment only in the image area on the stone. By alternately moistening and inking the stone, he could build up a layer of pigment sufficient to transfer a perfect image to a sheet of paper.

It is this concept of moisture and ink repelling each other that is the basis for all contemporary lithographic printing.

Objectives for Chapter Eleven

After completing this chapter you will be able to:

- Describe the basic components of a plate-maker.
- Explain what is meant by actinic light and tell why platemakers produce this type of light.
- Explain how a sensitivity guide can be used to calibrate a platemaker.
- Describe the characteristics of an offset printing plate.
- Define the term *grain*.
- Explain how offset plates are grained.
- Explain the basic components of light sensitive coating for offset plates.
- List and describe three major classifications of lithographic plates.
- Explain the difference between negative acting and positive acting plates.
- List various methods of imaging a direct image nonphotographic plate.
- Explain the process of preparing a wipe-on lithographic plate.
- List and describe two types of presensitized surface plates.
- List the steps involved in processing an additive lithographic plate.
- List the steps involved in processing a subtractive lithographic plate.
- State the advantages of a photopolymer surface plate.
- Describe the construction of a deep-etch and a bimetal plate.
- Explain how a diffusion transfer lithographic plate is exposed and processed.
- Discuss the basic procedure involved in making an electrostatic lithographic plate.
- Discuss the processes used to make projection plates, and the high production applications for this type of platemaking.
- Describe the operation of a laser plate exposure system.
- Explain the operation of a step-and-repeat plate-making system.

Introduction

The preparation and printing of most modern metal plates used in lithographic printing is based on the original concepts of stone printing developed by Alois Senefelder nearly two hundred years ago. Senefelder's invention was intended and used as an industrial process. Printers used this technique to reproduce images such as advertisements, business forms, maps, and many other printed products.

Lithography developed a reputation as a fine arts process in America through the products of the Currier and Ives Company that operated from 1835 to 1895. Today, stone lithography remains an art process; historically it has formed the foundation for a major portion of the commercial printing industry. A brief review of the steps taken by a stone lithographer will help you understand all industrial approaches.

A slab of lithographic stone (generally, limestone) is first cleaned and ground to a perfectly flat surface with a smaller stone and water mixed with carborundum. This process is called "graining." Once the stone is grained and dry, the artist-printer begins to draw on the surface with a lithographic grease crayon (a refinement of Senefelder's original correction fluid). This forms the printing image. The grease is absorbed into the pores of the stone. A gum arabic solution (generally mixed with a small quantity of nitric acid), called an etch, is then worked into the entire stone surface. The gum is absorbed into the nonimage areas and solidifies the grease, or image, areas. Etching seals the open parts of the stone against grease but keeps them receptive to water. After the residue crayon is removed with turpentine, the stone is ready to print.

A roller of ink is prepared and a layer of water is wiped on the stone with a damp cloth. The water is repelled by the grease cra-

yon image, but it remains in the nonimage areas. As the ink roller moves over the stone, the film of water acts as a buffer that repels ink. Wherever there is no water (as on the crayon image), the ink remains.

If a prepared piece of paper is carefully positioned over the stone and pressure is applied, the image will be transferred to the sheet. A skillful stone lithographer can prepare a stone and pull one print every ten minutes.

Equipment for Proofing and Plating

Exposure Systems

Most proofing materials and most offset plates contain photoemulsion surfaces, which are exposed to light to form an image. During plate making, light passing through a transparent image carrier, such as a film negative or film positive, strikes the plate or proofing material emulsion. The areas effected by the light become the image or the nonimage areas, depending upon the type of photoemulsion used on the proofing or plate material. Most proofing materials and offset plates can be exposed in the same type of exposure unit.

Whether they are used for plate making, proofing, or daylight-handling film exposures, most exposure systems are referred to as **platemakers.** The simplest sort of exposure system is made up of a vacuum frame and some high-intensity light source. Some platemakers have the vacuum frame and light source set within a cabinet (figure 11.1). Other designs have the frame and lights on rolling stands that can be moved closer or farther

Figure 11.1. A fliptop platemaker
Courtesy of nuArc Company, Inc.

apart, or use an overhead light source. The vacuum frame holds the film or flat in contact with the proofing material, film, or plate; the light source provides the light needed for exposure.

Most proofing and plate photoemulsions have peak sensitivity in the blue and ultraviolet end of the visible spectrum, and little sensitivity in the remaining areas of the spectrum (see "Light Sources," Appendix A). Light in the blue and ultraviolet end of the visible spectrum is referred to as **actinic** light. Because most proofing, daylight film, and plate photoemulsions are primarily sensitive to actinic light, they can be handled in room light, or in room light filtered through yellow filter material, which blocks actinic light.

The most efficient light sources for exposing proofing materials and offset plates produce light that is high in the actinic end of the spectrum. The two most commonly used light sources for plate making are metal halide and pulsed xenon. Carbon arc lamps are sometimes used; however, the emission of fumes and dirt, which must be removed from the plateroom with a ventilation system, is a major disadvantage with carbon arc lamps.

Processing Systems

The equipment for processing printing plates varies. The simplest type is merely a smooth, slanted hard surface set in a sink with a water source (figure 11.2). This type, called a **plate-making sink,** is generally used for hand processing lithographic plates, but it can also be used for developing several types of photomechanical proofs. Also available are several

Figure 11.2. A plate-making sink
Courtesy of nuArc Company, Inc.

types of automatic processing units that produce plates ready for press without any hand finishing. A variety of special purpose plate-makers and processing units are designed to be used with a specific process (such as an electrostatic platemaker for the electrostatic plate-making process).

Light Source Calibration

The control of exposure is the most important variable in the plating and proofing processes. The simplest form of platemaker control has a toggle switch that can be plugged into an automatic timer or manually controlled by an operator with a watch. The problem (as with line photography) is that accurate exposure is not necessarily related to time. Such variables as line voltage variation, the position of the light source, and the age of the lamp can all influence exposure. The most accurate technique for exposure control is a light integrator (figure 11.3). With a phototube sensing unit mounted on the platemaker vacuum frame, the integrator automatically controls the units of light reaching the plate or proof and alters exposure time with any line or light source variation. Such a system ensures that there will be no more than a 0.5% difference in the amount of light that strikes the plate from any two exposures made at the same time setting.

Whether you are using a simple toggle switch or an integrated system, the initial problem is to determine the quantity of exposure needed to produce a quality plate or proof image. Most plate or proofing material manufacturers will provide recommended exposures for general lighting situations. However, the actual exposure will differ for each working situation. To calibrate or to determine this actual exposure, you must use a transparent **sensitivity guide.**

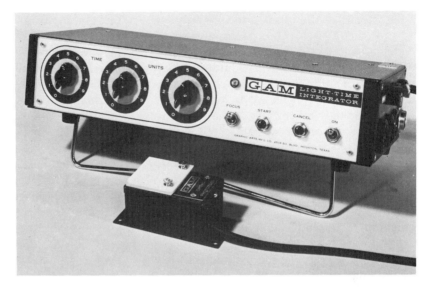

Figure 11.3. A light-time integrator
Courtesy of Graphic Arts
Manufacturing Co.

The sensitivity guide is a continuous-tone density scale (in effect, a transparent gray scale). The density of each step increases from step 1 (around 0.0 density) to the last step (generally around 3.0 density). There is generally a 0.15 density difference between steps. The scale passes progressively less light to the plate or proof as the step number becomes larger.

In addition to a suggested exposure, plate or proofing material manufacturers will also indicate a specific step reading that the exposure should record on the sensitivity guide.

To determine the actual exposure for a specific working situation, place a test sheet of the plate or proofing material in the platemaker, emulsion positioned as specified by the manufacturer. Place a transparent gray scale over the sheet with the right-reading side of the gray scale facing the exposure lamp. Mask all other areas of the emulsion with a masking sheet. Make an initial exposure by using the manufacturer's recommendations. Then process the material with appropriate

procedures and controls. If the resulting image shows a step reading less than required, increase the exposure. If a higher step is recorded, decrease the exposure and run another test. Continue this trial-and-error technique until the desired step is reached. The exposure that produces the desired step density becomes the actual exposure for that specific material.

For greatest consistency of results, a sensitivity guide should be stripped into the flat in a nonimage area for every plate. If variation occurs, each processing step should be reexamined for any variation, or the entire system should be recalibrated.

Lithographic Printing Plates

The basis of all industrial lithography today is a combination of photography and Senefelder's original observation that oil and water do not mix. Almost all modern lithographic presses employ the offset principle and use as an image carrier a thin paper, plastic, or metal sheet, called a **plate,** that can be wrapped around the plate cylinder. When prepared for printing, the plate surface consists of two areas: image areas, which repel water (thus they remain dry and accept ink) and nonimage areas, which accept water. Therefore, the basic requirement of almost all lithographic printing plates is the ability to produce a plate surface which will have image areas that are "hydrophobic"; that is, they repel water. The nonimage areas of the plate must be "hydrophilic"; that is, they must accept water. A large amount of the differences between offset plates is the method they use to separate the image from the nonimage areas.

Base Plate Materials

The great majority of plates used in offset lithography are made of thin sheets of metal. Metal plate thicknesses range from 0.005 inches to around 0.030 inches, depending on the size of the plate and the type of press. The entire plate must be of uniform thickness. It is generally held to a gauge tolerance of ± 0.0005 inches. Most metals for plates are cold-rolled to the final plate gauge or thickness to produce a hard printing surface.

Zinc was the standard plate material of the industry for years, but it has been almost totally replaced by aluminum for all but special purpose plates. Some types of plates are made from such materials as steel, stainless steel, chromium, copper, and even paper, but aluminum enjoys the most widespread use.

Just as Senefelder had to prepare, or **grain,** the stone surface before an image could be added to it, modern lithographic plates must also be grained. On metal surface printing plates, this is a roughening process that

must be performed so that a uniform layer of photoemulsion will adhere to the plate. All graining processes can be classified as either mechanical or chemical.

Mechanical Graining.   The simplest form of mechanical graining is accomplished by placing the plate in a rotating tub filled with steel ball bearings, water, and some form of abrasive material. Assembly-line techniques have been applied to the process so that a continuous row of plates passes under a series of nylon brushes with a spray of water and pumice. Sandblasting has also been used, but this procedure presents some problems because small pieces of abrasive become embedded in the metal plate surface.

Chemical Graining.   Chemical graining of lithographic plates is similar in operation to Senefelder's first trial acid etch of a piece of stone. The plate is submerged in an acid bath that causes surface roughness. One technique uses an electrolytic reaction in a solution of hydrofluoric acid. Almost all presensitized surface plates (see following sections) are formed from anodized aluminum. The surface is chemically treated and then sealed. The anodized surface is unaffected by almost all acids but remains water receptive.

Coating Materials

All photosensitive lithographic metal plates have a photoemulsion surface consisting of some form of light-sensitive material combined with a collodion coated on a grained metal surface. A **collodion** is an organic compound that forms a strong, continuous layer. When mixed with the light-sensitive solution and then exposed to light, the colloid becomes insoluble and forms a strong, continuous coating on the printing plate.

Ammonium bichromate combined with egg albumin was previously used as the photoemulsion in the photolithography process. Albumin has gradually been replaced by other solutions, until it is now very nearly obsolete. Popular industrial coatings are polyvinyl alcohol (PVA), diazo, and photopolymers.

Gum arabic is a collodion commonly used with deep-etch and some forms of bimetal plates (see following sections). It is also used for a variety of other purposes in the lithographic process.

Classifying Lithographic Plates

Lithographic plates can be classified in several ways. The most common method is to apply labels according to structure and action.

Lithographic plate structure can be described as surface, deep-etch, or bimetal. **Surface plates** can be visualized as being formed from a colloid sitting on the surface of the metal (figure 11.4). **Deep-etch plates** are formed by the actual bonding of the colloid material into the plate surface (figure 11.5). **Bimetal plates** function through the adhesion of two dissimilar metals—one ink-receptive and the other water-receptive (figure 11.6). There are, of course, special-purpose plates that defy classification with any one of these three. Surface, deep-etch, bimetal, and special-purpose plates are discussed in detail in the following sections.

A second way to classify plates is by action. Almost all industrial lithography uses the photographic process to produce the image area on the plate. Plate emulsions can be formulated for use with either negatives or positives. When the plate image is formed by passing light through the clear areas of a negative, the plate is called **negative acting.** When a positive is used to expose the plate, the plate is called **positive acting.** Plate action is not

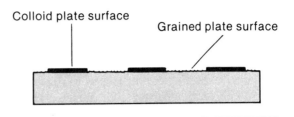

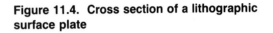

Figure 11.4. Cross section of a lithographic surface plate

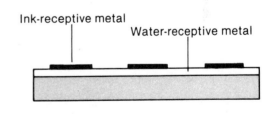

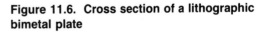

Figure 11.5. Cross section of a lithographic deep-etch plate

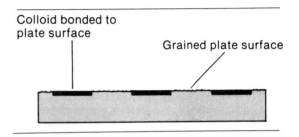

Figure 11.6. Cross section of a lithographic bimetal plate

necessarily associated with plate structure. Surface plates can be designed for use with either negatives or positives, but only positives can be used with deep-etch plates.

Surface Plates

Direct Image Nonphotographic Surface Plates

The **direct image nonphotographic surface plate** is the closest remaining industrial link to the original Senefelder craft. Most current direct image base materials are either paper, acetate, plastic-impregnated paper, or thin aluminum foil adhered to a paper base. Whatever the base, however, almost all such plates have surfaces that are chemically treated to be especially grease receptive. For that reason, dirty or moist fingers touching the plate will reproduce as fingerprints or smudges on the printed sheet.

Any oil-based substance can be adhered to the surface of a direct image plate. Images may be hand drawn with a lithographic crayon, a pencil, a pen and brush, or even a ballpoint pen. Probably the most common process is to type directly on the plate while using a carbon ribbon in an electric typewriter.

In the actual running of a direct image plate, the plate is placed on the press and a special liquid etch is rubbed into the surface. The etch serves to make the image areas somewhat permanent and the nonimage areas water-receptive.

The quality of direct image nonphotographic plates ranges according to their potential length of run. The most inexpensive are projected to yield a maximum of 50 press sheets before the plate image begins to break down. The highest-quality plates boast of up to 5,000 quality copies.

Wipe-On Surface Plates

A refinement of the early attempts to sensitize a lithographic stone with a photographic emulsion is the **wipe-on metal surface plate.** With this process, an emulsion is hand or machine coated onto a pregrained plate immediately prior to plate exposure.

The base material is either aluminum or zinc. Aluminum has gained the widest acceptance. All plates are supplied to the printer with a fine-grain surface and are treated with a protective coating that acts as a link between the future emulsion coating and the base metal. The emulsion is generally mixed in small quantities shortly before it is to be applied. All current emulsions are formed by mixing a dry diazo powder and a liquid base.

There are two techniques for coating the light-sensitive emulsion onto the plate: by hand and with a mechanical roller. With the hand process, the liquid is applied with a damp sponge (or cheesecloth). The goal is to place a fairly uniform layer of emulsion over every portion of the plate surface.

The mechanical roller approach for wipe-on plates employs a dual roller device (figure 11.7). As the plate is passed between the two rollers, a perfectly uniform layer of emulsion is distributed over one side. The gap between the rollers can be adjusted to put the desired thickness of emulsion on the plates, and there is no problem with consistency of coating or with streaking, major difficulties with the hand process.

Work has been done in the past several years to develop a positive-acting wipe-on plate, but almost all systems now in use for actual production are negative acting (some positive-acting plates are currently used as image carriers for press proofing). Most wipe-on plates are exposed through a film negative, with the use of a vacuum frame and a high-intensity light source. Specific times vary according to the individual plate and emulsion, and the working situation. Manufacturers' specifications should always be followed.

Wipe-on plates are processed by one of two methods. The first technique is a two-step process. A pool of desensitizer gum is

Figure 11.7. Coating a wipe-on surface plate
Courtesy of Western Litho Plate and Supply Company

ink and could be used on the printing press. But adhering a layer of lacquer to the exposed areas greatly increases the number of copies that can be made from the plate. With the two-step process, a final layer of desensitizer gum is generally buffed into the entire surface until dry. This last step serves to protect the plate until the job is run on the press and also ensures that all unexposed emulsion has been removed.

The alternative wipe-on processing technique is a one-step process using a lacquer developer that removes the unexposed emulsion at the same time that lacquer adheres to the image areas. After being washed with water, the plate is buffed with a coating of gum arabic until the entire surface is dry.

Presensitized Surface Plates

Presensitized surface plates are by far the most widely used plates for commercial offset lithography. These plates are supplied from the manufacturer with the emulsion surface already coated on the metal base, thus they are called "presensitized." The first presensitized metal plates were introduced by the 3M Company in 1950. Since that time, several manufacturers have developed similar plates. Presensitized plates offer many advantages. Because they are precoated with a photoemulsion, the platemaker need not be concerned with mixing and wiping on the emulsion, or using and maintaining emulsion-coating equipment. Presensitized plates are used by the platemaker directly from the manufacturer's wrapper with no surface preparation. In addition, the plates are processed with ease, have a reasonably long shelf life (generally up to six months), and can be produced for high-quality, long-run press situations.

The base material for presensitized plates

first poured onto the plate and rubbed into the entire surface with a damp sponge. The gum solution serves the dual function of removing any unexposed emulsion and making the nonprinting area water-receptive. The excess desensitizer is removed. A second solution, made up primarily of lacquer, is then rubbed over the entire plate. Then the plate is washed with water.

The image area, which was hardened during exposure, would theoretically accept

can be paper, aluminum foil laminated to paper, or a sheet of aluminum. Paper and foil plates are generally used only for short-run situations. As discussed previously, the metal plates are typically grained and then anodized. The term *graining* is actually misleading, because relatively little roughness is imparted to the surface. Aluminum plates can be sensitized on one or both sides.

Almost all presensitized emulsion-coating materials used today are of diazo formulation. The specific makeup of the solution varies from manufacturer to manufacturer, but the primary ingredient of all types is nitrogen. When the plate emulsion is exposed to a sufficient quantity of light (UV sensitive), the nitrogen is released and the material becomes insensitive to additional light. The insensitive emulsion then can readily accept dyes that become the printing, ink-receptive surface.

Presensitized plates are available in a wide range of capabilities, from short runs of less than 1,000 copies to emulsions that can easily produce as many as 300,000 impressions. With the anodized metal surface, the diazo emulsion, and mass production techniques, presensitized plates easily compete in quality and cost with other types of surface plates.

In addition to being either negative or positive acting, presensitized plates can also be classified as additive or subtractive. Recall that for wipe-on plates a lacquer was adhered to the image areas in order to increase potential plate life. The lacquer, then, is the surface that actually accepts the ink. The same concept is used with preparing the image areas for presensitized plates. When the printer applies a lacquer-like material to the image areas during plate processing, the plate is **additive.** When the printing surface is built into the emulsion by the manufacturer and the printer merely desensitizes the unexposed areas, the plate is **subtractive.**

Processing Additive Plates. Additive materials can be processed with a one- or two-step technique. With the two-step process the plate, after exposure, is first desensitized with a gum-acid solution. The chemical is distributed over the carrier with a moist sponge in order to remove the emulsion and/or make the unexposed emulsion area water-receptive. The entire plate is then rubbed with a gum-water-lacquer mixture (plate developer) to build up the image areas. Finally, the plate is washed, squeegeed, coated with a light layer of gum arabic, and buffed dry (figure 11.8). With the one-step technique, the desensitizer and lacquer-developer functions are combined. The plate is developed with the single solution, washed, squeegeed, gummed, and then buffed dry.

Negative-acting presensitized emulsions are exposed by light passing through the open or image areas of a film negative.

Processing Subtractive Plates. With negative-acting subtractive plates, only one developing step is used. After exposure, a special developer, supplied by the plate manufacturer, is used to remove the unexposed lacquer emulsion that was added during the presensitizing process. Again, the plate is washed and squeegeed. Often, a special subtractive gum must be used to coat the plate for storage (figure 11.9).

Positive-acting presensitized plates are exposed by light passing through the open or nonimage areas of a film positive. Positive-acting presensitized plates can also be classified as either additive or subtractive. In general, after exposure, the exposed emulsion of an additive plate is removed by wiping it with a special developer supplied by the manufacturer. The unexposed or image area remains in place. The developing action is then halted by a fixing agent. As with negative-acting additive plates, lacquer is rubbed into the plate.

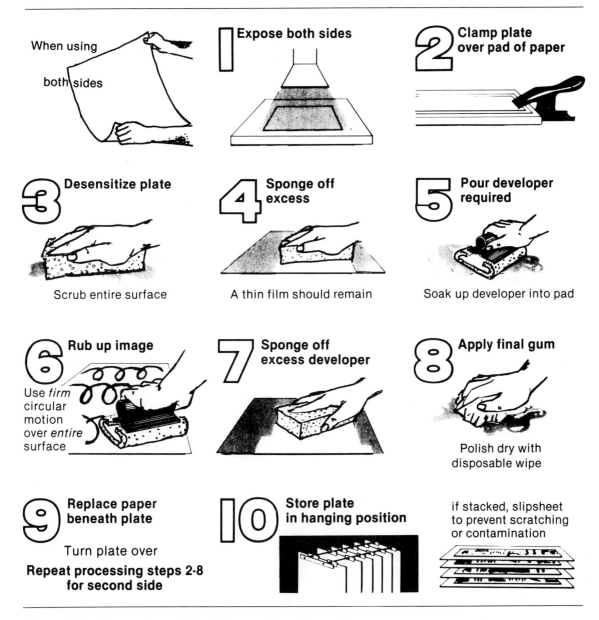

When using both sides

1 **Expose both sides**

2 **Clamp plate over pad of paper**

3 **Desensitize plate**
Scrub entire surface

4 **Sponge off excess**
A thin film should remain

5 **Pour developer required**
Soak up developer into pad

6 **Rub up image**
Use *firm* circular motion over *entire* surface

7 **Sponge off excess developer**

8 **Apply final gum**
Polish dry with disposable wipe

9 **Replace paper beneath plate**
Turn plate over
Repeat processing steps 2-8 for second side

10 **Store plate in hanging position**

if stacked, slipsheet to prevent scratching or contamination

Figure 11.8. Processing additive lithographic surface plates
Courtesy of Printing Products Division, 3M Company

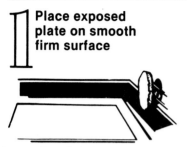

1 Place exposed plate on smooth firm surface

Use yellow lighting in work area

2 Pour developer smoothly

Apply liberally to Pad and Plate

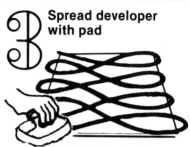

3 Spread developer with pad

Pause briefly to allow chemicals to work

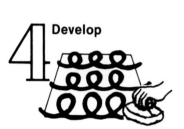

4 Develop

Use firm pressure and tight circular motion

5 Clean pad

Remove loose coating particles

6 Squeegee plate and sink area

Remove *all* visible developer from *plate surface*

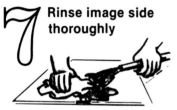

7 Rinse image side thoroughly

Use *disposable* paper wipe to mop surface while rinsing

8 Rinse under plate

To wash away developer and sensitizers

9 Squeegee plate

Face   Backside

10 Gum plate
- Place plate on dry surface
- Dry plate if still wet
- Pour on liberal amount of Gum
- Spread with disposable wipe

- Buff dry with fresh disposable wipe
- Turn plate over on clean dry surface
- Dry backside with wipe

Storage — Slipsheet processed plates to prevent scratching or contamination.

Figure 11.9. Processing substractive lithographic surface plates
Courtesy of Printing Products Division, 3M Company

The lacquer adheres to the image areas and increases the potential length of the press run. After the plate is washed and squeegeed, it is coated with gum arabic and buffed dry. Subtractive positive-acting plates are processed in a similar manner, but without the lacquer step.

Several plate manufacturers have developed automatic processing units for presensitized plates (figure 11.10). Although the specific configuration varies from unit to unit, all systems provide for the exposed plate to be inserted at one end, use automatic drive rollers for uniform feeding, and deliver a finished, gummed, and dried plate at the other end. Automated processing has virtually eliminated the possibility of an uneven printing emulsion. This can be a problem with hand-lacquered additive plates.

Photopolymer Presensitized Surface Plates

One disadvantage of presensitized surface plates with diazo emulsions is that they cannot be used for extremely long press runs. Until the development of photopolymer presensitized plates, only deep-etch or bimetal plates (explained later in this chapter) could be used for offset press runs of a million or more copies. When properly exposed and processed, photopolymer emulsions produce image areas that are extremely hard and wear-resistant, which means that they can be used for press runs that are much longer than plates with diazo emulsions. At the same time, the exposure and development process for photopolymer emulsions is far less involved and time consuming than that for deep-etch or bimetal plates.

Negative-acting photopolymer emulsions consist of molecules called **monomers.**

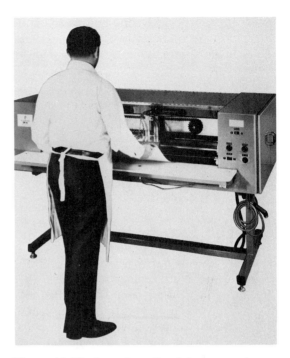

Figure 11.10. An automatic plate-processing unit
Courtesy of Western Litho Plate and Supply Company

When exposed to actinic light, these monomers chemically link and cross-link with each other to form polymers. Polymers can be thought of as complex chains of monomers which are linked so strongly that they behave as a single, hard, wear-resistant molecule. Photopolymer plates are developed in a manner similar to presensitized diazo emulsion plates. The developer removes the unexposed plate coating but leaves the exposed coating (image area) on the plate.

Positive-acting photopolymer plates can be baked in large ovens for a specific time, at a specific temperature. The baking firmly adheres the image to the plate surface, as well as adhering a special baking gum to the non-image portions of the plate. Plate life of more than a million impressions is possible. Newer negative-acting photopolymer plates are now available that reach this plate life without the need for baking.

Deep-Etch Plates and Bimetal Plates

Deep-Etch Plates

There is basically only one category of deep-etch plates. All are defined by the fact that the emulsion areas are bonded or etched into the base metal—unlike surface plates, where the emulsion is merely adhered to the surface. This single characteristic permits a deep-etch plate to hold more ink than any other type of lithographic plate, which results in a greater ink density on the printed sheet. Halftones appear more brilliant with a superb tonal range representation.

The base material for deep-etch plates can be aluminum, zinc, or even stainless steel. The plate is fine grained, by a mechanical or chemical process. Some manufacturers have refined techniques that can use an anodized aluminum plate surface. Some types of plates can be regrained after one use and used a second time with no decrease in image quality.

The basic concept of the deep-etch plate is that of a stencil formed on the plate that covers the nonimage areas with a resist but leaves image areas as open base metal that can be etched with a special solution. Two types of coating materials are commonly used to form the stencil: a bichromate gum solution and a bichromate polyvinyl alcohol (PVA) formulation. The gum compound provides greater exposure latitude, but the PVA is easier to process.

After the base plate is coated with the light-sensitive emulsion, a right-reading film positive is registered with the carrier in a vacuum frame and a high-intensity light source is projected through the clear, or nonimage, areas on the positive. The actinic light hardens the emulsion in the nonimage areas; but in the image areas, no light reaches the plate and the coating remains soft.

Deep-etch plates are unrivaled for high-quality, extremely long-run press jobs. Runs of 500,000 impressions are common, and longer editions have been printed on quality machines run by experienced craftspeople.

Bimetal Plates

Bimetal plates function through the adhesion of two dissimilar metals—one ink-receptive and the other water-receptive. Bimetal plates appear similar to deep-etch plates in that there is an apparent difference of levels between the printing and the nonprinting areas. A common image metal is copper. Chromium is often used as the nonimage surface.

The operation of bimetal plates is due to the chemical properties of only two metals. However, there are plates that have been formed from three or more different metals. Zinc and aluminum are often used as a base to hold the image and nonimage metals. The basic advantage is a decrease in weight and cost over the copper-chromium combination.

Bimetal plates are more expensive to prepare and process than nearly any other form of lithographic plate. Their main attractions are the potential length of run and high image quality. More than a million impressions are commonly made from a single bimetal plate and up to 3 million impressions are not rare.

Special Purpose Lithographic Plates and Plate-Making Systems

Diffusion Transfer Plates

Diffusion transfer lithographic plates are formed from a light-sensitive coating on an intermediate carrier that is exposed and then transferred to the actual printing plate. The advantage of the technique is that the usual film and stripping steps are bypassed because the intermediate sheet can be exposed in a process camera or contact print frame, or even on a special purpose electronic scanner. Several types of transfer systems are commercially available. The PMT (photomechanical transfer) Metal Litho Plate by the Eastman Kodak Company is one example.

Recall from Chapter 6 that the diffusion transfer process is a method used to produce quality opaque positives (either enlarged, reduced, or same size) from positive opaque originals on a process camera. The copy is positioned on the copyboard and the reproduction size and camera exposure are adjusted. A sheet of diffusion transfer negative material is placed on the filmboard and an exposure is made. A sheet of receiver paper is then positioned emulsion to emulsion with the negative and both are passed through an activator bath. After a short period of time the sheets are separated. A positive image is formed on the opaque receiver sheet and it is ready for paste-up.

In the diffusion transfer plate-making process, an aluminum plate can be substituted for the paper receiver sheet. The fine-grained plate need only be fixed and gummed before it is placed on the press. The plate can produce up to 25,000 press copies with a quality that rivals a medium-run presensitized metal plate.

Electrostatic Plates

The process of making **electrostatic transfer plates** is based on the concept of xerographic image reproduction. The idea is commonplace in the office copier now marketed by the Xerox Corporation and others. The basic procedure involves the formation of an image by light striking a photoresponsive surface that has been charged with static electricity (hence the name "electrostatic").

In actual practice, some type of material is coated (selenium and zinc oxide compounds are two patented coverings) on the plate and then positively charged. When light (generally reflected light through a process type of camera) strikes the plate, the positive charge is lost in the nonimage areas, which leaves only the positively charged image area. The remaining charged area is then dusted with negatively charged resin powder. The powder, which clings only to the image area, is then fused to the plate to be run on lithographic presses (figure 11.11).

One interesting feature of the electrostatic system is that corrections can be made directly on the plate. The negative pole of a magnet is used to remove the resin powder from unwanted areas before the powder is fused to the plate. Resin powder can also be added in areas where it was not deposited during the initial process.

In recent years, several manufacturers have developed plate materials that can directly carry the photoresponsive surface. One such manufacturer, the Addressograph-Multigraph Corporation, has linked an electrostatic platemaker to an offset lithographic press. The original copy is inserted into the copier, and the plate is automatically prepared and delivered to the plate cylinder by a belt delivery system that attaches it to the press. The press automatically runs the required number of sheets, removes the plate,

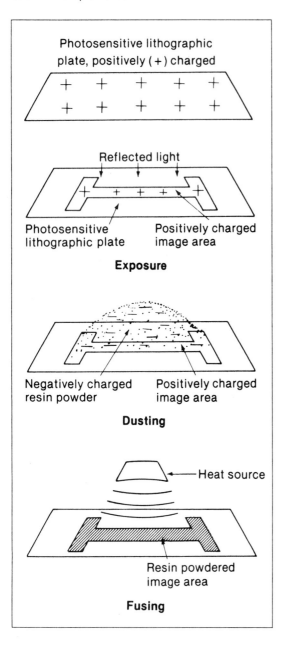

Photosensitive lithographic
plate, positively (+) charged

+ + + + +
+ + + + +

Reflected light

Photosensitive   Positively charged
lithographic plate   image area

Exposure

Negatively charged   Positively charged
resin powder   image area

Dusting

Heat source

Resin powdered
image area

Fusing

**Figure 11.11. Electrostatic printing
process** Electrostatic printing uses a positively
charged image to attract negatively charged resin
powder. The resin powder is then fused in place
with heat.

cleans the blanket cylinder, and turns the whole system off (figure 11.12).

The electrostatic process is receiving widespread acceptance for systems work in the printing industry. Although intended for low- to medium-quality short runs (up to 5,000 copies), the low cost makes it a viable plate-making system for many printers who print one color of ink, usually black, on standard sheet sizes (8½ × 11 inches or 8½ × 14 inches).

Projection Plates

Two types of projection plate making are commonly used. Small projection plate-making systems are often used in quick print or in-plant operations to reproduce a single original on a single printing plate for short-run

**Figure 11.12. A lithographic printing system
with an electrostatic platemaker**
Courtesy of Multigraphics, a Division of AM International, Inc.

applications. Most projection plates for these systems are designed to receive an image directly from a positive original, by using a special camera-platemaker. In practice, an opaque, camera-ready original is mounted on the copyboard. Light reflected from the original is passed through a lens which can enlarge or reduce the copy size. Most systems store the plate material in roll form and automatically advance and cut the required plate length prior to exposure. Plate development is accomplished automatically in the camera-platemaker.

The camera lights for projection plates do not produce intense actinic light characteristic of platemakers, thus projection speed plates contain silver halide emulsions which react to light more quickly than the diazo or bichromate solutions used for most plate photoemulsions. Small projection plate systems often use paper or plastic as the plate base material. Plastic is generally used for plates requiring higher resolution capabilities or longer press runs than paper plates will provide.

A typical projection speed plate is structured with four separate layers: the base material, a developer emulsion layer, a sensitized emulsion layer, and a top fogged emulsion layer. The reflected light passes to the second layer and exposes the sensitized emulsion. Where light is not reflected from the copy (the image areas), the emulsion remains unexposed. The plate is then passed through a bath that activates the bottom chemical layer and causes the developer to begin to travel toward the top layer. The exposed portions of the second layer exhaust the developer, and the process is halted in the nonimage areas. Where the sensitized emulsion in the second layer was not exposed, the developer is allowed to pass to the top fogged area and changes the fogged layer to black metallic silver. Finally, the plate is delivered through a

stop-bath, which halts the entire developing process.

The top surface of the plate, then, is made up of a hardened image area that is ink-receptive and an undeveloped nonimage area that is water-receptive. Most direct image photographic plate systems are totally automatic, self-contained units that deliver finished plates within seconds after the exposure has been made.

The advantages of this technique are speed and low cost. The entire film-stripping operation is eliminated because no film is made. The position of the original on the exposure unit determines the position of the image on the plate. Small projection plate-making systems are intended for work where short-run, low- to medium-quality copies are to be run on presses set up for a standard paper size.

A second type of projection plate-making system is designed to expose metal-based projection plates. These systems are widely used in book, newspaper, and directory work, where single-color page images must be imposed into signatures consisting of several pages. These projection plate-making systems combine stripping, imposition, and plate making in one operation. Rather than photographically reproducing each original directly on a single plate through a camera lens, these systems record a number of opaque originals onto photographic film from which the images are exposed in the correct imposition onto a plate to make up a signature. In practice, opaque originals of each page in the job are photographed as individual frames on a roll of photographic film. As each original page is photographed, a code is included with each frame to indicate the sequence of the frame in the job. The film is then processed and loaded into a projection platemaker, where it is exposed one frame at a time, directly onto a printing plate. In most systems the plate exposure unit is mounted on a carriage, which moves across the plate. A computer is used to control image placement so that the correct frames are exposed on the plate in the correct imposition (figure 11.13).

Because projection plate making combines stripping and plate making into one operation, it greatly increases the speed with which images can be plated: A typical newspaper page can be assembled and plated in a few minutes. In addition, because image placement is controlled by computer, image location and imposition problems can be virtually eliminated.

Laser Exposure Systems

Laser plate exposure systems are ideally suited for exposing plates from digitized information contained in computer memory. Most laser plate-making systems contain two laser beams, one of which reads the copy while the other exposes a printing plate. During operation, the "read" laser scans across an opaque original, projecting light onto the copy. Areas that reflect light back from the copy are treated as nonimage areas; areas that absorb light are treated as image areas. The read laser then passes this scanned information to the computer as digitized input. The computer uses this digitized information to activate a "write" laser which exposes the plate.

The write laser exposes only a tiny area of the plate at one time—the area immediately beneath the small laser beam. Exposure times are extremely short, typically only one or two milliseconds. However, laser light is much more intense than the light produced by traditional platemaker light sources (over 1,000,000 times more intense), thus the plate is properly exposed, even with such a short exposure.

Almost any type of photoemulsion plate can be used with a laser plate-making system. After exposure, the plate is processed with

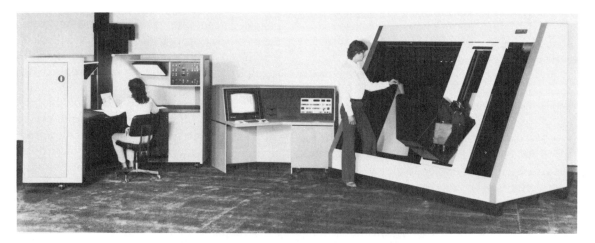

Figure 11.13. A projection platemaker This direct-to-plate system eliminates mechanical make-up and stripping. With this system copy can be plated up to 90% faster than through traditional operations.
Courtesy of Rachwal Systems

the same procedures that would be used had it been exposed with a traditional light source. Positive or negative film images can also be produced with most laser systems.

Laser plate-making systems offer several advantages over traditional systems. Even though the plate exposure process involves thousands of individual exposures, these exposures proceed so rapidly that the overall speed of plate production is greatly increased. In addition, complete pages or signatures consisting of several pages can be scanned and plated in one operation, eliminating stripping. One final advantage is that, because the scanned information is digitized, it can be stored for reuse or telecommunicated to several remote locations for simultaneous plating.

Step-and-Repeat Plate Making

Often a number of identical images must be placed on a single printing plate. One solution is to prepare a separate mechanical layout for each image and gang them all up on one illustration board. A second method is to pre-

pare only one original image but produce a film conversion for each desired plate image. All pieces of film can then be stripped onto one flat. Unfortunately, both of these methods would take far too much time. To meet the need of identical multiple plate images, the industry has developed the **step-and-repeat platemaker** (figure 11.14).

With this approach, one paste-up and film conversion is prepared. The single negative (or positive) is then masked and fitted into a special frame or chase. When the chase is inserted in the step-and-repeat platemaker, the device can be manually or automatically moved to each required position on the plate and an exposure made. During each exposure, all areas of the plate except the portion under the chase are covered and receive no light.

Image exposure and placement is computer controlled on most modern step-and-repeat plate-making systems. With computer-controlled systems, information about plate and press sheet size, the number of images to be repeated, and their positioning is pre-programmed into a computer. The computer then causes the carriage that carries the chase

Figure 11.14. A step-and-repeat platemaker
Courtesy of Royal Zenith Corporation

to automatically position the chase, make the exposure, then reposition the chase in the next required location. Step-and-repeat operations are typically used in the printing of labels, and for other printing jobs where the printing of several duplicate images on a single press sheet is the most efficient procedure.

Key Terms

platemaker
actinic light
offset plate
plate-making sink
sensitivity guide
grain
collodion
negative-acting plate
positive-acting plate

surface plate
direct image
   nonphotographic plate
wipe-on surface plate
presensitized surface plate
additive plate
subtractive plate
photopolymer plate
monomer

polymer
deep-etch plate
bimetal plate
diffusion transfer plate
electrostatic plate
projection plate making
laser plate making
step-and-repeat plate making

Questions for Review

1. What is the basis of all industrial lithography?

2. Describe the basic components of a platemaker.

3. What is meant by actinic light, and why is actinic light important in plate making?

4. How is platemaker exposure calibrated for plate production?

5. What is the purpose of lithographic plate graining?

6. What are the three most basic types of lithographic plates?

7. What is the difference between a negative-acting and a positive-acting lithographic plate?

8. How is a direct image nonphotographic plate prepared?

9. Describe two methods of preparing a wipe-on surface plate.

10. How do presensitized surface plates differ from wipe-on plates, and what are the advantages of presensitized plates?

11. What is the difference between an additive and a subtractive plate? How is each processed?

12. How does a photopolymer emulsion differ from a diazo emulsion?

13. Describe how deep-etch and bimetal plates differ from surface plates.

14. How are diffusion transfer lithographic plates made?

15. What is the advantage of electrostatic plates?

16. Describe the operation of two types of projection plate-making systems.

17. How does a laser plate exposure system work, and what are the advantages of this type of system?

18. Describe the process of step-and-repeat plate making, and give two examples for the use of this process.

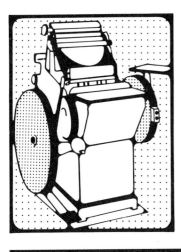

Chapter Twelve

Printing Presses: An Overview

Anecdote to Chapter Twelve

The first high-speed printing press was designed around 1450 by Johann Gutenberg in Germany. Gutenberg tried several different designs, but he settled on the basic form of a wine press. He changed the bed around so that it could be rolled out from under the plate, activated the screw by a lever, and added a frame, or tympan, to hold the paper. With this device he printed his famous forty-two-line Bible (called the Gutenberg Bible). It took him just over three years to print two hundred copies.

The press worked so well that three hundred years later Benjamin Franklin used a similar device (see illustration). In practice, two men operated the press. The type was locked in place on the bed, the raised portions were inked, and the paper was positioned on the tympan frame and swung into place over the type. The bed was then rolled under the platen and the lever activated to press the sheet against the type. The press was then opened, the printed sheet was hung on a line to dry, and the entire process was repeated. Using this method, the press operators could make about three hundred impressions in a single twelve-hour workday. The basic steps of feeding the paper, registering the paper to the form, printing, and finally delivering the sheet remain to this day. Modern processes, however, are more accurate and more rapid than the wine press.

A replica of Benjamin Franklin's press
Courtesy of Smithsonian Institution, Photo No. 17539-B

Objectives for Chapter Twelve

After completing this chapter you will be able to:

- Recall the four units that make up any printing press.
- Discuss the development of press designs, from platen presses to rotary presses.
- Explain the principle of offset printing.

- Diagram the cylinder configuration of an offset perfecting press.
- Explain the operation of the feeder unit, registration unit, printing unit, inking unit, dampening unit, and delivery unit on an offset lithographic press.
- Give a general description of the operation of a web offset press.

Introduction

A printing press is a machine that transfers an image from some sort of plate or image carrier to a substrate, such as paper. It is certainly possible to transfer images from a plate surface without the use of a machine—consider a rubber stamp or a stencil—but printing presses are much faster and print more accurately than hand methods.

Gutenberg's refinement of a wine press could be operated at the then fantastic rate of one copy every three minutes. Contemporary automatic presses operate at a medium speed of around 125 copies each minute (6,000 to 8,000 copies per hour). When the paper is fed from a continuous roll (called "web feeding"), the paper can pass under a printing plate as rapidly as 1,800 feet per minute.

The design of Gutenberg's original press has been refined a bit, but presses still perform the same basic operations of feeding, registration, printing, and delivery that Gutenberg's press performed more than five centuries ago. It is important to understand that every printing press is built from these four basic units (figure 12.1). Relief, gravure,

screen, and lithographic presses all have a feeding system, registration system, printing unit, and delivery system. A firm understanding of press systems and component parts will simplify the task of running any type of printing press.

The **feeding** system can be as simple as a human hand picking up a sheet of paper or as complex as an air-vacuum device that automatically fans the top sheets of a paper pile and lifts a sheet with mechanical fingers. Whatever the method, the concern is to feed stock into the press rapidly and uniformly.

The **registration** system is designed to ensure that the sheet is held in the same position each time an impression is made. It is important that the printed image appear in the same spot on every sheet. Registration is especially important for color printing, which requires two or more impressions on each press sheet. The different colored images made during each impression would not line up if the position of the paper were not controlled during printing.

Once the sheet is held firmly in the proper position, the image is transferred from the plate to the paper in the printing unit. The placement of the plate or image carrier might vary with the type of printing (relief, screen, gravure, or lithography), but there are general similarities with all presses.

After printing, the completed sheet must be removed from the press by the **delivery** system. Gutenberg picked up each printed copy and hung it on a wire line to dry. Modern presses generally deliver a uniform stack of sheets that can be easily folded, collated, packaged, or cut.

In this chapter we will discuss the development of printing presses and the operation of the four press systems. Much of this

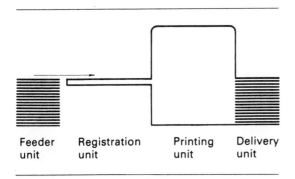

Figure 12.1. The four units common to all presses

discussion will center around the systems used on offset lithographic presses, as offset lithographic printing is the printing method most used industrially. Gravure, screen, and flexographic presses are discussed in more detail later in the text.

Press Development

Since Gutenberg developed his first press, major improvements have been made in press design. These improvements have increased both the speed and the quality with which work can be printed. Modern press designs are the result of changes in the method used to move paper through the press and in the method used to transfer an image. A brief look at press development will help you understand the operation of a modern offset press.

Platen Press

If it were in operation today, Gutenberg's converted wine press would be labeled a **platen press.** On this type of press, the paper is placed between the typeform and a flat surface, called a "platen" (figure 12.2a). The typeform and the platen are then brought together, and an image is transferred to the sheet (figure 12.2b). Although the feeder, registration, and delivery units have been automated, the basic problems inherent in the platen design remain. The paper must be inserted, held in place, and printed, and it must remain in place until the platen opens sufficiently for the sheet to be removed. The process is slow.

In addition to being slow, the process is limited to the page size that can be printed. The platen press requires 175 pounds of pressure per square inch (psi) to transfer ink from the type form to paper. A press capable of printing an 11- × 14-inch image must be able

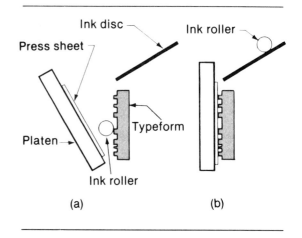

Figure 12.2. Diagram of a platen press A press sheet is positioned on a platen when the device is open (a), and the image is transferred when the press is closed (b).

to produce 26,950 pounds of pressure. (This is why early wooden printing presses were built in the basement or first floor of a two-story building. The press was the main support for the floor above.) Speed and size were the two factors which lead to the development of the flat bed cylinder press.

Flat Bed Cylinder Press

An improvement on the platen press, the **flat bed cylinder press** is constructed so that the sheet rolls into contact with the typeform as a cylinder moves across the press (figure 12.3). Mechanical fingers, or "grippers," hold the paper in place during the trip and automatically open at the end of one rotation. Ink rollers are usually attached to the cylinder assembly so that as an image is being printed, the form is also being re-inked. After each impression, the cylinder is automatically raised and rolled back to the starting point to receive

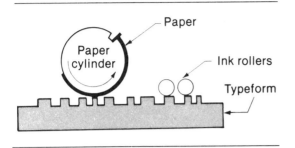

Figure 12.3. Diagram of a flat bed press A flat bed cylinder press rolls the paper sheet over the plate carrying the image.

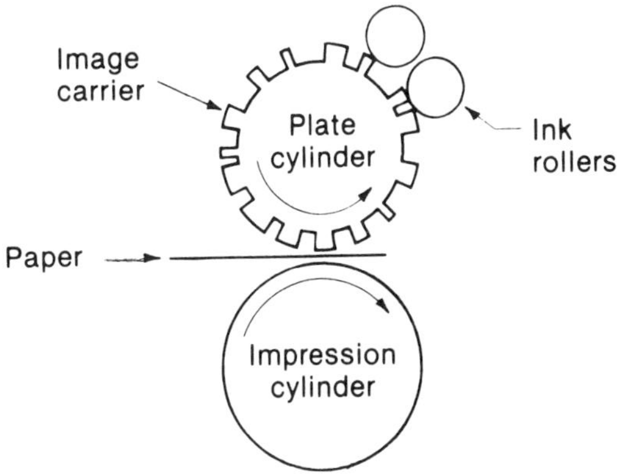

another sheet. On some models the cylinder is stationary and the form moves.

One advantage of the flat bed cylinder design is that, because only a very narrow portion of the sheet is being printed at any given instant, much less pressure is required to transfer the image than for the platen design. A slight modification is to place the form in a vertical position so that both the bed and the cylinder rotate in opposite directions. This cuts the printing time in half because the cylinder makes only a 180° turn for each impression. However, there is still wasted motion when the cylinder and/or the form return to their original position and no image is being transferred.

Rotary Press

The **rotary press** is formed from two cylinders. One holds the typeform while the other acts as an **impression cylinder** to push the stock against the form (figure 12.4). As the cylinders rotate, a sheet is inserted between them so that an image will be placed in the same position on every piece. Ink rollers continually replace ink that has been transferred to the press sheet. The impression cylinder

Figure 12.4. Diagram of a rotary press A rotary press moves the paper sheet between two cylinders—the plate cylinder, which holds the image carrier, and the impression cylinder, which pushes the piece against the plate.

can usually be moved up or down to adjust impression pressure for the weight or thickness of the material being printed.

The rotary press is an efficient design. Because one impression is made with each cylinder rotation, there is no wasted motion. It is the only press design that can transfer an image onto a continuous roll of paper (called "web printing"). The rotary configuration can easily be adapted to multicolor presswork. One common design is to place several **plate cylinders** around a single impression cylinder (figure 12.5). All modern offset lithographic presses are rotary presses.

Offset Principle

The term **offset** is generally associated with the lithographic process, but the offset principle can be applied to a variety of printing processes. An offset image is produced by

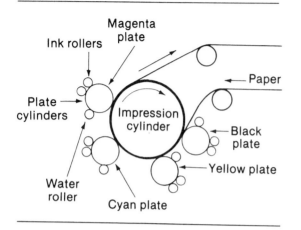

Figure 12.5. Diagram of a multicylinder rotary press A rotary web-fed press can be adapted to place several plate cylinders around a single impression cylinder.

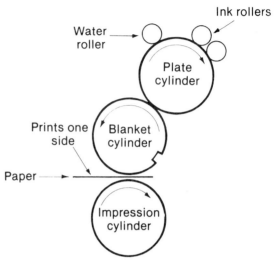

Figure 12.6. Diagram of an offset rotary press With the offset principle, the image is transferred (or offset) from the plate to the blanket cylinder, which reverses the image. The image is then passed to the press sheet as it moves between the blanket and impression cylinders.

transferring the image from an inked printing plate onto a rubber blanket, then transferring the image from the blanket to the paper (figure 12.6).

Transferring an image from a blanket to the paper, rather than transferring directly from the plate to the paper, has several advantages. Paper has an abrasive effect on printing plates. If the paper were allowed to come in contact with the printing plate throughout the press run, the plate would soon be too worn to print properly. Having the plate contact a rubber blanket, instead of the printing paper, lengthens the life of the plate. In addition, whenever an image is transferred from one carrier to another, the symbols are reversed (recall that foundry type is cast in reverse). When a blanket cylinder is used on an offset press, the characters on the printing plate must be right-reading. The characters will be printed in reverse on the blanket, then reversed again (back to right-reading) on the press sheet. Right-reading characters are more convenient for people to work with and assemble during the com-

position and stripping processes. A rubber blanket also tends to diminish unwanted background detail or "scum" that might accumulate on the printing plate.

A **perfecting press** can print simultaneously on both sides of the paper as it passes through the printing unit (figure 12.7). The most common perfecting presses use the rotary configuration and can be designed for either sheet-fed or web-fed reproduction.

Classifying Offset Lithographic Presses

Offset printing presses can be classified by feeding method, by registration method, by whether the device is a perfector, by the num-

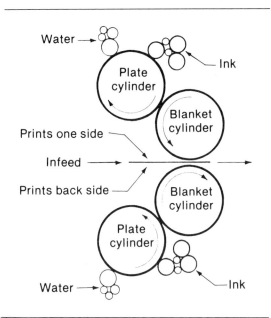

Figure 12.7. Diagram of a blanket-to-blanket configuration for a perfecting press

Figure 12.8. A common pedestal type of duplicator
Courtesy of Multigraphics, a Division of AM International, Inc.

ber of printing units, by speed, and by delivery method, among other characteristics. Offset lithographic presses are labeled as either duplicators or presses, based on the size of the press sheet that can be printed.

Offset Duplicators. **Duplicators** are any offset lithographic presses that can feed a maximum sheet size of 11 by 17 inches. A duplicator is assumed not to have the degree of control found on a larger offset press, although the feeder, registration, printing, and delivery units will always be present.

Table-top duplicators are designed for short-run work and can be operated by office personnel. Most models have friction paper feed, control registration by the position of the paper pile, and use a simple gravity delivery system. Figure 12.8 shows a common pedestal type of duplicator. Pedestal dupli-

cators are usually more rugged than table model duplicators and have a few more sophisticated controls than the table-top design.

An offset duplicator can do any job a larger press can handle, but there are differences in sheet sizes that can be handled. Modern duplicators are available that can print on a variety of stock thicknesses at speeds of 5,000 to 10,000 impressions per hour. They are also available with a web-fed design and multicolor printing units.

Duplicators are versatile machines that meet the short-run demands of the industry. They have the same basic controls as offset presses yet are significantly less expensive. Duplicators are commonly used for introductory press training because of their similarity to larger offset presses.

Offset Presses. A true offset press can feed a sheet size greater than 11 by 17 inches. Presses are generally identified by the maximum sheet size that they can print. Sheet-fed presses are available in sizes from 12⅝ by 18 inches to 54 by 77 inches. Figure 12.9 shows a common offset press.

Although "presses" and "duplicators" are technically different, the word *duplicator* is rarely used. Rather, both duplicators and larger presses are referred to as "presses."

Understanding Offset Press Operation

As mentioned, all presses are composed of four basic units: feeder, registration, printing, and delivery. It is crucial that you understand the process a sheet of paper goes through in its trip from the infeed pile through the registration system to the printing unit and finally to the delivery table, in order to understand the adjustments necessary for press operation.

Figure 12.9. A lithographic offset press
Courtesy of Miller Printing Equipment Corp.

The Feeder Unit

One method of classifying presses is by the form of the material sent through the feeder system. When a roll of paper is placed in the feeder unit, the press is classified as **web fed** or simply web (figure 12.10). When the feeder unit picks up individual sheets from a pile, the press is classified as **sheet fed.** Our primary concern at this point is sheet-fed presses. Web presses will be discussed later in the chapter.

The feeder unit for a sheet-fed offset press must separate the top sheet of paper from the infeed pile, pick it up, and deliver it to the registration unit. This process must be done consistently for each sheet in the pile. Only one sheet can be fed at a time, and each must reach the registration unit at a precise moment to be registered and sent to the printing unit.

Loading Systems

The simplest and most common sheet-feeding system is **pilefeeding** (figure 12.11). With this system a pile of paper is placed on a feeder table while the press is turned off. The table

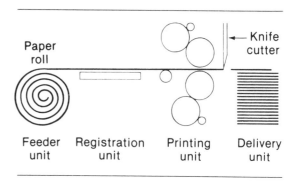

Figure 12.10. Diagram of a web-fed press

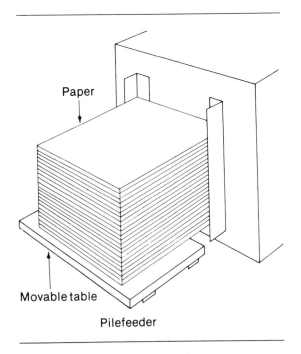

Figure 12.11. Diagram of a press with a pile feeder

is then raised to a predetermined feeder height and the press run begun. As each sheet is removed from the pile, the press moves the table up so that the top of the pile remains at a constant height.

Pilefeeding presents no difficulties when all the sheets for a single job can be placed in one pile. However, when the press must be stopped and started several times during an extremely long run to add more paper, problems are often encountered. When a job is first set up on a press, a certain amount of paper spoilage occurs during **make-ready** (or preparation work) to obtain a quality printed image. During a steady press run, it is relatively easy to maintain consistent quality. Whenever the press is stopped, however, not only is production time lost, but more wast-

age could occur before the quality impression is again obtained.

Continuous feeding provides a means of adding sheets to a feeder system without stopping the press in the middle of a run. There are two common continuous-loading designs. The oldest generally has a feed table located over the registration unit (figure 12.12). The printer fans the paper, and the pile is spread on the infeed table. A continuous belt then moves the pile around and under the feeder table to the registration unit. Additional paper is fanned and added to the moving pile as it is needed.

A second system provides continuous feeding by loading new paper under an existing pile while the press is running (figure 12.13). Before the pile has run out, temporary rods are inserted, and the fresh pile is elevated into position. The rods are removed, and a single stack of paper is again in the feeder unit.

Types of Feeders

The most common type of mechanical feeder is the **successive-sheet-feeding** system (figure

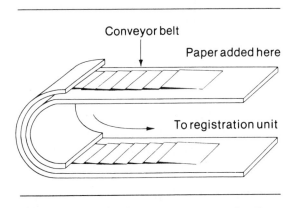

Figure 12.12. Diagram of a continuous-feeding system

Figure 12.13. Example of a continuous-feeding system that uses dual tables
Courtesy of Miller Printing Equipment Corp.

Figure 12.14. Diagram of a successive-sheet-feeding system

12.14). Mechanical fingers pick up one sheet from the top of the paper pile and direct it into the registration unit.

Usually, an **air blast** is used to separate the top sheet from the rest of the pile. This blast can be adjusted for papers of different weight and for different atmospheric conditions. On dry days, when the sheets tend to cling together because of static electricity, the air blast can be increased. Heavy papers require a stronger air blast than is needed for light papers. Coated papers, too, generally require a stronger air blast than is needed for uncoated papers. The air blast must be strong enough to "float" the top piece of paper above the pile at a specified height below the sucker feet.

The **sucker feet** are small vacuum tubes that grab the floating top sheet and send it down the registration board, where the reg-

istration unit takes over. The amount of vacuum in the sucker feet can be adjusted for the weight of paper being printed. Heavy papers generally require more vacuum than is needed for light papers. The object is to adjust the vacuum so that only a single piece of paper is picked up by the sucker feet and delivered to the registration unit.

In actual operation, the sucker feet grab the top sheet from the pile and move it forward a short distance where it is picked up by pull-in wheels (or some other device) that put it squarely on a conveyer belt system on the registration board. The press automatically controls the precise moment when the sucker feet grab the top sheet, their movement toward the registration board, and the precise moment when the vacuum is cut off and the sheet enters the registration unit.

As the press removes paper from the infeed table, the height of the paper pile decreases. Yet the paper pile must be maintained at a constant distance from the sucker feet. This requirement is accomplished automatically by the press. As the press removes paper from the infeed pile, the infeed table is automatically moved up, which moves the infeed pile closer to the sucker feet.

The feeder system must be adjusted for air blast, vacuum, paper pile height, and upward movement of infeed table as the paper is used.

The paper feed must be synchronized

with the printing unit—each time an impression is made, the feeder must be ready to insert a fresh sheet. For high-speed presses with a successive-sheet-feeding system, the paper is literally flying through the registration unit in order to keep up with the printing unit. It is not easy to hold accurate registration when high-speed printing with a single sheet feeder. There is a possibility of the paper misaligning as it enters the registration board at a high rate of speed.

A **stream feeder,** on the other hand, overlaps sheets on the registration board, and the rate of sheet movement is significantly slower (figure 12.15). With a stream feed, sheets move through the registration unit at a fraction of the speed of the printing unit. This makes accurate registration control less difficult.

Automatic Feeder Controls

Whatever the method of paper loading or feed, there are common feeder system controls on all sheet-fed presses. When the paper pile is loaded into the feeder system, it is centered on a press. A scale is usually provided somewhere on the feeder to ensure accurate paper position. Once the pile has been centered, movable side and back guides are put into position just touching the paper so that the pile will not shift position during the press run (figure 12.16).

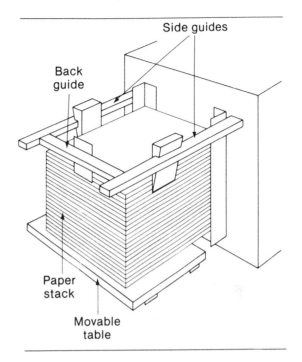

Figure 12.16. Diagram showing movable guides The movable side and back guides hold the pile in position.

Figure 12.15. Diagram of a stream-feeding system

The height of the pile can usually be adjusted and automatically maintained by the press. Usually some type of sensing bar touches the top of the pile immediately after a sheet has been fed and directs a gear-and-chain pile height control. The actual pile height required depends on such factors as the weight of paper, environmental conditions, and method of feed. The top of the pile must be as nearly level as possible for consistent feeding. This is usually a problem only with large press sheets. Wedges or blocks are often placed under the pile to keep it level.

To ensure that only one sheet is fed into the registration unit at a time, the top sheet must be separated from the rest of the pile.

Various mechanisms are used on different machines, but they are all called **sheet separators.** The most common is a blast of directed air. Blower tubes, which can be directed at the front, side, or rear of a pile, place a blanket of air under the first few sheets (figure 12.17). Another common approach is to combine a blast of air with a mechanical **combing wheel,** which curls one edge of the paper above the rest of the stack (figure 12.18). With either technique, a sucker foot telescopes to the top sheet and forwards it into the registration unit. Most sheet separators have at least two sucker feet. Both the volume of air to separate the top sheet and the amount of vacuum pull in the sucker feet can be adjusted for different paper characteristics.

The final consideration is to ensure that only one sheet is fed into the press from the feeder at a time. Multiple sheets can jam the press, give poor image impression, fail to be held in register, and even do damage to the printing unit. Most presses have a **double-**

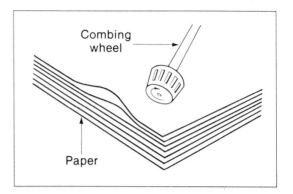

Figure 12.18. A mechanical combing wheel

sheet detector (figure 12.19) to check for multiple sheets and either eject the double sheets from the registration system or stop the press when double sheets are detected. Usually the mechanism merely gauges the thickness of the material passing under a sensing switch. The gap under the switch can be set to any thickness. When the allowable gap is exceeded, the switch is tripped and the double sheets are ejected. On some presses, the paper feed shuts down when a double sheet is detected. If all paperfeed adjustments have been properly made, the feeder should rarely feed multiple sheets.

The Registration Unit

Importance of Registration

Registration is the process of controlling and directing the sheet as it enters the printing unit. The goal of registration is to ensure absolute consistency of image position on every sheet printed. When one color is to be printed over another on a single sheet, the image will not fit unless registration of all sheets is held throughout the press run. The ideas of registration and fit are often confused. **Fit** refers to the image position on the press sheet. The

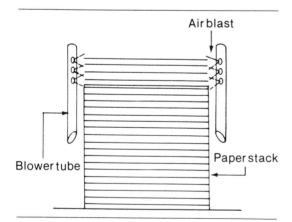

Figure 12.17. Diagram showing blower tubes Blower tubes force a blanket of air under the first few sheets of paper and float them above the rest of the pile.

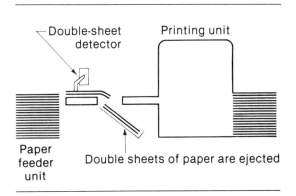

Figure 12.19. Diagram showing a double-sheet detector

term is often used when discussing flat color work. Two colors that are printed adjacent to each other in the proper positions are said to have proper fit. Fit can be affected by a variety of factors, including the original mechanical, the camera operations used to reproduce it, and the stripping of the job. **Registration** refers to the consistency of the position of the printed image during printing. An image which had the proper fit in stripping can be made to register properly. However, if the fit was wrong in stripping, no amount of adjustments on press will bring the image into correct register.

Typical Registration Systems

After leaving the infeed pile, the press sheet is moved along the registration board. The registration board consists of a conveyer belt system and some type of registration system. The conveyer belts carry the paper to the registration unit, where it is momentarily stopped and squared to the plate cylinder along the top edge by a headstop. At the same time, it is either pushed or pulled slightly sideways and placed in the proper printing position. It is important to understand that before each

sheet is printed, the registration system places it in exactly the same position as the preceding sheet. This position determines where the image will be printed on the press sheet. The registration unit must be adjusted for paper width and image location.

The actual operation of registering the sheet is performed just before it enters the printing unit. There are basically only two types of sheet-fed automatic registration systems: "three-point guides" and "rotary" or "roller guides."

In a three-point guide system, the sheet is advanced along the registration board and is halted against movable front guides, called **"headstops"** (figure 12.20). Side guides then push the sheet into the proper position, the

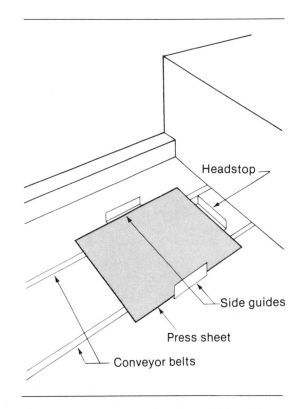

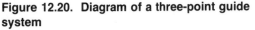

Figure 12.20. Diagram of a three-point guide system

front guides move out of the way, and the sheet is moved into the printing unit. There is sometimes a tendency for heavy stock to bounce back as it comes into contact with the headstops. Extremely lightweight materials easily buckle with the push system. Either condition can lead to misregistration.

The two-point pull rotary system reduces the possibility of the sheet misregistering (figure 12.21). The headstops still swing into position at the head of the registration board, but a single side guide is locked into position and does not move. As the sheet meets the headstops and comes to rest, a finger or roller is lowered against the stock and it is pulled by a rolling, or rotary, motion

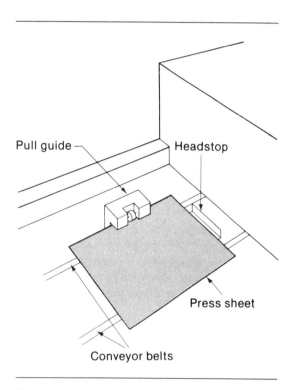

Pull guide

Headstop

Press sheet

Conveyor belts

Figure 12.21. Diagram of a two-point pull rotary system

against the stationary side guide. Once in register, the sheet is moved into the printing unit.

The Printing Unit

The printing unit places a water solution and ink on the plate, transfers the image to the paper, and delivers the paper to the delivery unit. The printing unit must be adjusted so that the proper amount of ink and water solution is deposited on the printing plate and so that the image is transferred accurately, evenly, and consistently to the printing paper. Every offset printing unit is made up of the following three parts:

- The cylinder system
- The dampening system
- The inking system

Each serves an important function in the total image transfer process and thus will be examined in detail.

Cylinder System Configurations

The cylinder system for any offset lithographic press has three functional groups: a plate cylinder, a blanket cylinder, and an impression cylinder. The function of the plate cylinder is to hold the plate and revolve it into contact with the blanket cylinder during the printing process. The plate cylinder generally has some form of clamping system that holds the plate squarely and firmly in place. Ink and water **form rollers** contact the plate while it is attached to the plate cylinder, thereby causing the image areas to be inked. The plate image is transferred to the blanket cylinder, and the image is reversed. The press sheet is then passed between the blanket and impression cylinder, where the image is offset back to right-reading. The impression cylinder applies the necessary pressure against the blanket and paper to transfer the image from the blanket to the paper.

Figure 12.22 shows one common configuration of plate, blanket, and impression cylinders, called the **three-cylinder principle.** Notice that because the blanket is above the impression cylinder, the paper travels in a straight line from feeder to delivery. Note also the direction of rotation of each cylinder and the logical placement of water and inking systems (remember that the plate must be moistened before it is inked).

Figure 12.23 illustrates an alternative cylinder configuration called the **two-cylinder principle.** With this design the plate and impression functions are combined on a main cylinder with twice the circumference of the blanket cylinder. During the first half of the main plate/impression cylinder rotation, the image is offset from the plate section of the

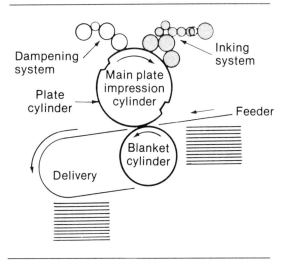

Figure 12.23. Example of a two-cylinder configuration

main cylinder to the blanket. During the next half-revolution, the press sheet is passed between the impression section of the main cylinder and the blanket cylinder. Because the blanket is beneath the impression cylinder, the paper must be flopped by the delivery system in order to have the printed image face up on the outfeed table. This means that the sheets to be fed into the press must be placed on the infeed table upside down.

The three-cylinder configuration is commonly found on both duplicators and presses. The two-cylinder design is rarely used on offset presses.

Impression Cylinder Adjustments

The gap between the blanket cylinder and the impression cylinder affects the final image quality. The pressure must be sufficient to transfer a dense ink image but not great enough to smash either the blanket or the

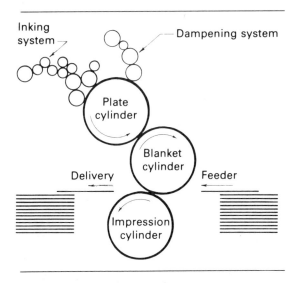

Figure 12.22. Example of a three-cylinder configuration

press sheet. Controlling the amount of gap is referred to as adjusting **impression.** Each time the thickness of the paper being printed changes, the impression must be readjusted. Heavier papers need a wider opening than lighter papers.

On most duplicators, the impression cylinder can be raised or lowered by a simple set screw arrangement. On presses, impression is controlled by adding or removing packing from behind the blanket cylinder or by a cam adjustment attached to the impression cylinder. On some presses, both the impression and the blanket cylinders require packing.

The Inking Unit

The goal of any inking system is to place a uniform layer of ink across every dimension of the printing plate. The lithographic process is unique in that it requires the ink form rollers to pass in contact with the nonimage areas of the plate without transferring ink to them.

Inking Unit Configurations

All lithographic inking systems are made up of three main sections:

- Ink fountain and fountain rollers
- Ink distribution rollers
- Ink form rollers (figure 12.24)

The ink fountain stores a quantity of ink in a reservoir and feeds small quantities of ink to the rest of the inking system from the fountain roller. The ink distribution rollers receive ink and work it into a semiliquid state that is uniformly delivered to the ink form rollers. A thin layer of ink is then transferred to the image portions of the lithographic plate by the ink form rollers.

Inking Unit Operation

The ink **fountain** (figure 12.24a) holds a pool of ink and controls the amount of ink that enters the inking system. The most common

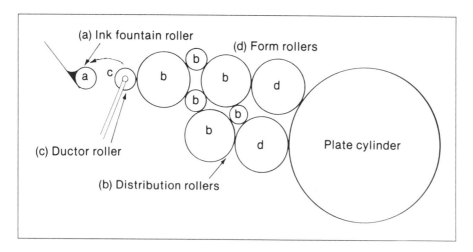

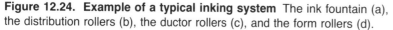

Figure 12.24. Example of a typical inking system The ink fountain (a), the distribution rollers (b), the ductor rollers (c), and the form rollers (d).

type of fountain consists of a metal blade that is held in place near the fountain roller. The gap between the blade and the fountain roller can be controlled by adjusting screw keys to vary the amount of ink on the fountain roller. The printer adjusts the keys in or out as the fountain roller turns to obtain the desired quantity of ink. If the image to be printed covers only half the plate, half the fountain keys will be closed. If the plate image is even across the whole plate, all keys will be moved to place a uniform layer of ink on the ink fountain roller.

The ink distribution rollers spread the ink out to a uniform layer before it is placed on the plate (figure 12.24b). There are generally two types of distribution rollers: rotating distribution rollers and oscillating distribution rollers. **Rotating distribution rollers** rotate in one direction. **Oscillating distribution rollers** rotate and also move from side to side.

The ink is transferred to the ink distribution rollers by a **ductor roller** (figure 12.24c). The ductor is a movable roller that flops back and forth between the ink fountain roller and an ink distribution roller. As the ductor contacts the fountain roller, both turn and the ductor is inked. The ductor then swings forward to contact a distribution roller and transfers ink to it. The rate of rotation of the ink fountain roller and the gap between the fountain blade and roller control the amount of ink added to the distribution system. The rollers that actually ink the plate are called form rollers (figure 12.24d).

A simple indication of the quality of a printing press is the number of distribution and form rollers it has. The greater the number of distribution rollers, the more accurate the control of ink uniformity. It is difficult to ink large solid areas on a plate with only one form roller. With three (generally the maximum) it is relatively easy to maintain consistent ink coverage of almost any image area on the plate.

The Dampening Unit

Recall that most lithographic plates function on the principle of water- and ink-receptive areas. In order for ink to adhere only to the image areas on the plate, a layer of moisture must be placed over the nonimage areas before the plate is inked. The dampening system accomplishes this by moistening the plate consistently throughout the press run.

Dampening Unit Configurations

There are no radical differences among the basic designs of most conventional, direct dampening systems (figure 12.25). Like ink-

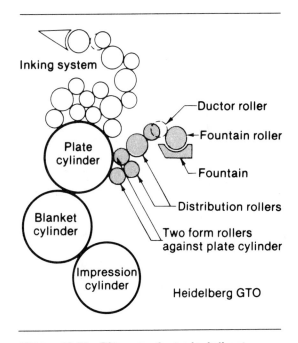

Figure 12.25. Diagram of a typical direct dampening system

ing systems, they all contain some form of fountain, a fountain roller, a ductor roller, distribution rollers, and one or more form rollers.

Not all manufacturers use direct dampening systems where the ink and water rollers are separate. An indirect dampening system, such as the "aquamatic system" found on A. B. Dick duplicators, combines the ink and dampening rollers and carries the water solution to the plate on the ink-covered form rollers (figure 12.26).

Dampening Unit Operation

In a direct dampening system, the dampening fountain roller sits in a pool of fountain solution stored in the dampening fountain. As

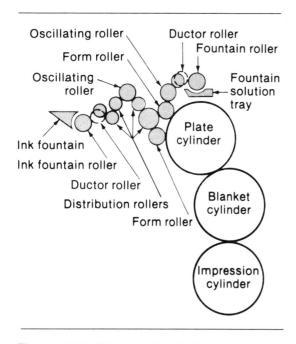

Figure 12.26. Diagram of an indirect dampening system

the press runs, the dampening fountain roller turns, picking up fountain solution from the fountain and holding it on its surface. A ductor roller jogs back and forth touching the fountain roller, where it picks up fountain solution, then touching a dampening distribution roller. The distribution roller(s) takes the fountain solution from the ductor roller to the dampening form roller(s), where it is transferred to the plate.

As mentioned above, in an indirect dampening system, the dampening distribution and form rollers are also the inking distribution and form rollers. In this system all the rollers in the **ink and water train** are inked; then fountain solution is added to the fountain. Because the dampener fountain roller and every other roller in the roller train is inked, the fountain solution literally rides on the surface of the inked rollers and is carried to the plate.

On both systems, the rate at which the dampener fountain roller rotates in the fountain can be varied. The faster the fountain roller turns, the more fountain solution it delivers to the dampening system. In this way, the quantity of moisture reaching the plate can be adjusted.

The Delivery Unit

The delivery unit takes the paper from the printing unit and places it on an outfeed table. There are two common designs for sheet-fed press delivery units: gravity delivery and chain gripper delivery. **Gravity delivery** is the simpler and less dependable of the two. As the sheet leaves the printing unit, it is dropped into a delivery pile. The basic limitation is that paper cannot be delivered faster than gravity can pull it into place. With lightweight papers, air resistance reduces the possible press speed even more. Gravity delivery is usually found on only the smallest, least expensive duplicators.

The most popular design for delivery units is the **chain gripper system** (figure 12.27). With chain delivery, the paper can be either pulled through the printing and delivery unit by the same chain system or transferred from the paper grippers on the impression cylinder in the printing unit to a different set of grippers on the delivery chain.

As the sheet leaves the printing unit, a set of mechanical fingers (grippers) grabs the leading edge of the sheet and pulls it out of the printing system. The gripper bar is attached to a continuous chain that moves the printed sheet to a paper pile, releases it, and moves the grippers back to receive another sheet. The chain moves at the same rate and in synchronization with the feeder, registration, and printing units. As one sheet is delivered, another sheet is being placed onto the registration board. Presses with chain gripper delivery systems can print at high speeds because the gripper chain moves the sheet and does not depend on gravity to remove it from the printing unit.

Delivery Pile Controls

Ideally, the delivery system will form a perfectly neat stack of paper on the outfeed table. If a perfect pile is formed, the printer can easily move it back to the feeder system to print another color, can stack it in a paper cutter to trim it to a finished size, can collate it with other sheets, or can punch, drill, fold, or package it.

Jogging side and back guides are usually used to control the outfeed pile (figure 12.28). As a sheet is dropped onto the stack, the guides are open. As the sheet drops into position, the guides begin to close until they gently push the stock in place. Most systems are designed so that two stationary guides can be adjusted to the paper extremes. The jogging guides are adjusted to touch the remaining two paper sides on their innermost stroke. As the press operates, the delivery pile is continually touched by all four guides. This keeps the stack straight. The entire outfeed table is typically lowered automatically as the height of the delivery pile increases.

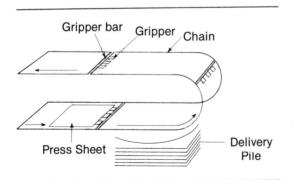

Figure 12.27. Diagram of a chain gripper delivery system

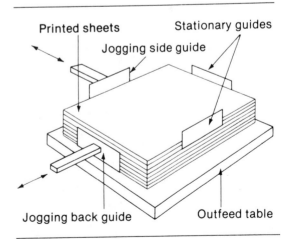

Figure 12.28. Diagram showing jogging side and back guides

A static electric charge is frequently built up on a sheet as it passes through the printing unit. Charged sheets tend to cling to each other and often do not stack properly in the delivery system. The most common **static eliminator** is a piece of copper tinsel attached to a thin copper wire. A length of tinsel is stretched across the delivery unit so that each sheet must brush against it. The wire is grounded through the press and removes the static electricity from the sheet.

Multicolor Sheet-Fed Presses

The demand for multicolor printing is constantly increasing. In an effort to meet this demand, press manufacturers have developed many types of multicolor presses. **Multicolor sheet-fed presses** operate in the same manner as single-color sheet-fed presses, but they are equipped with two or more color printing units arranged in-line (one following the other). Each printing unit is capable of delivering a single color of ink to the press sheet. Most multicolor presses are designed with two, four, or six printing units. Two-color presses are ideal for jobs that require spot color, such as a page of text in which the text is printed in one color, and the display type or graphic elements (rules, boxes, decorative borders, or illustrations) are printed in another color. Four-color presses are designed especially for four-color process printing. A five- or six-color press (figure 12.29) increases printing possibilities even further by allowing a sheet to be printed with four process colors, followed by a flat or match color, or a varnish. Varnish is a clear ink-like substance which changes the reflectance characteristics of the printed piece in the area where the varnish is applied, causing that area to stand out visually and to have a different texture than the rest of the press sheet.

The primary advantage of a multicolor press is that more than one color can be printed in a single pass through the press. Without a multicolor press, the press sheet would have to be printed with one color, then replaced on the infeed table and run through the press again for each additional color required. Not

Figure 12.29. A five color sheet-fed offset press Five printing units are arranged in-line on this press. Note the press controls on the infeed table. These controls can be used to adjust paper feed, along with a variety of press operations, making it possible for the operator to control the press from the infeed end.
Courtesy of Miller Printing Equipment Corp.

only is this a time-consuming operation, but it can lead to misregister problems. As has been mentioned, paper is not dimensionally stable. When passed through the press, each piece of paper is subjected to both ink and water. Moisture from the dampening system tends to make the paper stretch, then shrink as it dries. Absorption and drying of ink on the printed sheet can have a similar effect. Further, when a single-color press is used for a multicolor job, some time will elapse before the paper is put through the press for the next color. During this time the paper may shrink, stretch, or warp slightly owing to humidity and other environmental conditions in the printing plant. The overall effect is that on the second pass through the press, the paper is not exactly the same size as it was on the first pass through the press. This makes critical registration, such as is required for process color, difficult and sometimes impossible. A multicolor press can reduce this problem.

One additional advantage of a multicolor press is that the press operator can judge the quality of the printed sheet immediately as it comes off the press, and he or she can make press adjustments based on this evaluation. When printing process color, all four colors must be printed with the correct press settings if the colors on the final job are to be correct. When a single-color press is used to print process color, improper press adjustments during the printing of the first color may only be discovered as the fourth color is being printed. By this time, all of the sheets have been printed with three colors, and it is too late to make any corrections. The whole job will have to be scrapped and reprinted.

Perfecting Transfer. To increase press flexibility, the press shown in figure 12.29 is equipped with a perfecting transfer system. The system on this press is designed and patented by the Miller Printing Equipment Corporation, though other press manufacturers offer perfecting presses which operate on a similar principle. A schematic of a two-color press equipped with a perfecting transfer system is shown in figure 12.30. With this system it is possible for a two-color press to print two colors on one side, or one color on each side, in one pass through the press. A four-color press equipped with the perfecting transfer system has even greater printing flexibility. It can print four colors on one side, or three colors on one side and one color on the other side, or two colors on each side. Five- or six-color presses can also be equipped with a perfecting transfer system, again increasing printing flexibility.

The perfecting transfer system introduces several additional cylinders which work in conjunction with the impression and blanket cylinders commonly found on an offset press. As shown in figure 12.31, the Miller system uses two transfer cylinders and a perfecting cylinder. The second transfer cylinder is twice the diameter of the first transfer cylinder. Together, these cylinders can pass a press sheet from one printing unit to another so that it reaches the second printing unit with either the printed side facing the second blanket cylinder (multicolor mode) or with the unprinted side facing the second blanket cylinder (perfecting mode). The cylinders are especially designed so that freshly printed ink is not smeared when the printed side of the sheet is pressed against them.

In the perfecting mode, the printed sheet is passed from the first impression to the first transfer cylinder. At this point the printed side is against the face of the first transfer cylinder. The first transfer cylinder passes the sheet to the second transfer cylinder, inked side up (away from the cylinder face). The perfecting cylinder is equipped with two sets of grippers. In the perfecting mode, the perfecting cylinder grips the *tail* edge of the sheet

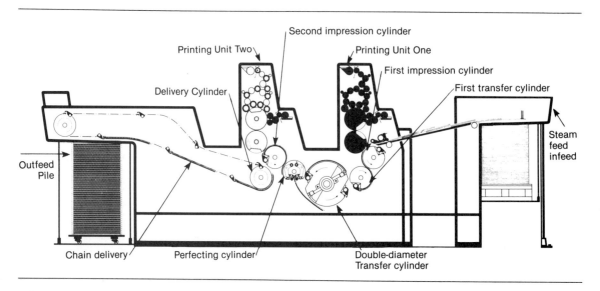

Figure 12.30. A two-color sheet-fed offset press equipped with a perfecting transfer system The two transfer cylinders and the perfecting cylinder in this press allow for printing one color on each side or two colors on one side.
Courtesy of Miller Printing Equipment Corp.

with one set of grippers, and passes it to the second impression cylinder, inked side down (against the cylinder face), with the second set of grippers, to be printed on the opposite side. Thus the sheet leaves the press printed on both sides. In the multicolor (nonperfecting) mode all of the cylinders still handle the sheet, but only one set of grippers is activated on the perfecting cylinder. In this mode the perfecting cylinder grips the sheet on the *lead* edge and passes it to the second impression cylinder inked side up (away from the cylinder face). Thus the sheet is printed with two colors on the same side.

Multicolor Press Monitoring and Control Systems

It is a relatively easy task for a single operator to control infeed, registration, ink and water balance, and outfeed on a single-color press. However, as the number of color units increases and registration becomes more critical, press control becomes a bigger problem. Until recently, the answer to this problem has been to provide each press with enough operators to monitor all press functions. Thus a six-color press might require four to six operators. Even with the required number of operators, press control still presented problems, not the least of which was the inability of the press operators to react quickly enough to make needed press adjustments without a great deal of spoilage.

The use of computers has reduced this problem and has greatly improved the quality of printed products while, at the same time, reducing make-ready time and spoilage. A typical automated press control system is shown in figure 12.32. The system involves the use of a **plate scanner** and a press console.

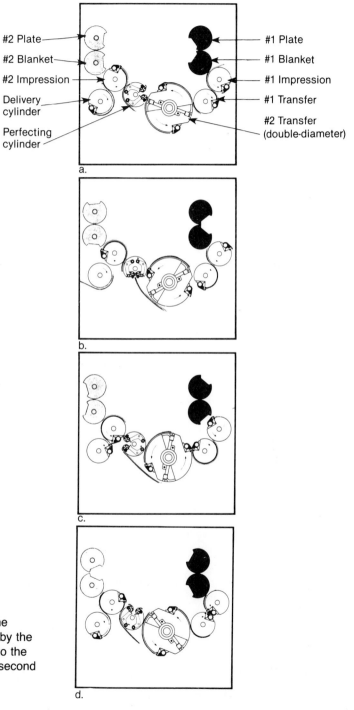

#2 Plate

#2 Blanket

#2 Impression

Delivery cylinder

Perfecting cylinder

#1 Plate

#1 Blanket

#1 Impression

#1 Transfer

#2 Transfer (double-diameter)

a.

b.

c.

Figure 12.31. Schematic of the Miller perfecting transfer system, perfecting mode Note the two-gripper system on the perfecting cylinder which grips the sheet by the tail edge (a), with one gripper, passes it to the second gripper (b and c), then on to the second impression cylinder (d).

Courtesy of Miller Printing Equipment Corp.

d.

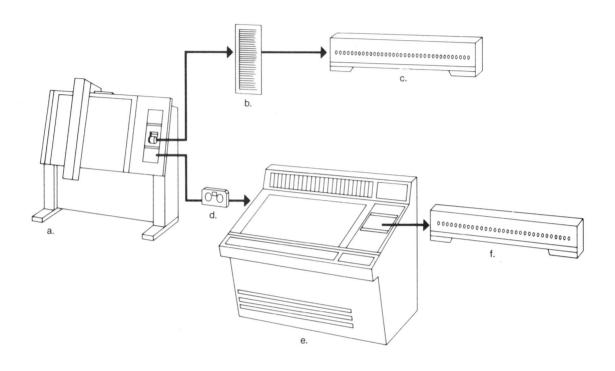

**Figure 12.32. Schematic of a typical automated press control
system** The plate scanner (a) scans the plate and prints information needed
to set the press ink system on paper output (b) for manual ink system setting
(c) or on cassette tape (d) for automatic system setting (f) through the press
console (e).
Courtesy of Miller Printing Equipment Corp.

The plate scanner (figure 12.33) is typically
installed in the plate-making room. After a
plate is made, it is scanned. The scanner moves
across the plate, optically measures the image
area of the plate, and calculates the settings
needed on the press ink keys and the amount
of **roller stroke** needed (the stroke length required on the ink fountain roller). This information can be stored on cassette tape and/or
on a printout. The tape or printout is then
passed, along with the plate, to the pressroom. On fully automated systems, the in-

formation from the cassette tape can be fed
directly into the press from the press console.
Adjustment of the ink system will be made
automatically when the press reads the information on the tape. Where the press is not
equipped with this fully automatic feature,
the press operator can use the information on
the printout to preset the ink system. A plate
scanner significantly reduces both make-ready
and spoilage because presetting produces almost the final ink settings required for the job
with the first sheet off the press.

Figure 12.33. A plate scanner Note the printout tape in the center of the control panel and the slot for cassette tape at the top of the panel. The scanner is built into the vertical bar positioned over the plate.
Courtesy of Miller Printing Equipment Corp.

The **press console** is really the heart of an automated press system (figure 12.34). At the start of the job, the press operator enters parameters about the job into the press console. These parameters include ink density and other job specifications. As the job is printed, the operator pulls sample press sheets from the outfeed table and places them on a scanning densitometer which reads a **color bar** printed on each press sheet (figure 12.35). Color bar images can be seen recorded on the plate shown in figure 12.33. From the color bar, the console computer gathers information about density values, register, dot gain, doubling, ink trapping, and print contrast (see Chapter 13). This information can be used by the console computer to correct for press problems automatically, or to alert the operator to problems through the CRT screen for manual press adjustments.

Automated press systems offer several major advantages. Not only do they reduce spoilage during make-ready, but they keep spoilage down throughout the job by allowing for fast, accurate press adjustment. Because the press console is preprogrammed with parameters for the job, printing problems can be recognized instantly and the job quickly returned to the quality standards established on the "OK" sheet (the sheet approved by the printer or press operator). It takes only a few seconds for a press operator to scan a press sheet at the computer console and make press adjustments. Even if the adjustments are made manually, they can be made from the computer console. This is an additional advantage, because fewer operators are required to run the press. Thus the printer can deliver more acceptable quality faster, and at less cost. This makes the printer more competitive in a highly competitive printing market.

Though the introduction of automated press operations means that fewer press operators are required to run a press, computer systems have not reduced the overall number of press operators required in the industry. Instead, they have increased the amount of quality color printing being done, and greatly increased the knowledge needed and the type of skills required by press operators.

While few educational institutions are equipped with computer-controlled presses, the knowledge gained in school from manual press operations is still valuable. No matter how automated press systems become, there will always be a need for skilled operators who understand the basics of press operation

Figure 12.34. A press console Note the CRT tube (right-hand side of the console). The sheet scanner is located below the CRT tube. The switch controls on the right-hand side of the console are used for actual press adjustment.
Courtesy of Miller Printing Equipment Corp.

and the concepts of print quality. This is the type of knowledge that is gained during manual press operation, and it provides a firm foundation on which to build the skills needed to operate an automated press.

Web Offset Presses

A detailed description of web offset press operation is beyond the scope of this text. However, the growth of web offset printing—particularly for printing books, newspapers, business forms, magazines, directories, and packaging—has made the process a major part of the commercial printing industry. The fol-

lowing information will give you a brief introduction to the web offset process, and to the types of web presses and auxiliary equipment commonly used in the industry.

As has been mentioned, web printing refers to printing on a continuous roll of paper (or some other substrate) rather than printing on individual sheets. The actual method of image transfer in web offset does not differ from the offset printing method used for sheet-fed work. The image is transferred from a printing plate to a blanket, and from the blanket to the printing substrate. However, because the substrate is wound on a roll and travels continuously through the press, the infeed, registration, and delivery systems used

GATF COMPACT COLOR TEST STRIP

Figure 12.35. One type of color bar Colors printed on this test strip can be read by a scanning densitometer and used to monitor press operation.
Courtesy of Graphic Arts Technical Foundation

on web presses are different from those used on sheet-fed presses. The major sections of a typical web press, shown in figure 12.36, are the infeed unit, the printing unit, and the delivery unit.

Infeed.   Paper is delivered to the press by the infeed section. The infeed section typically contains a **roll stand** to hold the paper rolls; a **splicer** which automatically splices the end of one web to the beginning of another web; a **web-steering** device which controls the **sidelay** (side-to-side position) of the infeeding web; and a **tensioner** which maintains the proper tension on the web as it enters the press.

Printing.   The printing section is made up of one or more printing units. Each printing unit contains one or more **printing couples.** A printing couple contains an inking system, a dampening system, a plate cylinder, a blanket cylinder, and an impression cylinder. Each printing couple can print one color of ink.

Delivery.   The first major component of the delivery section is an ink drying device. After the ink dryer, the delivery section can consist of a variety of devices, from a simple sheeter, which cuts the moving web into sheets of the required size, to a combination sheeter and folder, which can both fold the web into final signatures and trim the signatures to size. Where no folding or cutting is required, the delivery section can contain only a rewinder which winds the web into a roll for later processing.

Types of Web Presses

The most popular web presses for commercial printing are the **blanket-to-blanket** and the **common impression cylinder** presses. A

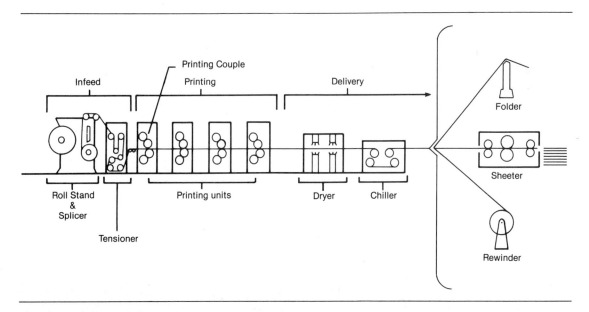

Figure 12.36. Major sections of a web offset press

blanket-to-blanket web press uses two printing couples to print simultaneously on both sides of the web. Thus it is a perfecting press. However, as you will note from figure 12.7, each blanket cylinder serves a dual function; it serves as a blanket for one printing couple, and as the impression cylinder for the other printing couple. Thus impression pressure is developed between two blanket surfaces, rather than between a blanket and an impression cylinder.

Common Impression Cylinder (CIC). Common impression cylinder presses use one large, central impression cylinder in conjunction with a number of printing couples (figure 12.37). The web travels around the common impression cylinder, passing under one or more blanket cylinders, each of which is part of a printing couple. The advantage of a CIC press is that the paper or other substrate will

have a uniform stretch around the large impression cylinder. This uniformity makes obtaining proper register, and keeping register consistent, much easier than it is on a blanket-to-blanket press.

In-Line. In addition to blanket-to-blanket and CIC presses, in-line web presses are also common, particularly for forms printing (figure 12.38). The major feature of an in-line press is that each printing unit consists of only one blanket and impression cylinder combined with an inking and dampening system. Thus in-line presses are not perfecting and are used mostly for work that needs to be printed on one side only, such as business forms and labels. However, some in-line presses provide for printing on both sides by inserting a **turn bar** between printing units. The turn bar turns the web over so that it can be printed on the back side by the remaining printing

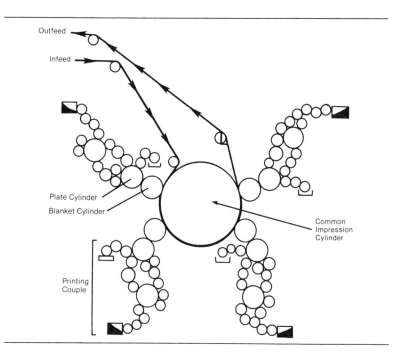

Figure 12.37. Schematic of a common impression cylinder press

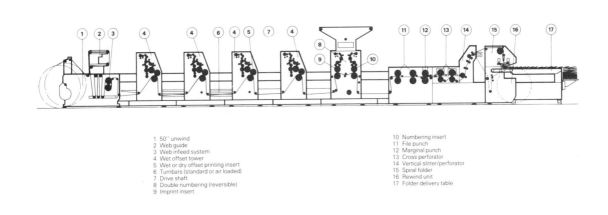

1 50'' unwind
2 Web guide
3 Web infeed system
4 Wet offset tower
5 Wet or dry offset printing insert
6 Turnbars (standard or air loaded)
7 Drive shaft
8 Double numbering (reversible)
9 Imprint insert

10 Numbering insert
11 File punch
12 Marginal punch
13 Cross perforator
14 Vertical slitter/perforator
15 Spiral folder
16 Rewind unit
17 Folder delivery table

Figure 12.38. An in-line forms press This press is specially designed for printing business forms, checks, lottery tickets, envelopes, data mailers, and other direct mail applications. Equipped with four printing couples and a rewinder, the press can print from one to eight colors.
Courtesy of Müller-Martini Corporation

units. Typical presses can print two to four colors on one side of the web or one to two colors on both sides.

Components of a Web Press

The major components of the printing couple for offset printing (the plate and blanket cylinder, and associated ink and water systems) have already been discussed in this chapter. We will confine our discussions here to the components of a web press which are not typically found on a sheet-fed offset press.

Roll Stand.   The **roll stand** holds one or two webs of paper, and it meters the paper feed into the press. On most presses, the roll stand

is placed in-line with the printing couples. However, it is possible to locate the roll stand to one side of the press or beneath the press to conserve space or to keep paper roll-handling operations out of the press room (figure 12.39). Many presses are equipped with auxiliary roll stands so that more than one web can be fed to the press at a time (figure 12.40). This provides great flexibility on a multiprinting unit web press, in that an individual paper web can be printed by one, two, three, four, or more printing couples. Thus on a six-color web press, a two-color job can be printed by two printing units at the same time that a four-color job is printed on the remaining four printing units.

Control of the web as it unwinds from the roll stand and enters the printing unit is

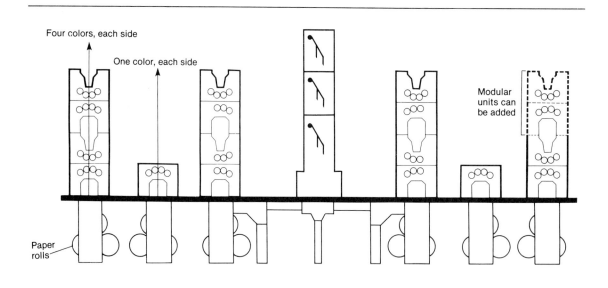

Figure 12.39. Web press flexibility This multiunit web press is supplied with four base units to which other vertical printing couples can be added. With a modular unit design, the press can be configured for the type of job to be printed, and press flexibility is greatly increased. Note that the paper is fed from rolls below the press room floor.
Courtesy of Graphic Systems Division, Rockwell International Corporation

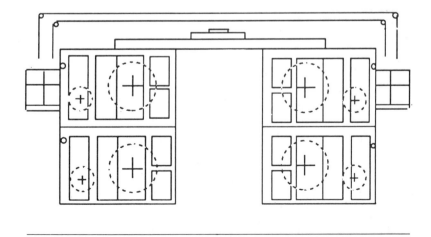

Figure 12.40. Roll stands This web press is equipped with four roll stands to increase press flexibility. The schematic below the photograph shows roll-stand configuration.
Courtesy of Enkel Corporation

established by a **dancer roller** which operates in conjunction with a brake on the roll stand. The infeeding web wraps around the dancer roller which actually rides on the moving web, pressing its weight against the moving paper. The dancer is free to move up and down; this movement controls a brake on the roll stand. As shown in figure 12.41, if the web feeds too rapidly, the paper under the dancer roller becomes slack and the dancer roller drops, which automatically applies a brake to the roll stand, slowing paper feed. If the web feeds too slowly, just the opposite occurs. The paper under the dancer becomes taut, lifting the dancer, which releases the brake on the roll stand, allowing the web to feed more rapidly.

Splicer. In addition to the dancer roller, it is common for a roll stand to include a splicer, sometimes called a "paster." The splicer automatically positions a new web for infeed, and splices the lead end of this new web to the tail end of the web being printed. There are two types of splicers: **flying splicers** and **zero speed splicers.** Both operate automatically, and both use adhesives to connect the two webs. The difference between them is that a flying splicer connects the two webs while each is rotating at press speed. It does so by pressing both the adhesived lead edge of the new web and the tail edge of the printing web against a splicing arm (figure 12.42). The zero speed splicer uses a **festoon,** consisting of several rollers. As shown in figure 12.43, the festoon holds enough paper to feed the press during the splice. Thus the splice can be made while both the old and new web are stationary, without stopping the press.

Web Tensioner. While the roll stand and dancer roller work together to meter the web as it enters the printing units, they cannot completely control web tension. Several factors, such as the tension with which the web was rolled at the mill, the type of the paper or other substrate on the web, and the configuration of the press itself affect web tension during printing. The dancer and break mechanism cannot adequately compensate for all of these factors to maintain proper web tension. Yet web tension is critically important. Improper tension can lead to improper image registration. In the worst case, improper tension can cause a web break, forcing the operator to shut the press down.

Most presses employ a tensioner to maintain consistent web tension. The tensioner consists of a series of rollers over which the infeeding web passes. As the infeeding roll passes over the tensioner rollers, it "recovers" from the tension with which it was wound at the mill, and is regulated to the proper, even tension for the press run. Many tensioners consist of a series of variable speed rollers, followed by a second dancer roller. This configuration ensures proper web tension, with minimum variation (figure 12.44).

Dryer and Chill Rolls. The dryer and chill rolls work together to ensure that the ink on the printed sheet is dry and set as it comes off the web. If the web were allowed to leave the press with wet ink, ink setoff would be a problem, and the wet ink would be almost certain to smear as the web passed through the folder, cutter, or rewinder. Most web printing inks are heat-set inks. A web printed with heat-set ink is passed from the last printing unit through a dryer, which brings the moving web up to a temperature of about 300° F in a few seconds. This temperature is high enough to evaporate most of the ink solvent. It also softens the resin which will bind the ink pigments together during chilling. Drying is immediately followed by chilling, which is accomplished by passing the web over a series of water-cooled chill rolls. During chilling, web temperature is reduced to about 90°

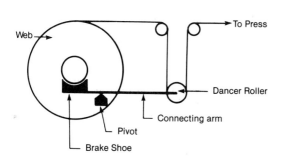

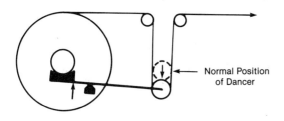

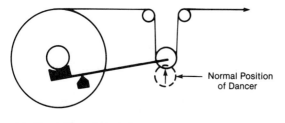

c) As Dancer Rises, Brake is Released

Figure 12.41. Schematic showing operation of dancer roller and roll brake Up or down movement of dancer roller controls brake on roll stand.

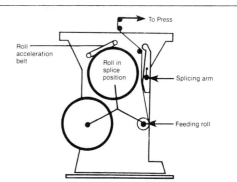

a) Splice in preparation, new roll accelerated and splicer arm in position.

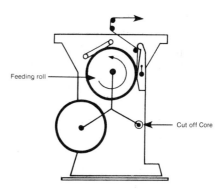

b) Splice made, new roll feeding and old roll cut, leaving core.

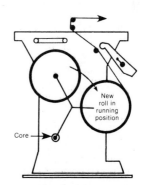

c) New roll moved into running position; splicer arm and acceleration belt moved aside.

Figure 12.42. A flying splicer After the splice is made, the core is removed and a new web is mounted.

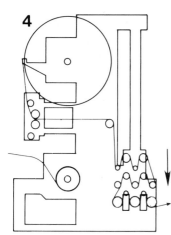

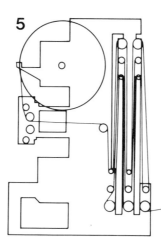

(1) The roll is feeding into the press, and the festoon has begun rising. (2) The festoon has expanded to store a full 80 ft. of paper; a new roll has been mounted, and its lead edge prepared for the splice. (3) The expired roll has been stopped, and paper feeds into the running press from the collapsing festoon. The lead edge of the splice roll has been placed close to the surface of the expiring web.

Detail view of actual splice

(A) Top roll running with bottom roll being prepared

(B) Top roll running with bottom roll ready for splice

(C) Moment of splice

(D) Bottom roll running with top roll being prepared

(4) The splice has been made, the expiring web severed, and the newly spliced roll accelerated up to press speed. The festoon starts rising and storing paper. (5) The festoon is fully expanded, and the roll stand is ready for the mounting of a new roll.

1—Idler rolls	3—Cutoff knives
2—Web clamping brushes to hold severed web	4—Nip rolls
	5—Cutoff brush
	6—Vacuum blade

Figure 12.43. Splicing on a zero speed splicer

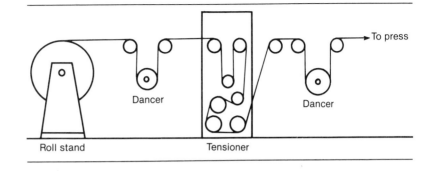

Figure 12.44. A web tensioner The dancer rollers before and after the tensioner help maintain proper web tension.

.F, which is cool enough to set the binder and pigment, producing a dry print.

Folding and Cutting. Owing to the nature of the work done on web presses, most web presses are equipped with one or more folders which fold work into signatures as the web leaves the press. The type of folder required depends to a large extent on the type of work being printed on the press. There are three basic types of folders: former folders; jaw folders; and chopper, or quarter, folders. Often, all three folding devices are incorporated into a **combination folder,** as shown in figure 12.45.

A **former folder** folds the web by pulling it over a triangular-shaped former board. This action makes a "with-the-grain" fold by folding the web along its length. Additional folds after the former fold are made with jaw and chopper folders. A **jaw folder** folds the web across its width (cross grain) by allowing it to travel around a cylinder equipped with a tucker blade which forces the paper into a jaw (opening) on an opposing cylinder. After passing through the folding jaw, the web is automatically cut into individual signatures and, if necessary, passed to a chopper folder. In the **chopper folder** each signature is forced between two rotating fold rollers that make the final fold, again with the grain.

Press Console. Most modern web presses will print on a moving web at speeds as great as 1,800 feet per minute. Much paper would be wasted if the press operator had to examine printed signatures while the press was running in order to determine if press adjustments were needed, and then had to go to the appropriate printing unit and make the required adjustments. High-speed web presses are equipped with press consoles similar to those used on automated sheet-fed presses, which provide electronic control for register and image quality on the moving web (figure 12.46). Information such as web side-lay, register, color consistency, and backup (the relative position of the image being printed on the top and bottom of the web) is computer controlled. Press adjustments can be made "on the fly" (as the press is running at printing speed). Settings for each printing unit or couple—such as ink and dampening settings, and horizontal and vertical register—can be made directly from the console. Once the press operator has the press set properly, computers continually monitor press performance and make adjustments to maintain the initial settings. The press operator monitors the console and, if necessary, makes press adjustments by adjusting switches on the console, which cause the appropriate adjustments to be made on the press itself. Thus

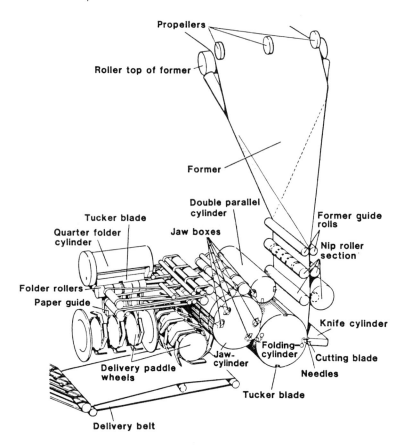

Propellers

Roller top of former

Former

Double parallel cylinder

Tucker blade

Quarter folder cylinder

Jaw boxes

Former guide rolls

Nip roller section

Folder rollers

Paper guide

Knife cylinder

Delivery paddle wheels

Jaw-cylinder

Folding-cylinder

Cutting blade

Needles

Tucker blade

Delivery belt

Figure 12.45. A combination roller
Courtesy of Solna, Incorporated

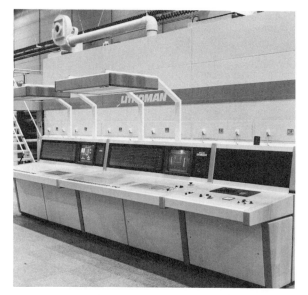

Figure 12.46. A web press console This press console is designed for complete press control in a single location. Note CRT graph display of operating conditions, color-balanced overhead lighting. Web drying unit is located behind the console.
Courtesy of M. A. N.-Roland, ISA, Inc.

the console greatly reduces wastage by reducing the amount of misprinted material and by reducing the amount of press downtime. Some presses even have automatic blanket washing units that are controlled from the press console. Consoles also reduce the number of people required to operate the press.

Key Terms

feeder unit
registration unit
printing unit
delivery unit
platen press
flat bed cylinder press
sucker feet
stream feeder
sheet separator
double-sheet detector
registration
fit
headstop
three-cylinder principle
two-cylinder principle
impression
fountain roller

rotary press
impression cylinder
plate cylinder
offset printing
perfecting press
duplicator
distribution roller
ductor roller
form roller
chain delivery
static eliminator
roll stand
web splicer
web tensioner
printing couple
common impression cylinder

web-fed
sheet-fed
pilefeeding
make-ready
continuous feeding
successive-sheet-feeding
in-line press
dancer roller
flying splicer
zero speed splicer
chill rolls
combination folder
former folder
jaw folder
chopper folder
press console

Questions for Review

1. What are the four units common to all presses?

2. How does a platen press differ from a flat bed cylinder press?

3. Why is the design of a rotary press efficient for printing?

4. Explain the offset principle.

5. Draw the cylinder configuration for a blanket-to-blanket perfecting press.

6. Describe the differences between an offset duplicator and a true offset press.

7. How does a successive-sheet-feeder feed paper to a press, and what controls are available on such a feeder?

8. What is the difference between registration and fit?

9. How is registration controlled on a sheet-fed offset press?

10. Describe the three- and two-cylinder configurations used on offset presses.

11. Why must adjustment be made to control impression?

12. Describe the roller train for the inking and dampening systems on a press equipped with a conventional direct dampening system.

13. Explain the operation of a chain delivery system.

14. What are the major units of a web offset press?

15. How does a common impression cylinder press differ from a blanket-to-blanket press?

16. How do the roll stand and dancer roller control web travel?

17. Describe the method used to make a splice with a flying splicer and with a zero speed splicer.

18. Why are a dryer and chill rolls needed on a high-speed web offset press?

19. Describe the three types of folders commonly found on a web offset press.

20. What is the purpose of a press console?

Chapter Thirteen

Offset Press Operation

Anecdote to Chapter Thirteen

Original drawing of Senefelder's lithographic press design

Alois Senefelder, the inventor of lithography, designed the first lithographic press sometime between 1798 and 1800. He borrowed the basic idea of a press that was used to reproduce copperplate engravings—a relief process. Senefelder took what was basically a flat bed cylinder design and added a tympan frame and frisket to hold the paper, a flexible blade instead of a roller to apply the pressure, and a lever-counterweight system to control the blade tension.

In actual production, two workers operated the device. They drew a design by hand on a slab of limestone with a grease crayon-like material and placed the "plate" on the movable bed of the press. They then covered the stone with a water and gum arabic solution. The liquid flowed off of the greasy image but covered the nongreasy stone surface. Then they vigorously rolled an ink-covered leather roller back and forth over the stone. The ink was repelled by the water film but attached to the grease image. The stone was ready to print after the workers carefully wiped it with a clean cloth to remove any excess moisture.

They mounted a sheet of previously dampened paper on the tympan, closed the frisket to hold it in place, and lowered the frame into contact with the stone. Then they lowered the blade against the back of the tympan. One worker stood on the pressure lever while the other slowly turned a wheel to slide the bed under the blade. It was this scraping pressure that actually caused the ink to be transferred from the stone to the paper. There was always danger that too much pressure would be applied by the blade and the stone would be broken or that the sheet would slip under the scraping action. After one pass, they released the blade, hinged the tympan frame out of the way, and hung the sheet on a line to dry. Then they repeated the whole process.

Senefelder's press was considered a marvel of its time. In an average twelve-hour day, two craftsmen could produce perhaps fifty acceptable copies. His later designs included an automatic dampening and inking system and a lever scraper blade that moved across the stone instead of the stone moving under the blade.

Although steam power was applied to a litho press around 1866, Senefelder's basic design was not changed until the offset press was introduced in 1907.

Objectives for Chapter Thirteen

After completing this chapter, you will be able to:

- Recall the most common inking unit configuration and describe setup operations.
- Recall the most common dampening unit configuration and describe setup operations.

- Describe the basic steps in setting up and operating an offset lithographic press.
- Recall press concerns when printing process color on sheet-fed offset lithographic presses.
- Describe several quality control devices commonly used in offset printing.

– Recall common roller and blanket problems and solutions, and describe mechanical adjustments that are possible on most presses.
– Recall common press concerns.

– Recognize a troubleshooting checklist and be able to use it to suggest solutions to press problems.
– List common press maintenance steps.

Introduction

There are so many different offset presses on the market today with so many minute operational differences that it is easy for the reader to become bogged down trying to learn press operation by the "which-switch-does-what" method. The problem with this approach is that the operator is lost if moved to another type of machine.

An operation manual prepared by the press manufacturer is unexcelled for teaching "switches." Such a manual can provide more detailed on-the-job information for a production situation than any textbook could ever hope to provide. The purpose of this chapter is not to provide a "general operation manual," but to deal with fundamental understandings that will enable the reader to run any offset duplicator or sheet-fed press after a review of the manufacturer's operation manual.

This chapter is divided into two sections. The first section covers the information necessary to run an offset press. The second section gives important information on press-troubleshooting concerns.

SECTION 1

The purpose of this section is to examine the general operation of any sheet-fed offset press or duplicator. Refer to an operation manual for the details of operation for a specific machine.

Offset Press Operation

Experienced printers typically set up the ink and water sections of the printing unit before adjusting the paper feed. In an industrial situation each machine is usually assigned one operator (or group of operators). Whoever is assigned to a press knows its characteristics and typically runs only a few standard sheet sizes. Novice printers, however, do not have the same advantages. In a learning situation the student is not familiar with the machine, is not aware of the sheet size previously run, and is generally hesitant when confronted with a machine as complicated as an offset press. For these reasons, the authors recommend that when learning press operation, students adjust the paper feed before adding ink or fountain solution to the printing unit. When the sheets are consistently passing through the press without jam-ups or misfeeding, students can direct their attention to obtaining proper ink-water balance.

Feeding the Paper

It is important that the pile of press sheets be accurately cut to the same size, be of the same thickness (paper weight), and not be wrinkled or stuck together. Begin by fanning the pile to remove any static electricity that might be holding individual sheets together (figure 13.1). Place the pile in the feeder section of the press, slightly off center. When the sheet passes through the registration unit, it is generally jogged or pulled from ⅛ to 3⁄16 inch and is then centered on the registration board.

Push the pile forward so that it is squarely seated against the front plate of the feeder when held by the side and back guides (figure 13.2). The top of the paper pile must be perfectly level and parallel to the registra-

Figure 13.2. Adding paper to the feeder section Seat the pile of paper squarely against the front plate of the feeder.

tion board. If the stock sags, place a heavy board (such as a binder board cut slightly smaller than the paper size) under the pile. If the stock is curled, insert wedges at several points into the pile to make the top surface level (figure 13.3).

Next adjust the pile height below the feeding mechanism (generally, sucker feet) (figure 13.4). Heavy paper must be closer to the sucker feet than is necessary for lighter material. To set the paper height, turn the machine on and allow the automatic pile height control to raise the stock to the previously set position. Turn the machine off and check the distance between the pile and the sucker feet when they are in the lowest position. If the distance is not between ⅛ and ¼ inch, lower the pile manually, readjust the pile height control, and allow the press to run and lift the paper pile to the new setting. Feeding problems will result if the pile height is not properly set. If the paper pile is too high, the sucker feet will pick up double sheets, or jam-ups will result because the air

Figure 13.1. Fanning the press sheets The press sheets are fanned to remove any static electricity.

Figure 13.3. Using wedges to level the paper Push wedges under the pile of paper to level the top surface of curled stock.

and vacuum system is not allowed to do its job. If the pile is too low, the sheets will not be picked up or misfeeds will occur.

The purpose of the air blast is to float the top few sheets above the rest of the pile on a blanket of air. The amount of air blast needed will vary depending on the weight and size of the stock being printed. In general, the air blast should be adjusted to the point that the sheets do not vibrate and the topmost sheet nearly contacts the sucker feet (figure 13.5). Too much air blast will cause the top sheets to press together, rather than separate. Vacuum should be sufficient to draw the top sheet the short distance into contact with the sucker feet but not great enough to pick up more than one sheet.

Before allowing the feeder mechanism to send a sheet to the registration unit, the pull-in wheels (not on all machines) and the double-sheet detector must be set. Adjust the pull-in wheels to a uniform pressure so that each sheet is pulled squarely from the feeder onto the registration board. Double-sheet detectors either open a trap door and eject multiple sheets to a tray below the registration board or they mechanically (or electronically) cause the press to stop when a double sheet is detected. Set the device to pass the thickness of one sheet but to trip the press if more than one sheet is fed.

Next allow the press to feed a sheet into the registration unit and to stop it in contact with the headstop (figure 13.6). Line up the conveyer tapes, straps, or skid rollers to the

Figure 13.4. Adjusting the pile height

Figure 13.5. Adjusting the air blast

Figure 13.6. Adjusting the registration system Adjust the registration system by allowing a sheet of paper to move into contact with the headstop, and position the sheet jogger or pull guide.

Figure 13.7. Adjusting the delivery side guides

sheet size. Then adjust the sheet jogger or pull guide to push or pull the sheet about ⅛ inch. The sheet should lie flat without binding or curling. Inch the sheet into the grippers that pull it between the impression cylinder and the blanket cylinder and allow it to be transferred to the delivery system.

Move the sheet to the delivery unit, but adjust the delivery table side guides before the sheet is released from the chain grippers (figure 13.7). Allow the sheet to drop onto the delivery table and position the table end jogger.

In order to check the entire system, start the machine and allow paper to pass from feeder to delivery. The sheets should be smoothly and consistently fed to the registration board. Each sheet should be uniformly registered and transferred to the printing unit. The delivery system should remove each sheet and stack a perfect pile on the outfeed table. Final adjustments for image registration will

be made after the printing unit has been inked and the first few proof sheets have been checked.

It is wise to place a quantity of make-ready sheets on top of the press sheet pile. Be certain that the make-ready sheets are of the same weight and surface finish as the final sheets (figure 13.8). These make-ready sheets can be used for initial press setup.

Preparing the Printing Unit

Recall that basically two different systems are used to put water solution and ink on the printing plate: the direct system and the indirect system. In the direct system, moisture is transferred to the plate directly from a dampener form roller. In the indirect system, the water is transferred to the plate from the ink form rollers. The major difference in printing unit preparation for these two presses is that with the indirect system, the fountain solution cannot be added to the water fountain until after the press is completely inked. In the direct system, the ink and fountain so-

Figure 13.8. Using make-ready sheets Notice that a marker is placed between the make-ready or scrap sheets and the clean press sheets on the infeed table.

Courtesy of SUCO Learning Resources and R. Kampas

Figure 13.9. The ink fountain The fountain holds a pool of ink that is passed to the inking system and controlled by ink fountain keys.

lution can be put into the ink and water fountain during the same step. It is important to keep in mind which system you are working on as you read the following.

Adjusting the Ink Feed. Ink is transferred from the ink fountain reservoir by a ductor roller that contacts the fountain roller. The consistency of the ink layer over the fountain roller directly influences the amount of ink fed to the distribution section.

Many ink fountains are set up with ink fountain keys that allow the press operator to adjust the ink feed to allow for variation in ink coverage needed on the plate (figure 13.9). If large solids or halftones cover one section of the plate, it will be necessary to feed an additional quantity of ink to that area of the plate (figure 13.10).

When you are setting up an ink fountain, assume that the ink feed needs adjustment. Begin by loosening all the fountain keys, which will bring the ink fountain doctor blade

out of contact with the fountain roller (figure 13.11). Reverse the process by gently tightening each key until you feel blade pressure against the roller. Then move the keys out slightly, allowing a small gap between the blade and fountain roller.

When the doctor blade is straight and parallel to the fountain roller, you can add ink to the ink fountain. To check for uniform ink distribution, manually rotate the press until the ink ductor roller touches the ink fountain roller. Then turn the ink fountain roller and observe the appearance of the ink coverage on the ductor roller. If the surface is evenly covered, the keys are properly set. If heavy or light areas are noticeable across the system, make set-screw adjustments until the ink layer is consistent. If some areas of the plate require more ink than others, open the fountain keys in line with those sections to allow more ink to pass to the plate.

Once the first rough ink adjustments have been made, without bringing the water or ink form rollers into contact with the plate

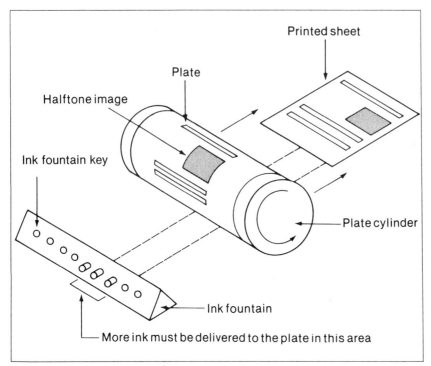

Figure 13.10. Adjusting the ink fountain In areas where large halftones or other kinds of dense copy are to be printed from the plate, the ink fountain keys must be adjusted to deliver more ink.

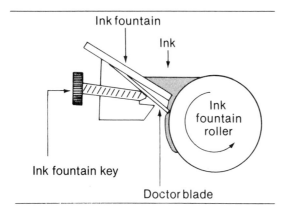

Figure 13.11. Diagram of an ink fountain key As the ink fountain key is adjusted, it moves the doctor blade either toward or away from the ink fountain roller, and thereby decreases or increases the amount of ink that is deposited on the roller.

cylinder, turn the machine on and allow the systems to ink up. As the distribution rollers work the ink to a fine layer, make small adjustments to ensure ink train uniformity. Do not overink the system. It is easier to add ink as needed than it is to remove ink from the system.

Adjusting the Water Feed. Fountain solution is added to most presses and duplicators from a storage bottle that keeps the water fountain full by gravity feed. This bottle should be located and tipped into place at this time. Remember, if you are operating an indirect dampening system, the fountain solution should not be added until the whole roller train is inked. In contrast, the fountain solution can be added to a direct dampening system before, after, or during ink adjustments.

Indirect systems have no covers on any of the ink and dampener rollers. Direct systems generally have cloth or fiber covers on the dampener ductor and form rollers. If these dampening covers are bone dry (as may occur after a long period of press shutdown), turn on the press, bring the dampener ductor roller into contact with the fountain roller, and turn the fountain roller by hand to add extra fountain solution to the water ductor. This action will speed up the dampening process. Be careful not to soak the ductor roller, however, as this will overdampen the press.

Another way to speed up the dampening process is to soak a cotton wipe in the fountain tray and squeegee the dampening solution onto the ductor roller. The form roller cover should be damp to the touch but not dripping wet. Once the unit is adequately inked and moistened, stop the press and insert the plate.

Attaching the Plate.   Mount the plate on the press by inserting the front edge of the plate into the lead clamp of the plate cylinder and tightening it into position (figure 13.12). If

Figure 13.12. Mounting the plate on the press

packing is required, select and cut the appropriate material. Position the packing sheets between the plate and cylinder (if necessary) and rotate the cylinder forward so that the plate is curved into contact with the plate cylinder. When the rear plate clamps are exposed, insert the tail edge of the plate and tighten the clamp. The plate should be tight around the cylinder but should not be distorted or stretched.

Starting Up and Proofing

Most lithographic plates have had some form of gum preservative coating applied to protect the surface for the time between development and placement on the press. Moisten a sponge with plain water or fountain solution and wipe the entire plate to dissolve the coating. If a direct image plate is used, it is at this point that a special etch or starter solution must be used.

Inking the Plate.   If you are operating an *indirect* system, start the press and allow it to operate for a moment; then move the form rollers into contact with the plate. The plate should pick up ink in the image areas and no ink in the nonimage areas. If no ink is picked up anywhere on the plate after several press revolutions, check to make sure that the form rollers are in contact with the plate. If they are, you must either cut back on the moisture or add ink until the image appears on the plate. To determine which adjustment is necessary, stop the press and observe the plate. If the plate is moist with only a thin film of fountain solution (not dripping), more ink is probably called for. If the plate is overdampened, adjust the water fountain to deliver less moisture.

If you are operating a *direct* dampening system, start the press, let it operate for a moment, and lower the dampener form rollers into contact with the plate. Release the rollers, stop the press, and check the plate. The surface should be moist, but dampening solution should not drip from the plate. If the plate is not moist, adjust the fountain system to deliver more moisture and repeat the process of dampening and checking. When the dampening form rollers are delivering enough moisture to the plate surface, lower the ink form rollers into contact with the plate. Ink should be transferred to only the image areas. If ink is deposited in nonimage areas, the problem is probably lack of moisture. Place additional fountain solution onto the dampener form roller in the scumming area.

Press Proofing.   Once the plate is properly inked, place the press on "impression" (the plate cylinder lowered into contact with the blanket cylinder) and allow several make-ready sheets to pass through the printing unit.

The initial concern is only with image position, not with image quality. Examine the first few sheets for consistency of image placement, and compare the image position with the proofs or layout specifications for the job. All offset presses allow the image to be raised or lowered on the sheet by moving the position of the plate image on the blanket. On most presses you can skew the plate on the plate cylinder or the paper on the registration board to square the image on the press sheet. Before final side-to-side and up-and-down adjustments are made, the image must be square to the lead edge of the press sheet. The side-to-side image position can be adjusted by moving the registration system.

After obtaining the desired image position, start the press, lower the dampening and ink form rollers into plate contact, and begin the run with the make-ready sheets. As the sheets pass through the press, examine the image quality and make appropriate ad-

justments to the ink or water system and the impression cylinder. As the first clean sheets begin to be fed, set the sheet counter to zero and begin the press run.

Achieving Proper Ink-Water Balance.   The ink-water balance is crucial in offset printing. If not enough moisture is on the plate, the image will scum on the press sheet. If too much moisture reaches the plate, the image will appear light and washed out (not dense enough) on the press sheet. Adding ink to an overdampened plate will not correct the problem. In fact, it will make matters worse because once the correct amount of moisture is delivered to the plate, the press will be overinked.

It is important to remember that small changes made at the fountain rollers take a while to work their way through the distribution and form rollers to the plate. Most fountain rollers are adjusted by a ratchet arrangement. A lever is moved forward or back so many "clicks" along the ratchet to make the fountain roller turn faster or slower. Often the lever has a scale printed next to it. This scale does not refer to any specific quantity of ink or moisture, but rather is relative to the rate of fountain roller rotation at any given time. Moving the lever up the scale makes the fountain roller rotate more rapidly. Moving it down the scale causes the roller to rotate slower.

The water fountain roller alone controls the amount of moisture placed on the plate. However, on the inking system both the opening of the ink fountain keys and the rotation rate of the ink fountain roller control the quantity of ink reaching the plate. In order to achieve proper ink-water balance, the ink fountain keys, ink fountain roller rotation rate, and water fountain roller rotation rate must all be properly adjusted. When they are adjusted properly and the press can be run through several thousand impressions without the press operator touching the ink or water adjustments, the ink and water systems are said to be "in balance."

Ink-water balance can be achieved only while the press is actually printing. An inexperienced press operator may have to print quite a few make-ready sheets to achieve this balance. Even experienced press operators allow up to 6% spoilage for a run of 1,000 sheets. In other words, an experienced operator expects to print up to 60 press sheets before getting the press to feed properly and reaching the correct ink-water balance. These sheets, called the "spoilage allowance," are added to the 1,000 sheets needed for the final run and are paid for by the customer as part of the job.

The ink and water settings necessary to achieve proper ink-water balance differ with each job printed. One job may have large, dense image areas and require more water and ink than needed for another job. When colors are printed, whether process or flat color, proper ink-water balance must be achieved for each separate color. Thus the spoilage allowance is increased for color work.

The mark of an experienced press operator is the ability to get the press feeding and to reach ink-water balance with the least amount of spoilage. This takes practice and familiarity with a particular press. Novice printers do not have these advantages. However, the following considerations may make achieving ink-water balance a bit easier for the novice:

1. Remember that the gauge of the printing job is the actual press sheet. Experienced press operators watch the *outfeed table*, pulling out every twenty-fifth, fiftieth, or one hundredth press sheet and comparing it to their initial acceptable press proof. A quick check of the press sheet should show consistent density across the image area, no scumming or ink in the nonimage areas, and no "set-off" (printed image on the back of the press sheet). Watching the ink rollers and registration board will not help you determine whether the printed image is acceptable.

2. On direct system presses, the ink and water form rollers can be lifted off the plate separately. It is always a good idea to raise the form rollers off the plate when the ink or water system is being adjusted. This will help keep the plate from becoming overdampened or overinked while the adjustment is being made.

3. Most ink and water fountain rollers can be stopped without stopping the ductor or distribution rollers. If the press appears underdampened, but the ink quantity seems right, stop the paper feed, lift the form rollers, and turn off the ink fountain roller before adjusting the water fountain roller. It may take 50 to 100 press revolutions for a small change in the ink fountain roller adjustment to work its way down to the plate. If the press is inking all this time and no paper is being printed, the ink will build up on the ink rollers. Once the water system is properly adjusted, the press will be overinked.

4. Feed jam-ups are a frequent problem for inexperienced press operators. Generally a jam-up can be corrected in a short time simply by shutting off the press and removing the jammed paper. Occasionally, however, jam-ups take longer to clear. If the press is shut down for much more than two minutes during a run, ink-water balance will have to be reachieved before final sheets are again printed. This will increase spoilage unless new make-ready sheets are placed on the infeed table after the jam-up is cleared.

Remember that all the time the press is shut down, the dampener rollers are drying out. If the shutdown is lengthy, it may take several press revolutions before the dampening system is back up to proper moisture level. After a long shut down, it is best to run the press for a few minutes with the ink system shut off, the form rollers lifted off of the plate, and the dampening system on. Once the dampening system is back up to proper moisture, the dampening form roller(s) can be engaged to moisten the plate, the press briefly stopped, and the plate examined for moisture content.

Cleanup Procedures

With the availability of rubber-based inks, many small job shops clean the ink and water systems only once a week. Some operators only cover the press with a cloth to keep out dust; others spray the ink fountain and rollers with a commercial antiscum material that coats the ink with a thin layer of lacquer and, in effect, forms a seal that prevents drying. The disadvantage of this approach is that the buildup of paper lint and other impurities in the ink and water systems will eventually reach a level that affects production quality. Therefore, the most common procedure is to give the entire printing unit a thorough cleaning at the end of each workday.

Before the inking system is cleaned, the water fountain is generally drained. A tube leading from the water fountain is used for this purpose.

The ink cleanup system on all but the smallest offset duplicators is almost totally automatic. One common design moves a squeegee or "doctor blade" against an ink roller (figure 13.13). If the wash-up solution is applied to the press while it is running, the ink is dissolved and passes across the squeegee into a sludge tray.

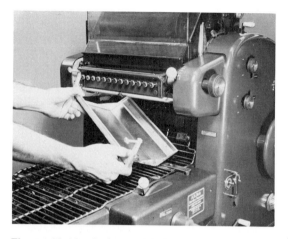

Figure 13.13. A doctor blade

There are specific procedures to follow when cleaning the inking system. First, remove as much ink as possible from the ink fountain. Next, remove the ink fountain and clean it by hand with ink solvent. On most presses, the rest of the system is cleaned almost automatically. While the press is turned off, attach or engage the squeegee or transfer roller cleanup device. Then start up the press and apply wash-up solution to one side of the distribution rollers (figure 13.14). Most of the ink rollers are driven by friction against two or three geared rollers. If solvent were applied across the entire system, friction would be reduced and not all the rollers would turn. Apply wash-up solution until half the system becomes clean and dry. Then apply the solvent to the remaining inked portion. Continue the procedure of applying solvent to one side of the system at a time until the entire system is clean.

The cleanup attachment will function more efficiently if the leading edge of the squeegee blade is wiped clean after each use. If ink dries and hardens on the blade, it will not contact the roller properly. Some cleanup attachments are completely removed from the

Figure 13.14. Applying wash-up solution

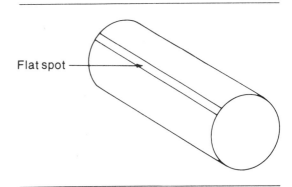

Figure 13.15. A roller with a flat spot

press after cleanup. Others merely hinge out of contact with the press rollers.

An alternative to the mechanical cleanup system is a blotter pad. Blotter pads are absorbent paper sheets that are cut and punched to the exact plate size for the press being used. To clean up the inking system, mount a pad on the plate cylinder, turn on the machine, and lower the ink form rollers into contact with the pad (take special care to raise the water form roller out of contact with the plate cylinder). Apply solvent much the same as you would when using a mechanical cleaning device, but with this approach the dissolved ink will be transferred to the blotter pad.

Many presses and duplicators have systems (often called "night latches") that separate the distribution rollers when the press is shut down. If the rollers are left in contact during lengthy shut-down periods, they will develop "flat spots" where they rest together (figure 13.15). Flat spots can cause uneven ink distribution throughout the roller train. Consult the operating manual for the press that you are running to determine whether there are night latches that should be set after the press is cleaned.

Printing Process Color on Sheet-Fed Offset Presses

Most offset lithographic presses can be used to reproduce quality process color work as long as good separations, plates, paper, ink, and, most important, a skilled operator are available.

Press Concerns

The concerns when working with four-color process printing are the same as for any quality single-color job: the sheets must be fed, registered, printed, and delivered. However, it becomes important that accurate and consistent registration be held throughout the entire run.

There is a simple method to check registration controls prior to printing a four-color job. Print a separate job that includes both line and halftone copy with the press set up for the most consistent feeding and registration. Without changing the press settings, remove the printed sheets from the delivery system and move them to the feeder system to be fed back through the press a second time. The goal is to print a second layer of ink—both halftone dots and line copy—over the first image with **dot-for-dot registration.** If, after two separate printings, only one sharp image is observed, quality registration is being held. If the image is blurred or if there is a double image, either the system is not properly adjusted or the press is incapable of quality color reproduction.

When a single press is used to reproduce four-color work, color contamination between runs is always possible. Even though an ink unit is thoroughly cleaned, residue ink may interfere with the purity of the next color. This is more of a problem when a dark color, such as black, is followed by a light color, such as yellow.

One solution is to ink the press first with a small quantity of the new ink and, after a uniform ink layer is obtained on all rollers, wash up the press. The press is then re-inked with the same color in proper quantities for the production run. With this procedure the press actually gets cleaned twice and there is little chance for color contamination. This technique, called a "color wash-up," is unnecessary when a light color is followed by black.

Sequence of Colors

Recall that process color involves the overprinting of four separate images whose combination can approximate the appearance of nearly any color in the visible spectrum. During printing, the sequence of colors can vary depending on the type of ink, paper, or press or the preference of the operator. There are, however, several common approaches.

The sequence of first cyan, then yellow, then magenta, and finally black is often used. Yellow, magenta, cyan, and black is another frequent order. The cyan printer generally resembles a normal halftone reproduction. In other words, if process blue (cyan) is the first color placed on the sheet, detail will usually be carried across the sheet wherever the final image will appear. Using progressive color proofs, it is possible to compare press sheets with each color to match density and detail positions, and it is relatively easy to fit all colors after cyan into their proper positions. One disadvantage with using cyan as the first color is with the quantity of ink laid down on the first pass through the press. With so much ink detail, all following colors tend to dry rather slowly because the paper has already absorbed ink over much of its area. With this technique there is also the possibility that as the paper becomes more ink saturated with each added color, adhesion can build up between the sheet and blanket.

Many printed jobs are made up of process color on the same page with other line copy, such as printed headlines or paragraph composition, which must appear in black. Often the color position on the page is defined by the location of this black detail. In this situation, it is necessary to print the black printer first and then fit all other colors in their correct position on the sheet. The typical sequence is black, yellow, magenta, and cyan. With this approach there is the added advantage that adhesion between the stock and blanket can be reduced because the colors typically carrying the least amount of ink detail are printed first. In instances where progressive proofs are not available, this sequence also enables the press operator to correct any color deviations on the first three colors by adjusting the cyan printer.

Quality Control Devices

While visual inspection of the press sheet can be used effectively to determine print quality of single-color line images, the quality of halftone images, or images which require critical registration, is best determined with quality control devices. Many companies have developed quality control devices which can be stripped, plated, and printed in an off-image area of the press sheet. Under magnification, these images can aid the press operator in determining overall press sheet image quality and in making press adjustments. In the following, we will discuss only a few of the many quality control devices available. All of the devices we will discuss have been developed by the Graphic Arts Technical Foundation (GATF), which for years has been at the forefront of research and development in the graphic arts. Readers who desire further information about these and other quality control devices can write to GATF directly (4615 Forbes Avenue, Pittsburgh, Pennsylvania 15213). We would like to note here that the following reproductions of GATF quality control devices are for illustration only. As supplied by GATF, these devices are of extremely high quality and fine line detail. The reproductions of the quality control devices shown in the following illustrations in no way reflects that of the original film images provided by GATF.

The GATF T-Mark

The GATF T-Mark consists of a configuration of thin, accurately ruled lines which, during printing production, are used to identify image centers, folds, trims, and bleeds (figure 13.16). The T-shaped center lines signify final trims, folds, or center-of-image. During stripping, the cross stroke of the "T" is positioned ⅛ inch (3 mm) outside of the final image area so that the mark will be trimmed off after printing. The set of outer marks indicate standard bleed or trim allowance. In negative form, these marks provide an accurate reference for film assemblers when cutting masks for bleeds. When printed on the press sheet, these

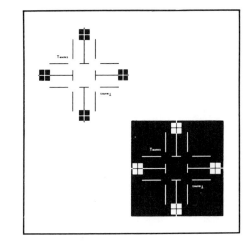

Figure 13.16. GATF T-mark for trims, centers, and bleeds
Courtesy of Graphic Arts Technical Foundation

marks guide the press operator in lineup for image fit and aid bindery operators when trimming press sheet signatures before folding. The reverse image crossmarks that appear in the small squares at the end of the T-marks indicate vertical and horizontal center-of-image on film sheets. These marks are especially useful for image alignment during step-and-repeat operations.

In addition to the above aids, film negative T-mark images can be positioned on master flats during four-color stripping so that they will be reproduced in identical locations on each of the plates used to print the job. During printing, the press operator checks to see that these marks line up for each press sheet color. These checks provide an aid in achieving initial color register and in monitoring register during the press run.

The GATF Star Target

The GATF Star Target is a small circular pattern of solid and clear pie-shaped wedges (fig-

Figure 13.17. Same-size image of the GATF Star Target as it appears on a press sheet
Courtesy of Graphic Arts Technical Foundation

ure 13.17). When printed on a press sheet, the Star Target gives the press operator a quick and effective measure of the following:

- **Ink Spread**: The edges of ink dots and lines on the press sheet spreading in all directions beyond their corresponding areas on the plate
- **Ink Slur**: Smearing of the trailing edges of dots, resulting in a tapering of ink film into the white areas

- **Doubling**: Printing of double images consisting of a full solid and a weak second image, slightly out of register with the full solid

In practice, the Star Target is stripped into the flat so that it will be plated in the trim areas at each corner of the trailing edge of the press sheet. These corner areas are usually the most sensitive in showing any slur or doubling. The image of the target on the press sheet shows the amount of ink spread and its direction by the way the center wedges of the target fill in with ink. Figure 13.18a shows a press sheet image with very little ink spread. Note that the wedge-shaped images are open almost to the white center. Compare this result to figure 13.18b, in which ink spread has caused the wedges to fill in and create a central disk of considerable size.

Slur can be recognized by a star target

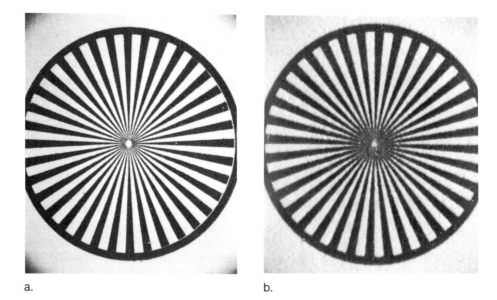

a.   b.

Figure 13.18. Photomicrographs of Star Target images on press sheets (6x) Target (a) shows very little ink spread. Target (b) shows considerable ink spread.
Courtesy of Graphic Arts Technical Foundation

in which image spreading is not uniform in all directions. In figure 13.19, note that the ink spread in the center of the target is greater in one direction, producing an oval shaped center. Doubling of an image is clearly shown in figure 13.20, where each wedge shows a double, and the center of the target forms an oval or figure eight.

The GATF Quality Control Strip

The Quality Control (QC) Strip is a pattern that helps the press operator control print quality throughout the press run (figure 13.21). The QC strip is stripped and plated to print parallel to the gripper edge. The press operator follows standard procedures to produce a properly printed sheet, which is called the "OK" sheet. During the press run, the operator pulls inspection sheets from the out-

Figure 13.20. Photomicrographs of Star Target image showing doubling (6x) Note weak double image adjacent to full printed image in target.
Courtesy of Graphic Arts Technical Foundation

Figure 13.19. Photomicrographs of Star Target image showing slur (6x) Press slur in vertical direction has caused the center of the target to spread to an oval shape.
Courtesy of Graphic Arts Technical Foundation

Figure 13.21. 10x enlargement of a segment of a GATF QC strip
Courtesy of Graphic Arts Technical Foundation

feed pile, compares the QC strip printed on the OK sheet to the QC strip printed on the inspection sheet, and looks for a perfect matchup. As shown in figure 13.22, under enlargement, the QC strip provides a quick and effective method of comparing image quality on the inspection sheet to image quality on the OK sheet. If the images do not match up, press adjustments are made until a new inspection sheet is produced with a QC image that matches the OK press sheet image.

The GATF Dot Gain Scale and Slur Gauge

The GATF Dot Gain Scale is used to determine if the dot areas of printed halftones match the dot areas on the halftone negatives or pos-

itives used to produce them. Fine screen tints are more sensitive to dot gain than coarse screens. The GATF Dot Gain Scale is designed to give numerical values to any dot sharpening (uniform loss in dot size) or dot gain (uniform gain in dot size). The scale is made up of ten steps of 200-line screen tints which are graduated in density from step to step. These steps are in the form of numbers from 0 to 9 on a background of a 65-line tint of uniform density. When reproduced along with halftone copy, some of the numbers will appear darker than the background, and some lighter. Since the density differences from one number to the next are not great, there will usually be one number that is about as dense as the background. This number, therefore, will not be visible to the naked eye on the OK press sheet. In using the dot gain scale, the

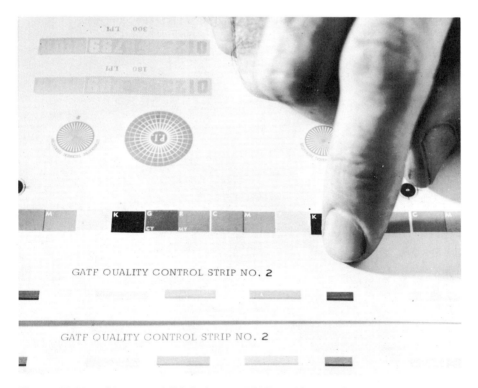

Figure 13.22a. Closeup of QC Strips on "OK" and inspection press sheets.

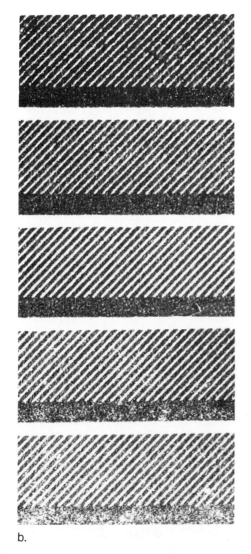

b.

Figure 13.22b. 10x enlargements of a QC Strip segment used to compare five different press sheets.

Figures 13.22a and 13.22b Courtesy of Graphic Arts Technical Foundation

press operator compares the numbers on the inspection sheet to those on the OK sheet to make sure that the same number remains invisible throughout the press run. If, for example, the number 3 were invisible on the OK sheet, but began to appear during the press run, the press operator would be alerted to a dot gain condition and could make adjustments accordingly (figure 13.23).

Dot gain results in the growth of dots in all directions, and can be caused by improper exposure or development in plate making, excessive cylinder pressures on press, too much ink, or a variety of other press factors. However, slur or doubling, which is directional, can also appear as dot gain. GATF has developed a Slur Gauge to help the press operator determine whether slur is occurring (figure 13.24). The Slur Gauge consists of fine horizontal lines that form the word "SLUR" on a vertical line background. Since the horizontal and vertical lines have the same density value, the word "SLUR" is invisible when all lines are printed with equal thickness. But

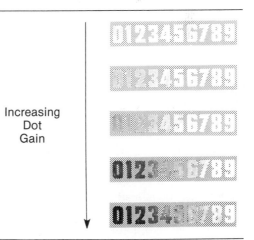

Increasing
Dot
Gain

Figure 13.23. GATF Dot Gain Scales showing increasing amounts of dot gain

Courtesy of Graphic Arts Technical Foundation

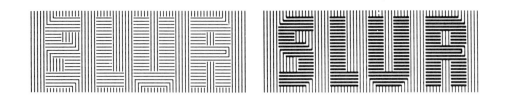

Figure 13.24. Enlarged GATF slur gauge Image on left shows no slur; image on right shows slur.
Courtesy of Graphic Arts Technical Foundation

if slur occurs, the horizontal or vertical lines will thicken, and the word "SLUR" will appear darker than the background, alerting the operator to the slur condition and indicating slur direction. Because slur can often be confused with uniform dot gain, GATF has combined their Dot Gain Scale with their Slur Gauge (figure 13.25). This combined scale allows the press operator to determine the cause of apparent dot gain quickly so that the problem can be corrected with minimum paper waste.

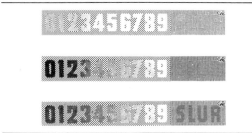

Figure 13.25. Combined Dot Gain Scale and Slur Gauge The top scale is sharp, the second scale shows dot gain without slur, and the bottom scale shows dot gain caused by slur.
Courtesy of Graphic Arts Technical Foundation

SECTION 2

This section covers some common press problems and concerns. Like all machines, presses need occasional adjustments in order to operate correctly. It is impossible to achieve proper ink-water balance or to print a quality image on a press that is not adjusted correctly.

Roller and Blanket Problems and Adjustments

Press operators often encounter several roller and blanket problems. Many of these problems can be corrected by relatively simple adjustments. Others require roller or blanket replacement. A press operator should be familiar with the adjustment procedures for most of the rollers in the roller train and be able to recognize solutions for many of the more common roller and blanket problems.

Blanket Considerations

Most offset blankets are formed from vulcanized rubber bonded to a fiber support base. Within the basic materials, however, a wide range of different blanket quality is available. There are special purpose formulations designed to be used with specific materials, such as ultraviolet drying inks or coated stock. Most printers do not change blankets every time a different ink or paper is fed through the press, but the importance of blanket compatibility with special materials must be stressed. Lithographic suppliers are prepared to identify the appropriate blanket for any press situation.

Blanket Problems

There are two common problems that occur with offset blankets that the press operator must be able to recognize and correct: glazing and smashes.

Glazing. Blankets become glazed as a result of long periods of improper cleaning or because of age. A very smooth, hard, glossy surface is created when the pores of the blanket fill with ink, ink solvent, and gum. A glazed blanket will lose its ability to transfer enough ink to produce an acceptable ink density on the press sheet. Commercial deglazing compounds are available that will clear blanket pores, but the best measure is to prevent the problem by properly washing the blanket after each press run.

A good technique for keeping the blanket clean is to dampen the blanket with water and to use a good blanket wash while it is still wet. The water will loosen any dried gum that will not be dissolved by the blanket wash, and the blanket wash will remove dried ink.

A properly washed blanket should have the appearance of smooth velvet.

Smashes. Blankets become smashed when more material is passed between the impression and blanket cylinders than the gap will permit. Each time the press sheet is wrinkled or folded as it travels through the printing unit, the blanket becomes smashed or creased. If enough pressure is applied, the smashed areas will be pushed in too far to receive ink from the plate cylinder and unable to transfer an image to the press sheets. If the smash is small, a commercial "blanket fix" is available. When this is painted over the smashed area, it causes the surface to swell. Do not "fix" a blanket in a halftone or tint area. The swelling caused by blanket fix is not uniform and will not print a uniform halftone or tint pattern. In such situations, the blanket should be replaced for quality printing. If there are actual tears in the surface, the blanket should also be replaced. If a large area has been smashed but there are no visible breaks, the blanket might be returned to a usable condition by removing it from the press and soaking it in a water bath for several days.

New blankets should not be stored near excessive heat. If a blanket is exposed to high temperatures, the rubber may lose its "give" or elasticity. Blankets should be stored in a flat position with a cover sheet to protect the surface from damage.

Plate-to-Blanket Packing and Adjustments

When the paper being printed passes between the impression and the blanket cylinders, the amount of pressure among the three must be uniform and sufficient to transfer ink. At the same time, it cannot be so great that the action becomes abrasive to the plate when the image is offset from the plate to the blanket.

The uniformity of the plate-to-blanket pressure can be easily checked by the operator. Turn off the dampening system and ink the entire surface of a used plate while it is mounted on the press. Stop the press and lower the plate cylinder into contact with the blanket cylinder (on "impression"). Separate the two cylinders and inspect the ink band that was transferred to the blanket. If the band is approximately ⅛ inch wide across the entire width of the blanket, the system is properly aligned. If the image is light, heavy, or irregular, consult the press manual for specific recommendations.

On most offset duplicators, plate and blanket cylinder pressure is either automatically controlled by spring pressure or can be changed by a manual screw adjustment.

On presses, plate-to-blanket pressure is usually adjusted by packing under the blanket and/or the plate. Improper packing of press cylinders could cause serious registration problems. Press manufacturers will specify appropriate packing for their equipment. Refer to the press manual for detailed procedure on plate-to-blanket packing.

Glazed Rollers

Even with the most efficient cleanup procedures, ink rollers can eventually become glazed with dried ink. **Glaze** is a buildup on the rubber rollers that prevents the proper adhesion and distribution of ink. Commercially prepared deglazing compounds are available that can be easily used to remove any dried ink from the rollers. One common technique is to apply a pumice compound to the rollers in the same manner as applying ink. Allow the pumice to work into the rollers

by running the press for 5 to 10 minutes. Then wash the system with a liquid deglazing solution. Both the compound and the solution can then be removed by using wash-up solution and standard cleanup procedures. Many press operators deglaze their rollers on a regular basis as a part of a preventive maintenance system.

Dampening Rollers

Water does not readily adhere to smooth roller surfaces. Therefore, several dampening rollers are covered with some material that will easily carry usable quantities of the water fountain solution to the plate. The ductor and form rollers are typically covered. Two types of dampening covers are commonly used: molleton covers and fiber sleeves.

Molleton covers are thin cloth tubes that slip over the rollers and are tied or sewn at each end. It is important that the molleton uniformly cover the entire roller. If the ends are so tightly tied that a taper is formed in the roller, insufficient moisture will be delivered to the plate and the outside edges of the plate will scum with ink. A new molleton cover placed on a roller should be broken in. Soak the cover with water and squeeze out any excess water by rolling the covered roller over a sheet of uncoated paper. The breaking-in process removes any lint or loose threads.

Dampening sleeves are thin fiber tubes that, when dry, are slightly larger in diameter than the roller. To apply the sleeve, slide the dry sleeve over the clean roller and soak it with warm water. Within minutes the fibers shrink into position on the roller and the roller is ready to be installed on the press. Dampening sleeves are generally used only on form rollers. Because the tubes are exceptionally thin (when compared to molleton covers), the rollers must be oversize compared to those usually supplied with the press. Dampener sleeves are, however, easy to install, lintless, and easy to keep adjusted to the plate cylinder.

Thin cloth sleeves that can be used to cover badly inked molletons are also available. Thin cloth and fiber sleeves react more readily to operator adjustments and make maintenance of consistent moisture control easier than with the traditional molleton cover.

At the end of each work day, remove the dampening solution from the water fountain tray. If the metal fountain roller becomes coated with ink, it can be cleaned with pumice powder and water. An occasional coating with any commercial desensitizing etch will ensure continued water transfer during the production day.

Cloth and fiber dampener covers can be cleaned with a commercial dampener roller cleaner. To clean the covers, first saturate the material with water so the cleaner will not soak into the fabric, then scrub the surface with a stiff brush and roller cleaner. Rinse the roller cover with water and allow the material to dry.

It is best to have two sets of dampener rollers for each press so a clean, dry roller will always be available. If the press has only one set and it is needed immediately after cleaning, roll the roller against blotter paper or cleaner sheets until no more water can be removed. Covers need not be cleaned on a daily basis, but only as necessary. They should be changed when the material in the cover will no longer accept water.

Distributor Roller Adjustment

All distribution rollers in the ink and water systems must be in uniform contact with each other to get proper ink and water distribution.

Most rollers are adjustable in at least one direction and are relatively simple to move.

A common method for setting distribution rollers involves the use of strips of 20-pound paper. Cut six pieces, 8 or 9 inches long, four approximately 2 inches wide and two 1 inch wide. To check for uniform pressure between the two rollers, roll a set of three strips between a set of rollers at each end and then gently pull the middle pieces out (figure 13.26). The strips should slide with slight uniform resistance, but should not tear.

Form Roller Adjustment

The ink and water form rollers must all be adjusted so that they touch the plate with the correct amount of pressure, and so that the pressure is uniform across the width of the plate. Form rollers all have some type of easy adjustment for skew and pressure.

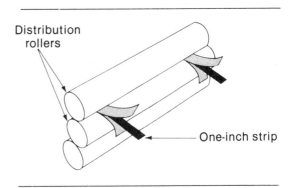

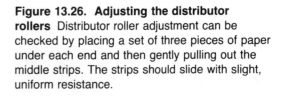

Figure 13.26. Adjusting the distributor rollers Distributor roller adjustment can be checked by placing a set of three pieces of paper under each end and then gently pulling out the middle strips. The strips should slide with slight, uniform resistance.

Dampening Form Roller Adjustment. If the dampener roller is not parallel to the plate cylinder, moisture will not be distributed evenly across the plate. If all portions of the plate surface are not uniformly moistened, ink scumming will occur on the plate. Dampening form roller-to-plate alignment and adjustment is often indicated when one side of the plate scums and the other side does not. This adjustment must be made with the roller in place on the press.

Cut two 1-inch-wide strips of 20-pound bond paper and place one under each end of the dampening form roller (figure 13.27). Lower the dampening form roller into position against a plate. Slowly pull each paper strip while checking for uniformity of resistance. If unequal pull is observed, the roller is not parallel to the plate cylinder and must be reset. Both duplicators and presses have adjustments to control form roller-to-plate alignment.

Ink Form Roller Adjustment. Ink form roller-to-plate pressure is critical. Too much pressure will result in a blurred or enlarged image. Too little pressure will not transfer ink. Proper adjustment requires not only that you have the proper amount of pressure, but that the pressure be even across the width of the plate. Form roller pressure is checked by first inking the press and then turning the press off in such a way that the plate is located beneath the form rollers. With the plate in this position, bring the form rollers into contact with the plate by moving the press to the "print" mode. Immediately bring the press off ink and rotate the plate to a position where you can examine the ink tracks left on it by the form rollers (figure 13.28). As shown in figure 13.29, the first roller to contact the plate should have the heaviest ink line (⅛ to 3/16 inch) and the last should have the lightest (3/32 to ⅛ inch). All rollers should transfer a uniform width of ink across the plate. Figure 13.30a shows proper form roller positions against a distri-

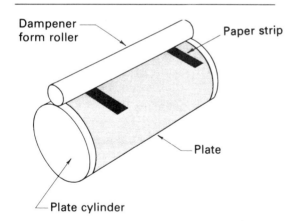

Figure 13.27. Checking the dampening form roller adjustment Dampening form roller adjustment can be checked by placing two strips of paper under each side and comparing resistance.

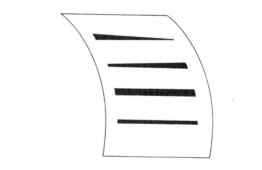

Figure 13.28. Example of test strip checks for ink form roller-to-plate pressure The top two strips show rollers that are contacting the plate with uneven pressure. The third strip indicates too much pressure. The last strip is uniform and not too wide, indicating correct pressure.

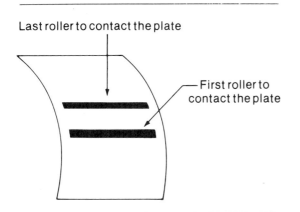

Last roller to contact the plate

First roller to contact the plate

Figure 13.29. Examples of difference in tracks left by the first and last roller The ink track left on the plate by both rollers should be even across the width of the plate. The track of the first roller should be slightly wider than the track of the last roller.

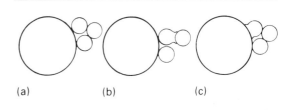

(a)　　　　(b)　　　　(c)

Figure 13.30. Diagram of ink form roller adjustment The proper adjustment of form rollers is shown in (a). Misalignment of form rollers is shown in (b) and (c).

bution and plate cylinder. Figures 13.30b and 13.30c illustrate two possible adjustments that will diminish image quality on the final sheet.

Common Press Concerns

Many concerns are common to all press designs or models. This section does not contain an exhaustive list, but it should help you understand some basic press problems.

The Dampening Solution and pH

The moisture applied to the surface of a lithographic plate actually serves two functions. First, the presence of water in the nonimage areas repels ink. However, if only pure water were used as the dampening solution, the action of the ink would rapidly cause the nonimage areas to become ink-receptive. The second purpose of the moisture, then, is to ensure that the nonimage areas of the plate remain water-receptive. Alois Senefelder recognized the dual role of the moisture layer on the stone and used a solution made from a combination of water, acid, and gum arabic.

Dampening solutions are available ready-mixed from a commercial supplier or can be purchased as separate components and mixed by the printer. Most solutions are now made from an acid concentrate, gum arabic, and a gum preservative.

For lithographers, the most meaningful measure of dampening solution usability is the level of acidity of the liquid. The numeric scale that measures acidity in a range from 0 (very acid) to 14 (very alkaline, or a base) is called a **pH scale** (figure 13.31). The midpoint 7 is considered neutral. Plate manufacturers specify a recommended pH level to be used with their plates. A reading between 5.5 and 4.5 is acceptable for most plates.

The printer can measure pH in several ways. Litmus paper pH indicators are available from printing suppliers and give an acceptable reading of the level of acidity for most production situations (figure 13.32). To make a test, remove a small piece of litmus paper from the roll and dip it into the fountain so-

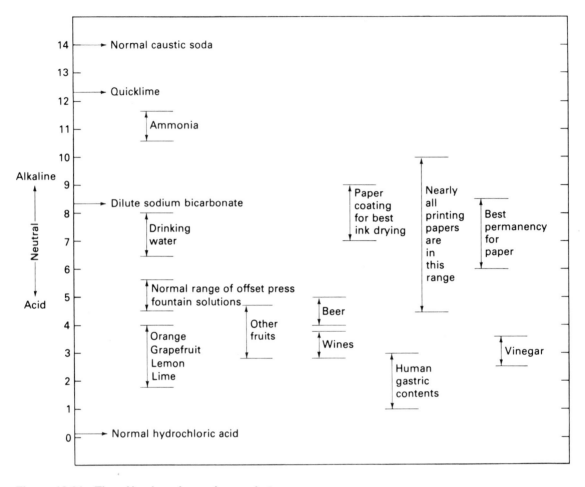

Figure 13.31. The pH values for various substances
Courtesy of Mead Paper

lution. The wet paper will change color and can be matched to color patches supplied with the roll. A pH number will be identified next to each color patch. If the pH is not in the recommended range, remix the fountain solution.

Some presses have built-in sensors that continually monitor the pH level of the dampening solution. With such sensors, the required pH is dialed into the unit, and the device automatically compensates for any variation by adding water or acid concentrate.

A variety of problems can occur as a result of too acid a fountain solution (pH readings from 1 to 3). A strongly acidic solution can greatly shorten plate life. The acid tends to deteriorate the image area of all surface plates and can eventually make the image "walk off the plate." When the pressroom humidity is high, the action of acid with ink will cause drying problems on the press sheets (especially when running high-acid content papers). A high-acid bath will also break down the ink. The ink is attacked by the high acid

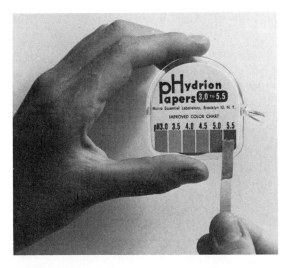

Figure 13.32. Example of a litmus paper pH indicator Litmus paper pH indicators are used to check the water fountain solution in most working situations.
Courtesy of Micro Essential Lab., Inc.

content of the fountain solution, and the ink becomes paste-like, or **emulsified.** The rollers will appear glazed, and no quantity of ink that is added to the system will correct the problem. The rollers must be cleaned and the unit re-inked.

If the acid level of the dampening solution is too low (pH readings from 7 to 14), the action of the moisture layer on the nonimage areas will decrease water receptivity, and the plate will scum with ink.

Ink and Paper Considerations for Lithographic Printing

Ink and paper are probably the two most common ingredients for any printing job. The customer doesn't want to be bothered with the details of production problems, but the printer must live with ink and paper problems on a day-to-day basis. Some characteristics of these

two important ingredients of offset litho press operation are worth examining.

Working with Lithographic Ink. Ink is affected by the paper it is put on. Many printers indiscriminately add materials, such as a drier or an extender, to their ink at the beginning of each workday, believing that they are improving the ink. There is a trend in ink manufacturing to supply inks that require no special mixing and that match each different type of press sheet and job characteristic. Under no circumstances should additives be mixed with any ink without consulting an ink supplier.

Troubleshooting Ink Difficulties. Beyond mechanical problems caused by inexact press adjustments, there are often difficulties resulting from ink characteristics that can be easily corrected by appropriate additives. Three common problems are tinting, picking, and slow drying.

Tinting is identified by a slight discoloration over the entire nonimage area—almost like a sprayed mist or the pattern created by a 5% or 10% screen tint. Generally, the situation is caused by a reaction between the ink and the water fountain solution. If the ink is too water soluble, it will bleed back into the water fountain through the dampening system. If tinting occurs, both the ink and the water systems should be cleaned and a different ink formulation used.

Picking is similar in appearance to small hickies over the entire image area of the press sheet (see figure 13.33). It can be caused by linty or poorly coated paper, but it is more commonly a result of ink that is too tacky. Small particles of paper are literally torn from the surface of each press sheet and fed back into the inking system. If picking is observed, the inking system should be cleaned and the ink mixed with a small quantity of reducer or nonpick compound.

Figure 13.33. Example of a printer's hickey Hickies are defects in a printed image caused by small particles of ink or paper attached to the plate or blanket.

Slow ink drying can be an elusive problem unless all possible causes are recognized. Simple drying problems can generally be eliminated with the addition of a drier compound to the ink, but too much drier can actually increase drying time. Overinking on a coated (nonabsorbent) stock can significantly increase drying time. On humid days, too high an acid content in the dampening solution (low pH) can cause difficulties. This combination of problems is almost impossible to solve without moving the sheets to a humidity-controlled environment. Delayed drying can be a special problem when the sheet must be flopped or turned to receive an image on the second side.

Paper Acid Content. In general, uncoated papers will not dry properly in a humid atmosphere if the pH is below 5 (see figure 13.31). Most coated papers have a pH of above 7.5. Coatings with a pH of between 6 and 7 would also cause ink-drying problems when linked with high humidity.

The pH testing of papers can be a cumbersome and time-consuming process. Acid content information for any paper lot is available from the manufacturer. If the room humidity is high and ink drying is a problem,

consult the paper supplier for testing or information.

Paper Grain. Paper grain direction is an important characteristic that is most closely related to the ability of the individual sheets to be run through a sheet-fed lithographic press. Most paper is formed from the combination and interlocking of cellulose fibers. As paper is formed on the moving wire belt of the paper-making machine, a majority of the fibers are turned parallel to the direction of travel. Press sheets are defined as **grain long** when most of the paper fibers are parallel to the longest dimension of the sheet. **Grain short** means the paper fibers are at right angles to the longest dimension of the sheet.

A distinction should be made between feeding and printing as they relate to grain direction. Grain long feeding is with the grain direction parallel to the direction of travel through the press. Grain short feeding is with the grain direction at right angles to the direction of travel (figure 13.34). Grain long printing takes place when the grain of the paper is parallel to the axis of the plate cylinder. Grain short printing is when the paper grain is at right angles to the plate cylinder axis.

The Mead Paper Corporation suggests that cellulose fibers expand as they absorb moisture. The expansion can be up to five times as great across the width of a fiber as along its length. This fact should suggest to lithographers that the direction of grain feed could present significant registration problems when multicolor runs are printed on a single sheet-fed offset press. In other words, on a litho press, press sheets come into contact with moisture from the fountain solution. The individual fibers in the paper sheets can then change size, with the greatest increase in the dimension across the grain. If the sheet has to be run through the press several times

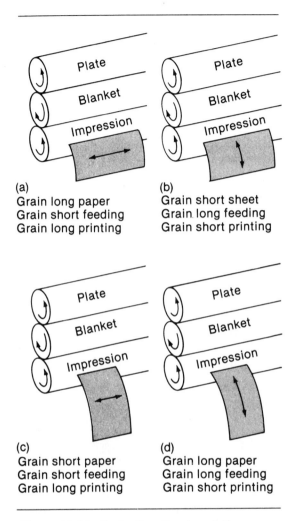

(a)
Grain long paper
Grain short feeding
Grain long printing

(b)
Grain short sheet
Grain long feeding
Grain short printing

(c)
Grain short paper
Grain short feeding
Grain long printing

(d)
Grain long paper
Grain long feeding
Grain short printing

Figure 13.34. Grain direction in printing

to receive different ink colors, each pass can add more moisture to the fibers and can cause different changes in sheet size. These changes can make it extremely difficult to fit one color image to another.

Almost all offset paper is supplied grain long. It is to the printer's advantage, when involved with multicolor runs, to print with the grain parallel to the axis of the plate cylinder. For most presses, the printing plate is longer across the cylinder dimension than it is around it. If the greatest paper expansion is going to take place across the grain, it is wise to feed the sheet so that the greatest change takes place across the smallest plate or image dimension. Also, on most presses, it is far simpler to make registration adjustments by rotating the printing cylinders than by moving the infeed pile.

It is important to understand that not all lithographic press work is done with grain long printing. Grain is of little importance for simple single-color runs or for multicolor images that do not have critical registration requirements. There are also instances when a multicolor job *must* be printed short grain. For example, when printed sheets are to be folded, grain direction is very important. Such jobs must generally be printed so that the fold is made parallel to the paper grain.

Surface Texture. A wide variety of textures can be formed on the surface of all papers. This texture is generally referred to as **finish.** Because lithography transfers an image from a flat printing plate, it is difficult to print a detailed design on a very rough paper surface. Ink would never reach the bottom valleys of rough textures. For this reason, almost all offset materials are relatively smooth. Lithographers are concerned with two main classifications of finish: coated and uncoated papers.

Almost all papers are formed by the interweaving of cellulose fibers. The surface of **uncoated paper** is made up of nothing more than the raw interlocking fibers. Although the fibers can be polished by **calendering** (pressing them between rollers or plates to smooth or glaze them), the ink image sits on and is often absorbed into the fibers. A **coated paper** surface has an added layer of pigment bonded to the original paper fibers to smooth out the rough texture of the natural material. Coated papers generally carry more printed detail and produce a better finished image, but they are more difficult to print than uncoated papers. Coated materials are available coated on one side (C1S) or coated on both sides (C2S). Both are made in at least two grades, and the surface appearance can vary from a dull to a high gloss.

There are several areas that lithographers have learned to watch when printing coated stocks. Most jam-ups occur because of static electricity between the coated sheets on the infeed table. The pile of paper should be carefully fanned and the feeding adjusted with start-up sheets before the actual run is begun. The blanket should be carefully checked for quality—specifically glaze buildup. Glaze has a tendency to pick and split or tear coated paper. Ink quantity is more critical with coated materials than with uncoated ones. Too much ink will cause **set-off** (the transfer of an image from the printed face of one sheet in the pile to the bottom face of the next sheet in the pile) of the image in the delivery pile. Overinking could also cause the paper to stick to the blanket cylinder and generally increases drying time. Roller and cylinder alignment is also more critical with coated stock and should be carefully checked.

A Troubleshooting Checklist

In theory, press setup and operation are simple. Unfortunately, difficulties may develop in every situation and prevent a quality image from printing on the final press sheets. The true craft of the printer is to identify and correct the problems. This process is called "troubleshooting." The following sections identify common press and duplicator difficulties and outline probable causes and solutions.

Scumming

Too Much Ink. **Scumming** is a condition in which nonimage areas accept ink. If the press is overinked, the ink system rollers will appear highly textured and a hissing sound will often be heard from the rollers as the press is idling. To remove excess ink without a wash-up, turn the machine off and manually roll scrap sheets of paper between two of the upper ink distribution rollers. Repeat the procedure until the required amount of ink is removed.

Dampening System Difficulties. Scumming could also be caused by insufficient moisture, dirty dampener covers, dampener covers tied too tightly, light dampener form roller pressure to the plate, or low acid level of the fountain solution.

First carefully study the pattern of the scum and trace its position back to the dampener form roller. If the scumming covers the entire plate, it could be from overall lack of moisture (increase the fountain feed), poor form roller pressure (readjust), or a dirty dampening form roller cover (clean with a commercial dampener roller cleaner or replace). If the scumming pattern is on the outer edges of the plate, the form roller cover could be tied too tightly or the ductor roller cover may have slipped (retie or replace covers). If the plate is scumming in a band that extends around the circumference of the cylinder, that area of the dampener form roller might be inked and will not allow the moisture to pass to the plate (clean the form roller). Scum on the plate can also be caused by improper plate making or gumming.

Blurred Copy (Double Image)

Loose Blanket. As blankets are broken in, and during a press run, they are pressed against the plate cylinder and tend to flatten or stretch out. If the blanket is new, immediately check for tightness.

Excessive Impression. Too much impression will tend to roll the blanket ahead of the impression cylinder and cause a set-off from the press sheet back to the blanket, resulting in a blurred image (back off impression).

Too Much Ink. Refer to the solution under "Scumming" above.

Gray, Washed-Out Reproduction

Too Much Moisture. If moisture is dripping off the plate or spraying onto the press sheets, water is flooding into the image areas and the plate cannot accept sufficient quantities of ink. Turn off the fountain ductor roller, lower the dampener form roller into contact with the plate, and allow the press to run. The process will allow the excess fountain solution to coat the plate and evaporate. If an extra set of dampener form rollers is available, it could replace the overmoistened ones. The rollers could also be removed from the press and rolled against clean, absorbent paper.

Not Enough Ink. If the inking system is carrying too little ink, a dense image cannot be transferred to the press sheet. Check the appearance of the ink coating and increase the ink feed if necessary. However, always check for too much moisture before increasing ink feed.

Incorrect Plate-to-Blanket Pressure. If the blanket image is light but the plate is inking well, the plate-to-blanket pressure is insufficient and should be readjusted or the packing should be increased.

Incorrect Impression-to-Blanket Pressure. If the ink and water systems are set correctly and the blanket is receiving a good image, the impression cylinder position should be checked. Increase impression until a dense, sharp press sheet image is obtained.

Gray, Washed-Out Reproduction and Scumming

Glazed Ink Rollers. If the inking system rollers appear shiny and hard, glazed ink rollers are interacting with the moisture system and passing inconsistent or inadequate amounts of ink to the plate. Use a commercial deglazing compound to clean the ink system.

Glazed Blanket. If the blanket surface appears shiny and hard, clean it with deglazing compound.

Too Much Form Roller Pressure. If the ink and/or dampener form rollers are set too close to the plate cylinder, then sufficient ink or water solution transfer will not take place. Readjust the pressure.

No Reproduction on Press Sheet

Check for insufficient ink form roller pressure (readjust), not enough plate-to-blanket pressure (reset), not enough impression (increase impression), or too much moisture and glazed blanket and ink rollers (decrease moisture and deglaze blanket and rollers).

Printer's Hickey

Hickeys are caused by small particles of ink or paper attached to the plate or blanket (figure 13.34). The solution is to stop the press and clean the plate and blanket.

Press Maintenance

Maintenance is unfortunately often viewed as an activity that takes place after a problem occurs. Manufacturers always provide a recommended maintenance program for their specific machine. But several general areas of concern should be considered for every press.

The motor that provides motion for the press is often concealed in a position that would seem to challenge a professional contortionist's skills. The fact that it is out of sight does not diminish its importance. Check for lubrication points and examine the belt and pulley systems often.

Chains on infeed and outfeed tables need to be kept greased and free from paper pieces or dirt. Infeed rollers become smooth from use. A piece of fine-grit abrasive paper can be used to roughen and remove any dirt from the surface. Vacuum pumps usually have an oil reservoir that should be kept filled. The pump itself should be flushed out several times a year.

All roller and cylinder bearings must be lubricated, usually on a daily basis. Some presses have a single oil reservoir that continually delivers lubrication to bearing surfaces.

The importance of a consistent maintenance schedule cannot be overstated. It is far cheaper to spend time each day doing preventive maintenance than to wait until a major malfunction takes place and the press is "down" for several days waiting for new parts.

A printing press is a machine that is controlled by humans. Many printers claim that each press has a distinctive personality and accordingly assign human names and characteristics: "It's Monday and Harold is kind of sluggish" or "Mabel is mad at me today—she's throwing paper all over the place." However, a mechanism cannot perform "tricks" beyond what a human programs it to do. Every press problem has a cause and a solution. The printer works with a press, but it is the person, not the machine, who controls the situation.

Key Terms

dot-for-dot registration	doubling	dampening sleeves
T-Mark quality control device	Dot Gain Scale	pH scale
Star Target	Slur Gauge	tinting
ink spread	glaze	scumming
ink slur	molleton covers	hickey

Questions for Review

1. Discuss the steps and procedures for setting up the paper feed on an offset press.

2. Explain how the printing unit is prepared for printing, including adjustments for ink and water for both direct and indirect dampening systems.

3. Describe the method for achieving proper ink and water balance.

4. How is press cleanup accomplished?

5. What is a solution to possible color contamination when running process colors on a lithographic press?

6. Describe the T-Mark, Star Target, QC Strip, Dot Gain Scale, and Slur Gauge produced by GATF, and tell what quality control checks can be made with each.

7. What causes a lithographic blanket to become glazed?

8. What is the purpose of dampening covers in the dampening system of a lithographic press?

9. Why is accurate alignment of form rollers against the image carrier (printing plate) so important?

10. How are printing inks formed?

11. What does the term *pH* mean?

12. What generally causes tinting on a lithographic press sheet?

13. What is the difference between grain short and grain long press sheets?

14. What are two possible causes of scumming on a lithographic press?

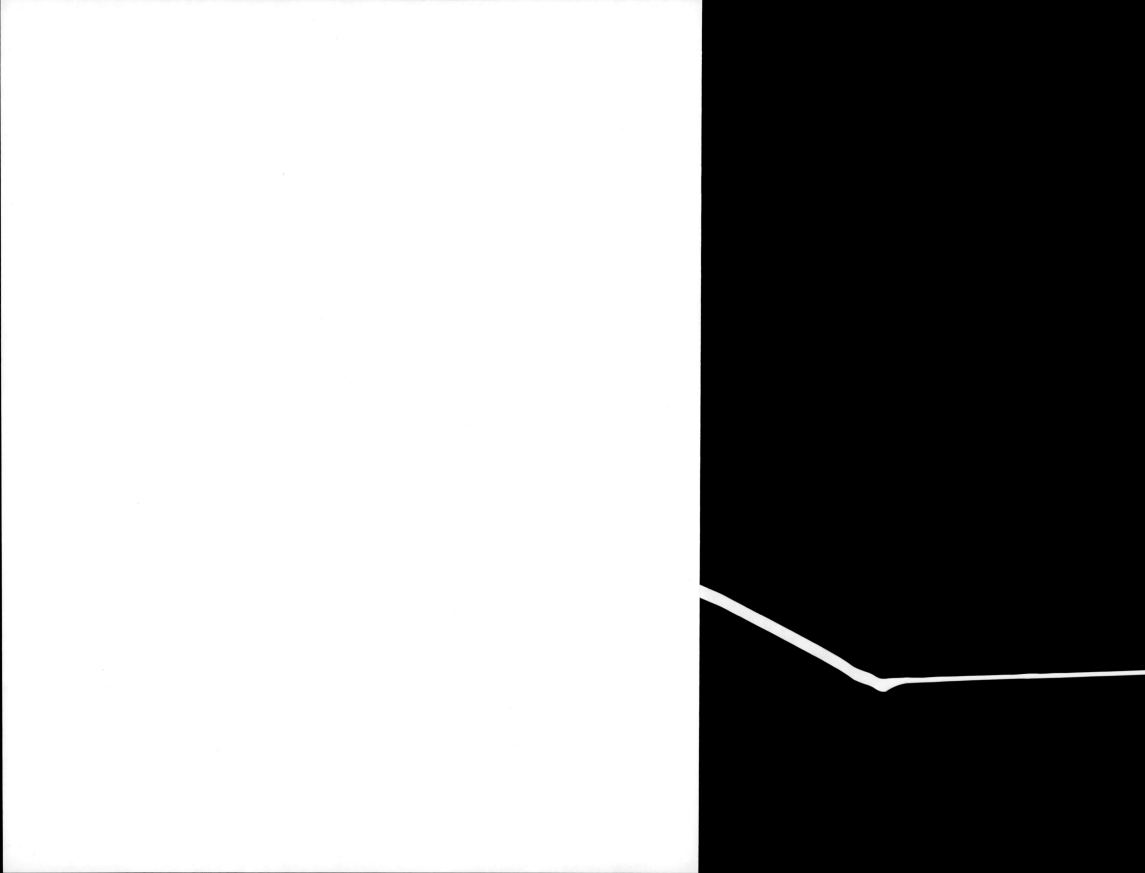

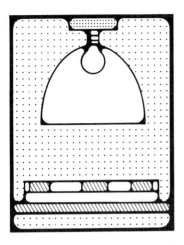

Chapter Fourteen

Screen Printing Stencils

Anecdote to Chapter Fourteen

It is possible that observations of insects eating holes through leaves suggested stencil printing to primitive people. Examples of this idea can be seen in the early work of the natives of the Polynesian Islands. Designs were cut into green banana leaves, and dyes were forced through the openings onto bark cloth, or *tapa*.

In Asia, the earliest existing stencils were produced during the Sung dynasty (A.D. 960–1280). Many examples of stencil printing that date from the same period are found in Japan. The Japanese have been extremely skillful in cutting detailed stencils from specially treated rice paper. It was easy to cut large open areas in the paper, but problems arose when the artist wanted to block out a portion of the open area. One solution was to glue center pieces or loose parts of the stencil together with strands of human hair. These strands were called "ties" because they tied the different parts of the stencil together. Fine pieces of silk

fiber were later substituted for hair because of their greater strength.

In England during the late 1700s, stencils were used to decorate wallpaper, which had become popular in upper-class homes. European screen printers still used ties to hold the stencil pieces together, and it was difficult to create especially intricate designs.

During the early years of our own country's history, the stencil was a well-guarded secret. Traveling teachers often sold the idea to local printers and signmakers. The price depended on what the market would bear, but most printers were happy to pay almost any price for a process that was low cost and could be used to reproduce nearly any size image without being limited by the size of the available type or printing press.

In 1907, Samual Simon of Manchester, England, was granted a patent on his revolutionary new concept called a "tieless" stencil. His design used a piece of coarsely woven

Japanese stencil
Courtesy of the Art Institute of Chicago

silk fabric to hold the stencil pieces in place. With the silk as a base, extremely intricate designs could be cut and then glued on the fabric. When ink was passed through the openings in the design, it would flow around the fabric threads and leave an image of the opening on the print.

It wasn't until the outbreak of the First World War that the method became a significant industrial process. It was ideal for rapid, high-quality, short-run signs and illustrations. With the development of photographic stencils, the process has been used for almost every conceivable application from printing tiny microcircuits in electronics to labeling cardboard cartons and even reproducing halftone photographs.

What began as a simple stencil probably more than thirteen centuries ago has moved into a position of significance in the printing industry. Many labels have been applied—stencil printing, silk screen serigraphy, and even mitography—but the term *screen printing* is now commonly accepted as the proper name for the process.

Objectives for Chapter Fourteen

After completing this chapter, you will be able to:

- Explain the basic concepts of screen printing.
- Classify types of screen stencils.
- Classify types of screen fabrics.
- Describe methods of stretching screens.
- List the steps in preparing and mounting hand-cut stencils.

- Describe the steps in preparing and mounting indirect photographic stencils.
- Describe the steps in preparing and mounting direct photographic stencils.
- Describe the different techniques of masking the stencil.
- Select the appropriate type of stencil, screen, and ink for different screen printing jobs.

Introduction

Of all the major printing processes, screen printing is undoubtably the oldest. The process was shrouded in mystery for centuries and remained a well-guarded secret until the first part of the twentieth century.

Screen printing is a generic term that today includes a wide range of techniques and applications. Although such terms as "silk screen," "mitography," "serigraphy," and "selectine" might be classed within this framework, "screen printing" is the general label that the industry recognizes and uses.

Basic Concept and Classification of Stencils

The Stencil

The basic concept of screen printing is simple and is based on the idea of a stencil. By taking a piece of paper, drawing some outline or sketch of an object, and then cutting out the sketch, we can make a stencil (figure 14.1).

By placing the stencil over another sheet, it is possible to paint, spray, or otherwise force ink through the opening (figure 14.2). When the stencil is removed, all that remains on the printed sheet is a reproduction of the opening on the stencil (figure 14.3). This process can be repeated as long as the original stencil holds its shape.

Figure 14.2. Spraying ink through a paper stencil
Courtesy of SUCO Learning Resources and R. Kampas

Figure 14.1. Paper stencil cut with Ulano swivel knife
Courtesy of SUCO Learning Resources and R. Kampas

Figure 14.3. A stenciled image
Courtesy of SUCO Learning Resources and R. Kampas

Today the advantages of screen printing are impressive. It is ideally suited for the low-cost production of high-quality short-run printed materials. Screen printing is extremely versatile. It is possible to print on nearly any surface, texture, or shape. The process is limited only by the size of the screen frame available. Fine line detail and even halftones may be reproduced by screen printing. Many types of ink are available, from acid etches to abrasive glues. Ink densities on the printed page are such that any color may be overprinted (printed over another color) without the first color showing through.

Types of Stencils

All stencil preparation can be classified into three groups:

- Hand-cut stencils
- Tusche-and-glue stencils
- Photographic stencils

As the name implies, **hand-cut stencils** are prepared by manually removing the printing image areas from some form of base or support material. **Tusche-and-glue,** an art process, involves drawing directly on the screen fabric with lithographic tusche (an oil-based pigment) and then blocking out nonimage areas with a water-based glue material. **Photographic stencils** are generally produced by the use of a thick, light-sensitive, gelatin-based emulsion that is exposed and developed either on a supporting film or directly on the screen itself. Only hand-cut and photographic stencils are used in commerical printing.

Screen printing preparation involves the selection and control of screen fabrics, screen frames, fabric stretch on the frame, fabric treatment to accept a stencil, stencil preparation, and stencil masking. As with all print-

ing processes, it is most important to control every variable to produce a quality image on the final sheet.

Fabric and Frame Preparation

Screen Fabrics

There is no one fabric that can be used for all screen printing applications. The type of ink to be screened, the fineness of line detail, the quality of the material that is to receive the image, the number of impressions, and the type of stencil must all be considered when selecting the screen fabric.

Screen fabrics are made from either natural fibers, such as silk, or man-made fibers, such as polyester or nylon. They are all classified as either multifilament or monofilament materials. **Multifilament screens** are made up of strands of fibers twisted together into threads (figure 14.4). **Monofilament screens**

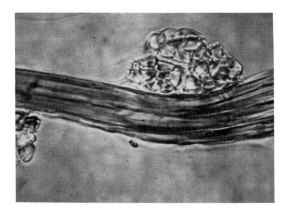

Figure 14.4. Magnified view of cross section of silk strand Notice that the strand is made up of individual fibers.
Courtesy of J. Ulano Company, Inc.

are woven from single round strands (figure 14.5).

Silk was the first fabric used to carry screen printing stencils. Multifilament silk strands provide greater cross-sectional area than monofilament strands and allow for the strong adhesion of nearly any hand-cut or photographic stencil (figure 14.6). However,

silk is not dimensionally stable, which makes it unsuitable for work requiring critical registration. Moreover, many special purpose inks, such as abrasives or chemical resists, can quickly destroy the silk fibers.

Although man-made multifilament fibers, such as multistrand polyester, do not have the natural coarseness of silk, they are stronger and can be woven more uniformly. Polyester is useful for critical registration work because it can withstand many abrasive materials and pass a uniform layer of ink.

Monofilament fabrics, such as single-strand polyester, nylon, or wire cloth (copper or stainless steel), have a uniform weave and freely pass pigments through the mesh openings. Because of the smooth nature of the fibers, it is generally necessary to treat or roughen the filament surface to obtain good stencil adhesion (figure 14.7). Each fabric type has its own characteristics. Nylon tends to absorb moisture and will react to changes in room humidity. Metal screens absorb no moisture but react to temperature changes and will pass nearly any abrasive pigment with

Figure 14.5. Magnified view of cross section of man-made monofilament strands
Courtesy of J. Ulano Company, Inc.

Figure 14.6. Magnified view of stencil applied to silk fibers
Courtesy of J. Ulano Company, Inc.

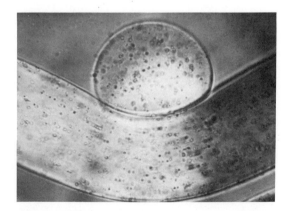

Figure 14.7. Magnified view of stencil applied to monofilament fibers
Courtesy of J. Ulano Company, Inc.

little difficulty. Monofilament polyesters have low moisture absorption rate, stability, and strength. They are also less expensive than most other screen materials, so they are rapidly becoming the main material for commercial work.

Screen fabric is purchased by the yard. Two systems of classification are used. Silk and multifilament polyesters are classified according to the ratio of open area to thread area per inch. Numbers ranging from 0000 to about 25 are assigned. The smaller the number, the larger the percentage of open or ink-passing area per inch. These materials are also assigned a strength indication. A 12XX fabric

is stronger than a 12X. Most other fabrics, such as nylon and metal cloth, are classified according to the number of threads per inch. These materials are available in a range from about 60 threads per inch to a maximum of around 500 threads per inch. The two classification systems can be compared so that equivalent opening sizes can be identified (table 14.1).

Specific recommendations cannot be made here about the type of fabric and mesh count to use in a given situation. Many variables can influence that decision. The first consideration is to identify the type of ink to be used and to consult the manufacturer's data

Table 14.1. A Comparison of Mesh Classification Systems

XX system used for silk and multi- or monofilament polyesters	Silk	Multifilament polyesters	Nylon	Monofilament polyesters	Stainless steel	Silk	Multifilament polyesters	Nylon	Monofilament polyesters	Stainless steel
6XX	74	74	70	74	70	47	43	45	34	55
8XX	86	86	90	92	88	45	32	42	42	48
10XX	109	109	108	110	105	40	20	43	39	47
12XX	125	125	120	125	120	32	28	45	30	47
14XX	139	139	138	139	135	30	26	47	35	47
16XX	157	157	157	157	145	31	25	41	24	46
18XX	166	170	166	175	165	31	31	38	34	47
20XX	173	178	185	—	180	28	29	43	—	47
25XX	200	198	196	200	200	23	26	44	32	46
			230	225	230			42	42	46
			240	245	250			39	38	36
			260	260	270			36	35	32
			283	280	—			37	34	—
			306	300	—			34	29	—
			330	330	325			30	27	30
			380	390	400			22	18	36

for the screen material the manufacturer suggests be used with that ink. Manufacturers specify minimum screen mesh sizes based on the maximum pigment particle sizes in the ink (the particles naturally must be able to freely pass through the screen openings). Manufacturers also indicate whether the ink vehicle will interact with any commercial screen fabrics. The next step is to consider the fineness of the line detail of the image to be screen printed. A coarse screen mesh will pass a heavy layer of ink, but it will not hold a fine line stencil. In general, use a 12XX fabric for hand-cut and indirect photographic stencils with normal images and a 14XX and finer for photographic stencils containing images with fine line detail. Multifilament fibers are generally not suitable for halftone or extremely fine line reproduction.

Organdy is often used for short-run situations where bold line detail is wanted and reclaiming the fabric is not important. Organdy is an inexpensive, loosely woven cloth that can be purchased from any fabric shop. It has a strength of around 10X. Although its replacement cost is about one-tenth that of a commercial screen material, it does have certain drawbacks. The fabric is not as strong as silk or a monofilament fiber, so the squeegee action can rapidly wear away or fray the cloth. Also, because the weave is not perfectly uniform, some fine line detail might be lost.

Frames

There is no standard size or shape for a screen printing frame. The frame must hold the fabric without warping, be deep enough to hold the quantity of ink being printed, and be at least 4 inches wider and longer than the largest stencil to be reproduced.

Commercially constructed frames are available, but they are certainly not a requirement. Frames that are custom-made by the printer to meet individual needs are often better than their commercial counterparts. Most custom-made frames are made from wood because it is inexpensive, fairly stable, and easily cut to any dimension. The high tension developed when modern synthetic fabrics are stretched on a frame will warp wooden frames constructed with common butt joints, so the joint must be such that the frame cannot be sprung in any direction (figure 14.8). Wood frames are not recommended for close registration work because wood does have a tendency to swell and shift if it gets damp. When exact registration is required, as in printed circuits or color process reproductions, steel or aluminum is a preferable frame material.

Fabric-Stretching Techniques

Fabric manufacturers recommend the amount of tension that should be placed on their material. Generally, silk should be stretched 3% to 4% of its original dimensions in two directions, nylon from 4% to 7%, and polyesters from 1% to 4%. Most suppliers recommend the use of a mechanical stretching system. With this system it is easy to control the exact amount of tension for any frame.

The simplest method of attaching screen fabric is by tacking or stapling the material to the underside of the frame. Use number 4 carpet tacks or ¼-inch staples in a general purpose industrial staple gun. Space the fasteners approximately ½ inch (1.27 cm) apart in two rows. Start by placing the loose fabric over the frame so that the strands are parallel to the frame edges. The rough cut fabric should be at least 2 inches (5.08 cm) larger in each direction than the dimensions of the frame. Place three fasteners in the upper right-hand corner. Pull the fabric diagonally and fasten a second corner in place. Then stretch the upper left-hand corner and next the lower

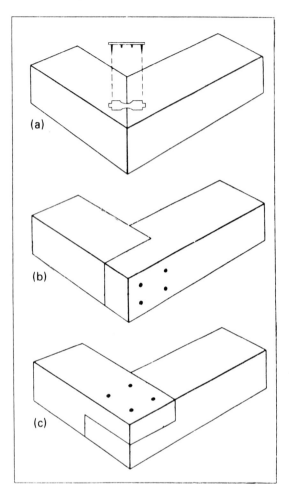

Figure 14.8.   Common wooden frame joints Common joints used for custom-made wooden screen frames are a reinforced miter joint (a), a rabbet joint (b), and an end-lap joint (c).

right. Now begin at the center of a long edge and space a row of fasteners completely around the frame. As you fasten, pull the material with fabric pliers so that all warps are removed from the screen surface. Go back and alternate a second row of fasteners just inside the first. (If staple tape is used, it will

be easy to remove the staples when the fabric is replaced.) Finally, cut the surplus fabric from the frame with a sharp razor blade and mask over the staples with gummed tape (figure 14.9).

An alternative method for hand stretching fabric on a wooden frame is a starched cord and groove technique. Cut a single notch partially through each frame side with a saw (figure 14.10). The inside groove may have to

Figure 14.9.   Cutting away surplus fabric
Courtesy of SUCO Learning Resources and R. Kampas

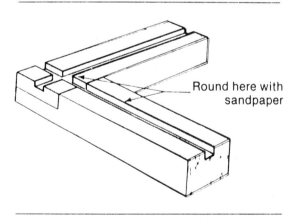

Round here with sandpaper

Figure 14.10.   Wooden frame with sawed notch

be rounded to prevent cutting the fabric. An inexpensive piece of 3/16-inch woven clothesline will nearly perfectly fill the groove left by a standard table saw blade. By carefully working from one corner, you can stretch the fabric by forcing both the cord and the fabric into the groove (figure 14.11). Special tools have been developed to insert the cord (figure 14.12), but any device that will not tear the cloth is acceptable. Whatever method is used, the fabric should be "drumhead" tight, without warps or tears.

Fabric Treatment

Monofilament fabric, such as nylon or polyester, must be treated before a stencil can be adhered. A **tooth** must be produced on the smooth monofilament fibers so the stencil can be held in place.

To do this, slightly dampen the fabric with water and pour half a teaspoon of 500-grit silicon carbide for each 16- × 20-inch (40.64- × 50.8-cm) area on the back, or stencil

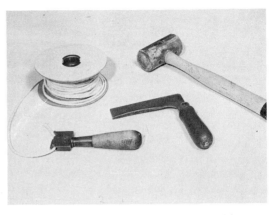

Figure 14.12. Tools used to insert cord into notch
Courtesy of SUCO Learning Resources and R. Kampas

side, of the screen. Carefully scour the fabric with a wet rag for 2 to 3 minutes. Scrub the entire screen surface. Then thoroughly rinse both sides of the screen with a strong water spray. The 500-grit silicon carbide will not clog even the smallest mesh screen opening. This operation must be repeated each time the screen is to be used.

Some printers use a very fine waterproof silicon carbide paper (sandpaper) to treat monofilament fabrics. Wet the screen and lightly rub the entire surface of the stencil side for 4 to 5 minutes. Then thoroughly rinse both sides of the screen with a strong water spray. This technique is recommended only if no alternative method is available.

All fabrics, whether new or used, must be cleaned and degreased to ensure proper film or emulsion adhesion. If it is an old screen, be sure that all ink has been removed and no foreign particles are clogging the mesh openings (figure 14.13). Ink manufacturers recommend the proper degreaser for their products. First, wet the screen with cold water and sprinkle both sides with powdered trisodium phosphate. Thoroughly scrub both

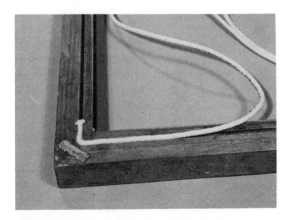

Figure 14.11. Cord forced into the notch to secure the screen
Courtesy of SUCO Learning Resources and R. Kampas

Figure 14.13. Magnified view of a clogged screen
Courtesy of J. Ulano Company, Inc.

sides with a soft bristle brush. Then rinse the screen with a powerful water spray. Allow the screen to drain and dry, but do not touch the fabric—skin oils on the fibers might prevent stencil adhesion. *Do not use* any commercial abrasive cleansers, such as "Ajax," because the cleanser particles can clog the screen on fine mesh fabrics and cannot be removed by the water spray. If trisodium phosphate is not available, use a commercial nonsudsing automatic dishwashing detergent.

After the fabric has been cleaned, it is ready to accept the stencil. It is important not to store the clean screen for a long period before attempting to adhere the stencil.

Hand-Cut Stencil Methods

The hand-cut process was the earliest method used to make screen stencils. Originally, pieces of thin paper were cut and glued to the underside of a screen. The process was tiring and time consuming, and it offered the printer only a limited number of impressions before the stencil simply wore out. Later, the paper

was coated with shellac or lacquer to increase the stencil's durability, but the process was still slow.

In the early 1930s Joseph Ulano (founder of J. Ulano Company, Inc., now a leading screen printing supplier) made an interesting observation. He found that if a layer of lacquer was sprayed over a hard surface and allowed to dry, a thin sheet of lacquer could be pulled from the surface in one piece. This lacquer could be used as a stencil by coating it onto a support sheet and then cutting away the design, leaving a thin, clean stencil on the sheet. The lacquer could be applied to a screen and the support sheet pulled away. This method is the basis for nearly all hand-cut stencils in the industry today. It has the advantage of speed combined with sharp, crisp line detail.

The basic process of creating a hand-cut stencil is relatively simple. It involves only three steps:

- Cutting the stencil
- Applying the stencil to the screen
- Removing the support sheet

Cut-film stencils are made up of two layers: a support sheet and a lacquer- or water-based emulsion. The problem is to cut away the emulsion without embossing or cutting the support sheet. As with all stencils, only the areas to be printed are removed from the base material.

Hand-Cutting Techniques

Place a line drawing of the desired stencil under a piece of cut-film material. Be sure that the emulsion side of the stencil material is up and that there are at least 2 inches of stencil film around all edges of the image. Tape the drawing and cut-film material securely in place.

A variety of tools are used in the industry to cut the film. A frisket knife is the cheapest and the most popular. Other useful tools are a swivel knife, bicutters (for cutting parallel lines), and a beam compass (figure 14.14). But none of these is absolutely necessary.

Several general techniques will ensure success with a hand-cut stencil. A razor-sharp blade is very important. The extra pressure needed with a dull blade rounds the film edge by forcing it down into the emulsion. A round edge will not properly adhere to the screen. Place the stencil material on a hard, flat surface. Apply light pressure while holding the blade at nearly a right angle to the film. The lower the angle of the cutting blade, the more danger of rounding the edges of the stencil material. Begin by practicing on a piece of scrap film. Cut only through the emulsion. A cut in the base will hold excess adhering solvent during the adhering step, which could dissolve part of the stencil material. Cut every line in a single stroke. It is extremely difficult to recut over a line. Where lines meet, always overlap the cuts (figure 14.15). This measure

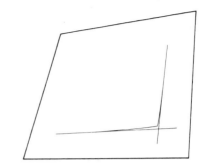

Figure 14.15. Overlapping cuts

will produce sharp corners on the final print. The overcuts will always fuse together when the stencil is applied to the screen. As each image area is cut, remove the emulsion. Don't wait until all lines have been cut. The easiest method to remove a layer of cut emulsion is to stab it with the point of the knife and lift (figure 14.16). Remember to remove the emulsion only in the areas where ink is to appear on the final print.

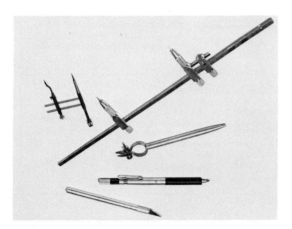

Figure 14.14 Common cutting tools From bottom counterclockwise: exacto knife or frisket knife, Ulano swivel knife, parallel bicutters, beam compass cutters.

Figure 14.16. Removing cut emulsion Stab a layer of cut emulsion with the point of a knife and lift it off the support base.

Adhering Water-Soluble Hand-Cut Stencils

There are two methods of adhering water-soluble hand-cut stencils. The first (figure 14.17a) uses a buildup board that is smaller than the inside dimensions of the frame. Place the hand-cut stencil emulsion-side up on the center of the board. Position the screen over the stencil and buildup board so that the screen fabric is against the emulsion of the stencil material. Saturate a sponge or cloth with water and slowly wipe the stencil in overlapping strokes until the entire surface is wet. Do not rub the stencil with the sponge. Allow only

enough contact to moisten the stencil emulsion. With the frame still flat, dry the emulsion with a cold-air fan. To reduce drying time, excess moisture can be blotted out of the stencil with newsprint. The base material may be peeled off when the emulsion is dry. (See "Masking the Stencil" in this chapter.)

The second method (figure 14.17b) is to thoroughly wet both sides of the fabric with a clean sponge dampened with water. Roll the emulsion side of the stencil against the bottom of the wet screen. Using light pressure, move the wet sponge over the entire surface of the base material to adhere the stencil to the fabric. With the frame flat, dry the

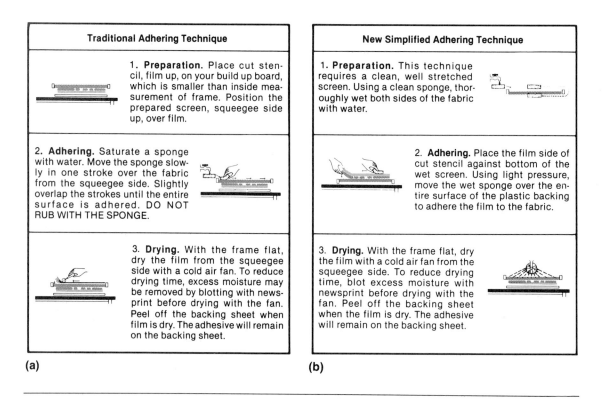

Traditional Adhering Technique
1. Preparation. Place cut stencil, film up, on your build up board, which is smaller than inside measurement of frame. Position the prepared screen, squeegee side up, over film.
2. Adhering. Saturate a sponge with water. Move the sponge slowly in one stroke over the fabric from the squeegee side. Slightly overlap the strokes until the entire surface is adhered. DO NOT RUB WITH THE SPONGE.
3. Drying. With the frame flat, dry the film from the squeegee side with a cold air fan. To reduce drying time, excess moisture may be removed by blotting with newsprint before drying with the fan. Peel off the backing sheet when film is dry. The adhesive will remain on the backing sheet.

(a)

New Simplified Adhering Technique
1. Preparation. This technique requires a clean, well stretched screen. Using a clean sponge, thoroughly wet both sides of the fabric with water.
2. Adhering. Place the film side of cut stencil against bottom of the wet screen. Using light pressure, move the wet sponge over the entire surface of the plastic backing to adhere the film to the fabric.
3. Drying. With the frame flat, dry the film with a cold air fan from the squeegee side. To reduce drying time, blot excess moisture with newsprint before drying with the fan. Peel off the backing sheet when the film is dry. The adhesive will remain on the backing sheet.

(b)

Figure 14.17. Adhering water-soluble stencils
Courtesy of J. Ulano Company, Inc.

emulsion with a cold-air fan. To reduce drying time, blot up excess moisture with newsprint. The base material can be peeled off when the emulsion is dry. (See "Masking the Stencil" in this chapter.)

Adhering Lacquer-Solvent Hand-Cut Stencils

Lacquer-based hand-cut stencils use a commerical adhering fluid to soften the lacquer emulsion long enough to allow the stencil to adhere to the screen. The specific fluid used should match the specifications provided by the stencil manufacturer. To attach a lacquer stencil to the screen, place the stencil emulsion-side up on a buildup board. Position the screen over the stencil and board so that the screen fabric is against the emulsion of the stencil material. Place several weights on the frame to keep the stencil from shifting or, if possible, actually clamp the frame in place.

Take two clean, soft cloths and roll one into a tight ball. Moisten the cloth ball with a small quantity of adhering fluid. The cloth should not be so wet that the liquid drips from the ball. Begin in one corner of the stencil and moisten about a 4-inch square with the wet cloth. Use a blotting motion to saturate the area and then immediately wipe it dry with the second cloth. The moistened area should become darker in color than the rest of the stencil. That area is now adhered to the screen. Continue blotting and drying 4-inch squares over the rest of the stencil. Be extremely careful not to dissolve the lacquer with too much solvent, but use enough so that the entire stencil is a single uniform color. Lacquer-based materials dry rapidly. When the stencil is completely dry, the backing sheet may be peeled away. (See "Masking the Stencil" in this chapter).

Photographic Stencil Methods

The primary reason for the growth of the screen printing industry has been the development of the photographic stencil. The idea is not new. The basic process was developed in Great Britain in1850 by William Henry Fox Talbot. He found that certain materials, such as gelatin, egg albumin, and glue, mixed or coated with a potassium bichromate solution hardened when exposed to light. The areas not exposed remained soft and could readily be washed away. Talbot actually was concerned with a continuous-tone negative/positive process. It wasn't until 1914 that someone applied his work to the screen printing industry.

Today photographic emulsions far more sophisticated than egg albumin are available through commerical suppliers. However, whatever type of emulsion is used, the method is the same. Printers expose the light-sensitive material through a positive transparent image, and unhardened areas on the stencil are washed away. The stencil is fixed or made permanent, masked, and then printed.

The primary advantage of photographic stencils is the possibility for intricate and high-quality line detail. Step-and-repeat images, halftones, exact facsimile reproductions, and high-quality process color stencil prints are all possible and commonplace. The introduction of photographic screen printing allowed the screen printer to enter the field of packaged product illustration. A color image can be screen printed with any ink on any surface shape (flat, cylindrical, or irregular).

All photographic stencil processes are divided into three types:

- *Indirect* or transfer image method
- *Direct* image method

– Film emulsion or *direct/indirect* image method

The **indirect process** uses a dry emulsion on a plastic support sheet. The stencil emulsion is sensitized by the manufacturer and is purchased in rolls or sheets. The stencil film is exposed through a transparent right-reading positive and is then treated with a developer solution. The areas that light reaches (the nonimage areas) are hardened during exposure. The remaining areas are washed away with a warm-water spray to form the image or printing areas. The stencil is adhered to a clean screen while it is wet, and the support sheet is removed after the stencil dries (figure 14.18).

The **direct process** uses a wet emulsion that is coated directly on a clean screen. The emulsion is exposed through a transparent positive to harden the nonimage areas. The image areas are washed away with a warm-water spray. When the emulsion is dry, the stencil is ready to print (figure 14.19). Direct emulsions have a limited shelf life when compared to indirect material.

The **direct/indirect process** combines the techniques of both the indirect and the direct photographic processes. An unsensitized film material is placed under the stencil side of the screen on a flat table. The stencil emulsion is stored in two parts, a liquid emulsion and a sensitizer. When the two are mixed together, they become light sensitive and are coated through the screen to the film support. When the emulsion is dry, the backing sheet is removed and normal direct exposure techniques are carried out (figure 14.20). The main advantage of the process is the uniformity of the emulsion thickness. Because the direct/indirect process uses the procedures of both the direct and the indirect stencil methods, it will not be discussed in detail in this chapter.

Determining Photographic Stencil Exposures

Most photographic stencil emulsions have a spectral sensitivity that peaks in the ultraviolet-to-blue region of the visible spectrum (see "Light Sources" in Appendix B). Because the stencil emulsion must be exposed through a transparent positive, good contact is important to ensure accurate line detail. Vacuum frames are generally used to hold the stencil and film in place during exposure.

Proper exposure is important for photographic screen stencils. An underexposed stencil will produce an emulsion that is too thin. A thin emulsion will have difficulty adhering to the screen material, with the possibility of passing ink in a nonimage area. An overexposed stencil will result in an emulsion that is too thick. A thick emulsion will close in the fine line detail and, if on an indirect stencil, might not adhere properly to the fabric.

A commercial **step wedge** manufactured by the J. Ulano Company, Inc. (figure 14.21, p. 422) can be used to calibrate correct stencil exposure. An alternative calibration device is a transparent positive made up of normal and hard-to-reproduce copy. The step wedge is preferable because it contains identified line weights.

In practice, a series of exposures is made through the step wedge to the photographic stencil. Most stencil manufacturers make time recommendations, but it is best to calibrate the exposure for a specific working condition. Begin with the manufacturer's recommended exposure time for the specific light source and distance. If no recommended time is identified, start with 60 seconds. From the recommended time, determine exposures that are 50%, 75%, 100%, 125%, and 150%. For example, if 60 seconds is the recommended time,

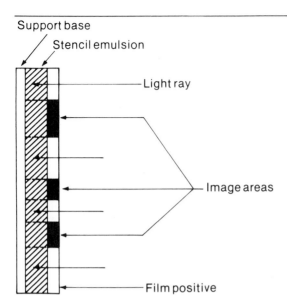

1. Exposure
No light strikes the photographic screen emulsion under the image areas on the transparent positive.

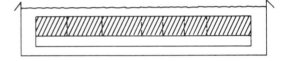

2. Development
Areas exposed to light during exposure are hardened during development.

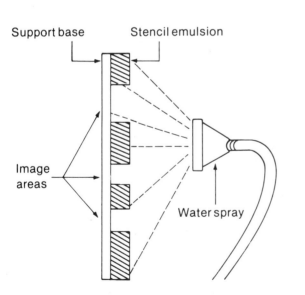

3. Wash
Unhardened areas (image areas) are washed away leaving open areas in the stencil.

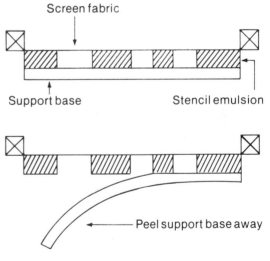

4. Adhesion
Adhere stencil emulsion to screen fabric, let dry, and peel support base away.

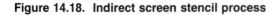

Figure 14.18. Indirect screen stencil process

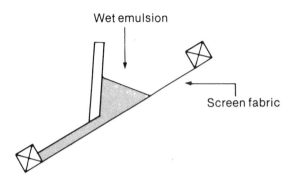

Wet emulsion

Screen fabric

1. Coating
A wet emulsion is coated onto a clean screen.

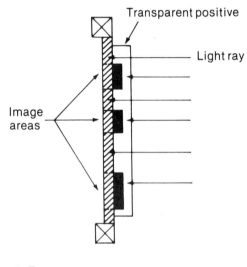

Transparent positive

Light ray

Image
areas

2. Exposure
Areas where light strikes the emulsion
(nonimage areas) become hardened during
exposure.

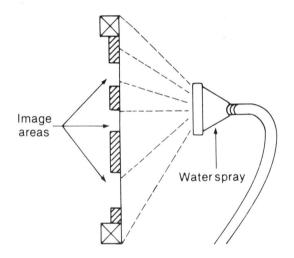

Image
areas

Water spray

3. Wash
Unhardened areas (image areas) are washed
away leaving open areas in the stencil.

Figure 14.19. Direct screen stencil process

then five separate exposures would be made
through the step wedge: 30 seconds, 45 seconds, 60 seconds, 75 seconds, and 90 seconds.

If an indirect stencil is used, the emulsion must be exposed through the base material (figure 14.22). If a direct stencil is used,
the transparent positive is exposed through
the bottom side of the screen (figure 14.23).

A test exposure is easy to make if these
time percentages are used. Place the transparent positive in contact with the stencil. First

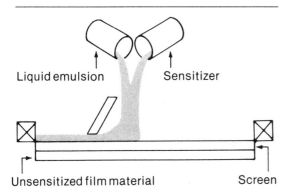

1. Coating
The two parts of the emulsion are mixed and coated on the screen material. Note the piece of unsensitized film material under the screen.

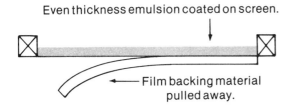

2. Removing the backing
The film backing is removed after the emulsion has dried.

Figure 14.20. Direct/indirect screen stencil process

expose through the positive for the shortest exposure (for this example, the exposure would be 30 seconds). Then mask off ⅕ of the step wedge with opaque paper or masking film and expose the remaining uncovered portion for 15 seconds. Move the masking sheet to cover ⅖ of the wedge and again expose the uncovered area for 15 seconds. Continue this procedure until the entire step wedge has been exposed. Develop and wash out the stencil. (See the following sections

outlining the specific procedures for each type of stencil.)

Mount the stencil on the screen that will be used in the shop, allow it to dry, and make a print with the desired ink. Examine the image in detail. First identify the step that has most faithfully reproduced the original line detail. Consider the narrowest line that was reproduced, then select the exposure that has the thickest emulsion but has held that line dimension. If no step appears ideal, expose another stencil with a smaller percentage difference (such as 80%, 90%, 110%, and 120% of the recommended time).

Indirect Photographic Stencil Process

The indirect photographic stencil process is known by several terms in the industry: "transfer," "carbon tissue," and "pigment paper" are a few. The process is also identified by several trade names representing indirect stencil material that is supplied by individual dealers.

The indirect photographic stencil is exposed through a transparent film positive. Where light strikes the stencil, the emulsion is hardened. Where light does not strike the stencil, the emulsion remains soft and can be washed away. Logically, the better the positive, the better the reproduction. Chapter 6 provides detailed information on the production of positive film images.

An indirect stencil is the easiest of all the screen stencils to produce. It involves the following six steps:

1. Exposure
2. Development
3. Washing
4. Application of the stencil to the screen
5. Drying
6. Removal of the base material

Figure 14.21. Ulano step wedge The Ulano step wedge is a precision tool that can be used to determine the correct exposure time for any type of photographic stencil. The illustration shown is only an approximation and in no way attempts to duplicate the quality of the original instrument.
Courtesy of J. Ulano Company, Inc.

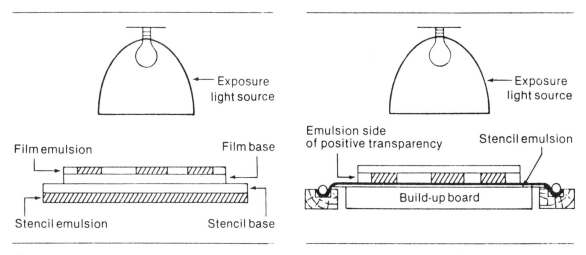

Figure 14.22. Exposing indirect stencils Indirect stencils must be exposed through the base side of the stencil material.

Figure 14.23. Exposing direct stencils A direct stencil is set up to be exposed through the bottom of the screen.

Exposure. All indirect emulsions are coated onto a transparent support sheet by the stencil manufacturer. It is always necessary to expose the stencil through the support material. Some sort of contact frame is generally used to bring the positive into intimate contact with the presensitized sheet. It is important that the right-reading side of the positive be against the base side of the stencil. Place the positive on a table top so that the image reads exactly as it would on the final print. Place a sheet of stencil material over the positive so that the emulsion side is up. Be sure that the stencil extends at least 1 inch (2.54 cm) beyond all image extremes (figure 14.24). Then pick up

the sandwich of both pieces and turn them over. To expose the stencil, the light must pass through the clear areas of the positive. Place the two sheets in the contact frame and expose the stencil for the time that was determined from the test exposure.

Development and Washing. The process of developing removes all areas not hardened by exposure to light. Any area covered by the positive image will be washed away. Depending on the type of emulsion, indirect stencils are developed by one of two techniques: a hydrogen peroxide bath or plain water.

Some emulsions require a hydrogen peroxide bath to harden the exposed areas. The stencil is placed in the solution emulsion-side up and is constantly agitated for 1 to 3 minutes, depending on the manufacturer's recommendations. The sheet is then removed and is sprayed with warm water (95°–105°F). The spray washes away the unhardened stencil areas, leaving a stencil outline of the image.

Other emulsions are developed in plain water immediately after being removed from the contact frame. A cool-water (70°F) spray is directed over the entire emulsion surface until the image areas are washed away.

With both methods the concern is with stopping all development as soon as the image areas are clear. Excess warm-water spray will remove the hardened emulsion and can create a thin stencil. All indirect stencils are fixed by a stream of cold water (gradually decreasing the temperature).

Application. Indirect stencils adhere very easily to the screen fabric. Place the chilled stencil emulsion-side up on a hard, flat buildup board (figure 14.25). Position the clean screen over the stencil so that the clear printing area is in the center of the screen frame (figure 14.26). Do not move the screen once it has contacted the stencil and do not use excessive

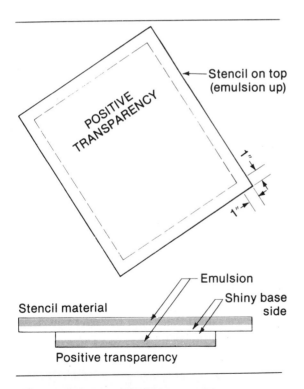

Figure 14.24. Positioning the positive transparency The right-reading side of the positive must be placed against the base side of the stencil.

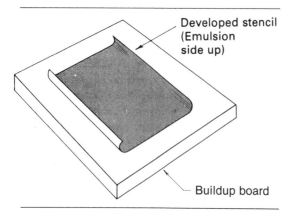

Figure 14.25. Placing the indirect stencil on a buildup board

pressure—merely allow the weight of the frame to hold it in position. Excess moisture is removed from the stencil by blotting it with clean newsprint or inexpensive paper towels (figure 14.27). Gently wipe the newsprint with a soft, clean rag; *do not use pressure.* Keep changing the newsprint until it does not pick up moisture from the stencil. Excessive pressure during blotting will push the fabric threads into the emulsion, which could cause pinholes or a ragged sawtooth edge during

Figure 14.26. Positioning the screen over the stencil
Courtesy of SUCO Learning Resources and R. Kampas

Figure 14.27. Removing excess moisture
Courtesy of SUCO Learning Resources and R. Kampas

printing. The function of blotting is to remove excess moisture and to "blot up" through the fibers the soft "top" of the emulsion.

Drying. Indirect stencils should not be forced dry with hot or warm air. Rapid drying could result in poor adhesion or could warp the stencil. To dry the emulsion properly, place the entire frame in a position so that air is allowed to flow over both sides—a gentle room air fan may be used. A spotty appearance of light and dark areas indicates that the stencil is drying. The emulsion is completely dry when the entire stencil area is uniform in hue.

Removal of the Base Material. When the emulsion is dry, the clear support base can be peeled off (figure 14.28). After printing, all indirect photographic stencils can generally be removed from the screen fabric with a high-pressure hot-water spray. For difficult materials, enzymes are available that will help to dissolve the old material (on metal or synthetic screens, bleach is commonly used).

Direct Photographic Stencil Process

With the direct method of stencil preparation, a wet photographic emulsion is applied di-

2. Application of the emulsion to the screen
3. Drying the emulsion
4. Exposure
5. Development

Preparation. Unsensitized, direct screen emulsions are provided by the manufacturer in two parts: a liquid unsensitized emulsion and a dry powder sensitizer. The dry sensitizer is first dissolved in warm water according to the manufacturer's recommendations. The liquid sensitizer is then added to the liquid emulsion to create an active solution. The mixture may be stored in a closed amber or light-tight bottle, but it usually must be applied to the screen as soon as possible.

Application. The screen should be coated with the liquid emulsion in a yellow or subdued light situation. One technique is to pour a quantity of the emulsion on one edge of the bottom side of the frame rather than on the screen itself, because then the liquid would rapidly seep through the screen mesh. With a round-edged scoop coater, squeegee the emulsion to the other end of the screen with smooth, continuous strokes (figure 14.29). Turn the frame over and immediately squeegee the inside of the screen until it is smooth. The quantity of liquid to apply for the first coat depends on the length of the screen, but it is better to apply too much and squeegee off the excess than to use too little and not totally cover the screen.

Drying. Store the frame flat in a dark place. A circulating air fan can be used to hasten drying. When the first coat is dry, apply a second coat to the inside of the screen and allow it to dry. The thickness of the ink deposit can be somewhat controlled by the number of emulsion layers. If a thick ink deposit

Figure 14.28. Peeling off the support material
Courtesy of SUCO Learning Resources and R. Kampas

rectly to the screen fabric by the printer. The entire screen is then exposed to a positive image, developed, and printed.

The main requirement of the direct process is some form of liquid light-sensitive emulsion. All currently used emulsions fall into the following types of chemical formulations:

- A synthetic-based material, such as polyvinyl alcohol
- A gelatin-based chemical material
- A combination of both synthetic and gelatin materials

Most printers use commercially prepared emulsions rather than prepare their own. Commercial emulsions are more economical, higher in quality, and can be formulated by the supplier to meet any printing requirements. Commercial emulsions are available in two forms: presensitized and unsensitized liquids.

The steps in preparing a direct photographic stencil are relatively simple and involve five steps:

1. Preparation of the sensitized emulsion

Figure 14.29. Using a scoop coater on the emulsion
Courtesy of SUCO Learning Resources and R. Kampas

is desired, a third emulsion coating should be placed on the bottom side of the frame.

Exposure. Special contact frames must be used to hold the screen frame and film positive during exposure. Place the right-reading side of the transparent positive against the outside surface of the screen (see figure 14.23). The light must pass through the positive to expose the screen emulsion. Expose the screen stencil material through the positive for the time determined from the test exposures.

Development. The stencil image is developed by first wetting both sides of the screen

in warm (95°–105°F) water, then gently spraying both sides with warm water until the image areas are completely clear (figure 14.30). Allow the frame to drain and blot the emulsion dry with newsprint.

Masking the Stencil

Preparing a Paper Mask

The idea of a stencil is that ink passes through any open areas on the screen. It is necessary to block out or mask those open areas of the screen not covered by the stencil material and not intended to print. There is generally a gap between the edge of the stencil and the screen frame that must be covered to prevent ink passage.

A paper mask works very well for short runs for blocking nonimage areas. Cut a piece of kraft paper slightly smaller than the inside dimensions of the frame. Lay the paper on the screen and with a pencil trace the rough outline of the image area. Remove the paper

Figure 14.30. Developing the image Gently spray both sides of the screen with warm water.
Courtesy of SUCO Learning Resources and R. Kampas

and cut out an area that is about 1 inch (2.54 cm) larger than the image extremes. Replace the masking sheet and apply gummed tape around the edges of the frame. Then tape the opening of the masking sheet to the stencil material. It is important that the tape be at least ¾ inch (1.91 cm) from the nearest image and in perfect contact with the solid stencil.

Preparing a Liquid Block-Out Mask

A second method of masking employs a liquid block-out fluid (figure 14.31). These fluids are usually water based and are easy to use. Materials such as LePage's glue will work, but specially formulated commercial products are inexpensive and work much better. Brush or scrape one coat on the underside of the screen wherever the fabric is exposed but an image is not desired. Allow it to dry and apply a second coat on the inside area of the screen.

It is often necessary to touch up any imperfections, such as pinholes, that are in the

Figure 14.31. Using a liquid mask
Courtesy of SUCO Learning Resources and R. Kampas

stencil. The liquid block-out is ideal for small corrections and should be applied to the underside of the screen.

The processes of printing and cleaning the screen and stencil are discussed in detail in Chapter 15.

Key Terms

screen printing
stencil
hand-cut stencils
tusche-and-glue

photographic stencils
multifilament screens
monofilament screens
tooth

indirect process
direct process
direct/indirect process
step wedge

Questions for Review

1. What is the basic concept of screen printing?

2. What are the three groups of stencil preparation methods?

3. How are screen fabrics classified?

4. Which mesh count will pass a coarser ink pigment, a 6XX or a 14XX fabric?

5. Why must a tooth be produced on a monofilament fabric and not on a multifilament one?

6. Why should commercial household abrasive cleaners *not* be used to clean or degrease a screen?

7. What are the three basic steps in creating a hand-cut stencil?

8. What is the primary advantage of photographic stencils?

9. What are the three types of photographic stencils?

10. Briefly outline the six steps necessary to prepare an indirect photographic stencil.

11. Briefly outline the five steps necessary to prepare a direct photographic stencil.

12. What is the purpose of masking?

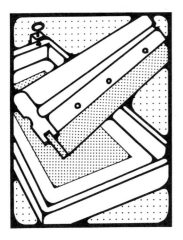

Chapter Fifteen

Screen Printing

Anecdote to Chapter Fifteen

The "Knave of Bells" A printed playing card from about A.D. 1500.

The illustration is a famous playing card called the "Knave of Bells" that dates from before the year 1500. There is some debate as to how the card was actually printed, but it was probably printed from a stencil. The "Knave" was a part of a set of forty-eight playing cards found in the inner lining of a book cover that was printed and bound sometime around the turn of the sixteenth century. Paper was such a precious commodity that discarded or inferior sheets were often used to stiffen book bindings. Many valuable early pieces of printing have been found in such hiding places.

As we understand the process today, the stenciled card was made by using a perforated metal plate. To create a stencil, many small holes were punched through the thin metal in the shape of the desired image. The "illuminator," as he was called, positioned the plate over the paper and applied the ink with a brush. The brush forced the ink through the small openings onto the page. Several different colors were often used, with a separate plate for each color.

No one knows exactly when playing cards were invented, but the first documented evidence of their existence can be found in a 1392 account book kept by the treasurer of King Charles VI of France, in which a notation was made on the purchase of three packs of cards for the king. Several scholars, however, have found references to "games of hazard," as cards were called, in French poetry as early as 1328.

It is also difficult to trace the exact evolution of the printed card design. It is known that by 1550 printers had nearly universally adopted the four suits we know today as symbols of the four classes of society. Hearts symbolized the clergy. Spades were a refinement of the Italian *spada,* a sword, and were for the nobility. Clubs meant the peasantry. Diamonds symbolized the citizens or burghers.

There are some experts who suggest that playing cards were the first printed product ever produced in Europe. Some even believe that it was the widespread use of games of hazard that started an interest in learning for many of the uneducated peasants of the Continent. There is little doubt that a demand was created for a printed product.

Objectives for Chapter Fifteen

After completing this chapter, you will be able to:

- Identify important considerations when selecting a squeegee and ink.
- Explain basic screen printing techniques, including registration, on- and off-contact printing, printing, and clean-up.

- Recall multicolor printing techniques.
- List methods of ink drying.
- Recall methods of screen printing halftones.
- Classify high-speed production screen printing presses.
- Recognize special screen printing machine configurations.

Introduction

The basic process of screen printing has changed little in the last several hundred years. The standard printing device remains a stencil attached to a piece of fabric stretched over a wooden or metal frame. A flexible **squeegee** is used to force the ink through the stencil opening. Even though the basic printing device has changed little, the printer's understanding of the variables that affect image quality has substantially increased.

The term **printing press** might sound strange when associated with the most basic screen printing unit, but the screen printing frame is in every sense a press. The receiver must be fed and registered under the stencil. The ink must be transferred to the receiver. The printed product must be removed and stored for later distribution. Screen printing presses can range in complexity from an elementary homemade, hand-operated wooden frame (figure 15.1) to a sophisticated system that automatically inserts, registers, prints, and removes any material, including cylindrical surfaces.

Figure 15.1. Basic screen printing unit The wooden frame is hinged off of a particle base board.
Courtesy of SUCO Learning Resources and R. Kampas

Squeegee and Ink Considerations

Selecting Proper Squeegee

It is the squeegee (figure 15.2) that actually causes the image transfer to take place, because it is the squeegee that forces the ink through the stencil and fabric openings onto the receiver. All squeegees have two parts: a handle and a blade. The handle can be of any design that is comfortable for the printer and meets his or her particular needs, but great care must be taken when selecting the squeegee blade. Three primary blade considerations must be examined prior to printing:

– Shape
– Chemical makeup
– Flexibility
– Length

Shape. The blade shape generally determines the sharpness and thickness of ink deposit. There are six basic blade shapes (figure

15.3). A *square* blade (figure 15.3a) is the most common and is a good general purpose design that can be used to print on flat surfaces with standard poster inks. A *double-bevel, flat-point* design (figure 15.3b) is good for working with ceramic materials such as glazes or slip. The *double-bevel* shaped form (figure 15.3c) is

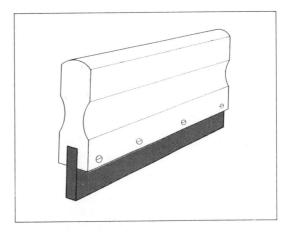

Figure 15.2. Printer's squeegee

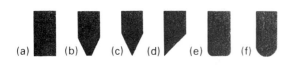

Figure 15.3. Basic shapes of squeegee blades The six basic shapes are square (a), double-bevel, flat point (b), double-bevel (c), single-bevel (d), square-edge with rounded corners (e), and round-edge (f).

used for printing on uneven surfaces or for placing a fine layer of ink on a surface when stenciling extremely fine line detail. The *single-bevel* (figure 15.3d) is generally used when printing on glass. The *square-edge with rounded corners* (figure 15.3e) is generally used when screening light colors over dark backgrounds. The *round-edge* (figure 15.3f) works well with printing on fabrics. The round-edge design has the advantage of forcing an extra-heavy amount of ink through the screen. All but the special purpose printer will find the square form acceptable for almost every job.

Chemical Makeup. The chemical makeup of the squeegee blade is important. The base for some inks could actually dissolve the blade if the wrong type of blade were used. Most squeegee blades are cast from rubber or plastic. Blades that are designed for vinyl or acetate printing are water soluble and cannot be used with a water-based pigment. Synthetic blades, such as polyurethane, retain their edges longer and have more resistance to abrasion than do blades of any other material, but they are significantly more expensive. A good general purpose blade is neoprene rubber. It can be used for vinyl, lacquer, oil, poster enamel, and ethocel inks. When selecting the specific chemical makeup of the blade, decide on the type of ink to be used, identify

the ink base, and determine which blade formulation is acceptable.

Flexibility. The third consideration for squeegee blade selection is flexibility. Rubber hardness is measured in terms of **Shore Durometer** readings—an average blade for general use has a rating of 60 Shore A. Most squeegee manufacturers translate the value into the terms *hard*, *medium*, and *soft*. Soft blades (around 50 Shore A) will deposit a fairly thick layer of pigment. Hard blades (around 70 Shore A) will deposit a sharp, thin ink layer. A medium squeegee blade (60 Shore A) will meet most shop needs.

Length. The length of the squeegee is also an important consideration. As a rule of thumb, the blade should extend at least ½ inch beyond the limits of the stencil image, but it should be able to pass freely between the edges of the screen frame.

Squeegee Preparation

Whatever the shape, makeup, or hardness of the blade selected, the major factor controlling image quality is blade sharpness. Several types of commercial squeegee sharpeners are available that can be used to prepare any shape of edge (figure 15.4). Most machines operate with a moving abrasive belt or drum. The squeegee is mounted with a series of clamps, and the blade is passed against the cutting surface.

If a sharpening machine cannot be obtained, 6- and 8-inch widths of garnet cloth are suitable for sharpening square-edge blades. The cloth is mounted (generally with staples) on a hard, flat surface. The squeegee is held in a perfectly vertical position and is dragged back and forth over the abrasive cloth until a sharp edge is formed.

It is important that the squeegee be ab-

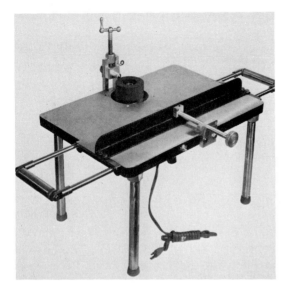

Figure 15.4. Commercial squeegee sharpener
Courtesy of Naz-Dar Company

There are so many different materials intended for so many different applications that both novice and experienced printers become easily confused. Choosing the appropriate ink becomes easier to understand if all elements of a particular job are examined in detail and several specific questions are answered.

Product Characteristics. The first area of concern should be the characteristics of the printed piece. What is the function of the final product? Will it be exposed to harsh weather conditions (as is a billboard)? Will it be in contact with harsh chemicals (as is printing on a detergent bottle or even a cola container)? Should the appearance of the image be a gloss or a flat finish? What will be the surface of the image receiver? Will the ink have to dry by absorption into the material? Will it need to be heat set? Will it have to air dry?

Production Limitations. After considering the characteristics of the printed piece, the printer must deal with the limitations of the production situation. Any material that can be ground into a fine powder can be mixed with a liquid vehicle and used as a screen ink. Ink manufacturers will recommend a minimum **screen mesh count** (or opening) that can be used with each of their materials. If the openings are smaller than the recommended minimum, no ink will pass through the screen. The solvents for the stencil and for the ink must not be the same. For example, if a water-based ink is used with a water-based stencil, the entire image carrier will rapidly become a puddle of ink and stencil on the screen.

By making a list of both product and production limitations, it is possible to eliminate all but a narrow category of possible ink choices. More information about screen inks for specific applications is given in Chapter 18.

solutely clean prior to printing. Any dry ink left on a blade from previous printing runs will contaminate the pigment used with other printing jobs. This is especially important when a dark color is to be followed by a light color.

Ink Selection

The pigment and vehicle must freely pass through screen fabric and still place an image of acceptable density on the receiving surface. Screen inks are thinner than letterpress or lithographic inks. Early screen inks were very similar to ordinary paint. The creation of new fabrics and stencil materials, the growth of printing on nontraditional materials (anything but paper), and the application of screen printing to specialized industrial needs (such as printed circuits) resulted in the development of a wide variety of screen inks.

Ink Preparation

Many manufacturers advertise that their inks are "ready to use directly from the can," but rarely does the printer not have to prepare the ink before printing. **Ink viscosity** (resistance to flow) is of major importance. The goal is to keep the ink as dense as possible to form an acceptable printed image. But at the same time, it must be thin enough to pass freely through the screen openings without clogging. The difficulty is that the required viscosity can be different for every job. The higher the mesh count, the thinner the ink must be. In very general terms, the ink should "flow like honey" off the ink knife. It should move slowly and smoothly and should not hesitate to flow when the knife is tipped.

Many different additives can be mixed with screen inks to yield certain ink characteristics. Viscosity can be decreased by adding a compatible thinner and/or reducer. The addition of a transparent base will make the ink somewhat translucent. An extender base will increase the quantity of usable ink without affecting density. The function of a drier is to hasten the drying of the ink on the receiver, but it can also increase the possibility of the ink drying in the screen fabric. A binder can be added to increase the adhesion of the ink to the stock. Individuals inexperienced with additives should always consult a screen ink supplier for information.

The Basic Printing Process

The basic techniques for screen printing will be discussed in terms of a hand-operated hinged-frame system. For this section it will be assumed that the printing frame is held with a pair of heavy-duty hinge clamps to a wooden or particle-board base. The hinges can be common butt hinges, or special hinges can be purchased from a screen printing supplier.

The sequence of steps, as with any press system, is to feed, register, print, and deliver the stock. Because the simple screen system is hand fed and delivered, this section will consider only registering the stock and printing the image. The processes of drying the image, cleaning the screen, and removing the stencil will also be discussed.

Basic Registration Techniques

As with all printing systems, registration is concerned with placing the image in the same position on every press sheet. Recall from Chapter 2 ("Controlling Image Position on the Press Sheet") that three metal gauge pins were used on the tympan of a platen press to hold the sheet in place. It is possible to form "gauge pins" from a narrow strip of paper. These gauge pins will hold the sheet in register during printing. Cut three pieces of 20- to 40-pound paper ½ inch by 2 inches and make a simple Z fold. Tape the tabs to the base under the screen frame (figure 15.5).

Commercial printers use several methods to locate the image in the appropriate printing position. A simple method is to place the original drawing or film positive used to produce the screen stencil right reading on a piece of the printing stock. Tape it to the stock so that the image is in the desired printing position. Place the stock, with the taped image, on the base board and lower the screen frame into the printing position over the stock. Move the stock until the taped image aligns with the stencil opening, then carefully hinge the screen up out of the way. Without moving the stock, carefully insert the "gauge pins" and tape each one to the base (figure 15.6). The tabs should be positioned so that there are two pins on a long side of the paper and

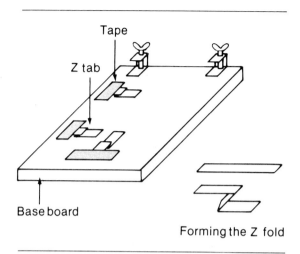

Figure 15.5. **Making gauge pins** Three Z tabs taped in place serve as gauge pins used to register the paper.

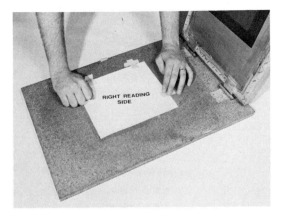

Figure 15.6. Setting the image position The Z tabs are placed against the positioned stock and carefully taped in place.
Courtesy of SUCO Learning Resources and R. Kampas

a single one on a short side. It is also important that the tabs be placed as far away from the image areas as possible. Remove the printing sheet and tape the inside portion of the Z tabs to the base. If every piece of stock is seated against the inside of the three tabs, the image will be printed in the same position on each sheet.

On- and Off-Contact Printing

Two common printing methods are used for hinged-frame printing: on-contact and off-contact printing. With **on-contact printing,** the screen and stencil contact the printing material throughout the transfer process. With this method the press sheet sticks to the screen. After the image is transferred, the frame must be hinged up and the stock carefully peeled away. On-contact printing is the most common technique for small job shops or for short-

run jobs that do not require an extremely sharp impression. However, off-contact printing should always be done if possible to avoid the problem of sticking. One method of preventing the stock from sticking to the screen with the on-contact approach is to place several pieces of thin double-backed adhesive in non-image areas on the base board.

In **off-contact printing,** the screen and stencil are slightly (generally no more than ⅛ inch) raised away from the printing material by small shims, or spacing material, under the hinge and frame. With this technique the stencil touches the stock only while the squeegee passes over the screen. Once the image is transferred across the squeegee line, the screen snaps back away from the receiver (figure 15.7). Off-contact printing helps keep the press sheet from sticking to the screen and usually prevents image smearing. It is often used as a technique to produce sharp impressions on smooth surfaces.

A vacuum frame base can be used with either on- or off-contact printing to help keep

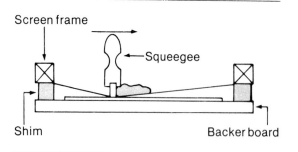

Figure 15.7. Diagram of off-contact printing In off-contact printing, the screen touches the paper only when the image is transferred by the squeegee.

the stock from sticking to the screen. Vacuum bases are available as single units or tables and are found on most semiautomatic machines.

Printing the Stencil

Chapter 14 outlined several procedures for masking the nonimage portions of the screen. Before printing, two tasks remain. First check to ensure that there are no pinholes or other unwanted openings in the stencil. Block out any areas with the recommended block-out solution for the type of stencil being used. Second, seal off the inside edge, between the fabric and the frame. Sealing can be done with any wide commercial tape (a 2-inch width is recommended). If the run is exceptionally long or if special inks (such as water-based) or abrasive materials (such as ceramic glaze) are used, a plastic solvent-resistant, pressure-sensitive tape should be used. Otherwise, a water-moistened gummed tape will be sufficient.

Begin the printing operation by positioning a piece of stock in the registration sys-

tem on the base and lowering the screen frame into position. Pour a puddle of prepared ink at one end of the screen, away from the image and in a line slightly longer than the width of the image (figure 15.8). Hold the squeegee at about a 60° angle to the screen surface and, pressing firmly, draw the puddle of ink across the stencil opening with one smooth motion (figure 15.9). It is important that the move-

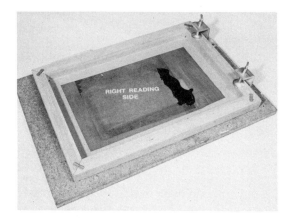

Figure 15.8. Adding ink to the screen
Courtesy of SUCO Learning Resources and R. Kampas

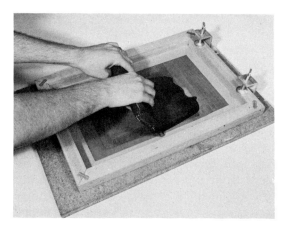

Figure 15.9. Distributing the ink
Courtesy of SUCO Learning Resources and R. Kampas

ment be uniform and that the motion not stop until the squeegee is out of the image area. Make only one pass. Remove the squeegee, raise the frame, prop the screen away from the image surface, and remove the stock sheet (figure 15.10).

Examine the printed image for correct position, ink uniformity, and clarity of detail. If necessary, readjust the registration tabs for proper registration. Ink clogging or drying in the fabric can cause the layers of ink on the image to be nonuniform or can actually cause loss of line detail. To correct this problem, remove as much ink from the screen as possible and add thinner to the ink. Clean the clogged portions of the screen by gently wiping the underside of the stencil with a rag moistened with thinner. Then re-ink and pull a second impression. Once an acceptable image is obtained, continue the process of inserting stock, passing the squeegee across the stencil, and removing the printed sheet until the job is completed.

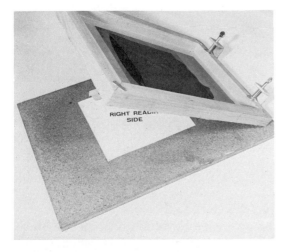

Figure 15.10. Removing the stock sheet
Courtesy of SUCO Learning Resources and R. Kampas

Multicolor Printing

Multicolor screen printing presents no great difficulties. The primary concern is the method of registration. It is important that the first color be accurately placed. If the first image is printed with variation in page placement, it will be impossible to fit the second image to it.

A two-color job requires two separate stencils. Multicolor runs require careful planning of the sequence of printing and overlapping of the colors to eliminate gaps between them. When opaque colors are used, the images must overlap by at least 1/16 inch. It is not necessary to overlap transparent colors except where a third color is desired.

Several techniques can be used to control accurate color fit. Register the first color by using standard positioning methods, but mark the first sheet as a proof. While the proof sheet is still held by the Z tabs, mark the position of the tabs with a pencil. Most press sheets are cut with some slight variation on the edges. If, for the second color, the tabs are placed in the same position as for the first color, the possibility of misregistration is lessened.

To position the second color over the first, mount a sheet of clear acetate over the base board and tape it from one edge so it can be hinged out of the way when necessary. With the acetate in place, swing the second stencil down into the printing position and pull an impression. When the frame is removed, the second image position will have been defined on the plastic. Slip the proof sheet from the first color under the acetate and line up both colors. Carefully hinge the plastic out of the way and mount the register tabs on the base board in line with the pencil marks. The two colors should now fit for the second printing. Any number of additional colors may be registered with this technique.

Problems with registration are not always the operator's fault. Fabrics that are loosely stretched on the frame tend to cause problems with multicolor registration. Frame hinges can become loose. If not taped securely, register tabs move out of position. Whatever the reason, when colors do not fit, all possible variables should be carefully examined.

Drying the Image

Most screen printing inks dry by absorption, aerial oxidation (air drying), a combination of both absorption and aerial oxidation, or by heat-setting action. Screen prints cannot be delivered from the press and stacked because all types of screen inks require some drying time. To save worker motion and conserve production space, a drying rack is often used to receive press sheets (figure 15.11). Racks are available in a wide variety of sizes, and commercial models come equipped with a spring system attached to floating bars that swing each shelf down into position as needed.

Inks that dry by absorption into the stock or by aerial oxidation can generally be stacked, dried, and shipped within 30 minutes. It is possible to hasten drying time by passing the sheet through a heat oven.

Heat-setting inks require an intense direct heat source. Some form of commercial curing or baking batch oven is generally used (figure 15.12). Most types are rated to about 320°F, have forced air circulation and a temperature control device, and are equipped with a variable-speed conveyer belt feeder system.

Cleaning the Screen

To clean the screen, first remove any large deposits of ink remaining on the screen and

Figure 15.11. Floating bar print drying rack
Courtesy of Naz-Dar Company

squeegee with an ink knife. It is generally wise to discard the ink from the screen surface and thereby avoid contaminating any fresh ink remaining in the can. Place ten to fifteen open sheets of newspaper on the base board and lower the screen into the printing position. Place a quantity of compatible solvent

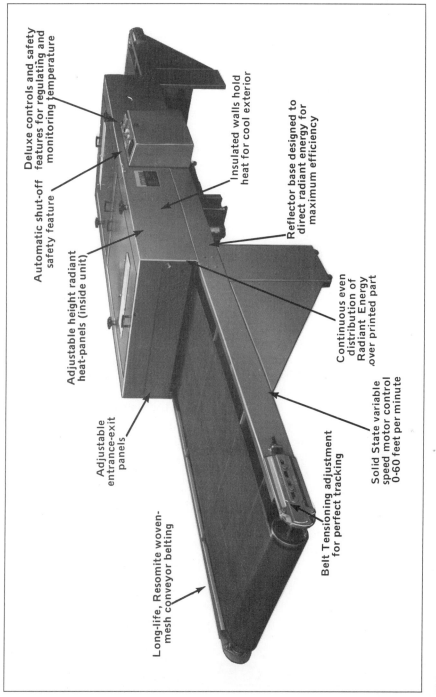

Deluxe controls and safety features for regulating and monitoring temperature

Automatic shut-off safety feature

Adjustable height radiant heat-panels (inside unit)

Insulated walls hold heat for cool exterior

Reflector base designed to direct radiant energy for maximum efficiency

Continuous even distribution of Radiant Energy over printed part

Adjustable entrance-exit panels

Solid State variable speed motor control 0-60 feet per minute

Belt Tensioning adjustment for perfect tracking

Long-life, Resomite woven-mesh conveyor belting

Figure 15.12. Commercial batch oven A commercial batch oven is used to dry heat-setting inks.

Courtesy of Advance Process Supply Company, Chicago

on the squeegee side of the screen. It is important to dissolve all the ink before any solvent is removed. If a rag were immediately applied to the screen, the solvent would be absorbed but no dissolving action would take place. Using your hand, rub the solvent into the entire surface of the screen. (Plastic gloves are practical during this process.) After all ink is dissolved, remove both the ink and the solvent with a dry cloth rag. Lift the screen and remove several layers of newspaper. Repeat the same operation until all ink has been removed. As a final step, moisten a clean rag with solvent and rub the underside of the screen to remove any remaining ink.

Commercial screen cleaning units (figure 15.13) are available that will dissolve all ink and leave the fabric perfectly clean. The frame is placed on a washing stand and a solvent spray is directed over it. The solvent drains back into a container where the ink and dirt settle or are filtered out, and the clear solvent is recirculated through the system.

There is a tendency for novice printers to mix dissimilar solvents during the cleanup operation. Stencil material and printing inks are chosen so that their bases will not dissolve one another. If the stencil is water based and the ink lacquer based, and water is accidentally mixed with the ink, problems occur. The stencil may not wash away, but the ink will become emulsified and hopelessly clogged in the screen. It is important that the printer have a clear understanding of the printing materials and their solvents before starting any cleanup.

Removing the Stencil

After all ink has been cleaned from the screen and any remaining ink solvent has evaporated, the stencil can be removed. One of the great advances in recent years is the devel-

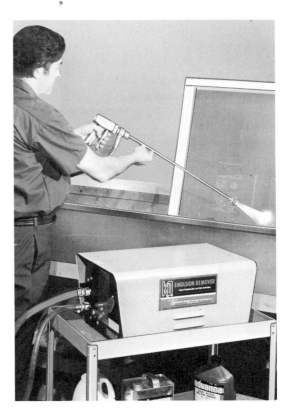

Figure 15.13. Commercial screen cleaning unit
Courtesy of Advance Process Supply Company, Chicago

opment of a quality water-based stencil material. Whether hand cut or photographic, most water-based stencils are designed to be removed with a hot-water spray. With some materials, a commercial enzyme is recommended.

Wet both sides of the stencil and sprinkle on the enzyme. After letting the material stand for 5 minutes (or whatever time is recommended by the manufacturer), spray the screen with hot water. It is necessary to neutralize the enzyme remaining on the wet screen by wiping the fabric with a 5% acetic acid or white vinegar solution. Thoroughly rinse the screen with cold water and allow it to air dry.

If nylon, polyester, or stainless steel fabrics are used with a water-based stencil, you can use a household chlorine bleach presoak in place of the enzyme. One method is to wet both sides of the stencil with a sodium hypochlorite solution (bleach) and allow it to stand for 5 minutes. Carefully rinse off the bleach solution (avoid splashing or contact with the eyes) and spray with hot water. The technique should *not* be used if a natural fiber, such as silk, is used.

Lacquer stencils must be removed with lacquer thinner. Lay several layers of newsprint on a flat surface and pour lacquer thinner on both sides of the stencil. Allow the thinner to set for several minutes before rubbing with a cloth. Lacquer thinner has a tendency to dry very rapidly, so several applications of the solution might be necessary before the screen is clean.

Troubleshooting Clogged Screens

A clean screen is the first requirement when preparing to print. A clogged screen should not be used because a stencil will not adhere well; if adhered, the quality of the printed image will be very poor. In a learning situation, with many different individuals using the same equipment, it is not always possible to identify what material is clogging a screen. It could be stencil emulsion, block-out material, ink, or even some foreign substance.

There are several steps to follow to clean a clogged screen when you do not know what is causing the problem. First try the household chlorine bleach mentioned in the preceding section (as long as the fabric is not silk) or a commercial enzyme (this should remove any water-based substance). Next try the solvent for the ink that was used for the last printing. If the screen is still clogged, try scrubbing the area with lacquer thinner, and finally try alcohol. It is important that the screen be thoroughly dried after each step. If, after all attempts, the fabric remains clogged, discard the material and restretch the frame.

Halftone Reproduction

Screen printing halftone images has several advantages over relief or lithographic processes. It is ideal for short-run posters or illustrations. It is less costly than any other method in terms of both time and materials. It can print extremely large image sizes. In addition, a wide range of inks can be used that have a brilliance, opacity, and texture unmatched by any other method.

There are, however, special considerations associated with screening halftones. Although 85- and 110-line halftones are commonly screened in the industry, a small job shop without critical controls with stencil preparation and printing should stay with rather coarse halftone screen rulings (85 lines per inch or coarser). Whatever ruling is used, however, the highlight and shadow dot structure must be carefully controlled and a film positive must be produced.

The reproducible halftone dot sizes of the final film positive should be 10% to 15% for highlights and 85% to 90% for shadows. Anything not within this limit will probably not reproduce on the final printed sheet.

Methods of Halftone Preparation for Screen Printing

The basic problem when preparing halftone images for screen printing is to work within the limit of production facilities. Although a 65-line contact screen is readily available from printing suppliers, it is not a common commodity in shops other than those preparing illustrations for newspaper production or screen companies that specialize in halftone printing.

Basically four methods can be used to prepare film halftone positives within a shop situation:

1. If a 65-line halftone screen is available, first make a film halftone negative to the reproduction size. Then make a contact film positive of the halftone negative.

2. Using an available halftone screen (such as 133-line screen), make a reduced halftone negative that can fit into a film enlarger (as used for making continuous-tone prints). Then project through the negative in the enlarger onto a fresh piece of high-contrast film to make a film positive at the reproduction size.

3. Using the available halftone screen, make a same-size film halftone negative from the original. Then place the negative on a backlighted process camera copyboard and enlarge it to the required reproduction size on a fresh piece of high-contrast film.

4. Using an available diffusion transfer halftone screen (usually 100-line), make a diffusion transfer opaque halftone positive samesize from the original. Then enlarge the positive on a process camera to the required reproduction size by using either a second set of diffusion transfer materials with a transparent receiver sheet or high-contrast film to make a film negative. Then contact print a film positive.

If any but the first method is used, it is necessary to be able to calculate percentage changes in order to make halftones of the required screen ruling with available in-plant materials.

Assume, as an example, that a 5-× 7-inch continuous-tone photograph is required to be printed as a 9- × 12-inch halftone reproduction with a 50-line ruling. The available screen is a 133-line negative gray contact screen. It is decided to produce the final film positive by projection, with an enlarger (method 2).

First determine the necessary enlargement of a 133-line ruling to obtain 50 lines per inch by using the following equation:

$$PE = \text{Percent Enlargement}$$

$$= \frac{\text{Available screen ruling}}{\text{Desired screen ruling}} \times 100$$

$$= \frac{133}{50} \times 100$$

$$= 133 \times 2$$

$$= 266\%$$

In other words, it is necessary to enlarge a halftone with a ruling of 133 lines per inch 266% in order to obtain a 50-line ruling.

An enlarger is to be used for this example, so it is necessary to determine the size of the first halftone negative. The easiest method is to refer to a proportion wheel. Set the wheel at 266% enlargement. Then read across from the required size (9″ × 12″) to obtain the size negative to be placed in the enlarger. For this example, the first halftone negative must be reduced to 3⅜″ × 4½″ from a 5″ × 7″ original. Calculations for all four methods can be made in similar manner.

Fabric Selection

When selecting the fabric for screening halftone images, the major concern is with the cloth mesh count. In general, monofilament fabrics should be used with halftones. Choice of a specific mesh count depends on the halftone ruling of the film positive. The Ulano Company recommends that the halftone ruling be multiplied by 3.5 to 4.0 to obtain a usable fabric mesh range. For example, if the halftone ruling is 60 lines per inch, any mesh count between 210 and 240 can be used.

Whatever screen mesh is used, the smallest halftone dot must be attached to at least four fiber intersections (figure 15.14). For example, if a 133-line halftone stencil is attached to a number twelve fabric, which has approximately 125 threads to the inch, many individual dots would drop through the screen during the printing operation because there would be insufficient fabric support.

Moiré Patterns

A moiré pattern (an objectionable optical pattern discussed in Chapter 8) may be formed when two screen patterns are overlapped (such as a halftone image on the fabric screen pattern). This is a particular problem when the fabric mesh count is too coarse for the halftone screen ruling. A way to avoid the moiré pattern is to place the clean, stretched screen over the film halftone positive on a light table before making the stencil. Rotate the position under the screen until the moiré pattern disappears. Then mark the location or angle of the positive so that the stencil can be adhered in the same position.

Printing Considerations

Special inks designed for halftone reproduction are available from screen printing suppliers. Halftone ink is made from fine-ground pigment and can be purchased as either transparent or opaque ink. As with normal ink preparation, the material should be able to form a dense image on the receiving surface but should not be so thick that it clogs the screen. If the ink is too thin, the halftone dots may bleed together on the sheet, resulting in a loss of image detail in the shadow areas.

A double-bevel squeegee blade (see figure 15.3c) is recommended for halftone work. A sharp, square blade (see figure 15.3a) can be used, but the amount of pressure should be less than is typically applied for normal production runs.

When screening halftones, a vacuum base or off-contact printing will diminish the possibility of a blurred image as a result of the stock sticking to the bottom of the screen.

High-Speed Production Presses

The basic problem with any hand-operated hinged-frame screen printing system is the small number of impressions that can be made per hour. Production is limited by how rapidly the printer can feed the stock, close the frame, position the squeegee, pull the impression, remove the squeegee, and deliver the

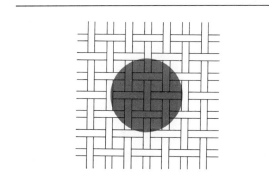

Figure 15.14. Halftone dot on screen printing fabric

stock. Even the most rapid operator is hard-pressed to screen print more than fifty impressions an hour with only a small stencil.

Low output was no problem with the early slow-drying inks. Most printers could not store an output of several thousand wet prints an hour that required overnight drying. With the introduction of fast-drying inks, however, greater production speeds became more important. High-speed screen printing presses can be classed as hand-operated, hand-fed, and hand-delivered; semiautomatic; or automatic units.

Lever-Action Hand-Operated Presses

Figure 15.15 illustrates one type of lever-action screen printing press. The advantage of the press is that a single operator can screen print images of nearly any size. The screen frame is counterbalanced over a vacuum frame that holds the paper. With light pressure the frame will swing down into position. The squeegee is attached to a lever that automatically springs up, out of contact with the screen. By grasping the lever handle, the operator lowers both the screen and the squeegee and, with a simple motion, drags the blade across the stencil.

Although the press is still hand operated, the action of lowering the screen, positioning the squeegee, and pulling the impression is significantly shortened. Large images are also easy to handle with the device because the lever action ensures uniform pressure across the stencil.

Semiautomatic Presses

Semiautomatic screen printing presses (figure 15.16) are generally hand fed and delivered by the operator, but the actual image transfer

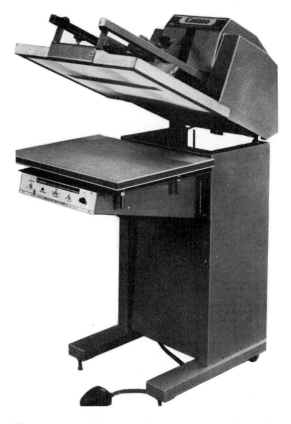

Figure 15.15. Lever-action screen printing unit
Courtesy of Advance Process Supply Company, Chicago

is automatic. The operator inserts and positions (registers) the stock. The machine then lowers the frame, draws the squeegee across the stencil, and raises the frame. Some devices have a 5- to 30-second built-in time delay for the stock to be fed. Others have a foot switch that is controlled by the printer to activate the squeegee. As with lever-action units, the speed of a semiautomatic machine is limited by the speed of the operator.

Figure 15.16. Semiautomatic screen printing press
Courtesy of Naz-Dar Company

Figure 15.17. Automatic screen printing press This press is used to produce screen printed electronic circuits.
Courtesy of Electronic Products Division, E. I. Du Pont de Nemours and Company, Inc.

Automatic Presses

True high-speed screen printing is not achieved until the responsibility for feeding and removing each individual press sheet is taken from the operator and given to the machine. The techniques for the automatic screen printing press are the same as for any automatic press, except that the press uses no rollers or cylinders. The actual image transfer concerns are the same as for the hand-operated hinged system discussed earlier in this chapter.

One area of special importance, however, is the delivery system. Because wet sheets are being removed from the press at a high rate of speed, their handling becomes a problem. Devices are available that can be synchronized with any production press speed to deliver dry sheets that can be stacked or packaged.

Special Machine Configurations

Screen printing has been applied to a wide variety of nontraditional materials and uses. One example is the production of printed circuits for the electronics industry (figure 15.17). Major machine designs have been developed since World War II to meet the special demands of the screen industry and its customers.

Screening Cylindrical Surfaces

One major area of growth has been the printing of labels directly on cylindrical or conical containers such as bottles, cans, and drinking cups.

Whether automatic or hand operated (figure 15.18), all devices function according to the same basic principle. The familiar flat screen is always used as the stencil carrier.

Figure 15.18. Hand-operated cylindrical screen printing press
Courtesy of Naz-Dar Company

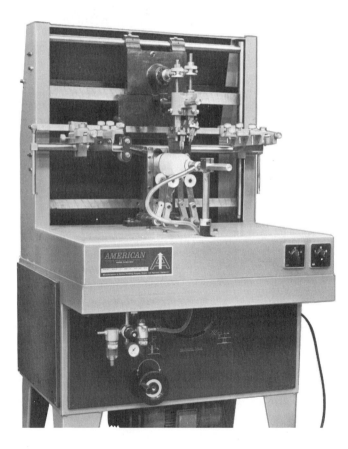

Figure 15.19. Automatic conical-shaped screen printing press
Courtesy of Advance Process Supply Company, Chicago

Figure 15.20. Multicolor rotary screen printing press
Courtesy of Naz-Dar Company

The cylindrical object is positioned beneath the screen and rests on ball bearings or some other system that allows the object to rotate. A squeegee is lowered into contact with the screen and the cylindrical object and is locked into position. To transfer the image, the screen frame is moved along a track. The pressure of the squeegee (which is not moving) pressing the screen against the cylindrical object also rotates the object.

Figure 15.19 shows a totally automatic screen printing press that can feed, print, and deliver 6,000 cone-shaped containers per hour. It operates with the same stationary squeegee and moving-screen idea.

Cylindrical Screens

There is a need for continuously repeating images on long rolls of such materials as wall-

Figure 15.21. Single-unit multicolor wet-on-wet screen printing press
Courtesy of Naz-Dar Company

Figure 15.22. Automatic carousel printing system
Courtesy of Advance Process Supply Company, Chicago

paper or bolt fabrics. A single flat screen stencil was traditionally used to meet this need. The stencil was carefully prepared so that the printer could step the image down the sheet. This method is still used with specially designed equipment, but it is a slow and costly process. Figure 15.20 shows a multicolor rotary screen printing press that is designed for continuous web printing. The stencil is carried by rigid screen mesh cylinders. Both the ink and squeegee ride inside the cylinders, which rotate as the line of material passes beneath them. With this approach a continuous multicolor image (up to sixteen colors with this model) can be placed on a roll of paper, plastic, or fabric at a rate of 240 feet a minute.

Carousel Units

A popular method of screening multicolor images, such as T-shirts, is **wet-on-wet printing** (figure 15.21). With this technique the individual pieces are mounted on **carousel carriers** that sequentially rotate under each different stencil color. The wet ink from the first color contacts the bottom of the second stencil, but because it touches in the same place each time, no blurring or loss of image detail occurs.

Registration is generally controlled with a pin system that accurately positions each screen stencil. Because the material is not moved until the entire printing cycle is complete, color fit should be perfect.

Some printers use automatic printing units with the carousel design (figure 15.22).

Key Terms

squeegee	carousel carriers	ink viscosity
on-contact printing	wet-on-wet printing	screen mesh count
off-contact printing	Shore Durometer	

Questions for Review

1. Why is the chemical makeup of the squeegee blade important?

2. Why must the solvent for the ink be different from the solvent for the stencil base?

3. What is the difference between on-contact and off-contact screen printing?

4. Briefly describe the techniques that can be used to control accurate color fit when doing multicolor screening.

5. How do most screen printing inks dry?

6. What are the highlight and shadow reproducible dot sizes when screening halftone images?

7. How can a moiré pattern be prevented when mounting a stencil with a halftone image?

8. What is the advantage of a lever-action hand-operated screen press?

9. Briefly describe the operation of a semi-automatic screen press.

10. What is the advantage of a cylindrical screen?

11. What does the term *wet-on-wet printing* mean?

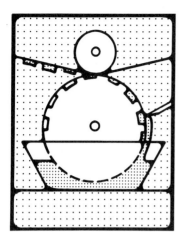

Chapter Sixteen

Gravure

Anecdote to Chapter Sixteen

The history of gravure printing begins with the work of creative artists during the Italian Renaissance, in the 1300s. Fine engravings and etchings were cut by hand in soft copper. The designs were cut away, leaving a channel, or sunken area, to hold the ink during printing. The term *intaglio,* which we use today to describe a class of printing, is an Italian word meaning to print with a sunken pattern or design.

The process quickly gained widespread recognition as a rapid, high-quality printing process that could be put to many different uses. The French artist Jacques Callot devel-

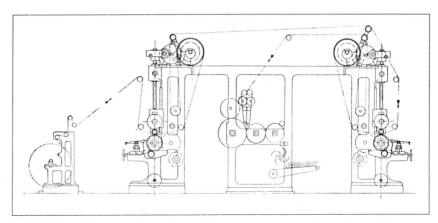

An early patent design for a French rotogravure press

oped his reputation by sketching the fighting on battlefields and then rushing back to his studio to print etchings of the scenes. He would sell the etchings only a few days after the battle. Callot is sometimes called the first photojournalist because of the speed with which he distributed copies of his sketches.

The first photographic intaglio prints were made by Joseph Nicephore Niépce in about 1814. Niépce, who called his process heliography, printed the products on a copperplate press. Fox Talbot refined Niépce's work and, in addition to developing the first film negative, also worked on heliography.

The recognized inventor of modern gravure printing, however, is Karl Klič (born Klitsch). Klič began experimenting with photographic copper etching in 1875. By about 1879 he had refined the process and made a formal announcement of his "heliogravure" process to the Vienna Photographic Society. He produced very high-quality reproduction for art collectors but gained little recognition outside his own country because he wanted to keep the techniques secret. He eventually sold his "secret," but continued to refine the process, even to his death in 1926. He made the revolutionary move from flat printing plates to printing from a cylinder. He developed the first doctor blade and even designed a method of printing color on a web press. He is the one who originated the term *rotogravure* for printing from a cylinder.

After Klič shared his methods, other individuals became interested in rotogravure and began designing and building equipment for the process. By the beginning of this century, rotogravure had developed a relatively widespread reputation for fine reproductions. By 1920 huge presses were in use with four or five units for color gravure. Postcards, calendars, illustrations for books, and even magazines were being printed in full color.

One of the major uses of the process that began in the 1920s was the printing of the supplement section of the Sunday newspaper. The section carried human-interest stories, many advertisements, and lots of color photographs. The section was, and continues to be, a favorite item that readers look forward to each week. The supplement section and rotogravure printing gained such widespread public recognition that a Broadway play was even produced that used the two as a theme.

Irving Berlin was one of America's most famous songwriters. Few people, however, remember his 1934 Broadway play, *As Thousands Cheer.* However, almost everyone remembers the play's opening song, called "Easter Parade." The most famous lines mention both rotogravure printing and the Sunday supplement because the two terms had come to mean the same in the public's eye:

On the Avenue, Fifth Avenue, the photographers will snap us, and you'll find that you're in the rotogravure.

Objectives for Chapter Sixteen

After completing this chapter, you will be able to:

- Understand the organization of the gravure industry and the importance of professional associations in its growth.
- Recall the major methods of cylinder preparation, including diffusion etch, direct transfer, electromechanical, and laser cutting.
- Recognize the variables in gravure printing, including well formation, film positive quality, etching and plating techniques, cylinder balance, cylinder and doctor blade considerations, and impression rollers.
- Recall the major steps in cylinder construction and preparation.
- Recall the major steps in placing an image on a cylinder by using the conventional gravure techniques.
- Recognize the parts of a gravure press and recall cylinder, doctor blade, and impression roller functions.

Introduction

Intaglio is a term that was introduced in Chapter 1 in a simple comparison of the following four major printing processes (figure 16.1):

- *Relief*, which forms an image from a raised surface
- *Screen*, which passes ink through openings in a stencil
- *Lithography*, which prints photochemically from a flat surface
- *Intaglio*, which transfers ink from a sunken surface

Terms associated with intaglio include *etching, engraving, drypoint,* and *collagraphy*. Artists use these terms to describe images printed from lines cut into the surface of metal or plastic.

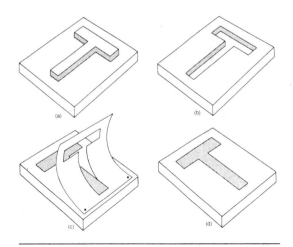

Figure 16.1. The four major printing processes Relief printing (a), intaglio printing (b), screen printing (c), and lithographic printing (d).

Industrial intaglio is called **gravure** printing, or **rotogravure.** *Roto* means "round." All industrial intaglio transfers an image from sunken areas cut into the surface of a cylinder (figure 16.2). Except for small proof presses, most industrial gravure presses are web-fed (figure 16.3). As the plate cylinder turns, a continuous roll of paper, foil, or plastic is passed through the press to receive the image. After printing, the paper is either rewound onto a roll for shipment to the customer or cut into sheets at the end of the press by a device called a slitter.

The Gravure Industry

Gravure is a major printing process. Twenty percent of all printing in this country is done by gravure. The gravure industry has enjoyed a steady growth rate and, with recent technical advances, will continue to gain a larger share of the printing market. Several important characteristics make gravure an ideal process for jobs requiring high quality and extremely long press runs:

Figure 16.3. A web-fed gravure press Almost all production gravure presses are web-fed.
Courtesy of the Morrill Press

Figure 16.2. A gravure press cylinder
Rotogravure means printing from a cylinder.

– Gravure is the simplest of all printing systems, with the fastest press start-up and the most direct press controls.
– Gravure's easy press control results in very little paper waste. Gravure has less than half the paper spoilage rate of lithography.
– Gravure press speeds are extremely fast. The largest gravure presses can operate as rapidly as 45,000 impressions an hour.
– Gravure cylinders are especially hardy. Several million impressions from the same cylinder are common. Some printers report press runs as long as 20 million copies without the cylinder wearing out.
– Gravure gives the highest-quality image of the four major printing processes. It has the reputation of delivering excellent color and ink density even on low-quality printing papers.

The only significant disadvantage of gravure is the length of time required to prepare the printing cylinder. New equipment has been developed to automate much of the process, but most cylinders are still produced by the specialized craft of gravure engravers. Jobs with press runs of less than 60,000 to 70,000 impressions are generally not considered an effective use of the process. The cost of cylinder preparation is so much higher than other processes that some companies refuse jobs of less than a million copies.

Industry Organization

Gravure printing is divided into three broad product areas, each with its own special problems and solutions. The first group is **packaging printing.** This area includes folding cartons, bags, boxes, gift wrappers, labels, and flexible materials that will eventually be formed into containers.

The second area is **publication printing.** Publication printing includes newspaper supplements, magazines, catalogs, and mass mailing advertisements. Gravure is ideally suited for the long press runs required for the Sunday newspaper supplement sections that are distributed on a national basis.

The third area of gravure printing is **specialty printing.** In this area gravure is used to print such materials as wallpaper, vinyl, floor coverings, and even textiles for both decoration and clothing fabrication.

Companies have found that they become more efficient and cost-effective by limiting the jobs they accept to a specific product area.

The Gravure Association of America

One reason for the steady growth of gravure printing in the United States has been the cooperative efforts of gravure printers, suppliers, and manufacturers, focused through the **Gravure Association of America** (GAA). GAA provides consultative assistance, publishes a wide range of technical materials related to all phases of gravure production, has worked to establish industry standards, supplies technical aids, and has a tradition of collegial efforts to educate printers and to disseminate information on gravure printing. Much of the information contained in this chapter was compiled through the courtesy and cooperation of the Gravure Association of America. Individuals interested in using GAA's services or in becoming affiliated with the organization should write to the Gravure Association of America, 60 East 42nd Street, Suite 2201, New York, N.Y. 10017.

Key Ideas

Gravure differs in several ways from other printing processes. Before the techniques of cylinder preparation are explained in detail, it is important to review several key ideas.

Methods of Cylinder Preparation

There are basically four ways to prepare a gravure cylinder:

- By diffusion etch
- By direct transfer
- By the electromechanical process
- By laser cutting

Diffusion-Etch Process. In the **diffusion-etch process** (figure 16.4), a special mask is prepared by exposure first through a special gravure screen and then through a film positive of the printing image. Next the mask is applied to a copper gravure cylinder and is developed on the cylinder. After development, the mask is thick in the nonimage areas of the

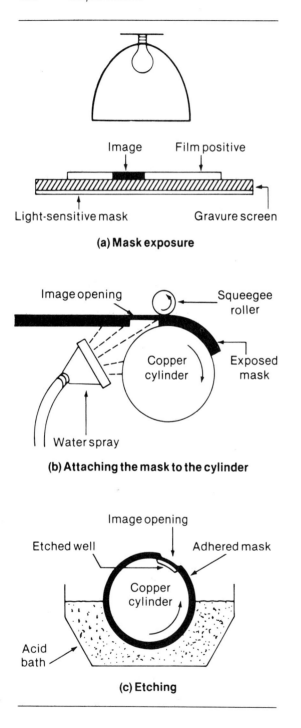

(a) Mask exposure

Image   Film positive

Light-sensitive mask   Gravure screen

(b) Attaching the mask to the cylinder

Image opening   Squeegee roller

Water spray   Copper cylinder   Exposed mask

(c) Etching

Image opening

Etched well   Adhered mask

Copper cylinder

Acid bath

cylinder and is thin where an image is to carry ink. The cylinder is then placed in an acid bath. The acid penetrates through the thin areas of the mask and eats or etches away the copper. The last step is to apply a thin layer of chrome over the entire cylinder by an electroplating process. The purpose of the chrome is to extend the life of the surface areas.

Direct-Transfer Process. The second method of cylinder preparation is called **direct transfer.** The main difference between diffusion etch and direct transfer is the way in which the cylinder mask is exposed. In direct transfer, a light-sensitive mask is sprayed or applied over the cylinder surface. The mask is exposed by directing light through a halftone positive as it moves past the cylinder, which turns the same rate that the positive is moving (figure 16.5). The final steps of developing, etching, and chrome plating are the same as in the diffusion-etch technique.

Electromechanical Process. Another way of preparing a gravure cylinder is by the **electromechanical process.** In this process, a clean copper cylinder is mounted in a special engraving machine. Like a scanner used in color separation (see Chapter 9), the original copy is read by a beam of light. The information from the light is stored in a computer and is then translated into the motion of a cutter head (figure 16.6). A special diamond stylus actually cuts into the surface of the copper as the cylinder rotates. After cutting, the cylinder is chrome plated and is then ready for the press.

Figure 16.4. Cylinder preparation: diffusion etch The three main steps in the conventional gravure process are mask exposure (a), attaching the mask to the cylinder (b), and etching (c).

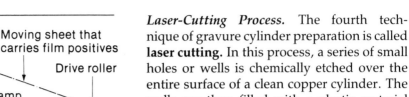

Mask exposure

**Figure 16.5. Cylinder preparation: direct
transfer** In the direct-transfer process, the light-
sensitive mask is exposed by passing light
through a halftone positive as it moves in contact
with the rotating cylinder.
Courtesy of Southern Gravure Service

Laser-Cutting Process. The fourth technique of gravure cylinder preparation is called
laser cutting. In this process, a series of small
holes or wells is chemically etched over the
entire surface of a clean copper cylinder. The
wells are then filled with a plastic material
until the cylinder again has a smooth, uniform surface. Like the electromechanical
method, the original copy is scanned by a
beam of light. This process, however, uses
the narrow beam of a laser to remove parts
of the plastic from individual wells rather than
a diamond tool to cut away metal. The cylinder can be sprayed with a special electrolyte
and plated with chrome.

Of the four cylinder preparation processes, diffusion etch is the oldest and is still
the one most widely used by the industry.
Recent advances with the laser process, and
techniques still in the early research stages,
point to changes in the near future that will
revolutionize gravure cylinder preparation.

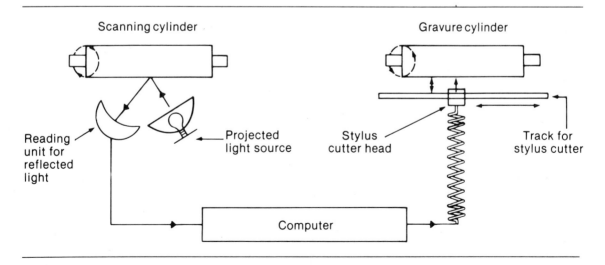

Figure 16.6. Diagram of the electromechanical process The cylinder is
cut by using a diamond stylus in the electromechanical process.

Well Formation

Gravure transfers ink from the small wells that are etched or cut into the surface of the cylinder (figure 16.7). On the press, the cylinder rotates through a fountain of ink. The ink is wiped from the surface of the cylinder by a doctor blade. The cup-like shape of each individual well holds ink in place as the cylinder turns past the doctor blade. The formation of perfect wells is the main concern of the gravure engraver. There are several important ideas to understand about gravure wells.

Every **gravure well** has four variables (figure 16.8):

 – Depth
 – Bottom
 – Opening
 – Bridge

The *depth* is measured from the *bottom* of the well to the top surface of the cylinder. The *opening* is the distance across the well. The **bridge** is the surface of the cylinder between wells. The doctor blade rides against well bridges as it scrapes ink from the cylinder.

Within the diffusion-etch technique are two basic types of well design:

 – Conventional gravure design
 – Lateral hard-dot process design

In the **conventional gravure** design, every well on a cylinder has exactly the same opening size (figure 16.9a). The amount of ink to be transferred to the paper is controlled only by the depth of the well. When reproducing photographic material, a continuous-tone film positive, rather than a high-contrast halftone, is used to expose the mask.

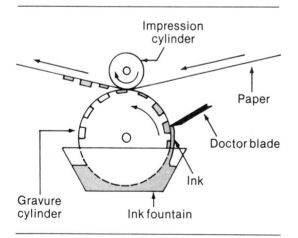

Figure 16.7. Diagram of the gravure printing process Etched wells in the printing cylinder pick up ink from the fountain. The excess ink is wiped from the surface of the cylinder by the doctor blade before the ink is applied to the press sheet.

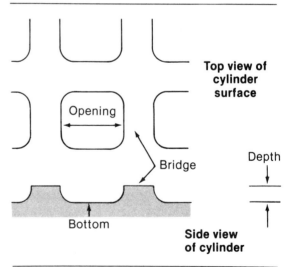

Figure 16.8. Diagram of gravure cylinder wells A gravure well has four variables—depth, bottom, bridge, and opening.

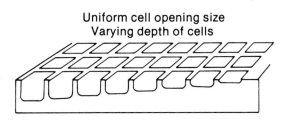

(a) Conventional Gravure

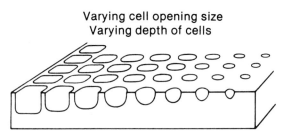

(b) Lateral Hard Dot

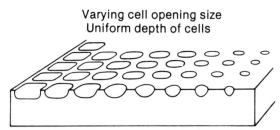

(c) Direct Transfer

Figure 16.9. Three examples of gravure wells Conventional gravure wells vary in depth, but all have the same opening size (a). Lateral hard-dot wells vary in both depth and opening (b). Direct-contact wells vary in opening size, but all have the same depth (c).
Courtesy of the Southern Gravure Service

The second major type of well design with diffusion etch is called the **lateral hard-dot process** (sometimes called **halftone gravure**) design. Two separate film positives are used to expose the mask with the lateral hard-dot process. The first is a continuous-tone film positive, as with conventional gravure. A second exposure is then made with a halftone film positive that falls in the same position on the mask as that of the first exposure. The result is a well formation that varies in both opening size and depth (figure 16.9b).

The direct-transfer method of cylinder preparation produces yet another well design. A single halftone positive is used to expose the mask. The dot formation in the halftone defines the opening size of each well (figure 16.9c). The depth of each well is the same.

Electromechanical well formation is a bit different from diffusion etch or direct transfer. In the electromechanical process, each gravure well is created by the action of a diamond stylus as it pushes into the soft copper surface of the cylinder (figure 16.10). A direct relationship exists between the depth of cut and the opening size. As the stylus pushes deeper, it also increases the opening. This action influences the volume of ink that the well can carry. In photographs, shadow area wells are much deeper than highlight wells.

Film Positives

Most artwork is delivered to the gravure engraver in the form of film positives. The characteristics of film images used by gravure are somewhat different from those used in other printing methods. The main difference is the image density range (see Chapter 6 for a review of densitometry). Wells are etched or cut in proportion to the density of the corresponding area on the film positive.

There is a minimum depth that will hold ink during the printing process. If the well is too shallow, the action of the doctor blade and the rapidly spinning cylinder can actually pull

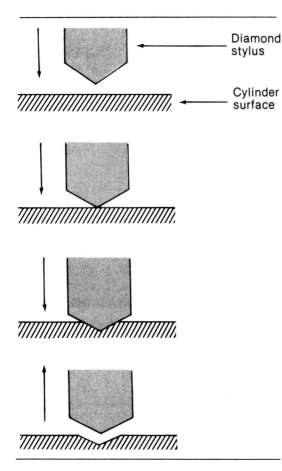

Figure 16.10. Cutting a cylinder surface In the electromechanical engraving process, wells are cut in the cylinder as a diamond stylus moves into the copper and then moves back.

ink from the well. Film positives must be prepared with a minimum density so that each well will be deep enough.

For continuous-tone images, the Gravure Association of America recommends a density range of 0.30 to 1.65. This range means that the highlight areas of the positive will have a transmission density of 0.30 and a shadow reading of 1.65. The difference between the two measurements produces a basic density range of 1.35, which is acceptable to commercial photographers and still exceeds the range of most halftone negatives used in lithography.

Line images, such as type, ink, or line borders, are also supplied in positive form. Line image density should be near the same 1.65 shadow area density for continuous-tone images. Positives are often supplied to the engraver with both continuous-tone and line images on the same piece of film. The most common approach is first to prepare each type of image separately, in negative form, and then to make several contact exposures onto a new sheet of film to create a single film positive.

Cylinder Construction and Preparation

The quality of the final gravure image depends first on the construction of the cylinder. Almost all cylinder cores are made from steel tubing. Some packaging printers prefer extruded aluminum cores because they are much lighter, less expensive, and easier to ship than steel is. A few companies use solid copper shells, but steel remains the most popular core material.

A steel cylinder is used when printing with adhesives or other corrosive materials. In most gravure printing, however, a thin coating of copper is plated over the steel core to carry the image. Copper is easier to etch than steel and can easily be replaced when the job is finished.

Cylinder Design

There are five important parts to identify on a gravure cylinder (figure 16.11):

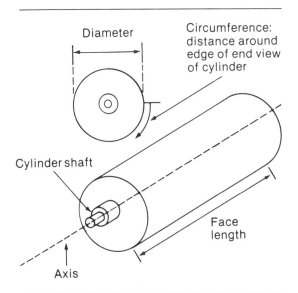

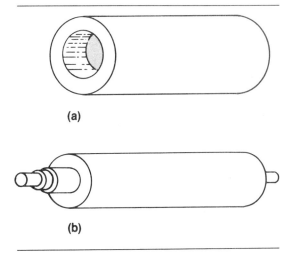

(a)

(b)

Figure 16.12. Two forms of gravure cylinders There are two basic forms of cylinder construction—mandrel (a) and integral shaft (b).

Figure 16.11. Parts of a gravure cylinder The most common identification parts of a gravure cylinder are diameter, circumference, shaft, axis, and face length.

- Axis
- Shaft
- Diameter
- Circumference
- Face length

The *axis* is the invisible line that passes through the center of the length of the cylinder. The *shaft* is the bearing surface as the cylinder rotates in the press. If you look at the end view of a cylinder, it appears as a circle. The *diameter* is the distance across the circle, through the center of the shaft. The *circumference* is the distance around the edge of the end view. The *face length* is the distance from one end to the other, along the length of the cylinder.

The face length of the cylinder limits the width of paper to be printed. The circumfer-

ence limits the size of the image. One rotation of the cylinder around its circumference is called one **impression.** Continuous images can be etched on a cylinder, without a seam, so the design is repeated without a break. Wallpaper designs are commonly printed by this technique.

There are two basic cylinder designs (figure 16.12):

- Integral shaft
- Mandrel

In the integral shaft design, the shaft is permanently mounted on the cylinder. The cylinder is first formed, and then the shaft is either pressed or shrunk in place. The shaft is permanently attached by welding and is not removed during the life of the cylinder.

A mandrel cylinder (sometimes called sleeve or cone cylinder) is designed to have a removable shaft. Most holes are tapered so that the shaft can be pressed in place and then easily removed.

Integral shaft cylinders are more expensive than mandrel cylinders but are generally considered to produce higher-quality images.

Balancing the Cylinder

A major concern during printing is vibration caused by an unbalanced cylinder (figure 16.13a). A great deal of vibration can bounce the cylinder against the doctor blade and result in a poor image. Vibration can also damage the press. GAA identifies two types of imbalance: static and dynamic.

Static imbalance occurs when the cylinder is not perfectly round or has different densities within a cross section (figure 16.13b). Static imbalance can be caused by such defects as air holes, impurities in the steel core, or improper copper plating and polishing.

Dynamic imbalance occurs when the cylinder differs in density or balance from one end to the other (figure 16.13c). Dynamic imbalance is the greatest cause of cylinder vibration at high press speeds. Both static and dynamic imbalance can be corrected by either cutting away from or adding weight to each end of the cylinder.

Copper Plating and Polishing

Electroplating is the process of transferring very small bits (called **ions**) of one type of metal to another type of metal. The process takes place in a special liquid **plating bath.** The ions are transferred as an electrical current is passed through the liquid. The longer the current flows, the more new metal will be plated onto the cylinder.

The first step in the gravure electroplating process is to thoroughly clean the surface of the cylinder. The cylinder is cleaned by

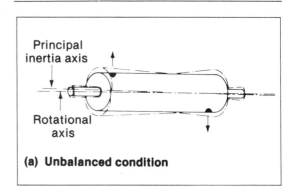

(a) Unbalanced condition

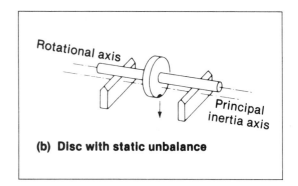

(b) Disc with static unbalance

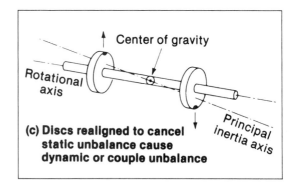

(c) Discs realigned to cancel static unbalance cause dynamic or couple unbalance

Figure 16.13. Examples of cylinder imbalance
Courtesy of Gravure Association of America

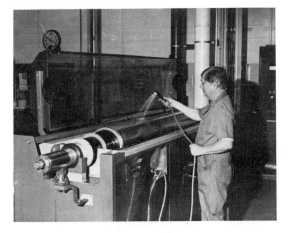

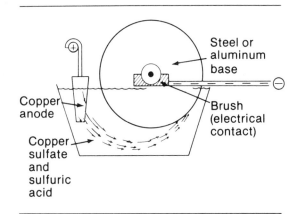

Figure 16.14. Cleaning the cylinder surface It is important to remove all spots of grease, rust, or dirt so that a perfect layer of copper can be applied to the cylinder surface.

Figure 16.15. Diagram of the electroplating process An electric current passes from the copper anode through the plating solution to the steel or aluminum cylinder until the desired thickness of copper is plated on the cylinder. Courtesy of Southern Gravure Service

brushing or rubbing it with special cleaning compounds and then rinsing with a powerful stream of hot water (figure 16.14). Some plants use special cleaning machines. The goal is to remove all spots of grease, rust, or dirt so that a perfect coating of copper can be applied over the entire surface. Areas not to be plated, such as the cylinder ends, can be coated with asphaltum or other staging materials.

To add a layer of copper, the cylinder is suspended in a curved tank and then rotated through the plating bath (figure 16.15). The electric current is allowed to flow from the copper anode (the plating metal) through the bath to the cylinder (base metal). Zinc sulfate, copper sulfate, or cyanide solutions are common plating-bath liquids. Six-thousandths inch (0.006″) to thirty-thousandths inch (0.030″) is the common thickness range for the copper layer on a gravure cylinder.

A **newage gauge** is a device used to test the hardness of copper. Copper hardness is measured by pushing a diamond point into the copper surface. The diagonal length of the opening created by the diamond is measured and then compared with the amount of force required to push the diamond into the copper. The result is expressed in D.P.H. (diamond point hardness). Most printers look for a D.P.H. between 93 and 122.

The last step in the construction of a gravure cylinder is to bring the diameter (and circumference) to the desired size and at the same time to create a perfect printing surface. The cylinder must be not only perfectly round but also perfectly smooth and uniform across its length. If the cylinder is not uniform, the doctor blade will not be able to remove excess ink from the nonprinting surface (figure 16.16).

The newly plated cylinder is mounted in a lathe and prepared for final turning. Some plants use a diamond-cutting tool to bring the

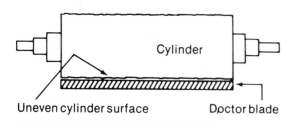

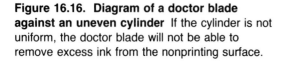

Figure 16.16.   Diagram of a doctor blade against an uneven cylinder If the cylinder is not uniform, the doctor blade will not be able to remove excess ink from the nonprinting surface.

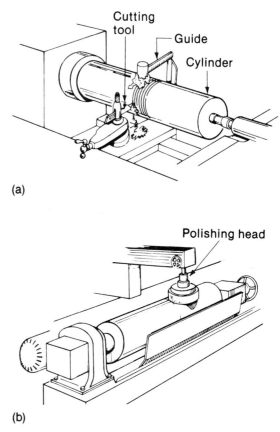

(a)

(b)

Figure 16.17.   Final turning of a plated cylinder The cylinder is first cut to rough dimensions (a), and then it is ground or polished to the final size (b).
Courtesy of Southern Gravure Service

cylinder into round; then they use separate grinding stones to polish the surface (figure 16.17). Other plants use specially designed precision machines to both cut and polish at the same time. With this method, cylinders can be cut within one ten-thousandths inch (0.0001") of the desired size and surface. After the final turning, the cylinder is ready for image etching.

Reuse of Cylinders

Gravure cylinders can be reused many times. One approach is to cut away the old image on a lathe. This involves removing only two- to three-thousandths inch. The cylinder is then replated with copper and again cut or ground to the original diameter.

Another technique is simply to dissolve the chrome coating (added as the final step in cylinder preparation to protect the soft copper on the press) and then to plate over the old image with new copper. The replating process fills in the image areas above the level of the original surface. Excess copper is then cut or ground away, and the cylinder is returned to the desired diameter size.

Ballard Shell Cylinders

The **ballard shell process** is a special technique used by many publication printers that allows easy removal of a copper layer after the cylinder has been printed. The cylinder is prepared in the usual manner, including copper plating, except that it is cut twelve- to fifteen-thousandths-inch undersize in diameter. The undersized cylinder is coated with a special nickel separator solution and returned to the copper plating bath. A second layer of copper is plated onto the cylinder over the first layer. The cylinder is then cut or ground to the desired size, given an image etch, and printed.

The difference between most gravure cylinders and ballard shell cylinders is seen when the cylinder has been printed and is ready to receive another image. The second copper layer can be simply ripped off the ballard shell cylinder base. A knife is used to cut through the copper to the nickel separator layer, which allows the shell to be lifted away. The cylinder can then be cleaned, a new nickel separator solution applied, and another shell plated to receive the image.

Conventional Gravure

There are several different ways to prepare a gravure cylinder. Four techniques were briefly described at the beginning of this chapter (diffusion etch, direct transfer, electromechanical, and laser cutting). A detailed explanation of the steps for each method is beyond the scope of this chapter. It is valuable, however, to examine one technique as an example of methods used in the gravure industry.

While diffusion etch is not the most widely used process, it does allow easy understanding of all etching processes. Diffusion etch is still used in the industry, and the steps involved in cylinder preparation are somewhat similar to those used in direct transfer. The following sections detail the procedures of etching a cylinder by diffusion etch, using conventional gravure with carbon tissue.

Cylinder Layout and Film Assembly

Most jobs arrive at the gravure printer in film format, with a dummy showing final page position. (See Chapter 3 for a review of signature layout and use of a dummy.) The first step in gravure printing is to lay out the cylinder and identify page or image positions.

Figure 16.18 shows the layout for the

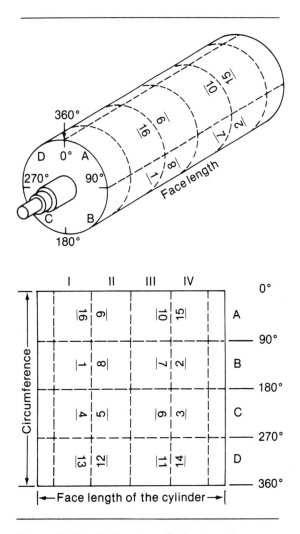

Figure 16.18. A 16-page cylinder layout

first two cylinders that will be used to print a 16-page advertisement. The face length of the cylinder is one dimension of the layout, and the circumference is the other. The pages are identified by Roman numerals (along the face length) and by letters of the alphabet (around the circumference). For example, position III–C is page 6 of the job. Page positions are determined by how the job will be folded and are always provided with the job materials. Notice that for this job a second cylinder will be used to print the other side of the paper. The web will then be slit and folded to form two separate rolls. The layout will be used as a guide for assembling the different pieces of film.

If the job arrived as film negatives, then the printer must prepare contact positives. To make film positives that will fall into the correct position on the cylinder, special carriers or cabs (cabriolets) are used. **Cabs** are special film masks that are punched and marked so they can be used as guides for the images (figure 16.19).

Each cab carries special registration marks and has a clear, open area to receive the negative image. The negatives are stripped to the cab's registration marks and then contact printed to a new sheet of film. The unexposed film is punched on the same device used to punch the cab (figure 16.20). When contacting is done, both the cab and the film are dropped onto registration pins (figure 16.21). The processed film positive will then fall into place on register pins mounted on a master plate.

The **master plate** is a frame with register pins that hold the film positives in correct printing position during exposure to the cylinder masking material. For color printing,

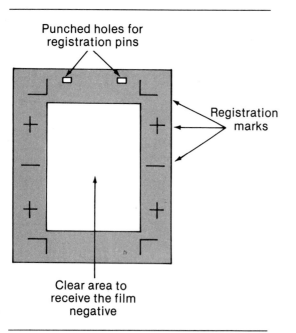

Punched holes for registration pins

Registration marks

Clear area to receive the film negative

Figure 16.19. Diagram of a cab (cabriolet) A cab is used to register the film negative.

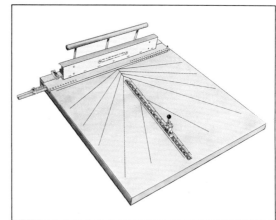

Figure 16.20. A Berkey stripper punch A two- or three-hole punch is used to punch both the cab and the unexposed film.

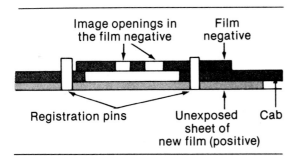

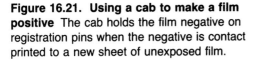

Figure 16.21. Using a cab to make a film positive The cab holds the film negative on registration pins when the negative is contact printed to a new sheet of unexposed film.

each set of separations is exposed to the cylinder mask with the same master plate to ensure perfect color fit.

When the positives are completed and in position on the master plate, several additional positives are added before exposure to the cylinder masking material. Registration on many gravure presses is monitored by special electronic eyes that sense misfit and automatically make press adjustments. **Electronic-eye mark** film positives are added to the master plate so that the marks will be etched into the cylinder, out of the image area on the paper web.

Some jobs require blank pages. Where no image is required, pieces of film, called burner film, are added to the master plate. **Burner film** is a piece of transparent film that allows full passage of light to the cylinder mask. This hardens the light-sensitive mask and does not allow acid to reach the copper cylinder. If acid does not reach the surface, the area is not etched and will not carry ink to the paper.

With all positives in position on the master plate, the job is ready for carbon printing.

Carbon Printing

The process of transferring the positive image to the cylinder mask is called **carbon printing.** The point of the process is to create a resist that can be adhered to the cylinder. A **resist** is material that will block or retard the action of the acid on the copper. There are two basic types of resist material for diffusion etch: carbon tissue and rotofilm.

Carbon tissue is a gelatin-based material coated on a paper backing. The emulsion can be sensitized so that it "hardens" in proportion to the amount of light that strikes it. Carbon tissue must be made light sensitive by the engraver. The second material is called rotofilm and is manufactured by the DuPont corporation. Rotofilm has the same characteristics as carbon tissue but comes to the engraver presensitized and ready for use.

Carbon tissue is sensitized by immersing the material in a 3% to 4% potassium bichromate solution. The sheet is placed in the solution, emulsion-side up, for 3½ to 4 minutes and then squeegeed onto a plexiglass sheet to dry. The squeegeed sheet is dried under circulating cool air for several hours and is then placed in storage for 8 to 10 hours to "cure."

The sensitized carbon tissue is placed emulsion-side up on a vacuum frame for exposure. In conventional gravure, the carbon tissue will receive two separate exposures. The first is a screen exposure, and the second is the image exposure.

Recall that with conventional gravure the well openings are all the same size and vary only in depth (see figure 16.9). A special gravure screen is used to create the outline of each well (figure 16.22). A sharp screen pattern is formed on the carbon tissue by allowing an intense light to harden the outline of the well bridges (figure 16.23).

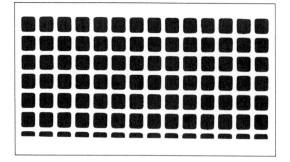

Figure 16.22. A cross-line gravure screen A cross-line gravure screen is used to create the well openings in conventional gravure.

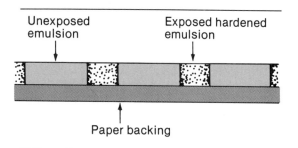

Figure 16.23. Side view of carbon tissue after exposure to a cross-line screen

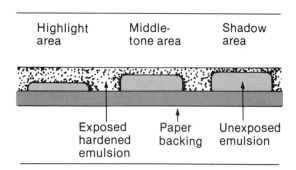

Figure 16.24. Side view of carbon tissue after exposure to a continuous-tone film positive

For most work, printers use a 150-line screen (150 wells per inch). Gravure printers are also concerned with the ratio of opening to bridge dimensions. A ratio of 2½ or 3 to 1 (3 : 1) is common. This means that for each unit of well thickness there will be 2½ or 3 units of opening.

Carbon printing is done by exposing the master plate (with the film positives in place) to the carbon tissue. Registration to the cylinder is commonly controlled by a lug system. Both the carbon tissue and the master plate are dropped over special lugs or pins on the vacuum frame. The punched carbon tissue can then be mounted on the cylinder with a corresponding lug system.

The gelatin compound hardens in direct proportion to the amount of light that reaches the emulsion. The emulsion hardens first at the top of the gelatin layer. As light continues to reach the carbon tissue, the emulsion hardens down toward the paper base.

With line work, little light reaches the carbon tissue, so the emulsion is hardened only at the top layer. The varying densities of a continuous-tone photograph affect the emulsion differently. Highlight areas pass a great deal of light, so the hardened emulsion is very thick in those areas. Shadow areas pass little light, so the hardened emulsion is thin in those areas (figure 16.24). A highlight area on the positive, with a density of 0.35, passes 50% of the light that strikes the film; 50% is absorbed by the image density. In the middle tones, an area with a density of 1.0 will pass 10% of the light. At a density of 1.65 (a shadow area), only 2½% of the light reaches the carbon tissue.

Tissue Laydown and Development

The process of attaching the carbon tissue to the copper cylinder is called **tissue laydown.**

The tissue can be laid down as a single piece of the same size as the cylinder. More commonly, however, tissue is applied to the cylinder in several separate pieces.

Before laydown the cylinder must be cleaned. Any traces of tarnish or grease will prevent tissue adhesion. Most companies use an electrolytic degreasing machine (see figure 16.25).

Most laydown is done on a special laydown machine. The clean cylinder is placed in the device and positioned by a special control gauge. A fixed metal lug bar holds the carbon tissue in register with the cylinder position (emulsion side of the carbon tissue against the cylinder) (figure 16.25a). A layer of distilled water is poured on the cylinder, and a rubber squeegee roller is brought into contact with the carbon tissue, against the cylinder (figure 16.25b). The carbon tissue is cut from the lug bar, and distilled water is poured between the tissue and cylinder as the rubber squeegee roller turns. After one rotation the carbon tissue is adhered to the cylinder. If several pieces of tissue are to be applied to the cylinder, the operation is repeated for each section. After all pieces are mounted, the paper backing is soaked with cold water and then gently squeegeed by hand. The backing is then allowed to dry thoroughly (usually from 5 to 10 minutes with fan driers). This method is called **dry laydown.**

When the paper backing is completely dry, development can begin. The first step is to swab the paper with an alcohol solution. This solution rapidly soaks through the backing and begins to loosen it from the gelatin emulsion. The cylinder is then partially submerged in a water bath and slowly rotated so that all parts of the surface are kept uniformly wet. As the water temperature is gradually raised, the paper loosens from the cylinder and can be pulled away.

The goal in development is to remove

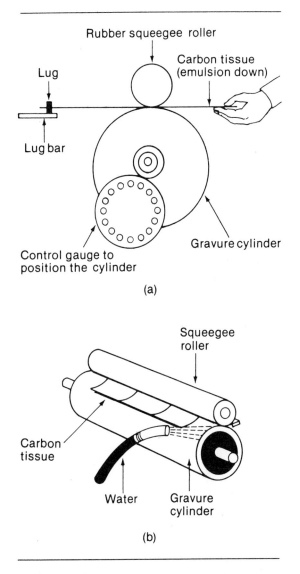

(a)

(b)

Figure 16.25. Mounting the carbon tissue on the gravure cylinder A special laydown machine is used to mount the carbon tissue on the gravure cylinder.

all portions of the unhardened gelatin emulsion (figure 16.26). Some engravers gently spray the cylinder as it turns in the warm-water bath. Others use an automatic system that changes the water in the bath by a low-pressure water spray located in the bottom of the tray.

Development is completed when no more gelatin can be removed and the surface is hard to the touch. The emulsion is fixed by first cooling the cylinder below room temperature and then pouring an alcohol solution over the surface. A soft rubber squeegee is then used to remove all alcohol from the cylinder, and the emulsion is allowed to dry.

Staging and Etching

Some areas of the cylinder often are not covered after laydown and development. The edges and ends of the cylinder must be protected from the action of the acid. Other areas must be also protected. When two or more pieces of tissue are applied to the cylinder, the area where they meet often shows bare

metal. If acid reaches the metal at this union, a line will be etched and will appear as an image on the press.

The process of covering bare metal or thin areas on the tissue is called **staging**. The most common staging material is asphaltum. **Asphaltum** is a tar-like material that is acid resistant. The engraver paints the stage in unprotected areas by hand with a small brush or pen. After etching, the asphaltum can be dissolved with turpentine.

In etching, an acid bath penetrates through the resist to the copper (figure 16.27). When the acid reaches the surface, it dissolves a portion of the copper metal. The highlight areas of the resist are thick and therefore allow little acid to reach the cylinder. Highlight wells are shallow. The shadow areas of the resist are thin and allow a great deal of acid to penetrate to the copper. Shadow wells are deep.

Etching a cylinder is as much an art as a technical process. Conventional gravure typically involves five or six separate etching solutions, each of different acid strength. The acid used in the etching bath is perchloride

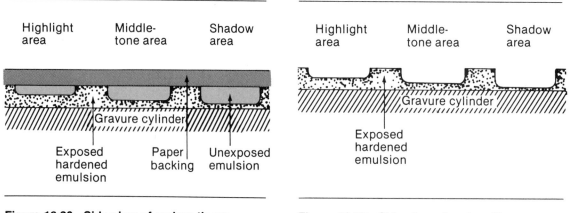

Figure 16.26. Side view of carbon tissue attached to a gravure cylinder showing unexposed emulsion to be removed.

Figure 16.27. Side view of carbon tissue attached to a gravure cylinder showing emulsion that the acid bath must penetrate.

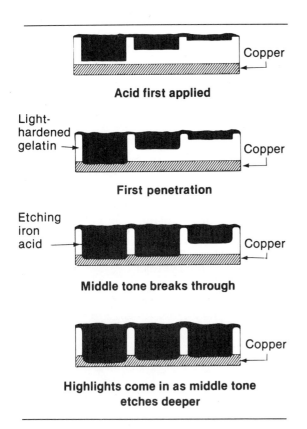

Acid first applied

First penetration

Light-hardened gelatin

Etching iron acid

Middle tone breaks through

Highlights come in as middle tone etches deeper

Figure 16.28. Stages of acid etch of a cylinder The several different etching solutions gradually penetrate through the gelatin emulsion to form the wells.
Courtesy of Southern Gravure Service

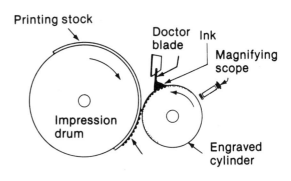

Figure 16.29. Diagram of a proof press Special proof presses are used to duplicate the quality of the production press.
Courtesy of Southern Gravure Service

fectiveness. Figure 16.28 shows the action of the acid as it gradually penetrates through the carbon tissue to cut highlight, middle-tone, and shadow wells. Some efforts have been made to automate the process, but successful etching of a cylinder still requires the practiced eye of a skilled engraver.

The last step in the etching process is to remove the carbon tissue and staging material. The cylinder is rotated through a hot acetic acid saltwater bath. The action of the hot bath dissolves all traces of the carbon tissue layer. The staging is dissolved with turpentine.

Cylinder Proofing, Correction, and Chrome Plating

The final steps in gravure cylinder preparation (with conventional gravure) involve proofing, correction, and chrome plating.

Proofing. The cylinder is mounted in a special proof press that duplicates the quality of the production press (figure 16.29). Ink is applied, and several proofs are pulled from the

of iron. The acid arrives at the engraver in large containers, usually at 48° Baumé (pronounced "48 degrees bomb-a"). Recall that Baumé is a system of measuring the density (or specific gravity) of a liquid. As the degrees Baumé fall, so too does the acid concentration, or strength. A 48° solution is much stronger than a 38° solution. For conventional gravure, separate etching solutions of 46°, 44°, 42°, 40°, 39°, and 37° Baumé are commonly used. The action of each bath penetrates the gelatin emulsion with different degrees of ef-

cylinder. Color proofs are always judged under special viewing lights—usually 5,000° K (see Chapter 6 for a discussion of color viewing).

Correction. Several methods are used to correct defects in the cylinder or to improve image quality to meet the customer's approval. It is possible to do hand tooling on a cylinder. A skilled engraver can reduce contrast by using an abrasive to rub away well walls. It is also possible to burnish or cut new wells into the cylinder with tools called a graver and a roulette wheel.

Sometimes it is necessary to fill in etched wells with new copper and then re-etch a new image. This is accomplished by spot plating. A **spot plater** is a machine that passes an electric current to the cylinder through a handheld electrode. The electrode is covered with cotton or gauze and then soaked in a plating solution. As the electrode is held against the cylinder, a small area of copper is built up on the surface. Spot plating can be used only to correct small areas.

Sometimes the entire cylinder must be re-etched to increase overall well depth. A technique called **rollup** is used to cover the cylinder in the nonimage areas. A special brayer is carefully rolled over the surface to apply a layer of rollup ink (figure 16.30). After rollup, the cylinder can be returned to the etching room or the engraver can apply an etch to selected areas by using cotton soaked in acid.

Chrome Plating. After the press sheets have been approved by the customer, the cylinder is ready for chrome plating. Several different machines are used for chrome plating. All are designed to place a thin layer of chrome over the surface of the cylinder.

The cylinder is first cleaned to remove all traces of ink or grease from the proofing operation. The edges are staged or a special cover is applied to protect the cylinder shaft

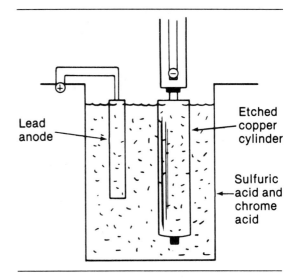

Figure 16.31. Plating the cylinder Electric current passes from the anode through the chrome plating solution to the cylinder.
Courtesy of Southern Gravure Service

Lead anode

Etched copper cylinder

Sulfuric acid and chrome acid

Figure 16.30. Rollup of a gravure cylinder

and face edge. The cylinder is then suspended in a solution of chrome and sulfuric acid (figure 16.31). Lead is commonly used as the anode. Electric current is passed from the anode through the plating bath to the cylinder. By controlling both time and amperage, a layer of chrome is deposited over the copper surface. Most chrome layers are between 0.0002″ and 0.0007″ thick. The desired thickness is determined by the type of screen and the depth of well etch.

After all traces of the plating bath are washed away and the cylinder is dry, the cylinder is ready to be sent to the pressroom.

Gravure Presswork

Gravure presswork is similar to press operations for both relief and lithography. Almost all gravure printing is done on web-fed presses (figure 16.3). Paper or some other material (called a substrate) is fed from large rolls to the printing unit through an intricate system of tension and registration controls (figure 16.32). The paper passes between the image cylinder and an impression cylinder. Some companies use offset gravure, but most transfer the image directly from the cylinder. After the paper leaves the printing area, it might pass through a set of driers to set the ink or it might follow an intricate set of rollers to dry by aerial oxidation and absorption. As the paper enters the delivery end of the press, it might be slit (figure 16.33), cut into sheets and folded (figure 16.34), or rewound onto a roll for shipment to the customer (figure 16.35).

Figure 16.33. Slitting the printed paper Some jobs require that the web be slit into smaller rolls at the delivery end of the press.
Courtesy of the Morrill Press

Figure 16.32. A printing unit of a web-fed press
Courtesy of the Morrill Press

Figure 16.34. Folding unit of a web press Some jobs are cut into sheets and folded in line on the press.

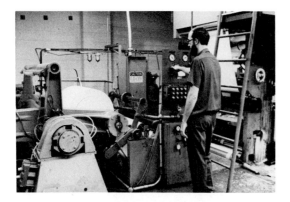

Figure 16.35. Rewinding printed paper Some jobs are rewound back onto a roll after printing.
Courtesy of the Morrill Press

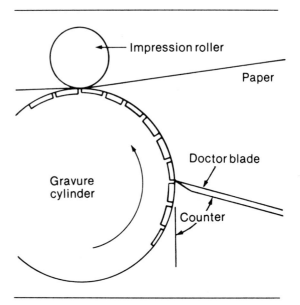

Figure 16.36. Diagram showing the counter The counter is the angle between the doctor blade and the cylinder surface.

Many of the concerns in gravure web-press operation have already been discussed in previous chapters. Chapter 12 dealt with press design and operation, which are applicable to the basic procedures for any printing method, including gravure. Chapter 18 deals with ink and paper and discusses the special characteristics of gravure ink. Some elements, however, are unique to gravure press operation. The two main areas of cylinder and doctor blade adjustment and impression rollers will be examined to complement the information presented in other chapters.

Cylinder and Doctor Blade Considerations

The function of the doctor blade is to wipe ink from the surface of the plate cylinder, leaving ink in only the recessed wells. A great deal of research has been done on materials, angles, and designs for doctor blades.

Several different materials are used for blades. The goal is to minimize blade wear and reduce heat generated by the rubbing of the blade against the turning cylinder. Plastic,

stainless steel, bronze, and several other metals have been used with success. The most common blade material, however, is Swedish blue spring steel. Blades are usually between 0.006" and 0.007" thick. The blades must be relatively thin to reduce wear on the cylinder, but strong enough to wipe away ink.

Blade angle is an important consideration. The angle between the blade and the cylinder is called the **counter** (figure 16.36). There is much discussion on the proper counter for the best image quality. The "best" counter depends on the method used to prepare the cylinder. For example, with electro-mechanically engraved cylinders, image quality decreases as the counter increases. Most angles are set between 18° and 20°. After the blade is placed against the cylinder and production begins, the counter generally increases to around 45°.

Another way to set the blade angle is by using the reverse doctor principle. With this approach the doctor blade is set at a large enough angle to push the ink from the surface (figure 16.37). The principle is not widely used, but it is gradually gaining acceptance in the industry.

Several different doctor blade designs are used by gravure printers (figure 16.38). The most popular are called conventional and MDC/Ringier. Care must be taken to keep the conventional design sharp and uniform. Most printers hone the blade by hand with a special stone and then polish it with a rouge or emery paper to get a flawless edge.

The MDC/Ringier design has a longer working life than the conventional form has and requires much less press downtime for blade cleaning and repair.

The action of the doctor blade against

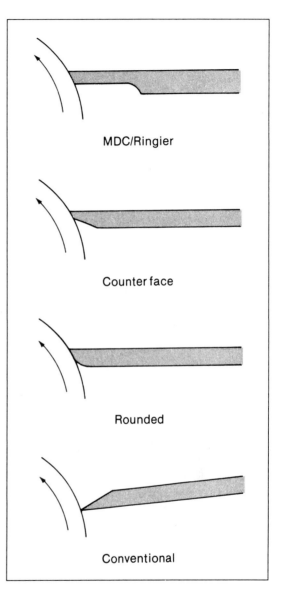

Figure 16.38. Examples of different doctor blade designs

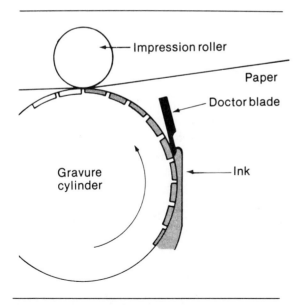

Figure 16.37. Diagram showing a reverse doctor blade A reverse doctor blade pushes ink from the cylinder surface.

the cylinder is of special concern. The blade rides against the cylinder with pressure. Pressure is necessary so that the ink does not creep under the blade as the cylinder turns. The most common method of holding the blade against the surface is by air pressure. The blade fits into a holder, which in turn is mounted in a special pneumatic mechanism. Most printers use a pressure of 1¼ pounds per inch across the cylinder length.

Most doctor blades are not stationary. As the cylinder rotates, the blade oscillates, or moves back and forth, parallel to the cylinder. The oscillating action works to remove pieces of lint or dirt that might otherwise be trapped between the cylinder and the blade. Dirt can nick the blade, which then allows a narrow bead of ink to pass to the cylinder surface. Blade nick is a major defect that can ruin the image or scratch the surface of the cylinder.

A **prewipe blade** is commonly used on high-speed presses to skim off excess ink from the cylinder (figure 16.39). This device prevents a large quantity of ink from reaching the doctor blade and ensures that the thin metal blade will wipe the surface perfectly clean.

Impression Rollers

Use of an impression roller is the second main difference between gravure presses and other web-fed machines. The purpose of the impression roller is to push the paper against the gravure cylinder to transfer ink from the image wells (see figure 16.18). The major considerations for impression rollers are pressure, coating and hardness, and electrostatic assist.

Most impression rollers are formed from a steel core coated with rubber or a synthetic material, such as DuPont's Neoprene. Rubber hardness is measured by a Shore Durometer (discussed in Chapter 15). Values are given in "Shore A" readings. Hardness increases as Shore A numbers get larger. Different types

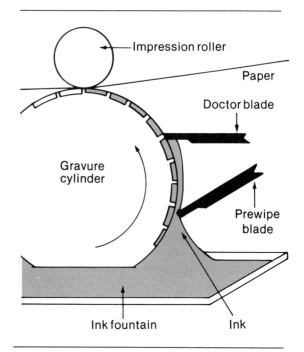

Figure 16.39. **Diagram of a gravure cylinder showing prewipe and doctor blades** Most presses use a prewipe blade to skim off most of the ink before the cylinder reaches the doctor blade.

of paper or substrates require different degrees of hardness for the impression roller. Material such as cellophane might require 60 Shore A, but Kraft paper or chipboard might need 90 Shore A.

Ink is transferred to the web by pressure of the impression roller. More pressure does not always give better image quality. Pressure might vary from 50 to 200 pounds per linear inch (p.l.i.). The amount of pressure the operator sets is determined by previous tests for the kind of paper being printed. Whatever setting is selected, it is critically important that uniform pressure be applied over the entire length of the cylinder.

The area of contact between the impression roller and the cylinder is called the **nib width,** or flat (figure 16.40). The amount of nib width is determined by the hardness of the impression roller and the amount of pressure. The nib width is important because it is the area of image transfer to the paper or plastic web. The nib width is adjusted to give the best-quality image on the web stock.

A great advantage of the gravure process is that it allows the printing of high-quality images on low-grade papers. Problems do occur when the paper surface is coarse and imperfect. Ink transfers by direct contact. If a defect in the paper prevents the contact, then no image will be transferred (figure 16.41). The Gravure Research Association designed and licensed a special device, called an **electrostatic assist,** to solve this problem and improve image transfer. With this technique, a power source is connected between the cylinder and the impression roller (figure 16.42).

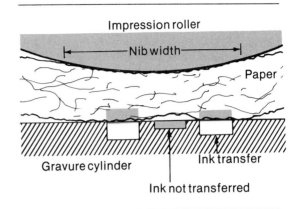

Figure 16.41. Diagram showing inking on defective paper If defects in the paper prevent contact with the gravure cylinder, ink will not be transferred.

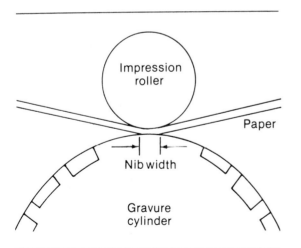

Figure 16.40. Diagram showing the nib width The nib width is the area where the paper contacts the cylinder by the compression of the impression roller.

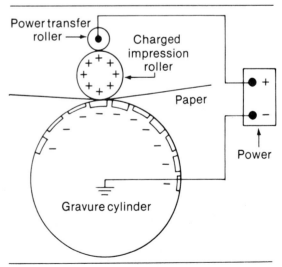

Figure 16.42. Diagram of electrostatic assist printing Electrostatic assist printing charges the impression roller and gravure cylinder so that the ink is electrostatically lifted from the cylinder to the paper.

A conductive covering must be added to the impression roller, but no special problems are caused by this addition. An electric charge is created behind the web, which forms an electrostatic field at the nib. The charge pulls the ink around the edges of each well, which causes the ink to rise and transfer to the paper. Most presses are now equipped with electrostatic assist devices.

Gravure printing presses are sophisticated devices that have a wide range of controls to ensure high image quality. New presses are in use that reach speeds as high as 2,500 feet per minute. It is this high speed, linked with outstanding image quality, that makes gravure printing one of the major printing processes in this country.

Key Terms

gravure
rotogravure
packaging printing
publication printing
specialty printing
diffusion etch
direct transfer

electromechanical process
gravure well
bridge
lateral hard-dot process
electroplating
master plate
electronic-eye mark

conventional gravure
carbon printing
resist
carbon tissue
staging
counter
electrostatic assist

Questions for Review

1. What are the main characteristics of rotogravure printing?

2. List four characteristics of gravure that make it ideal for high-quality long-run jobs.

3. What is the Gravure Association of America?

4. List the four basic methods of gravure cylinder preparation.

5. What are the most common identification parts of a gravure cylinder?

6. What is the difference between static and dynamic balance?

7. What are the two basic forms of cylinder construction?

8. What is electroplating?

9. What is a newage gauge?

10. What is the ballard shell process?

11. What is the purpose of a cab in cylinder layout?

12. What is a master plate?

13. What is carbon printing?

14. What is a resist?

15. What is "tissue laydown"?

16. What is the purpose of staging?

17. What is the purpose of chrome plating prior to printing a gravure cylinder?

18. What is the purpose of a doctor blade on a gravure press?

19. What is the difference between a conventional doctor blade design and a MDC/Ringier?

20. What is the purpose of an impression roller in gravure presswork?

21. What does "electrostatic assist" refer to in gravure presswork?

22. What is the "nib width" on a gravure press?

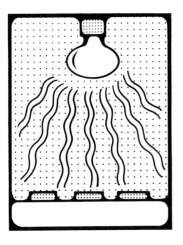

Chapter Seventeen

Other Printing Processes

Anecdote to Chapter Seventeen

An image scanner Using an image scanner to store graphics in computer memory can greatly reduce the lead time needed to produce printed matter.
Courtesy of Scangraphic

All modern printing processes have been developed to meet a human need for information. Gutenberg invented printing to meet Europe's increasing need for printed records in the late 1400s. The effect of Gutenberg's invention was to expand knowledge. This expansion of knowledge quickly lead to an increasing demand for more printed material. The development of the rotary relief press and the Linotype in the 1800s helped meet this demand. In doing so, they too increased demand, so that inventors keep looking for methods of producing printed information faster and faster.

In the 1950s, when the phototypesetter was introduced, many people felt that we now had a device which could set type faster than would ever be necessary. But within a few short years, the speed of the typesetter was outstripped by the printing speed of the offset lithographic process. And so it has gone throughout history, with each new technological innovation increasing demand and leading to other, related innovations, which themselves have produced more demand, which in turn has sparked the development of newer technologies.

Probably the technological innovation that has had the greatest impact on the modern printing industry is the computer. Computers have made it possible to produce printed matter faster, easier, and more efficiently than was ever thought possible. Printers use computers not only to set type but to control and to monitor almost every task in the printing plant. In addition, the computer has made possible a completely new type of printing, known as "on-demand" printing. All traditional printing processes rely on a time-consuming and costly process which involves designing an image, generating camera-ready copy from which negatives are made, using the negatives to produce printing plates, and then using the plates to produce printed reproductions. The problem with this approach is that production of the final copy requires a great deal of lead time. On-demand printing, in which copy is reproduced directly from computer memory, without negatives or plates, reduces the lead time needed for printed matter from months to minutes.

The invention of plastic materials is another innovation which has had a profound effect on printing, by greatly expanding the type of substrates on which printing is required. Before the development of plastics, printers were primarily called upon to print on paper. Printing presses, inks, plates, and all developments in printing were centered around printing on a paper substrate. The development of cellophane in the 1930s represented a major breakthrough in the packaging industry. Here was a material which, when used for food packaging, would keep foods fresh far longer than paper wrappers. The material was easy to use, because it would stretch and seal itself to the food surface. It could be made clear, so the customer could see the product inside the package. Above all, it was inexpensive to produce, store, and handle. In all aspects, it provided the answer to the food processor's dreams. In all aspects, that is, but one—it was almost impossible to print on cellophane. Here, then, was a material which, in answering a need, created yet another need. Aniline printing, which was introduced to this country in the early 1900s rushed in to meet this need, and the aniline process, which today is known as flexography, provides the primary means for printing on plastic materials.

Will we ever have a printing process that can print instantly on any material? Probably not. As long as people can think, they will be creative. And as long as people create, they will produce a need for even more printing processes which will print at even greater speeds. It is this cycle of innovation leading to innovation that makes technology so interesting and that guarantees a future for us all, not only as printers, but as members of the human race.

Objectives for Chapter Seventeen

After completing this chapter, you will be able to:

- Discuss the development of flexographic printing.
- Describe the major components of a flexographic press.
- Discuss the function of an anilox roll.
- Describe a two- and three-roll flexographic inking system.
- Explain how sheet and liquid photopolymer plates, and how rubber flexographic plates are made.
- Describe the six steps in the xerographic process.
- Explain how a laser printer exposure system operates.
- Discuss the resolution capabilities of laser printers.
- Explain the difference between a continuous spray and a drop-on-demand ink-jet printer.
- Discuss the major advantages of an ink-jet printer, and give an example of where an ink-jet printer would be used.

Introduction

This chapter introduces four printing processes which are becoming increasingly important in the printing industry. Flexography, the first process we will discuss, has long been a significant relief process used in the package printing industry. Xerography has been used for about fifty years, but for most of these years it remained no more than an office photocopying process. Only recently has high-speed xerography been applied for on-demand printing in which unique documents are created as they are needed, rather than being preprinted and inventoried for later use. Laser printing, a near cousin to xerography, is one of the most recently developed printing processes. Ink-jet printing is a specialty printing process, designed for relatively low-quality printing of unique images at exceptionally high speeds. Both laser and ink-jet printing rely on the computer for their operation, and both are useful in situations where no traditional printing method would be appropriate.

Flexographic Printing

Flexographic printing, commonly referred to as **flexo printing,** is a rotary relief printing process in which the image carrier is a flexible rubber or photopolymer plate with raised image areas. The process was first introduced in the early 1900s, at which time it was called **aniline printing** because the inks used were made from synthetic, organic aniline dyes. A variety of packaging products including foil, tissue, paper, paperboard, corrugated board, and plastic film can be printed with flexo. In fact, flexographic printing owes its wide acceptance in the packaging industry to the invention of cellophane, which became popular in the 1930s because it proved an ideal material for food packaging. However, cellophane cannot be printed with the offset process; and while it is possible to print on cellophane with gravure, the cost of gravure cylinder making is so high that only extremely long press runs are economical.

It is ironic that the flexo process, which was ideal for printing on cellophane food packaging, got off to a slow start in commercial printing because of a mistaken belief that aniline dyes were poisonous and that they would contaminate food products. Even though the U.S. government approved the use of aniline inks for food packaging in 1946, the name, "aniline printing," still caused many package printers and food processors to reject the process. To overcome this problem, the aniline printing industry formally changed the name of their process to "flexographic printing" in 1952. Since the name change, the use of flexography has grown to the point where the process currently represents about 15% of the commercial printing market.

Components of a Flexographic Press

A flexographic press consists of three major units: the infeed, printing, and outfeed units (figure 17.1). As we discuss these units, it should become apparent that one of the greatest benefits of flexography is simplicity, from infeed to delivery.

Infeed Unit. The majority of flexographic printing is done on roll-fed materials such as film, foil, and laminates used for food, med-

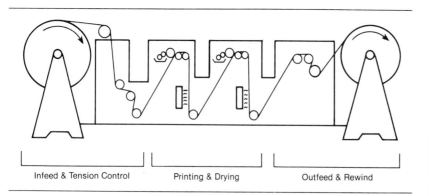

| Infeed & Tension Control | Printing & Drying | Outfeed & Rewind |

Figure 17.1. Schematic of a typical web-fed flexographic printing press.

ical, and sanitary packaging materials. Sheet-fed flexo is also possible, and is the only practical solution for the printing of thicker materials such as corrugated board. As with other web systems (Chapter 12), the flexo infeed system consists of a roll stand with some type of tensioning device. The roll stand typically operates in conjunction with a dancer roll and brake to control web tension.

Sheet-fed flexographic infeed units are not far different from those found on sheet-fed offset presses, except that a sheet-fed flexo infeed system must be designed to feed heavier stock than is generally fed through an offset press.

Printing Unit. The major advantage of flexographic printing lies in the printing unit, both in its simplicity and in its ability to deliver ink to a wide variety of substrates. Offset ink trains are designed to take relatively thick, viscous inks from an ink fountain and spread the ink to a thin consistency by passing it through a number of distribution rollers and eventually to form rollers which ink the plate. Flexographic inks are much thinner than offset inks and require a much simpler inking system.

The heart of the flexo inking system is a roller with a cellular surface, called the **anilox roll.** The process of manufacturing an anilox roll involves engraving a steel roller to form individual cells (from 10 to 550 cells per linear inch) on the roller surface. After the cells are formed on the steel roller, the roller is chrome plated, or plasma coated with a ceramic material to protect it from corrosion and wear. The cells collect ink from the ink fountain and transfer it to the plate. A great deal of research has gone into the development of the particular cell structure, size, and number of cells needed for particular printing applications. Two cell structures are commonly used. Under magnification, the **pyramid cell** structure appears as a number of

inverted pyramids with sharply sloping walls that form cells which are pointed at the base (figure 17.2a). The **quadrangular cell** structure appears as four-sided cavities with relatively straight walls that form cells which are relatively flat at the base (figure 17.2b). The number, shape, and size of the cells required on the anilox roll depends on a variety of fac-

a. Pyramid Cell Structure

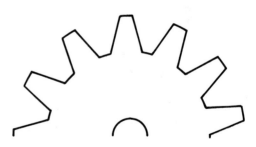

b. Quadrangular Cell Structure

Figure 17.2. Cell structures The pyramid cell structure has a sharply pointed base (a); the quadrangular structure produces a cell with a flat base (b).

tors, among which are the type of ink to be used, the amount of ink to be transferred, the material to be printed on, the actual image to be printed, and whether the ink train is a three- or two-roller system.

Three-roller ink systems consist of an ink fountain roller, typically made of rubber, which passes ink to the anilox roll (figure 17.3). On such systems the fountain roll speed is kept constant; the anilox roll speed is variable. Thus the fountain roll not only passes ink to the anilox roll but slips against it, wiping excess ink from the anilox roll. Ink metering is established in a three-roller ink system by controlling the rotating speed of the anilox roll.

Two-roller systems have no fountain roller. Instead, the anilox roll turns directly in the ink fountain and a doctor blade is used to remove excess ink from the anilox roll (figure 17.4). The steel doctor blade is positioned parallel to the anilox roll and at a 30° angle to it. The doctor blade arrangement provides more precise and consistent ink metering, but it tends to produce more wear on the anilox roll than does the two-roller system. This excess wear is compensated for to some extent by using quadrangular cells on anilox rollers

designed for doctor blade ink systems. Because they are square at the base, rather than pointed, quadrangular shaped cells can tolerate more wear without significant reduction in cell capacity than can the pyramid-shaped cells used on three-roller systems (figure 17.5).

The plate cylinder is designed to hold the flexible plate through the use of an adhesive. Unlike offset plates, flexographic plate size varies with the job to be printed. The plate cylinder selected has a circumference that matches the size of the plate to be used. Generally, several repeat images are printed in succession from several plates mounted on the same cylinder. Thus the size of the plate cylinder is chosen to match the repeat image size. That is, if the image to be printed is 6 inches, a 12-inch plate cylinder can be used to print two repeat images. However, a 10-inch plate cylinder could not be used to print a 6-inch job. Because the plate cylinder must be changed to match the plate, and the anilox roll must also match the job, flexo presses are designed so that the plate cylinder and ink train can be easily removed and installed as a unit in the press each time a new job is run.

Many flexographic presses are configured with several printing units in-line, so

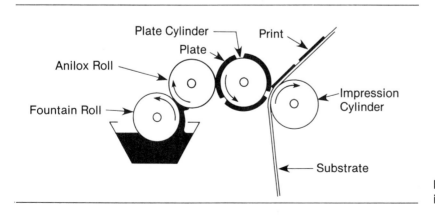

Figure 17.3. Three-roller ink system

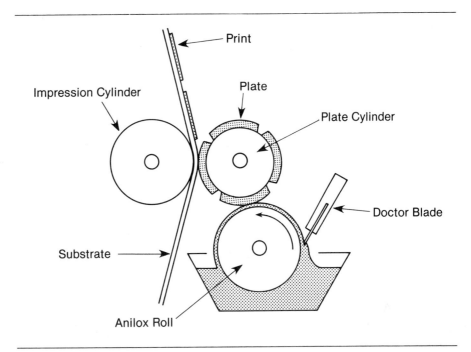

Figure 17.4. Two-roller ink system

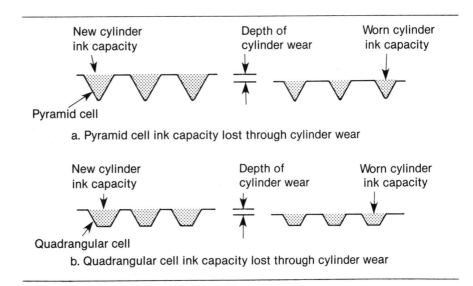

a. Pyramid cell ink capacity lost through cylinder wear

b. Quadrangular cell ink capacity lost through cylinder wear

Figure 17.5. Comparison of cell capacity after cylinder wear Because of their shape, the ink capacity of quadrangular cells, which are wider at the base than pyramid cells, contain more ink in the base of the cell and are less affected by cylinder wear at the cell surface.

that four or more colors can be printed in a single pass through the press. Drying units are located between each color head to dry the substrate before the next color is applied. Changing jobs on such a press requires removing and replacing the printing units for each color. This operation takes some time, but the time lost changing units is more than compensated for by the fact that new plates are mounted and proofed off-press, thus reducing on-press make-ready time.

Pressure between the polished metal impression cylinder and the plate is adjusted to deliver what is termed a "kiss impression." Owing to the thinness of the film and laminate materials often printed with flexo, and also owing to the fact that the plate and image areas are flexible, the lightest possible impression pressure needed to transfer the image must be used. If the pressure is too great, it will cause the image to spread and lose quality. Far too much impression will damage the plate or the substrate being printed.

Outfeed Unit. Outfeed units vary considerably with the type of work being printed. Many outfeed units consist only of a rewinder which rewinds the substrate into a roll for later processing. A rewinder might be used for foil-laminated, printed candy bar wrappers, for example. After rewinding, the roll of printed wrappers is sent from the flexo plant to the candy manufacturer. There it is remounted and fed into the manufacturing line, where each wrapper is filled with a candy bar, sealed, and placed in a carton. Often flexo presses are designed in-line with the manufacturing production line so that printing and packaging can be done as one continuous operation. In the same manner, a sheet-fed flexo press for printing corrugated board may be configured in-line with a converting machine that turns the printed board into folded cartons.

It is difficult to check for proper image register on substrates that are rewound for further processing. Stopping the press to check for register would destroy the image quality on the part of the web that was stopped in the printing unit(s). One approach to checking register on a moving web is to pass the web vertically under a large magnifying glass. The web is illuminated by a strobe light that flashes in time with the speed of the press. Synchronization of the strobe light with the press speed makes the image appear to be stationary in front of the magnifying glass. With this technique, the press operator is able to view register at web speed, and to make appropriate adjustments on the fly.

Flexographic Plates

Flexographic-plate composition must be matched to some extent to the type of ink to be used and to the substrate to be printed. Both rubber and photopolymer plates are used.

Rubber Plates. Natural and synthetic rubber plates were the first type of flexo plates developed, and they are still used for some applications. The actual process of producing a rubber plate is not far different from the process used to produce photoengravings used in the hot type letterpress process (figure 17.6). A sheet of metal alloy coated with a light-sensitive emulsion is placed in a specially designed vacuum frame. The emulsion is not only light-sensitive, it is also an acid resist. A negative of the job is placed over the coated sheet and light is passed through the negative. Where light strikes the emulsion the acid resist is hardened. During processing, the unhardened resist in the nonimage areas is washed away, leaving hardened resist only on the image areas. The metal sheet is then

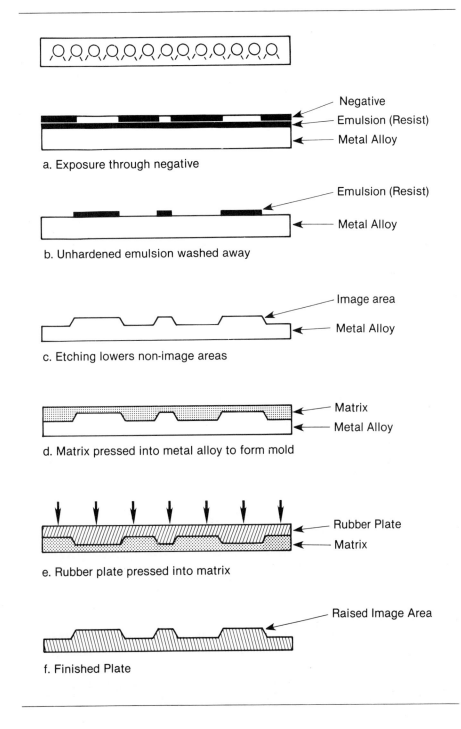

a. Exposure through negative

b. Unhardened emulsion washed away

c. Etching lowers non-image areas

d. Matrix pressed into metal alloy to form mold

e. Rubber plate pressed into matrix

f. Finished Plate

**Figure 17.6.
Steps in
producing a
rubber plate**

etched, which lowers the nonimage areas, leaving the image areas raised. The remaining resist is washed off. The completed engraving is then moved to a molding press where a matrix (mold) of the engraving is made by pressing matrix material against the engraving with controlled heat and pressure. The matrix material sinks into the metal engraving to form a mold. The rubber plate is made from the matrix by pressing a rubber sheet into the matrix, again under controlled heat and pressure. Preformed sheets for rubber plates are available in a variety of thicknesses. The thickness selected depends on the job to be printed and the press to be used.

The major disadvantage of rubber plates is that they are more costly to make than photopolymer plates. Also, because they are made from an engraving, any plate problems identified during proofing must be corrected by remaking the engraving, which further increases the expense of the process.

Photopolymer Plates.   Photopolymer plates eliminate many of the disadvantages of rubber plates. These plates are made from light-sensitive polymers (plastics) which are hardened by ultraviolet light. Photopolymer plates are made from both sheet and liquid materials.

Sheet photopolymer plates are supplied in a variety of thicknesses for specific applications. The plates are cut to the required size and placed in an ultraviolet light exposure unit (figure 17.7). One side of the plate is completely exposed to ultraviolet light to harden or "cure" the base of the plate. The plate is then turned over, a negative of the job is mounted over the uncured side, and the plate is again exposed to ultraviolet light, which hardens the plate in the image areas. The plate is then processed to remove the unhardened photopolymer from the nonimage areas, thus lowering the plate surface in the nonimage areas. After processing, the plate is dried and given a postexposure of ultraviolet light to cure the whole plate.

Liquid photopolymer plates are made in a special ultraviolet light exposure unit. In the process, a clear plastic protective cover film is mounted over a negative transparency which is placed emulsion-side up on the exposure unit (figure 17.8a). A layer of liquid photopolymer is then deposited by a motorized carriage over the transparency and cover film. The carriage deposits the liquid evenly over the cover film and controls the thickness of the deposit. As the liquid is deposited, the carriage also places a substrate sheet over the liquid (figure 17.8b). The substrate sheet is specially coated on one side to bond with the liquid photopolymer and to serve as the back of the plate after exposure. Exposure is made first on the substrate side of plate. This exposure hardens a thin base layer of the liquid photopolymer and causes it to adhere to the plate substrate. A second exposure through the negative forms the image on the plate (figure 17.8c). As with sheet materials, the image areas are hardened by this exposure. The nonimage areas remain liquid. Processing removes unwanted liquid in the nonimage areas, leaving raised image areas. A postexposure is then made to cure the whole plate.

The **Cameron Belt Press** is a unique flexo press that makes use of liquid photopolymer plates. The Cameron press is used to produce a variety of publications such as softcover pocket books and coloring books. In the plate-making process, liquid photopolymer is coated on a belt of nylon. The length of the nylon belt is determined by the number of pages in the book. All of the pages of the book are exposed on the belt in the proper page imposition. One half of the belt contains the odd-numbered pages, and the other half contains the even-numbered ("back up") pages. The web is printed on one side from the half of

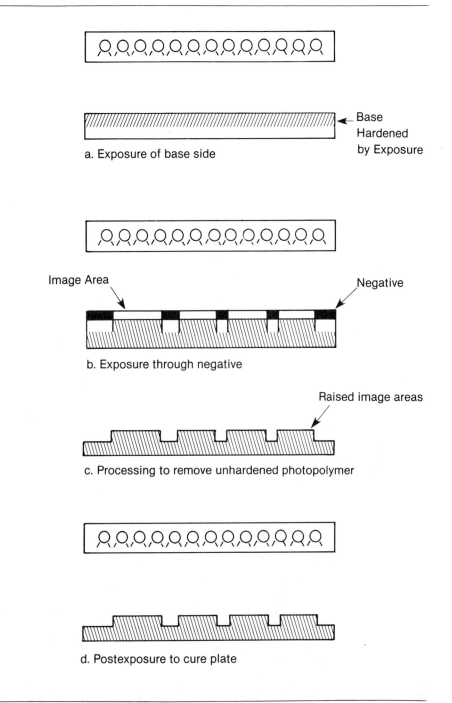

a. Exposure of base side

Base
Hardened
by Exposure

Image Area — Negative

b. Exposure through negative

Raised image areas

c. Processing to remove unhardened photopolymer

d. Postexposure to cure plate

**Figure 17.7.
Steps in
producing a sheet
polymer plate**

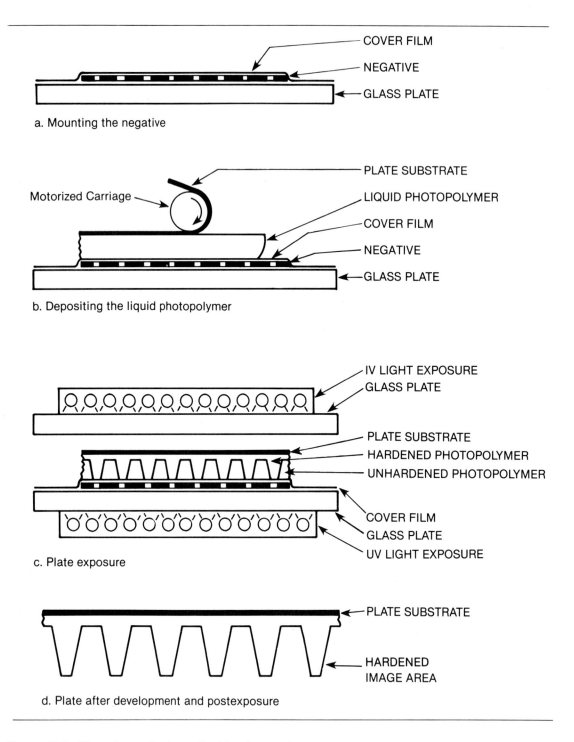

Figure 17.8. Steps in producing a liquid polymer plate

the belt with the odd-numbered pages, turned over with a turn bar, and printed on the back side of the web with the even-numbered pages by the other half of the belt. The web runs continuously through the press, thus the entire book is printed in one pass. An in-line finishing operation folds, cuts, adds a preprinted cover, and glues and trims the book. The completed book is loaded into shipping boxes directly from the press outfeed section.

The Future of Flexography

In relation to offset printing, flexographic printing offers two major advantages: long-run capabilities and relatively low waste during make-ready. Flexo can be used for press runs exceeding five million impressions. The flexible plate wears very little during a press run because of the low pressure used for impression. All make-ready is done off press; this eliminates waste because the plate is proofed and produces quality copy after a few impressions once it is mounted on the press. In addition, ink and water balance does not have to be achieved as it does in offset lithography; thus, press start-up is quicker and, once the ink metering system is adjusted, image quality remains constant throughout the press run. In relation to gravure, which can also be used for long press runs, flexographic printing offers low plate cost. Even if rubber plates which require engraving are used in the process, the cost of plate making for flexography is only a fraction of the cost of producing a gravure cylinder.

For years flexography had the reputation of producing relatively low-quality printed images, suitable only for package printing on nontraditional substrates such as foil and corrugated board. With the developments in inks and plates that are taking place today, this reputation is rapidly changing to the point

where flexography is increasingly being used for halftone, critical line work, and four-color printing on paper stock.

One other reason for the bright future of flexography is the fact that the process is suitable for printing with water-based as well as solvent-based inks. Solvent-based inks have long been used for quality printing because they produce excellent color fidelity and are quick drying. This makes solvent-based inks extremely suitable for four-color process printing on coated papers. Their major disadvantage is that during drying the evaporating solvent produces environmental pollution. Over the last several years, the U.S. government has established environmental pollution guidelines which have forced many printers to install complex and expensive fume recovery systems. Water-based inks, which do not produce environmental pollution, eliminate this problem. The result is that flexography is being used increasingly for color printing on a variety of papers, particularly for comic books and for medium-quality color inserts in newspaper printing. Several newspapers, including the *Pittsburgh Press*, the *Miami Herald*, and the *Providence Journal*, use the flexo process. As environmental controls become more stringent, and as research continues in flexographic plates, ink, and register systems, there is no doubt that the move toward flexo will continue. Some researchers believe that flexo's share of the printing market will increase from its current 15% of the market share to well over 20% by the year 2000.

Xerographic Printing

The word "xerography" comes from a combination of two Greek words: *xeros*, which means "dry," and *graphos*, which means "writing." The invention of the xerographic process was a response to the need for printing on demand. The process, commonly known as photocopying, was developed in 1937 by Chester Carlson, a patent attorney and physicist who was seeking a method for copying patent drawings without using photography. All xerographic processes in use today rely on the fundamental principle that Carlson applied in his original device: Unlike electrical charges attract; like electrical charges repel.

Many developments have occurred in xerography since Carlson's original invention, but all common xerographic processes involve six steps: charging, exposure, development, transfer, fixing, and cleaning (figure 17.9).

Charging. The image carrier in xerography is a photoconductive surface. In most systems, the photoconductor is a selenium-coated drum. Other photoconductors, such as zinc oxide and cadmium sulfide are used, but selenium is the most common photoconductor used because it is readily available and relatively inexpensive. Whatever photoconductor is used, it must have the ability to retain an electrical charge when in darkness but to lose the electrical charge when exposed to light. During charging, a charge of static electricity is placed on the photoconductor, while the photoconductor is in complete darkness. After charging, the photoconductive surface is completely charged (figure 17.9a).

Exposure. During exposure the image to be copied is illuminated. The dark image areas on the original absorb light, and they reflect no light to the charged photoconductive drum. Thus the drum retains its charge in the image areas. Nonimage areas of the original reflect light to the drum, causing it to lose the charge in these areas. Thus, after exposure, there is

a latent image on the drum consisting of electrical charges in the image areas (figure 17.9b).

Exposure on small, low-speed office copies is accomplished in one of two ways. One method exposes the drum by placing the original on a glass surface under which a light is moved to make the exposure (figure 17.10). Other models move the glass and original over a fixed light source. Both of these methods provide acceptable results, but both are relatively slow. Modern high-speed copiers generally use a segmented drum or a photoconductive belt on which several individual images can be exposed in rapid succession (figure 17.11). A flashing strobe light is used to make the actual exposure.

Development. Toner is applied to the drum during development (figure 17.9c). Several types of toners are available, but the most common is a dry powder toner consisting of tiny particles of metallic powdered resin. The toner must be capable of receiving an electrical charge, because it is electrical attraction which transfers the toner to the photoconductor and to the final paper printing surface. Resin is needed to make the toner adhere to the paper after transfer. The color of the toner determines the color of the final printed image.

Two common methods exist for applying toner to the photoconductive surface. The cascade development process (figure 17.12a), as the name implies, allows toner to flow over the whole photoconductor. Magnetic brush development (figure 17.12b) utilizes a specially designed brush to apply the toner. In either case, the toner, which is given a charge opposite the charge on the photoconductor, is attracted to the photoconductor and clings to the drum only in the charged image areas. It falls free of the drum in the uncharged nonimage areas. Thus, after development the photoconductive drum is covered with toner

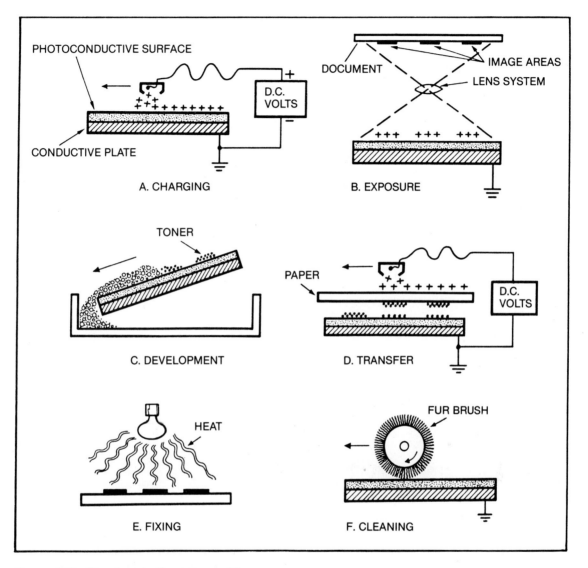

Figure 17.9. Six steps in the xerographic process

only in the image areas and is ready for the transfer step.

Transfer. During transfer, a piece of paper is passed close to the drum. The paper is given a charge of the same type (negative or positive) as the drum, but the charge placed on the paper is stronger than the charge placed on the drum. The stronger charge on the paper attracts the toner from the drum to the

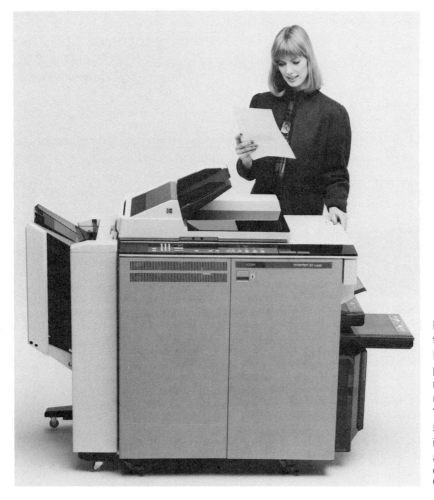

Figure 17.10. An office-type photocopier
Exposure on this photocopier is made by moving an exposure light under the glass surface. This machine can produce 50 copies per minute and is capable of enlargement and reduction.
Courtesy of Eastman Kodak Company

paper, transferring the toner image to the paper (figure 17.9d).

Fixing. The toner must be "fixed" so that it will adhere permanently to the paper. Most toners are heat set and are fixed by passing the paper under heat lamps or heat rollers that cause the toner to melt and combine with the paper through absorption (figure 17.9e). After fixing, the printed piece is ejected from the machine into an outfeed device.

Cleaning. The last essential step in the xerographic process is cleaning the photoconductor. If the photoconductor were not made perfectly clean between each image printed, small toner particles would remain on the photoconductor surface. These particles would be transferred to the next sheet printed, causing a ghost image of the previous image produced and eventually darkening the overall image. Another reason for cleaning is toner recovery. Toner which was not transferred to

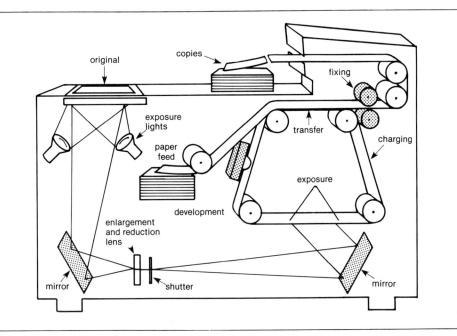

Figure 17.11. Schematic of a high-speed photocopier

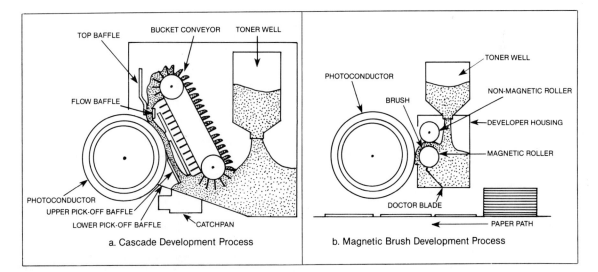

a. Cascade Development Process

b. Magnetic Brush Development Process

Figure 17.12.   Cascade and brush development

the paper can be reused to produce the next image. Brush and wiper systems are both used to clean the photoconductive surface. On some machines these mechanical cleaners are aided by vacuum heads, which help draw toner off the drum.

Importance of the Xerographic Process

Once viewed only as a low-quality short-run reproduction method, xerography has become the mainstay of the growing quick-print industry. As we have seen in this text, all of the major printing processes are ideally suited for high-speed reproduction of the same image. However, xerography, which requires no photography or plate making, lends itself to the rapid reproduction of multiple copies of unique images.

Recent advances in xerographic technology have led to the development of color copying, making short-run color work possible at an affordable price. Color copiers employ three developing units which have toner colored to match the three process colors, yellow, magenta, and cyan (figure 17.13). While the current state of this technology cannot rival the color produced by process color printing with any of the major printing processes, color copying can produce color which is suitable for a variety of applications.

In addition to producing color, many xerographic devices are equipped with automatic feeders, two-sided copying on sheets

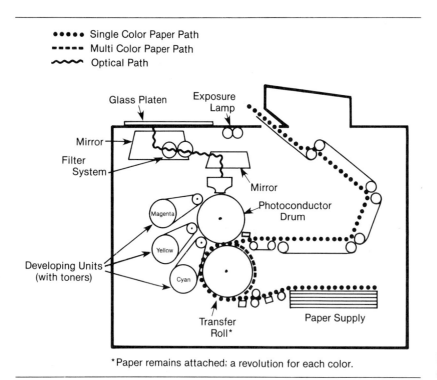

* Paper remains attached; a revolution for each color.

Figure 17.13. Schematic of a color xerox machine

up to 11 inches by 17 inches, enlargement and reduction capabilities, collating devices, and binding systems (figure 17.14). These copiers allow an operator to feed in a stack of originals and output bound copies in a matter of minutes. Most important, the xerographic process can be configured directly with computerized word processing equipment to produce images directly from digitized information. This feature is especially important in the field of electronic printing using laser printer output, as explained in the next section.

Laser Printing

Laser printing is a marriage between the technology of xerographic printing and the computer. The word "laser" is an acronym for the phrase "Light Amplification by Stimulated Emission of Radiation." Simply stated, a laser beam is a concentrated beam of light. The beam can be made so small that it is capable of microscopic precision. The main feature of the laser light source in relation to xerography is that the laser beam can be controlled by digitized information sent from a computer.

A laser printer operates in every way exactly as does a xerographic printer, except for the exposure system. That is, a laser printer employs the six basic xerographic steps of charging, exposure, development, transfer, fixing, and cleaning. However, the exposure step is accomplished by imaging the photoconductor with a laser light source, rather than through reflection from an original (figure 17.15). Thus a hard copy original is not needed for the process, which is why laser printers are often referred to as "intelligent copiers."

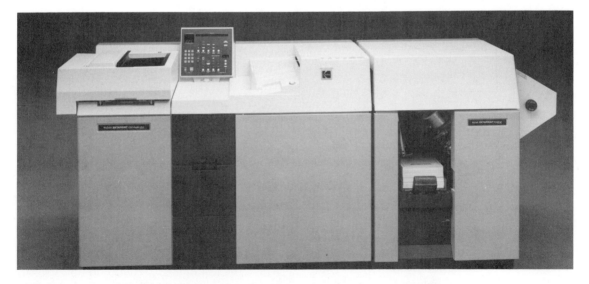

Figure 17.14. A high-speed photocopier This machine can produce over 5,000 copies per hour, "duplex" copy (copy on both sides), enlarge, reduce, collate, print on paper up to 110-pound index, and staple automatically. Note wire spool for staples above outfeed stack and computer controlled keyboard.
Courtesy of Eastman Kodak Company

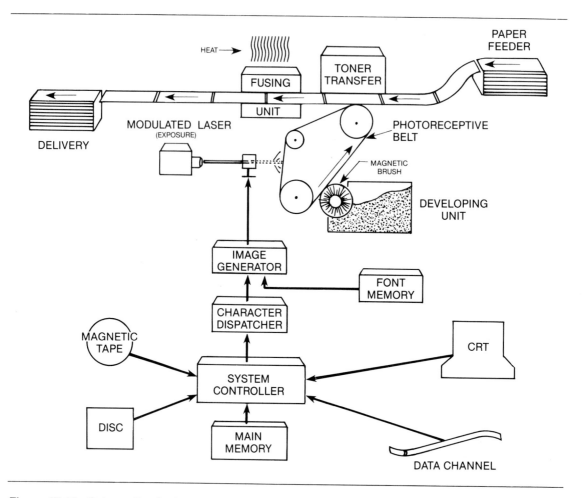

Figure 17.15. Schematic of a laser printer

Laser Exposure. A laser printer exposure unit receives digitized character or graphic information from a computer (see Chapter 5). The computer passes the character and graphics information to the printer along with code instructions indicating which fonts are to be used for character display. The printer then combines the character and graphics information passed to it with the font information it contains. Font memory, the information needed to actually form the characters in the required fonts, is stored in the laser printer. In most laser printers, font information is stored as a mathematically expressed formula which the laser image generation unit uses to build an outline of the bit map that will generate the appropriate character. Based on the font formulas, the image generation unit causes the laser light beam to pulsate (flash repeatedly) and build the character outline.

Characters of various sizes can be produced by mathematically manipulating the formula used to produce character outlines.

An alternative character formation process is being used by some manufacturers of laser printers. Instead of storing font information as mathematical formulas, these printers store font information for each character in each size, as individual bit maps. This storage method increases the speed with which individual characters can be formed. However, because they must hold bit map information for each character in each size, these printers require far more font memory, which limits the number of fonts that they can have available on-line. To overcome this limitation, such printers typically provide a means for temporally storing and changing available fonts. The most common system uses font cartridges which can be easily plugged into and removed from the printer (figure 17.16).

Regardless of how font information is stored, the individual flashes produced by the laser during exposure are reflected from a mirror to the photoconductive drum or belt to produce the required dot matrix image (figure 17.17). The flashes produce the image outline first, then "fill in" the character by flashing the photoconductor in the nonimage areas. This causes the electrical charge placed on the photoconductor during charging to be drained from the photoconductor in the nonimage areas. The remaining charged areas pick up toner during development, transfer the toner to a paper receiver, and fuse the toner in a fusing unit.

Figure 17.16. Laserjet printer The Hewlett-Packard Laserjet printer uses font outlines rather than mathematical formulas to generate characters. Note font cartridge (top right). Courtesy of Hewlett-Packard Corporation

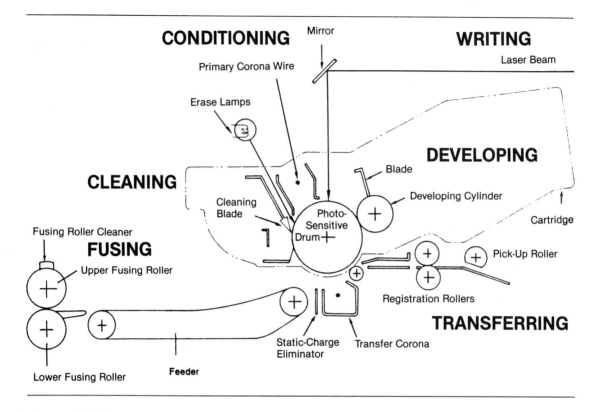

Figure 17.17. Laser exposure of the photosensitive drum The laser
beam is reflected from a mirror onto a photosensitive drum.
Courtesy of Hewlett-Packard Corporation

Printer Speed. Unlike traditional printing processes, in which an image carrier such as a plate is made once, then used repeatedly to transfer an image to a substrate, in laser printing the image carrier is remade for each image transferred. If several copies of the same page are required, the page must be re-imaged on the photoconductor for each copy. This re-imaging process affects the overall speed of image reproduction. In fact, there is little difference in speed whether each new image produced is a duplicate page or a new page with a different image. A small laser printer, such as the one shown in figure 17.18 can

produce up to ten 8½- × 11-inch pages per minute. Larger printers equipped with high-speed exposure units and continuous belt photoconductors can produce copies at much faster rates of speed. However, while these high-speed laser printers can make copies faster, their major advantage is the speed with which they can generate original copy from digitized computer information. Generally, they are reserved for just that purpose. If multiple copies are required, the original copy, generated on the high-speed laser printer, is placed in a high-speed photocopier that can automatically feed originals, make the re-

Figure 17.18. A tabletop laser printer
Courtesy of Apple Computer, Inc.

quired number of copies, and collate them for binding.

Resolution. As mentioned in Chapter 5, laser printing units cannot produce copy with the same resolution as phototypeset output. One of the reasons for this limitation is that the toner particles used to produce xerographic images are much larger in size than the black metallic silver particles on a typical film emulsion. Thus the edges of an image produced by a laser printer appear "fuzzy" compared to those produced on phototypeset output.

Additionally, the dot matrix images produced on a laser printer consist of a much lower number of dots per inch than those produced by high-quality phototypesetting equipment. Recall from Chapter 5 that dot matrix image formation is accomplished by dividing an image up into a grid, called a matrix which consists of individual pixels (picture elements). The number of individual pixels used to reproduce this matrix greatly affects image resolution. A quality photo-

typesetter can produce dot matrix output with a resolution of over 2,000 dots per inch. Even the highest quality laser printers currently being introduced cannot expose an image with a resolution much greater than 400 dots per inch. This difference in resolution is closely related to the ability of a selenium photoconductor to receive a charge of static electricity and to differentiate between charged and uncharged areas. Development of cadmium sulfide photoconductors, which are far more light sensitive and can hold much higher resolutions than selenium, may help eliminate this problem.

One final limitation to laser printer resolution results from the manner in which the image is recorded on the photoconductor. Image areas retain a static electrical charge and nonimage areas have no charge. Thus image and nonimage areas are only differentiated by this charge, no-charge situation. If we were to measure the charge across an individual pixel on a photoconductor, we would find that the charge is strongest in the center of the pixel, and weakens toward the pixel extremes. Thus, when toner is applied, the pixel created is somewhat rounded, rather than square, because of the stronger electrical attraction at the pixel centers. This creates a slight "fuzziness" of the printed image, which is increased by the fact that some toner particles tend to overlap into the edge between the charged image and the uncharged nonimage areas.

Future of Laser Printing. Even with these limitations, laser printing represents an important step in the future of office automation and on-demand electronic printing and publishing. While no laser printing system yet developed can produce duplicate copies at the speed of most traditional printing processes, its major advantage lies in its ability to pro-

duce unique originals much faster than any other printing process. Not only does it receive its information directly from computers, but all of the traditional printing steps of camera work, stripping, plate making, and press operation are eliminated with laser printing. There can be no doubt that new developments in toner technology and in laser imaging science will increase both the speed and the resolution of laser output.

Ink-Jet Printing

Ink-jet printing produces an image by transferring individual drops of ink from an orifice (opening) through a small air gap to a printing surface (figure 17.19). The process can be used to print on a variety of substrates, including

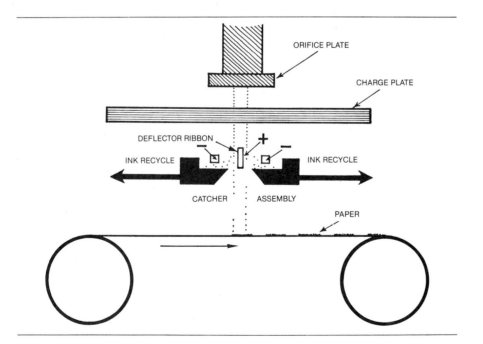

Figure 17.19. Ink-jet printing

corrugated board, plastics, fabric, and paper. The primary use for the process in the printing industry is in addressing equipment. Indeed, many people maintain that the current direct mail industry has been made possible largely through the invention of ink-jet printing.

All ink-jet processes rely on computer input to form a dot matrix image made up of individual drops of ink. The major difference between the different systems available is whether the ink spray is "continuous" or "drop-on-demand."

Continuous-Spray Systems. In continuous systems, each ink orifice sprays ink drops continuously toward the printing surface. Ink drops not needed to form the image are deflected so that they do not hit the printing surface, and are accumulated in an ink recy-

cling unit for reuse. The most common continuous ink-jet printing unit in use is the Videojet system, developed by the A. B. Dick Company (figure 17.20). The Videojet print head consists of an ink chamber which continuously emits a small stream of ink through a single ink orifice. When forced through a small orifice at high speed, liquid ink tends to break up into a spray containing drops of various sizes. To control individual drop size and direction, the ink is given a frequency by a vibrating piezoelectric crystal. This frequency makes the emitted drops regular in size, shape, and spacing. As the drops leave the jet orifice, they are subjected to electric charges, which vary in strength, based on digitized information sent from the computer. The electric charges of various strengths deflect the ink drops from a straight path, and move them in the appropriate directions to

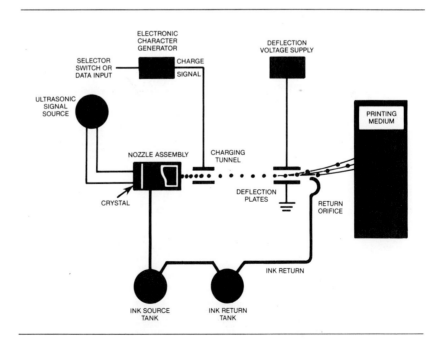

Figure 17.20. A. B. Dick's Videojet printing process

produce the desired dot matrix image. Drops not needed in the matrix are given a charge that deflects them into the ink recycling system.

An alternative continuous-spray system is the Mead Dijit system (figure 17.21). The Dijit system provides an array of ink orifices in a single ink head. All of these orifices feed from the same ink chamber, which is given a frequency by a crystal. Only the drops needed

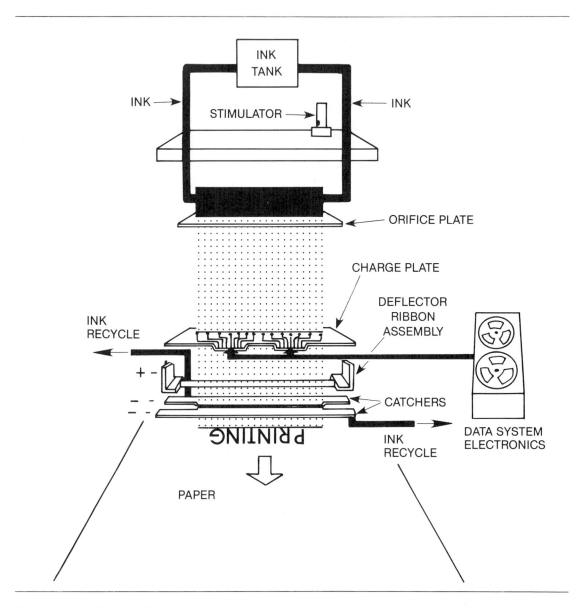

Figure 17.21. Mead's Dijit printing process

to form the image are charged when they leave the chamber. These drops travel in a relatively straight line from the orifice array to strike the paper and form the image. Unwanted drops receive no charge and are deflected to the ink recycling system by a charged deflector ribbon. Because a number of ink orifices, called an "orifice array," are used with the Mead system (120 per inch), characters can be printed many times faster than by a single-orifice system. Over 50,000 characters per second can be produced with an orifice array; only about 13,000 characters per second can be produced with a single-orifice system.

Drop-On-Demand Systems. A drop-on-demand, or **impulse,** printer produces a drop from the ink orifice only when a drop is needed to form the matrix image. The ink drops are given a frequency in a manner similar to that of continuous drops. However, instead of being continuously sprayed, electrical impulses, based on digitized information from the computer, cause individual drops to be squeezed out of the ink orifice and propelled toward the printing surface. On-demand units have the advantage of being less complicated because they do not require a dot deflection system for dot placement or to remove unwanted drops. They are also economical because ink is only provided where it is needed to form the image. Their major disadvantage is that they are much slower than continuous-spray systems.

Disadvantages of Ink Jet. The major disadvantage of ink-jet printing is the low resolution of the images printed. In part, this low resolution is the result of the minimum size ink drop that can be produced at the ink orifice. Drop size affects the size of the matrix divisions that can be used to produce the image, and ultimately affects the number of dots per inch that make up the image. The highest quality ink-jet printers currently available can provide images with resolutions no greater than 300 dots per inch. In addition, with all systems there is a certain amount of drop misplacement during printing. Misplaced ink drops further reduce the overall quality of the image. Finally, the inks used in ink-jet printing dry primarily by absorption, which tends to spread out the individual dots that make up the image. The combination of all of these factors means that the image quality produced by ink-jet printing is not even close to the quality that can be produced by any of the major printing processes. However, in fairness to the process, we should point out that for the applications in which ink jet is used, high-quality imaging is not the primary concern.

Advantages of Ink Jet. The major advantage of ink-jet printing is the speed with which unique character images can be generated. This is the reason ink-jet printing is so widely used for addressing and for producing variable information on repeat forms.

Ink-jet printers can be configured in-line with web-fed presses and high-speed bindery equipment for automated addressing of printed newspapers, magazines, catalogs, and other direct mail items at web speeds. This completely eliminates a separate addressing step in the direct mail operation. The publication leaves the press printed, bound, sorted in zip code order, and addressed, ready to deliver to the post office. Ink-jet printers are also used in manufacturing plants to print unique bar codes and batch codes, at assembly-line speeds, on products such as cans, bottles, and boxes.

Another high-speed printing application for ink jet is in check-printing operations. Large corporations produce thousands of payroll checks every week, each with a different name and dollar amount. Ink-jet printing is ideally suited to this application. Check blanks with the company name and bank identification information are preprinted as continuous, perforated rolls or sheets by off-set printing. The variable information (name, address, and amount) is added by running the preprinted checks through an ink-jet printer.

One final advantage of ink-jet printing is that the process is non-impact. That is, the image carrier is not forced against the printing substrate. This feature makes it possible to print with ink jet on almost any surface, regardless of surface texture, shape, or resistance to pressure. Ink-jet printing can place an image on a plastic container or bubble package (or even an egg yolk) as easily and as quickly as it can on paper, on a textured surface as rough as sandpaper, or on a curved surface such as a pill or capsule.

Key Terms

flexographic printing	rubber plate	laser printing
aniline printing	photopolymer plate	ink-jet printing
anilox roll	sheet photopolymer	continuous-spray system
pyramid cell	liquid photopolymer	drop-on-demand system
quadrangular cell	xerographic printing	impulse printer

Questions for Review

1. What type of products are printed primarily with flexography?

2. What are the major components of a flexographic press?

3. What is the purpose of the anilox roll, and why does it have surface cells?

4. What is the difference between the pyramid and the quadrangular cell structure?

5. Why is the quadrangular cell structure used on ink systems which require a doctor blade?

6. How are rubber flexographic plates made?

7. Describe the process for producing a sheet photopolymer plate and a liquid photopolymer plate.

8. List and describe the six steps in the xerographic process.

9. What is meant by "on-demand" printing?

10. Why can laser printing be considered a marriage between xerography and the computer?

11. Describe the operation of a laser exposure unit.

12. What factors limit laser printer resolution?

13. Name two applications for ink-jet printing.

14. What is the difference between continuous-spray and drop-on-demand ink-jet printing?

15. What are the advantages and disadvantages of ink-jet printing?

Chapter Eighteen

Ink and Paper

Anecdote to Chapter Eighteen

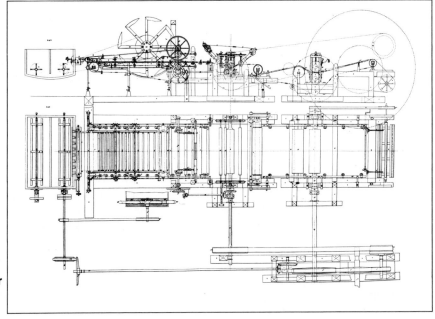

The patent drawing for the Fourdrinier papermaking machine

Throughout the history of printing, demand for paper has constantly increased. The paper industry has evolved to meet this growing demand. It is the craft of early papermakers that allows us today to hold Gutenberg's first Bible, five hundred years after the sheets left his press.

The first paper-like material, called papyrus, was invented by the Egyptians about five thousand years ago. Their "paper" was made from the papyrus plant, which grew along the banks of the Nile River. The pith, or center of the plant, was cut into strips. These were then glued together in thin, crosswise layers to form sheets. After pressing and drying, the sheets were ready to use. They are still readable after more than five millennia.

The first truly modern paper was invented in China by a eunuch named Ts'si Lun in A.D. 105. He first shredded cloth fibers into a special hot-water solution. The fiber solution was then poured into a frame covered with a loosely woven cloth screen. The water drained through the cloth, leaving fine interwoven fibers on the screen. The frame was then placed in the sun to dry. The remaining water evaporated from the fibers, and the result was paper. Later, Ts'si created "laid" papers by immersing the screen in the fiber solution and gently raising the frame to the surface. The laid technique produced a better quality of paper than the earlier method did. This basic hand process was used to produce all paper until around 1800.

The first automated process was developed in 1798 in the paper mill of M. Didot, a member of a famous printing-publishing family, in Essonnes, France. Nicolas Louis Robert, a superintendent in Didot's mill, developed the idea of making paper by pouring the fiber solution onto a continuously moving wire belt. After the water drained through the wire, the paper was passed between felt-covered rollers. The machine worked very well and, with time for improvements, would have been a commercial success. However, the French Revolution, and several lawsuits with his employer, prevented Robert from reaching his goal.

In 1801 an associate of the Didot family, John Gamble, joined the brothers Fourdrinier in a partnership to develop Robert's idea in England. By 1807 they had designed and constructed the first fully automated, continuous paper-making machine.

The fiber solution, called "stuff," was deposited from a special box onto a finely woven copper wire belt. The belt moved both forward and side to side. The belt's copper web was 54 inches wide and 31 feet long. The full length of the machine, including driers, was almost 100 feet. It took seven workers to operate and could produce a continuous roll of paper at the rate of more than 600 feet an hour.

The machine operated better than expected and created great excitement. At long last, here was a way to meet the ever-growing demand for printing papers. Like so many other creative people, the men who perfected one of the greatest contributions to modern printing died in poverty. The Fourdriniers lost a fortune in attempting to market their device. Although by 1860 thousands of tons of paper were being produced on automated machines all over the world, none of the paper-making machine pioneers ever benefited financially from the effort.

While many refinements and improvements have been made, the basic design of the 1807 machine is still used today to produce all paper. The machine is called a fourdrinier in honor of the brothers and the partnership that gave the world the supply of paper it needed.

Objectives for Chapter Eighteen

After completing this chapter, you will be able to:

- Classify paper into four common groups and recognize the characteristics of each.
- Recognize and define common paper terms, such as ream, M, M weight, substance weight, and equivalent weight.
- Calculate press sheet cuts from standard paper sizes.
- Use a paper merchant's catalog to calculate the cost of paper for a job.

- List and define the properties of ink, including viscosity, tack, and drying time.
- List the common groups of ingredients of printing ink, including pigment, vehicle, and additives.
- Describe the characteristics of lithography, screen printing, letterpress, flexographic, and gravure inks.
- Recognize the Pantone Matching System as a tool in selecting inks.

Introduction

Two of the most important ingredients for the printing processes are ink and paper. Traditionally printing consisted of images set in dense black ink on white paper. For many years, the problems of creating the ink and paper were so troublesome and time-consuming that no one bothered about using different colors.

Today, however, the printer and printing customer are faced with another problem. There are so many different kinds of paper—with different colors, textures, finishes, thicknesses, and weights—that it is hard to make a choice. So many different kinds of ink, each formulated for a specific process, problem, or paper, are available in any color of the spectrum that the printer is hard-pressed to understand even a fraction of the possible choices (table 18.1).

The purpose of this chapter is to organize the information on paper and ink into an understandable form. It is divided into two sections. The first deals with paper; the second, with ink. Each classifies materials and examines ideas that are important for a novice printer to understand.

SECTION 1: PAPER

Classifying Paper

There is no standard way to categorize the thousands of different papers available to the

Table 18.1 Ink Mileage chart

Grade of Stock	Black	Purple	Haven Blue	Sky Blue	Kelly Green	Yellow Lake	Opaque Orange	Fire Red	Antique Red	Opaque Base	White
Enamel	360	320	330	330	200	275	250	300	250	310	250
Litho Coated	300	300	280	300	175	240	180	240	200	265	200
Label	240	250	250	220	155	190	160	190	165	195	165
Dull Coated	205	200	200	205	120	160	130	170	140	190	140
Newsprint	150	155	150	140	160	110	140	130	105	110	104
Antique Finish	135	120	130	120	140	95	115	110	90	95	90
Machine Finish	180	170	180	170	180	100	140	130	125	120	120

The numbers indicate the approximate number of thousand square inches of area that one pound of offset litho ink will cover on a standard sheet-fed press.

average printer through a supplier. One workable way is to classify all types under one of the following five headings: book, writing, cover, bristol, and an "other" category. Table 18.2 lists these five categories with a further breakdown.

Book paper is the most common type of paper found in the industry. It is used as a general purpose material for such things as catalogs, brochures, direct mail, and books. **Writing paper** is generally a high-quality material that was originally associated with correspondence and record keeping. Today it includes a wide range of qualities and uses, such as stationery, inexpensive reproduction (such as for the ditto or mimeograph processes), and tracing or drawing. **Cover paper** is commonly used for the outside covers of brochures or pamphlets and is generally thicker than both book and writing paper. Common applications are booklets, manuals, directories, and announcements. **Bristol paper** comprises stiff, heavy materials that find wide usage for such things as business cards, programs, menus, file folders, and inexpensive booklet covers. The "other" category is a holding bin for anything that cannot be classified under the first four headings. Common examples are newsprint, lightweight mate-

Table 18.2 One Way to Classify Types of Paper

Book Papers
　Offset
　Opaque
　Converting

Writing Papers
　Bond
　Duplicator
　Mimeograph
　Ledger
　Tracing

Cover Papers
　General Purpose Cover
　Duplex

Bristol Papers
　Tag
　Index
　Post Card

Other
　Groundwood (newsprint)
　Lightweights
　Special Purpose

rials such as onionskin, or items that meet a special purpose, such as NCR (no carbon required) paper.

All papers within each category are further classified (and sold) according to weight.

The system is called basis weight. **Basis weight** is the weight in pounds of one **ream** (500 sheets) of the basic sheet size of a particular paper type. Unfortunately, all paper types do not use the same basic sheet size to determine weight. The **basic sheet sizes** of the four common paper classifications are:

- Book paper: 25 × 38
- Writing paper: 17 × 22
- Cover paper: 20 × 26
- Bristol: 22½ × 28½

Most papers are available in a variety of basis weights. For example, the most common weights for uncoated book papers are basis 40, 45, 50, 70, and 80. One ream of basis 40 book paper measures 25 by 38 inches and weighs 40 pounds. A basis 80 book paper has the same dimensions, but one ream weighs 80 pounds. Within each category, then, the greater the basis weight, the heavier the sheet. It is not possible, however, to make the same generalization when dealing with different categories (such as book and cover) because the sizes of the sheets to be weighed are not the same.

Sometimes a basis weight is converted to **M weight,** which is the weight of 1,000 sheets (rather than 500) of the basic sheet size of a particular paper type. A paper's M weight is twice its basis weight. M weight is used merely as a convenience for paper calculation.

Although the basic size of book paper is 25 by 38 inches, other sizes are available to the printer. If the order is large enough, the printer can specify the required size to the manufacturer. In order to meet the needs of small jobs, local paper suppliers generally stock a variety of sizes within each paper type. These common sizes are called **standard sizes.** The left column in table 18.3 shows some regular sizes for book papers. Regular sizes are also stocked in each of the common basis weights.

Although a ream of basis 40 paper of the basic sheet size weighs 40 pounds, a ream of the same paper in any other sheet size (regular size) will not weigh the same. The weight of these regular size reams is defined in terms of **equivalent weight.** Equivalent M weight is twice the equivalent ream weight. Table 18.3 is a chart that printers and paper manufacturers use to determine equivalent M weights for regular sizes of book papers.

As an example, locate the basic sheet size for book paper (25″ × 38″) in table 18.3. Notice that the M weight for basis 40 is 80 pounds. One ream (500 sheets) weighs 40 pounds, and 1,000 sheets weigh 80 pounds. Now find the 38″ × 50″ regular sheet size (which is double the basic sheet size of 25″ × 38″) and find the equivalent weight of 160 pounds. One thousand sheets of 38 × 50 basis 40 book paper have an equivalent weight of 160 pounds.

There are two general exceptions to this vocabulary of papers when dealing with the four main types. Some bristol and cover papers are described not by weight but rather in terms of thousandths of an inch—called "points." An 11-point bristol is a sheet that is 0.011 inch thick. Common thicknesses are 8, 10, and 11 points. Most bristols and covers, however, are classified by the more common basis weight designation.

The second general exception deals with writing papers. Within this category, the term *substance weight* is used instead of *basis weight*, but the terms mean the same thing. **Substance weight** is the weight in pounds of one ream of the basic sheet size (17″ × 22″) of one particular type of writing paper. Table 18.4 shows some equivalent M weights of a list of regular sizes of writing papers.

When printers buy paper for a job, they order it from the supplier according to total pounds, type, and basis weight.

Table 18.3. Regular Sizes for Book Papers and the Corresponding Equivalent Weights

Basis	40	45	50	60	70	80	90	100	120
Sizes	Equivalent M Weights								
17 × 22	31	35	39	47	55	63	71	79	94
17½ × 22½	33	37	41	50	58	66	75	83	99
19 × 25	40	45	50	60	70	80	90	100	120
22½ × 29	55	62	69	82	96	110	124	137	165
22½ × 35	66	75	83	99	116	133	149	166	199
23 × 29	56	63	70	84	98	112	126	140	169
23 × 35	68	76	85	102	119	136	153	169	203
24 × 36	72	82	90	100	128	146	164	182	218
25 × 38	80	90	100	120	140	160	180	200	240
26 × 40	88	98	110	132	154	176	198	218	262
28 × 42	100	112	124	148	174	198	222	248	298
28 × 44	104	116	130	156	182	208	234	260	312
30½ × 41	106	118	132	158	184	210	236	264	316
32 × 44	118	134	148	178	208	238	266	296	356
33 × 44	122	138	152	184	214	244	276	306	366
35 × 45	132	150	166	198	232	266	298	332	398
35 × 46	136	152	170	204	238	272	306	338	406
36 × 48	146	164	182	218	254	292	328	364	436
38 × 50	160	180	200	240	280	320	360	400	480
38 × 52	166	188	208	250	292	332	374	416	500
41 × 54	186	210	234	280	326	372	420	466	560
41 × 61	210	236	264	316	368	422	474	526	632
42 × 58	206	230	256	308	358	410	462	512	616
44 × 64	238	266	296	356	414	474	534	592	712
44 × 66	244	276	306	366	428	490	550	612	734
46 × 69	268	300	334	400	468	534	602	668	802
52 × 76	332	374	416	500	582	666	748	832	998

Determining Paper Needs

When printers deal with sheets on the press, they do not deal in pounds. Suppose we had a job that required 500 sheets of substance 40, 28- × 34-inch writing paper. How many pounds must be ordered from the supplier? By referring to table 18.4 we see that the equivalent M weight (remember, that means 1,000 sheets) is 204 pounds. Half of 1,000 is 500. Therefore, if we multiply 204 pounds by one-half, we get a paper weight of 102 pounds. If an identical job required 715 sheets, the paper would weigh 145.86 pounds (715 is 0.715 of 1,000, 204 × 0.715 = 145.86).

Not every job will use regular size press sheets that are easily obtained from the paper supplier. Most printers stock only a few sizes of each type and then cut them to meet the needs of individual jobs. Others purchase the most efficient regular sizes but often have to gang several jobs together on a single press

Table 18.4. Regular Sizes for Writing Papers and the Corresponding Equivalent Weights

	Substance Weights								
	13	16	20	24	28	32	36	40	44
Sizes	Equivalent M Weights								
8½ × 11	6.50	8	10	12	Sizes and weights normally				
8½ × 14	8.25	10.18	12.72	15.26	used for business papers—				
11 × 17	13	16	20	24	often called cut sizes				
16 × 21	23	29	36	43	50	57	65	72	79
17 × 22	26	32	40	48	56	64	72	80	88
17		41	51	61	71	81	92	102	112
18 × 23	29	35	44	53	62	71	80	89	97
18 × 46	58	70	88	106	124	142	160	178	194
19 × 24	32	39	49	59	68	78	88	98	107
19 × 48	64	78	98	118	136	156	176	196	214
20 × 28	39	48	60	72	84	96	108	120	132
21 × 32	46	58	72	86	100	114	130	144	158
22 × 34	52	64	80	96	112	128	144	160	176
23 × 36	58	70	88	106	124	142	160	178	194
24 × 38	64	78	98	118	136	156	176	196	214
28 × 34	66	82	102	122	142	162	184	204	224
34 × 44	104	128	160	192	224	256	288	320	352

sheet. In either case, the printer is faced with the task of calculating the most efficient method of cutting smaller pieces from available stock sizes.

To illustrate the process, consider an example. A printer is to cut a press sheet size of 8½ × 11 inches from a regular sheet that measures 28 × 34 inches. What is the maximum number that can be cut from the larger piece? Figure 18.1 shows the two common ways of figuring the problem. In the first case, the width and length of the stock sheet are divided by the corresponding width and length of the press sheet. The two answers are then multiplied to show that 9 sheets are possible. The same result can be obtained by simply drawing a picture of the large sheet and blocking out the maximum number of press sheets. In the second case, the width

and length of the larger sheet are divided by the length and width of the smaller sheet. The result with this method is only 8 sheets. The printer would obviously cut the paper to obtain 9 press sheets to gain the maximum number of press sheets from the regular sheet.

In the example above, the maximum number of sheets is really 9. The procedure of dividing corresponding dimensions and then alternate dimensions of the stock and press sheets is rather straightforward, but paper calculation is not always that simple. Drawing a picture of the calculations can make the process easier and often can show where additional gains can be made.

Drawing and working with the placement of press sheets on the stock reveals that the example above (figure 18.1) can be cut to obtain 10 instead of 9 sheets (figure 18.2). It

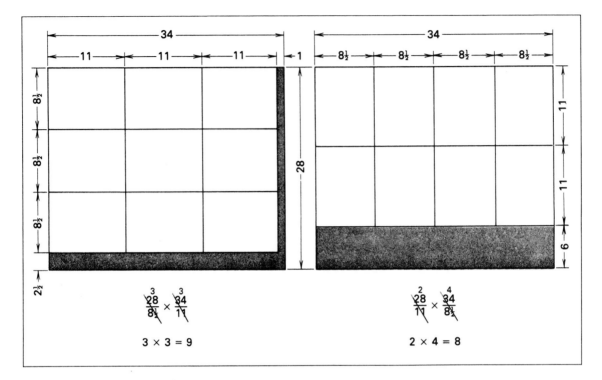

Figure 18.1. Example for calculating the number of sheets to be cut from a stock sheet by dividing or by drawing

is necessary, though, to tell the paper cutter the sequence of cuts. This process of manipulating the positions and order of cuts to gain an additional sheet is called making a **nonstandard cut** or **dutch cut**. In an era when paper and other material can account for more than half the cost of a job, a nonstandard cut can often mean the difference between profit and loss.

A very important consideration when calculating the paper needs of a specific job is spoilage. All printing processes require some start-up to get the press feeding properly and the printed press sheets up to proper ink density. This is called make-ready. Beyond this, it is a rare job that does not have some waste because of something as frustrating as a machine jam-up or as foolish as spilled coffee on

a finished pile. It is necessary, then, to give the press or bindery operators more sheets than the job actually requires to allow for start-up and printing problems. These extra sheets are called the **spoilage allowance.**

Table 18.5 shows a typical spoilage allowance chart that an estimator might use to calculate the average number of wasted sheets for different types of jobs.

For example, if 5,000 copies, two colors on one side, are to be run on a two-color lithographic press, the operator must begin the run with 5% more press sheets than the job requires (see table 18.5)—or (5,000 × 5%) + 5,000 = 5,250 press sheets.

Many printing presses are designed to print from rolls of paper that are cut into sheets after printing. This is called web printing. Even

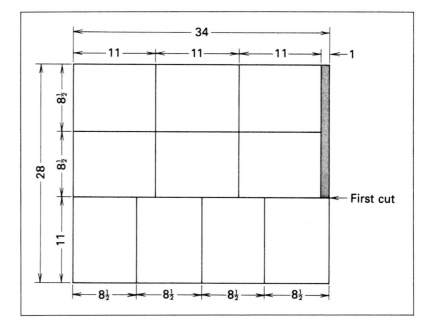

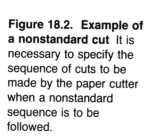

Figure 18.2. Example of a nonstandard cut It is necessary to specify the sequence of cuts to be made by the paper cutter when a nonstandard sequence is to be followed.

if their presses use sheets, many printers feel it is more economical to buy paper by the roll and have a machine (a slitter) that cuts individual sheets attached to their press.

The problem, again, is that rolls are sold by the pound, but the printer wants to count sheets. When estimating a job, the printer must determine the number of finished press sheets that can be obtained from a given roll.

Assume that a printer has an 800-pound roll of 25-inch-wide basis 50 book paper wound on a 3-inch wooden core. The printer wants to know how many 17- × 24-inch press sheets can be cut from the roll. To find the number of linear feet in the roll, use the following formula:*

linear feet =

$$\frac{(\text{weight of roll}) \times (\text{basis size}) \times (500 \text{ sheets})}{(\text{width of roll}) \times (12 \text{ inches}) \times (\text{basis weight})}$$

or to find linear inches:

linear inches =

$$\frac{(\text{weight of roll}) \times (\text{basis size}) \times (500 \text{ sheets})}{(\text{width of roll}) \times (\text{basis weight})}$$

The basis size of book paper is 25″ × 38″, so for this example:

linear inches =

$$\frac{800 \times 25 \times 38 \times 500}{25 \times 50} = 304,000$$

Because the press sheet size is 17″ × 24″, the printer can cut the 24-inch dimension out of the 25-inch roll width.** To determine the number of press sheets, divide the 17-inch sheet width into the total number of linear inches in the roll:

$$\frac{304,000}{17} = 17,882 \text{ press sheets}$$

*This formula applies only to rolls with a 3-inch core. Consult your paper salesperson for alternative formulas for other core diameters.
**The decision on which dimension to choose depends on grain direction (see "Paper Grain," Chapter 13).

Table 18.5. Paper Spoilage Allowances
(Percentage Represents Press Size Sheets, Not Impressions)

Lithographic	1,000	2,500	5,000	10,000	25,000 and over
Single-Color Equipment					
One color, one side	8%	6%	5%	4%	3%
One color, work-and-turn or work-and-tumble	13%	10%	8%	6%	5%
Each additional color (per side)	5%	4%	3%	2%	2%
Two-Color Equipment					
Two colors, one side	—	—	5%	4%	3%
Two colors, two sides or work-and-turn	—	—	8%	6%	5%
Each additional two colors (per side)	—	—	3%	2%	2%
Four-Color Equipment					
Four colors, one side only	—	—	—	6%	5%
Four colors, two sides or work-and-turn	—	—	—	8%	7%
Bindery Spoilage					
Folding, stitching, trimming	4%	3%	3%	2%	2%
Cutting, punching, or drilling	2%	2%	2%	2%	2%
Varnishing and gumming	7%	5%	4%	3%	3%

The figures above do not include waste sheets used to run up color, as it is assumed that waste stock is used for this purpose.

Use the next higher percentage for the following papers:
1. Coated papers when plant does not usually run coateds.
2. Papers that caliper .0025 and less.
3. Difficult papers such as foil, cloth, plastic, etc.

Letterpress	1,000	2,500	5,000	10,000	25,000 and over
Single-Color Equipment					
One color, one side	7%	5%	4%	3%	3%
One color, two sides or work-and-turn	13%	9%	7%	5%	5%
Each additional color (per side)	6%	4%	3%	2%	2%
Two-Color Equipment					
Two colors, one side	—	—	4%	3%	2%
Two colors, two sides or work-and-turn	—	—	7%	5%	5%
Each additional two colors (per side)	—	—	3%	2%	2%
Four-Color Equipment					
Four colors, one side	—	—	—	6%	5%
Four colors, two sides or work-and-turn	—	—	—	8%	7%
Bindery Spoilage					
Folding, stitching, trimming	4%	3%	3%	2%	2%
Cutting, punching, or drilling	2%	2%	2%	2%	2%
Varnishing and gumming	7%	5%	4%	3%	3%

These paper spoilage allowance charts have been reproduced through the courtesy of the ''Printing Industries of Metropolitan New York'' and demonstrate how paper spoilage is calculated by printers belonging to this association.

A Sample Problem

In order to tie together the ideas presented so far, let's consider a sample problem of paper estimating.

A printer has been asked to bid on a job that requires 15,000 copies of a two-color poster to measure 9 by 12 inches. The printer has in stock a basis 60 book paper in a 25- × 38-inch regular sheet size left over from a previous job. The printer has only a single-color lithographic press and wants to run the job in the 9″ × 12″ size. How many pounds of paper must be purchased to bid on the job?

How many press sheets must be given to the press operator?

The printer must deliver to the customer 15,000 sheets plus a 6% spoilage allowance (4% for the first pass through the press plus 2% for the second color) of 900 sheets.

$$15,000 \times 0.06 = 900$$

$$15,000 + 900 = 15,900$$

1. A total of 15,900 press sheets must be given to the press operator to ensure getting 15,000 good sheets for the customer.

2. How many basic sheets will be needed in order to cut 15,900 press sheets (figure 18.3)?
    If 8 press sheets can be cut from each stock sheet, then:

$$15,900 \div 8 = 1987.5$$

But because partial sheets cannot be bought, we must always go to the next full sheet, or 1,988 regular sheets.

3. How many pounds does 1,988 sheets

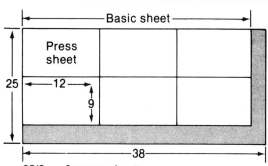

25/9 = 2 press sheets
and 38/12 = 3 press sheets

2 × 3 = 6

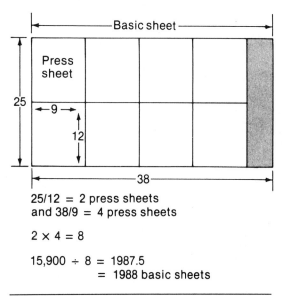

25/12 = 2 press sheets
and 38/9 = 4 press sheets

2 × 4 = 8

15,900 ÷ 8 = 1987.5
= 1988 basic sheets

Figure 18.3. Calculations to determine number of basic sheets needed to cut 15,900 press sheets.

of basis 60, 25- × 38-inch book paper weigh?
Referring to table 18.3, the equivalent weight is 120 pounds per 1,000.
We need 1.988 M (thousand sheets).

$$120 \times 1.988 = 238.56$$

Adams Brilliant Book

Shown in Sample Book number two.

Processes-- Offset and Letterpress
Color-- White
Finish-- Vellum and Coral
Packed-- Unsealed in Cartons
Basic Size-- 25 x 38

					16 Ctns	4 Ctns	1 Ctn	Less Ctn
BA	Size, M Wt		G	Per Ctn	Per 1,000 sheets			
Vellum Finish								
50	17.5x22.5-	41M	L	3600	14.04	15.09	17.26	25.89
50	23 x 35 -	85M	L	1800	29.11	31.28	35.79	53.68
50	38 x 50 -	200M	L	800	68.50	73.60	84.20	126.30
60	17.5x22.5-	40M	L	3200	17.13	18.40	21.05	31.58
60	19 x 25 -	60M	L	2400	20.55	22.08	25.26	37.89
60	23 x 29 -	84M	L	1800	28.77	30.91	35.36	53.05
60	23 x 35 -	102M	L	1500	34.94	37.54	42.94	64.41
→ 60	25 x 38 -	120M	L	1200	41.10	44.16	50.52	75.78 ←
70	17.5x22.5-	58M	L	2400	19.87	21.34	24.42	36.63
70	19 x 25 -	70M	L	2000	23.98	25.76	29.47	44.21
70	23 x 29 -	98M	L	1600	33.57	36.06	41.26	61.89
70	23 x 35 -	119M	L	1200	40.76	43.79	50.10	75.15
70	25 x 38 -	140M	L	1000	47.95	51.52	58.94	88.41
70	35 x 45 -	232M	L	600	79.46	85.38	97.67	146.51
80	23 x 35 -	136M	L	1100	46.58	50.05	57.26	85.88
80	25 x 38 -	160M	L	1000	54.80	58.88	67.36	101.04
80	35 x 45 -	266M	L	600	91.11	97.89	111.99	167.98
Coral Finish								
70	17.5x22.5-	58M	L	2400	21.66	23.26	26.59	39.90
70	19 x 25 -	70M	L	2000	26.15	28.07	32.10	48.16
70	23 x 35 -	119M	L	1200	50.80	54.54	62.36	93.57
70	25 x 38 -	140M	L	1000	52.29	56.14	65.19	97.64

Figure 18.4. A sample tear sheet from a print catalog for paper

To bid the job, the printer must determine the purchase cost of 238.56 pounds of book paper, basis 60, measuring 25 by 38 inches.

The task of calculating paper needs can become more complex than in this example, but the basic procedures are always the same:

1. Determine the spoilage allowance and find the total number of press sheets to run the job.

2. Calculate the most efficient method of cutting the stock sheets and figure the number of stock sheets required.

3. Find the total weight by referring to the paper's equivalent M weight.

Determining the Price of Paper

It is sometimes necessary to refer to a manufacturer's or distributor's price schedule to estimate the cost of the paper for the job without contacting a salesperson. Figure 18.4 shows a typical tearsheet from a price catalog. (The prices here are samples only and do not represent current paper costs.) It is important that the estimator have an understanding of price differences according to the quantity of paper ordered. It is often economical to buy more paper than is needed for the specific job. Consider an example.

Assume that we need 1,100 sheets of 25″ × 38″ size for a job we are to print. The line from figure 18.4 that interests us most is:

	16 Ctns	4 Ctns	1 Ctn	less Ctn
25 × 38	41.10	44.16	50.52	75.78

Just as with most manufactured products, the more we buy, the less the unit cost. If the supplier has to split open a carton to meet our needs, we pay more because of handling and the storage of the unused portion.

This is basis 60 paper, so the weight is 120 M (120 pounds per 1,000 sheets). There are 1,200 sheets per carton. We require 1,100, so we will figure the split-carton price. If the price is $75.78 per M, the cost per pound is $0.6315 ($75.78 divided by 120 pounds per M). The 1,100 sheets we need weigh 132 pounds (120 pounds per M × 1.1M). The cost of 1,100 sheets when purchased from a broken carton is $83.36 (132 pounds × $0.6315 per pound).

A quick glance at the carton price, however, shows that the price of an unbroken carton is over $30 less and we would get 100 more sheets if we bought a full box. The estimator must be aware of such price differentials and must spend time to calculate potential differences.

SECTION 2: INK

It is ink that forms the images you see as words and pictures in this book. Whatever the printing process, ink is transferred to the paper in the shape of the lines on the image carrier.

Not all ink images, however, are transferred to paper. While paper is the most common printing material, many other surfaces are used, such as metal foils, sheet laminates, plastics, and even wood veneers. Since surfaces other than paper are also used to receive ink, a special term is employed. A **substrate** is any base material used in printing processes to receive an image transferred from a printing plate. The term *substrate* will be used throughout the rest of this chapter.

Properties of Ink

Three properties of ink that control the ease and quality of image transfer are viscosity, tack, and drying quality.

Viscosity

The term **viscosity** is used to accurately describe the "body" of ink. Some inks are heavy (offset and letterpress inks) and some are light (flexographic and gravure inks). Viscosity, or resistance to flow, can be measured and is a term universally accepted in the printing industry.

Tack

Tack, or stickiness, is a property of ink that must be controlled in order to transfer images and deliver the sheet through the press. Tack can cause paper (especially coated paper) to adhere or stick to the blanket of an offset press. Ink that is excessively tacky may also pick the surface of the paper and cause misfeeding. (Recall that to pick means to lift or tear small pieces of the paper's surface.) Tack increases as one color is printed over another. When printing multicolor and process color work, decrease the amount of tack on successive runs. The first run should have the most tack. Each successive run should be printed with ink of less tack.

Drying Quality

The final, and extremely important, property of ink is its drying quality. There are two stages in the drying process. First, ink should instantly **set** or stick to the paper. When ink on the press sheet is set, it can be handled without smearing. If ink does not set as it is stacked in the delivery side of a press, the image will transfer to the bottom of the next sheet. This transfer of wet ink from sheet to sheet is called **set-off.**

The second stage in the drying process is called **hardening.** When ink has hardened, the vehicle (or solvent) has completely solidified on the paper surface and will not transfer. The time it takes for liquid ink to harden to a solid state is called the **drying time.**

Most natural or synthetic inks that contain a drying oil set and harden by a chemical process called **oxidation.** To oxidize is to combine with oxygen. By combining with the ink's drying oil, the oxygen of the air changes the vehicle of the ink from a liquid to a solid.

When an ink is printed on an absorbant substrate, drying results from a physical process called penetration. When ink dries by **penetration,** most of the vehicle is absorbed into the substrate. The ink vehicle is not changed to a solid state in this drying process. Inks that rely heavily on drying by penetra-

tion are not popular because the ink never hardens. Handling work printed with penetrating-drying ink usually results in ink transfer to the hands.

Some inks dry by **evaporation.** Resinous and other film-forming solutions in the ink vehicle pass off as vapor during the drying process. Drying by evaporation is much like drying by penetration. The volatile solutions disappear (by evaporating instead of penetrating), leaving an ink film on the surface of the substrate.

Ingredients in Ink

All printing inks are made from three basic ingredients: pigment, vehicle, and special additives. The **pigment** is the dry particles that give color to ink. The **vehicle** is the fluid that carries the pigment and causes it to adhere to the substrate. **Additives** are compounds that control ink characteristics such as tack, workability, and drying quality.

Pigments

The same basic pigments are used to produce all inks for the various printing processes. To some degree the pigment type determines whether the ink will be transparent or opaque. It also determines image permanency when exposed to various solvents such as water, oil, alcohol, and acid. Pigments are divided into four basic groups: black, white, inorganic color, and organic color pigments.

Black Pigments. Black pigments are produced by burning natural gas and oil onto a collecting device. The by-products from the burning process are called *thermal* black and *furnace* black. Furnace black, the most popular pigment, is made from oil in a continuous furnace. Sometimes furnace black is combined with thermal black, which is made from natural gas. Each type of black pigment has unique properties. The pigments are used individually or mixed to produce the best pigment for the specified printing process.

White Pigments.   White pigments are subdivided into two groups: opaque pigments and transparent pigments. White ink containing "opaque" pigments (through which light cannot pass) is used when transferring an image to cover a substrate or when overprinting another color. Opaque whites are also used for mixing with other inks to lighten the color or hue.

"Transparent" white pigments (through which light can pass) are used to allow the background material or ink to be seen. Transparent whites are used to reduce the color strength of another ink, to produce a tint of another color, and to extend or add to some of the more costly materials in the ink's formula. Transparent pigments are often referred to as "extenders" or "extender base."

Organic pigments.   Organic pigments are derived from living organisms. All organic pigments contain carbon and hydrogen, and most are made from petroleum; however, coal, wood, animal fats, and vegetable oils are also used in organic pigment manufacture. The major advantages of organic pigments over inorganic pigments is that organic pigments provide a wider selection of colors, tend to be richer in color, brighter, more transparent, and purer than inorganic pigments. These qualities are important, particularly for four-color process printing.

Inorganic pigments.   Inorganic pigments are chemical compounds, typically formed by precipitation. In the process, chemical solutions are mixed together and a chemical reaction takes place that produces an insoluble pigment (one which cannot be broken down into the primary chemicals from which it was formed). The insoluble pigment is then allowed to precipitate (settle), filtered out of the mixture, and dried. Eventual pigment color is determined by the proportions of the chemicals placed in solution. Cadmium yellow, for example, may contain the chemical cadmium sulfide in a compound with zinc sulfide. Inks made with inorganic pigments are less expensive to produce than those made with organic pigments. However, though they have good opacity, they lack some of the qualities of organic pigment inks, such as transparency.

Vehicles

The printing process and drying system determine the vehicle used in the manufacturing process. The vehicle of an ink is the liquid portion that holds and carries the pigment. It also provides workability and drying properties and binds the pigment to the substrate after the ink has dried.

Each vehicle used in the manufacture of ink has a slightly different composition. Nondrying vehicles used in newspaper and comic book production are made from penetrating oils such as petroleum and rosin. Resins are added to the oil base to control tack and flow.

Most letterpress and offset inks dry by oxidation. Linseed oil and litho varnish are the most widely used drying vehicles for these inks. The way in which the oil and varnish are "cooked" or prepared determines the viscosity of the final ink.

Gravure inks for paper consist of hydrocarbon solvents mixed with gums and resins. This combination causes rapid evaporation with or without heat. Naturally, evaporation rate increases with the use of heat.

Plastic, glassine, foil, and board inks are made with lacquer solvents and resins.

Alcohol and other fast-evaporating solvents combined with resins or gums are used to produce flexographic inks. Flexographic and gravure printing are capable of imaging many substrates. The substrate's surface characteristics will actually determine the final ingredients of the vehicle.

Screen printing inks dry by evaporation and oxidation. Therefore, a solvent-resin vehicle is used in their manufacture.

Offset and letterpress "heat-set" inks are made from rosin ester varnishes or soaps and hydrocarbon resins dissolved in petroleum solvents.

"Quick-setting" inks used for offset and letterpress consist of resin, oil, and solvent. During the drying process the solvent is absorbed by the substrate, leaving an ink film of resin and oil that dries by oxidation.

Additives

Some materials are added to ink during the manufacturing process, and some in the pressroom, to give the ink a special characteristic. Additives can reduce ink if it is too stiff. They can make ink less tacky or shorten its drying time. Additives should not be used carelessly. Many inks are "ready to use" and in normal situations will image best as they are. When you do use additives, be sure they are compatible with the ink's vehicle. The following list identifies major additives and describes their uses:

- *Reducers:* Varnishes, solvents, oils, or waxy or greasy compounds that reduce the tack or stickiness of ink. They also aid ink penetration and setting.
- *Driers:* Metallic salts added to inks to speed oxidation and drying of the oil vehicle. Cobalt, manganese, and lead are commonly used metallic salts. Cobalt is the most effective drier.
- *Binding varnish:* A viscous varnish used to toughen dried ink film. Can increase image sharpness, resist emulsification, eliminate chalking, and improve drying. Emulsification occurs in offset lithography when excessive fountain solution mixes with the ink. The result of emulsification is an ink that actually appears to break down and becomes greasy looking.
- *Waxes:* Usually cooked into the vehicle during the manufacturing process or can be added to the ink later. Paraffin wax, beeswax, carnauba wax, microcrystalline, ozokerite, and polyethylene are commonly used. Wax helps prevent set-off and sheet sticking. Wax also "shortens" the ink—that is, limits its ability to stretch or web.
- *Antiskinning agents:* Prevent ink on ink rollers from skinning and drying. If these agents are used excessively, the ink will not dry on the paper.
- *Cornstarch:* Can be used to add body to a thin ink. Also helps prevent set-off.

Lithographic Inks

There are many ink formulations to serve lithographic printers. Table 18.6 charts various ink formulations for different presses and substrates. Lithographic inks are used on sheet-fed and web-fed presses. A variety of vehicles are required because of the differences between sheet and web feeding and because of the many substrates on which the printer must transfer images.

Table 18.6. Lithographic Inks and Substrates

Lithographic Inks	
Sheet-Fed Presses	**Web-Fed Presses**
Substrates	*Substrates*
Paper	Mostly Paper
Foil	
Film	
Thin Metal	
Ink Vehicle Class	*Ink Vehicle Class*
Oxidative—Natural or synthetic drying oils.	Oxidative—Drying oil varnish.
Penetrating—Soluble resins, hydrocarbon oils & solvents, drying and semidrying oils and varnishes.	Penetrating—Hydrocarbons, oils & solvents, soluble resins.
Quick Set—Hard soluble resin, hydrocarbon oils and solvents, minimal drying oils and plasticizers.	Heat Set—Hydrocarbon solvents, hard soluble resins, drying oil varnishes, and plasticizers.
UV Curing—Highly reactive, cross-linking proprietary systems that dry by UV radiation.	UV Curing—Highly reactive, cross-linking proprietary systems that dry by UV radiation.
Gloss—Drying oils, very hard resins, minimal hydrocarbon solvents.	Thermal Curing—Dry by application of heat and use of special cross-linking catalysts.

The viscosity of lithographic ink varies according to the vehicle and pigment formulation. Viscosity means resistance to flow. Some inks appear fluid, while others are stiff and viscous. An ink that appears stiff does not necessarily require an additive such as a reducer. Some inks are "thixotropic": they become stiff and heavy when left standing in their containers. The ink is conditioned and milled by the ink train of the press before it reaches the printing unit. The ink that reaches the substrate is not as stiff and heavy as it was when it came from the can. The thixotropic phenomenon is typical in rubber-base ink formulations.

Rubber-Base Offset Ink

Rubber-base ink is a heavy formulation that gives quick setting and drying on both coated and uncoated paper. A good all-purpose offset and letterpress ink, it can remain on the press for long periods without skinning. It is also compatible with aquamatic or conventional dampening systems (see Chapter 13).

Rubber-base ink can be left on the press and will stay open overnight. After standing overnight, the ink on the rollers might appear to be setting or stiffening. To overcome this problem, leave a heavy ink film on the rollers. This can be accomplished by simply placing extra ink on the large oscillating roller and running the press. When starting up again after the long shutdown, run the press at idle speed. If the press is an aquamatic type, remove the dampening solution. If the press is slightly overinked, **sheet off** the excess with scrap sheets of paper. Sheet off ink by manually feeding paper in and out of the ink train. The paper will collect the excess ink and bring the ink train to a normally inked condition.

Rubber-base ink works well with aquamatic dampening systems in which the ink and water travel on the same rollers. The high tack and viscosity of rubber-base ink are well suited to this system. When inking-up, use just enough ink to cover the ink rollers and run low on the dampening solution. Then increase both ink and water to acquire the desired density. Do not overink and/or overdampen. It is also important to keep the pH (acid content) of the fountain solution between 4.5 and 5.5. The pH factor keeps the nonimage area of the plate clean. The use of additives with rubber-base inks is not recommended under normal conditions.

Nonporous Ink

Ink such as Van Son's Tough Tex is an example of an ink with a nonporous formulated vehicle. This ink is suited for plastic-coated or metallic types of papers. It dries by oxidation rather than by absorption. It is important not to overdampen this ink. Since the substrate is nonporous, the fountain solution remains in the ink. Excessively dampened ink will not dry or set and will easily smear or set off to the adjacent sheet. An acid level of less than 4.5 will also retard drying. Ink additives are not recommended with this ink formulation. To prevent set-off, do not allow a large pile to accumulate in the stacker and use small amounts of spray powder.

Quick-Set Ink

Quick-setting, low-tack ink is formulated with the color and process printer in mind. Quick-set ink is usually available in a full range of process colors that will trap in any sequence. **Trapping** refers to the degree of ink transfer onto wet or dry ink films already present on the substrate. Successful trapping depends on the relative tack and thickness of the ink films applied. Quick-set ink usually has very good drying qualities. It also produces an accurate color and is scuff and rub resistant.

Additives for Litho Ink

The five ink characteristics that can be controlled with ink additives include tack, flow or lay, drying quality, body, and scuff resistance. The following list identifies major litho ink additives and describes their effects and use:

- *Smooth lith:* A liquid that controls lay and set-off. Smooth lith also reduces tack, which prevents picking. Since it is a colorless solution, it will not change the hue of the ink. It will also aid in the drying process. Use approximately one capful per pound of ink. If you are using small amounts of ink, add smooth lith with an eyedropper.
- *Reducing compound:* Cuts the tack of ink without changing its body. This compound is used to alter the ink's viscosity. About ½ ounce of reducer to each pound of ink is a starting recommendation (a heaping tablespoon is approximately ½ ounce).
- *#00, #0 litho varnish:* A thin-bodied compound that rapidly reduces the ink's

body. Use approximately ¼ ounce of varnish to each pound of ink (a teaspoon is about ¼ ounce).

- *#1 litho varnish:* Reduces tack and body. It is used as a lay compound and prevents picking.

- *#2, #3, #4, and #5 litho varnishes:* Increase ink flow without changing the ink's body. Use about ¼ ounce of varnish to each pound of ink.

- *Overprint varnish:* A gloss finish used to print over already printed ink. Also used as an additive to help prevent chalking on coated paper. When overprinting with varnish, use it directly from the can. When using overprint varnish as an additive to prevent chalking, add 1½ ounces to each pound of ink.

- *Cobalt drier, concentrated drier, and three-way drier:* Basic types of driers. Cobalt and some concentrated driers are recommended for jobs that will be cut or folded soon after printing. These driers should not be used for process colors or inks that will be overprinted. Some concentrated driers are rub proof or binding. They are excellent for package printing where rough handling is anticipated. The ink's body can be built up with additives such as luster binding base, aqua varnish, and body gum.

- *Luster binding base:* Builds up viscosity, gives ink a luster finish, and makes ink more water repellent. Mix about 1½ ounces of binding base to each pound of ink.

- *Aqua varnish:* Builds up body and tack of ink. Works well for inks used in aquamatic types of press. Aids the ink in repelling water and helps prevent emulsification (ink breakdown). Use approximately ¼ ounce of aqua varnish to each pound of ink.

- *Body gum:* A heavy varnish that increases the ink's body, tack, and water repellency. Use ¼ ounce of body gum for each pound of ink.

- *Gloss varnish and wax compound:* Increase the ink's resistance to scratching and scuffing. Gloss varnish gives ink a bright finish and helps prevent chalking on coated papers. Use about ½ to 2 ounces of gloss varnish to each pound of ink, depending on the ink's color strength. In addition to improving scratch resistance, wax compound also reduces tack and picking. It should not be used when ink is to be overprinted. This additive is good for package or label printing. Use about ¼ to 1 ounce of wax compound to each pound of ink.

Troubleshooting Litho Ink Problems

Many problems that occur on press are ink related. Set-off, scumming, slow drying, chalking, hickies, and scuffing are just a few. There is seldom a single cause for each problem. Table 18.7 outlines common problems and their possible solutions.

Screen Printing Inks

Inks for screen printing are available in a rainbow of colors. Each type of screen printing ink has a binder suited to a specific class of substrate. Screen inks are formulated to be short and buttery for sharp squeegee transfer. Ink solvents should not evaporate rapidly. Rapid solvent evaporation would cause screen clogging during the printing process. Table 18.8 lists the many types of ink and substrates available to the screen printer.

Table 18.7. Troubleshooting Litho Ink Problems

Problem	Cause	Cure
Set-off in delivery pile	Acid fountain solution	Test pH; keep between 4.5 and 5.5
	Overinking	Adjust fountain roller speed or fountain keys
	Not enough drier	Add three-way or cobalt drier
	Ink not penetrating paper	Add smooth lith or #00 varnish
	Too much paper in delivery pile	Remove small piles from press
	Paper pile being squeezed before ink sets	Handle with care
	Using wrong ink	Consult literature, manufacturer or vendor
Scumming or Tinting	Bad plate	Make a new one
	Overinking/ underdampening	Adjust ink/water balance
	Incorrect pH	Keep between 4.5 and 5.5
	Too much drier	Change ink; use less drier
	Dirty molleton or dampening sleeve	Change cover or sleeve
	Soft ink	Add binding base, body gum, and aqua varnish
Slow ink drying	Incorrect pH—too acid	Test pH; keep between 4.5 and 5.5
	Bad ink/stock combination	Check with your paper or ink vendor
	Too little drier	Add drier
	Acid paper	Use different grade
Chalking	Too little drier	Add three-way or cobalt drier
	Wrong ink used	Overprint with varnish
	Ink vehicle penetrated too quickly	Add body gum or binding base
Hickies	Dust from cutting paper	Jog and wind paper before printing
	General dirt and dust	Clean, vacuum, and sweep press and press area
	Dried ink particles	Do not place drier or skinned ink into ink fountain
Scratching and scuffing	Overinked	Adjust ink fountain roller or keys
	Too little drier	Add drier concentrate or cobalt
	Wrong ink used	Overprint with varnish
	Ink not resistant enough	Add wax compound or scuff-proof drier

Table 18.8. Screen Printing Inks and Substrates

Ink Types	Substrates
Water soluble	Paper
Lacquer	Cardboard
Plastics	Textiles
Enamels	Wood
Metalic	Metal & foil
Ceramic	Glass
Electrical conducting	Lacquer-coated fabrics
Etching	Masonite
Luminescent	All Plastics
Fluorescent	

Poster Ink

Inks whose end use is to produce "PoP" (point-of-purchase) displays, posters, wallpaper, outdoor billboards, greeting cards, and packaging materials are classified as poster inks. The following list identifies major poster inks and describes their uses:

- *Flat poster ink:* Recommended for printing on paper and board stocks. Dries by solvent evaporation in about 20 minutes or can be force dried with special driers in seconds. Produces a flat finish and is used for displays, posters, and wallpaper.
- *Satin poster ink and halftone colors:* Recommended for printing on paper and cardboard displays. Dry by solvent evaporation in about 20 to 30 minutes or can be force dried in seconds. Are used to print "PoP" displays, posters, outdoor billboards, greeting cards, and packaging materials. Standard colors are opaque, and halftone colors are transparent.
- *Gloss poster inks:* Produce a hard gloss finish and are formulated for paper and

board stocks. Are used to print "PoP" displays, posters, greeting cards, corrugated displays, and packaging materials. Dry by evaporation in about 15 to 20 minutes or can be force dried in seconds.

- *Economy poster inks:* Much like flat poster ink series but lack the outdoor durability of flat poster ink. Made for supermarket and chain store applications. Dry to a flat finish in about 20 to 30 minutes by evaporation or can be force dried in seconds.
- *24-sheet poster ink:* Formulated mainly for outdoor use. Are waterproof and flexible and can withstand finishing processes such as die cutting, creasing, and folding. Recommended for poster, outdoor displays, sign cloth, and bumper stickers. Dry by evaporation in about 20 to 30 minutes or can be force dried.

Enamel Ink

Enamels are inks that flow out to a smooth coat and usually dry slowly to a glossy appearance. Since they penetrate the substrate less than poster inks do and dry mainly by oxidation, drying times are much longer. Enamel inks include gloss enamel (normal and fast dry), synthetic gloss enamel, and halftone enamel.

Gloss Enamels. Gloss enamels are used to image substrates such as wood, metal, glass, paper, cardboard, and fiber drums and as an adhesive base for flocking or beads as a decoration on a variety of products. Normal gloss enamels dry by oxidation and should be allowed to stand overnight. Fast-dry gloss enamels are commonly used to image polyethylene bottles and lacquer-coated fabrics in addition to the substrates listed for gloss enamel. This formulation will air dry in approximately 60 minutes or can be cured (dry and usable) in about 5 minutes at 180°F (82°C).

Synthetic Gloss Enamels. Synthetic gloss enamels have high durability and are excellent outdoor inks. The synthetic vehicle adheres to a wide variety of surfaces. These enamels are great for imaging metal, wood, masonite, glass, anodized aluminum, some types of plastics, novelties, synthetic decals, and packaging containers. They dry by oxidation in 4 to 6 hours or can be cured at 180°F (82°C) in about 30 minutes.

Halftone Enamels. Halftone enamels are formulated to give the special hues required for halftone process work. They are made to be durable under outdoor conditions. Halftone enamels are used on the same substrates as synthetic gloss enamels. Halftone vehicles dry to a satin finish (instead of a gloss finish) in 4 to 6 hours or can be cured in 30 minutes at 180°F (82°C). All halftone enamels are transparent inks.

Lacquer Ink

There are basically two types of lacquer inks:

- A general industrial lacquer ink that can produce a gloss or flat, hard finish with excellent adhesion to a wide variety of finishes
- A lacquer ink specifically formulated for making decals or printing on a specific substrate

Industrial Lacquer Inks. Industrial lacquer inks have numerous applications where chemical and abrasion resistance is important. They are used to image enamel, baked-urea or melamine-coated metal parts, and many polyester finishes. Because of their high opacity, lacquer inks are also popular for printing on dark-colored book cover stock. In addition, they are used to image lacquer and pyroxylin surfaces, many plastics (cellulose acetate, cellulose acetate butyrate, acrylics, nitrocellulose, ethyl cellulose) and many polyesters. Wood, paper, and foils can also be imaged with lacquers. Lacquer ink dries by solvent evaporation in about 30 minutes or can be jet dried in seconds. It can be cured for 10 minutes at 250°F (93°C) for industrial applications.

Decal Lacquers. Decal lacquers are made for printing decalcomanias. **Decalcomania** is the process of transferring designs from a specially printed substrate to another surface. Decalcomanias can also be printed on any surface where a flexible lacquer ink is needed. Consult the manufacturer's literature on printing procedures. Decal lacquer dries by solvent evaporation in 1 to 2 hours.

Printing on Plastic

Because so many plastics are being manufactured, a complete line of special inks is needed by screen printers. Plastic materials are either thermoplastic or thermosetting. A **thermoplastic** material is one that can be reformed. A **thermosetting** plastic cannot be altered once it has been formed and cured. Table 18.9 lists several thermoplastic and thermosetting materials and some of their uses. Inks used to print on plastic include acrylic lacquer, vinyl, mylar, and epoxy resin inks.

Acrylic Lacquer Inks. Acrylic lacquer inks are general purpose formulations for imaging thermoplastic substrates such as acrylics, cellulose butyrate, styrene, vinyl, and ABS (acrylontile, butadiene, and styrene). They are

Table 18.9. Screen Printing Inks, Plastic Substrates, and Uses

Screen Printing Inks	
Print on Thermoplastic Substrates	**For End Use**
ABS (Acrylontile, Butadiene, & Styrene)	Safety helmets, automotive components, refrigerator parts, & radio cases
Acrylics	Outdoor signs
Cellulose Acetate	Packaging, toys, book cover laminations, lampshades, & toothbrush handles
Cellulose Acetate Butyrate	Outdoor signs & packaging materials
Polyethylene	Cosmetic packaging
Polypropylene	Housewares, medicine cups, luggage, & toothpaste and bottle caps
Polystyrene	Construction, insulation, packaging, signs, displays, & refrigerator liners
Vinyl	PVC bottles, book covers, decorative tiles, & building components
Thermosetting Substrates	
Melamine and Urea	Cosmetic packaging & electrical components
Phenolics	Electronics and appliance industry (excellent insulators)

used to image vacuum-formed products; in fact, adhesion and gloss are improved by vacuum forming. They dry by solvent evaporation in about 30 minutes or can be force dried.

Vinyl Inks.   Vinyl inks are naturally formulated for both rigid and flexible vinyl substrates. These include novelties, inflatables, wall coverings, and book covers. They dry by evaporation in approximately 30 minutes or can be force dried. The vehicles can be formulated to produce a flat, a fluorescent, or a gloss finish. Gloss vinyl inks can be vacuum formed.

Mylar Inks.   Mylar inks are formulated to image untreated mylar and other polyester films. They dry by solvent evaporation in about 30 minutes or can be force dried.

Epoxy Resin Inks.   Epoxy resin inks are formulated for difficult-to-print surfaces such as phenolics, polyesters, melamines, silicones, and nonferrous metals and glass. Epoxy inks dry by a chemical process called **polymerization** and require a catalyst prior to use. Once the catalyst is properly added, the ink must stand approximately 30 minutes. This period of time allows the catalyst to become part of the solution and to activate the polymerization process. The polymerization drying process takes approximately 2 to 3 hours and about 10 days for maximum adhesion and chemical resistance. The ink can be cured in 30 minutes at 180°F, 10 minutes at 250°F, or 4 minutes at 350°F. Epoxy inks that require no catalyst must be cured or baked and are not recommended for outdoor use. They are used on thermosetting plastic, glass, and ceramics. They dry to a flat finish and must be baked at 400°F for 3 minutes or 350°F for 7 minutes. This type of epoxy ink is very suitable for nomenclature printing on circuit boards that must be soldered.

Ink for Printed Circuits and Nameplates

Resist inks include alkali removable resist, solvent removable resist, vinyl plating resist, plating resist, and solder resist inks.

Alkali Removable Resist Inks. Alkali removable resist inks are ideal for print-and-etch boards. They are less expensive than solvent removable resist ink and can reproduce fine lines. They cure at 250° to 265°F (120° to 130°C) in about 3 or 4 minutes. Air drying takes about 4 or 5 hours. Alkali removable ink can be removed from the board after etching with a 1% to 4% solution of sodium hydroxide.

Solvent Removable Resist Ink. Solvent removable resist ink, only black, is formulated for plating etch-resistant operations such as circuit boards or nameplates. It has excellent adhesion and printability and resists acids such as ferric chloride, ammonium persulphate, and other common etchants. Removable etch resist air dries in 30 minutes or can be dried in 5 minutes at 200°F (93°C).

Vinyl Plating Resist Inks. Vinyl plating resist inks are also formulated for plating or etch resist operations. They air dry in approximately 30 minutes or in 10 minutes at 200°F (93°C). They can be removed after etching with trichlorethylene or xylol.

Plating Resist Inks. Plating resist inks are formulated specifically for plating operations.

The inks are recommended for long plating cycles. Curing takes about 30 minutes at 200°F (93°C). The resist can be removed from the substrate with trichlorethylene or xylol.

Solder Resist Inks. Solder resist inks are alkyd melamine formulations for printing on copper or copper-treated coatings. Solder resist inks cure in 20 minutes at 250°F (140°C), 10 minutes at 300°F (150°C), and 5 minutes at 350°F (160°C).

Textile Ink

The three basic inks available to the textile printer are standard textile, plastisol, and dye inks.

Standard Textile Inks. Standard textile inks are formulated for cotton and other nonsynthetic fabrics. Ease of application makes these the most widely used inks for natural fabrics. They dry to a flat finish in about 45 minutes or can be cured in 5 minutes at 275°F (135°C).

Plastisol Inks. Plastisol textile inks are formulated for woven or knitted cotton and some synthetic fabrics. These inks can be printed directly onto the fabric or onto a coated release paper. When printing directly onto the fabric, cure for 3 minutes at 300°F (150°C). When printing onto release paper, cure for 1½ to 2 minutes at 225° to 250°F (107° to 120°C). Images on release paper can be transferred to fabric with an iron or a heat transfer machine. Be sure to allow the release paper and fabric to cool before peeling away the paper backing.

Dye Inks. Dye textile inks are water-in-oil concentrated pigments that must be mixed with a clear extender. The proportions in the mixture determine the color strength. These inks are used to image cotton, rayon, linen, some nylon, and other synthetic blends. Dyes dry in 3 minutes at 300°F (150°C) and in 5 minutes at 250°F (120°C). Water-soluble stencil material cannot be used with dyes because of the water content of the dyes. For best results use knife-cut lacquer or a direct emulsion when preparing the stencil.

Letterpress Inks

Letterpress was once the major printing process. Much of what is known about ink today was discovered for the letterpress process. Although letterpress is gradually being replaced by other processes, it is still used to produce newspapers, magazines, packaging, and some commercial printing.

Some letterpress inks are much like offset inks. They are viscous, tacky compositions that dry mainly by oxidation. Letterpress inks include job, quickset, gloss, moisture-set, and rotary inks.

Job Ink

Job inks are standard items kept in most shops. They must be formulated to be compatible with a wide variety of presses and papers. By using additives, their characteristics can be altered to be short-bodied for platen press work, to flow well on faster automatic presses, or to set properly on different papers. In many shops a rubber-base offset ink is a common job ink for both general printing on platen letterpresses and small duplicator machines.

Quick-Set Ink

Quick-set inks are used when it is necessary to immediately print another run or color or to subject the substrate to finishing operations. They are used mostly on coated papers and boards. The ink's vehicle is a resin-oil combination. It dries by a combination of oxidation, absorption, and coagulation. When printed, the oil penetrates the stock and leaves the heavy material on the surface to dry by oxidation and coagulation (thickening).

Gloss Ink

Gloss inks are made of synthetic resins (modified phenolic and alkyd) and drying oils that do not penetrate the substrate as other inks do. This resistance to penetration is what produces the high gloss. A combination of gloss ink with a paper that resists penetration will produce the best ink finish. Since the ink does not penetrate the substrate rapidly, it must dry mainly by oxidation and coagulation.

Moisture-Set Ink

Moisture-set inks are used mainly in printing food packaging. Because they are free from odor, they are used to print wrappers, containers, cups, and packaging materials. The ink vehicle is actually a water-insoluble binder dissolved in a water-receptive solution. The ink sets as the water-insoluble binder adheres to the paper when the water-receptive solvent is exposed to humidity. Atmospheric humidity or the moisture in the stock might be sufficient to cause setting on some substrates.

Rotary Ink

Rotary inks are used mainly to print newspapers, magazines, and books. These publications require different substrates. Book papers range from soft to hard and are coated or uncoated. Rotary book-printing inks flow well and are quick setting to be compatible with these substrates. Magazines are usually printed on coated or calendered paper, which often requires a quick-drying heat-set ink. Heat-set inks are composed of synthetic resins dissolved in a hydrocarbon solvent. Presses using heat-set inks must be equipped with a heating unit, cooling rollers, and an exhaust system.

Flexographic Ink

Flexography is a relief process much like rotary letterpress. This economical process is now printing a variety of substrates with a fast-drying volatile ink. "Flexo" printing is commonly used to transfer an image to plastic films for laminating to packaging, glassine, tissue, kraft, and many other paper stocks. It is also a popular process for printing wrapping paper, box coverings, folding cartons, and containers.

Flexographic ink is formulated with alcohols and/or esters and a variety of other solvents. Plasticizers and waxes are used to make the ink flexible and rub resistant. These volatile ingredients cause the ink to dry extremely rapidly by evaporation.

Water-base inks are also used to print paper, board, kraft, and corrugated substrates. There are many different water-base vehicles, such as ammonia and casein. Water-base inks are limited, however, to absorbent stocks, rather than nonabsorbent materials such as foil or plastic, because of the ink's slow-drying and low-gloss characteristics. Water-base inks are popular because of ease of use and low cost.

Gravure Inks

Gravure printing uses two major kinds of ink: publications ink and packaging ink. Both are available in a full range of colors and properties. Publications ink basically consists of modified resins, pigments, and hydrocarbon solvents. Most packaging ink is formulated with nitrocellulose and various modifiers.

Because of the increased popularity of gravure printing on a variety of substrates, ink making and ink classification has become confusing. Many resins and solvents are used to make the ink, and most are not "compatible" or cannot be mixed together. In order to know which solvents are to be used with the inks purchased, a major ink supplier initiated the classification of various types of inks by using letters. In this system, all inks of a single type are compatible. Types of inks are identified by letters as follows:

- A-type inks are low-cost aliphatic hydrocarbons
- B-type inks use resins and aromatic hydrocarbons
- C-type inks are made up of modified nitrocellulose and an ester class of solvent
- D-type inks consist basically of a polyamide resin and alcohol
- E-type inks are based on binders thinned with alcohols
- T-type inks consist of modified chlorinated rubber reduced with aromatic hydrocarbons
- W-type inks use water and sometimes alcohol as a reducing solvent

This method of classification indicates which solvents should be used to obtain the proper viscosity. When you are mixing ink, carefully examine the technical data sheets, since ink suppliers frequently use trade names rather than "type" classifications.

The Pantone Matching System (PMS)

The **Pantone Matching System (PMS)** is a method universally accepted for specifying and mixing colors. Using this technique, artists and customers can select any of the more than 500 hues from a "swatch book." The printer can then mix the desired color by using the swatch number and referring to a "formula guide." The guide gives the formula for making the color. It identifies the basic colors involved and indicates how much of each to mix together. The ten basic colors in the PANTONE MATCHING SYSTEM are rhodamine red, purple, reflex blue, yellow, warm red, rubine red, process blue, green, black, and transparent white.

Key Terms

basis weight
ream
M weight
equivalent weight
substance weight
nonstandard cut
spoilage allowance

substrate
viscosity
tack
set-off
oxidation
penetration
evaporation

pigment
vehicle
additives
trapping
thermoplastic
thermosetting
Pantone Matching System

Questions for Review

1. What are the three major expenses in the printing industry?

2. What are the five main paper types?

3. What is basis weight?

4. What is M weight?

5. Why is spoilage always considered when calculating paper needs?

6. Briefly outline the general procedures for calculating paper needs.

7. Define the word *substrate*.

8. List six factors that will slow down the ink-drying process.

9. Define the words *chalking* and *polymerization*.

10. Describe the difference between an inorganic and an organic ink pigment.

11. What is an ink vehicle? List an example for each of the following inks:
    a. Offset
    b. Screen
    c. Letterpress
    d. Flexographic
    e. Gravure

12. Define the words *emulsification* and *thixotropic*.

13. Match the cure to the following ink-related problems:

    —Set-off   a. Jog paper and clean press area well.

    —Scumming   b. Adjust ink/water balance.

    —Chalking   c. Remove small piles from the press.

    —Hickies   d. Add wax compound or scuff-proof drier.

    —Scratching   e. Add body gum or binding base.

14. What screen printing ink or inks would be best for printing an outdoor sign on the following substrates?
    a. Paper
    b. Plastic
    c. Metal
    d. Wood

15. What plastic ink or inks would be used for printing the following substrates or products?
    a. Dark book cover
    b. Polyester film
    c. Drinking glasses
    d. Printed circuit
    e. Iron-on for a T-shirt made of woven cotton and polyester
    f. Directly onto a sweatshirt

16. Briefly describe the properties of the following inks:
    a. Letterpress
    b. Flexographic
    c. Gravure

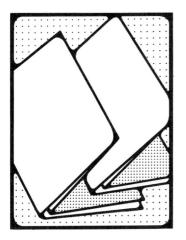

Chapter Nineteen

Finishing Operations

Anecdote to Chapter Nineteen

Around A.D. 800, Charlemagne, the Frankish king who ruled from 742 to 814, ordered every abbot, bishop, and count to keep in permanent employment a copyist who would reproduce books by hand, writing in only roman letters. The bound books that the scribes let-

An industrial binding operation from around 1880

tered were to be stored in special rooms called "scriptoriums," which later evolved into what we know today as libraries.

Binding the finished pages together was a process nearly as important as copying. It was felt that just as each page of a manuscript needed to be decorated, so too did the case that held the pages together. The more valuable works were often encased in bindings of precious metal, such as gold and silver. They were sculptured works of art. These books were often so cumbersome that special lecterns were built just to hold them while they were being read. There is even a recorded instance when a reader accidently dropped a well-bound, sculptured book and was seriously injured. He almost had to have his leg amputated.

By the 1400s, bookbinding had grown into a profession with several special subdivisions. The person who sewed the pages and built the cover was called the "forwarder." The binding was passed to a "finisher," who ornamented the cover. When a book was destined for a great deal of use, hog skin was frequently used as the binding. If it was to be a more expensive, carefully handled volume, calf or goat skin was often the choice. Large, inexpensive works were often bound in thin planks of wood.

The process of binding books remained a slow, specialized craft until the eighteenth century. The illustration shows one part of an industrial binding operation from around 1880. Several activities are taking place in this room. The women at the right are hand folding press sheets that will become signatures. Each is using an "ever-in-hand paper-folder," which today we would call a bone knife, to crease each edge as a fold is made. The two rows of tables hold the folded signatures, which are piled in the proper sequence as they will appear in the finished book. The women gather the book together as they walk down the rows, picking up one signature from each pile. After the signatures are gathered, three holes are punched through the edge of each one by the "stabbing-machine." The seated women in front of the large power wheel are all involved with hand sewing the signatures together by passing thread through the punched holes. On the floor below, the sewed books are trimmed, glue is applied to the backs, and covers are put in place.

The bindery of 1880 looks a bit crude to us today, but it was a big step beyond the tedious book work of five hundred years before. The work that took months to complete in 1400 took only days in 1880. The same job can be done today in only a few minutes.

Objectives for Chapter Nineteen

After completing this chapter, you will be able to:

– List the steps in safely operating an industrial paper cutter, including identification of machine parts, safety steps, size adjustment, and actual cutting.

– Describe the basic folding devices, including the differences between knife and buckle folders.

- List and define the common assembling processes, including gathering, collating, and inserting.
- List and define the common binding proc-

esses, including adhesive binding, side binding, saddle binding, self-covers, soft covers, and casebound covers.

Introduction

Few printing jobs are delivered to the customer in the same form as the one in which they leave the printing press. Some work, such as simple business forms or posters, requires no additional handling other than boxing or wrapping. But the vast majority of printed products require some sort of additional processing in order to meet the job requirements. Those operations performed after the job has left the press are called **finishing.** Finishing might be performed by a separate company specializing in those operations; it might be handled by "in line" equipment that receives each piece as it leaves the press; or it might be handled in a special section of the shop.

The most common finishing operations are cutting, folding, assembling, and binding. Techniques such as embossing, perforating, scoring, and die cutting were discussed in Chapter 2, but they are often called finishing procedures. The tasks do not follow any certain order or sequence and are not necessarily all performed on the same job (although it is certainly possible). The following sections examine some basic techniques within each of the four common operations. Because paper is the most widely used printing receiver, the discussions will be restricted to devices and techniques used to finish paper materials.

Cutting

The Basic Device

The basic paper-cutting device used in the industry is called a **guillotine cutter,** or simply a "paper cutter" (figure 19.1). Guillotine cutters are manufactured in all sizes and degrees of sophistication. Size is defined by the widest cut that can be made. Sophistication is described by the speed with which the machine can be set up and a cut taken.

The bed of the cutter is the flat table that holds the paper pile. The back guide, or fence, is movable and is usually calibrated with some measurement system that tells the operator the distance of the guide from the knife (figure 19.2). The side guides are stationary and are always at perfect right angles to the edge of the bed. The clamp is a metal bar that can be lowered into contact with the paper pile before a cut is made. Its purpose is to compress the pile to remove air and to keep the paper from shifting during the cut. The cutter blade itself is usually mounted up away from the operator's view and hands. When activated, the blade moves down and across to cut the pile in one single motion.

The simplest sort of guillotine cutter is

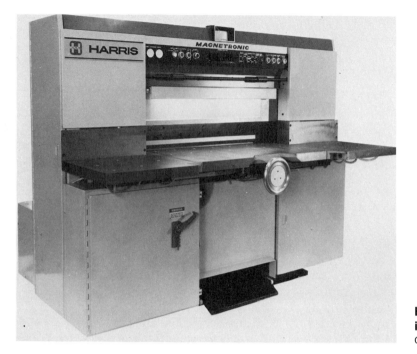

Figure 19.1. An industrial paper cutter
Courtesy of Harris Corporation

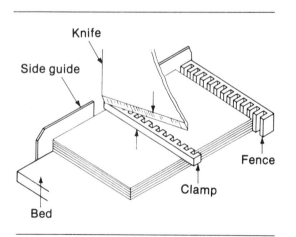

Figure 19.2. Diagram of a guillotine cutter The blade of a guillotine cutter moves down and across to cut the paper pile.

called a **lever cutter** and obtains its power from the strength of the operator. The worker moves a long lever that is directly linked to the cutter blade. The most common device is a power cutter, which automatically makes the cut at the operator's command. A frequent source of power is an electric motor, which operates a hydraulic pump.

The mere movement of paper onto and off the bed of the cutter is the most fatiguing part of the paper cutter's job. Consider that a single ream of paper might weigh 200 pounds and that several tons of paper are usually cut in a single day. Many devices are equipped with air film tables that work to reduce the fatigue factor. With this system, the paper is supported by a blanket of air that escapes from small openings in the table to allow for easy movement of any size of paper pile over an almost frictionless surface (figure 19.3).

One of the most time-consuming actions when making a series of different cuts is resetting the fence, which controls the size of cut to be made. Automatic spacing devices can be programmed to "remember" the order and setting for as many as twenty different cuts. As the operator removes a pile, the machine readjusts the back fence and is ready for the next cut by the time the new pile is in place. Some cutters can split the back fence into three sections and then independently control each position so that three different lengths can be cut with one motion of the cutter blade.

Cutting Safety

The guillotine cutter is named after the infamous "guillotine" that so efficiently removed

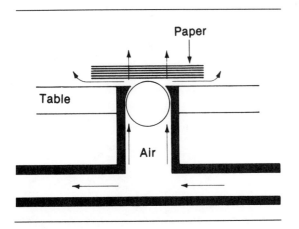

Figure 19.3. Side view of an air film table A sketch of the side view of an air film table shows one of the small openings that release air onto the table surface.

heads in times past. Today's guillotine cutter is intended to cut only paper. But, like its ancestor, it will easily cut almost anything placed in its path.

Today's paper cutters require an operator to use both hands to activate the cutter blade. Early machines had no such safety feature. As a result, many operators lost fingers or hands. No device is foolproof, so it should be a standard procedure to keep hands away from the blade and blade path at all times.

It is also a wise practice never to place anything but paper on the bed of a cutter. A steel rule or paper gauge can cause damage by chipping the blade's cutting edge. This will require resharpening the blade.

Operating a Paper Cutter

Paper cutting is a critical operation. The time and effort that go into every job can be made useless by a single sloppy cut. The fence and side guide of a paper cutter are similar in function to the side guide and headstop of a printing press. If the pile is in contact with both guides, the sheet will be cut square and to the proper length.

Every job delivered to the paper cutter should have a cutting layout attached to the pile. The **cutting layout** is generally one sheet of the job that has been ruled to show the location and order of the cuts. Sequence does not seem important at first thought, but if the cutting layout is not faithfully followed, some part of the main sheet will be damaged and a job will have to be done over.

Determine the length of the first cut from the cutting layout and adjust the back fence to that dimension. Place a pile on the cutter table and seat it carefully against both the fence and the side guide. Activate whatever control system the machine uses and make the cut.

Remove the scrap (generally to be binned and sold back to the paper mill) and pull the cut pile free. If the job is large and the cutter is not equipped with automatic spacing, the same cut might be repeated for the entire pile. Then the fence would be adjusted for the next cut, and the entire pile would be cut again. If automatic spacing is used, the cutter goes to the next position at the operator's command.

Folding

The Basic Devices

The most basic type of folding device is called a **bone folder.** Printers have used it for hundreds of years to do hand folding. The process is simple. The printer registers one edge of the sheet with the other and then slides the bone folder across the seam to make a smooth crease (figure 19.4). Bone folders are used today only for very small, prestige jobs. Nearly all industrial folding is now done by high-speed machines. The two common folding devices are called knife and buckle folders.

Knife folders operate by means of a thin knife blade that forces a sheet of paper between two rotating rollers. The action takes place in two steps. First the sheet is carried into the machine and comes to rest at a fold gauge (figure 19.5a). Just as in a press, the sheet is positioned by means of a moving side guide. Next the knife blade is lowered between the two rotating rollers until the knurled (ridged) surfaces catch the sheet, crease it, and pass it out of the way so the next sheet can be moved into register (figure 19.5b). If sets of rollers and knives are stacked one over the other, many folds can be made on the same sheet as the piece travels from one level to the next.

Buckle folders (figure 19.6) operate on a similar notion of the sheet passing between two rotating rollers. The technique that directs the piece, however, is a bit different. Instead of a knife or some other object contacting the paper and causing the crease, the

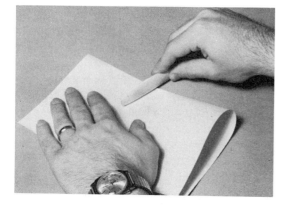

Figure 19.4. Example of a bone folder
Courtesy of SUCO Learning Resources and R. Kampas

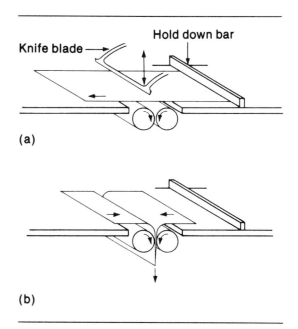

(a)

(b)

Figure 19.5. Diagram of a knife folder operation

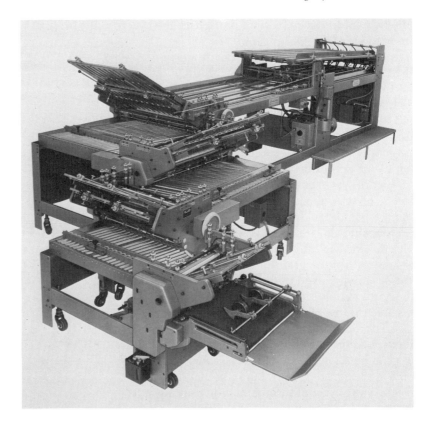

Figure 19.6. A buckle folder
Courtesy of Bell and Howell/ Baumfolder Division/Philipsburg Division

sheet is made to buckle or curve and passes by its own accord into the rollers. The sheet is passed between two folding plates by a drive roller until the sheet gauge is reached. The gap between the plates, however, is so slight that the paper can do nothing more than pass through the opening. As the piece hits the sheet gauge, the drive roller continues to move the sheet, which buckles directly over the folding rollers and passes through the two to be creased and carried on to the next level.

Sequence of Folds

Two important terms must be understood when discussing the sequence of folding. They are "right-angle" and "parallel" folds. Figure 19.7a shows a traditional formal fold, called

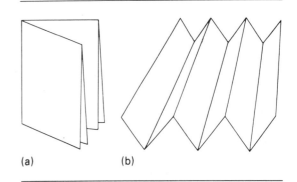

(a)   (b)

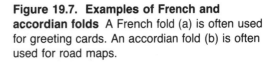

Figure 19.7. Examples of French and accordian folds A French fold (a) is often used for greeting cards. An accordian fold (b) is often used for road maps.

a **French fold,** that is frequently used in the production of greeting cards. To make a French fold, first fold a sheet across its length. Then make a second fold at a right angle to the first across the width. A French fold is a **right-angle fold** because it has at least one fold that is at a right angle to the others. Figure 19.7b illustrates an accordion fold that is commonly used in the preparation of road maps. An **accordion fold** can be made in a number of ways, but each fold is always parallel to every other crease and is therefore called a parallel fold.

Ideally, all parallel folds should be made with the crease running in the same direction as (parallel to) the grain of the paper. Great stresses are involved with folding, and grain direction should be considered whenever possible (figure 19.8).

The final folding product is a result of the use of either parallel or right-angle creases or a combination of the two. The sequence of folds is an important consideration that must be taken into account throughout the printing process.

In Chapter 10 the ideas of signature, work-and-turn, and work-and-tumble imposition were discussed. When laying out for imposition, the order of folds in the bindery room dictates the position of each paper or form on the press sheet. Figure 19.9 reviews four different ways that a single sheet can be folded to produce a sixteen-page signature. It also shows the page layouts for one side of the sheet. If the job is laid out for one sequence of folds but another sequence is actually used, the final result will be unusable. The wisest procedure is always to prepare the dummy by using a signature that has been folded on the piece of equipment and in the same sequence that will be used on the final press sheets.

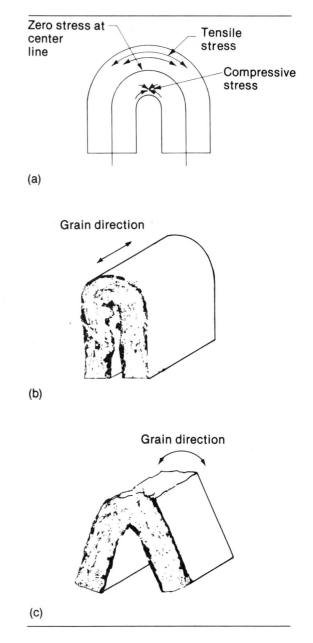

(a)

(b)

(c)

Figure 19.8. Diagram showing areas of stress in folding Fibers bend easily with the grain (b), but tend to bread break because of the stresses when folding against the grain (c).
Courtesy of Mead Paper

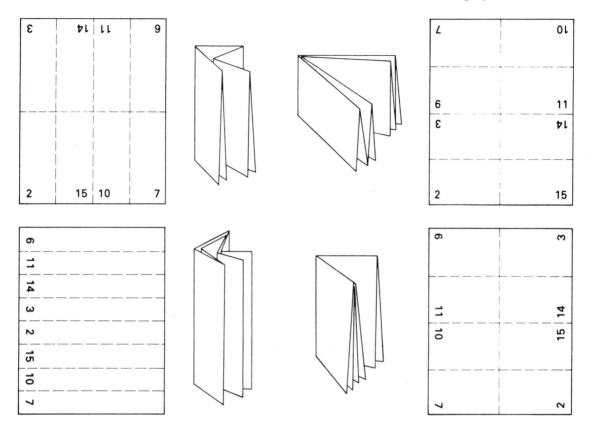

Figure 19.9. Four ways to fold a sixteen-page signature

Assembling

Understanding Terms

Assembling is a term that is generally used to describe several similar operations that have the same final goal. Before a printed product can be bound, the separate pieces must be brought together into a single unit. For a case-bound book, the unit might be made up of ten signatures; for a pile of NCR forms, it might be only two sheets. Whatever the size

of the unit, assembling generally includes gathering, collating, and inserting.

Gathering is the process of assembling signatures by placing one next to the other (figure 19.10a). Gathering is commonly used to prepare books whose page thickness will be greater than ⅜ inch (0.95 cm).

Collating once meant checking the sequence of pages before a book was bound, but now it means gathering individual sheets instead of signatures.

Inserting is combining signatures by

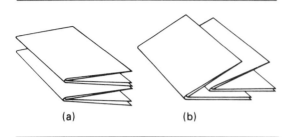

(a)   (b)

Figure 19.10. Two ways of assembling signatures Gathered signatures are placed next to each other (a). Inserted signatures are placed one within another (b).

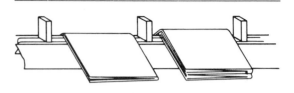

Figure 19.11. Diagram of open signatures placed at saddlebars on a conveyor

placing one within another (figure 19.10b). Inserting can be done for pieces whose final page thickness will be less than ½ inch (1.27 cm).

Basic Assembling Techniques

Assembling procedures are either manual, semiautomatic, or totally automatic.

Manual Assembly. Manual assembly is exactly what the term implies. Piles of sheets or signatures are laid out on a table, and workers pick up one piece from each stack and gather, collate, or insert them to form bindery units. Equipment is available that improves the process a bit by having the worker stationary and moving the piles of a circular table. But the process is still slow and clumsy. Manual assembly is reserved for either extremely small jobs or for work so poorly planned that it cannot be assembled in any other way. Nearly all contemporary industrial assembly is done with semiautomatic or automatic equipment.

Semiautomatic Assembly. Semiautomatic assembly machines require no human interaction with the devices except to pile the sheets

or signatures in the feeder units. In semiautomatic inserting, a moving chain passes in front of feeder stations. At each station an operator opens a signature and places it on the moving conveyor at "saddlebar" (figure 19.11). The number of stations at the machine will be the same as the number of signatures making up the unit or book. By the time each saddlebar has moved past every station, an entire unit has been inserted or assembled and the saddle pin pushes the unit off the machine. The unit can then be moved in line with a bindery unit for fastening or can be stacked for storage and later binding. Little gathering or collating is done with semiautomatic equipment, but the same general principle is used as for inserting.

Automatic Assembly. Automatic assembling machines use a conveyer device moving past feeder stations. But a machine instead of a person delivers the sheet or signature (figure 19.12). Almost all automatic systems are in line with bindery equipment so that assembly and fastening are accomplished at the same time.

Two designs of feeder mechanisms are used on automatic gathering devices (figure 19.13). Both allow for continuous loading of signatures because pieces are delivered from the bottom of the stack. With the swinging arm device, a vacuum sucker foot lowers one

Figure 19.12. Automatic gathering during assembly Courtesy of Muller Martini Corporation

signature into position to be received by a gripper arm. The arm, with signature in hand, swings over the conveyer system and drops the piece in place on the belt. The rotary design uses the same suction system, but a rotating wheel with gripper fingers removes the signature and delivers it to the moving chain. With each rotation, the device can gather two signatures and is therefore considered a faster system than the swinging arm mechanism.

Automatic collating equipment is similar in design to gathering machines, except that feeding is generally done from the top of the pile, as with most automatic printing presses. Even though the machine must be stopped to load the feeder units, the device is nearly as efficient as continuous devices because a great many single sheets can be placed in the same area that only a few large signatures would take up.

Automatic inserting devices are almost always linked with a closed system of operations that extends from the composition room through plate preparation, press, on past assembly to fastening, trimming, labeling for mailing, and even bundling of piles by zip code order. Magazines such as *Time* and *Newsweek*, with editions of sometimes a million copies and little allowance for production time, require accurate planning, speed, accuracy, and a tightly controlled closed system of production. High-speed inserting is done by a combination of vacuum and grippers that removes the signature, opens it, and places it in the proper sequence with the other signatures in the job.

Binding

It is difficult to categorize neatly all the methods used by the printing industry to fasten together the assembled unit into its final form. The type of cover used on the printed piece is often confused with the actual method of attaching the pages. Sheets or signatures can

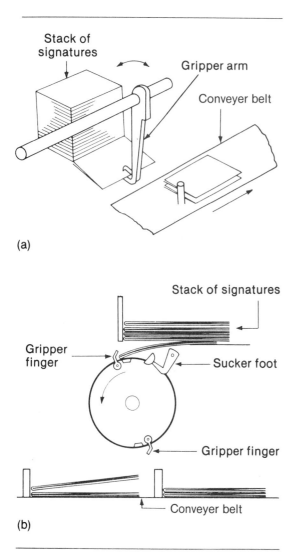

(a)

Stack of
signatures

Gripper arm

Conveyer belt

Stack of signatures

Gripper
finger

Sucker foot

Gripper finger

Conveyer belt

(b)

Figure 19.13. Two types of feeder mechanisms used on automatic gathering machines A swinging arm mechanism and suction action are used to move signatures onto a conveyer belt (a), or a rotating wheel with gripper fingers serves the same purpose (b).

be fastened together by using such techniques as adhesive, side, or saddle binding. The fastened pages can be covered with self-, soft, or casebound covers.

Adhesive Binding

The simplest form of **adhesive binding,** called **padding,** is found on the edge of the common notepad. In the adhesive binding process, a pile of paper is clamped together in a press and a liquid glue is painted or brushed along one edge. The most common material is applied cold and is water soluble while in a liquid state, but becomes insoluble in water after it dries. Individual sheets can be easily removed by pulling one away from the padding compound.

The popular "paperback" or "pocket" book is an example of an adhesive binding technique called perfect or **patent binding.** The perfect fastening process is generally completely automatic (figure 19.14). If signatures rather than individual sheets are combined, the folded edge is trimmed and roughened to provide a greater gripping surface. The liquid adhesive (generally hot) is then applied, and a gauze-like material called

Figure 19.14. An automatic perfect fastening machine
Courtesy of Gane Brothers and Lane, Inc.

crash is sometimes embedded in the pasty spine to provide additional strength.

Adhesive binding offers many advantages in both book and magazine publishing. Not only is the process relatively fast and inexpensive, but it can be used to combine a number of different printing substrates in the same publication. In addition to the printed signatures used for most of the publication, special signatures or single pieces of paper, printed plastic sheets, and other printed substrates can be added to the publication. Paper of different thickness and different finishes may also be added without affecting the binding process.

Side Binding

A common office stapler is probably the most familiar method of **side binding**. With this technique, the fastening device is passed through a pile at a right angle to the page surface. In addition to the wire staple, side binding can be accomplished by mechanical binding, looseleaf, or side sewing.

Mechanical Binding. Mechanical binding is a process that is usually permanent and does not allow for adding sheets. One of the most common forms is a wire that resembles a spring coil. The wire runs through round holes that have been punched or drilled through the sheets and cover. The coil is generally inserted by hand into the first several holes of the book. Then the worker pushes the wire against a rotating rubber wheel that spins the device on the rest of the way.

Looseleaf Binding. Looseleaf binding devices are considered permanent, but they allow for the removal and addition of pages. The casebound three-ring binder is a popular item, but there are a great many other forms.

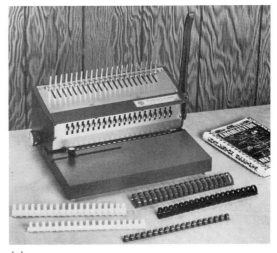
(a)

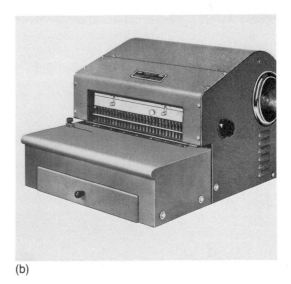
(b)

Figure 19.15. A hand-operated plastic punch and binder (a) and a power-operated punch (b)
Courtesy of Plastic Binding Corporation

Binder posts, spring back, and expansion posts are only three examples. An increasingly popular technique is a plastic comb binder (figure 19.15). With this system, a special device is used to punch the holes, and another device expands the plastic clips so the pages can be inserted on the prongs. The binder can be opened later to add sheets or it can be removed completely and used to fasten another unit.

Side-Sewn Binding.   One pattern for the side sewing of a book is shown in figure 19.16. With hand sewing, the pile is drilled (always an odd number of holes) and then clamped in place so the individual pages will not shift. A needle and thread is passed in and out of each hole from one end of the book to the other and then back again to the last hole, where the cord is tied off. Automatic equipment has been designed that produces a side-sewn book rapidly and accurately, although with a different thread pattern than the hand technique (figure 19.17). The main drawback to side-sewn or wire-stapled side binding is that the book does not lie flat when open.

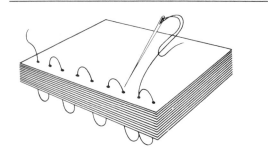

Figure 19.16. Diagram of hand side sewing of a book

Saddle Binding

Saddle binding is the process of fastening one or more signatures along the folded or backbone edge of the unit. The term comes from the fact that a signature held open at the

Figure 19.17. An automatic side-stitching device
Courtesy of Harris Corporation

fold resembles—with some imagination—the shape of a horse's saddle.

Popular news magazines are fastened by saddle wire stitching. With large editions, the stitching is done automatically in line with the inserting of signatures. Saddle wire stitching can also be done by hand with large staple machines. It can be performed semiautomatically: the operator merely places the signature over a support, and the wire is driven through the edge, crimped, and then delivered (figure 19.18). This method of wire fastening is generally restricted to thicknesses of less than ½ inch (1.27 cm).

Smyth sewing is commonly considered the highest-quality fastening technique in the world today. Sometimes called "center-fold" sewing, the process produces a book that will lie nearly flat when it is opened. Nearly all Smyth sewn books are produced on semiautomatic or completely automatic equipment. Semiautomatic devices require an operator to open each signature and place it on a conveyer belt that moves it to the sewing mechanism and combines it with the rest of the book. Automatic machines are usually in line with a gathering mechanism that delivers a single unit to the sewing device.

Self-Covers

Self-covers are produced from the same material as the body of the book and generally carry part of the message of the piece. Newspaper and some news magazines have self-covers. The method requires no special techniques to assemble or attach the cover to the body of the work. The process is generally restricted to the less expensive binding techniques, such as wire side or saddle fastening.

Soft Covers

Soft covers are made from paper or paper fiber material with greater substance than that used for the body of the book. Soft covers rarely carry part of the message of the piece. They are intended to attract attention and to provide slight, temporary protection. Paper-

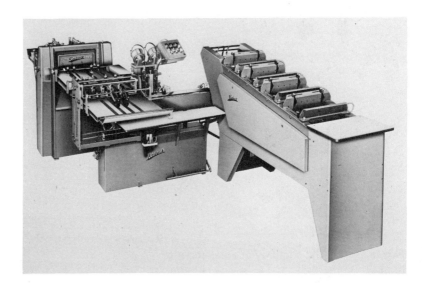

Figure 19.18. A semiautomatic saddle-stitching device
Courtesy of F. P. Rosback Company

back books are one example of their use. Soft covers can be glued in place, as with perfect binding, or can be attached by stitching or sewing. The covers are generally cut flush with the pages of the book.

Casebound Covers

A **casebound cover** is a rigid cover that is generally associated with high-quality bookbinding. The covers are produced separately from the rest of the book and are formed from a thick fiber board glued to leather, cloth, or some form of moisture-resistant impregnated paper (figure 19.19). A casebound cover extends over the edge of the body of the book by perhaps ⅛ inch (0.32 cm). This "turn-in" provides additional protection for the closed pages.

In order to casebind a book, several operations, called forwarding, are necessary. First, the signatures are trimmed, generally by using a three-knife device that cuts the three open sides in a single motion (figure

19.20). The back or fastened edge of the book is then rounded. Rounding gives the book an attractive appearance and keeps the pages within the turn-in of the cover (figure 19.21). Backing is accomplished by clamping the rounded book in place and mushrooming-out the fastened edges of the signatures (figure 19.22). The purpose of backing is to make the

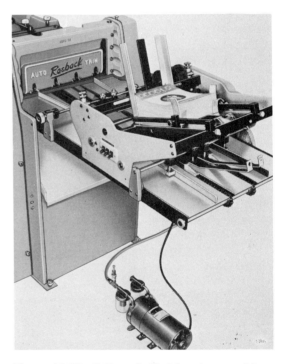

Figure 19.20. A three-knife trimming machine
Courtesy of F. P. Rosback Company

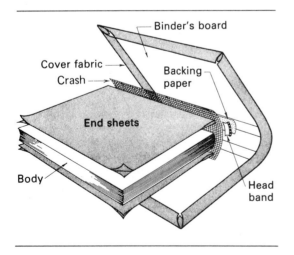

Figure 19.19. The anatomy of a casebound book

Figure 19.21. Rounded signatures of a book

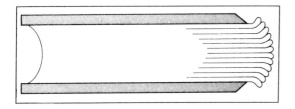

Figure 19.22. Backing the edges of the signatures

rounding operation permanent and to provide a ridge for the casebound cover. Next the book goes through a "lining-up" process, which consists of gluing a layer of gauze (called "crash") and strips of paper (called "backing paper") to the backed edge. The crash and backing paper are later glued to the case and provide additional support for the book. A headband is a decorative tape that can be attached to the head and tail of the back of the book to give a pleasing appearance. This is not always done. All forwarding can be completed on automatic equipment.

The actual case is made from two pieces of thick binder's board glued to the covering cloth. The cloth can be printed before gluing to the board or after by such processes as relief hot stamping or screen printing. The binder's board is cut so that the piece will extend over the body of the book by at least ⅛ inch (0.32 cm) on each open edge and will miss the backed ridge by the same distance. The cloth is cut large enough so that it will completely cover one side of both boards and will extend around the edges by at least ½ inch (1.27 cm) (see figure 19.19). The positions of the two boards on the cloth are critical and must be carefully controlled. Automatic equipment exists that cuts both the board and the cloth and joins the two pieces in their proper positions.

The final process of joining the forwarded book with the case is called casing in. The two parts of the case are attached by two sheets called **end sheets** (see figure 19.19). End sheets can be the outside leaves of the first and last signatures or can be special pieces that were joined to the pages during the assembling and fastening operations.

To case in a book, the end sheets are coated with glue, the case is positioned in place, and pressure is applied. The pressure must be maintained until the adhesive is dry. This was traditionally accomplished by stacking the books between special "building-in" boards (figure 19.23). This technique has been gradually replaced by special heat-setting adhesives that dry in a matter of seconds as the end sheets contact the case.

When the book is complete, it can be jacketed (put in a protective paper cover) or boxed and delivered to the customer. Equipment exists that automatically case binds books from the forwarding operations to the final steps of sealing and labeling the cases used to ship the final product.

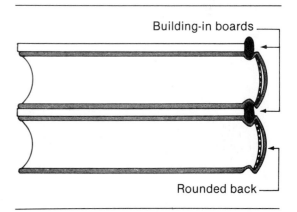

Figure 19.23. Diagram of the use of traditional building-in boards

In-Line Finishing

Traditionally, the post-press operations of collating, gathering, binding, and finishing have been costly, labor-intensive operations handled by trade shops with specialized equipment. Today, many printers are investing in in-line finishing equipment which links post-press operations directly to the press room. In-line finishing reduces the amount of labor required and speeds up the finishing process (figure 19.24). A typical operation will pass printed matter directly from the press to an in-line finisher (figure 19.25). Many in-line devices are equipped to fold, trim, stitch, and address each publication in zip code order. After addressing, the publications are automatically placed on pallets and shrink-wrapped for storage and delivery (figure 19.26).

At the heart of any in-line finishing operation is a computer which not only controls the printing finishing equipment but provides addressing information to a label or ink-jet printer which addresses each publication in zip code order. In addition to addressing publications, the computer makes demographic binding possible. With **demographic binding,** the computer selectively assembles publications, based on address information. Thus it is possible for local advertisers to place advertisements in a national magazine, such as *Newsweek,* and have their advertisements appear only in the magazines received by customers within their selling area. Magazines delivered to Chicago, for example, will contain advertisements for Chicago merchants; those delivered to New York, will advertise New York merchants.

Demographic binding meets advertis-

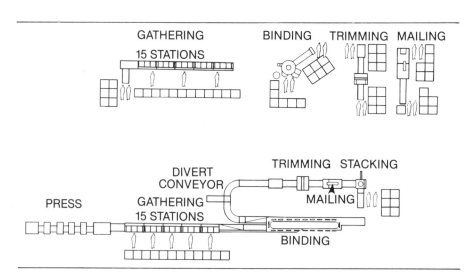

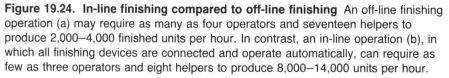

Figure 19.24. In-line finishing compared to off-line finishing An off-line finishing operation (a) may require as many as four operators and seventeen helpers to produce 2,000–4,000 finished units per hour. In contrast, an in-line operation (b), in which all finishing devices are connected and operate automatically, can require as few as three operators and eight helpers to produce 8,000–14,000 units per hour.

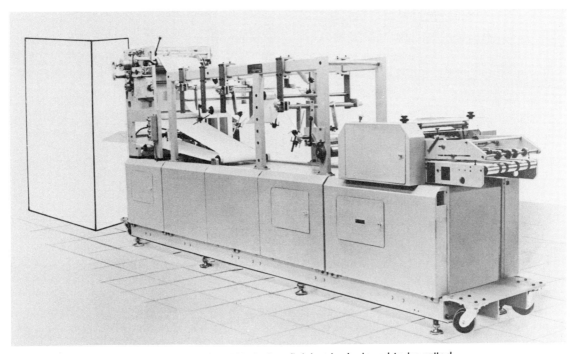

Figure 19.25. In-line finishing system This in-line finisher is designed to be rolled into place and set up at the outfeed side of the press. The machine can fold, cut, trim, glue, slit, score, perforate, and stack in one continuous operation. Additional folders can be added as modular units to produce multiple folds. Stacked items can be delivered directly to additional in-line equipment for further finishing and addressing. Courtesy of Custom-Bilt Machinery, Inc.

Figure 19.26. In-line finishing A six-color web offset press equipped with an in-line folder, trimmer, and stitcher. Note the computer console which controls the operation. Courtesy of Hantscho, Inc.

ers' and publishers' demands for personalized printing and, because products are addressed in zip code order, allows printed products to qualify for lower postal rates. Savings of up to 4½ cents per magazine have been reported through demographic binding. This sounds like a small sum, but when you consider an edition of several million magazines or catalogs, it becomes quite significant.

Key Terms

finishing
guillotine cutter
knife folders
buckle folders
French fold
right-angle fold
accordion fold

parallel fold
assembling
gathering
collating
inserting
adhesive binding
perfect binding

patent binding
side binding
saddle binding
self-covers
casebound covers
in-line finishing

Questions for Review

1. What are the most common finishing operations?

2. How is the size of a guillotine paper cutter defined?

3. Explain the difference between the operation of a knife folder and that of a buckle folder.

4. What do the terms *right-angle fold* and *parallel fold* mean?

5. What is the difference between gathering, collating, and inserting?

6. What does the term *perfect binding* mean?

7. Give three examples of side binding.

8. What is the process of saddle binding?

9. Explain the differences between self-covers, soft covers, and casebound covers.

10. What does the term *forwarding* describe?

11. Describe a typical in-line finishing operation.

Chapter Twenty

Estimating and Production Control

Anecdote to Chapter Twenty

Printing has made many contributions to our written and spoken language. Before printers came on the scene, there was no consistency of spelling or punctuation. When books were hand written by medieval scribes, words, sentences, and even paragraphs could be run-togetheronthe whim of the artist. They could become very difficult to read. Spaces between words, commas, periods, and other marks were invented by early printers to act as signals to

One of two news cases necessary to store a complete alphabet
Courtesy of Mackenzie and Harris, Inc.

the reader. There are also many examples of printers' language used in everyday conversation. One example is the use of the terms *uppercase* and *lowercase* to describe capital and small letters in our alphabet.

One of the early methods of storing pieces of foundry type was in a case of individual bins called a "news case" (see illustration). Two cases were necessary to store a complete alphabet. There was one case for the minuscule, or small letters, and another for the majuscule, or capitals. In actual practice, the printer placed one bin or case over the other. The case hold-

ing the capitals was placed above the case containing the small letters.

When the master printer wanted a certain letter, he would call out to his "devil" (a worker with less status than an apprentice) "get me a *C* from the upper case." When he was trying to save time he would shout, "Get me an upper case *C*."

The terms *uppercase* and *lowercase* have been accepted as the nicknames for the capital and small characters in our alphabet and are a direct result of the language of the early relief printers.

Objectives for Chapter Twenty

After completing this chapter, you will be able to:

- Explain how estimates are determined for the length of time required to complete a task and how to use a unit/time standards form.
- Explain how fixed costs are identified and determined in production costs.

- Outline the basic job estimating process.
- Discuss the use of a job work order to direct a job through scheduling and production control.
- Describe the major components of an automated data collection and management of information system.

Introduction

Both novice and experienced printers sometimes become so concerned with the craft that they lose sight of what is involved in operating any company beyond the manufactur-

ing of the product. The purpose of this chapter is to examine the important problem of determining operating costs.

Determining the Cost of Labor

No industry can function by guesswork. At each level in a printing organization, it is important that the supervisor or manager know how long it takes to perform a specific task and how much it costs. Without information on time and cost standards, it is impossible to predict accurately the cost of a job. A bid would be either so low that the company loses money or so high that a competitor gets the job.

A variety of techniques are used by the printing industry to determine these important standards. The complexity or simplicity of the procedures depends on the size and diversity of the business. A small "quick print" company that uses only one sheet size sold in units of 100 will have a single standard— a set amount of dollars per hundred sheets. A large job shop, on the other hand, might need to set labor requirements and prices for as many as a thousand different operations. This section deals with the procedures that a medium-sized job shop might use to determine labor costs.

Figure 20.1 shows a typical form used in any section to determine unit/time standards. The section supervisor would maintain a form for each piece of equipment or operation. Every job or only a random sample of each week's work could be recorded on the

Standards Sheet

Description	Section	Equipment	Unit Quantity
Labor	Press	17x22 offset	1,000 sheets

No.	Date	Employee	Units	Total Hours	Average Hours per Unit
1	5/8	Faux	5	1.13	.23
2	5/11	Adams	7	1.44	.21
3	5/19	Roehrich	2	.38	.19
4	5/22	Gartner	4	.82	.21
5	5/23	Roehrich	10	2.10	.21
6	5/26	Faux	5	.98	.20
7	6/1	Gartner	2	.90	.18
8	6/2	Adams	6	.44	.22
9	6/3	Faux	5	1.20	.20

Total   1.85

Total (1.85)/No. of Entries (9) = .21

Standard = .21 hrs/1,000 shts

Figure 20.1. A typical unit/time standards form

sheet. In each instance, the standard is nothing more than the average time to complete an operation.

The example in figure 20.1 is concerned with determining the average labor time to print 1,000 sheets of paper in the press section on a 17- × 22-inch offset press. On May 8, press operator Faux ran 5,000 sheets in 1.13 hours. That averages to 0.23 hours per 1,000 sheets. The press supervisor has taken a random sample of work on the 17- × 22-inch press for four different press operators. In each case the average time per 1,000 sheets was determined.

Industry has found that it is more convenient to record time in units of hundredths instead of hours, minutes, and seconds. It is far simpler to multiply $5.00 per hour times 1.13 rather than 1 hour, 7 minutes, and 48 seconds.

1 hour, 7 minutes, 48 seconds
$$48/60 = 0.8 \text{ minutes}$$

1 hour, 7.8 minutes
$$7.8/60 = 0.13 \text{ hours}$$

1.13 hours

When the labor standards sheet was full, the "average hours per unit" column was totaled (1.85 in figure 20.1) and then divided by the number of entries (9) to give the standard time needed to print 1,000 17- × 22-inch sheets (0.21 hours per 1,000).

This procedure can be duplicated in each section, or cost center, of the company, and then a master list can be compiled for the estimator to use when preparing job bids (figure 20.2). Some companies continually keep track of production standards and update their master list on a weekly basis. Others merely spot-check their standards on a monthly or quarterly basis.

Determining Fixed Costs

It is relatively easy for a manager to determine the cost of the materials and labor that go into a given job, but in any business there are expenses that are hard to determine when making a job estimate. How many paper clips should be charged to that job? What was the cost of the electricity used to operate the camera lights for five negatives? How much water was used to wash the press operators' hands at the end of the day, and what job should be charged? All of these items are small alone. But when they are summed over the span of a year, they become significant. They are expenses and must be considered in the total cost of each job.

One approach is to add a certain percentage, called **overhead,** to each job. If the management had determined that 4% of their yearly costs were a result of these "unmeasurable" expenses and a job was calculated to cost $1,000, the 4% or $40 would be added to the bid.

An alternative procedure to the single overhead figure is to add a fixed amount to each productive hour spent on every job. The determination of that fixed amount is a bit involved, but it is a fairly accurate method of accounting for difficult-to-measure expenses of any business. It is necessary to use an example to illustrate the process.

Consider figure 20.3, a floor plan of Spartan Graphics, a typical—although imaginary—medium-sized printing company. From the accounting office, the president has determined that they have $8,000 fixed building costs each year. By measuring the plant, the president finds that there are 2,000 square feet in the building, which means that it costs the business $4 per square foot each year just to operate the building.

If the square foot area of each section is determined from the floor plan, it should be

STANDARD LABOR PER UNIT		
SECTION	UNIT	STANDARD
Composing	Body composition, 35 square inches, 6–10 point	0.10 hour
	Headlines, 50 inches	0.15 hour
Camera	Negatives up to 17 × 22 17 × 22 and up	 0.12 hour 0.18 hour
	Halftones up to 4 × 5 4 × 5 to 8 × 10	 0.23 hour 0.32 hour
	Contacts	0.09 hour
Stripping	Flats, single color 12 × 19 19 × 24	 0.25 hour 0.48 hour
	For each added color 12 × 19 19 × 24	 0.34 hour 0.58 hour
Plate	Plates, surface 12 × 18½ (1 side) 19 × 24 (1 side)	 0.20 hour 0.22 hour
	For each added exposure	0.09 hour
Press	11 × 17 press, 1,000 sheets	0.18 hour
	17 × 22 press, 1,000 sheets	0.21 hour
	For each added color 11 × 17 press 17 × 22 press	 0.22 hour 0.27 hour
	Wash-up per color	0.35 hour
Bindery	One fold and staple, 1,000 sheets, saddle	0.15 hour
	Two folds and staple, 1,000 sheets, saddle	0.19 hour
	Trim, wrap and carton, 1,000 sheets 11 × 17 17 × 22	 0.09 hour 0.11 hour
	Trim and skid only, 1,000 sheets 11 × 17 17 × 22	 0.05 hour 0.06 hour

Figure 20.2. Example of a master list used by estimators to prepare job bids

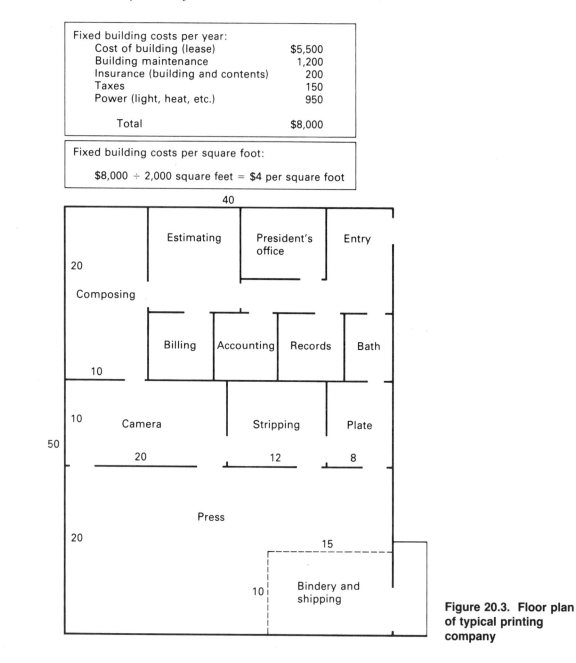

Fixed building costs per year:
Cost of building (lease)	$5,500
Building maintenance	1,200
Insurance (building and contents)	200
Taxes	150
Power (light, heat, etc.)	950
Total	$8,000

Fixed building costs per square foot:

$8,000 ÷ 2,000 square feet = $4 per square foot

Figure 20.3. Floor plan of typical printing company

possible to assign a portion of the fixed building costs to each. The first three columns of table 20.1 have determined the "fixed building costs per square foot by department."

Another cost that is difficult to proportion out to each job is **depreciation.** Somehow the cost of the presses, platemakers, cameras, and all the other equipment must be paid for;

Table 20.1. Determining Fixed Costs

Department	Sq. Feet of Dept	× Cost per Sq. Foot	= Fixed Bldg. Cost per Sq. Foot by Dept	+ Equip. Deprec. by Dept	= Total Fixed Costs per Dept per Yr	÷ Total Prod. Hrs per Yr	= Fixed Hour Cost	+ Fixed Office Factor	= Total Fixed Cost per Prod. Hour
Office	600	× $4 =	$2,400	+ $1,400 =	$3,800	÷ 9,150 hrs =	$ .42	+ $.07 =	$ .62
Composing	200	× 4 =	800	+ 1,200 =	2,000	÷ 3,660 =	.55	+ .07 =	1.10
Camera	200	× 4 =	800	+ 1,100 =	1,900	÷ 1,830 =	1.03	+ .07 =	.34
Stripping	120	× 4 =	480	+ 500 =	980	÷ 3,660 =	.27	+ .07 =	.79
Plate	80	× 4 =	320	+ 1,000 =	1,320	÷ 1,830 =	.72	+ .07 =	.89
Press	650	× 4 =	2,600	+ 6,400 =	9,000	÷ 10,980 =	.82	+ .07 =	1.81
Bindery	150	× 4 =	600	+ 2,600 =	3,200	÷ 1,830 =	1.74	+ .07 =	
Totals	2,000 sq ft		$8,000	+ $14,200 =	$22,200				

but their cost is so great that no single job could cover it. Depreciation is arrived at by dividing the total cost for each piece of equipment by the number of years it should be productive. Table 20.2 shows the annual depreciation in the press section. The equipment manufacturers have determined that with proper maintenance and service the four presses that the business owns will last ten years. The total cost is then divided by ten to determine the annual charge that must be set so that at the end of the life of each press a new press can be purchased.

Column four in table 20.1 lists the equipment depreciation for each section. This is added to the fixed building cost in column five. The total represents the amount that must be distributed throughout the entire year for each productive hour worked in each section.

In table 20.3 the total number of available productive hours per worker per year has been calculated. (It is interesting that more productive hours are lost through coffee breaks than by two weeks of paid vacation.) In table 20.4 that number has been multiplied by the number of employees in each section to determine the total productive hours each year. Those figures have been transferred to column six in table 20.1. If the total fixed costs are divided by the total productive hours, the fixed hour cost has been determined (table 20.1, column seven).

A difficulty arises with the fixed hour cost for the office area. It is not possible to identify how much office time was devoted to each individual job. Also, time is spent estimating jobs that the company does not get, and that cost must be absorbed somewhere

Table 20.2. Depreciation, Press Section

Equipment	Original Cost	Annual Depreciation
17 × 22 press (2)	$40,000	$4,000
11 × 17 press (2)	23,000	2,300
Miscellaneous Tools	1,000	100
		$6,400

Table 20.3. Productive Hours Per Year

(40 hours per week) × (52 weeks) = 2,080 hours

less:

1) 2 weeks paid vacation	80 hrs	
2) 5 paid holidays	40 hrs	
3) 1 paid sick day (average)	8 hrs	
4) 30 minutes paid break per day (2½ hrs per week × 49 weeks minus 30 min for sick day)	122 hrs	
		− 250 hours
Maximum productive hours		1,830 hours

Table 20.4. Productive Hours per Year by Section

Section	Number of Employees	×	Productive Hours/Year	=	Total Productive Hours/Year
Office	5	×	1,830	=	9,150
Composing	2	×	1,830	=	3,330
Camera	1	×	1,830	=	1,830
Stripping	2	×	1,830	=	3,660
Plate	1	×	1,830	=	1,830
Press	6	×	1,830	=	10,980
Bindery	1	×	1,830	=	1,830

in the operation. Much office time is either nonproductive or not associated with particular jobs. To solve the problem, the fixed office cost is divided equally among all the other sections. In this case, $.42 was divided by 6 (six sections), and $.07 was added to the fixed hour cost for each section. When all these calculations have been completed, a total fixed cost per productive hour is determined that can be added to each estimate according to the number of hours worked in each section.

Preparing the Job Estimate

Each company uses those estimating procedures that work best for its type of organization. There are published pricing guides, such as the *Franklin Printing Catalog,* that give "average" costs for nearly all operations or products of a typical printing company. Computerized programs are available that require sales personnel only to enter information on the job into a computer terminal. The estimated costs are displayed on a television-like screen above the keyboard. Some companies prepare price schedules for items that they frequently work with to avoid re-estimating every job. Whatever the method—computer, pencil and paper, or published guide—certain procedures are always followed to obtain a final price estimate. The following are the eight basic steps for making any estimate. Some authors might expand or reduce the number by combining or separating items, but the basic process will always remain the same.

1. Obtain accurate specifications.
2. Plan the job sequence.
3. Determine material needs and convert to standard units.
4. Determine time needed for each task.
5. Determine labor costs.
6. Determine fixed costs.
7. Sum costs and add profit.
8. Prepare formal bid contract.

The Basic Estimating Process

It is important, when predicting the cost of a job, to have all the information about what the customer wants. It is the job of the sales personnel to obtain all job specifications and to ensure that the company meets the job requirements, all within the final formal price estimate.

It is impossible to estimate printing costs without knowing how the job is to be produced. <u>It is necessary to outline the sequence of operations so time and material requirements can be easily determined.</u> If an operation is forgotten or estimated incorrectly, the cost of that operation must come out of the profits. Customers will not pay more than the contracted bid price unless, of course, they contract for extras after accepting the bid.

Once the sequence of operations has been determined, it is a simple task to determine the quantities of materials needed for each task. These are then converted to unit amounts. From the standard units (see figure 20.2), the estimator can calculate the amount of time necessary to complete each operation. Labor costs, which are usually paid on a per hour basis, are then determined for each operation. Fixed costs, or overhead, are then added, usually based on the time needed for each task. All of these figures are then summed, and a fixed percentage of profit is added to the total. This final sum is the proposed cost of the job.

As a last step, the estimator usually prepares a formal bid that acts as a binding contract for the company, stating that the company will print a specific job for the stated amount. The customer commonly has a fixed number of days to accept the bid before the contract offer becomes void.

A Sample Job Estimate

For the sake of clarification, it is valuable to follow through the procedures of estimating a sample job. Assume that a salesperson for our hypothetical company—Spartan Graphics—has called on a customer who would like to have an information brochure printed to explain the details of their training program to employees. They would like to know how much the job will cost before Spartan Graphics gets the job. Our salesperson records all

the important information about the job on a standard estimate request form (figure 20.4). Spartan has found that it is valuable to have the standard form so the sales personnel do not forget an important fact that might influence the job's final cost.

From figure 20.4, it can be seen that the brochure is to be an eight-page saddle-stitched booklet printed in one color on both sides of the page and trimmed to 8½ by 11 inches. The customer will supply only the manuscript and a rough layout of the job. Spartan Graphics will compose, print, fold, staple, and trim and will pack the paper-wrapped final product, 1,000 copies to the carton. Markert Enterprises, the customer, will pick up the boxes on or before November 4.

Will all this information, the salesperson returns to the office to calculate the job's cost. Either alone or with the production manager, the salesperson plans out the sequence of steps. The list of steps is as follows:

1. Composing:
   set body type
   set headlines
   paste up camera-ready copy
2. Camera: shoot negatives of paste-up copy
3. Stripping: strip flats
4. Plate making: burn plates
5. Press:
   print job
   wash-up press
6. Bindery:
   fold and staple brochure
   trim and box wrapped brochures

A decision must be made as to which press will be used because that will influence the sheet size and how the job is to be pasted up, folded, and stapled. In this case, the 17- × 22-inch lithographic press is to be used, with

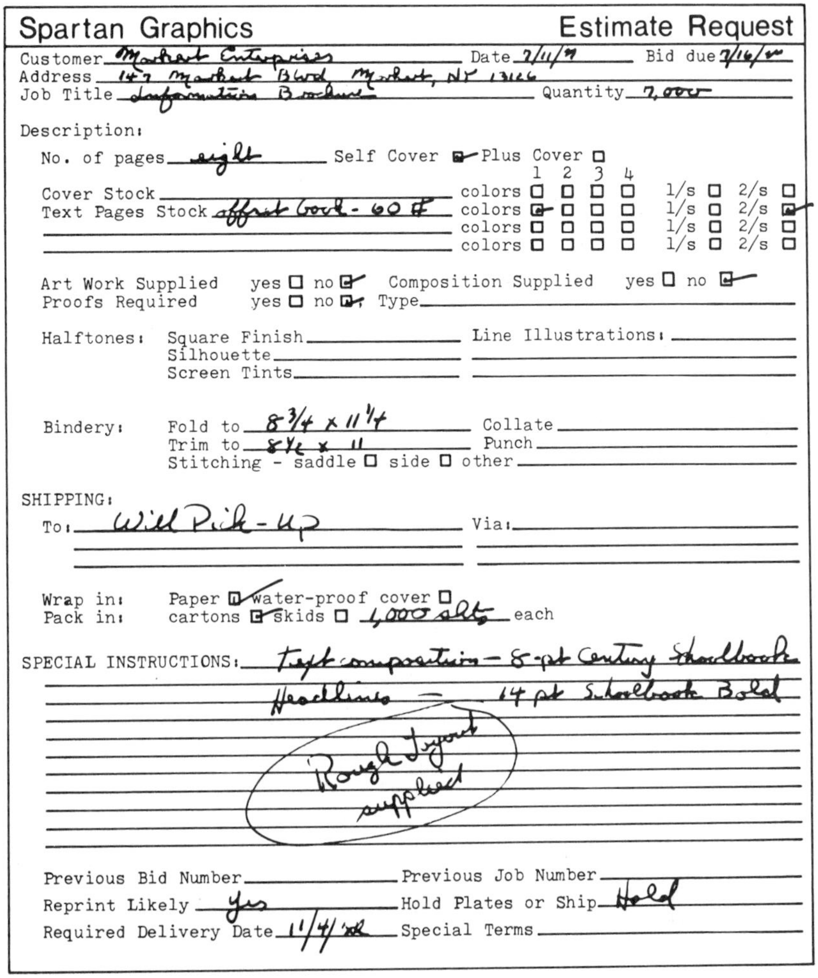

Figure 20.4. Sample estimate request form

a sheet size of 17½ × 22½ inches. All of this information is then recorded in the first three columns of the Spartan Graphics standard estimate sheet (figure 20.5).

The next step is to determine the materials needed for each stage of production. Columns three through six on the estimate sheet identify the number of units of work and the total cost for each step. Refer to figure 20.2 and table 20.4 to recall where the units came from. The salesperson obtains the cost per unit from the suppliers' current price lists. The total material cost is determined by multiplying the number of units by the cost per unit. Figure 20.6 shows how the number of paper units is determined.

The labor necessary to complete each unit is obtained from figure 20.2. The total labor units are a product of the labor standard times the number of units. For the sake of simplic-

Spartan Graphics												Estimate Sheet
Sequence	Section	Description	No. of units	Cost/ unit	Material cost	Standard labor/unit	Total labor units	Labor cost/ hour	Total labor cost	Fixed cost/ hour	Total fixed cost	Total operation cost
1	Composing	Body Comp	8	$1.05	$8.40	.10 hrs	.80 hrs	$5.00	$4.00	$.62	$.50	
		Headlines	1	.25	.25	.15	.15	5.00	.75	.62	.09	
		Paste-up	2	1.40	2.80	.25	.50	5.00	2.50	.62	.31	
					$11.45				$7.25		$.90	$19.60
2	Camera	17x22 negs	2	$5.40	$10.80	.18 hrs	.36 hrs	$5.00	$1.80	$1.10	$.40	
					$10.80				$1.80		$.40	$13.00
3	Stripping	19 x 24 flats	2	$2.10	$4.20	.48 hrs	.96 hrs	$5.00	$4.80	$.34	$.33	
					$4.20				$4.80		$.33	$9.33
4	Plate	19x24 plates	2	$21.00	$42.00	.22 hrs	.44 hrs	$5.00	$2.20	$.79	$.35	
		(Single Exposure)			$42.00				$2.20		$.35	$44.55
5	Press	17½ x 22½ - offset book - 60#	7.77 M			.21 hrs	1.63 hrs	$5.00	$8.15	$.89	$1.45	
		388.5 lbs			$142.60							
		ink			5.60							
		Wash-up	1	$2.10	2.10	.35	.35	$5.00	$1.75	$.89	$.71	
					150.30				$9.90		$1.76	$160.96
6	Bindery	Fold & Staple	7	$.60	$4.20	.19 hrs	1.33 hrs	$5.00	$6.65	$1.81	$2.41	
		Trim & Box	7	1.10	7.70	.11	.77	5.00	3.85	1.81	.20	
					$11.90				$10.50		$2.61	$25.01

sub-total ($272.45) x profit (.12) = $32.69   sub-total $272.45
plus profit 12%   32.69
total $305.14

Estimate made by J. Mitchell Arlin | Checker BK | Date 7/12/4 | File No. 196-24

Figure 20.5. Sample estimate sheet

ity, in this example we have assumed that all labor is paid at the rate of $5 per hour. It should be understood that in the actual industry the rate of pay depends on the type of job and the level of individual skill, but generally far exceeds this amount. The printing industry pays very competitive wages, and the authors use $5 per hour only for ease of arithmetic. Also, assume that the office labor costs have been averaged into the $5 figure. The total labor cost for each production step can be found by multiplying the total number of labor units by the labor cost per hour.

Next the fixed operations cost must be determined. From table 20.2, the fixed cost per hour for each section is recorded on the estimate sheet (figure 20.5, column eleven). The total fixed cost is found by multiplying column eleven by column eight (total labor units).

For each step in the production sequence, the material, labor, and fixed costs are totaled and recorded in the last column of the estimate sheet. The total operation costs for each step are then summed and entered in the subtotal blank at the bottom of the page.

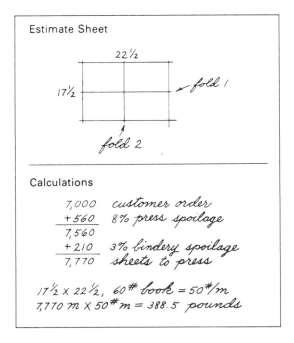

Figure 20.6. Sample estimate calculations

Spartan Graphics has set 12% as its desired rate of profit. Therefore, multiply 0.12 times the subtotal to obtain the actual dollar amount. This quantity is then added to the subtotal to find the total estimated cost of the job.

The final step is to prepare a formal bid contract to be sent to the customer. In the contract letter used by Spartan Graphics, the details of the job are again specified so that both parties understand the conditions, and the total price is given (figure 20.7). The actual estimate sheet is generally not sent to the customer. It is retained by the printer to be used at a later date if the job contract is received.

Implementing Printing Production

Before any job can go into actual production, it is necessary to carry a bit further the pre-liminary work done with the estimate. Work does not automatically flow through the shop. Every job requires continual planning, guidance, and follow-up. The following list outlines the typical steps involved in actually implementing printing production:

1. From estimate request sheet and estimate, prepare production work order.
2. Determine in-house availability of materials and order if necessary.
3. Prepare detailed job schedule.
4. Merge detailed schedule into production control schedule.
5. Coordinate materials with job's arrival in each section.
6. Put job into production.
7. Check quality control and production as necessary.
8. Reschedule as necessary.
9. Remove job from production control schedule and send all records to accounting.

To follow through with the logic of a typical printing job, let us assume that the brochure that was bid in the previous example was awarded to Spartan Graphics.

The Work Order

After the customer has accepted the bid and any legal contracts have been signed, the production manager takes control of the job. The first step is to transfer the information from the estimate request and estimate sheet to a production work order or "job ticket" (figure 20.8). The work order will be the road map that will chart the job through all the production steps. It will also be used by the production control section to check on the progress of the job. Each supervisor will log

Spartan Graphics
1359 West Third Street
Athens, New York 11476
July 14, 1982

Ms. L. Markert, President
Markert Enterprises
147 W. Markert Blvd
Markert, New York

Ms. Markert:

In reference to your request for an estimate, we are
pleased to submit the following information:

Job Title: Information Brochure

Quantity: 7,000

Format: 8½ x 11 inches, 8 pages, printed two
                sides, saddle stapled on 11 inch side.

Composition: Manuscript to be supplied by Markert
                Enterprises; Spartan Graphics to set
                body in 8 point Century Schoolbook,
                headlines in 14 point Century School-
                book Bold--according to layout
                specifications previously supplied by
                Markert Enterprises.

Packaging: Brochures to be wrapped in paper and
                boxed, 1,000 copies per carton.

Shipping: To be supplied by Markert Enterprises.

Terms: Net thirty days.

Total Cost: $305.14 plus applicable local tax.

We are looking forward to your acceptance of this bid.
If additional information can be provided please do not
hesitate to call on me personally.

Sincerely yours,

J. M. Adams

J.M. Adams
Sales Manager

**Figure 20.7. Sample
letter of bid**

the time that the job arrives and the time it leaves the section. The form can also serve as a means of updating the labor standards (see figure 20.1) if the actual time varies significantly from the standard or estimated time.

At the same time that the work order is completed, the inventory control staff should check to determine that all the required materials are on hand and are not committed to another job. If they are in storage, they are reserved. If the supplies are not available in-house, they are ordered, and information about the expected delivery date is sent to those responsible for job scheduling.

Job Scheduling and Production Control

Job scheduling is a problem of coordinating the most efficient combination of materials, machines, and time. The skillful production manager will schedule jobs in a sequence that will require minimum machine changes. For example, if four jobs are to be run on a single press next Tuesday—two with black ink, one with yellow, and another with red—it would

be wise to schedule the order to run the yellow first, then the red, and then the two black. The lightest colors should be run first (which makes for an easier roller cleanup), and the two black runs paired together. Likewise, it would be foolish not to schedule jobs with the same sheet sizes back to back.

The first step in the orderly scheduling of individual jobs is to prepare a detailed job schedule sheet (figure 20.9). Again the sequence of operations is listed, with the number of estimated hours in each section identified. A sort of diagram of times is then laid out so the planner can get a visual impression of the required times and sequence. If the job requires more than one day, additional sheets are used.

The individual job diagram is then merged into the overall shop production control schedule (figure 20.10). The goal is to match time blocks efficiently with available personnel, materials, and common sizes, colors, or types of jobs. The production manager will prepare detailed production control schedules well in advance for each day's work. With a job scheduled as far as a week in advance, it is possible to coordinate the required

Figure 20.8. Sample production work order

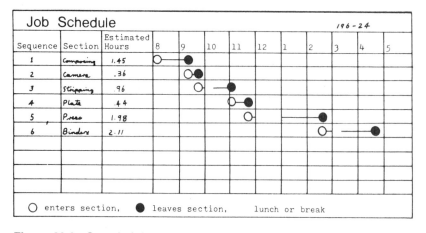

Figure 20.9. Sample job schedule

materials with each section as the job flows through the shop.

The frustration of production control is that jobs do not always conform to the estimated time. Perhaps the camera burns out a bulb, which must be immediately replaced. Paper might jam in the press, and thirty minutes are wasted removing the scrap. Materials might not arrive in the section on schedule, and time is wasted checking on the problem. At any rate, a delay at one point in the schedule is felt throughout the shop. It is therefore necessary continually to alter and adjust the flow of jobs to make up for time gains or losses.

With the work order, manuscript copy, and rough layout, our sample job enters production on the appropriate day and should emerge as a completed brochure at day's end. If there are problems, the production manager must make adjustments. It is also the production manager's task to know the stage of each job at almost every moment in the day. When customers call and want to know how their material is progressing, it is important to be able to give an immediate and accurate answer.

When the job has reached the last production step and is waiting to be picked up or is on its way to the customer, all records are sent through the production control office to the accounting or billing office. The job is removed from the production control schedule, and any materials that are to be stored, such as the original paste-up copy, negatives, or printing plates, are filed and new jobs enter the system. A bill is sent to the customer, and payment is received.

Computer-Aided Production Control

The development of computer-aided production control systems is a natural outgrowth of the entrance of the computer into almost every phase of printing operations. For years, larger printing firms have been using computer-based **management of information systems (MIS)** software to compare and assess business data. However, until recently, true MIS systems have only been available to the larg-

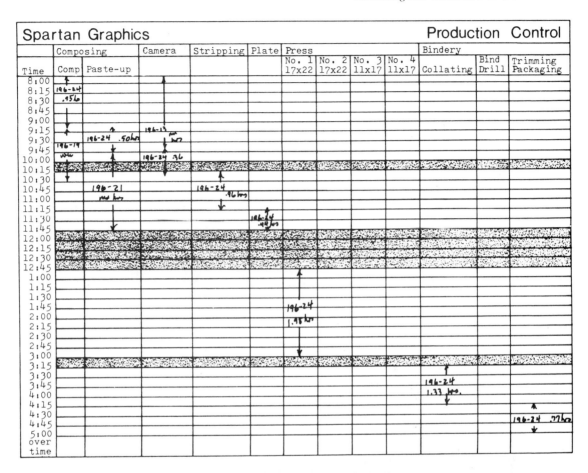

Figure 20.10. Sample production control sheet The control sheet shows
the example job sequenced across a single workday.

est printing firms capable of making a considerable investment in computer hardware and software. Current developments in microcomputer technology and considerable reductions in the price of microcomputer-based systems now make it possible for all but the smallest printers to take advantage of computer-aided production control.

At the heart of any MIS system is the accurate and timely gathering of information. Traditionally, information on inventory, job status, operating costs, and other expenses related to a specific job was gathered at the end of a shift, a workday, or a work week. Such information proved valuable in assessing expenses, and in isolating high-expense areas, but was historical in nature. Thus it was not useful for correcting problems as they occurred, because all information was collected only after the job was printed. **Automated data collection (ADC)** is a response to this problem. With ADC, data is collected through computer input as soon as it is known, rather than at the end of a specific time frame. This "real time" collection of data greatly enhances the plant's ability to assess the status of any particular operation and correct problems as they occur.

The actual operating procedures and software for data entry and information management on any ADC/MIS system are different for systems supplied by different manufacturers. Thus it would be impractical in this text to give more than an outline of how an overall system works. Procedures specific to different manufacturers' systems can be learned from system manuals supplied with the software.

All ADC/MIS systems contain a method of data entry, as well as software which processes data and provides screen or printer display, or both, for operations monitoring (figure 20.11). In most systems, data entry terminals are provided at all workstations where relevant data can be collected. Thus input stations would be installed in the pre-press areas for typesetting, camera, stripping, and assembling; in the press area; and in the post-press areas for binding and finishing. Data is entered by the operator who is doing each specific task, as the task is being done. At the typesetting station, for example, the compositor would enter information about when the job was received, the amount and type of supplies used to produce the typeset copy, and the amount of time taken by typesetting. The job would then be passed along to the camera department, where all information about the expenses for camera work would also be entered. This process would be followed through all of the workstations that came in contact with the job as it passed through the plant.

Actual data entry about every operation is accomplished in a variety of ways. One method is to have the person doing the operaton simply keyboard information about the

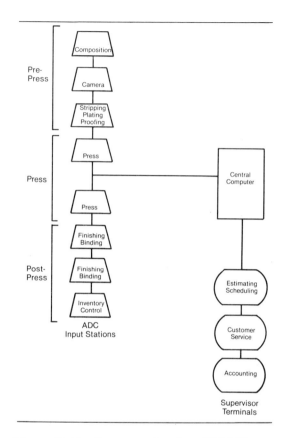

Figure 20.11. Components of an ADC/MIS system

job at the workstation terminal. Many systems use bar codes for information entry. With these systems, a bar code is attached to the job jacket containing the job. When operators receive the job jacket and start to work on the job, they read the job information from the job jacket into the ADC/MIS system by moving a light pen pointer over the bar code on the job jacket. The bar code sends information identifying the job to a central computer. Based on this information, the central computer provides a screen menu that prompts the operator for additional job information. The menu might display a list of questions for the operator to answer. For example, questions about the start time, the type and amount of materials needed, and other specifics about the job would appear as questions on the computer screen. The operator would respond to these questions through the keyboard. These responses give the computer the data it needs for job tracking and control. When the job is complete, the bar code is again scanned to indicate that work is finished at that station on that particular job.

Bar codes can also be used to identify supplies used. Most paper, for example, is supplied with bar code information directly from the manufacturer. The ADC/MIS system can read this bar code information from the paper box or roll and relate it to the job information from the job jacket. In this way the printer can keep track of the type and amount of paper used for the job and the inventory conditions for that particular type of paper. The ADC/MIS system will alert the plant management when inventory of that particular paper runs low, so that paper orders can be placed before the paper is needed again.

The beauty of a computer-based ADC/MIS system is that whatever information is known about a particular job is available immediately. Thus the customer service representative, in response to a customer's question, can look up the status of any printing job instantly on the computer screen and tell the customer how far along the job is in its progress through the plant, whether there have been any delays, and when the job can be delivered. ADC/MIS systems also greatly reduce the amount of paperwork to be done by workers at each individual workstation. With an ADC/MIS system, operators at each workstation need only enter data on the computer and check it on the screen, rather than writing all information out longhand on a form or on the job jacket. This makes data entry faster and more accurate.

In addition, job data entered about the job as it passes through the plant can be compared to the original estimate and used to update estimating information so that estimates are more accurate and can more closely reflect the actual cost to the plant of producing the job. This feature is most appealing to plants which use computer-aided estimating programs. The software for such programs is typically designed on the basis of a "generalized" printing business. Such software must be modified to reflect the specifics of a particular printing plant. ADC/MIS systems can provide the type of accurate information needed to continually update and correct estimating programs so that they provide accurate estimating information which will let the printer bid competitively and still make a profit.

It is important to understand that the printing industry is more than just the production tasks of running a printing press or operating a process camera. Planning printing production requires a thorough understanding of production, but it also demands individuals with many skills beyond the manipulation of ink and images. This chapter gave you a brief overview of those skills.

Key Terms

overhead
depreciation
Franklin Printing Catalog
job estimate

work order
job scheduling and
    production control
job schedule

management of information
    systems (MIS)
automated data collection
    (ADC)

Questions for Review

1. What is the advantage of a uniform price schedule?

2. Why is a review of the sequence of operations an important part of the estimating process?

3. What is the purpose of a production work order?

4. What is job scheduling?

5. What is a production control schedule?

6. What type of printing company is likely to use a uniform price schedule?

7. Explain why timely and accurate record keeping by production workers is important to accurate estimating.

8. What is a unit/time standards form?

9. Explain how fixed costs are identified and are added to production costs.

10. List the eight steps of the estimating process as outlined in the text.

11. List the major components of an ADC/MIS system, and explain the purpose of each.

Appendixes

Calibrating and Using Graphic Arts Tools

Appendix A

Determining Proper Film Exposure

Proper exposure for all film images has always been important, but with the increased use of film processors and rapid access type films it is becoming even more critical. In the past, camera operators have been able to compensate for improper exposure by adjusting development time or agitation. With film processors development time and agitation are controlled, therefore knowing the correct exposure is more essential. There is only one correct exposure for any given type of film with a given type of copy. Most film manufacturers recommend a solid step four for normal copy. It is important to realize that, due to the characteristics of the original copy, the correct exposure may be adjusted. One such example would be fine line copy in which a solid step three is recommended. The development should stay the same and the exposure should change to produce a solid step three. Once the copy has been evaluated and the exposure needs established, one must determine the proper exposure.

Determining the proper exposure is a systematic task and should never be approached by guessing, a hit-or-miss technique. To begin, it is important to review just what exposure is and what the basic elements are that affect exposure. **Exposure** can be defined as the total quantity of light that strikes the film. The two key elements that control exposure are the length of time light is allowed to strike the film and the amount of light that is available. A simple analogy to explain this point would be filling a bathtub with water. If you want to fill the bathtub with 20 gallons of water and you turn the faucet on full, it will take 6 minutes; if you were to install a second faucet on the other side of the bathtub and turn both faucets on full, it should take only half the time since twice as much water is available. When dealing with process cameras or other exposure equipment, the exposure time is regulated by different devices (timers or integrators) and the amount of light is controlled by the light source (wattage and/or number of bulbs). The light source can be further regulated by either a controlled opening (such as an aperture f/stop) or a light intensity control box (changes the current to the bulb). The choice of these depends upon the exposure equipment being used, such as a process camera or a contact frame. The correct exposure is also determined differently depending upon the exposure equipment used. The following outlines the process for determining the proper exposure for both a process camera and a contact frame. There are many ways to determine the proper exposure times and what is described in this appendix is only one of a variety of successful techniques. This method is fast, accurate, and uses a minimal amount of film.

Basic Process Camera Exposure Test

It is always a good idea to include a gray scale when doing any work on a process camera whether you are processing film in a tray or a film processor. Once you have used it to determine the proper exposure, it will act as a control device to assure quality and consistency. This testing method requires the use of a 12-step reflection gray scale. When working with process camera photography, most film manufacturers recommend a solid step four with a standard amount of development. The true variable, and problem at hand, is what exposure should be used. A good test exposure time to start with is two f/stops down from wide open at 15 seconds. In other words, if your camera has four f/stop openings (f/11, f/16, f/22, and f/32), you would begin with an exposure of f/16 at 15 seconds. There is no guarantee that this is the right f/stop or exposure time, but it will produce an image that can be adjusted according to the information outlined in the following paragraphs. If you are not putting your film through a film processor, it is important that you process the film in fresh chemistry and for precisely the length of time that the film manufacturer recommends; this is typically 2-1/2 or 2-3/4 minutes (if you are unsure, use 2-3/4 minutes). Once the film is processed you are ready to evaluate it and make compensations as needed according to a process referred to as **Gray Scale Math.**

Gray scale math is based upon the laws of physics and how they relate to film emulsions. In simpler terms, it is based upon the fact that wherever light hits the film emulsion, the emulsion turns black after processing, and the more light that strikes the film, the darker (denser) the emulsion will become. If the light is adjusted in a controlled manner, we can predict the density change on the film. There are three key elements needed to predict and control the change when dealing with a process camera: a timer or integrator, a diaphragm control board (f/stop dial), and a gray scale. Figure 6.10, "Camera F/stops," illustrates the relationship that each f/stop has to another. Looking again at that chart we can put this into a simple mathematical relationship. Whenever you move to a different f/stop above or below your original setting, you are changing the amount of light by a factor of two. This means that if you were to start with, say, f/22 and move to the next larger f/stop opening (f/16), you would be letting in exactly twice as much light. If you were to move to the next smaller f/stop opening (f/32), you would be letting in exactly half as much light. This relationship becomes even more important when it is recognized that a change of two steps on the gray scale is equal to a factor of two as well. This means that if your test piece of film shows development to a solid step two and you want a step four, you must increase your exposure by a factor of two. This can be achieved by moving to the next larger f/stop opening as just mentioned or by doubling the exposure time. If the test works out to be a solid 6, then you will need to decrease your exposure time by a factor of two (cut the exposure in half). This can be done by either changing to the next smaller f/stop opening or by cutting the exposure time in half. This simple technique can be expanded to include changes in any number of steps on the gray scale. Figure A.1. goes into detail on the rules and procedures for using gray scale math. Figure A.2. illustrates two examples of working with gray scale math that could resemble the result of your initial test exposure.

The basic procedure for running an exposure test can be summarized into the following steps:

1. Determine an initial test exposure for the camera being used. Expose and process a piece of film according to the manufacturer's recommendations.

A PRACTICAL APPROACH TO GRAY SCALE MATH

Moving up two steps on the gray scale -	Increase the exposure by 100%: This can be done by moving to the next larger f/stop opening or by multiplying the exposure time by 2.00
Moving up one step on the gray scale -	Increase the exposure by 50%: This can only be done by changing the exposure time. Multiply the exposure time by 1.50
Moving down one step on the gray scale -	Decrease the exposure by 25%: This can only be done by changing the exposure time. Multiply the exposure time by 0.75
Moving down two steps on the gray scale -	Decrease the exposure by 50%: This can be done by moving to the next smaller f/stop opening or by multiplying the exposure time by 0.50

Rules for Gray Scale Math:
1. Moving down on the gray scale is moving from a large number to a smaller number, moving up on the gray scale is moving from a small number to a larger number.
2. When making a change of two steps on the gray scale, the f/stop or exposure time can be changed.
3. When making a change of one step on the gray scale, only the exposure time can be changed.
4. Change only the f/stop or exposure time, not both (except when making equivalent exposures).
5. Due to reciprocity problems - large changes on the gray scale may require a second adjustment (such as moving from a solid step 9 to a solid step 4).

Figure A.1. Gray scale math procedures

A. A piece of test film was exposed at f/16 for 15 seconds and processed out as a solid step 2 on the gray scale. Since a solid step 4 is desired, the exposure must be increased by a factor of two using either the f/stop or the time as diagramed below:

= F/16 at 15 seconds

= F/16 at 30 seconds
(when doubling exposure time)

or

F/11 at 15 seconds
(when doubling f/stop opening)

B. A piece of test film was exposed at f/16 for 15 seconds and processed out as a solid step 2 on the gray scale. Since a solid step 4 is desired, the exposure must be increased by a factor of two using either the f/stop or the time as diagramed below:

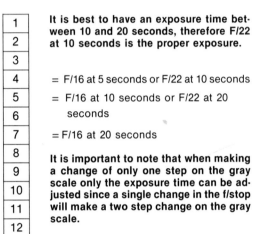

It is best to have an exposure time between 10 and 20 seconds, therefore F/22 at 10 seconds is the proper exposure.

= F/16 at 5 seconds or F/22 at 10 seconds

= F/16 at 10 seconds or F/22 at 20 seconds

= F/16 at 20 seconds

It is important to note that when making a change of only one step on the gray scale only the exposure time can be adjusted since a single change in the f/stop will make a two step change on the gray scale.

Figure A.2. Sample gray scale math problems

2. Evaluate the processed film and determine what step on the gray scale was reached using the test exposure.
3. Using the reference chart (figure A.1.) in this appendix, determine what adjustments should be made to the exposure time and/or f/stop. Reshoot the image.
4. Process and evaluate the second piece of film to see if the proper amount of exposure compensation was calculated. This piece of film must be developed exactly the same as the first test negative.

It is important to recognize that if any element in the exposure process changes, a new test may need to be run, since the exposure time may have changed. This is true regardless of the exposure equipment (process camera, contact frame, etc.) being used. Some of the common elements that might affect the exposure would be: a new brand or even a new batch of the same chemical or film, a different camera, new lights on the camera, or a change in the angle of the lights to the copyboard.

Since this method of testing can be done in under five minutes (once you are experienced) and using as little as one quarter of a sheet of 8 × 10 film, there is no reason to waste full sheets of film if you are not completely sure of the correct exposure for a box of film.

This procedure will work just as well for duplicating film on the process camera. The only difference is what you want to see on the gray scale. If on line film you want a solid four, which means that you can slightly see through the four when the negative is on a light table, then you should see the opposite on duplicating film. The four should have a slight bit of gray. Regardless of the step you are trying to achieve, gray scale math works the same as long as you keep in mind that more light increases the amount of clear area on duplicating film. If step 7 was clear and you desired a step 4 clear, you would move down 3 steps as illustrated in example B of figure A.2. Once again the important concept to remember when working with duplicating film is that light controls the quantity of clear area on the film—the more light, the more clear area. Gray scale math works equally well on duplicating film when approached from this perspective.

Contact Frame Exposure Test

Determining the proper exposure time in a contact frame follows the same rules of physics and light that we dealt with on the camera. Again in simple language, contact film (or line film) becomes darker as the amount of light striking it increases; duplicating film does just the opposite—it becomes lighter. The key in contacting is determining the proper exposure to get the exact opposite of the original when working on contact film or the exact same reproduction when working on duplicating film. You must realize that no matter how good a reproduction may be, there will always be some loss in the copy. There is a tremendous amount of exposure latitude when contacting, as compared to exposing on the process camera. This cannot be interpreted as meaning that there is not a best exposure. If you hope to achieve the best possible reproduction, you must work in a systematic manner with an appropriate testing device. A contacting test target is available

from most film manufacturers and, if used properly, can accurately establish the exposure time that will provide the best reproduction of the image for the film and processing methods you are using. The test target illustrated in figure A.3. has five identical images to allow you to make exposure step-offs to save film and time. Some test targets available come only as a single image. Once the correct exposure time has been established it is a good practice to make five duplicates and create your own test target with five identical images.

The test target is easy to use. The one shown in figure A.3. has seven areas; from left to right they are: clear, 2% dot, 5% dot, 50% dot, 95% dot, 98% dot, and solid black. Some versions have fewer dot percentages represented and, although it may be slightly harder to see the subtle changes in exposure, they can still produce very accurate results. To run a test, you expose the test image to a piece of film, stepping off in equal increments

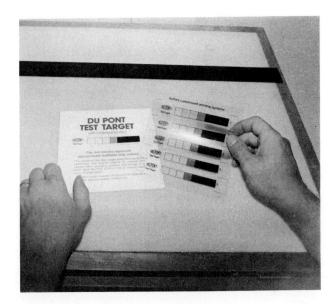

Figure A.3. A contact test target

(if you will be contacting emulsion-to-emulsion or emulsion-to-base, be sure to run your test the same way since there can be a difference). Determining the increments depends on the light intensity and film used. It is best to work with final exposure times of between 10 and 20 seconds; therefore you should try to adjust the light intensity (either raise or lower the light or change voltage regulator, if available) to produce an acceptable test with five 5-second step-offs (as illustrated in figure A.4.). If, in your initial test on contact film (or line film), it is too dark in all steps, decrease the intensity of the light. If you have an image that is not even black on the film, increase the exposure. Since duplicating film is used

a great deal in contacting work, keep in mind that these statements are reversed for duplicating film.

Once you obtain a test piece of film that has a range of exposures on it, look at the extreme dots; in the case of the test image shown here, these would be the 2% and the 98% dots. Decide which exposure best reproduced each as dot percentage (see figure A.5.). As in the example shown the two areas reproduce best at different exposure times. The best overall reproduction is therefore halfway between the two.

If you are working with materials where a test target is not available, such as contacting through paper (the example shown in fig-

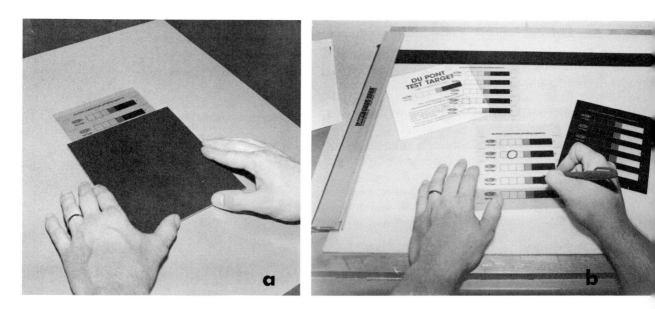

Figure A.4. a. Stepping off the test target in the contact frame.
b. Evaluating the test film— on the lower left in a duplicating film test, the right is a contact film test.

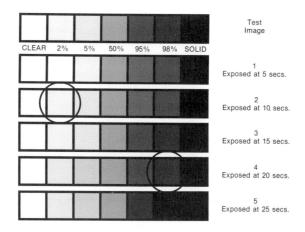
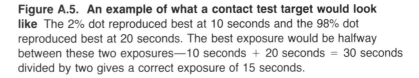

| | CLEAR | 2% | 5% | 50% | 95% | 98% | SOLID | |

Test Image

1
Exposed at 5 secs.

2
Exposed at 10 secs.

3
Exposed at 15 secs.

4
Exposed at 20 secs.

5
Exposed at 25 secs.

Figure A.5. An example of what a contact test target would look like The 2% dot reproduced best at 10 seconds and the 98% dot reproduced best at 20 seconds. The best exposure would be halfway between these two exposures—10 seconds + 20 seconds = 30 seconds divided by two gives a correct exposure of 15 seconds.

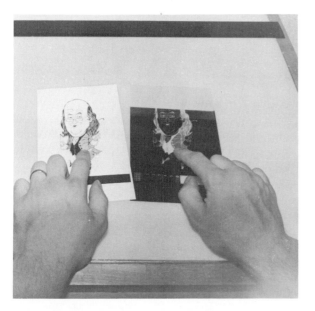

Figure A.6. Comparing original to stepped-off test image to determine the exposure that held the best detail

ure A.6. is diffusion transfer receiver paper contacted to line film), you can still do an exposure step-off.

Use as the "test target" an image on the same base material as the actual working material. This is best done with an image with fine detail, such as illustrated in figure A.6. or a halftone image. Follow the step-off procedures used for any exposure test. Several attempts may be necessary to determine the range of exposure needed to pass light through the base. As before, the key is to have a series of steps that can be compared with the original image. The best reproduction becomes the contact exposure time for that material and type of film.

Appendix B

Light Sources and Color Temperature

It is the radiation of light that causes the chemical reaction on a sheet of film. As printers, we are concerned with the quantity and quality of light that creates that reaction. The sun is an ideal source of white light. For years it was the only source printers used to produce photographic images. In line photography, huge rooms were set aside with large overhead windows and mirrors that could direct sunlight onto the movable cameras below. Quality photographs were produced—unless it rained or was cloudy or was night or was the wrong time of year. It was difficult to control and predict the sun, so artificial light sources were developed. Although more controllable, these artificial devices were far from perfect. Improvements have been made, but the printer now is even more concerned about how to control the quality of light that reaches the film through the camera lens.

Light Sources

If we were to plot a graph of the relative intensity of natural white light across the visible spectrum, it would look something like figure B.1a. There would be nearly equal amounts of energy from all wavelengths of the spectrum. Contrast the natural white light curve with a similar distribution of energy emitted by a 40-watt white tungsten lightbulb (figure B.1b). The artificial source is not made up of equal amounts of energy from the visible spectrum. Tungsten light is composed of much more red light than blue. This imbalance of radiation can cause significant problems for

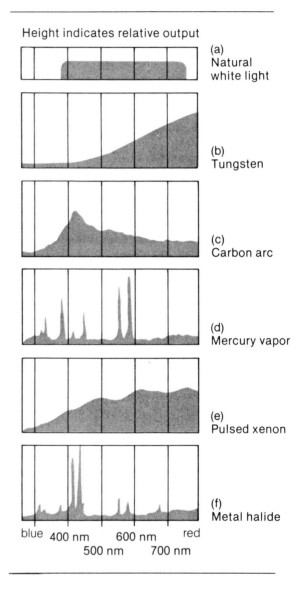

Height indicates relative output

(a) Natural white light

(b) Tungsten

(c) Carbon arc

(d) Mercury vapor

(e) Pulsed xenon

(f) Metal halide

blue 400 nm 600 nm red
500 nm 700 nm

Figure B.1. Electromagnetic energy distribution of five artificial light sources and natural white light

the line photographer if the sensitivity of the film does not match the emission of the light source.

Carbon arcs have been used as a light

source for nearly every photographic application in the graphic arts industry. Light is generated by passing an electric current between two carbon rods, much as in the arc-welding process. The electromagnetic emission of carbon arc light is continuous across the visible spectrum, but it is heavy in blue and violet light (figure B.1c). The quality of light is controlled by the inclusion of metallic salts in the core of each carbon rod. This peaking of energy in the blue end is actually an advantage because the sensitivity of most printing films and plates is greatest in that area. However, carbon arcs have several disadvantages. Voltage changes can cause unstable variation in color temperature and light output. Noxious fumes are released and must be ventilated. A great deal of dirt is generated in an area that must be kept as clean as possible. A brief warm-up period is required (60 seconds) before peak intensity is reached. There is always a potential fire hazard because of the open carbon flame. Owing to these limitations, carbon arcs find little application in modern printing operations.

Mercury vapor lamps operate by passing a current through a mercury gas in a quartz envelope. The vaporization and ionization of the gas generate light. The electromagnetic distribution is discontinuous across the visible spectrum (figure B.1d). There are massive peaks of emission in the blue-violet (b-v) and ultraviolet (u-v) regions, but radiation is practically nonexistent in all other areas. If images with colors other than b-v or u-v are being photographed, it is very difficult to record a film image. This characteristic makes it useless for color separation but causes no problems for blue-sensitive emulsions, and plate making. The lamps require a 2-to-3-minute warm-up time and are generally operated on a dual exposure system—a standby voltage and a full-intensity voltage. A shutter system is usually included to contain the light until an exposure is made. During the exposure the light is powered at full intensity and the shutter opens allowing the light to expose the plate. Once the lamp is extinguished, it has to cool down before it can be started again. However, additives to the mercury vapor can improve its light quality and significantly extend the lamp life.

Because of the 2-to-3 minute warmup period for this type of light source, it is seldom, if ever, used for camera lights. To do so would require the extra expense of using a shutter over each camera light.

Pulsed xenon lamps were first introduced in 1958. They were developed as an application of photographic electronic flash techniques. The lamp is formed by filling quartz tubing with low-pressure xenon gas. The xenon is charged and discharged at the rate of the power line frequency—120 times each second. Even though the lamp is pulsed, the frequency is such that the light appears continuous across the visible spectrum, with no radical peaks of emission (figure B.1e). Although lower in blue-violet output, it has several overriding advantages for line photography. The lamp reaches peak intensity instantly, has constant color temperature, has a spectral output very close to sunlight, is economical to operate, and is very clean. Pulsed xenon lamps are also used for plate making; however, longer exposure times are required as compared to metal halide lamps of the same wattage.

The **metal halide** is a recent development. It is basically a mercury lamp with metal halide additives. The electromagnetic emission peaks extremely high in the blue-violet area (figure B.1f). This output matches the maximum sensitivity of many printing materials. It has been successfully applied in plate making, proofing, photofabrication, screen emulsion exposures, and gravure work. It provides at least four times more **actinic output** (energy that activates or hardens light-sensitive coatings) than any other light source.

Color Temperature

Color temperature is a term bandied about by both printers and photographers, often without accurate understanding. Light sources are often classified according to color temperature (table B.1), which makes people think that it is a primary concern for all photography—which it is not. Color temperature is not a concern in black-and-white process photography, but it is of paramount importance for color work, whether original photography or color separation.

Color temperature is a measure of the sum color effect of the visible light emitted by any source. The blue end of the visible spectrum is rated as having a higher color temperature than the red end. Color temperature is theoretically defined by heating a perfect radiator of energy or "black body." As the temperature increases, the color of the body changes. Each color of the visible spectrum is then assigned a temperature that corresponds to the temperature of the black body for that color. Color temperature is measured in degrees Kelvin (°K), which is derived by adding 273 to the temperature in degrees Centigrade. Color temperature is not such an unusual idea. Blacksmiths for centuries visually judged temperature by the color a piece of metal displayed as it was heated.

It is important to realize that color temperature describes only the visual appearance of a light source and does not necessarily describe its photographic effect. Both a tungsten and a fluorescent light source might be rated at the same color temperature. But because of difference in spectral emissions, they might produce totally different results on a piece of film.

Most color films are balanced for a particular color temperature. In other words, they are designed to record images accurately under certain color conditions. If a film is rated around 5000°K, it should faithfully record color balance as viewed under natural sunlight. If rated around 3000°K, it is designed to be used under artificial incandescent light, as found in the average home.

Graphic arts films are rarely identified as being balanced for a particular color temperature. However, when working with color originals, the graphic arts photographer has to be certain that the reflected light that reaches the film is faithfully describing the color balance of the copy being reproduced. For that reason the industry has even adopted a color temperature standard for viewing and judg-

Table B.1. Color Temperature of Various Light Sources

Light Source	Color Temperature
Clear blue sky	15,000°K to 30,000°K
Sun	5,100°K
Partly cloudy sky	8,000°K to 10,000°K
Fluorescent lights, daylight	6,500°K
Pulsed xenon	6,000°K
Quartz-iodine (high level)	3,400°K
Carbon arcs, white flame cored	5,000°K
Incandescent, 100-watt	3,000°K

Source: *Handbook of Tables for Applied Engineering Science*, CRC, 1970.

Figure B.2. Color transparency viewers
Courtesy of Kollmorgen Corp., Macbeth Color and Photometry Division

ing color proofing and printing (5000°K) to ensure consistent human color perception. Figure B.2 is an example of a standard view-ing device. It ensures that each transparency viewed will be illuminated with a light source used throughout the industry.

Key Terms for Appendix B

carbon arcs	pulsed xenon	actinic output
mercury vapor	metal halide	color temperature

Appendix C

How to Use Basic Resources in the Graphic Arts to Locate Technical Information

There are many times when the student, manager, or technician needs to locate information about some aspect of the graphic arts but is at a loss as to how to find it. Perhaps a student has been assigned a research paper and needs to locate everything that has been published on a specific topic. A manager might want to read about a new system of production flow. The shop foreman might be having problems with some process and is trying to learn more about alternative approaches. Whatever the reason, locating information is a common problem, and unfortunately most people don't know how to solve it. The purpose of this appendix is to outline the procedures and resources available to help you find that information.

To begin any search, you need to get an idea of how much information is available on the subject. To do this, you need to have a quick overview. Any basic printing text (such as this one) can give you a summary of what is known in the field. Use the index to locate your topic in the book and then skim it for information. Then examine the bibliography for other basic works on the subject.

Another way to find an overview of a subject is to use one of the encyclopedia-like books on printing. *The Lithographers Manual*, published by the Graphic Arts Technical Foundation, is one example. It is brought up to date every five or six years and is a very technical treatment of every area of lithography. Use the index to find your information.

A more comprehensive approach is *The Printing Industry: An Introduction to Its Many Branches, Processes and Products* by Victor Strauss. It has sections on all phases of printing and is less technical than *The Lithographers Manual*. To date, only the first edition, published in 1969, is available. For each chapter a list of books is included for more detailed study.

If you find there are additional books that cover your area of concern, the next problem is to locate them. Many printers have them in their personal libraries. Almost any large library should have them as well. Some possibilities might be the library of a college or community college, a technical institute with a program in printing, the library of a large printing company, or a public library in a large city. Many small libraries can borrow books from larger ones, so if you can't find exactly what you are looking for, ask a librarian.

You may have enough information from the additional books you found in such sources as *The Printing Industry*. If you want more information, look in the card catalog in a library. Card catalogs can be difficult to use. One reason is that the word you think describes your topic might not be the word the cataloger used. Most large libraries use the same subject headings as the Library of Congress in Washington, D.C. Here are some useful headings from that system:

- Printing (used for general books about the whole industry)
- Printing, practical (used for books that are about technical aspects)
- Lithography (used for books concerned primarily with lithography for artists)
- Offset Printing (used for books that are about technical aspects of industrial lithography)

– Screen Process Printing (used for books that are about technical aspects of industrial screen printing)
– Serigraphy (used for books about screen printing for artists)

You might also find information under:

– Advertising layout and typography
– Book Industries and Trade
– Color Printing
– Color Separation
– Chromolithography
– Electrostatic Printing
– Flexography
– Handpress
– Intaglio Printing
– Linotype
– Map Printing
– Newspaper Layout and Typography
– Paper—Printing Properties
– Photolithography
– Printing Industry
– Printing on Plastics
– Proofreading
– Stereotyping
– Type and Type Founding
– Typesetting

If at any time you're having trouble finding what you need, be sure to ask a librarian for help. That's what librarians are there for!

There are over two hundred magazines concerned with printing in one form or another. Printing shops or schools may receive many of them. Sitting down and thumbing through many issues of magazines, however, is not an efficient way to obtain information. Indexes can be helpful. An index is a list of all the articles in a number of different magazines or journals. All the titles of articles that relate to the same subject are grouped together, with the name of the publication, date, and page number included for each one. Most indexes are compiled so that by looking in one book you will find everything under a subject heading that was published in a single year. The *Business Periodicals Index* indexes *Graphic Arts Monthly* and *American Printer* (as well as a few other magazines concerned with publishing) and can lead you quickly to some technical information.

Graphic arts abstracting services are probably the best sources of technical information. An abstracting service tries to keep up with all the literature in a certain field. It indexes articles so you can find them and gives a summary (called an abstract) of the article so you can tell whether the article will actually be helpful to you.

Graphic Arts Literature Abstracts is published by the Graphic Arts Research Center (Rochester Institute of Technology, 1 Lomb Memorial Drive, Rochester, NY 14623). This service abstracts international as well as American sources and is a guide to and summary of current research. The Graphic Arts Technical Foundation (4615 Forbes Avenue, Pittsburgh, PA 15213) publishes *Graphic Arts Abstracts*, which abstracts both books and articles.

Figure C.1 shows a sample entry from *Graphic Arts Abstracts* that was found under the subject heading of "Stripping—Image Assembly." There is a great deal of information here. The title of the article is "Alternative Ways from Mechanical Paste-up to Plate." It was written by P. Little. You can find the article on page 14 of the November 1975 issue of the *Kodak Bulletin for the Graphic Arts*, Number 33. The article is two pages long. Also included is a short paragraph that describes the scope and content of the material. The number "C1557–2" is a GATF reference number. If you cannot locate the publication, *Graphic Arts Abstracts* will send you a photo-

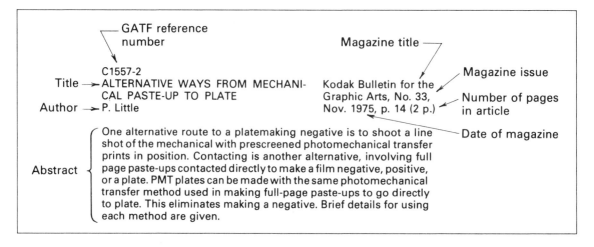

Figure C.1. A sample entry from *Graphic Arts Literature Abstracts*
Courtesy of Graphic Arts Technical Foundation

copy if you provide the reference number. *Graphic Arts Literature Abstracts* provides similar information and service.

In addition to using these publications as an index to find information, you can keep up with what is currently happening in the printing field by regularly reading the summaries and then reading the complete articles if you have time. The only difficulty with these abstracting services is the cost. Because they are highly specialized, only very large libraries or libraries that cater to the printing industry will have them.

Many fine magazines about printing and the graphic arts are available. Below is a list of some of the major magazines in the field, and addresses which can be used for subscriptions.

American Printer
300 W. Adams Street
Chicago, IL 60606

Graphic Arts Monthly
875 Third Avenue
New York, New York 10022

In-Plant Reproductions & Electronic
    Publishing
North American Building
410 N. Broad Street
Philadelphia, PA 19108

Printing Impressions
401 North Broad Street
Philadelphia, PA 19108

Publishers Weekly
205 East 42nd Street
New York, New York 10017

Quick Printing
3225 South U.S. 1
Fort Pierce, FL 33482

In addition to libraries and publications, technical associations provide an excellent source of information on the graphic arts. There are literally hundreds of graphic arts related technical and trade associations in the United States. The list below is only partial, and focuses on national associations. Most states and many major cities also have local associations. All of these associations can provide information to people interested in the area of the industry represented by their membership; many publish books, newsletters, and other educational materials; and most of them offer educational membership at a reduced cost to students and teachers in the graphic arts. Association membership can be an important part of your career in the graphic arts. Often the people that you meet through an association will remain your friends for a lifetime, broadening your perspective and increasing your opportunities for advancement.

American Business Press
205 East 42nd Street
New York, N.Y. 10017

American Newspaper Publishers
Association
11600 Sunrise Valley Drive
Reston, VA 22091

American Newspaper Publishers
Association Research Institute
P.O. Box 598
Easton, PA 18042

American Paper Institute
260 Madison Avenue
New York, NY 10016

American Printing History Association
P.O. Box 4922
Grand Central Station
New York, NY 10163

American Quick Printing Association
1324 West Clay
Houston, TX 77019

Direct Marketing Association
6 East 43rd Street
New York, NY 10017

Education Council of the Graphic Arts
Industry
4615 Forbes Avenue
Pittsburgh, PA 15213

Engraved Stationery Manufacturers
Association Inc.
1000 17th Avenue South
Nashville, TN 37212

Fibre Box Association
5727 East River Road
Chicago, IL 60631

Flexographic Technical Association
95 West 19th Street
Huntington Station, NY 11746

Graphic Arts Technical Foundation
4615 Forbes Avenue
Pittsburgh, PA 15213

Graphic Preparatory Association (PIA)
415 East Hitt Street
Mount Morris, IL 61054

Gravure Research Institute
22 Manhasset Avenue
Port Washington, NY 11050

Gravure Technical Association
60 East 42nd Street
New York, NY 10017

International Association of Printing House
Craftsmen
7599 Kenwood Road
Cincinnati, OH 45236

International Press Association
552 West 167th Street
South Holland, IL 60473

Magazine Publishers Association
575 Lexington Avenue
New York, NY 10022

National Association of Diemakers &
Diecutters
P.O. Box 2
Mount Morris, IL

National Association of Litho Clubs
P.O. Box 1074
Passaic, NJ 07055

National Association of Printers and
   Lithographers
780 Palisade Avenue
Teaneck, NJ 07666

National Association of Printing Ink
   Manufacturers, Inc.
550 Mamaroneck Avenue
Harrison, NY 10528

National Association of Quick Printers
1 Illinois Center
Suite 600
111 East Wacker Drive
Chicago, IL 60601312-644-6610

National Business Forms Association
433 East Monroe Avenue
Alexandria, VA 22301

National Newspaper Association
1627 K Street N.W.
Washington, DC 20006

National Paper Trade Association
111 Great Neck Road
Great Neck, NY 11021

National Printing Equipment and Supply
   Association
6849 Old Dominion Drive
McLean, VA 22101

Paper Industry Management Association
2400 East Oakto Street
Arlington Heights, IL 60005

Printing Industries of America, Inc. (PIA)
1730 North Lynn Street
Arlington, VA 22209

Affiliates of PIA:
   Binding Industries of America
   Conference Board of Major Printers
   Financial Printers Association
   Graphic Arts Employers of America

Graphic Arts Marketing Information
Graphic Communications Association
International Business Forms
   Industries, Inc.
International Thermographers
   Association
Label Printing Industry Section
Magazine Printers Section
Master Printers of America
National Association of Book
   Manufacturers
National Association of Lithographic
   Plate Manufacturers
National Composition Association
Non-Heatset Web Unit
PAIS Users Group
Web Offset Section

Printing Platemakers Association
501 North Wesley Avenue
P.O. Box 2
Mount Morris, IL 61054

Screen Printing Association International
10015 Main Street
Fairfax, VA 22031

Suburban Newspapers of America
111 East Wacker Drive
Chicago, IL 60601

Tag and Label Manufacturers Institute
P.O. Box 1333
Stamford, CT 06904

Technical Association of the Graphic Arts
P.O. Box 3064
Federal Station
Rochester, NY 14614

Typographers International Association
2262 Hall Plaza N.W.
Washington, DC 20007

Glossary

Accordion fold. Several folds made parallel to each other.

Acetate sheet. Clear (or frosted) stable-base plastic material commonly used for overlays in paste-up.

Actinic light. Any light that exposes light-sensitive emulsions.

Actinic output. Energy that activates or hardens light-sensitive coatings; consists of shorter wave lengths of visible spectrum.

Additive colors. Colors that make up white light; red, blue, and green are the additive primary colors.

Additive plate. Presensitized lithographic plate on which ink-receptive coating must be added to exposed area during processing.

Additives. Compounds that control such ink characteristics as tack, workability, and drying time.

Adhesive binding. Fastening together of printed sheets or signatures with glue.

Agitation. Flow of solution back and forth over film during chemical processing.

Alphanumeric code. A unique code symbol system for each letter of the alphabet, both uppercase, lowercase, and numbers, as well as some common punctuation and symbols.

Aniline process. An early term for flexography.

Anilox roll. A cellular surfaced inking roller on a flexo press.

Antihalation dye. Dye that is generally coated on back of most transparent-based film to absorb light that passes through emulsion and base during exposure.

Aperture. Opening through which light passes in the lens of a camera.

Ascender. Any portion of a letter that extends above the x-height.

ASCII (pronounced "As-Key"). An alphanumeric code used in telecommunication.

Asphaltum. Tar-like material used as an acid resist in gravure printing.

Assembling. Finishing operations that bring together all elements of a printing job into final form; common operations are gathering, collating, and inserting.

Back-lighted copyboard. Equipment in some process cameras for photographing transparent copy; light is projected through the back of the copyboard and the lens to the new film.

Balance. Equilibrium of the visual images on a sheet.

Ballard shell process. Special technique used by many gravure publication printers for easy removal of copper layer after cylinder has been printed.

Basic density range (BDR). Range of detail produced from halftone screen by main exposure.

Basic exposure. Camera aperture and shutter speed combination that will produce a quality film image of normal line copy with standardized chemical processing.

Basic sheet size. Basis from which all paper weights are determined by the manufacturer; differs for each of the four paper classifications: book paper (25″ × 38″), writing paper (17″ × 22″), cover paper (20″ × 26″), and Bristol paper (22½″ × 28¼″).

Basis weight. Weight in pounds of one ream (500 sheets) of the basic sheet size of a particular paper type.

Baumé. Density scale used by Antoine Baumé, a French chemist, in graduating his hydrometers.

Bimetal plate. Plate manufactured with two dissimilar metals; one forms the ink-receptive image, and the other the solution-receptive area.

Bit. A binary digit, either a zero or a one.

Blanket cylinder. Part of a rotary press that transfers the image from the plate cylinder to the press sheet.

Bleed. Extension of a printing design over the edge of a sheet.

Blueline flat. Special flat prepared as part of one multiflat registration system; carries all important detail, including register marks.

Blueprint. Inexpensive photomechanical proofing material; is exposed through the flat on a platemaker, developed in water, fixed in photographic hypo, and then washed to remove fixer stains.

Blue-sensitive material. Photographic material that reacts to the blue part of a white-light exposure.

Body-height. Distance from the base line to the top of a lowercase letter x in a given font; varies depending on alphabet design; also known as x-height.

Bone folder. Most common type of hand-folding device; consists of a long, narrow blade of bone or plastic.

Book paper. Most common type of paper found in the printing industry; available in a wide range of grades and noted for easy printability.

Bridge. Surface of a gravure cylinder between wells.

Bristol paper. Stiff, heavy material used for business cards, programs, file folders, inexpensive booklet covers, and the like.

Brownline. Inexpensive photomechanical proofing material; is exposed through the flat on a platemaker, developed in water, fixed in photographic hypo, and then washed in water to remove fixer stains; the longer the exposure, the more intense the brownline image.

Buckle folder. Paper-folding machine that operates by forcing a sheet between two rollers and causing it to curve.

Bump exposure. No-screen image exposure made through the lens; used to change contrast by compressing the screen range.

Burner film. Piece of transparent film that allows full passage of light to the cylinder when preparing a gravure mask.

Burnisher. Tool used to apply pressure to a small surface; usually has a long handle and a hard, smooth ball or point.

Cab. Special film mask used in gravure printing; is punched and marked to be used as a guide for stripping negatives prior to making a gravure cylinder.

Calendering. Paper-making process that passes paper between rollers to smooth or polish the paper surface.

California job case. Most popular case for holding foundry type; contains all characters in a single drawer.

Camera-ready copy. Finished paste-up used to create the images of the final job.

Cameron press. Web-fed printing machine used in book production; prints from rubber plates imposed on a flexible belt; designed to rapidly mass-produce an entire book.

Carbon arcs. Rods whose electromagnetic emission is heavy in blue and violet light; were commonly used as a light source for the graphic arts industry.

Carbon printing. Process of transferring the positive image to the cylinder mask in conventional gravure.

Carbon tissue. Gelatin-based material coated on a paper backing and used in gravure printing.

Carousel carrier. Multicolor screen printing equipment that holds individual screen frames, one for each color; rotates around a central axis and sequentially moves each screen into position over object to be printed.

Casebound cover. Rigid cover generally associated with high-quality bookbinding.

Center lines. Lines drawn on a paste-up in light-blue pencil to represent the center of each dimension of the illustration board.

Chain gripper delivery. Press delivery unit technique in which sheets are pulled onto the delivery stack by a mechanical system.

Characteristic curve. Visual interpretation of a light-sensitive material's exposure/density relationship.

Chase. Metal frame used to hold forms during relief plate making or printing.

Chaser method. Method of arranging furniture around a relief form when it is not a standard dimension.

Checking for lift. Procedure that checks all elements within a locked chase; determines whether they are tightly fixed in position and will not move or fall out during handling or printing.

Clip art. Art supplied in camera-ready form; copyright given with purchase; available from a number of companies that specialize in providing the service to printers.

Closed shop. Shop that requires craftspeople to join a union to maintain employment.

Coated paper. Paper with an added layer of pigment bonded to the original paper fiber surface to smooth out the rough texture.

Cold type composition. Preparation of any printing form intended to be reproduced photographically.

Collating. Finishing operation in which individual printed sheets are assembled into the correct sequence.

Collodion. Viscous solution of cellulose nitrates and ether and alcohol used as a coating for photographic plates.

Colloid. Any substance in a certain state of fine division.

Color sensitivity. Chemical change response in a particular silver halide emulsion to an area of the visible electromagnetic spectrum.

Color temperature. Measure of the sum color effect of the visible light emitted by any source.

Combing wheel. Type of sheet separator.

Commercial printing. Type of printing in which nearly any sort of printing job is accepted.

Common edge. Method of multiflat registration in which two edges of each flat are positioned in line with each other; if edges are lined up with corresponding edges of the plate, all images should be in correct position.

Complementary flats. Two or more flats stripped so that each can be exposed singly to a plate but still have each image appear in correct position on final printed sheet.

Composing stick. Instrument in which foundry type is assembled in lines for printing.

Composition. Process of assembling symbols (whether letters or drawings) in the position defined on the rough layout during image design.

Comprehensive. Artist's rendering that attempts to duplicate appearance of final product.

Contact printing. Process of exposing a sheet of light-sensitive material by passing light through a previously prepared piece of film.

Continuous-sheet-feeding system. Technique on a press that adds sheets to the feeder system without stopping the press in the middle of a run.

Continuous-tone photograph. Image created from many different tones or shades and reproduced through photography.

Continuous-tone photography. Process of recording images of differing density on pieces of film; continuous-tone negatives show varying shades of gray or different hues of color.

Contrast. Noticeable difference between adjacent parts in tone and color.

Control strip. Piece of film used in automatic film processing to gauge the activity level of solutions in the machine; several times a day the photographer sends a preexposed control strip through the machine and then examines the processed piece to determine whether machine adjustments need to be made.

Conventional gravure. Method of preparing gravure cylinders that delivers well openings of exactly the same opening size.

Copy. Words to be included on a rough layout; final paste-up; or, in some situations, final press sheet.

Copyboard. Part of a process camera that opens to hold material to be photographed (the copy) during exposure.

Copy density range (CDR). Difference between the lightest highlight and the darkest shadow of a photograph or continuous-tone copy.

Counter. In gravure printing, angle between the doctor blade and the cylinder; in relief printing, sunken area just below the printing surface of foundry type.

Counting keyboard. Operator-controlled keyboard that requires end-of-line decisions as copy is being typed.

Cover paper. Relatively thick paper commonly used for outside covers of brochures or pamphlets.

Crash. Gauze-like material that is sometimes embedded in the perfect binding adhesive to increase strength.

Creasing. Process of crushing paper grain with a hardened steel strip to create a straight line for folding.

CRT (cathode ray tube) character generation. Third-generation typesetting system that generates images by utilizing a computer coupled with a cathode ray tube.

Ctn weight. Weight in pounds of one carton (ctn) of paper.

Cursor. A term used to describe a blinking line or rectangle on a computer screen that marks the next point of data entry.

Curvilinear type generation. A computer image generation technique that produces letters and symbols by a complex mathematic expression, rather than as a series of points.

Cutting layout. Drawing that shows how a pile of paper is to be cut by the paper cutter.

Cylinder line. Area of a printing plate that marks the portion used to clamp the plate to the plate cylinder; always marked on the flat before stripping pieces of film.

Dampening sleeves. Thin fiber tubes that, when dry, are slightly larger in diameter than the water form roller; when moistened, they shrink to form a seamless cover.

Dark printer. One of the halftones used to make a duotone; usually printed with the use of black or another dark color; often contains the lower middle tones to shadow detail of the continuous-tone original.

Darkroom camera. Type of process camera designed to be used under the safelights of a darkroom; can be either vertical or horizontal.

Dead form. Any form that has been printed and is waiting to be remelted or distributed (if hot type).

Decalcomania. Process of transferring designs from a specially printed substrate to another surface; products are sometimes called decals.

Deep-etch plate. Offset plate with the emulsion bonded into the base metal.

Default parameters. Parameters supplied by the computer when the operator fails to provide them.

Delivery. Unit on a printing press that moves the printed sheet from the printing unit to a pile or roll.

Demon letters. In foundry type composition, lowercase *p*, *d*, *q*, and *b*.

Densitometry. Measurement of transmitted or reflected light with precision instruments and the expression of these measurements in numbers.

Density. Ability of a photographic image to absorb or transmit light.

Depreciation. Financial technique of spreading the cost of major purchases, such as equipment or a building, over several years.

Descender. Any portion of a letter that extends below the base line.

Design. Process of creating images and page layouts for printing production.

Desktop publishing. A term used to describe a process of preparing full-page images, on a microcomputer, generally intended to circumvent traditional composition and page makeup processes.

Developer. Chemical bath used to make the image on a light-sensitive emulsion visible and useful to the printer; some developers are used in the darkroom to process line film; others are used in proofing, plate making, stencil preparation in screen printing, and some areas of masking in gravure.

Developer adjacency effect.   Underdevelopment caused by chemical exhaustion of small, lightly exposed areas when surrounded by large, heavily exposed areas.

Diagonal line method.   Technique to determine size changes of copy.

Diaphragm.   Device that adjusts the aperture, or opening size, in the camera lens.

Diazo.   Light-sensitive material developed by exposing to ammonia fumes; also, a material used in one of the proofing processes.

Die cutting.   Finished technique used to cut paper to shape.

Diffusion-etch process.   Process used in gravure printing to transfer an image to a gravure cylinder; involves the preparation of a photomechanical mask that is applied to the clean cylinder; acid is used to eat through the varying depths of the mask into the cylinder metal.

Diffusion transfer.   Photographic process that produces quality opaque positives from positive originals.

Direct image nonphotographic plate.   Short-run surface plate designed to accept images placed onto its surface with a special crayon, pencil, pen, typewriter ribbon, and the like.

Direct image photographic plate.   Short- to medium-run surface plate exposed and processed in a special camera and processor unit; used mainly in quick print area of printing industry.

Direct/indirect process.   Method of photographic screen printing stencil preparation in which stencil emulsion is applied to clean screen from precoated base sheet; when dry, base is removed and stencil is exposed and developed directly on fabric; see also **Photographic stencils.**

Direct process.   Method of photographic screen printing stencil preparation in which stencil emulsion is applied wet to screen fabric, dried, and then exposed and developed; see also **Photographic stencils.**

Direct screen color separation.   Color separation method that produces a color-separated halftone negative in a single step.

Direct transfer.   Process used in gravure printing to transfer an image to a gravure cylinder by applying a light-sensitive mask to the clean cylinder; light is passed through a halftone positive as it moves in contact with the rotating cylinder; acid is used to eat through the varying depths of the mask into the cylinder metal after the mask has been developed.

Dominance.   Design characteristic that describes the most visually striking portion of a design.

Dot area meter.   Transmission or reflection densitometer designed to display actual dot sizes.

Dot etching.   Chemical process used to change dot sizes on halftone negatives and positives.

Dot-for-dot registration.   Process of passing a sheet through the press twice and fitting halftone dots over each other on the second pass.

Double dot black duotone.   Reproduction of a continuous-tone original made by printing two halftones, both with black ink; its purpose, when compared with a halftone, is to improve quality in tone reproduction.

Drafting board. Hard, flat surface with at least one perfectly straight edge that is used to hold the board during paste-up.

Dressing the press. Process of placing standard packing on the platen of a press.

Drying time. Time it takes for something to dry or for liquid ink to harden.

Dry offset. Printing process that combines relief and offset technology; in dry offset, a right-reading relief plate prints onto an intermediate blanket cylinder and produces a wrong-reading image, and the wrong-reading image is then transferred to paper as a right-reading image.

Dry transfer. Cold type method of producing camera-ready images in which pressure-sensitive material carries a carbon-based image on a special transparent sheet; the image is transferred to the paste-up by rubbing the face of the sheet.

Ductor rollers. Any press roller that moves ink or water from the fountain to the distribution rollers.

Dummy. Blank sheet of paper folded in the same manner as the final job and marked with page numbers and heads; when unfolded, can be used to show page and copy positions during paste-up or imposition.

Duotone. Reproduction of a continuous-tone image that consists of two halftones printed in register and that adds color and quality to the image.

Duplicate plates. Relief plates made from a (master) form that was not intended to be used as a printing surface.

Duplicating film. A film designed to produce either duplicate film negatives from original negatives or duplicate film positives from original positives.

Duplicator. Any offset lithographic machine that makes copies and can feed a maximum sheet size of 11 by 17 inches.

Dynamic imbalance. Defect in the cylinder balance on a press such that the cylinder differs in density or balance from one end to the other.

EBCDIC (pronounced "Ebsee-dick"). An alphanumeric code used in telecommunication.

Electric-eye mark. Mark added to the gravure cylinder as an image to be read by special electronic eyes to monitor registration.

Electromechanical engraving. Method of producing a relief plate by actually cutting an image into a material with a device that is electrically controlled.

Electromechanical process. Technique used in gravure printing to place an image on a gravure cylinder by cutting into the metal surface of the cylinder with a diamond stylus.

Electroplating. Process of transferring very small bits (called ions) of one type of metal to another type of metal.

Electrostatic assist. Licensed device (by the Gravure Association of America) that pulls ink from the cylinder wells in gravure printing by using an electronic charge.

Electrostatic transfer plate. Transfer plate produced by electrical charges that cause a resin powder to form on the image area; the powder is then fused and forms the ink-receptive area of the plate.

Electrotypes. High-quality duplicate relief plates made by producing a mold from an original form; the final printing plate, which is made from silver and copper or nickel, is then produced in the mold by an electrochemical exchange.

Embossing. Finishing operation that produces a relief image by pressing paper between special dies.

Em quad. Basic unit of type composition; physical size varies with the size of type being set (for 12-point type, an em quad measures 12 points by 12 points; for 36-point type, it measures 36 points by 36 points).

Emulsified. Condition in which something has become paste-like from contact with a highly acidic substance.

Emulsion. Coating over a base material that carries the light-sensitive chemicals in photography; emulsion in mechanical masking film and hand-cut stencil material is not light-sensitive.

En quad. Unit of type composition whose physical size varies with the size of type being set; two en quads placed together equal the size of the em quad for that size of type.

End sheets. The two inside sheets that hold the casebound cover to the body of the book.

Equivalent weight. Weight, in points, of one ream of regular size paper; see **Regular sizes.**

Evaporation. Conversion that occurs when a liquid combines with oxygen in the air and passes from the solution as a vapor.

Exacto knife. Commercial product with interchangeable blades.

Excess density. Density difference after the basic density range of the screen is subtracted from the copy density range (CDR).

Fake color. One-color reproduction printed on a colored sheet.

Fake duotone. Halftone printed over a block of colored tint or a solid block of color.

Feathering. Tendency of ink on a rough, porous surface to spread out.

Feeding. Action of a unit on a printing press that moves paper (or some other substrate) from a pile or roll to the registration unit.

File. A term used in computer storage to describe information contained in a distinct area.

Fillet. Internal curve that is part of a character in alphabet design.

Filmboard. Part of a process camera that opens to hold the film during exposure; a vacuum base usually holds the film firmly in place.

Film speed. Number assigned to light-sensitive materials that indicates sensitivity to light; large numbers (like 400) indicate high sensitivity; low numbers (like 6 or 12) indicate low sensitivity.

Final layout. See **Mechanical.**

Finish. Texture of paper.

Finishing. Operations performed after the job has left the press; common operations are cutting, folding, binding, and packaging.

Fit. Relationship of images both to the paper and, if multicolors, to each other; often confused with the term *registration*, which refers to position of the sheet.

Fixing bath. Acid solution that removes all unexposed emulsion in film processing; is the third step in the process and follows the developer and stop-bath; also called fixer.

Flare. Exposure problem caused by uncontrolled reflection of stray light passing through the camera's lens.

Flash exposure. Nonimage exposure made on the film through a halftone screen; regulates detail in the shadow area.

Flat. Assembled masking sheet with attached pieces of film; is the product of the stripping operation.

Flat bed cylinder press. Press designed so that the sheet rolls into contact with the typeform as a cylinder moves across the press.

Flat color. Ink the printer purchases or mixes to order for a specific job.

Flexography. A rotary relief printing process in which the image carrier is a flexible rubber or photopolymer plate.

Floppy disk. A magnetic storage system usually used in micro- and minicomputers.

Focal length. Distance from center of lens to filmboard when lens is focused at infinity.

Focusing. Process of adjusting the lens so reflected light from the object or copy will be sharp and clear on the film.

Fold lines. Lines drawn on a paste-up in light-blue pencil that represent where the final job is to be folded; small black lines are sometimes drawn at the edge of the sheet to be printed and used as guides for the bindery.

Font. Collection of all the characters of the alphabet of one size and series.

Form. Grouping of symbols, letters, numbers, and spaces that make up a job or a complete segment of a job (such as one page set to be printed in a book).

Formal balance. Design characteristic in which images of identical weight are placed on each side of an invisible center line.

Form rollers. Any press rollers that actually contact the plate.

Fountain. Unit that holds a pool of ink and controls the amount of ink passed to the inking system on a press.

Four-color process printing. Technique using cyan, magenta, yellow, and black process inks to reproduce images as they would appear in a color photograph.

Franklin Printing Catalog. Privately published pricing guide for printers to use to determine average costs for nearly all operations or products.

French fold. Traditional paper fold made by first creasing and folding a sheet along its length and then making a second fold at a right angle to the first, across the width.

Frisket. Sheet of paper placed between two grippers to hold a press sheet while an impression is made; the form prints through an opening made in the frisket.

f/stop system. Mathematically based way of measuring aperture size in the lens of a camera; f/stop numbers predict the amount of light that will pass through any lens; moving from one f/stop number to another always either doubles the amount of light or halves it.

Furniture. Any line-spacing material that is thicker or larger than 24 points; used primarily in relief printing.

Furniture-within-furniture technique. Method of arranging furniture around a relief form when the form is of a standard furniture dimension.

Galley. Sheet-metal tray used to store hot type.

Galley camera. Type of process camera used in a normally lighted room; film is carried to the camera in a light-tight case, the exposure is made, and the case is carried to the darkroom for processing.

Galley proof. Proof taken from a hot type form on a device called a galley proof press.

Gathering. Finishing operation that involves assembling signatures by placing one next to the other.

Gauge pins. Mechanical fingers that hold sheets in position on the tympan of a platen press.

Glaze. Buildup on rubber rollers or blanket that prevents proper adhesion and distribution of ink.

Grain. Mechanical or chemical process of roughing a plate's surface; ensures quality emulsion adhesion and aids in holding solution in the nonimage area during the press run.

Grain long. Condition in which the majority of paper fibers run parallel to the long dimension of the sheet.

Grain short. Condition in which the majority of paper fibers run parallel to the short dimension of the sheet.

Graphic images. Images formed from lines.

Gravity delivery. Process in which sheets fall into press delivery stack simply by falling into place.

Gravure. Industrial intaglio printing in which an image is transferred from a sunken surface.

Gravure well. Sunken portion of a gravure cylinder that holds ink during printing.

Gray scale. Continuous-tone picture of shades of gray used by graphic arts photographers to gauge exposure and development during chemical processing; also known as step tablet or step wedge.

Grippers. Mechanical fingers that pull a sheet through the printing unit of a press.

Gripper margin. Area of paper held by mechanical fingers that pull sheet through printing unit of press.

Guillotine cutter. Device used to trim paper sheets; has a long-handled knife hinged to a large preprinted board, which can be used to accurately measure the size of each cut.

Halftone photography. Process of breaking continuous-tone images into high-contrast dots of varying shapes and sizes so they can be reproduced on a printing press.

Hand-cut stencil. Screen printing stencil prepared by manually removing the printing image areas from base or support material.

Hanger sheets. Major part of the packing on a platen press.

Hard disk. A magnetic storage system used for computer data storage.

Hardening. Stage in ink drying when vehicle has completely solidified on paper surface and will not transfer.

Headstop. Mechanical gate that stops the paper on the registration unit of a press just before the gripper fingers pull the sheet through the printing unit.

Hickey. Defect on the press sheet caused by small particles of ink or paper attached to the plate or blanket.

Highlight area. Lighter parts of a continuous-tone image or its halftone reproduction.

Holding lines. Small red or black marks made on a paste-up to serve as guides for mounting halftone negatives in the stripping operation; are carried as an image on the film and are covered prior to plate making.

Horizontal process camera. Type of darkroom camera that has a long, stationary bed; film end is usually in the darkroom, and lights and lens protrude through a wall into a normally lighted room.

Hot type composition. Preparation of any printing form used to transfer multiple images from a raised surface; examples include Linotype, Ludlow type, foundry type, and wooden type.

Hypo. Fixing bath of sodium thiosulfate.

Illustration board. Smooth, thick paper material used in paste-up to hold all job elements.

Image assembly. Second step in the printing process; involves bringing all pieces of a job into final form as it will appear on the product delivered to the customer.

Image carrier preparation. Fourth step in the printing process; involves photographically recording the image to be reproduced on an image carrier (or plate).

Image conversion. Third step in the printing process; involves creating a transparent film image of a job from the image assembly step.

Image design. First step in the printing process; involves conceptual creation of a job and approval by the customer.

Image guidelines. Lines used in paste-up to position artwork and composition on illustration board; are drawn in light-blue pencil and are not reproduced as a film image.

Image transfer. Fifth step in the printing process; involves transfer of the image onto the final job material (often paper).

Imposing stone. Metal surface on which letterpress forms are arranged and locked into a chase or metal frame.

Imposition. Placement of images in position so they will be in desired locations on the final printed sheet.

Impression. Single sheet of paper passed through a printing press; is measured by one rotation of the plate cylinder.

Impression cylinder. Part of a rotary press that presses the press sheet against the blanket cylinder.

Incident light. Light that illuminates, strikes, or falls on a surface.

India ink. Special type of very black ink used for high-quality layout.

Indirect process. Method of photographic screen printing stencil preparation in which stencil is exposed and developed on a support base and then mounted on the screen; see also **Photographic stencils.**

Indirect relief. Process that involves transferring ink from a relief form to an immediate rubber-covered cylinder and then onto the paper; often called dry offset printing.

Indirect screen color separation. Color separation method that produces a continuous-tone separation negative; requires additional steps to produce color-separated halftone negatives.

Informal balance. Design characteristic in which images are placed on a page so that their visual weight balances on each side of an invisible center line.

Ink-jet printing. A printing process that produces an image by directing individual drops of ink from an opening, through a small air gap to a printing surface.

Ink proofs. Press sheets printed on special proof presses, using the ink and paper of the final job; are extremely expensive and usually reserved only for high-quality or long-run jobs.

Ink train. Area from ink fountain to ink form rollers.

Ink viscosity. Measure of resistance to flow.

In-plant printing. Any operation that is owned by and serves the needs of a single company or corporation.

Input. A computer term used to describe entering information (data) into computer memory.

Inserting. Finishing operation that involves placing one signature within another.

Instant image proof. Proofing material that creates an image when exposed to light and does not require special equipment or chemicals.

Intaglio printing. Transferring an image from a sunken surface.

Intelligent Character Recognition (ICR). Similar to Optical Character Recognition, except that ICR has the ability to learn new fonts and new symbols.

Job estimate. Document submitted to printing customers that specifies the cost of producing a particular job.

Job schedule. Schedule prepared for each printing job as it passes through each production step; shows how long each step should take and the order of movement through the shop.

Job scheduling and production control. Section of most printing companies that directs the movement of every printing job through the plant.

Justification. Technique of setting straight composition in which the first and last letters of each line of type fall in vertical columns.

Knife folder. Paper-folding machine that operates by means of a thin knife blade that forces a sheet of paper between two rotating rollers.

Laser cutting. Process used in gravure printing to transfer an image to a gravure cylinder by means of a laser that cuts small wells into a plastic surface on the cylinder; the finished plastic surface is then chrome plated.

Latent image. Invisible change made in film emulsion by exposure to light; development makes latent image visible to the human eye.

Lateral hard-dot process. Type of well design used in gravure printing in which a cylinder is exposed by using two separate film positives: continuous-tone and halftone.

Lateral reverse. Changing of a right-reading sheet of film to a wrong-reading one.

Lead. Thin line-spacing material used in hot type composition; is lower than type high and is generally 2 points thick.

Lead edge. Portion of a sheet that first enters the printing press; for sheet-fed automatic presses, the gripper margin is the lead edge.

Lens. Element of a camera through which light passes and is focused onto the film.

Letterpress. Process that prints from a raised or relief surface.

Lever cutter. Hand-operated guillotine paper cutter.

Ligature. Two or more connected letters on the same type body.

Light integrator. Means of controlling film exposure by measuring the quantity of light that passes through the lens with a photoelectric cell.

Light printer. One of the halftones used to make a duotone; is usually printed with a light-colored ink and often contains the highlight to upper-middle tones of the continuous-tone original.

Light table. Special device with a frosted glass surface and a light that projects up through the glass for viewing and working with film negatives and positives.

Line photography. Process of recording high-contrast images on pieces of film; line negatives are either clear in the image areas or solid black in the nonimage areas.

Line work. Any image made only from lines, such as type and clear inked drawings.

Linen tester. Magnifying glass used for visual inspection.

Lithography. Transfer of an image from a flat surface by chemistry.

Live form. Any form waiting to be printed.

Lockup. Process of holding a relief form in a frame or chase.

Logo. Unique design created to cause visual recognition of a product, service, or company.

Logotype. Two or more letters not connected but still cast on the same type body in relief printing.

Lowercase. Letters in the alphabet that are not capitals.

Magnetic tape. Tape that stores keystrokes by recording electrical impulses; is a faster and more practical method of information storage than paper tape.

Main exposure. Image exposure made through the lens and a halftone screen; records detail from the highlights or white parts of a photograph to the upper-middle tones; also called a highlight or detail exposure.

Make-ready. All preparation from mounting the image carrier (plate, cylinder, typeform, stencil) on the press to obtaining an acceptable image on the press sheet.

Mask. Any material that blocks the passage of light; is used in paste-up, stripping, and plate making; is generally cut by hand and positioned over an image; photomechanical masks used in color separation are produced in the darkroom.

Masking. Continuous-tone photographic image that is used mainly to correct color and compress tonal range of a color original in process color photography.

Masking sheets. Special pieces of paper or plastic that block the passage of actinic light; are most commonly used in the stripping operation.

Master flat. In multiflat registration, the flat with the most detail.

Master plate. In gravure printing, a frame with register pins that hold the film positives in correct printing position during exposure to the cylinder masking material.

Mechanical. Board holding all elements of composition and artwork that meet job specifications and are of sufficient quality to be photographically reproduced; also called a paste-up, final layout, or camera-ready copy.

Mechanical line-up table. Special piece of equipment used in the stripping operation; comes equipped with roller carriages, micrometer adjustments, and attachments for ruling or scribing parallel or perpendicular lines.

Medium. Channel of communication; mass media are radio, television, newspapers, and magazines.

Mercury vapor. Popular light source for the graphic arts industry that operates when current passes through a mercury gas in a quartz envelope; a mercury vapor lamp emits massive peaks in the blue-violet and ultraviolet regions of the visible spectrum.

Metal halide. Recent development in light sources for the graphic arts; a metal halide lamp is a mercury lamp with a metal halide additive and is rich in blue-violet emissions.

Microcomputer. A small, general purpose computer, with the ability to accept a wide variety of software and additional components to increase power: much smaller and less powerful than a mainframe and not dedicated like a minicomputer; also called a personal computer or a PC.

Middle tone area. Intermediate tones between highlights and shadows.

Minicomputer. A small, dedicated computer, usually used for only one task; smaller and less powerful than a mainframe computer.

Moiré pattern. Undesirable image produced when two different or randomly positioned screen patterns (or dots) are overprinted.

Molleton covers. Thin cloth tubes that slip over water form rollers.

Monofilament screens. Fabrics made from threads composed of a single fiber strand, such as nylon.

Multifilament screens. Fabrics made from threads composed of many different fibers, such as silk.

M weight. Weight of 1,000 sheets of paper rather than of a ream (500).

Mylar sheet. Clear (or frosted) stable-base plastic material commonly used for overlays in paste-up.

Negative-acting plate. Plate formulated to produce a positive image from a flat containing negatives.

Newage gauge. Gauge used to test hardness of copper.

News case. Container formerly used to store foundry type; upper case held capital letters, and lower case held small characters.

Nib width. Area of contact between impression roller and plate (or image) cylinder on any rotary press.

Noncounting keyboard. Keyboard that can capture operator keystrokes without end-of-line decisions.

Nonstandard cut. In paper cutting, manipulation of positions and order of cuts to gain an additional sheet; always produces press sheets with different grain direction.

Occasional typeface. One of the six type styles; includes all typefaces that do not fit one of the other five styles; also known as novelty, decorative, and other typeface.

OCR (optical character recognition) system. Optical scanning device that converts, stores, and/or outputs composition from special typewritten information.

Off-contact printing. Screen printing in which screen and stencil are slightly raised away from printing material; stencil touches stock only while squeegee passes over screen.

Offset. Press design in which an image is transferred from a plate to a rubber blanket that moves the image to the press sheet; offset principle allows plates to be right reading and generally gives a better-quality image than do direct transfers.

Offset lithographic press. Any machine that can feed sheets larger than 11 inches by 17 inches.

Offset paper. Paper intended to be used on an offset lithographic press; surface is generally smooth and somewhat resistant to moisture.

On-contact printing. Screen printing in which screen and stencil contact material throughout ink transfer.

Opaque. Liquid used to "paint out" pinholes on film negatives; also used as adjective meaning not transparent or translucent under normal viewing.

Opaque color proofs. Proofs used to check multicolor jobs by adhering, exposing, and developing each successive color emulsion on a special solid-base sheet.

Open shop. Shop that does not require craftspeople to join a union to maintain employment.

Optical center. Point on a sheet that the human eye looks to first and perceives as the center; is slightly above true, or mathematical, center.

Orthochromatic. Condition in which photographic materials are sensitive to all wave lengths of the visible spectrum other than red.

Oscillating distribution rollers. Press rollers in ink and water systems that cause distribution by both rotation and movement back and forth parallel to other rollers.

Overcoating. Protective coating placed on most transparent-based film to protect film emulsion from grease and dirt.

Overhead. Cost of operating a business without considering cost of materials or labor; typically includes cost of maintaining work space and equipment depreciation.

Overlay. Sheet of packing added under tympan sheet during make-ready; composed of built-up and cut-out areas to increase or decrease pressure on final press sheet.

Overlay sheet. Sheet often used in paste-up to carry images for a second color; clear or frosted plastic overlay sheet is hinged over the first color and carries artwork and composition for the second.

Oxidation. Process of combining with oxygen; in aerial oxidation, a solution or ink combines with oxygen in the air to evaporate.

Packing. On hand-fed platen presses, material used to control overall impression; top packing sheet holds gauge pins that receive press sheet during image transfer.

Padding. Simplest form of adhesive binding and an inexpensive way of gluing together individual sheets to form notepads.

Panchromatic. Condition in which photographic materials are sensitive to all visible wavelengths of light plus some invisible wavelengths.

Pantone Matching System (PMS). Widely accepted method for specifying and mixing colors from a numbering system listed in a swatch book.

Paper lines. Lines drawn on paste-up board to show final size of printed piece after it is trimmed; are measured from center lines and are usually drawn in light-blue pencil.

Paper tape. Continuous band of paper (about 1" wide) that stores keystrokes when punched; punched holes can then be read by other machines to output characters.

Paste-up. See **Mechanical.**

Patent binding. See **Perfect binding.**

Penetration. Drying of ink by absorption into substrate (usually paper).

Perfect binding. Common adhesive binding technique to glue together signatures into a book, usually a paperback; also known as patent binding.

Perfecting press. Press that prints on both sides of the stock (paper) as it passes through the press.

Perforating. Finishing operation in which slits are cut into stock so a portion can be torn away.

Photoelectric densitometer. Instrument that produces density readings by means of a cell or vacuum tube whose electrical properties are modified by the action of light.

Photoengraving. Relief form made by photochemical process; after being exposed through laterally reversed negative, nonimage portion of plate is acid etched, allowing image area to stand out in relief.

Photographic stencils. Screen printing stencils produced by use of a thick, light-sensitive, gelatin-based emulsion that is exposed and developed either on a supporting film or directly on the screen itself; the three types include direct, indirect, and direct/indirect stencils.

Photomechanical proofs. Proofs that use light-sensitive emulsions to check image position and quality of stripped flats; are usually exposed through the flat on a standard plate-making device.

Photopolymer plates. Plates formed by bonding a light-reactive polymer plastic to a film or metal base; polymer emulsion is hardened upon ultraviolet exposure; and unexposed areas are washed away, leaving image area in relief.

Photostat. Photographic copy of a portion of a paste-up; images are sometimes enlarged or reduced and then positioned on the board as a photostat; also called "stat."

Phototypesetting. Cold type composition process that creates images by projecting light through a negative and a lens and from mirrors onto light-sensitive material.

pH scale. Measure of acidity of a liquid; numeric scale is from 0 (very acid) to 14 (very alkaline, or a base); midpoint, 7, is considered neutral.

Pica. Unit of measurement used by printers to measure linear dimensions; 6 picas equal (approximately) 1 inch; 1 pica is divided into 12 points.

Picking. Offset press problem identified by small particles of paper torn from each press sheet and fed back into the inking system.

Pigment. Dry particles that give color to printing ink.

Pilefeeding. Method of stacking paper in feeder end of press and then operating press so that individual sheets are moved from top of pile to registration unit.

Pinholes. Small openings in film emulsion that pass light; are caused by dust in the air during camera exposure, a dirty copyboard, or, sometimes, aciditic action in the fixing bath; must be painted out with opaque in the stripping operation.

Pixel. A dot or picture element in a computer scanned image; also one element in computer image resolution.

Plate cylinder. Part of a rotary press that holds the printing form or plate.

Platemaker. Any machine with an intensive light source and some system to hold the flat against the printing plate; light source is used to expose the film image on the plate; most platemakers use a vacuum board with a glass cover to hold the flat and plate.

Plate-making sink. Area used to hand-process printing plates; usually has a hard, flat surface to hold the plate and a water source to rinse the plate.

Platen press. Traditional design used almost exclusively for relief printing; type form is locked in place and moves into contact with a hard, flat surface (called a platen) that holds the paper.

Plates. Thin, flexible aluminum sheets for lithographic printing; can be purchased uncoated and then sensitized at the printing plant or obtained presensitized and ready for exposure and processing; specific characteristics may vary depending on end use.

Plating bath. Solution used for electroplating.

Point. Unit of measurement used by printers to measure type size and leading (space between lines); 12 points equal 1 pica; 72 points equal 1 inch.

Polymerization. Chemical process for drying expoxy inks.

Positive-acting plate. Plate formulated to produce a positive image from a flat containing positives.

Posterization. High-contrast reproduction of a continuous-tone image; usually consists of two, three, or four tones and is reproduced in one, two, or three colors.

Preprinted paste-up sheets. Sheets commonly prepared for jobs of a common size and layout specifications; are printed with blue lines to help paste-up artist position composition and artwork.

Prepunched tab strips. Strips of film punched with holes and used to hold flat in place over pins attached to light table.

Pressboard. Hard, heavy sheet used as packing material when dressing a platen press.

Prewipe blade. Blade sometimes used in gravure printing to skim excess ink from cylinder.

Primary plates.   Relief plates intended to be used as printing surfaces and capable of producing duplicate plates.

Printing.   The process of manufacturing multiple copies of graphic images.

Printing processes.   Relief, intaglio, screen, and lithographic printing.

Process camera.   Large device used by graphic arts photographers to record film images; can enlarge or reduce images from the copy's original size and can be used to expose all types of film.

Process color.   Use of ink with a translucent base that allows for creation of many colors by overprinting only four (cyan, magenta, yellow, and black).

Process color photography.   Photographic reproduction of color originals by manipulation of light, filters, film, and chemistry.

Proof.   Sample print of a job yet to be printed.

Proofing.   Process of testing final stripped images from flat on inexpensive photosensitive material to check image position and quality.

Proportion.   Design characteristic concerned with size relationships of both sheet size and image placement.

Proportionally spaced composition.   Composition made up of characters that occupy horizontal space in proportion to their size.

Proportion scale.   Device used to determine percentage of enlargement or reduction for piece of copy.

Publishing.   Category of printing services that prepare and distribute materials such as books, magazines, and newspapers.

Pulsed xenon.   Recently developed light source for the graphic arts; xenon lamps are made by filling quartz tubing with low-pressure xenon gas; output is similar to sunlight.

Punch-and-register pin.   Method of multi-flat registration in which holes are punched in the tail of the flat or in strips of scrap film taped to the flat; the punched holes fit over metal pins taped to light table surface and cause the flat to fall in correct position.

Quadding out.   Filling a line of type with spacing material after all characters have been set in a composing stick.

Quick.   Early term for a skilled compositor (esp. foundry type composition).

Quick printing.   Printing operation characterized by rapid service, small organizational size, and limited format of printed product.

Quoins.   Metal devices that hold or lock relief forms into chase.

Rapid access.   A process of preparing a film image using an emulsion and developer that allows for wide latitude in skill to produce an acceptable film image.

Ream.   Five hundred sheets of paper.

Reflectance.   Measure of ability of a surface or material to reflect light.

Reflection densitometer.   Meter that measures light reflected from a surface.

Register marks.   Targets applied to the paste-up board and used in stripping, plate making, and on the press to ensure that multicolor images fit together in perfect register.

Registration. Unit on a printing press that ensures that sheets are held in the same position each time an impression is made.

Reglets. Thin pieces of wood used to fill small spaces and protect larger furniture from quoin damage during lockup.

Regular sizes. Sizes other than basic sheet size in which paper is commonly cut and stocked by paper suppliers.

Related industries. Category of printing services that includes raw material manufacturers (ink, paper, plates, chemicals), manufacturers of equipment, and suppliers that distribute goods or services to printers.

Relief printing. Transferring an image from a raised surface.

Reproduction proof. Proof taken from hot type composition and of such a quality that it can be photographically reproduced.

Resist. Material that will block or retard the action of some chemical.

Resolution. A term used to describe the smoothness of the edges of an image output by a computer.

Retouching pencil. Special pencil used by retouch artists to add detail or repair continuous-tone images.

Reverse. Technique of creating an image by use of an open area in the midst of another ink image.

Right-angle fold. Any fold that is at a 90° angle from one or more other folds.

Right reading. Visual organization of copy (or film) from left to right so that it can be read normally; see **Wrong reading.**

Rollup. Technique used to cover an area on a gravure cylinder for re-etching.

Roman. One of the six type styles; is characterized by variation in stroke and by use of serifs.

Rotary press. Press formed from two cylinders, one holding the typeform and the other acting as an impression cylinder to push the stock against the form; as the cylinders rotate, a sheet is inserted so an image will be placed on the piece.

Rotating distribution rollers. Press rollers in ink and water systems that cause distribution by rolling against each other; see **Oscillating distribution rollers.**

Rotogravure. Printing by the gravure process from a round cylinder.

Rough layout. Detailed expansion of thumbnail sketch that carries all necessary printing information to enable any printer to produce final reproduction.

Rubber cement. Semipermanent adhesive sometimes used to attach artwork or composition to paste-up board.

Saddle binding. Technique of fastening together one or more signatures along folded or backbone edge of unit.

Safelight. Fixture used in the darkroom to allow the photographer to see, but not expose, film; color and intensity of safelight vary with type of film used.

Sans serif. One of the six type styles; is characterized by vertical letter stress, uniform strokes, and absence of serifs.

Scoring. Finishing operation that creases paper so it can be easily folded.

Screen mesh count. Measure of the number of openings per unit measure.

Screen printing. Transferring an image by allowing ink to pass through an opening or stencil.

Screen ruling. Number of dots per inch produced by a halftone screen or a screen tint.

Screen tint. Solid line screen capable of producing evenly spaced dots and of representing tone values of 3% to 97% in various line rulings.

Script. One of the six type styles; is characterized by a design that attempts to duplicate feeling of free-form handwriting.

Scumming. Offset press condition in which nonimage areas of the plate accept ink.

Self-covers. Covers produced from the same material as the body of the book.

Sensitivity guide. Transparent gray scale often stripped into a flat to be used as a means of gauging plate exposure; also used in one method of direct color separation.

Sensitometer. An instrument that exposes a step tablet or gray scale onto light-sensitive materials.

Series. Variations within a family of type; common series are bold, extra bold, condensed, thin, expanded, and italic.

Serif. One of three variables in alphabet design; refers to small strokes that project out from top or bottom of main character strokes.

Set. Ability of ink to stick to paper; properly set ink can be handled without smearing.

Set-off. Transfer of excess ink from one sheet to another when press is over-inked.

Set width. Distance across nick or belly side of foundry type.

Shadow area. Darker parts of a continuous-tone image or its halftone reproduction.

Shaft. Center support of a press cylinder.

Sheet-fed press. Press that prints on individual pieces of paper rather than on paper from a roll.

Sheet off. Process of removing excess ink from ink rollers by carefully hand rolling a sheet of paper through the ink system and then removing it.

Sheet separators. Elements used in the press feeder unit to ensure that only one sheet is fed into the registration unit at a time.

Sheetwise imposition. Arrangement in which a single printing plate is used to print on one side of a sheet to produce one printed product with each pass through the press.

Shore durometer. Device to measure rubber hardness in units called durometers; the lower the rating, the softer the rubber.

Short-stop. See **Stop-bath.**

Shutter. Mechanism that controls the passage of light through the lens by opening and closing the aperture.

Shutter speed. Length of time the lens allows light to pass to the film; is adjusted by use of a shutter.

Side binding. Technique of fastening together pages or signatures by passing the fastening device through the pile at a right angle to the page surface.

Signature imposition. Process of passing a single sheet through the press and then folding and trimming it to form a portion of a book or magazine.

Single-edge razor blade. Tool used to cut and trim materials during paste-up.

Slipsnake. Fine, abrasive stone or hard rubber eraser used to remove images from plates.

Slug. Thick line-spacing material used in hot type composition; is lower than type high and is generally 6 points thick.

Slur. Condition in which an image is inconsistent in density and appears to be unsharp or blurred; is usually caused by platen press roller condition or adjustment.

Snap fitters and dowels. Method of multiflat registration in which adhesive dowels are attached to the light table surface; plastic snap fitters that fit over the dowels are stripped into the tail of the flat; exact image position can be controlled, since the flats will always fall in the same position on the dowels.

Soft covers. Book covers made from paper or paper fiber material with greater substance than that used for the body of the book but much less substance than binder's board.

Software. Instructions that direct a computer to perform specific tasks.

Special purpose printing. Printing operation that accepts orders for only one type of product, such as forms work, legal printing, or labels.

Spectral highlight. White portion of a photograph with no detail, such as the bright, shiney reflection from a metal object.

Spoilage allowance. Extra sheets delivered to the press to allow for inevitable waste and to ensure that required number of products are delivered to the customer.

Spot plater. Machine used to build up the metal in small areas on a gravure cylinder.

Square serif. One of the six type styles; is characterized by uniform strokes and serif shapes without fillets or rounds.

Squeegee. Device used to force ink through the stencil opening in screen printing; also used in plate making.

Stable-base jig. Exposed piece of stable-base film containing register marks, with a density between 0.7 and 1.0; used as a carrier for color transparencies during color separation process.

Stable-base sheet. Sheet that will not change size with changes in temperature.

Staging. Process of covering bare metal in gravure printing.

Staging solution. Solution used as a resist in the etching process; prevents dots or tones from being etched.

Stain. Black liquid used by retouch artists to add detail on continuous-tone images.

Standing form. Form that is never destroyed, melted down, or distributed so that it can at some time be reprinted.

Stat. See **Photostat.**

Static eliminator. Piece of copper tinsel mounted in delivery system to remove static electric charge that makes it difficult to stack individual sheets of paper.

Static imbalance. Defect in cylinder balance on a press that occurs when a cylinder is not perfectly round or has different densities within a cross section.

Stencil. Type of mask that passes ink in the image areas and blocks ink passage in nonimage areas.

Step-and-repeat plate making. Method of making identical multiple plate images on a single printing plate with one master negative; special machines move the negative to the required position, expose it, and then move it to the next location.

Step tablet. See **Gray scale.**

Step wedge. See **Gray scale.**

Stereotyping. Process of producing a duplicate relief plate by casting molten metal into a mold (or mat) made from an original lockup.

Stone proof. Proof taken from a form in hot type composition without the use of a machine.

Stop-bath. Slightly acidic solution used to halt development in film processing; is sometimes called the short-stop.

Straight composition. Composition in which the first and last letters of each line of type line up in vertical columns; also known as justified composition.

Stream feeder. Press element that overlaps sheets on the registration table; allows registration unit to operate at a slower rate than the printing unit and gives better image fit.

Stress. One of three variables in alphabet design; refers to distribution of visual "heaviness" or "slant" of the character.

Strike-on composition. Cold type method of producing images by striking a carrier sheet with a raised character through an ink or carbon ribbon.

Stripping. Process of assembling all pieces of film containing images that will be carried on the same printing plate and securing them on a masking sheet that will hold them in their appropriate printing positions during the plate-making process.

Stroke. One of three variables in alphabet design; refers to thickness of lines that actually form each character.

Subjective balance. Design characteristic in which images are placed on white space in such a way as to create a feeling of stability.

Substance weight. Weight in pounds of one ream of the basic sheet size (17″ × 22″) of one particular type of writing paper.

Substrate. Any base material used in printing processes to receive an image transferred from a printing plate; common substrates are paper, foil, fabric, and plastic sheet.

Subtractive plate. Presensitized lithographic plate with ink-receptive coating applied by the manufacturer; nonimage area is removed during processing.

Subtractive primary colors. Colors formed when any two additive primary colors of light are mixed; subtractive colors are yellow, magenta, and cyan; yellow is the additive mixture of red and green light; magenta is the additive mixture of red and blue light; cyan is the additive mixture of blue and green light.

Successive-sheet-feeding system. Most common form of press-feeding system; feeder unit picks up one sheet each time the printing unit prints one impression.

Sucker foot. Element used in the press feeder unit to pick up individual sheets and place them into the registration unit.

Surprint. Technique of printing one image over another.

Tack. Characteristic of ink that allows it to stick to the substrate (usually paper).

Telecommunications. A method of sending data from one computer to another over telephone lines, or by satellite.

Text. One of the six type styles; is characterized by a design that attempts to re-create the feeling of medieval scribes.

Thermoplastic. Condition in which a material is capable of being heated and reformed after hardening and curing.

Thermosetting. Condition in which a material is not capable of being reformed after hardening and curing.

Three-cylinder principle. Most common configuration for most offset lithographic presses; the three cylinders are plate, blanket, and impression.

Thumbnail sketch. Small, quick pencil renderings that show size relationships of type, line drawings, and white space as the first step in the design process.

Tinting. Offset press problem identified by slight discoloration over entire non-image area, almost like a sprayed mist.

Tones. Values of white, black, or color.

Tooth. Roughening of the threads of mono-filament screen fabrics to increase the stencil's ability to hold on to the fabric; is applied prior to mounting a stencil.

Trade shop. Printing operation that provides services only to other printers.

Transfer lithographic plate. Plate formed from a light-sensitive coating on an intermediate carrier; after exposure, an image is transferred from the intermediate carrier to the printing plate.

Transmission densitometer. Meter that measures light passing through a material.

Transmittance. Measure of the ability of a material to pass light.

Transparent-based image. Any image carried on a base that passes light; transparent-based sheets can be seen through.

Transparent color proofs. Proofs used to check multicolor jobs; each color is carried on a transparent plastic sheet, and all sheets are positioned over each other to give the illusion of the final multicolor job.

Trapping. Ability of one ink to cover another.

Triangle. Instrument used to draw right-angle lines with a T-square; is also available in a variety of angles, such as 30°, 45°, and 60°.

Trim lines. Lines often added to a paste-up in black india ink so they will reproduce on the final job; are used to guide paper cutter in trimming the paper pile.

T-square. Instrument used to draw parallel lines.

Tusche. Lithographic drawing or painting material of the same nature as lithographic ink.

Tusche-and-glue. Artist's method of preparing a screen printing stencil by drawing directly on the screen fabric with lithographic tusche and then blocking out nonimage areas with a water-based glue material.

Two-cylinder principle. Offset lithographic duplicator configuration that combines the plate and impression functions to form a main cylinder with twice the circumference of a separate blanket cylinder.

Tympan sheet. Top oil-treated packing sheet that holds the gauge pins; often referred to as a drawsheet.

Typeface. Alphabet design used in a printing job.

Type family. Unique combination of stroke, stress, and serif created and named by a typographer; is generally made up of many different series.

Type high. Distance from the face to the feet of hot type; for English-speaking countries, type high is 0.918 inch.

Type-high gauge. Device that measures 0.918, or type high, is used to accurately adjust relief press form rollers to evenly touch the form.

Type specifications. Directions written on rough layout that informs compositor about alphabet style, series, size, and amount of leading or space between lines.

Type style. Grouping of alphabet designs; the six main type styles are roman, sans serif, square serif, text, script, and occasional.

Typographer. Craftsperson who designs typefaces.

Uncoated paper. Paper is made up merely of raw interlocking paper fibers; see **Coated paper.**

Underlay. Piece of tissue or paper pasted under the form in areas light in impression.

Unity. Design characteristic concerned with how all elements of a job fit together as a whole.

Uppercase. Capital letters in the alphabet.

Vectoring. A computer image generation technique that produces letters and symbols by drawing straight lines between points on the symbol's outline.

Vehicle. Fluid that carries ink pigment and causes printing ink to adhere to paper or some other substrate.

Velox. Prescreened halftone print used to mount on a paste-up board; looks like a regular photographic print but has been broken into small dots for reproduction.

Vertical process camera. Type of darkroom camera that is contained entirely in the darkroom; is a self-contained unit that takes up little space because the filmboard, lens, and copyboard are parallel to each other in a vertical line.

Vignetted screen pattern. Pattern made up of gradually tapering density and found in halftone screens; produces the variety of dots found in a typical halftone reproduction.

Viscosity. See **Ink viscosity.**

Visual densitometer. Instrument that helps the operator to measure density by visual comparison.

Wax coater. Device used to place a thin layer of wax over the back of a piece of artwork or composition so that the copy can be repositioned any number of times.

Web-fed press. Press that print on a roll of paper.

Wedge spectrogram. Visual representation of a film's reaction to light across the visible spectrum.

Wet-on-wet printing. Printing of one color directly over another without waiting for the ink to dry.

Window. Clear, open area on a piece of film created on the paste-up by mounting a sheet of black or red material in the desired location.

Wipe-on metal plate. Surface, pregrained metal plate coated at the printing plant with a diazo type of emulsion.

Work-and-tumble imposition. Printing on both sides of a sheet, with the tail becoming the lead edge for the second color by turning the pile for the second pass through the press.

Work-and-turn imposition. Printing on both sides of a sheet, with the same lead edge for both passes through the press.

Work order. Production control device that carries all information about a particular printing job as it passes through each step of manufacturing.

Writing paper. High-quality paper originally associated with correspondence and record keeping; is considered the finest classification of paper, except for some specialty items.

Wrong reading. Backwards visual organization of copy (or film) from right to left; see **Right reading.**

WYSIWYG (pronounced "wizzy wig"). "What you see is what you get."

x-height. Distance from the base line to the top of a lowercase letter x in a given font; varies depending on the particular design; also known as body-height.

Zeroing. Setting or calibrating a densitometer to a known value.

Index